I0138019

IN THE RING WITH JOHN L. SULLIVAN

Adam J. Pollack

Win By KO Publications
Iowa City

In the Ring With John L. Sullivan

Adam J. Pollack

(ISBN-13): 978-0-9903703-6-9

(hardcover: 50# acid-free alkaline paper)

Includes footnotes, appendix, and index.

Cover design by Gwyn Snider and Adam J. Pollack ©

Front cover lithograph courtesy of National Police Gazette Enterprises, LLC. Colorization by Corey Parker. Sullivan colorization by Corey Parker.

Back cover colorized lithograph of Sullivan before the Kilrain fight © 2011 National Police Gazette Enterprises, LLC. Used by permission.

Back cover colorization of Sullivan-Greenfield lithograph by Corey Parker.

Manufactured in the United States of America.

Win By KO Publications
Iowa City, Iowa
winbykopublications.com

Contents

The Transition

"I can knock out any man in this town within 4 rounds."

This was the boast that made John L. Sullivan famous. It was the first time that anyone had made such a claim. Sullivan would offer increasingly larger amounts of money to anyone who could last 4 rounds with him, as much as $1,000, which in the 1880s was more money than many folks earned in a year. What made Sullivan special was that he actually could back up his claims, even against trained and experienced fighters, and he could do it in a way that inspired awe in observers. Mouths dropped open when they saw the speed and ferocity with which he could knock out his opponents. No one had ever seen anything like him. John L. Sullivan was the world's first sports superstar.

Sullivan is a pivotal figure in the sport of boxing because he is the one who popularized and legitimized Queensberry rules gloved boxing, the type of boxing we watch today. Contrary to popular belief, Sullivan really was more of a gloved fighter than a bareknuckle fighter. He fought mostly as a gloved boxer. In fact, he only fought three bareknuckle bouts. However, there are reasons why his bareknuckle fights were amongst his most famous.

Imagine taking a well-known sport, one that had been in existence for well over a hundred years, and fundamentally changing its rules, so much so that it practically was a different sport. How would the sporting public treat that new sport? Usually, deviation from tradition is met with initial reticence or rejection. The mind often treats a new idea or way of doing things like the body reacts to a foreign substance – it rejects it. It would take some time for those new rules to gain acceptance from traditionalists, and it would require a hugely popular exciting advocate with star power to foster and promote such acceptance.

John L. Sullivan is the man who was so special that he made gloved boxing a popular national and international money-making sport. He was the man who started it on the path towards acceptance in the sporting world as *the* form of fighting that could determine a true boxing champion.

However, because gloved Queensberry rules boxing was a new thing, and many traditional fight purists were begrudging in their acceptance of it as the real deal, Sullivan occasionally, though rarely, engaged in bareknuckle fights in order to prove himself to the critical skeptics.

John L. Sullivan is a transitional figure in boxing. To understand his radical impact on the sport, you have to understand a little bit about the history of bareknuckle prizefighting. Bareknuckle prizefighting began its evolution in the 1600s in England, and existed for well over 150 years.

Hence, it had a deeply rooted history that gloved boxing rules had to overcome.

In 1743, Jack Broughton published the first set of bareknuckle boxing rules, known as Broughton's rules. In 1838, the London Prize Ring Rules (LPR) emerged, which for the most part were the same, but with some additional safety measures.

Imagine boxing today if a referee would never stop a bout simply because a fighter was hurt or down, and that fighter could recover for 30 seconds every single time he went down, and the fight continued indefinitely until one or the other simply could no longer continue after the rest period. There would be no points decisions, so it did not matter how many knockdowns one suffered. All one had to do was go down from any blow and he could obtain 30 seconds of rest each time. A sport where a round did not end until someone went down, a fighter could be thrown down, and he could hold and hit. Just imagine how different boxing would be. This was the world of boxing for well over a century.

Bareknuckle (LPR) boxing was vastly different from boxing as we know it today. Obviously, in bareknuckle boxing, boxers fought with their bare hands – no gloves, no handwraps for protection. This could be painful not only to the person being struck, but harmful to the hand doing the striking. One had to be careful about where one landed, and how one threw.

An LPR round was of unlimited duration. A round ended only once or as soon as someone either was knocked down or thrown down. A round could last a few seconds, or it could last an hour. Hence, the number of rounds an LPR bout lasted does not necessarily inform one about the bout's length. Above-the-waist Greco-Roman wrestling moves were legal, as was holding and hitting (including grabbing the hair – which is why so many fighters cut off their hair).

LPR fights were to the finish, meaning that they continued until someone was knocked out and could not continue after the rest period following a knockdown, or they retired, or a draw was declared because they were too exhausted to knock out one another. One could be disqualified for a breach of the rules, such as for low blows, grabbing below the waist, hitting a man who was down, or jumping on a man who was down (although when both fell down one could "accidentally" land on his opponent).

After a boxer went down, he would have up to 38 seconds to toe the scratch line at ring center and present himself ready to fight again. Even if he was knocked out cold, his handlers could pick him up, bring him to the corner, revive him using any means they desired, and then after 30 seconds elapsed, the boxer would have another 8 seconds to toe the scratch line and resume fighting again. Hence the origin of the phrase, to "toe the line."

Because of the rests allowed following knockdowns or falls, these fights often lasted quite a long time. A boxer could go down as many times as he liked, and therefore obtain needed rest and recovery. This could greatly extend a bout's length. Technically, it was against the rules to go down voluntarily or without being struck, but some fighters used any excuse to drop. Going down from slips or from weakness was not illegal. Hence, boxers could drop from light blows and argue that it was a matter of subjectivity regarding how much effect the blows had, and referees, loath to make a ruling based on subjectivity or a technicality, rarely issued disqualifications on such grounds. Therefore, many of these bouts were lengthy wars of attrition and endurance, and quite brutal. Top fighters often obtained a great deal of experience and knowledge from one fight, owing to the bout's great duration. LPR prizefighters required strength, endurance, toughness, wrestling skills, and yes, defensive and offensive boxing skills.

John Morrissey vs. John Heenan prizefight, October 20, 1858

Regardless of boxing's popularity and the fame and money that it could garner for its participants, LPR bareknuckle prizefighting was illegal. LPR contests were perceived to be barbaric human cockfights. Religious and civilizing forces which had the power to make laws considered the sport immoral. Fighters could be arrested and serve lengthy prison sentences for engaging in this sport, which was a felony in most states. If your opponent died, you could be charged with manslaughter or murder. The law was the number one impediment to the sport's ability to flourish.

Because they were illegal, the fights usually had to take place in secret locations, not in public halls, which made making money by selling tickets quite challenging. One could not advertise the fight's location. This could reduce attendance. It also could discourage participation.

Because these LPR fights were so brutal, debilitating, and long, requiring such a great deal of training preparation time and expense, and such a great recovery period after the fight, as well as entailed the risk of arrest and imprisonment, most fighters were not willing to engage in them unless there was a very tempting financial incentive. But with the reduced ability to earn money with gate sales, how then did fighters earn good money? The answer is that the sport attracted wealthy gamblers. It meant that fighters generally had to be good enough to convince financiers to back them and put up enough money in stakes and wagers so that a big money fight could be made. Hence, it was a gambler's sport, and championship fights only took place occasionally. Gamblers were not going to risk big money on just anyone. If they won, they won big, but if they lost, they lost it all. Pay depended on success. This meant that most fighters fought very hard so that they could win, earn money, and secure backers.

Despite the fact that they practiced an illegal trade, many fighters had a certain popular status. Throughout history, men always have loved to watch fights, and always have admired fighters and warriors. Because men want to fight, and want to see fights, they always have found ways to make fights happen, regardless of the law.

Because of its lengthy history, bareknuckle LPR prizefighting was considered to be the true test of a champion. It was *the* traditionally accepted form of fighting. This is the real reason why John L. Sullivan engaged in three bareknuckle and a few gloved prizefights under the London Prize Ring Rules, despite the fact that he could be subject to a prison sentence for engaging in fights to the finish under the LPR rules.

In 1866 - 1867, just after the U.S. Civil War ended and slavery was abolished, John Sholto Douglas, then the Marquis of Queensberry, published boxing rules written by John Graham Chambers. These modified rules formed the basis of the sport of boxing as we know it today. The rules required gloves, usually ranging from 2 to 5 ounces, but sometimes up to 8 ounces, rounds were three minutes in length with a one minute rest, wrestling moves and holding and hitting were made illegal, and a downed boxer only had 10 seconds to rise and immediately continue or the bout would be over. Points decisions could be authorized.

Because of their major differences from the accepted form of fighting which the world had been accustomed to for over a century, the Queensberry rules only gradually gained popularity and acceptance. Furthermore, these bouts simply were not considered fights. The Queensberry rules originally were intended for limited rounds sparring exhibitions of skill and amateur bouts, not "real" fights. To the purists, such bouts were watered down. A bareknuckle London Prize Ring Rules prizefight was a *fight*.

Unlike today, LPR fighters fought in fights to the finish, fights that were punishing and could last hours. They didn't have ten to fifteen fights at the start of their careers in limited rounds contests against easy opponents to pad their records. When they fought, it was in legitimate contests that had an aura of danger and brutality, which ended when someone was well beaten. Hence, it is a mistake to evaluate fighters' records from that era in the way we do today. Back then, one fight meant a lot.

It would require the advocacy of a star, in conjunction with legal circumstances and economics, to popularize the Queensberry rules.

Ironically, it was the perception of Queensberry rules boxing as not being real fighting that helped gain this form of fighting a foothold in society.

The Queensberry rules were perceived as more civilized than the London Prize Ring Rules, and were marketed as such in order to enable fighters to practice their skill with a reduced fear of imprisonment. Hence, even though Queensberry rules bouts were advertised as "sparring exhibitions of skill" for legal reasons, in fact, quite often they were competitive fights in the sense that we know them today. The bouts were just called "sparring exhibitions" so as to get around the anti-prizefight laws, but to some degree, most knew it was a legal fiction. That said, they were not the same as the brutal illegal prizefights.

The participants argued that at common law or under state statutes, illegal prizefights were LPR bareknuckle fights to the finish. A gloved limited rounds Queensberry rules bout did not fit the definition of a prizefight, and therefore was not illegal. Hence, depending on the jurisdiction, police and politicians often tolerated such bouts, at least to a certain degree.

The Queensberry rules gave boxers a way to practice their craft more often and enabled them to make more money, boxing in front of paying audiences in public inside theaters and arenas, instead of remote hidden secret locations with few spectators. They could do so without violating anti-prizefight laws, which helped the sport to flourish. Such bouts also gave boxers a way to demonstrate their abilities and convince financiers to back them in real LPR prizefights. Fighters could practice and improve their skills, get fight sharp, and earn money at the same time. Such exhibitions also could serve to foster and promote upcoming prizefights. Gamblers could scout the fighters and make their decisions about who they wanted to wager upon.

Contrary to popular belief, boxing skills that we are familiar with today have existed for a very long time. There are only so many ways to block, duck, or elude blows, or to move, or to clinch, and only so many ways to strike one's foe. These skills have existed for hundreds of years, and like today, have been employed in varying combinations, degrees, and styles, depending on the individuals and the rules. Fighting always has been popular among men. The fact is that a sport cannot exist for well over a century and its permutations not be known by the participants who rely on success to earn money. Just as the talented Mozart and Beethoven were effective successful musicians in the 1700s, they still would be successful musicians today, even though their music might sound different. And yet, their original music still resonates today. Likewise, the feel of fighting might change from era to era, but effective fighters are effective fighters, and they always will find a way to succeed. Hitting and not getting hit always has been the name of the game. Bareknuckle fighters knew how to fight.

That said, with the new Queensberry rules, the emphasis on various skills changed. Although clinching and infighting remained a part of the sport, there was less of an emphasis on wrestling and flagrant holding and hitting. With gloves, the fighters did not have to be quite as careful or particular about when or where they punched, because their hands were better protected, and they could fire more combinations. With a limited number of rounds, the fighters could throw more often and maintain a faster pace as well.

During the late 19th century, there was no radio, no television, and no movies. Folks sought entertainment in theaters, where plays and various vaudeville acts took place. The post-U.S. Civil War desire to enjoy life helped stimulate the popularity of entertainment and sporting events. Boxers wanted in on the money-making opportunities. Football only existed in colleges, and was not a pro sport until 1895. Basketball was not invented until 1891. Boxing had an advantage over baseball because it could be held outdoors or indoors, in the same theaters that were hosting plays and vaudeville, in the day or night. And it was exciting.

Despite the more civilized image that these Queensberry rules brought the sport, boxing had an odd relationship with the law for quite some time. Not everyone was convinced that the Queensberry rules were civilized, and legal acceptance lagged far behind social acceptance. Politicians and police had mixed and vacillating views about the sport of gloved boxing, and, throughout his career, Sullivan had to tangle with the law. Exhibitions of skill were legal, but pummeling an opponent into insensibility, Sullivan's forte, often was perceived as going beyond mere exhibition, and therefore illegal. Yet, it was that illegal style that made Sullivan rich and famous.

Throughout history, at the same time that hypocritical legislators would bar violent sports like boxing, they often were financing and/or supporting conquest and colonization, slavery, police and mob violence, lynchings, and warfare in civil wars, foreign wars, and the American Indian wars.

Sullivan's and boxing's popularity represented an internal social and legal division and contradiction within the country and world. Much of the population was utterly fascinated with and intrigued by boxing, while another faction was horrified by it and wanted it barred. The law could not and still cannot legislate away desire, or human nature. Despite the fact that humans have an aspirational desire for peace and civilization, there also is a certain part of us that admires warriors and realizes that backing every civilization is violence, or the threat of violence. It is inherent. Laws always are backed by the threat of police action, which means physical force. Kings and emperors got that way in part owing to success in battle. King David, Alexander the Great, Julius Caesar, Napoleon, etc. The first president of the United States was a warrior – General George Washington. General Ulysses S. Grant led the North to victory in the U.S. Civil War, the most brutal war in American history in terms of casualties. He became the 18th President of the United States, serving from 1869 to 1877. Hence, it is no surprise that a tremendously talented warrior like Sullivan would garner admiration.

John L. Sullivan actually preferred gloved bouts, for several reasons. First, gloves protected the hands. Ironically, this protection allowed fighters to hit harder and more often. Hence, some actually argued that despite its less brutal image, gloved boxing actually was more brutal. The ten-second rule caused bouts to end faster and in a more entertaining fashion, as opposed to bareknuckle fights that could continue ad-infinitum due to the lengthy recovery rules. Thus, the gloved rules were perfect for Sullivan's speedy, hard-punching, swarming style. He liked to end matters quickly. It was this style that the general public most admired and enjoyed.

However, Sullivan was willing to engage in either type of bout. It was the fact that bareknuckle LPR bouts were illegal that led to his participation in mostly gloved Queensberry rules bouts masquerading as sparring exhibitions in order to avoid the law, when really they were intended as fights. The Queensberry rules enabled Sullivan to fight before the paying public often, earn good money, not have to fight for hours on end, with a reduced fear of imprisonment.

Sullivan was such a phenomenal talent that he helped bring the Queensberry rules to prominence and make gloved boxing the norm rather than the exception. In Sullivan, the public really liked what it saw. He made people say, "Wow!" Everyone wanted to see Sullivan, which made him a lot of money, and achieved immense popularity for the sport of boxing. When young men saw that they could earn very good money as boxers, it attracted much greater participation. Hence, the sport flourished and grew exponentially. Theaters and arenas wanted to host boxing bouts because fights increased bookings and sold tickets. Sullivan became so popular that eventually it was said to be an honor to shake the hand that shook Sullivan's hand.

Technological advancements helped grow Sullivan's popularity. The Gilded Age was a time of unparalleled explosive growth in technology. Thomas Edison invented the light bulb in 1879, which made it easier for boxing exhibitions to take place at night. Wealthy entrepreneurs like Henry Flagler were building railroads and funding oil companies like Standard Oil, which helped power technology. By 1869, the two coasts were linked by rail. This enabled Sullivan to travel from town to town across the country, allowing everyone a chance to see him. Also, by 1861, the two coasts were linked by telegraph. This allowed newspapers to print reports of his bouts throughout the country, regardless of where he had boxed.

Boxing and the newspapers had a symbiotic relationship. The two helped build one another. The public enjoyed reading about Sullivan, and the explosion of boxing reports helped increase the circulation of newspapers and magazines like Richard K. Fox's *National Police Gazette.* Fox's focus on boxing made him financially successful. The savvy entrepreneur Fox, an Irish immigrant who had purchased the magazine in 1876, recognized what stimulated magazine sales, and boxing and sports certainly sold very well, as did stories of kidnappings, lynchings, executions, raids, shootouts, crooked police and politicians, sex scandals and crimes, and illustrations of scantily-clad women. It all was printed on pale pink stock. The *National Police Gazette* quickly became a favorite men's magazine in barrooms and barber shops. And the more folks read about boxing, the more popular the sport became. The telegraph, railroad, electric light, legal circumstances, and consistent press all fostered the development of America's first sports hero. Not all of that press was positive, but the sport's participants soon learned that any news was good news, from a promotional standpoint. That meant more money for everyone.

John L. Sullivan began boxing in 4-round gloved bouts in the late 1870s, and quickly developed a local Boston reputation as a coming talent who easily could obtain backers. Generally, in order to demonstrate their ability, boxers engaged in short 4-round gloved "exhibition" bouts as part of variety shows, which then secured for them financial backers for a "real" fight to the finish under London Prize Ring Rules.

The 5'10" 196-pound Sullivan was a vicious, strong, two-fisted slugger with huge power and very good speed. He maintained a fast pace, was quick on his feet, using fast rushing attacks, and knew how to accurately land his punches. He had an underrated defense and also took a punch very well. He could hurt his opponents, and no one could hurt him.

Before he was through, John L. Sullivan would turn boxing into one of the two most popular sports in the country (baseball being the other one), and he made it *the* most lucrative individual sporting profession in the world, one that was enjoyed by all classes of people.

The Rise

The son of Irish immigrant parents, in the year 1858, John Lawrence Sullivan was born, either on October 12 (birth certificate) or October 15 (Sullivan and family records), in the Boston, Massachusetts area. He was two years old when the U.S. Civil War began, and six years old when it ended.

Before they ever met, Michael Sullivan and Catherine Kelly, Sullivan's parents, had emigrated from Ireland to Boston, USA, to escape the potato famine in Ireland. They were part of a mass Irish exodus in the mid-1800s.

This wave of Irish Catholic immigration caused a rise in anti-Irish anti-Catholic prejudice, which limited their economic opportunities. The Irish were poor, and mostly earned money as manual laborers.

130-pound Michael and 180-pound Catherine met in Boston, and were married in St. Patrick's Church on November 6, 1856. Two years later, John Lawrence Sullivan was born in Boston's South End neighborhood. He was baptized in St. Joseph's Church.

Michael Sullivan supported the family as a mason and day laborer, earning a modest $15 a week. John's younger siblings, sister Annie and brother Michael Jr. were born in 1865 and 1866 respectively. Eventually they moved to a Boston neighborhood just east of the Roxbury border. Sullivan spent his youth in the South End and the Boston Highlands.

Like most fighters, Sullivan did not care for school. Some said he dropped out by the age of 13, while others said it was a bit later. In his autobiography, Sullivan said, "In school days I had many a fracas with the other fellows, and I always came out on top."[1]

For about six months, Sullivan made $4 a week as a plumber's apprentice. He and a journeyman wound up in a fistfight, with Sullivan coming out on top, naturally. He then worked as a tinsmith for a year-and-a-half, and again got into a fight with a fellow journeyman. He also worked as a trench digger for the city's sewer lines. For two years, he worked as a mason as well.

---

[1] John L. Sullivan, *I Can Lick Any Sonofabitch in the House!* (Carson City: Proteus Publishing Co., 1979), reprint of the 1892 autobiography, *Life and Reminisces of a Nineteenth Century Gladiator.*

A young Sullivan loved sports. His first passion was baseball, from which he discovered that he could earn $25 - $40 per week. Starting at age 16, he left home to pursue a brief baseball career, playing semi-pro ball, which he occasionally did during the years that he was working.

Sullivan learned that he had another talent. At around age 17, a 200-pound Sullivan was working in a tin factory. After playing baseball during his lunch break, Sullivan returned to work a bit late, and the foreman kicked him. "You're late. Get back to work." Sullivan was not one to turn away from a fight, and he defended himself. He nailed the foreman under the chin with a right uppercut, sending him through the glass window into the yard. John L. walked outside, and, fearing that the large foreman might recover sufficiently to attack him, Sullivan resumed his attack and pummeled him into insensibility. Everyone stood there, observing in shock and awe.

Word spread about the incident. Everyone started calling Sullivan the "strong boy." It was a nickname that stuck. The Boston Strong Boy Sullivan enjoyed the respect and admiration that fighting well earned him. It also brought him confidence, which eventually helped spur him on to turn to fighting as a way to earn money.

Years later, his nicknames would include the Boston Hercules, Knight of the Fives, Trip-hammer Jack, His Fistic Highness, the Famous Knocker-Out, Lord High Executioner, Champion of Champions, and several more.

Occasionally, variety entertainment shows contained Queensberry rules boxing exhibitions. One such exhibition was supposed to be held at a variety show (either at Roxbury's Institute Hall or the Dudley Street Opera House). A man named Jack Scannell was supposed to box someone who failed to show up. Instead, someone thought to ask a 19-year-old Sullivan to fill in, for already he had a local reputation as someone who could pound on the boys well. Sullivan agreed.

The more experienced Scannell attacked, and Sullivan dodged and moved about. Eventually he timed the attacking Scannell with a vicious right, and Scannell went through the ropes off the stage, landing on top of a piano, out cold. Once again, Sullivan had impressed.

As a result, Sullivan began taking part in more local gloved boxing Queensberry rules exhibitions, for which he was paid some money. The more people who turned up and paid to see him box, the more money he could earn. The more opponents he knocked out, the more people wanted to see him.

Sullivan's reputation grew to the point such that financiers wanted to back him in real competition, with a real fighter. Thomas Earley, who ran a boxing gym, and James Keenan, a turfman and sporting-house owner, became his financial backers.

On Thursday March 13, 1879 in Boston, a 20-year-old Sullivan was scheduled to fight Philadelphia's Jack Curley for a $250 purse. The late-night show went past midnight, so they actually started fighting at about 1 a.m. on Friday March 14.

The 6'1" 193-pound Jack Curley was an older, more experienced fighter. He had engaged in bareknuckle bouts as far back as 1869. This was no regular variety entertainment fight. The *Boston Daily Globe* reported:

> Both men appeared stripped to the waist, and both were bent on their work. After a hard-fought battle of 1 hour and 14 minutes Sullivan was declared the winner. It is the opinion of the sporting fraternity that Sullivan is the coming man, and it is understood that he will be backed by a well-known sporting man of this city for from $500 to $1000 against any heavy-weight pugilist in the prize ring.[2]

This likely was an LPR bout, though it is not clear whether they fought it with gloves or their bare hands, although for legal reasons it most likely was gloved. Already, Sullivan had proven his toughness and endurance.

After the hour-long fight, Sullivan went home and slept, but then returned that evening, on the 14th, to box in an exhibition, this time with John Woods, also known as "Cockey" Woods, who was "well known a dozen years ago among the patrons of the manly art in Boston." Sullivan stopped him as well, and the "encounter gave the spectators great pleasure."[3] Imagine someone fighting for over an hour, and then coming back within the same 24-hour span and boxing again. Clearly, Sullivan enjoyed fighting, he was good at it, and the money was good.

Sullivan continued boxing in local shows. He stopped Dan Dwyer, the Massachusetts champion. He defeated 36 or 37-year-old Tommy Chandler, an "old timer" with plenty of LPR experience dating back to the 1860s. John L. also was victorious against fighting veteran John "Patsy" Hogan, who had LPR experience going back to 1872.

In February 1880 at a benefit show at Boston's Howard Athenaeum, Sullivan boxed 3 rounds with the more seasoned boxing instructor, "Professor" Mike Donovan, a former Union soldier. The experienced middleweight champion Donovan had been boxing since the 1860s. He had participated in many gloved exhibition bouts as well as LPR prizefights. His fights included: 1866 LDQby59 Crowley Davis, W5 Patsy Curtin, and W30 Jim Conroy; 1867 W4 Pat McDermott, W62 Mike Conroy, and W1 Dan Carr; 1868 W23 John Boyne and W7 Pat Kelly; 1869 W10 John Shanssey; 1872 W2 Jack Curtin and W2 Jack Lawrence; 1873 D44 Jimmy Murray; 1874 ND4 Charley Burke; 1877 W5 Dick Liston; 1878 LDQby14 and W7 William McClellan, W2 Billy Costello, and W2 George Crockett; and 1879 W3 George "Deacon" Smith, D94 William McClellan, and WDQ6 Ed McGinchey.

Donovan said that Sullivan rushed at him "like a panther," and was as "quick as a cat and very strong." "In fact he was the strongest man I had

[2] *Boston Daily Globe*, March 15, 1879.

[3] *Boston Daily Globe*, March 15, 1879.

ever met, and I had boxed nearly every big man of reputation up to that time, Paddy Ryan included, and was considered the cleverest man in the ring."

Donovan had to use all of his knowledge, experience, and effort to last the 3 rounds, and was exhausted at the end. "[N]ever in my life did I have to do such clever ducking and side-stepping. … He hit me on top of the head several times, and his blows made me see stars of different colors." Even then, Donovan was convinced, "I had just fought the coming champion of the prize-ring."[4]

Mike Donovan

On March 6, 1880 in New York, Sullivan exhibited with Jerry Murphy as part of an exhibition show that contained several bouts.[5] Murphy was a Sullivan "side partner." Clearly they were making money giving exhibitions together. Years later, it was noted that the more Sullivan boxed, the more he improved.[6]

As of 1880, the U.S. was comprised of 38 states, with a population of 50,189,209. Massachusetts had a population of 1,783,085. New York was the biggest state with 5,082,871. California only had 864,694 people. Of the total U.S. population, 6,518,372 were black.

John L. Sullivan was living in a two-story wood frame house in the South End of Boston with his parents, siblings, aunts, cousins, and an uncle.

---

4 Sullivan at 23-24; Mike Donovan, *The Roosevelt That I Know* (New York: B.W. Dodge & Co., 1909), 37-43, 121.

5 *New York Clipper*, March 13, 1880.

6 *National Police Gazette*, April 26, 1884.

A New Kind of Champion

Veteran bareknuckle champion Joe Goss had been fighting since the 1850s, both in England and the U.S., the former being his native country. He had at least 14 known LPR fights, having lost only twice. This was a tremendous amount of experience, given that LPR fighters did not fight very often, because such bouts were so brutal and long, often lasting 1 - 3 hours. His late 1850s fight with Jack Richson lasted over 3 hours before the police stopped it. An 1859 64-round victory over Jack Rooke in England lasted 1 hour 40 minutes. In 1860, Goss defeated Tom Price in 15 rounds lasting 25 minutes, Charlie Paget in 18 rounds, and Dan Crutchley in 120 rounds lasting 3 hours 29 minutes. In 1861, Goss defeated Bill Ryan or Ryall in 37 rounds lasting 2 hours 30 minutes. Their 1862 rematch D36 lasted 3 hours 18 minutes. Goss defeated Posh Price in 66 rounds lasting 1 hour 40 minutes.

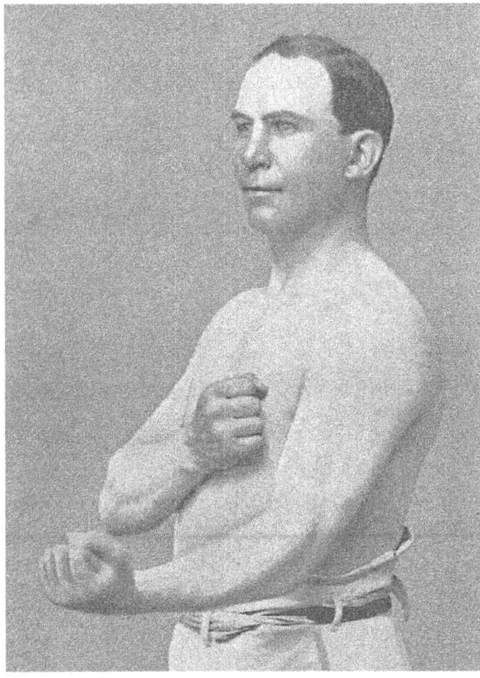

Joe Goss

Goss fought England's champion Jem Mace three times: L19 (1 hour 55 minutes)(1863), a draw after 1 hour 5 minutes (1866), and L21 (31 minutes)(1867).

Goss also fought British Tom Allen to a D31 (1 hour 52 minutes)(1866). Several other bouts took place in England during the 1860s.

In an 1876 rematch in Kentucky, ten years after they fought the first time, Goss defeated Tom Allen on a foul (struck while down) in 21 rounds (48 - 52 minutes) for a a $2,000 or $2,500 side-bet and the American championship. They were arrested and charged with violating the state's anti-prize-fight laws. Allen fled to England. Goss was tried, found guilty, and sentenced to 6 months imprisonment and a $250 fine.[7]

[7] *National Police Gazette*, May 22, 1880, January 20, 1883, January 27, 1883; *New York Clipper*, March 28, 1885.

Goss occasionally engaged in gloved sparring exhibition bouts as well, including with John Dwyer, William Miller, and Steve Taylor.

In 1880, Joe Goss was scheduled to fight "Trojan Giant" Paddy Ryan in a London rules bout for $1,000 a side and the world's championship, given that champion Jem Mace was 49 years old and retired.

In the meantime, both Goss and Ryan gave Queensberry rules exhibitions. Ryan had impressed backers by his performances in exhibitions with veterans Mike Donovan, Steve Taylor, and William Miller.

On Tuesday April 6, 1880 in Boston's Music Hall, the 5'9" 178-pound 42-year-old Joe Goss gave a gloved "exhibition" against the 5'10 ½" 190-pound 21-year-old Sullivan, "the coming man." 1,800 spectators witnessed the bout.

Sullivan dominated. In the 1st round, Sullivan exhibited skill and "planted blow after blow with his left on the face of the champion." Even when Goss occasionally landed, Sullivan countered him.

In the 2nd round, after several rapid exchanges, Sullivan landed "no less than four sledge-hammer-like blows upon the right ear of Goss, and the latter went reeling to the floor. He was assisted to his feet by the master of ceremonies, who, thinking that the champion had only slipped, left him to get to a seat upon the stage." However, "Goss went reeling like a drunken man about the stage, and the danger of his falling among the audience was so great that the master of ceremonies at last realizing his situation, at once caught him and assisted him to a sitting on the platform." Goss was wobbly and out of it. In today's world of boxing, it would be a technical knockout.

Goss was given time to recover, somewhat in LPR fashion. Sullivan promised to spar lightly with him for another round, so Goss agreed.[8]

Goss later was quoted as saying of Sullivan that a blow from "that damned savage is worse than the kick of a horse."

This bout really put Sullivan's name on the map. In essentially stopping Goss in 2 rounds, it was obvious that he was the best fighter in the country, if not the world. However, because it was a Queensberry rules exhibition and not a "real" fight to the finish under LPR rules, Sullivan was not considered the champion by the traditional fight purists, because he had not defeated Goss via the accepted championship rules. In truth, even at this point, he was the best gloved Queensberry rules fighter in the world. However, there were no gloved champions to defeat, because there was no such thing as a Queensberry rules champion.

Two months later, on June 1, 1880 in an LPR championship fight, 6'1" 28-year-old 182-pound Paddy Ryan of Troy, New York stopped Joe Goss after 87 rounds lasting 1 hour 27 minutes. The *National Police Gazette* had advertised the bout as being for the world's championship (although sometimes it said the fight was for the American championship). The bout's location had to be kept a secret, owing to the illegality of the proceedings,

[8] *Boston Daily Globe,* April 7, 1880; *New York Clipper,* April 3, 1880.

but apparently it took place just outside Steubenville, either in Ohio or in Brooke County, West Virginia, some saying Collier's Point, West Virginia.[9]

THE GOSS-RYAN PRIZE FIGHT.

The *National Police Gazette*, which had a national circulation of about 150,000, saw its circulation temporarily increase to over 400,000 in sales of its issues that covered the Goss-Ryan fight. Boxing was big business. Hence, backing and promoting boxing could earn its owner Richard K. Fox a lot of money. Plus, Fox was an admirer of the sport.

Paddy Ryan had refused to spar Sullivan, treating him with disdain, telling John L., "You go and get a reputation first."

Indeed, Sullivan continued building his reputation in Queensberry rules gloved bouts against experienced veterans. He also would fight a couple gloved LPR bouts, and travel around giving some actually friendly exhibitions.

In June 1880, Sullivan, whom the *National Police Gazette* called a boxer of "no mean pretensions," challenged to fight anyone in America with or without gloves for $500. Clearly, he had wealthy financial backers.[10]

On Monday June 28, 1880 in Boston, at the Howard Athenaeum, Sullivan fought George Rooke, an experienced LPR veteran. Since 1867, Rooke claimed the American middleweight championship. Born in England in 1843, Rooke came to New York when he was young. He stood 5'11", was 37 years old, and weighed about 160 pounds. He had boxed in both England and America. Rooke was "one of the finest sparrers in the country, as well as the cleverest of fighters that ever came to America. His victories in the mother country have been legion." Rooke was a local boxing

[9] *Wheeling Daily Intelligencer*, June 2, 1880. If legal authorities did not know the exact location that a fight took place, it made it harder to prosecute subsequently, because jurisdiction could not be proven.

[10] *National Police Gazette*, June 26, 1880.

professor. His record included: 1866 W14 Tim Hussey; 1867 LDQby16 Charles Collins and L25 Matthew Moore; 1868 D18 Tim Hussey; and 1878 L6 Denny Harrington. He also had participated in several sparring exhibitions, though he had been inactive in recent years.[11]

The audience included the upper classes and lovers of the "manly art."

In this contest, the very large "Highland boy" Sullivan treated Rooke like a "shuttle-cock." Sullivan decked him three times in the 1st round. He did the same in the next two rounds, knocking out Rooke in the 3rd round.

Many in the audience cried out, "Drunk-Drunk-Drunk." They believed that Rooke was intoxicated; his staggering about was so pronounced. However, the question was whether he was intoxicated with liquid courage before the fight or whether Sullivan's blows had rendered him so wobbly that many simply believed that he was drunk.[12]

GEORGE ROOKE.

Sullivan subsequently gave exhibitions with Dan Dwyer.

Some have claimed that on September 21, 1880, while in Boston, in a large private room before paying spectators, Sullivan was going to take on a black fighter named George Godfrey, but the police entered and prevented the fight.[13]

The local *Boston Daily Globe* listed Sullivan's measurements as 6' tall, 43" chest, 16" bicep, 14" forearm, 26" thigh, and 17" calf. "He is in excellent form, and has backers willing at any time to place him in the prize-ring against Paddy Ryan, or any other pugilist in the country."[14]

---

[11] *National Police Gazette*, May 15, 1880, December 17, 1881; *Boston Daily Globe*, June 28, 1880.
[12] *Boston Daily Globe*, June 29, 1880.
[13] *Boston Daily Globe*, September 22, 1880; *Referee* (Sydney), September 26, 1888, April 27, 1892; *San Francisco Chronicle*, July 30, 1888; *Daily Alta California*, December 31, 1888. The next-day *Boston Daily Globe* report did not list the fighters' names.
[14] *Boston Daily Globe*, September 23, 1880.

Sometimes Sullivan was just sparring in entertaining fashion to earn some money, while at other times he actually was fighting and trying to knock out his opponent. In November 1880, Sullivan sparred with John Kenny at Harry Hill's in New York.

On November 19, 1880, Boston's Boylston Museum featured a sold-out house that paid ten cents each to witness a vaudeville stage show as well as a 3-round gloved exhibition bout between "Boston's Champion" Sullivan and Brookline's 6'6" 225-pound Martin McMahon. Although McMahon was big and strong and tried to use some wrestling moves in addition to punches, Sullivan was quicker and cleverer. The bout was called "as clever an exhibition of the manly art as ever was given to a Boston audience."[15]

"Professor" John Donaldson

Demonstrating the increasingly strong relationship that newspapers had with the sport, the *Cincinnati Daily Enquirer*'s editor, John McCormick, whose pen name was "Macon," offered Sullivan $150 plus expenses to come to Cincinnati, Ohio to box the middleweight-sized local champion boxing instructor, "Professor" John Donaldson.

The 160-pound 5'10 ½" Donaldson had defeated at least four pugilists of note in LPR bouts, stopping Dan Carr in 7 rounds (23 minutes), Bryan Campbell in 3 rounds (11 minutes), Bluett Boyd in 2 minutes 45 seconds of the 1st round (May 1880), and Jim Taylor in 5 rounds (6 minutes)(August 1880).

On Saturday December 11, 1880 at Robinson's Opera House in Cincinnati, Sullivan and Donaldson boxed for the first time. The 212-pound Sullivan was "the hero of many sparring exhibitions, and is considered by the Bostonians as the best boxer living."

Both men had sculpted, well-proportioned bodies. They wore sleeveless athletic shirts.

[15] *Boston Daily Globe*, November 19, 20, 1880.

In the 1st round, they went right to work, "making exchanges and parries with a rapidity that could scarcely be followed. Not a blow was wasted or misdirected, as they danced around the stage as light as feathers." Sullivan exhibited "extraordinary strength and wonderful quickness" in attacking Donaldson.

Despite the local man's efforts to keep away, Sullivan dropped Donaldson with a right, some saying it was a slip and a hit combined. The result was obvious, for thereafter Donaldson showed a very healthy respect for Sullivan's punching power, fighting in a defensive manner, using his science to save himself.

Already in the 2nd round, Donaldson seemed fatigued by the constant pressure. Both feinted often. Sullivan was "self possessed and determined, showing an entire absence of the novice."

In the 3rd round, Sullivan landed left leads. They engaged in rattling exchanges. A right almost knocked out Donaldson, who ended the round under Sullivan's arm.

After the round, the Professor said, "I've had enough. I'm sick, and in no condition to spar." He retired, pulling off the gloves.

However, Sullivan and the crowd encouraged him to box one more round. John L. promised to work easily with Donaldson, who eventually agreed. Hence, they boxed a 4th round as well. "Sullivan went at him again like a flash and had it all his own way to the end."

The local newspaper said the entertaining exhibition was worth traveling miles to see.

Afterwards, with his reputation and pride having taken a hit, Donaldson said he would like to give it another go with Sullivan on another day, in an LPR fight with hard gloves for $500.[16]

Sullivan and Donaldson scheduled a rematch to be held just under two weeks later, on December 23. However, Donaldson's backers applied for a license for the technically illegal match, giving away its location. As a result, the mayor sent the police to prevent the contest. Even though it would be a gloved bout, since it otherwise was going to be using LPR rules and was a fight to the finish, it still was an illegal prizefight.

Either Donaldson's backers were foolish or they were trying to get the contest called off. The local *Cincinnati Daily Enquirer* questioned Donaldson's courage. Sometimes fighters wanted to give the impression of desiring a fight, but in actuality were happy to see it called off, and even facilitated its prevention. This paper suggested that Donaldson merely arranged the fight to counteract the poor impression he had made a couple weeks prior, arguing that his interest in a rematch was not genuine. The criticism might not have been fair.

Either motivated by having his courage questioned, or because his backers had learned their lesson, the bout was re-scheduled for the next day,

[16] *Cincinnati Commercial,* December 5, 12, 1880; *National Police Gazette,* January 8, 1881.

on Friday December 24, 1880, in a secret location – the recently closed Pacific Garden, a saloon.

They fought with hard gloves, which essentially were just leather gloves with no padding, usually weighing no more than a couple of ounces, as opposed to the heavier 5-ounce soft gloves that contained some padding inside. It was the closest thing they could get to being bareknuckle. Other than the hard gloves, they used LPR rules, which meant that above-the-waist wrestling was legal, holding and hitting was legal, the rounds only ended when someone was knocked down or thrown down, and the rest period following knockdowns lasted up to 38 seconds. The fight would continue until one or the other retired, was unable to come to the scratch, or was disqualified.

Only about 30 people witnessed the battle, because fear of police interference forced them to keep the illegal bout's date and location secret. The purse was $100, which was good money at that time, but not great.

They fought in a 20-square-foot room. There was no formal or official ring. The surrounding crowd and room walls formed the ring. Several trunks were used for the boxers and their seconds to sit upon. Donaldson provided the gloves. Both fighters wore knit shirts, tights, and shoes with rubber soles.

1 – Sullivan charged in like a mad bull, firing away with both hands until a right to Donaldson's neck "knocked him over against the wall." Sullivan kept blasting away until Donaldson went down in a heap. Already it was obvious that Donaldson had no chance. He took his 30 seconds of rest.

2 – A Sullivan left drew blood from Donaldson's mouth. Donaldson moved about, ducked, and dodged away as the aggressive Sullivan gave chase. Donaldson even illegally grabbed Sullivan by the leg, trying to no avail to lift him. Sullivan pounded away, until Donaldson went down from "a little clip" "in a very suspicious manner to avoid further punishment," meaning that he might have intentionally gone done to save himself, which technically was against the rules.

3 – Sullivan landed a telling uppercut squarely on the jaw. Donaldson tried to fight back hard, but Sullivan "rushed him back over a pile of rubbish, and eventually knocked him down over a couple of trunks." Donaldson rose and continued fighting until Sullivan again decked him near a straw heap. Donaldson's cornermen alleged that John L. had kicked him when he was down, but the claim of foul was not recognized.

4 – Donaldson tried to hold off Sullivan with a stiff-arm, but he was sent back against the wall, and as he slipped down, a hard right nailed him, some saying it landed once Donaldson was down. It was a close call, and even if it did land when he was down, it clearly was accidental, for the blow was in motion as Donaldson was falling, so the claim of foul was not allowed. Donaldson's lip was bloody.

5 – As he was recovering, Donaldson told his second that he wanted to retire. He had enough. However, his second refused to retire him and urged Donaldson to continue. Donaldson resumed and missed two blows. He moved about in an effort to evade the punches, but Sullivan landed a discouraging smash to the jaw, and then Donaldson either went down to avoid another punch or he was fought down "over the trunks."

6 – Donaldson ducked and ran away. One viewer said a sledge-hammer blow dropped him, while another said Donaldson slipped down from a light punch. Sullivan was laughing.

7 – Sullivan landed two rights in quick succession. He forced him back, and Donaldson slipped down against the wall without being struck. Sullivan's seconds claimed the fight on a foul, feeling that Donaldson was going down without being hit in order to survive. An argument between the seconds of both sides followed. Donaldson's seconds argued that Sullivan had hit their man while he was down. The referee decided that the fight would continue.

8 – Donaldson hit Sullivan on the nose, but when Sullivan rushed him, he went down over the trunks again, onto the planks.

9 – Sullivan "knocked him about like an old sack," and Donaldson quickly went down.

10 – Donaldson used his left hand to grab around Sullivan's neck, but John L. kept landing rights anyway. About 20 seconds into the round, a series of rights and lefts sent Donaldson down again.

After his seconds dragged him back to his corner, Donaldson told them, "I won't continue. I'm overmatched." He walked up to Sullivan and said, "I'm satisfied." No one criticized the retirement, for it was obvious to everyone that he had enough and could not win. The fight had lasted 22 minutes.

Afterwards, Donaldson said, "He was too big and strong. I knew that I couldn't lick him, but I was tired of being called a coward."

Instead of seeming joyous, Sullivan seemed somewhat disappointed that it had taken so long to win. "It took me a while to do him. But what could I do…he wouldn't stand up and fight, but would run away and even throw himself on the floor."

Regardless, the victory garnered a great deal of praise for Sullivan. The local newspapers lauded his victory, saying that Sullivan "has probably no equal in the prize-ring today." "If the days of the prize ring were not gone by, Sullivan would stand at the head and front of the fraternity." The *National Police Gazette* said that despite the fact that Donaldson put up a plucky fight, Sullivan was too much for him from the start, proving that he was "the best man in America."[17]

The day after the fight, on Christmas Day, December 25, 1880, the police arrested both fighters, took them to jail, and charged them with engaging in an illegal prizefight; a felony. They sat in jail for two days.

At their preliminary hearing, none of the witnesses would testify that a fight had occurred. When one potential witness was asked, "Did you see a fight?," he responded, "No; I've seen a foot race." When asked, "Who was ahead?" he replied, "Donaldson, and Mr. Sullivan was running after him but could not catch him." Another said they were not fighting but merely sparring. This continued, until the judge dismissed the charges, for the prosecution could not establish that a prizefight had occurred. Regardless, Sullivan had experienced first-hand how LPR-style prize-fighting could mean the loss of his liberty, even if only temporarily. No one wants to sit in jail for any period of time.[18]

Sullivan was very active in 1881 in Queensberry "exhibition" bouts. The popularity and renown he obtained from quickly stopping his opponents created a demand for his services, which enabled him to fight often. This afforded him the opportunity to gain valuable experience and improve as a fighter. Fighting frequently meant that he would earn enough money to make boxing his sole source of income, something no prior fighter had been able to do.

On Monday January 3, 1881, inside the Boston Music Hall, a mere 10 days after the Donaldson fight, Sullivan fought 28-year-old 6'1" 205-pound Canadian champion Jack Stewart, known as the Scotch Giant of Glasgow. The Scottish-born Stewart had been fighting since 1869, when he won an LPR bout in 17 rounds. Stewart drew with Tom Allen. After the police stopped an 1870 LPR bout in the 10th round, Stewart fled to Canada to avoid imprisonment. In 1880, he defeated Lon Wright.[19] Recently, Stewart

---

[17] *Cincinnati Daily Enquirer,* December 24, 25, 1880; *Cincinnati Commercial,* December 25, 1880; *National Police Gazette,* January 8, 1881, April 16, 1881.

[18] Sullivan at 32; Michael T. Isenberg, *John L. Sullivan and His America* (University of Illinois Press, 1994), 87-89; Cyberboxingzone.com.

[19] *National Police Gazette,* January 1, 1881, September 8, 1883; *Australian Sportsman,* May 28, 1881.

had been sparring with former Sullivan opponents Joe Goss and George Rooke.

The Sullivan-Stewart fight "attracted an audience such as has never before attended an exhibition of the kind in this city, and the hall was crowded to its utmost capacity." John L. could fill arenas, something no other boxer had been able to do. The bout was part of an exhibition benefit show.

JACK STEWART,
CHAMPION PUGILIST OF CANADA

The *Boston Daily Globe* said that Sullivan "managed to cross counter almost every blow from Stewart, in fact, in the first round, he knocked Stewart out of time." Hence, it appears that Sullivan stopped him in the 1st round. However, Stewart was allowed to recover, in London Rules fashion, and they sparred some more. "The second and third rounds were the same, Sullivan just playing with Stewart as a cat does with a mouse." It appears that Sullivan carried him to some degree. The *Boston Herald* said that at one point, Stewart turned his back to Sullivan, who viciously hit him twice more anyhow, giving Stewart a black eye. Some hissed him as a result.

The "Boston boy" followed the Stewart bout with a "grand wind-up" with Joe Goss, the "champion boxer of England." Sullivan sparred with Goss in a tame manner.

On the whole, it was said to have been the best exhibition show given in the city for some time. The show was quite orderly, contrary to the belief of those who claimed that boxing bouts only led to disorder and riots.[20]

In January 1881, the *National Police Gazette* advertised that Sullivan was willing to fight any man in the world for $2,500 a side.

Regarding the state of boxing, in February, the *Australian Sportsman* wrote,

[20] *Boston Herald, Boston Daily Globe,* January 4, 1881; Sullivan at 33; Isenberg at 89.

> Boxing is a sport which has lost much of its olden popularity, principally by reason of the low character of many of its professors, although it still retains a place in the list of athletic amusements in colleges and other institutions where physical training is encouraged. … In America, however, it is otherwise. In that country, boxing matches are extremely numerous.[21]

On Monday March 21, 1881 at another Boston exhibition benefit in the Music Hall, the 212-pound Sullivan again sparred 3 exhibition rounds with "middleweight champion" Mike Donovan. The local *Boston Daily Globe* called Sullivan the strongest man in the profession and "the coming champion."

Sullivan was brutal and unmerciful, sending forth savage pile-drivers, while the cautious Donovan used cleverness and speed to dodge and elude the blows. The clean punches that Donovan landed had no effect whatsoever. The local paper said of Sullivan,

> A well-directed blow from him has, seemingly, force enough to lay low a full grown Texas steer, and when he gets upon the stage he considers that it is the proper caper for him to immediately throw all the brutal force within him into his arm and launch it forth at his opponent.

Many hissed Sullivan for being too vicious against his smaller foe. They thought he should have been working with Donovan more, given that it was just an exhibition. "The affair was not at all satisfactory, the conduct of Sullivan being of such a brutal description as to invoke the hearty disapproval of the audience, who gave vent to their displeasure by prolonged hissing."[22]

John L. Sullivan's signature claim to fame began when he traveled to New York and offered $50 to anyone who could last 4 Queensberry rules rounds with him without being knocked out. John L. later said, "This was the first time that anything of this kind had been offered." Such tremendous confidence helped market Sullivan. That was more money than some families earned in a month. It wasn't uncommon to find poor families living on a $10 weekly wage. Some thought of him as a braggart, and wanted to see him get his comeuppance. Most wanted to see whether the fiercely confident man was good enough to back up his claims. Either way, the boast's market value at the gate was realized.[23]

On Thursday March 31, 1881 at the notorious Harry Hill's theater in New York, just 10 days after the Donovan exhibition bout, John L. Sullivan fought New Jersey heavyweight champion Steve Taylor (a.k.a. John Mahan), who accepted the offer to try to earn $50 for lasting 4 rounds with Sullivan.

---

[21] *Australian Sportsman,* February 12, 1881.

[22] *Boston Daily Globe,* March 20, 22, 1881; *New York Clipper,* April 2, 1881.

[23] Sullivan at 33.

Harry Hill's was located on Houston street, just west of Mulberry. A huge red-and-blue lantern and a golden eagle adorned its front entrance. Women were admitted into the popular dance hall for free. Hill's was a popular place of entertainment and drink.

Steve Taylor's significant experience included: 1876 D17 Billy Edwards (police interfered) and W18 Charles McDonald; and 1877 L15 John Dwyer. Some later called Taylor the ex-heavyweight champion of America. Taylor had sparred with Professor William Miller, John Dwyer, Joe Goss, and Paddy Ryan. He had helped prepare Ryan for the Goss fight. He also had sparred with Jem Mace all over the country. John L. described Taylor as a "six footer, of very powerful build, and as agile as a cat." By day, he was the Jersey City coroner.[24]

Steve Taylor

Sullivan weighed about 212 pounds, and his confident appearance "bordered on contempt." Taylor weighed around 200 pounds, but was soft and puffy, with many pounds of excess flesh.

The fighting space was about 20-feet square. They fought with hard gloves.

Taylor took a defensive position, while Sullivan "held his hands very low" and immediately attacked, delivering heavy rights and lefts in such rapid succession that "parrying them was an impossibility." "Taylor was knocked up against the wall, and there he stood

[24] *Seattle Daily Post-Intelligencer*, February 5, 1884; *Galveston Daily News*, April 10, 1884; Sullivan at 34; Cyberboxingzone.com.

taking hit after hit…without returning." With sledgehammer blows to the neck, Sullivan quickly decked Taylor onto his hands and knees. Already, the fight was a foregone conclusion. Some yelled "Foul," while others yelled, "Fair." Others called out, "Give it to him, Sullivan!"

After rising, a swinging left to the right ear knocked Taylor down to the stage again. In London rules fashion, his seconds assisted him to his feet (which was illegal, given that it was a Queensberry rules bout).

Taylor's fight had been pummeled out of him. "The severity of Sully's hitting had dazed him and caused him to forget all he knew about sparring." Sullivan turned him into a defenseless chopping block, decking him again.

Harry Hill's theater

Taylor rose and continued, but voluntarily went down twice more at the urging of his second who told him to go down, and each time after he followed the instructions, his second falsely called out a claim of foul, which the referee did not recognize. Taylor barely lasted the three minutes.

In the 2nd round, Sullivan repeatedly knocked down Taylor. Once again, at times Taylor "tried to get the verdict on a claim of foul, based on his being hit when on his knees, but, as the referee held that he went down without a blow, the claims were disallowed."

As soon as Steve rose to his feet, Sullivan rushed at him with both hands. Several blows knocked Taylor up against the stage scenery, which provided the only support to prevent him from going down. While there, Sullivan struck him multiple times. Nevertheless, a well-placed right to the head sent him down again. Taylor's second threw up his handkerchief and sponge to retire him. Taylor clearly had enough.

Some said Sullivan gave Taylor a gift of $5, while others said it was $25.

Those who criticized Sullivan said that although he was powerful, he threw mostly "round handed" blows. The *New York Herald* believed that he would not do as well with a good straight hitter, but, "As it is he is the champion." Already, some saw him as the real champion. The *New York*

Clipper opined that Sullivan was such a great puncher that even scientific men had little chance with him:

> Sullivan maintained the reputation he gained in former encounters of being a tremendously hard and punishing hitter and a quick fighter…but on the score of science he is not the equal of Taylor. … Unless a man is quick on his feet, coolheaded and possessed of good heart, the science of any man would not prevail against the batteries of so strong and earnest a fighter as Sullivan.[25]

On Monday May 16, 1881 in Yonkers, New York, just a month and a half after the Taylor fight, John L. Sullivan fought John Flood in a bout that, like the second Donaldson fight, used LPR rules with the lone exception that they wore small hard leather gloves instead of fighting with their bare hands. Sullivan engaged in the occasional LPR bout to prove himself in a "real" fight. However, he fought his LPR bouts with gloves.

Some have said that Sullivan weighed 196 pounds to Flood's 197, while others said that Sullivan had trained down to 180 or 183 pounds to Flood's 185 or 188 pounds. Fighters often reduced in weight for fights to the finish, for endurance and efficiency purposes. Flood was either 30 or 33 years old and stood 5'11 ½". Sullivan was 22 years of age.

John Flood, the Bull's Head Terror

Known as the "Bull's Head Terror," the Irish-American Flood had a local Five Points area reputation for "rough and tumble fistic engagements" without rules, which meant something, because the Five Points was known for being crime-and-gang-infested with New York's roughest toughest types. His background included bodyguard duty and forcing folks to pay their debts. Amongst vicious

[25] *New York Herald*, *New York Sun*, April 1, 1881; *National Police Gazette*, April 16, 1881; *New York Clipper*, April 9, 1881.

toughs, he was known as the toughest. His local reputation actually made him a 3 to 1 betting favorite. Right or wrong, the perception was that Flood had proven himself in real fights, whereas Sullivan primarily was a Queensberry rules boxer.

In order to escape the law, the illegal fight was held on the deck of a barge that was towed six miles up the Hudson River, just off of Yonkers. The incentive was financial. They fought for a $1,000 purse, of which the winner was to receive $750. Many Americans did not earn that much money in a year. About 400 patrons paid $10 each to enter the barge before it sailed away at 9 p.m. Torches helped light the barge deck and create the outline of a ring. Paddy Ryan was in attendance, probably scouting Sullivan. He said he would not fight for less than $5,000.

Joe Goss and Billy Madden seconded Sullivan. Barney Aaron and Dooney Harris seconded Flood. Al Smith refereed. The fight began at about 10 p.m.

1 - For about two minutes straight, they struck freely and fiercely up close with short rights and lefts, in exciting fashion, until Sullivan decked Flood. "This was the fiercest round ever seen in so short a time." In LPR fashion, they rested for 30 seconds following knockdowns and falls.

2 - While clinched, they hit rapidly with both hands "in the roughest and most unscientific manner until Flood again went down."

3 - They fought up close in give-and-take fashion for a minute, until Sullivan again decked the very game Flood.

4 - As was the fight's pattern, they fought up close in the clinches, throwing short inside blows for about 30 seconds, until as usual, Sullivan decked Flood.

5 - Flood illegally head-butted Sullivan, who then landed a swinging right to Flood's head, dropping him in a heap.

6 - In the clinch, Sullivan landed a few short blows that dropped Flood, who was bleeding from his mouth.

7 - After some inside punches were exchanged, "Flood went down completely used up."

8 - At the start of the round, Sullivan immediately decked Flood with a right to the side of the head. After the 30 seconds rest period, time was called for the fighters to approach the scratch and continue. However, Flood was not able to rise, and his corner said that he had enough and could fight no more.

The exciting and brutal fight had lasted 16 minutes.

Summarizing, the *National Police Gazette* said the first solid blow that Sullivan landed left Flood "groggy and no good from that moment." The *New York Clipper* agreed that Sullivan immediately dashed at Flood with both hands and quickly knocked him down with severe blows, "the effects of which he failed to shake off" for the rest of the fight. Sullivan had him at his mercy and administered severe punishment, while receiving little in return. Every round ended with Flood either being knocked down, fought down, or thrown down. A "jaw breaker" dropped Flood to end the 8th round, and his backer threw in the towel.

The *New York Herald* criticized both fighters, saying that neither "seemed to understand the first rudiments of the art of self-defense. It was all pull and haul and hitting at close quarters. Nothing but 'slugging' from the call of time to the end, Sullivan had the best of the fight from the start to the finish." However, the *Clipper* said of Sullivan, "What he lacks in science is fully made up by his tremendous strength and hitting power, coupled with a quickness of action not often found in big men."[26]

The *Police Gazette* drawing of the Sullivan – Flood fight failed to show the gloves.

Sullivan's reputation was spreading throughout the world. In May, the *Australian Sportsman* wrote,

> The American ring is characteristically represented by John Sullivan, who is stated to be a remarkable specimen of humanity. He is 22 years of age, stands six feet in height, and weighs 212 pounds. He has met all the heavyweight pugilists so far that dared meet him with the gloves in his native city, Boston, and made short work of them. He was recently sent for by McCormick, of the *Enquirer*, Cincinnati, to fight Donaldson. … In this battle Sullivan demonstrated that he was a clever two-handed fighter and a terrific hitter.

The *Sportsman* also said about the state of boxing,

---

[26] *New York Herald,* May 17, 1881; *New York Clipper,* May 21, 1881; *National Police Gazette,* February 18, 1882; Isenberg at 8; Sullivan at 34.

> Our English and American files furnish abundant testimony of the wholesale revival of boxing and pugilism in the two countries, the glove fighting being practically a modified form of pugilism, gloves of such thinness being used that the force of the fists is but slightly deadened. In England, however, the police authorities are unremitting in their attempts to suppress pugilistic displays, and one result of this is that the leading English pugilists are rapidly finding their way to the United States.[27]

Many of those traveling English pugilists would be future Sullivan opponents.

On Monday June 13, 1881 in New York City's Clarendon Hall, almost a month after they had fought, Sullivan and Flood engaged in a friendly 3-round exhibition that "was highly unsatisfactory to those who looked for anything but a very mild bout." Sullivan's usual pattern would be that after he had dominated a foe in a competitive match, he was willing to work more gently with him in follow-up money-making sparring exhibitions.[28]

Richard K. Fox's *National Police Gazette* admired Paddy Ryan for his willingness to demonstrate his manhood with his bare hands, under the pure, traditional rules. Fox criticized the modern boxer who wanted to fight with gloves. Naturally, this set the periodical at odds with a fighter like Sullivan, for there was an inherent tension between old-school tradition and the new rules.

> Time was when the laurels of fistiana were won by nature's weapons unadorned, backed by pluck and muscle. The modern gladiator would win them with gloves! Not so with Paddy Ryan, the present champion. He won his title from one of the gamest old warriors who ever put up his hands in the old-fashioned way, and does not propose to lose it or retain it on any other plan.

The *Police Gazette* further said that anyone who wanted to fight Ryan for $5,000 a side, in a true LPR bout, including Sullivan, simply had to show their money at the *Police Gazette* office at No. 183 William street, New York.

In its subsequent issues, the *Police Gazette* said there were positive indications that Sullivan would fight Ryan. Like Ryan, Sullivan said he would take the fight if the money was right.[29]

Paddy Ryan might have been the LPR champion, but gloved champion Sullivan was the one who was filling theaters and capturing the general public's interest and admiration. Financially, Sullivan did not need Ryan, but in order to gain full acceptance as the true champion, he needed the fight.

Sullivan followed the Flood fight with four pure Queensberry rules bouts, with most opponents attempting to win money for lasting 4 rounds.

---

27 *Australian Sportsman*, May 28, 1881.

28 *New York Clipper*, June 18, 1881.

29 *National Police Gazette*, June 25, July 2, 9, 1881.

Only one man was able to last more than a minute. Sullivan's performances were awe-inspiring.

On Monday July 11, 1881 in Philadelphia, at Arthur Chamber's Hall and Saloon, a couple months after the Flood fight, Sullivan fought English fighter Frederick Crossley, who stood 6'1" and weighed 200 pounds to Sullivan's 196 pounds. Although Sullivan had offered $25 to anyone who could last 4 Queensberry rules rounds with him, Crossley said he was willing to fight Sullivan without regard to the financial inducement. He was a true sportsman who simply wanted to test himself, and perhaps earn a reputation.

The aggressive Sullivan quickly "landed two sledge-hammer blows rapidly in succession on Crossley's head and face, and knocked him down."

The Englishman rose and fired a punch, but his blow was "warded off with the greatest ease," and Sullivan landed a stinging left smash to the nose, causing blood to flow from it. "Crossley showed the white feather at once." Crossley went to his corner and said, "Remove my gloves. I've had enough." However, they persuaded him to continue, and he did.

Sullivan pressed the taller Crossley to the ropes and delivered his "powerful shoulder blows," causing the discomfited and bloody Crossley once again to retire, acknowledging that "he was no match for his scientific opponent." The bout had lasted only one minute.

The disappointed crowd howled at how quickly Crossley had quit in the 1st round.

To give the spectators some further entertainment, Sullivan sparred lightly with trainer/manager Billy Madden, a former lightweight fighter.[30]

For the next week, Sullivan and Madden remained in Philadelphia and sparred with each other each night, giving exhibitions at John Clark's Olympic Boxing Academy.[31]

BILLY MADDEN.

On Thursday July 21, 1881, still in Philadelphia, in the Olympic Theatre, just ten days after the Crossley bout, John L.

[30] *Philadelphia Press, Philadelphia Record,* July 12, 1881; *New York Clipper,* July 16, 1881.
[31] *New York Clipper,* July 30, 1881.

Sullivan fought either Dan McCarthy (or McCarty) or John Buckley. The local press disagreed as to who he was. The *Philadelphia Record* said Baltimore's Dan McCarthy stood 5'9" and weighed 175 pounds. The *Philadelphia Press* said blacksmith John Buckley was the only one to accept Sullivan's offer of $50 to anyone who could last 4 rounds of sparring with him. The 5'11 ½" Sullivan weighed about 190 pounds.

The *Philadelphia Press* version of the bout said that after about four seconds, Sullivan landed a left fired from the shoulder and "Buckley dropped like a lump of lead on the floor. He fell all in a heap and instantly gave a convulsive shudder and stretched himself out like a dead man."

The *Philadelphia Record* version said Sullivan immediately drove McCarty back and dropped him with a left to the face. As soon as he rose, Sullivan decked him again with a tremendous right to the neck. McCarty was out cold. The combat had lasted just 40 seconds.

There was some nervous concern, because Buckley/McCarty did not wake up for quite a while. "For a few minutes there were grave doubts about resuscitating the defeated pugilist." They feared he might die. He was unconscious for several minutes, despite the application of restoratives. After being taken to the dressing room, finally he regained consciousness. "This incident brought the exhibition to a close, as no one else had courage enough to stand up before the pugilist from the Hub."

One greatly impressed observer said, "Well, I have seen all from Hyer down to the present day, but none could have beaten that young fellow Sullivan."

When word spread about Sullivan's opponent being knocked unconscious for quite some time, no one in Philadelphia wanted to step into the ring with him, regardless of the financial inducement. Sullivan's local offer increased to $100 to anyone who could last 4 rounds, but no one accepted, despite the additional incentive.

Whenever no one could be found willing to fight him, Sullivan often sparred in a friendly fashion with one or more regular sparring partners before paying audiences. This way he still could make money, train and improve his skill, and give audiences a chance to see him in action. During the next week in Philadelphia, Sullivan sparred Billy Madden nightly.[32]

On Saturday August 13, 1881 at Chicago's McCormick Hall, three weeks after the Buckley/McCarthy fight, Sullivan fought Captain James Dalton, the captain of a Lake Michigan tugboat called the *Ingram*. Dalton was about the same height as Sullivan, and weighed 175 pounds to Sullivan's 190 pounds. Dalton had fought "some of the crack ring men of the country." He held a victory over former Sullivan foe Professor John Donaldson, as well as John Dwyer and Tommy Chandler. Dalton also had sparred with

---

32 *Daily Arkansas Gazette* (Little Rock), April 29, 1884; *Philadelphia Record, Philadelphia Press*, July 22, 1881; *New York Clipper*, July 30, 1881; *National Police Gazette*, August 13, 1881; Isenberg at 98 – 100; Sullivan at 38.

Paddy Ryan and held his own. Known for his skill, Dalton was called the best man in the west. He was attempting to earn $50 for lasting 4 rounds.

It was the first boxing exhibition held in Chicago in two years, and at least 3,000 people were in attendance. After some preliminary bouts, the crowd began shouting, "Sullivan! Sullivan! Sullivan!" Eventually, Sullivan and Dalton appeared.

CAPTAIN JAMES H. DALTON,

THE CELEBRATED PUGILIST, WHO HAS WON HONORS FROM SOME OF THE BEST OF THEM.

1 - The fighters began cautiously, each sizing up the other. After about 30 seconds, Dalton landed a right and eluded a counter left. Throughout the round, in between clinches, they exchanged lively blows.

2 - Dalton forced matters and occasionally landed "a blow that would have knocked down an ordinary man, but which did not appear to effect Sullivan in the least." Whenever Sullivan tried to advance and fire, Dalton would rush in and clinch, doing so five times. He was very clever.

3 - Sullivan began forcing the pace. He appeared to have figured out Dalton's tactics. After two minutes, Sullivan's right to the temple knocked the captain to the ground "as though struck with a trip-hammer." Dalton struggled to rise, but did, and he survived by holding on to Sullivan. He even managed to throw Sullivan down in London rules fashion. Regardless, Dalton appeared to be very groggy and dazed.

4 - Sullivan dominated and quickly knocked out Dalton within the first minute of the round.

The *Chicago Tribune* and *Chicago Herald* summarized that Dalton did very well for the first 2 rounds, landing some good hard stiff punches, but Sullivan did not seem to mind. In the 3rd round, Sullivan "smashed him viciously a few times," and terribly pounded upon Dalton. In the 4th round, Sullivan "knocked him so stiff" that Dalton could not beat the ten-count.

Sullivan gave Dalton the $50 anyway, because he considered him to be the best man that he had ever met. The crowd applauded his generosity.

The Chicago writers were impressed. "Sullivan proved that he is capable of tackling the best in the ring. He stated that he is ready to meet any man in the ring, either in this country or England."

The *Chicago Times* said, "A good many people in Chicago were inclined to think him too much a talker; but he showed on last evening an extraordinary talent for hard hitting, as well."[33]

Sullivan would become known for engaging in occasional extra-curricular activity outside the ring as well. One evening, while in Mt. Clements, Michigan, a summer resort about 20 miles from Detroit, a bully tried to jostle him off a sidewalk. Sullivan asked, "What do you mean by doing that?" The bully used several vile epithets and said, "I will show you." He attempted to strike Sullivan, who was forced to put the man to sleep. The next day, a local druggist named Crane tried to give Sullivan a $250 present for teaching the bully a lesson, for he had been abusing everyone in town, but Sullivan refused to accept the money.[34]

On Saturday September 3, 1881, once again in Chicago's McCormick Hall, less than a month after the Dalton bout, Sullivan fought 29-year-old 6'3" 215-pound Canadian-born Englishman (now hailing from Michigan) Jack Burns (also called Byrne or Byrnes). Apparently, the "Michigan Giant" Burns had fought a number of LPR prize-fights. He was attempting to win $50 for lasting 4 rounds. At least 2,000 people were present in the hall.

Despite Burns' superior size and reputation, Sullivan lost no time, quickly decking Burns with a right to the jaw within the first 15 to 20 seconds. He went sprawling near the foot-lights. Burns rose from the stage and dashed forward with his head down, perhaps in an attempt to clinch and wrestle, but Sullivan immediately blasted him with a ferocious right uppercut to the jaw that lifted him off the stage and sent him into the audience. The local *Daily Inter Ocean* said "he was knocked a distance of twenty feet, going over the stage into the audience."

With the spectators' assistance, Burns climbed back up onto the stage, but his legs were unsteady. Sullivan attacked him with a hurricane half-dozen blows. Burns raised and waived his arms around in the air attempting to defend and block the punches, but it was futile, and he went down and out. "The audience was frantic with delight, the more so because the affair was something of a surprise." No one had expected big Burns to be knocked out so quickly in the very 1st round. However, Sullivan had the speed and power to knock out large men very quickly too.

---

33 *Chicago Times, Chicago Tribune,* August 14, 1881; *Chicago Herald,* August 13, 15, 1881; *Chicago Daily News*, August 13, 1881; *National Police Gazette*, September 3, 1881, November 12, 1881;
34 Sullivan at 39.

The *Chicago Tribune* and *Chicago Times* said the fight was over in less than a minute. The *Chicago Herald* said that Sullivan "pounded Burns with sledge-hammer effect," scoring three knockdowns in two minutes. Burns had been "completely demoralized."

The dazed Burns required half an hour "again to get fairly acquainted with himself," and even then he was so groggy that he did not quite know where he was. Attempting to last 4 rounds with Sullivan could be dangerous to one's health.

POLICE GAZETTE'S GALLERY OF FAMOUS SPORTING-MEN.
CAPT. JAMES DALTON.

Because of the bout's short duration, in order to provide the spectators with more entertainment, Sullivan's opponent from the previous month, Captain James Dalton, sparred Sullivan in a friendly 4-round sparring match that "demonstrated that Sullivan is as scientific as he is powerful."[35]

Sullivan next headed to Kansas City, sparring with Billy Madden, before heading back to New York.[36]

Sullivan had impressed enough folks with his performances such that wealthy financiers, including Charles "Parson" Davies and Mike McDonald, wanted to back him financially in a championship fight against Paddy Ryan. Discussions were ongoing.

On July 2, 1881, Charles Guiteau had shot U.S. President James A. Garfield in the back. Garfield subsequently died on September 19, and the next day, on September 20, 1881, Chester A. Arthur was sworn in as president. Intrigued by criminal celebrities, Sullivan visited Guiteau while he was in jail awaiting trial.

---

[35] *Chicago Tribune, Chicago Times,* September 4, 1881; *Chicago Herald, Daily Inter Ocean, Boston Daily Globe,* September 5, 1881.
[36] *National Police Gazette,* October 1, 1881.

Bareknuckle Champion

John L. Sullivan and Paddy Ryan had been building towards the era's version of a unification match. Ryan was the established traditional LPR bareknuckle champion. Sullivan was the popular gloved champion. It was old school vs. new school. The traditional fight purists would not recognize Sullivan as the true champion and world's best fighter unless and until he defeated Ryan in a pure LPR fight. Sullivan's reputation had been built up sufficiently over the past year such that large enough financial incentives and backing could be provided to induce Ryan to defend his crown against him, and for Sullivan to accept the fight as well.

RICHARD K. FOX.
Editor and Proprietor of the "Police Gazette" and "Fox's Illustrated Weekly."

Richard K. Fox, publisher of the very successful *National Police Gazette*, a weekly magazine which heavily promoted and discussed boxing in every issue, helped financially back, promote, and build the championship fight. Fox billed Ryan as the true champion after he defeated Joe Goss in an LPR fight back in June 1880 (87 rounds, 1 hour 27 minutes). 50-year-old former bareknuckle champion Jem Mace was retired and inactive for several years, so Fox had a good argument that Ryan was now the champion.

In Ryan's victory over the very experienced, tough, and tricky Goss, he proved to be "a game man and a hard hitter, and one of the best fighters and wrestlers of his time." The *Police Gazette* backed him owing to his "pluck, science, and stamina," and because he "proved he was a clever wrestler and an expert boxer." Ryan also had engaged in a number of sparring exhibitions, including some against Steve Taylor, Mike Donovan, William Miller, Joe Goss, Charlie McDonald, and Captain James Dalton, amongst others.

Although there had been challenges, discussions, meetings, and wrangling regarding the terms of a potential fight between them, on October 5, 1881, Billy Madden met with *Police Gazette* editor William E. Harding at the *Gazette's* New York office to iron out the details of a

Sullivan-Ryan fight. They agreed to an LPR fight for a wager of $2,500 a side, the fight to take place on February 7, 1882, to be held within 100 miles of New Orleans. The parties agreed to deposit a $500 performance guarantee immediately with Harry Hill, the final stakeholder. A second deposit of $1,000 was required in November, and the third deposit of a like amount by December. The big fight was on.[37]

Arranging the championship fight further stimulated public interest in the combatants' exhibitions, which made them more money. Sullivan sparred and exhibited with men such as Billy Madden, middleweight Pete McCoy, and lightweight Bob Farrell. Sparring exhibitions helped build further interest in the fight and allowed gamblers to assess the two men.

John L. Sullivan
Of Boston, Mass., the Famous "Strong Boy," Ryan's Antagonist in the Championship Fight

During October 1881 at a benefit at the New York Aquarium, no one accepted Sullivan's offer of $50 to anyone who could last 4 rounds with him. Instead, a crowd of 2,000 watched him spar former opponent Steve Taylor in tame and friendly fashion.

The disappointed crowd wanted more, and they responded with three cheers for Paddy Ryan. Usually Sullivan held back in these friendlier sparring exhibitions. He only showed his full power against those who attempted to last 4 rounds against him. An annoyed Sullivan addressed the crowd, offering any man in the house $250 to stand before him, but there were no takers. His next exhibition was scheduled for Philadelphia.[38]

On November 5 in New York, Sullivan sparred Billy Madden.[39]

---

[37] *National Police Gazette*, October 22, 29, 1881.

[38] *National Police Gazette,* October 29, 1881.

[39] *New York Clipper,* November 12, 1881. Sullivan was scheduled to travel to Boston, but would return to New York to spar Pete McCoy in Buffalo on November 16.

On November 28, 1881, a Cincinnati, Ohio audience paid to see Sullivan spar Pete McCoy and then Billy Madden, back to back, in a clever but tame fashion.

The local writer called Sullivan the heavyweight champion, and complimented his progress as a scientific fighter. "Since Sullivan was here in December last his improvement has been something wonderful." He always had done terrific work in round-arm hitting, but experts believed that round-house blows were a waste of time and force. Trainer Billy Madden had helped Sullivan correct his amateur habits. He had become a "skilled man in straight hitting." "He has acquired a great deal of 'science,' and he already had an almost unlimited quantity of strength and stay."[40]

All of Sullivan's 1880 and 1881 bouts had been fought with gloves, and except for the Donaldson and Flood fights, which were fought under the LPR rules (but with gloves), all other Sullivan bouts had been fought under the gloved Queensberry rules that we are familiar with today. He soon would be preparing for his first bareknuckle LPR contest.

In December 1881, Sullivan started formal training for the Paddy Ryan prizefight under coaches/sparring partners Billy Madden, Pete McCoy, and Joe Goss. At first, he trained in Bay St. Louis, Mississippi, 50 miles east of New Orleans, but later transferred his training quarters to New Orleans. Ryan trained at the Barnes Hotel in Mississippi City, Mississippi, but he too transferred venue and trained in New Orleans for a period of time as well. There was a reason for the moves. The exact fight location had to be a well-kept secret, given the contest's illegality. Even if there was no legal prohibition, politicians often would use their police power to prevent such fights from occurring. Hence, the fight camps had to keep folks guessing as to where the fight would take place.

Louisiana Governor Samuel McEnery told the fight organizers that the contest would not be allowed to take place in his state. Mississippi Governor Robert Lowry said the same. Both Louisiana and Mississippi had introduced bills in their state legislatures making prizefighting a felony, not just a common-law misdemeanor.

Ryan's training consisted of running 10 miles, rowing for 45 minutes, sparring for 30 minutes, shadow-boxing with 2.5-pound dumbbells, and walking.

In his training, Sullivan ran 100-yard sprints in 11 - 11.5 seconds. In the morning, he would take long walks. In the afternoon, he would run, and then strike a ball attached to a rope "with machine-like regularity."

As with most big fights, the press and public debated the fighters' relative merits and offered opinions on the likely result. New York wagering favored Ryan, while Sullivan was the Chicago favorite. Those who had seen Ryan spar recently said that he had "wonderfully improved in the use of his

---

[40] *Cincinnati Commercial,* November 28, 29, 1881. In December 1881, Sullivan sparred either Madden or McCoy in Cleveland, Chicago, and then New Orleans.

hands, and may now be called a clever man." Another said, "I consider Ryan a wonderful man. I saw him when he fought Goss, and his abilities as a wrestler and in fighting are immense. I don't know why I think so, but I am inclined to believe that if Sullivan gets a hot-facer he will have a fit of the sulks." A New Yorker said, "Ryan will fight cautiously from the start, and will not allow Sullivan to hit him. He is longer in the reach and can fight him at long range for a time. This will break Sullivan up, and then, when he loses his temper and rushes in, Ryan will cross him and get the best of it."

PADDY RYAN,

OF TROY, N. Y., BACKED BY THE "POLICE GAZETTE" OF NEW YORK, IN THE GREAT PRIZE FIGHT.

Purists liked the fact that Ryan was a proven commodity in a lengthy war of attrition with bare knuckles and legalized wrestling under LPR rules, the kind of fight they would be fighting. Sullivan was perceived as a limited rounds Queensberry rules gloved fighter, and many did not see that format as necessarily translating well when it came to a "real" LPR fight, which often required great endurance, something gamblers were not sure that Sullivan could demonstrate with his explosive style. They also wondered how Sullivan's bare hands and hard punching style would endure without the protection of gloves, and when it came to wrestling and holding and hitting. Of course, they overlooked the fact that Sullivan had defeated Flood and Donaldson using LPR rules, though with hard gloves, and had, very early in his career, in a lesser-known or perhaps unknown fight, defeated Jack Curley in a bout that lasted over an hour. Also, Sullivan had Goss groggy and out much more quickly than had Ryan, though of course it was with a totally different rule-set and not the same financial incentives. With 30 seconds of rest between falls, bare knuckles, with wrestling, and with big money on the line, a Goss contest could have had a different result, or so they thought.

Sullivan's supporters were supremely confident in his talents, feeling that he was a sure thing:

> Sullivan will down Ryan as sure as you live. I have seen a good many fighters, and I give you my word that I have never seen a man that I considered his equal. I saw him when he knocked Dalton out in Chicago, and his blows are like those struck with a sledge-hammer. He is a terrible hitter, and I believe he will stand to the scratch just as long as the other man will.

Another opined that Sullivan "is a tremendous hitter and the most perfectly built man that I ever saw. I regard him as a wonder and think that he will out fight Ryan from the start."

Joe Goss, who had fought both, was helping to train Sullivan. When asked what he thought of Ryan after seeing him in an exhibition on January 31, Goss said, "He looked very well, I thought, and has improved wonderfully in his sparring, but my man will lick him sure."

PETE M'COY, JOHN L. SULLIVAN AND JOE GOSS AT THEIR TRAINING QUARTERS BEFORE SULLIVAN'S FIGHT WITH PADDY RYAN AT NEW ORLEANS. SULLIVAN AT THIS TIME WAS IN THE PRIME OF HIS CAREER AND A PERFECT ATHLETE IN BUILD.

Although most of the general public supported Sullivan, most of the leading veteran sporting men were betting on Ryan, the slight favorite. Gamblers were wagering hundreds of thousands of dollars.[41]

On February 2, 1882 in New Orleans, five days before the fight, in front of an audience of 800 people, the "Boston Wonder" Sullivan sparred 3 rounds with Joe Goss. According to the local *Daily Picayune*, Sullivan had lost a lot of weight since starting his training, and against Goss, John L. appeared "quick and graceful and did not exert himself, getting in his blows

[41] *Times-Democrat* (New Orleans), February 2, 4, 6, 1882; *New York Herald*, February 8, 1882.

and warding off those of his adversary with ease. Goss showed that he had lost none of that science for which he has so long been justly celebrated."[42]

However, the local *Times-Democrat* was not as impressed, feeling that Goss was his superior.

> The Boston Boy's habit of ducking his head and shutting his eyes was very unfavorably commented upon by the sports present, and many stated that compared with Ryan, the Troy man is the better sparer of the two, being cooler in his judgment, quicker with both hands and fully as agile as his opponent. The friends of Sullivan were rather disappointed at the showing that he made and admitted that while he was a harder hitter than Ryan, yet the latter was the more scientific man of the two.[43]

A sportsman said that if Sullivan turned his head when striking at Ryan as he did with Goss, he would be in trouble. "People say that Sullivan is a wonder, but I can't see it."

Of course, they overlooked the fact that Sullivan was holding back on his trainer, and once before had blown through Goss. Skeptics might suspect that he was trying to look bad, so that he and his backers could shift the odds further and make even more money with better odds. Or, given the divergence of opinion regarding Sullivan's performance, perhaps the reporter was trying to shift the odds.

When asked if he felt any fear or nervousness, Sullivan replied, "No, sir; not a bit. There ain't a man in the world that I am the least bit afraid of, nor one that I wouldn't fight."

Ryan also was confident. One observer of his training said, "I think I shall have to walk home if Ryan is whipped, but I know he won't be. I have just seen him, and he is as quiet and confident as a man can be. Nothing worries him, and it would take tonight a man with a club to beat him. Put that in your diary."

Although the fighters were stationed in New Orleans, Louisiana, there was some suspicion that the fight might take place in a nearby southern state. Mississippi Governor Robert Lowry ordered the sheriffs of all counties to prevent the fight. Yet, technically, the anti-prizefighting bill had not yet passed through the Mississippi legislature.[44]

---

[42] *Daily Picayune* (New Orleans), February 3, 1882, February 8, 1882.

[43] *Times-Democrat* (New Orleans), February 3, 1882.

[44] *Times-Democrat* (New Orleans), February 4, 7, 1882.

Regardless of Governor Lowry's edict, the fight took place in Mississippi. A special train took the principals and spectators to Mississippi City, about 100 miles north of New Orleans. Over 2,000 patrons paid $10 for a special railroad ticket to the fight location, which reflected the cost of the train fare and a view of a fight. The railroad would take a cut, and the rest of the $20,000 would be apportioned amongst the backers and fighters. They left New Orleans at 5 a.m. on February 7.

On Tuesday February 7, 1882, the bareknuckle LPR Sullivan-Ryan championship fight took place in front of the Barnes Hotel in Mississippi City. Allegedly, the local sheriff had business in Biloxi that day. Some suspected that he might have been bribed, or simply decided to look the other way. Boxing was good for the local economy. Folks paid for food and beer, and even admission to watch the fight from nearby rooftops and the hotel's galleries.

At 11 a.m., the required 24-foot ring was pitched in the ground. It contained eight wooden posts or stakes – one in each corner, and one at the center/mid-point of each side. Two ropes surrounded the ring, as required for LPR fights. They fought on the turf.

The spectators were all eager to wager. Shouts of offers to bet at even money or 100 to 80 on Sullivan were accepted quickly.

The outdoor hotel galleries were so crowded that there was danger of their falling all at once. The branches of the low-spreading oaks were covered with men who had failed to secure good spots inside the hotel or around the ring.

At 11:45 a.m., Sullivan appeared. The audience greeted him with great applause and cheers. He threw his cap into the middle of the ring, a fight tradition. He was attended by Madden, Goss, and Arthur Chambers.

Ryan also received hearty applause upon his entrance. He was attended by Tom Kelly and Johnny Roche or Roach.

Sullivan was 23 years of age and weighed 178-182 pounds, while the 6'2 ½" 29-year-old "Trojan Giant" Ryan weighed 190-195 pounds. There were no official weigh-ins for heavyweight bouts back then, so most weights given out either were estimates or self-reports. Both men were much smaller than usual, as a result of the intense endurance training necessary for a fight to the finish. Sullivan usually weighed around 200 pounds, while Ryan usually weighed around 220 pounds.

Paddy Ryan

Ryan wore white pants, while Sullivan wore green pants. They both wore stockings and spiked shoes. Sullivan's white-silk handkerchief had a green border with Irish and American flags at the corners (one source claimed there was a Confederate flag). He also wore a white kid plaster protector, which concealed the small of his back and loins.

Although contractually they were fighting for a wager of $2,500 per side, just before the fight, confident Ryan backer Richard K. Fox, owner of the *National Police Gazette*, wired an offer of an additional $1,000 side-wager, a bet that Sullivan's backers immediately accepted.

Paddy won the toss of the coin for corner selection, and he took the corner with the sun to his back, which meant that the sun would be in Sullivan's face.

It took quite a while for them to agree upon a referee. Several were discussed and rejected. Some of those who were agreed upon declined the position. Finally, they agreed that two men would referee jointly - Alexander Brewster of New Orleans and Jack Hardy of Vicksburg.

In front of over 2,000 spectators, the bareknuckle fight began at 1 p.m.

1 - Ryan held his guard low, and from the start was defensive, wary of Sullivan's right. "Sullivan's guard was good, and his left hand was in constant motion as he moved around his adversary." They sparred. Ryan missed a hard right that fell short, and Sullivan countered him with a left on the mouth and nose that started a little bit of "claret" flowing. Sullivan then quickly landed a right that hurt, and Paddy closed in. Up close, Sullivan landed several more rights. Before Ryan could recover, Sullivan "swung his right like a sledge-hammer, catching Ryan under the ear and knocking him down." The round had lasted less than a minute. One said it had been only 30 seconds. Paddy rose and walked to his corner. After the 30 seconds of rest, time was called, and they had 8 seconds to resume fighting again.

Notice that the fighters were drawn into the photo subsequently to overcome blur.

2 - Blood slightly trickled from Ryan's nose and mouth. Sullivan forced the fighting and landed a couple of blows before Ryan countered, closed in and used his wrestling skills. They hit each other in close, but Ryan's blows lacked steam. After wrestling fairly evenly, with a great deal of effort Paddy managed to whirl John around and trip him, falling heavily on top of Sullivan, who landed on his back.

The cornermen rushed to their fighters, picked them up, and took them back to their corners, all of which was legal under LPR rules. The round only lasted about 25 seconds, and although Ryan threw and fell heavily on Sullivan, "the fatigue that the effort cost him seemed greatly to impair his strength."

3 - Ryan was cautious and moved around. Sullivan made a few lightning attacks, rushing towards him. Both feinted several times, until Sullivan landed a right to the mouth, causing Paddy to stagger and fall heavily on his back. The blow to the mouth had drawn more blood. A claim of first blood was made and granted. This was a typical betting point. Like the prior rounds, this round was quite short as well.

4 - Ryan was bleeding from his mouth and a cut on his nose. He was alert and wary, but "it appeared impossible for him to win, Sullivan's tremendous battering powers being more than Ryan could stand." Sullivan landed a right to the head but was countered with a blow to the neck. Ryan attempted counters, but Sullivan's blows were far more frequent. After some sharp infighting, Ryan retreated. Sullivan followed him about the ring, punching all the time. He landed body shots until Ryan clinched. "Ryan tried to back-

heel Sullivan, when the latter forced him to the ropes and both fell, Ryan being the most damaged by the fall." The round only lasted about 30 seconds.

THE BATTLE OF THE GIANTS.

Meeting of the *Police Gazette* Champion, Paddy Ryan, and John L. Sullivan, of Boston, in the Great Contest for the Heavyweight Championship of the World and Five Thousand Dollars Stakes

5 - Sullivan again forced and followed Ryan around the ring, firing punches all the time. Ryan fought back desperately. His neck was swelling and the blood was flying from his mouth. Ryan landed a couple of rights and clinched, and in the wresting that followed, Sullivan back-heeled and threw Paddy heavily. However, Sullivan also went down and landed on his own back as well.

The local *Times-Democrat* said that Ryan "was suffering terribly from the blows that no pugilist in the word but Sullivan can deliver, while it was plain to be seen he was gradually failing. Sullivan, on the other hand, was just as fresh as when he commenced the battle about six minutes before."

6 - Ryan bled profusely from his mouth and nose. The men feinted and exchanged blows. While in close, Ryan landed a nice uppercut. However, Sullivan did not flinch, but responded with the same blow in kind, with telling effect. Ryan staggered, and before he could recover, Sullivan rushed in, striking away with both hands, beating the wobbly Ryan down to the ground. The round lasted a little over 30 seconds.

7 - Sullivan forced the fighting, yet avoided Ryan's blows. John L. landed his punches in rapid succession. Eventually, Paddy landed a solid right, "which made Sullivan put down his hands for a moment and look at Ryan in a bewildered way." Sullivan resumed his attack and once again knocked him about with lefts and rights until Ryan clinched. Sullivan easily threw Paddy down. One said Ryan was "a wreck."

8 - Rapid blows were exchanged. Sullivan showed no fear. Ryan could not resist Sully's volley, being sent back to the ropes and almost over them.

Ryan closed in to a clinch and struggled for several seconds until he went down to one knee.

Sullivan released him, and they were about to return to their corners, but their seconds urged them to continue, which they did. John L. punished him until they clinched again. They struggled, until Sullivan threw him down to the turf, although because Ryan did not let go of him, they both went down together.

9 - Ryan struggled to rise and make it to the scratch on time to start the round. He closed in to clinch a couple times, but each time, Sullivan pushed him off. Sullivan pounded away. A heavy right to Ryan's chest made a sound so loud that it could be heard all over. Sullivan followed-up, administering a combination of blows as Ryan staggered back. Several rights to the jaw and temple knocked him around the ring, without being able to fire a return. Eventually Sullivan landed a final devastating left to the neck that sent Ryan down to the ground in a heap. Others said it was a right under the ear that did the trick. He was almost totally senseless.

His seconds carried Ryan to his corner. He was in poor condition. When time was called for the men to come to the scratch to start the 10th round, Sullivan walked to ring center, but Ryan had failed to regain consciousness sufficiently in order to rise. His second threw up the sponge, signifying acknowledgement of defeat.

The 9-round fight had lasted 10 ½ or 11 minutes. The *New York Herald* said the actual fighting time, excluding the rests, was about 6 minutes.

Ryan had to be carried to his quarters. A physician was called upon to attend to him.

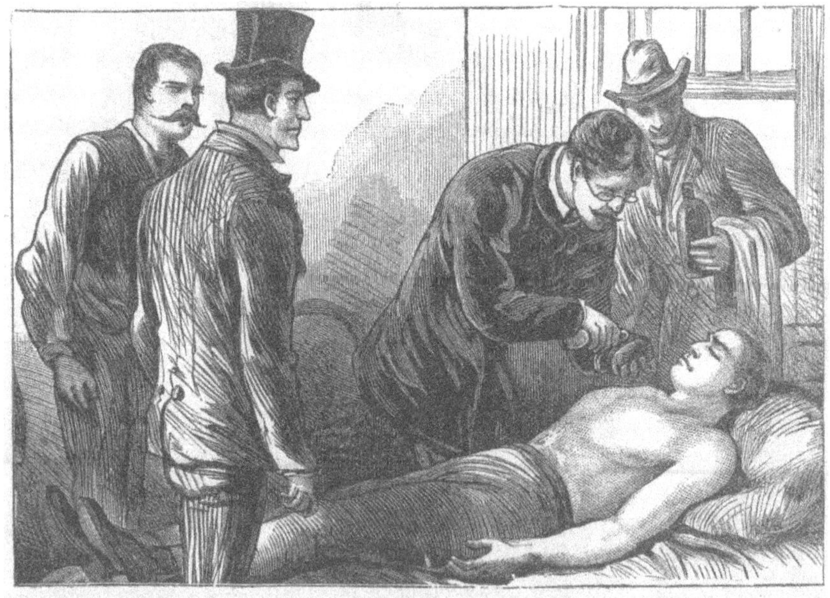

RYAN AFTER THE FIGHT.

The New Orleans-based *Daily Picayune* and *Times-Democrat* had reporters at the fight. According to the *Picayune*, from the start, Sullivan was fierce and aggressive, rushing in, delivering rapid combinations and following up with clinching or fighting inside. Sullivan knew no retreat, and rarely feinted, but instead tried to crush his opponent as quickly as possible, leaving Ryan no time to respond. From the start, Sullivan's hammering powers were too much. Paddy never did recover from Sullivan's ferocious rights.

The *Times-Democrat* said it was the greatest fistic battle of the past 20 years. Sullivan had been very impressive:

> It was short, sharp, and decisive. … [I]t is generally conceded that the Boston Boy is a wonder. His hitting powers are terrific, and against his sledge-hammer fists the naked arms of a man are but poor defense. He forced the fighting from the start and knocked his opponent about as though he were a football, receiving himself but little punishment in return. Ryan was dazed after the first round. … Nothing but his gameness kept him in the ring from that time on. …
>
> [Sullivan's] style of fighting differed from that of any pugilist that has entered the ring of late years. … He is a rusher, and it is this quality and his tremendous hitting powers that really make him a great pugilist. Beside, he is a skillful wrestler and a good in-fighter, quick to dodge and always on the alert for any opening that an opponent may leave.

The *Daily Picayune* said Ryan had gashed lips, a cut across the nose, and a large swelling on the left side of his neck. The *Times Democrat* added that Ryan had suffered a slight cut near the left eye and had contusions on his chest. The *New York Herald* claimed that Paddy's jaw had been broken in two places. Sullivan only had a slight swelling above his left eye.

The *New York Times* reported that Sullivan exhibited "remarkable skill as a two-handed fighter," attacking with ferocity from the start, and following his attack with clinching and wrestling, as allowed by the bareknuckle LPR rules. It was an easy victory. Each round only lasted between 4 and 30 seconds, most being only about 20 seconds long.

The *New York Herald* said that it was evident from the start that Sullivan was superior. Ryan's blows "appeared weak for a man of his great size. It was clear that the first blow he got in the neck dazed him." As a result, Ryan mostly resorted to wrestling tactics. However, Sullivan was too fast and Ryan quickly weakened.[45]

When he recovered, Ryan admitted that Sullivan had defeated him fairly. He had great respect for Sullivan. Paddy said,

---

[45] *Daily Picayune*; *Times-Democrat*; *New York Herald*; *New York Times*; *Boston Herald*; *Boston Daily Globe*, *New York World*, all February 8, 1882; *National Police Gazette*, March 11, 1882.

> I never faced a man who could begin to hit as hard, and I don't believe there is another man like him in the country. One thing is certain, any man that Sullivan can hit he can whip. … Some people have got very wild notions concerning Sullivan. I have heard it said dozens of times that he can't box. It is true that he is not what could be fairly called a brilliant boxer, but on the whole he spars about as well as the general run of pugilists. … He is a wonderful man, physically, and seems to have been built for a fighter, and he can hit hard enough to break down any man's guard that I know of.

JOHN L. SULLIVAN, CHAMPION OF THE WORLD.

Sullivan said, "I believe in giving every man his just due. Ryan is a game man but I was sure of downing him from the start. When the first round was over I knew I had him. … I had perfect confidence that I could win." The new champion said he was not injured at all.[46]

Boxing experts were very impressed. John Walsh said, "I think that Ryan is lucky to have escaped with his life. That boy from Boston is liable to kill a man with a blow." Another observer said, "I have seen all the big fighters in the ring, not alone in this country, but also in England, but never in my life saw such a hitter as Sullivan. So far as science is concerned, he has improved wonderfully in the past year." Yet another said, "I have seen Tom Hyer in his best days, Morrissey and others in the ring; all, as you know, were good ones, but I am satisfied that Sullivan could lick any of them." Although science was not Sullivan's strongest point, it did not matter. He rushed in and forced the fight, and all he needed was to land once, and his opponent would never again be the same. "The result of this fight must undoubtedly give Sullivan the highest place as the hardest hitter that is now to be found upon the American continent."[47]

---

[46] *National Police Gazette*, February 25, 1882.
[47] *Boston Daily Globe*, February 9, 1882; *New York Herald*, February 8, 1882.

As would be a theme in boxing's history, despite the accolades about Sullivan and the fight, some criticized prizefighting, saying that it was "nothing more or less than an exhibition of brute force in its most repellant form. … If the encounter yesterday is a sample of the latter-day prize fight, then the sooner the prize ring is abolished and the whole race of modern prize fighters swept out of existence the better."[48]

In his autobiography, Sullivan quoted a subsequent *Times-Democrat* report as saying,

> It is amusing to observe the style in which the newspapers now speak of the Sullivan - Ryan fight. They describe it contemptuously as a mere brutal hammering of Ryan by Sullivan. … [O]ne would suppose that Ryan was a helpless, old imbecile who had been inhumanly beaten by a cruel and callous giant. The fact is, however, that previous to the battle, nine tenths of the sporting men in the country looked upon Sullivan's pretensions with open derision. He was alluded to as a green and gawky boy, a chap who had never fought without gloves and who would give up at the first good blow. Ryan was lauded as a Hercules and a hero; a man who could endure any amount of punishment; who was a magnificent boxer and invincible wrestler, - in a word, a winner. … Experienced sports…bet their money on Ryan. … You must have thought the backers of Sullivan the most besotted fools upon the globe. …
>
> Sullivan won the fight by virtue of superior science and irresistible strength. … He cared nothing for Ryan's blows, and his own hitting is so tremendous that it seems beyond the power of man to recover from the shock of one of his hands let out from the shoulder.

Sullivan said that after the victory, "I was treated like a lord in New Orleans."[49]

Bostonians celebrated the news wildly, but no one celebrated the victory more than the Irish. Sullivan was one of their own, and he was the world's best fighter. He instantly had become an Irish-American hero and idol.

At this point, most Americans granted Sullivan recognition as the world champion, for the *National Police Gazette* had promoted Ryan as the world champion, although sometimes it also called him the American champion. After the fight, it called Sullivan the champion of the world. However, the *New York Times* and others billed the fight as being for the American championship. Regardless, if someone disagreed with the world championship claim, they certainly were welcome to challenge Sullivan, who seemed to love to fight. He clearly was the best fighter in the world.[50]

---

[48] *Times-Democrat*, February 8, 1882.

[49] Sullivan at 64 – 65, 71.

[50] *Times-Democrat* (New Orleans), *Boston Daily Globe*, February 2, 1882; *Daily Picayune*, *Daily Democrat* (Natchez), *New York Herald*, February 8, 1882; *National Police Gazette*, October 29, 1881, November 5, 1881; February 18, 1882; March 18, 1882.

Fox had lost thousands in wagers, but he made up for it many times over with magazine sales. In the wake of the fight, the *National Police Gazette*, with its extensive coverage of the contest, sold twice as many issues as usual - over 300,000 copies. Hence, the investment in boxing, and the hype surrounding the fight, had paid off. It was a marketing lesson that did not go unnoticed.

An upset Mississippi Governor Robert Lowry eventually would foster the passage of the Mississippi anti-prize-fight law. Seven years later, he would attempt to get his revenge on Sullivan.

A joyous and now wealthier Sullivan paid off the mortgage on his parents' house. During his career, he would help support them financially, and even purchased his parents a second house in Boston in 1885.

Championship Power

After defeating Paddy Ryan in a bareknuckle LPR fight in early February 1882, John L. Sullivan would not fight with his bare fists again for six years. Hence, in truth, he was more of a first gloved champion than anything. He simply fought a bareknuckle LPR title fight in order to legitimize and justify his championship claims, to gain acceptance and recognition as a true champion. Having proven himself a under the traditional format, he now had the power to dictate how future matches would be fought.

Sullivan preferred the Queensberry rules, saying, "They said that I was only a glove-fighter, and that I was afraid of the bare knuckles. For that reason I consented to fight Ryan as I did. I think I have proved that I can fight with my knuckles, and now anyone who wants to tackle me will have to do it my fashion."[51]

Sullivan would fight at least eight times in 1882.

After the Ryan fight, Sullivan, Madden, Goss, McCoy, and Bob Farrell exhibited in Chicago, Detroit, Cleveland, Cincinnati, Columbus, Pittsburgh, and Philadelphia. Sullivan's popularity had skyrocketed. He was lionized everywhere. Bostonians and the Irish saw him as their hero. Gamblers loved the money he earned for them. Strangers suffered from hero worship, wanting to shake the hand of the highly talked-of champion. They all wanted to buy him a drink, and the sociable Sullivan usually accepted. Drinking alcohol in saloons was a big part of the social culture, including the Irish culture. Admirers also lavished Sullivan with expensive gifts.[52]

On March 23, 1882 in Boston, Sullivan exhibited with Joe Goss. Sullivan said he would fight anyone for a wager of $5,000 a side in a Queensberry rules bout. "I will not fight again with the bare knuckles, as I do not wish to put myself in a position amenable to the law. My money is always ready, so I want these fellows to put up or shut up."[53]

Still, the begrudging traditionalist Fox and the *National Police Gazette* felt that Sullivan had a duty to defend his title under the bareknuckle LPR format, and in subsequent years, would harp on this point.

On March 27, 1882 in New York at the Third Avenue Rink, 6,000 - 8,000 spectators paid to watch Sullivan spar 6 rounds in friendly exhibition style, 3 with blacksmith Joseph Douglas and 3 rounds with Billy Madden. Sullivan accidentally hit Douglas with one solid right that turned him around, and Douglas wanted to retire, but Sullivan convinced him to continue. Thereafter, Sullivan handled him gently, blocking his blows and landing lightly.

---

[51] *National Police Gazette*, March 11, 1882.

[52] Sullivan at 71 – 72.

[53] *New York Clipper*, April 1, 1882; Sullivan at 72.

Observers of his subsequent sparring with Madden were impressed with Sullivan's science:

> [Sullivan's] quickness in hitting, the activity he displayed, and the improvement shown in his style of sparring, surprised the spectators, many of whom changed their previously unfavorable opinion regarding his scientific attainments after seeing him set to subsequently with Billy Madden, the pair making a very pretty and interesting display, wherein the champion held his punishing powers in reserve. … In hitting, guarding and evasive tactics, Sullivan displayed decided skill.

His performance changed the minds of those who previously had regarded Sullivan "as a bull like rusher, hitting round and at random."[54]

Sullivan continued giving money-making sparring exhibitions in various cities such as Jersey City and Hoboken, New Jersey, with Steve Taylor and Pete McCoy.

On Thursday April 20, 1882 at the Grand Opera House in Rochester, New York, Sullivan was scheduled to fight a black man named Johnson. That day, Sullivan said, "There are a great many boxers who are anxious to cope with me, but when they come to put the gloves on they seem to weaken. I hope Johnson will be on hand tonight, for I am anxious to give him a few points."[55]

However, that evening, Johnson failed to show up. "A darky named Johnson had agreed to undertake the job, but when the pinch came he weakened." Apparently, Johnson refused to appear when he learned that it would not be a friendly sparring bout, but a real contest.

Instead, local Rochester fireman John McDermott accepted the offer to try to win $100 for lasting 4 rounds. However, McDermott was only a welterweight, weighing about 147 pounds. Yet, he confidently believed that he could last 4 rounds with the 200-pound Sullivan.

1,800 men and boys packed the local opera house with the greatest crowd ever seen there.

Sullivan wore a light gauze shirt and green silk knee pants. He was a "model of physical beauty." McDermott wore a blue flannel shirt and some other heavy clothing.

1 - Despite his small size, McDermott was agile and strong, showing that he knew how to box. The crowd voiced its support for the local man. Mac was skillful and lively, more so than Sullivan (who might have been carrying him). McDermott "slipped" once and went down to his knees, but was up in an instant. The local press claimed that McDermott landed two telling blows that sent Sullivan backward and almost down. Sully appeared to be out of breath.

---

[54] *New York Clipper,* April 1, 1882; Sullivan at 72.
[55] *Rochester Daily Union and Advertiser,* April 20, 1882.

2 - Sullivan struck sledge-hammer blows, but McDermott demonstrated surprising agility, ducking and countering. Mac occasionally "slipped" down to the ground. However, eventually Sullivan knocked him down.

The *Rochester Democrat and Chronicle* said, "It was announced that the set-to was to be governed by the Marquis of Somebody's rules which limited the rounds to three minutes…[but the] master of ceremonies allowed the round to last 4 ½ minutes…and the reputation of the champion was saved." This local writer implied that the round was allowed to continue until Sullivan could score a clean knockdown. At the round's conclusion, both men appeared fatigued.

3 - Sullivan struck McDermott with a terrible blow in the face with the heel of this hand that sent him out amongst the scenery. Mac continued, and "it was necessary for the Bostonian to jump around and hit him in the back of the head with one of his sledge-hammer blows to send him to the floor." The local writers agreed that toward the end of the round, McDermott gave up, for he had enough. However, he "had not been touched in the face during any of the rounds."

The local Rochester newspaper accounts were fairly biased in favor of the local man.

The *New York Herald* and *New York Clipper* reported that in the 1st round, McDermott escaped all of Sullivan's blows with scientific dodging, ducking, and quick movement around the stage. In the 2nd round, Sullivan "clipped him twice, which sent him to the floor." Sullivan dropped him three times in the 3rd, and then knocked McDermott into the stage scenery and down. He rose and continued, but a sweeping left "used McDermott up, and he withdrew" and "gave up the unequal struggle."

The crowd sympathized with the local, smaller underdog, hissing and jeering at Sullivan during and after the fight.

The crowd's feeling against Sullivan "was intensified by a few words of his nauseating bombast" after the contest. With his "characteristic conceit," Sullivan gave a speech to the crowd, claiming that he had carried McDermott. "Despite opportunities to do so, I did not take advantage of this novice." In response, the crowd jeered at Sullivan, one saying, "You big duffer, you got all you wanted any how." Allegedly, privately Sullivan spoke highly of Mac's boxing skills.

Sullivan was going to follow up the McDermott bout by sparring with Billy Madden, but the crowd's ill treatment hurt his feelings, and he declined to entertain them further.

Sullivan's share of the receipts was $852, which was very good money.

The local papers were not impressed. "Sullivan showed nothing at all but brute force, and the assemblage was quite disgusted." Another said that Sullivan was a "so called champion," and overrated. "This man from Boston may be a mechanic in the pugilistic art…but if so, he did not give any evidence of it. … [Sullivan] could probably break a lamp-post with his fist if he got a fair blow at it, but it would be a clumsy lamp-post that did not dodge his blows." Regardless, McDermott had failed to make it out of the 3rd round, let alone last the full 4 rounds, so he did not earn the $100.[56]

On occasion, Sullivan was known to drink a bit too much. It was so easy, given the number of free drinks that fans offered him. However, sometimes the alcohol ignited a temper. Late at night on April 25, 1882 in a Boston barroom, Sullivan got into a fight with Charles Robbins, breaking his jaw. Sullivan faced charges of assault and battery. However, investigation revealed that Robbins had taunted and provoked John L. into the fight, so the charges were dismissed.[57]

On another evening in Boston, a drunken Sullivan was stumbling down the street, and his verbal abuse of a police officer with obscene language led to an $11 fine.

During this time, Sullivan was seeing a woman named Annie Bailey, who was a year older than he was. Bailey had married young and became a widow at age 16. Originally from Rhode Island, some said she was a chorus girl or a pianist on the Boston stages. She had caught Sullivan's eye, and quickly became his girlfriend.

On Independence Day afternoon, Tuesday July 4, 1882, outdoors in Washington Park in Brooklyn, New York, located on the East River at the foot of 69th street, Sullivan fought LPR veteran Jimmy Elliott, who had over 20 years of fight experience. A native of Ireland, Elliott was 37 years of age and had been fighting in the U.S. since 1861, winning an LPR fight against Nobby Clark in 1 hour (34 rounds). An 1862 LPR fight with Hen Winkle lasted 2 hours 15 minutes (99 rounds), resulting in a draw. In 1864, Elliott served one year of a two-year prison sentence for engaging in an illegal 1863 LPR fight against Jim Dunn in New Jersey, which he lost via 12th round disqualification. In 1867, Elliott knocked out Bill Davis in 9 rounds. In a grueling 1868 LPR fight, he defeated Charley Gallagher in 1 hour 17 minutes (23 rounds). In 1869, Elliott stopped British champion Tom Allen in 3 minutes (2 rounds). Elliott had been an American champion, but after an 1870 conviction for robbery and assault with intent to kill, he served 9 years in prison.

After serving his prison sentence, in 1879, Elliott lost to Joe Dwyer in a 12-minute (10 or 12 rounds) LPR fight. Most recently, on May 1, 1882, 179-pound Elliott defeated 205-pound "Troy Terror" Richard Egan/Eagan in the 4th round; a right uppercut doing the trick.[58]

---

56 *Rochester Morning Herald; Rochester Democrat and Chronicle; Rochester Daily Union and Advertiser,* all April 21, 1882, *New York Herald,* April 21, 1882, *New York Clipper,* April 29, 1882.

57 Isenberg at 118. In May, Sullivan exhibited with Billy Madden in Lynn, Massachusetts. On May 11 at Harry Hill's in New York, before a crowd of 700, Sullivan exhibited with Joe Goss. On June 5, Sullivan boxed Madden at Worcester, Massachusetts, and on June 9 at Holyoke, Massachusetts, he boxed Dan Dwyer.

58 *New York Daily Tribune,* July 5, 1882; *National Police Gazette,* December 25, 1880, April 15, 1882, September 23, 1882, October 7, 14, 1882, March 17, 1883; *Times-Democrat,* February 8, 1882; *Boston Daily Globe,* April 6, 1879; Cyberboxingzone.com.

It was a rainy day, and the grounds were muddy.

Tickets sold for 50 cents each, although ladies were admitted for free. At the gate, the ticket seller announced to patrons that they would see "one of your country's heroes."

Jimmy Elliott

Elliott was attempting to win $500 for lasting 4 rounds with Sullivan.

Located in the center of the park grounds, the outdoor ring was a 24-square-foot wood platform elevated 5 feet above the ground, with ropes stretched around it.

Over 5,000 people witnessed the fight. 100 policemen were present.

Just after 5 p.m., Sullivan and Elliott entered the dripping and slippery board ring.

The 6'1" 185-pound Elliott wore white tights and white stockings, but was bare-chested from the waist up. The 195-pound Sullivan wore blue stockings, green tights, and a white sleeveless undershirt. At Elliott's request, they fought with hard gloves.

Mike Cleary refereed, after Elliott had objected to Harry Hill. Billy Madden and Fiddler Neary seconded Sullivan. George Morton, Bob Smith, and Johnny Roche seconded Elliott.

They shook hands and the fight began at 5:30 p.m.

1 - Sullivan forced the fight with his irresistible attack, rushing upon him like a cyclone, firing heavy blows that put Elliott on the defensive. What blows Elliott did manage to throw, Sullivan quickly dodged. Elliott went down several times, sometimes from blows, while at other times he slipped on the wet boards. On some occasions, Elliott grabbed Sullivan's legs as he went down.

After being partially knocked down, Elliott rose and clinched. His mouth was bleeding. Sullivan knocked him down into his own corner. Upon the third knockdown, Elliott's fall against the ropes and ring post stripped off skin from his back. When the round was over, Sullivan smiled.

In the corner, Roche fanned Elliott and gave him something to drink from a bottle.

2 - Elliott tried but was not able to hit Sullivan, who crowded in and furiously rained blows upon him, forcing Elliott to the ropes and into corners, slugging him mercilessly, hitting him under the ear as with a mallet. Elliott was "choking from blood flowing inwardly from his nose." Jimmy stepped forward but slipped and fell as Sullivan stepped back. After Elliott rose, Sullivan landed a terrible blow to the neck that knocked him down in his corner.

Elliott rose again, but his breast, shoulders, and face were almost as red as blood. They exchanged furious blows, and Elliott landed a hard right to the chin that knocked Sullivan backwards to the ropes, but John L. rallied back and landed a crusher to the chin that again decked Elliott heavily onto the wood platform. His second, Johnny Roche, helped him to his chair.

Between rounds, in the corner, "Johnny Roche finding the blood in the nose interfered with his principal's breathing placed his mouth to that organ, sucked it clear and spit the blood so obtained upon the floor of the platform ring." That is what you call cornerman dedication.

3 - Sullivan practically ran across the ring, dealing out slashing blows with both hands, punishing Elliott, who kept retreating all over the stage. Sullivan's rights were magnificent, straight from the shoulder, full on the nose, neck, and chest, sending Elliott down.

Elliott quickly rose. After a few exchanges, a Sullivan right to the neck or chin "sent Elliott off his feet flying into his corner senseless. He was unable to speak or to move and lay limp and lifeless." He was hanging over the lower rope without moving, in danger of dropping to the ground several feet below. He was out cold. It required two men to lift the unconscious fighter into his chair. One source said the round had lasted only about 20 seconds, while another said it was 1 minute 30 seconds.

Elliott was slow to respond to restoratives. When he opened his eyes, he asked, "Where am I?"

Showing his generosity, Sullivan gave the LPR veteran Elliott $50.

The lines between Queensberry and LPR rules may have been blurred in this contest, and a form of hybrid rules utilized. There are some indications that the rounds were three minutes, but the rest periods only lasted 30 seconds. However, some said otherwise. The *New York Times* and *New York Tribune* said fight lasted 7 minutes 20 seconds. That would be two 3-minute rounds, two 30-second rests after the first 2 rounds, and a 20-second 3rd round. However, the *New York Sun* said Sullivan knocked him out in the 4th round. It said the battle had taken 13 ½ minutes, with 10 ½ minutes of fighting time. It clocked the last round at 1 minute 30 seconds. The stopping and re-starting again after some knockdowns in LPR fashion probably confused some reporters. Billy Madden said the fight was 7 minutes 20 seconds, but his explanation was that the 1st round was not more than 2 minutes, then there was 1 minute of rest; the 2nd round was 3 minutes, then another minute rest, and then Sullivan ended him after 20 seconds of the 3rd round. The *Sun* noted that would make 5 minutes 20 seconds of actual fighting time. Either way, Sullivan had stopped yet another veteran fighter very quickly, dominating him from the start.

ELLIOTT KNOCKED OUT.

THE CHAMPION PUGILIST, JOHN L. SULLIVAN, CELEBRATES THE FOURTH OF JULY BY VANQUISHING A NOTED HEAVY-WEIGHT FIGHTER IN NEW YORK CITY.

Summarizing, the *New York Sun* said, "Mr. Sullivan had more than satisfied his friends that he had improved greatly in the science of boxing. His rapid style of fighting was decidedly effective." He had closed in and slugged Elliott with such violent rapidity and force that "Mr. Elliott must have seen more stars than were to be seen in all the rest of the firmament."[59]

Although newsmen generally liked boxing, in part because fight reports helped stimulate newspaper and magazine sales, not everyone was thrilled about the sport's resurgence. The local *Brooklyn Daily Eagle* bemoaned the fact that since the Sullivan-Ryan fight, "the country has suffered an epidemic of prize fighting."[60]

Not pleased with the fact that Sullivan was accepting only Queensberry rules contests with gloves and was refusing challenges under LPR rules, the *National Police Gazette* withdrew its recognition of Sullivan as champion. It wanted Sullivan to fight the man it was backing, England's Tug Wilson. It sometimes called Wilson the "Police Gazette Champion." After some

---

[59] *New York Times*, *New York Daily Tribune*, *New York Herald*, *New York Sun*, *Boston Daily Globe*, July 5, 1882; *National Police Gazette*, October 14, 1882; Isenberg at 119-120; Sullivan at 74.
[60] *Brooklyn Daily Eagle*, July 1, 1882.

negotiations, "It was agreed that there should be a sparring match between Mr. Wilson and Mr. Sullivan before any arrangements for a prize-fight should be made." Wilson would need to prove himself sufficiently in a gloved bout in order to garner momentum and sufficient demand for an LPR fight.

Tug Wilson

On Monday July 17, 1882 in New York City's Madison Square Garden, just short of two weeks after the Elliott fight, 23-year-old John L. Sullivan fought middleweight-sized 34-year-old 5'8 ½" Englishman, Joe "Tug" Wilson (whose real name was Joseph Collins). Once source said that Sullivan, who had been eating and drinking more, and not training as much, weighed about 215 pounds. However, another source said that he had trained down from 231 pounds to 194 ½ pounds. It said Wilson had trained down from 184 to 157 pounds.

Tug Wilson's fight career began in 1866. In an 1881 LPR prizefight that lasted 1 hour 45 minutes (28 rounds), Wilson was superior to fellow 165-pound Englishman Alf Greenfield, until Greenfield's supporters entered the ring and stopped the fight. It technically was declared a draw.

Sullivan offered Wilson $1,000 plus half the gate receipts if he could last 4 rounds of gloved sparring under Queensberry rules, so everyone knew that Sullivan would be attempting to knock him out. At that time, for legal purposes, Sullivan was operating under the facade that a gloved fight was civilized and tame compared to the perceived-as-brutal bareknuckle prizefight. The *New York Herald* noted that it really was a fight rather than mere sparring, and the "pretence of calling it a glove contest was as thin as the gloves the men were expected to wear and deceived no one." The gloves they used weighed a little more than 2 ounces, and were "very small and almost as hard as wood."

The *New York Herald* and *New York Daily Tribune* called Sullivan the American champion and Wilson the English champion. The *National Police Gazette*, which backed Wilson, and called him the champion English pugilist.

The morning of the fight, Sullivan was the 10 to 6 favorite to stop him, although eventually wagers on Wilson closed the odds to 10 to 8 that Wilson would survive. No one wagered that Wilson would knock out Sullivan.

The Sullivan-Wilson fight generated a massive crowd of over 10,000 (one said 12,000). The building was not big enough to fit comfortably all those who purchased tickets, and about 5,000 folks remained outside, unable to obtain tickets. Reserved seats sold for $2, while ticket speculators sold those seats for $2.50, doing brisk business. Speculators sold $1 tickets for $1.25. The ticket scalpers thrived. Some young boys climbed the walls like lizards to obtain a view through the windows of Madison Square Garden.

All classes and professions were represented inside the arena. The fashionably dressed patrons wore tall white hats with broad black bands. Clearly, Sullivan had widespread crossover appeal. Boxing was big business, which is why Madison Square Garden owner and multi-millionaire William K. Vanderbilt had decided to host a boxing show featuring a popular champion. The *New York Tribune* noted that Sullivan's "short career in the ring had been so remarkable that it was generally believed that few if any of the past champions were his equals." Everyone wanted to see him.

The big and tall Police Captain Alexander "Clubber" Williams was on hand with his club and 80 men under him charged with keeping order. The short and stout but powerful Inspector Thorne was present as well.

The ring was a 24-foot square platform, raised 6 feet from the floor, with a post at every corner and one on each side's midpoint, with two ropes.

The house trembled from the storm of applause that greeted the fighters. At 9:30 p.m., Wilson stepped onto the platform, seconded by

Arthur Chambers and George Holden. Wilson wore white tights and pink stockings. Sullivan, seconded by Joe Goss and Billy Madden, wore white or flesh-colored drawers and dark green stockings. Their seconds fanned them with towels. Sullivan, who had large hands, had difficulty getting the small gloves on. The *Times* said the gloves were 2 ounces, but the *Tribune* said they were 4 ounces. The men shook hands, and the fight began at 9:38 p.m. Harry Hill refereed.

1 - As Sullivan threw his right, Wilson stepped in and hit him with a left on the neck. However, Sullivan doubled up on his right and dropped Wilson.

Wilson rose and hit Sullivan with a left to the nose, but in return Sullivan rushed in like a mad bull and beat down his guard, raining in several staggering blows in nonstop fashion with such velocity that they could neither be counted nor followed, until a right decked Wilson again.

After Wilson rose, Sullivan's subsequent onslaught sent him down for the third time.

Wilson escaped John L.'s attack and hit the champ in the body. Sullivan pushed him back until Wilson hit the ropes and fell. He rose and continued.

After Sullivan struck Wilson with several hard blows, Tug fell again.

The fight's pattern had been established - Wilson occasionally landed a decent punch, but inevitably Sullivan would deck him again, and again.

The *New York Herald* said, "In this manner, without the slightest display of science on Sullivan's part, he made his rush and downed Wilson every few seconds until at the ninth knockdown" the round ended. The *New York Times*, which was more critical of Sullivan, said that ten times during the 1st round, Wilson either was pushed down or fell down, but was not knocked down. The *New York Sun* said that eleven times in the round, Wilson was knocked down by blows that battered his head, beat upon his neck, cracked against his shoulders, and drove the wind out of his lungs. Conversely, Wilson's blows had no effect whatsoever, and Sullivan treated them as if they were mere snowballs. After the bell, Wilson was led to his corner, sponged and fanned, and he had a dazed, confused, and almost horrified look upon his face. "Such blows had never been seen here before." The crowd was wild with excitement.

2 - Wilson began the round with a smile. Sullivan promptly dropped him with a terrific right under the left ear. But again he rose. Throughout the round, several times Sullivan either knocked him down or Wilson intentionally "went down easily to kill time. Tug took advantage of the hit, no matter how light it might be, to go down." He was using survival tactics. Sullivan was wild, and sometimes grabbed Tug around the neck and illegally hit him in the back of his head.

The *Herald* said Wilson went down eight times in the round. The *Times* said the Englishman was crowded to the ropes and pushed down six times. Both men struck "heavy blows." The *Sun* said Wilson was knocked down ten times. The fifth time he fell heavily against the ropes and almost through them. Awful slugging beat him down again in his own corner. A clean left dropped him like a bowling pin. Sullivan dropped him three more times. Still, some thought that Sullivan was tiring, for he was breathing heavily.

3 - At the start of the round, Wilson hit Sullivan twice and then rushed in and kept close so that Sullivan's swings could not land. Tug's goal was to get under John's guard and clinch and crowd Sullivan and hold his neck, which he often did. Tug began laughing. Sullivan had lost some power. After wrestling, Sullivan threw Wilson and fell on top of him.

Shortly thereafter, "Tug went down rather suspiciously to avoid punishment and to kill time, and as he did so he took hold of Sullivan's leg and tried to pull him down." Tug was going down voluntarily without being hit, or when hit lightly, using it as an excuse to go down, get a rest, and avoid follow-up blows. Such tactics technically were against the rules, as was grabbing the leg.

Several times during the round, while they were clinched, they fell to the ground. Wilson was wrestling a lot, in LPR style. He either evaded or took Sullivan's blows well. After avoiding some punches, Wilson managed to strike John twice more.

However, despite Sullivan's appearance of fatigue, he still dropped Wilson two more times.

Wilson advocates who bet on him to last the distance admired his foxy tactics. Sullivan admirers who wagered that he would win by knockout used profanity and yelled at John L. to go in and finish him. The *Sun* said Wilson was down nine times in this round, but only once did he seem to be hurt, after receiving some blows to the back of his neck from the heel of Sullivan's hand.

4 - They again wrestled and twice fell down together, with Sullivan smartly landing on top of his opponent.

Wilson was hit by some less powerful rights, and dropped down to avoid another. Both went down during Sullivan's next rush. Wilson next went down from a push.

In order to kill the clock and avoid punishment, Wilson would go down any time he had an excuse, whether he was hit by a light blow or pushed. Towards the end of the round, Sullivan threw him down and again landed on top of him.

The *Sun* said that out of the seven times that Wilson dropped, fell, or was knocked down in the round, Sullivan fell on him three times. At the end of the fight, Sullivan appeared to be much more fatigued than Wilson. Of course, he had done most of the work.

Tug Wilson had managed to survive the full 4 rounds. It has been estimated that he was down anywhere from 21 to 24 times.

The *New York Herald* noted that from the bout's start, it was clear that Wilson's sole intention was to survive the 4 rounds, using whatever means were necessary to that end, even if his tactics might cast aspersions on his courage. Wilson went down incessantly, using whatever excuse he could to fall down and benefit from a count to kill time and prevent Sullivan from hitting him. He also held, wrestled, moved, and ducked. He fought a purely defensive fight in order to avoid being knocked out in 4 rounds.

However, the more critical *New York Times* account gave the impression that Sullivan's pushing, swinging, mauling, and fouling tactics were what caused Wilson to drop to the ground so often, rather than knockdown blows or Wilson's own tactics. The *Times* said that often throughout the bout, Sullivan "took an unfair advantage…by striking him before he was fully on his feet." Sullivan made little attempt to display "science," but was a "slugger," plain and simple. Wilson either evaded or took Sullivan's blows well.

The *New York Daily Tribune* agreed with the *Herald* version, saying that Wilson did everything that he could to last the full 4 rounds.

> Sullivan forced the fighting in tremendous style, raining crushing blows on Wilson's neck and head, and knocking him all about the platform, against the ropes and upon the floor. Wilson was down almost as much as he was up. The thundering strokes which he received again and again seemed enough to knock a dozen men senseless.

Sullivan kept knocking him down with "avalanches" of "thumps," but Wilson kept rising. "Very rarely in a prize-ring or out of it has a man been knocked down so often and got up again so many times in so few minutes. Sullivan could knock down Wilson easily enough, but he could not knock him out."

Noted was the difference between bareknuckle and gloved fighting. The "bare knuckles cut and bruise but the hard gloves shock and stagger fearfully."

Wilson technically was entitled to $1,000 and half the gate receipts because he lasted 4 rounds, but that is all he earned. There was little praise to be garnered for the performance, other than the fact that he proved that he could abuse the rules and survive Sullivan.

One man who bet on Wilson to last said, "Of course Tug couldn't stand up before Sullivan in a regular give and take, but I bet on Tug because I was confidentially told what his little game was to be." Another said Tug's tactics made sense, given their size disparity. "Sullivan is the hardest hitter I ever saw, and can handle two Tugs; but the Englishman was playing for a big stake, and his only chance was to prevent being knocked out by going down as often as possible."

Ex-Senator Tim McCarthy said, "Wilson went in merely for the money, and he got it by sticking to Sullivan as long as he could, and when he went to grass he took the full benefit of his knockdown."

Sullivan said it hardly could be called a fight, for Wilson was only interested in "floor-crawling and hugging," for which the Tug earned $7,000 according to one source, and $11,700 according to another.

Apparently, the gate yielded at least $16,000 according to one source, and between $20,000 and $25,000 according to another, so all parties involved earned a lot of money, including Sullivan.

"Police Gazette" champion Tug Wilson meets Sullivan at Madison Square Garden

1 – Tug lands the first blow. 2 – Wilson "takes kindly to his punishment," holding. 3 – Sullivan lands his "big licks." 4 – Tug goes down "smiling."

Afterwards, Wilson said, "I didn't try to fight at all. I kept on the defensive. But when he gets me before him with bare knuckles he will find a different man."

Tug Wilson After the Battle
How the Police Gazette Champion Pugilist Enjoyed His Honors and Raked In His Rich Stakes After His Gallant Glove Fight With John L. Sullivan in New York

Despite the *Police Gazette's* attempt to spin Wilson's performance as being meritorious, thereafter, whenever a boxer merely attempted to survive against Sullivan, going down easily and often, grabbing, moving, and falling down, they would be accused derogatorily of using "Tug Wilson tactics." Such tactics often were used in LPR fights, causing them to be exceedingly long.[61]

In the wake of the bout held in front of thousands of members of all classes, the *New York Times* addressed boxing's uncertain legal status. "In view of the prevailing public sentiment in regard to prize-fighting, it is surely time that the nearly obsolete law against this manly sport should be repealed." It noted that those in the crowd witnessing the Sullivan - Wilson bout "were by no means the lowest elements of our population." Boxing's reputation had been that of a sport that attracted only gamblers, ruffians from the lower class, and the criminal element. But Sullivan was changing that image. He had cross-over appeal, stimulating interest in the sport from all classes. The *Times* also noted that boxing bouts were allowed to occur, regardless of the law. Hence the law against fighting might as well be repealed.

> Now, when a man can thus violate...the law which forbids any person to set on foot or to promote a prize-fight, and when prize-fights...can take place in the heart of our City under the protection of a platoon of Police, and in the presence of thousands of people, why should we any longer retain in the statute-book any part of the law against prize-fighting?[62]

---

[61] *New York Herald, New York Daily Tribune, New York Times, New York Sun*, July 18, 1882; *New York Times*, June 29, 1882; *National Police Gazette*, July 8, 1882; Isenberg at 120-122; Sullivan at 75, 77; Cyberboxingzone.com.

[62] *New York Times*, July 28, 1882.

Sullivan and Wilson scheduled an August 14, 1882 rematch at the Garden, but the legal authorities prohibited it. The mayor's office had asked the city's legal counsel to offer an opinion regarding whether the proposed sparring match was legal. The lawyer opined that the first Sullivan-Wilson bout had not been legal sparring, but an illegal prizefight, and therefore so too would be the upcoming contest. City officials directed Captain Williams to apply for warrants for the arrest of Sullivan and Wilson, which warrants would be served if they again were present in New York. If arrested, the boxers would have to post bonds agreeing to keep the peace, meaning not fight. Hence, the contest was called off. The *Police Gazette*, which backed Wilson, proclaimed that the authorities' actions were arrogant, ignorant, and illegal.[63]

About a month after the Sullivan-Elliott fight, despite having been knocked out cold by Sullivan, Jimmy Elliott posted a monetary forfeit and challenged Sullivan to fight him according to the London Prize Ring rules. When Sullivan did not accept the challenge, Elliott claimed the American championship. Although the public still recognized Sullivan, who had knocked out Elliott with ease under Queensberry rules, the *National Police Gazette*, still an advocate of the LPR system as *the* form of true championship fighting, backed Tug Wilson to meet Elliott for the vacant championship. However, the Elliott-Wilson fight did not take place, for Tug left the U.S. and returned to England.[64]

The *National Police Gazette* was the first to try to "strip" Sullivan of his championship title. It continually insisted that the true test of a champion was an LPR fight, and wanted Sullivan to accept challenges to fight under the LPR rules. Sullivan did not want to do so unless very big money was on the line, particularly since such contests were illegal, and he was earning very good money with gloved contests.

Although reports on Sullivan's gloved bouts and his popularity stimulated its circulation, nevertheless, the *Police Gazette* often would hype prospective opponents, back them financially, promote their challenges, and criticize Sullivan if he did not fight them when, for how much, and under what format it wanted. This only served to promote fights, marketing from which Sullivan ultimately would derive a benefit. Perhaps that was the intention. The more buzz surrounding prospective opponents and potential fights, the greater the readership and money to be made for everyone eventually when they arranged a match and fought. That was the lesson learned from the Ryan fight.

On August 19, 1882 in North Adams, Massachusetts, Sullivan and Joe Goss gave one of their sparring exhibitions. A large crowd of nearly 1,000 people met their train at the depot, cheering themselves hoarse.

---

63 *New York Sun*, August 1, 1882; *New York Tribune*, August 3, 1882; *National Police Gazette*, August 26, 1882.

64 *National Police Gazette*, October 14, 1882.

Sullivan and Goss began sparring at 5:30 p.m. in a picnic grove. Proving his popularity, anywhere from 6,000 to 8,000 men, women, and children were present to witness the exhibition. Sullivan could draw large crowds even when he wasn't going to attempt to knock out someone.

Against Goss, Sullivan feinted often and landed some heavy blows to the eye and nose. After only 2 minutes 3 seconds, the master of ceremonies ended the round, either to save Goss from too much punishment or because the police were struggling to hold back the surrounding crowd, which was surging forward and encroaching onto the rope-less platform.

During the 2nd round, about a dozen spectators who were crowded near the stage began fighting one another. For the next several minutes, the police had to use their billy-clubs to restore order. The exhibition was terminated.

That evening, at 9:30 p.m. in a local hall, Sullivan and Goss again sparred in animated fashion, so animated that the master of ceremonies called time early for each of the 3 rounds.[65]

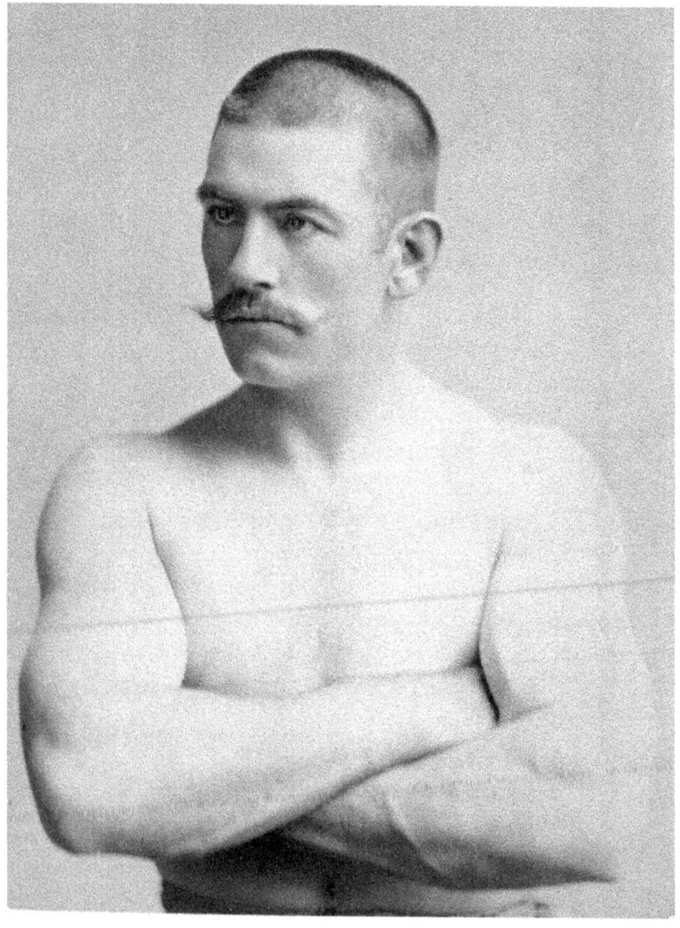

[65] *Boston Herald*, August 20, 1882; *Boston Daily Globe*, August 20, 1882.

A Tour

John L. Sullivan signed a contract to appear with a traveling variety company managed by Harry Sargent. He agreed to spar six nights a week for 20 weeks for $500 a night, starting in Newark, New Jersey on September 4, 1882. They would tour around the East and Midwest, and Sullivan would spar Billy Madden, Pete McCoy, and Bob Farrell as part of the variety entertainment show. During the tour, the champion would remain open to meeting all-comers, and would allow them to attempt to last 4 rounds with him to win some money. Occasionally, someone would accept the offer, but for the most part, Sullivan generally sparred in friendly fashion with his touring buddies.[66]

Regarding his sparring with Madden on September 22, 1882 in Buffalo, New York, the *Buffalo Courier* said, "Sullivan made many expert passes and showed remarkable quickness in dodging blows with his head."[67]

The next day, on Saturday September 23, 1882 in Buffalo, local native 194-pound Henry Higgins attempted to last 4 rounds with Sullivan. Higgins made one or two good passes, which brought the crowd's applause, but he was no match, for Higgins was "a plaything" in Sullivan's hands. Sullivan toyed with him for a couple of rounds, showing him some mercy. However, Higgins did not last past the 3rd round. Accounts vary regarding how it ended. The local newspaper simply said the 3rd round badly winded Higgins and time was called. This gave the impression that Higgins could not continue. Others said a tremendous right took him out in the 3rd round, and Higgins was out cold for 20 minutes.[68]

On Monday October 16, 1882 at Fort Wayne, Indiana, the tall, muscular, burly 175- or 180-pound amateur boxer-blacksmith S. P. Stockton attempted to win $500 if he could last 4 rounds against the now 24-year-old Sullivan. Stockton, who slung a sledgehammer all day for his work, claimed to be able to lift 800 pounds, and insisted that no fighter could whip him in 4 rounds, especially not with gloves.

---

[66] *National Police Gazette,* September 23, October 7, 1882; Sullivan at 78-79. The sparring combination appeared in several locations in September (4th to 21st), including Newark and Trenton, NJ; Lancaster, Reading, Allentown, Philadelphia, Pittston, Scranton, and Wilkes-Barre, PA; and Albany, Utica, Syracuse, and Batavia, NY.

[67] *Buffalo Courier,* September 23, 1882.

[68] *Buffalo Courier, New York Tribune, New York Herald,* September 24, 1882; *New York Clipper,* October 7, 1882; *National Police Gazette,* October 14, 1882. Subsequently, from September 26 to October 14, Sullivan, Madden and the touring buddies boxed in places like Oil City and Bradford, PA; Richburg and Olean, NY; Massilon, Columbus, Springfield, and Xenia, OH, and Richmond, IN.

In the 1st round, Sullivan felt him out, and Stockton showed great grit, punching away. However, in the 2nd round, "the champion knocked Stockton clean off his feet and he lay like a log on the stage." When he awoke, Stockton asked, "Did I fall off a barn?"[69]

At some point during the tour, Sullivan broke ties with both Harry Sargent and Billy Madden. The issue with Madden allegedly was both financial and the result of a personal dispute regarding one of the company's showgirls. Madden left with her. Sullivan took over the company's management.

On Monday October 30, 1882 in Chicago's McCormick Hall, just before Sullivan was about to spar with Pete McCoy; the short, chunky Charles O'Donnell, a Cleveland native, announced that he wanted to attempt to last 4 rounds with champion Sullivan. His wish was granted.

O'Donnell wore black pants, calico shirt, and a cotton handkerchief tied around his waist for a belt. Sullivan wore a scarlet costume.

In the 1st round, using only his left, Sullivan pounded him about the stage and decked O'Donnell five or six times. It was a total mismatch, and O'Donnell was forced to retire in the 1st round, saying that he wanted no more.

Pete McCoy

Sullivan then sparred with Pete McCoy in a playful fashion. Nevertheless, "it showed to advantage the matchless form of Sullivan and the cat-like agility of McCoy."[70]

The following evening, on the 31st in Chicago, the "champion of the world" again sparred a friendly 3-round bout with McCoy before a small crowd mostly comprised of the city's tough element.[71]

On Friday November 17, 1882 in the Theatre Comique in Washington, D.C., Georgetown blacksmith P. J. Rentzler (or Rensler) attempted to win the $500 offered to anyone who could last 4 rounds with Sullivan. The house was packed to suffocation with a crowd of 2,000. Many were turned away, for there was not enough room to house all those who wanted inside.

Rentzler was a well-built muscular 190

[69] *Indianapolis Sentinel,* October 17, 1882; *National Police Gazette,* November 4, 1882; Sullivan at 82. From October 18 to 28, Sullivan exhibited in Indianapolis and Evansville, IN; Louisville, KY; Lafayette, IN; and Bloomington and Streator, IL.

[70] *Chicago Herald, Daily Inter Ocean, Chicago Daily News,* October 31, 1882.

[71] *Chicago Herald, Daily Inter Ocean*, November 1, 1882. On November 4, they exhibited in Lancaster, PA, and from the 13th to 16th, they were in Washington D.C.

pounds and was about 30 years old. He wore a white knit shirt and plush-colored tights. Sullivan wore a complete suit of sleeveless blue tights with gaiters. They wore medium soft gloves, meaning that the gloves contained some padding inside.

After shaking hands, at the call of time, Rentzler raised his fists in "approved attitude" and fired a left, but Sullivan countered with a right, dropping Rentzler to his knees against the scenery. Sullivan stepped back, but after Rentzler rose, the champion immediately "sprang savagely forward" and dropped him again. Thereafter, P.J. only was able to hold up his arms in ineffective attempts to block. He had no time to punch back.

The local *Washington Post* said, "This brutal display continued until Rensler was knocked down eleven times, not having once struck Sullivan a blow, and a more sickening spectacle of brutality was never witnessed here before." The local *Evening Star* said Sullivan decked Rensler six times. After Rensler rose from the sixth knockdown, Sullivan landed a blow to the nose which drew blood. Seeing him bleeding from his mouth and nose, the crowd called upon the police to stop it, and they did, entering the ring and calling a halt to the bout, only 1 minute 33 seconds into the 1st round.

Some in the audience hissed Sullivan. He denounced them, saying, "Those that hissed are mules. I can knock out the best you have, and am willing to prove it. Just step right up." However, no one did. After that, they kept their mouths shut. The *Washington Post* opined that no man from the District of Columbia ever again would be willing to stand up against "Slugger Sullivan, the champion heavy weight."

Sullivan still gave the spectators some additional entertainment, closing the show by sparring McCoy 3 rounds.

Afterwards, Sullivan said that he had not used his greatest force, because he knew that Rensler was no match. Another newspaper quoted Sullivan as saying that he did not hit him as hard as he could because of the scenery standing about the stage which interfered with Rentzler's free movement.

The game Rentzler said that he could have continued, and wanted to meet Sullivan again the following night. However, the manager would not allow it, for he did not want to invoke the police's wrath. The *Post* opined that like many others, Rensler "had evidently sought the glory of standing up before the champion of the world."[72]

During Thanksgiving week, the sparring combination was in Cincinnati.

On December 10, 1882 in Chicago, they appeared at Charles "Parson" Davies' establishment, The Argyle. At that time, Sullivan signed with Davies to manage him for the next 6 months.

Sullivan was scheduled to fight a rematch with Jimmy Elliott (who was coming off of a late-November 46-second knockout victory over Captain James Dalton), in a 4-round bout to be held in Chicago on December 22, but the local authorities prevented it.[73]

On December 15, Sullivan sparred Joe Goss at Harry Hill's in New York.

While Sullivan was in New York, former American bareknuckle champion Joe Coburn joined his sparring troupe. The 47-year-old Coburn had been fighting since 1856. He had fought a 160-round draw with Ned Price. In 1863, he defeated Mike McCoole in 1 hour 10 minutes (67 rounds). In 1871, he fought world champion Jem Mace to a 3-hour 48-minute 12-round draw.

Joe Coburn

Coburn went to prison for 10 years for assault with intent to kill a policeman. He was released on December 7, 1882.[74] Allowing the experienced veteran to join the crew was a way to help him obtain some money and get back on his feet again. Plus, he was tough enough and experienced enough to absorb Sullivan's blows, which had some pop even when he threw them lightly.

On December 28, 1882 in Madison Square Garden in New York, Sullivan exhibited for the first time with Coburn. 3,000 people from all walks of life were in attendance, even though it was advertised as being only a strictly scientific exhibition.

[72] *Washington Post, Washington Evening Star*, November 18, 1882; *New York Clipper,* November 25, 1882. Sullivan exhibited in Pittsburg on November 19, 1882.

[73] *National Police Gazette*, February 10, 1883, September 20, 1884; Sullivan at 83.

[74] *National Police Gazette*, February 10, 1883; Cyberboxingzone.com.

The platform was raised a few feet from the ground, and draped with some old canvas. A single rope was drawn around it.

In the 1st round, Sullivan danced about the stage and landed leads to the head as Coburn mostly played defense, parrying blows. It was a tame exhibition of skill. The crowd grew a bit boisterous and encouraged the men to let each other have it.

> The men upon the platform seemed a trifle annoyed, ceased sparring, and then both stopped and advanced to the rope, while Pop Whittaker raised his voice.
>
> "You will remember, gentlemen, that this is a friendly exhibition with the gloves and that Mr. Sullivan has kindly come here to spar for Mr. Coburn's benefit."
>
> There was a moment's silence when Sullivan brushed past the speaker and sent this reminder ringing over the house: -
>
> "I came here to box with Mr. Coburn in a friendly wind-up. This is no knocking out business. On some future occasion I'll kill a man for you."
>
> There was an outburst of applause and the exchange of fisticuffs was interrupted no more.

At the conclusion of the 3-round scientific exhibition, the audience cheered.[75]

During December, Sullivan purchased a home at 4 Lovering Place in Boston's South End. He moved into it with his girlfriend Annie Bailey. They were not present all that often or for too long, because John L. was busy making very good money touring around giving sparring exhibitions, taking Annie along with him.

Although boxing soon would become very popular in Australia, in early 1883, the *Australian Sportsman* wrote,

> An attempt is being made to revive public interest in the departed glories of the prize ring. … We have not the slightest sympathy with the prize ring. Its surroundings have invariably been of the lowest kind. … Had pugilism possessed a little of the advantages claimed by its advocates it would never have lost its popularity, but its demoralizing influence has always proved too much even for those interested in its maintenance. It is a sport best left alone.[76]

In 1883, Sullivan would fight at least seven times, in addition to his many friendly sparring exhibitions. On January 11, 1883 in Boston, Sullivan sparred McCoy.

On January 20, 1883 in Buffalo, New York, before a crowd of 2,000,

---

[75] *New York Herald*, December 28, 29, 1882.

[76] *Australian Sportsman*, January 10, 1883.

Sullivan sparred Coburn in a lively bout.[77]

On January 23, 1883, the sparring combination appeared in Toronto, Ontario, Canada. The local hall was packed. Even standing-room was at a premium. Sullivan and Coburn sparred in a tame but scientific bout of "mutual forbearance." A local reporter said of Sullivan, "It is a very sure thing that light sparring is not his forte. … Of course Coburn is not a man who would care to stand up night after night and take the sledge hammer blows of Sullivan even with the soft gloves." Sully had to work with him.[78]

Despite its desire to see Sullivan face a man who could test him, and its desire to see him in another LPR bout, the *National Police Gazette* gave credit where it was due. One of its writers said of Sullivan,

> One thing is certain, and that is that neither Mace or Sayers ever encountered so hard or so quick a hitter as is John L. Sullivan. … It was the writer's fortune to see the fight between Heenan and Morrissey, and had Sullivan been on the boards that day as big, as capable, and in as good condition as when he fought Paddy Ryan, it is my opinion that he could have whipped both of them, one after another. Those who think that he is not a thoroughly scienced man, are somewhat mistaken. He has a far better knowledge of the fistic art than either Heenan or Morrissey possessed. He is stronger than either, and unquestionably he is the hardest hitter known to the records of the ring.[79]

Sullivan sparred Coburn in Rochester on January 24, Syracuse on the 26th, Troy on the 29th, and in Utica, New York on January 30.

Negotiations were ongoing for a potential LPR prizefight against 27-year-old (some say 32) Australian champion Herbert "The Maori" Slade, who was trained and backed by former champion Jem Mace, who in December 1882 had brought his pupil to the U.S. from Australia. Slade stood 6'2" and weighed around 220 pounds. Mace said Slade was the hardest hitter that he had ever seen, and a wonderful wrestler who threw the big and strong wrestler/fighter Professor William Miller like a baby. Slade could withstand punishment and was as active as a cat. Mace's backing and stamp of approval served to market Slade instantly. For the next several months, Mace and Slade gave exhibitions together.

The 52-year-old Mace claimed to be willing to fight Sullivan. However, Sullivan preferred to fight Slade, because there would be more credit associated with a victory over a young man, as opposed to one who was too old and past-it to do much against him.[80] There were some intermittent discussions of a potential Sullivan-Mace bout, but after Mace saw Sullivan in action, he changed his mind.

---

[77] *National Police Gazette,* February 10, 1883.

[78] *Toronto Globe,* January 24, 1883; see also *Toronto Evening Telegram,* January 24, 1883.

[79] *National Police Gazette,* January 27, 1883.

[80] *Billings Herald,* January 18, 1883.

Regardless of the rules that were to be used, a potential Slade-Sullivan bout encountered legal obstacles. New York authorities made known their displeasure even at the thought of such a contest. They made it clear that they would try to do everything they could to make things difficult.

HERBERT A. SLADE,

THE MAORI HERCULES, TO BE MATCHED BY THE "POLICE GAZETTE" AGAINST THE AMERICAN CHAMPION, JOHN L. SULLIVAN.

When *National Police Gazette* owner Richard K. Fox arranged a sparring bout between Slade and Mace in late January 1883, Fox and the two boxers were arrested in New York on a warrant charging them with violating the penal code by planning to participate in and promoting, aiding, and abetting prize-fighting, based on Fox's offer to put up $5,000 for a Slade-Sullivan match. Fox had to post a $1,000 bond and agree to keep the peace.[81]

Ultimately, Fox took the matter to court, and a fair judge ruled that the arranged sparring was not a violation of the law. The *Police Gazette* trumpeted its victory over "bigots and sneaks."[82] However, certainly the ruling made it obvious that a Sullivan-Slade bout, if it took place in New York, would have to be fought under the Queensberry rules. Sullivan and his manager Madden wanted the fight to be held in New York because it was the most populous and affluent state in the nation, which made it more likely that the fight would yield a bigger gate. Fox still wanted to find a location to host the fight using traditional LPR rules. Madden was concerned about their being arrested for such a contest. Eventually, in May, Mace and Slade went to England to give exhibitions there.

In February 1883, in Rochester, New York, Sullivan and Coburn gave another one of their exhibitions. 48-year-old Coburn had retained his

---

[81] *Toronto Globe,* January 31, 1883; Isenberg at 136.

[82] *National Police Gazette,* February 17, 1883.

scientific skill, but was "no match for his youthful opponent's ponderous muscles."[83]

On February 22, 1883 in Boston, Sullivan boxed 3 exhibition rounds with "middleweight champion" Pete McCoy. "Both men were in fine condition and gave a magnificent display of the science of boxing. Heavy blows and lightning-like parries and counters were the order of exhibition between them, and elicited frequent rounds of applause."[84]

On March 1, 1883 in New York's Madison Square Garden, as part of an exhibition benefit for recent Ohio valley flood survivors, Sullivan sparred 3 friendly rounds with well-known athlete Professor John Laflin. Sullivan was received with great cheering, for his presence "was sufficient to arouse the greatest excitement among the spectators. The applause was terrific."

Regarding the Sullivan-Laflin exhibition, the *New York Daily Tribune* said, "Both are finely-formed men, and both spar well, but Sullivan forced the fighting and got decidedly the best of the first two rounds. In the third round, however, Laflin rallied and held his own." The *New York Times* said, "Mr. Sullivan rapped the Professor on the nose, forehead, ears, and mouth, but the Professor never flinched." The audience was quite satisfied, for the exhibition had been sufficiently exhilarating.

As he left the stage, Sullivan savagely exclaimed, "If that was only the Maori, I'd show you more!" The crowd cheered long and loud. The band played "Hail to the Chief."

That same day, in Chicago, Jerry Dunn shot and killed Jimmy Elliott. Apparently, Dunn had insulted Elliott's courage, saying that Elliott feared another meeting with Sullivan, which led to their drawing guns on one another in a Chicago saloon. Eventually, Dunn, who earlier in his life had killed two other men, was successful with his self-defense claim, for a jury acquitted him.[85]

On March 13 at a benefit at Madison Square Garden in New York, showing his generosity, after Sullivan sparred Coburn before a crowd of 5,000, Sully announced that he would contribute $100 to the fund for Jimmy Elliott's mother.

On March 19, 1883 in Boston's Mechanics' Fair Building, over 12,000 people witnessed another Sullivan exhibition show. It was a sold-out house, standing room was packed, and thousands more were turned away, for there was not enough space. Tickets were scalped for $4 and $5, with plenty of buyers. It was "the largest assemblage of people ever gathered together to witness a sparring exhibition in Boston." Looked upon as "the champion of all champions," Sullivan could pack a house even for friendly sparring exhibitions. Sully said the benefit generated over $15,000 in net profits.

---

[83] *National Police Gazette,* February 17, 1883. Sullivan also exhibited with McCoy in Boston on February 22.

[84] *Boston Herald,* February 23, 1883.

[85] *New York Daily Tribune, New York Times,* March 2, 1883. Sullivan boxed McCoy on March 5 in Lawrence, Massachusetts, and on the 6th in New York.

They boxed on a 5-foot high platform in a 24-foot ring with two ropes, with stakes at the corners and at the midpoints. Police were stationed at each corner and at the mid-point of each side.

The "world champion pugilist" told the crowd that it would be a scientific exhibition with no knocking out.

Sullivan exhibited in three separate 3-round sparring sessions; with former opponent Steve Taylor, Joe Coburn, and Mike Cleary. The 5'8 ½" Cleary was born in Ireland a year before Sullivan and weighed around 175 pounds. He was known both for his science and power, in 1882 having knocked out former Sullivan opponent George Rooke in 3 rounds.

Mike Cleary

First, Sullivan sparred 3 rounds with Steve Taylor. Sullivan wore light orange tights and a white shirt. Taylor wore bright pink tights and a white shirt trimmed with blue. In the 1st round, Taylor did most of the leading. They both picked it up in the 2nd. The 3rd round was fairly even.

Other exhibitions followed, including one between Pete McCoy and future Sullivan opponent Jake Kilrain. "Some very scientific sparring was shown, and the boxers proved themselves very proficient in the science of self-defense." The first 2 rounds of Kilrain-McCoy were close, but Kilrain had the advantage in the 3rd with some short-arm hitting.

Years later, it was reported that Sullivan had exhibited with Kilrain in one or more of his various exhibition bouts during the early 1880s.

Sullivan next sparred with Joe Coburn. Despite his advanced age, Coburn "exhibited considerable strength and agility." They boxed evenly and well for 3 rounds, making "one of the most enjoyable displays ever witnessed in Boston." Of course, "Sullivan could have made a fool of old Joe Coburn, but he used his 'left' only." Still, Sullivan was "clearly the master of Joe in strength."

After some additional exhibitions, Sullivan and Cleary ended the show, sparring in friendly fashion, using only light blows, though they threw a fair number of them. "Sullivan maintained the manifest superiority he had shown in the two other meets."

Afterwards, the Commercial Athletic Club gave Sullivan a gold medal in a box which had written on it in gold letters, "John L. Sullivan of Boston." The medal said, "Champion of the World."[86]

Throughout his career, quite often Sullivan would spar several times in friendly fashion to entertain a crowd. He knew how to hold back and work with sparring partners. Essentially, he was being paid very well to train in front of an audience.

[86] *Boston Herald,* March 20, 1883; *New York Clipper,* March 24, 1883; *National Police Gazette,* November 4, 1882; Isenberg at 127-128.

International Title Challengers

On April 24, 1883, John L. Sullivan suffered a lung hemorrhage and coughed up so much blood that he fainted. He slipped in and out of consciousness. Sullivan was so concerned that he summoned a priest to perform last rites. His parents even came to his bedside. The clergyman who performed the sacrament suggested that if he recovered, Sully should stop living in sin and marry Annie.

Sullivan soon overcame the illness, and immediately thereafter, on May 1, 1883, he married Annie Bailey in St. Patrick's Church, the same parish where his parents wed.

A well-known Sullivan vice was and would be alcohol. Sullivan denied that his recent illness had been the result of alcohol. He said it was the result of a cold, and insisted that he limited himself to only four or five glasses of ale a day. Still, given his growing reputation for drinking to excess, most suspected that the true cause of his illness was alcohol.

What made matters more concerning was the fact that Sullivan had an upcoming bout set to be held in only two weeks. Despite having just recovered from his illness, the seemingly invincible Sullivan did not request a postponement. He trained just outside of Boston with Patsey/Patsy Sheppard, a former lightweight fighter.

Charles Mitchell

Sullivan's upcoming opponent was England's current champion, Charley Mitchell. The 22-year-old Mitchell had been fighting in England since 1878 at age 16. His parents were Irish. Although only 5'9" tall and a middleweight in size, he had proven his ability to defeat heavyweights. In an 1879 LPR fight, he stopped 176-pound Baily Gray, a black fighter, in 11 minutes (1 round). In February 1881, he won a 4-round glove fight against Continental champion 224-pound W. Caradoff (or Caryadoff). In a June 1881 LPR fight, Mitchell fought a 1-hour 17-minute 25-round draw against fellow Brit Jack Burke, the fight being stopped as a result of darkness. For having participated in this illegal contest, both men had to serve a 6-week jail sentence.

After Billy Madden and Sullivan had split, Richard K. Fox had financed Madden's journey to England to seek a man capable of defeating Sullivan. In late December 1882 in London, Madden hosted an all-comers boxing tournament, with the winner to be paid 40 pounds and to be brought to the U.S. to fight Sullivan. Mitchell won six 3-round bouts and emerged victorious from the tournament.

Subsequently, in January and February 1883, Mitchell was superior to Tug Wilson and Alf Greenfield in exhibition bouts. Mitchell then came to the U.S.

On April 9, 1883 in New York, Mitchell defeated Sullivan sparring partner Mike Cleary, dropping and beating him badly enough that the police stopped it in the 3rd round. To that point, Mitchell was undefeated in about 17 bouts. He was fast, powerful, clever, and skillful. New Yorkers were sold, and the Sullivan bout was arranged for the following month.[87]

The *New York Clipper* said that Mitchell was the champion of England by virtue of his victory in the all-comers tournament. The *National Police Gazette* also called Mitchell the champion pugilist of England. The *Clipper* said Sullivan was the "technical champion of America and virtual champion of the world." The local press typically called Sullivan the American champion and Mitchell the English champion, giving the bout an international world championship feel.

---

87 *National Police Gazette*, February 10, 1883, April 14, 1883, April 21, 1883; *Australian Sportsman*, May 9, 1883; Isenberg at 133.

On Monday May 14, 1883 in New York's Madison Square Garden, the scheduled 4-round Sullivan-Mitchell Queensberry rules gloved contest took place.

Mitchell allegedly weighed only about 154 pounds, while Sullivan weighed 194 pounds, 40 pounds more, though some believed that Sullivan was even bigger. Back then, they did not concern themselves with weight disparities. If two men wanted to fight, they fought. There were no weigh ins. Sullivan's trainer, Frank Moran, said that when John L. began training, he weighed 223 pounds. Two days before the fight, on May 12, Sullivan weighed 202 pounds, but after taking a hot Turkish bath, he weighed 194 pounds.

10,000 or 12,000 spectators packed Madison Square Garden "to its utmost limits." The newspapers reported that no soft glove sparring exhibition ever had attracted so much public attention. All classes attended, including politicians, judges, lawyers, theatrical celebrities, members of the sporting fraternity, and the police. Former U.S. Senator Roscoe Conkling, who once had been a bareknuckle fighter, was in attendance. Also present in the house was Harry Hill, Richard K. Fox, Billy Madden, Patsey Sheppard, Joe Coburn, Mike Donovan, Mike Cleary, Pete McCoy, Bob Farrell, Florrie Barnett, Arthur Chambers, Billy Edwards, and Dooney Harris. Patrons had come from all over the country to see the bout. "The event was the biggest of its kind."

Although for legal purposes it was claimed that they would be engaging in a "friendly spar of 4 rounds," everyone knew it was going to be a fight. "Probably all present would have been disappointed had they been assured, that the contest was in truth to be a 'friendly' one." However, after the authorities had prevented the Tug Wilson rematch and other contests, fight promoters had to be more careful about their sales language. In New York, no more could Sullivan advertise that he was going to knock out someone.

It was nearly 9:30 p.m. when the pugilists entered the ring for the main event. Sullivan entered first. He was stripped to the waist and wore tight-fitting pink salmon-colored drawers, white stockings, and gaiters. He appeared to be fatter than when he met Tug Wilson, though his trainer claimed that he weighed 20 pounds less. He sat in a chair in his corner, and rested his muscular arms on the ropes. His black hair was neatly combed. Pete McCoy was with him, as well as Patsy Sheppard and Al Smith.

Charlie Mitchell entered, wearing white drawers, socks ribbed in brilliant colors, a gauze sleeveless shirt, and calfskin gaiters. A white-and-blue kerchief fluttered over his left hip. Charley had pale white skin and blue eyes. He bowed slightly to the audience and sat down.

Police Captain Clubber Williams checked the gloves to ensure that they were soft and not hard. Inspector Thorne was present as well.

Alluding to Sullivan's drinking and illness the month before, a local newspaper said that John L. looked "none the worse for his reported illness and hard living." Sullivan said, "I haven't touched a drop today."

The 24-foot ring was pitched on a platform in the center of the great hall. A score of electric lights and over a thousand gas jets shed a bright light over the arena.

Mr. William Mahoney introduced them, and the noise was so great that his introduction barely could be heard. He waived his right hand towards one corner, and said, "Mr. John L. Sullivan." Then his left gyrated towards the opposite corner and he said, "Mr. William Mitchell." He then shouted "Time" to start the bout and the men quickly jumped to their feet. Al Smith refereed.

1 - Mitchell started the fight aggressively, striking Sullivan with a stiff left, but Sullivan responded by running forward with a left and right to the sides of the head that dropped Mitchell.

Charley rose and landed several strong left jabs, but Sullivan attacked and decked him again, although one paper said that Mitchell slipped and fell when dodging a blow. He rose and they engaged in some lively hitting.

In a surprise, Mitchell scored his own flash knockdown of Sullivan, each local paper giving its own version of how it happened:

New York Times – After a clinch, Mitchell backed and Sullivan followed.

> Suddenly however, the little man stopped, and making a quick stroke upward, caught his opponent a square blow in the face which knocked him clean off his feet. … Sullivan was on his feet again in an instant, and again the two clinched and Mitchell was borne down to the ropes, the heavy form of his opponent pressing against him. This ended the round.

This gave the impression that Mitchell landed either a right uppercut or a straight right thrown from low to high.

New York Tribune - As they worked towards the ropes, Mitchell "cross-countered and put in a left and right which sent Sullivan to the floor fairly on his back."

New York Herald - Sullivan landed a right which staggered Mitchell back into a corner, but when John followed-up, Mitchell hit him with "a terrific right-hander on the chin, which floored him as if he had been hit with a pole-axe. This seemed to enrage the Bostonian, for when he got on his pins again he dashed after the wily Englishman."

New York Clipper - "Mitchell planted his right straight and squarely on the chin, fairly knocking Sullivan onto his seat." Sullivan immediately rose and rushed at Mitchell, who retreated. They exchanged hard blows. Although Mitchell landed well and was demonstrating some good defense on the retreat, he still was receiving most of the punishment inflicted.

New York Sun – Sullivan made another mad rush at him, and Mitchell landed a right on the jaw with full force and capsized him.

In his autobiography, Sullivan claimed that he was standing with his feet close together and that he was dropped as a result of being off balance. He quoted a writer as reporting, "Sullivan says his legs got crossed, and Mitchell hitting him knocked him down as you would knock over a chair."

Sullivan immediately rose and attacked Mitchell like a bull, forcing the fighting. Mitchell was not able to keep away, so he closed in. Sullivan threw him off, but Mitchell grabbed around the waist. They fought up close in the clinches until the bell rang.

2 - Sullivan came out fighting furiously, like a wild beast, delivering sledgehammer blows that drove Mitchell against the ropes three times. Doing his best to parry and fight back, Mitchell landed a solid body shot and a left to the mouth that made a smacking sound that could be heard throughout the building. Nevertheless, Sullivan maintained his rapid pace, constantly coming forward like a locomotive, landing a tremendously powerful body blow that had its effect. He kept working, not allowing Mitchell any rest, beating down his guard. Sullivan landed a right to the jaw, and Mitchell clinched. After breaking free, a Sullivan left and right knocked Mitchell down near the ropes.

As soon as Mitchell rose, Sullivan sprang towards him again. They exchanged blows, interspersed with clinches. Sullivan ran at him and landed both hands on the head. A succession of three rights dropped Mitchell for the second time in the round.

Mitchell rose, and Sullivan landed two lefts and a right to the head that dropped him again. Upon rising, Mitchell looked weak and dazed.

Sullivan gradually pushed Mitchell to the ropes, and then the champ quickly sprang forward and landed a right to the jaw that sent Mitchell entirely over the top rope and out of the ring, falling head-first into the crowd and down to the floor below. He would have sustained severe injuries had his fall not been cushioned by the hands and arms of the spectators who tried to catch him and diminish his fall. The bell rang, saving him before he re-entered the ring with assistance from the crowd.

The *National Police Gazette* said that Sullivan had knocked him around and down in Tug Wilson fashion. It later claimed that Mitchell had injured his back in his fall to the floor below.

3 Mitchell moved around the ring, with Sullivan chasing after him. Sullivan fought him down at the ropes and fell on top of him.

After rising and resuming, a Sullivan left and right sent Mitchell down again.

Mitchell rose and managed to land a good body blow, but it had no effect. After a clinch, John twice hit him in the face with his left, and then a heavy right knocked Mitchell clean across the ring and down in a heap against the ropes.

The dazed Mitchell barely managed to beat the 10-count. At that point, Police Captain Alexander "Clubber" Williams mounted the stage with his nightstick, entered the ring, and held up his hand, informing the men that the contest had to stop. "This fight must stop right here." He was not about to allow matters to proceed any further. "The referee, who saw that Mitchell was beaten, declared that Sullivan had won the fight."

No one criticized the stoppage. Everyone agreed that it was prudent to end matters, for Mitchell was hurt badly. The *New York Times* said, "He was dazed, and it was evident that he could not sustain the unequal contest much longer." The feeling was that had Mitchell been allowed to continue, he would have been "knocked senseless before it was concluded." "As it was, Sullivan, with his trip-hammer blows, succeeded in dazing Mitchell so completely that he was quite willing, and even thankful, to have the fight stopped, and the Boston prize-fighter was declared the winner of the match." This writer claimed that the police captain asked him if he was satisfied, and Mitchell said that he was.

The *New York Herald* said that even the spectators were glad to see the contest stopped, which was a rare occurrence. "It was remarked that this is the first occasion on which police interference with a fight has not been hissed. … Every one admired the pluck of the Englishman, while they understood it was of no avail and were glad to see him exposed to no further punishment."

The *Brooklyn Daily Eagle* summarized that "but for the intervention of the police, Mitchell would unquestionably have been knocked out."

The *Sun* echoed that Mitchell was staggeringly weak and tottering, and without police interference, would have been knocked out.

The *New York Clipper* said Mitchell clearly was shaky, and "he had undertaken a task he was physically incapable of accomplishing." It was "apparent to all that he was not able to longer continue the unequal conflict." Nevertheless, Mitchell was game and willing to continue, and Sullivan wanted to finish him. However,

> [T]he action taken by Capt. Williams was probably best for all concerned, and no fault was found with it by the spectators, usually so strenuously opposed to any interference with their amusements, but who on this occasion recognized that to prolong the affair would only cause needless punishment to be inflicted upon a game man whose power to fight had gone.

Captain Williams said he had stopped the match because he thought Mitchell was completely done for, and if allowed to continue, just would have suffered needless punishment and been knocked down again. It no longer was a sparring match.

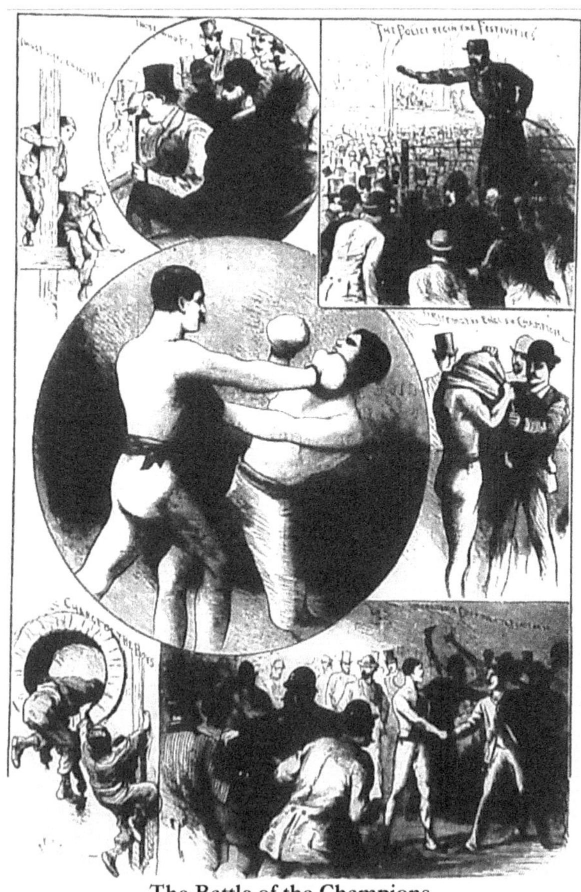

The Battle of the Champions
Sullivan and Mitchell, the American and English Champion Pugilists, Meet in the Arena at Madison Square Garden, on May 14. A Lively Contest With the Gloves Before a Throng of Excited Spectators

Mitchell said that he would have continued the bout if the police had not interfered. "There are many turns in a fight." He had a bump on his forehead and his arms were wrenched badly from stopping Sullivan's blows. "All I know is what people told me, and that is, that I got worsted."

Sullivan said, "I think Mitchell is a very game little man. There is no Tug Wilson about him. He stands up and takes his punishment well." He also said that Mitchell "is a good little man, but too small for me."

Regarding his future, Sullivan said, "I intend to retire from the ring, and will never fight again with the bare knuckles." He meant LPR fights. He still would meet any man with the gloves under Queensberry rules.

The *New York Tribune* said, "The general impression among 'sporting' men was that though Mitchell had shown his superior science, Sullivan was much too heavy and powerful an opponent for him to meet with bare knuckles." The *National Police Gazette* agreed that Mitchell was overmatched. The *Sun* said Mitchell was no match.

Sullivan received 60% of the proceeds, while Mitchell received 40%. The gate likely exceeded $15,000, though some said it was $11,000 or $12,000. Regardless of the exact numbers, it was a very nice payday.

In the days subsequent to the fight, Mitchell was less than pleased with the stoppage, saying,

> I was not hurt at all, and felt as well at the finish as I did at the start. … I was never knocked down, but was borne under by the superior weight of my opponent and the slipperiness of the stage. … I am sure had the rounds continued, he could not have knocked me out…but I must say, in justice to Sullivan, he is the strongest man, if not the cleverest, that I have ever met. … But I don't think he will be over-anxious to meet me again.

In his autobiography, Sullivan said that he had Mitchell helpless and completely at his mercy. He wanted to finish him, saying, "Captain, let me have one more crack at him." However, the police captain feared that he would be killed, asking, "John, do you want to kill him?" "When Mitchell recovered, he made all sorts of bluffs, and Capt. Williams said: - 'You go to your dressing-room. You are a lucky individual that I stepped in and saved Sullivan from killing you.'" Sully quoted ex-U.S. Senator Roscoe Conkling as saying, "Mitchell is a very good man, but he met another who is his superior all the way around. … Mitchell was unquestionably overmatched."[88]

Sullivan had defeated the champions of the U.S., Canada, and England.

Sullivan exhibited with John Flood on the 17th at Madison Square Garden. That same week, Sullivan also appeared on stage in Boston in a play called "Tom and Jerry."

On May 24, 1883, the Brooklyn Bridge opened. Richard K. Fox's *National Police Gazette* headquarters overlooked Franklin Square and the entrance ramp to the bridge. His lavishly-adorned office included a life-size portrait of Sullivan, as well as other sports memorabilia. When the bridge opened, he threw a huge and wild party that attracted thousands.

John L. Sullivan's first love was baseball. He had learned that he was so famous that folks would pay to see him, even if it wasn't inside a ring. He started making semi-pro baseball appearances, pitching and hitting for various teams, and being paid half the gate to do so. His appearances had a way of packing the house.

On May 28, 1883, 4,000 fans, including, men, boys, and even women, paid fifty cents each to watch Sullivan play baseball as a pitcher for the semi-pro New York Metropolitans at the Polo Grounds. He got three hits – all singles, scored a run, committed four errors, threw three wild pitches, struck out one batter, and gave up a lot of hits, although his team still won, 20 to 15. Sully earned half the gate, or $1,585.90.

A few days later, he pitched for the Philadelphia Athletics and won with a 15 to 2 score.

---

[88] *New York Times*, *New York Tribune*, *New York Herald*, *New York Sun*, *Brooklyn Daily Eagle*, May 15, 1883; *Boston Herald*, May 15, 16, 1883; *Boston Globe Supplement*, May 17, 1883; *National Police Gazette*, May 26, 1883, July 12, 1884; *New York Clipper*, May 19, 1883; Sullivan at 86-87, 178.

At various times throughout his career, Sullivan accepted baseball gigs, for he enjoyed playing the game, and he made money. Team owners realized that he boosted ticket sales. He also occasionally would umpire baseball games. His mere presence was a gate draw.

Outside the ring, the champion was continuing to drink a fair amount. Some reported that a drunken, angry Sullivan had smashed furniture in his home and struck his wife. Some later even suggested that he had assaulted his sister, who was married to a man named James Lennon. Both women publicly denied the reports, although his wife Annie admitted that her husband "is so lavish in entertaining his friends that he sometimes oversteps the bounds of prudence in his habits of sociability and is then a little morose and surly." Many knew that Sullivan's drinking habit was a problem.

Despite his faults, during this time, Sullivan was supporting his parents financially.

On June 21 in New Haven, before his scheduled boxing exhibition with Steve Taylor, Sullivan spent nearly the entire day sleeping, recovering from a bad hangover. He then proceeded to perform in a very mild and disinterested manner. Sometimes Sullivan's drinking even caused him to call off exhibition engagements.

A black fighter named Charles Smith challenged Sullivan, "but the champion objected to meeting Smith on account of his color." This was the first known time that Sullivan openly drew the color-line, the social and legal norm holding that the races should not compete with one another. Despite the fact that separation of the races was the general rule, the *National Police Gazette* said, "We do not see why Sullivan should refuse to arrange a match with Smith merely because he is a colored man. Bob Travers, the great pugilist, was a colored man, and he arranged matches with and fought some of the best pugilists in England." Eventually, on August 16, 1883, Jack Stewart, whom Sullivan had defeated, quickly knocked out Smith in six minutes.[89]

[89] *National Police Gazette*, August 4, September 8, 1883.

Although many fair-minded sportsmen and members of the press did not believe the color-line should apply in boxing, Sullivan was a reflection of his era. Slavery had ended in 1865. After the federal government withdrew troops from the South in 1877, most post-war advances in civil rights were in fact reversed completely, and many laws were passed mandating separation of the races. In late 1883, the United States Supreme Court would rule that race discrimination in public accommodations was perfectly legal, and Congress had no power to pass legislation requiring equal treatment.

Herbert Slade

Sullivan's next scheduled bout was the long-awaited fight with the large New Zealander Herbert "The Maori" Slade. Slade's father was Irish and his mother was Maori, which was a New Zealand native, thought to have migrated there from Tahiti or Polynesia. Slade's trainer/manager Jem Mace said the undefeated Slade had whipped every man he had faced at "rough-and-tumble fighting."

In early 1883 in the U.S., a 222-pound Slade gave several 4-round gloved exhibitions with Mace. Slade also exhibited with George Robinson and Joe Coburn. The *National Police Gazette* reported that Slade was both strong and clever.[90]

[90] *National Police Gazette*, January 27, 1883, February 24, 1883, August 18, 1883.

After a January 8, 1883 exhibition between Mace and Slade in San Francisco, it was reported that the general opinion was that Sullivan would find Slade "to be a harder man than he has met yet." Mace said of the 6'2" Slade, "He can outbox, outwrestle, and outjump any man in the world, and he ain't 28 years old."

Mace also said, "I wish I was 40 instead of 50, so that I could enter the lists for the championship." Mace was willing to spar Sullivan, but only if John L. would promise not to knock him out, which John L. refused to do.[91]

A reporter who saw a San Francisco exhibition between Slade and Olympic Club champion George Robinson was not all that impressed:

> [Slade's] sparring was neither as scientific nor as satisfactory as that of his opponent. Slade was not quick to counter and he missed almost every opportunity for cross-countering. ... The action of Slade gives rise to the suspicion that his success in the prize-ring will depend upon his ability as a wrestler. He certainly has failed to show any marked ability as a boxer.[92]

However, Mace and Slade countered the report by insisting that Slade had promised to go easy with Robinson, so he was holding back.[93]

Regardless, Slade had the backing, sponsorship, and marketing of Fox and Mace, and he was a large, strong-looking man touted as the Australian champion, so the contest had a big-fight aura.

Sullivan trained with Joe Goss and Pete McCoy, some saying that he had to train down from 230 pounds. He stopped drinking and got into fine physical condition.

On Monday August 6, 1883 in New York's Madison Square Garden, in a Queensberry rules fight scheduled for 4 rounds, John L. Sullivan fought Herbert Slade. The *New York Times* called Sullivan the heavyweight champion of the world and Slade the "half-breed Maori."

Anywhere from 10,000 to 13,000 people were crammed into the sold-out arena, making it the "largest crowd that ever gathered there." Even standing-room and the aisles were utterly packed. Present were U.S. Congressmen - Senators and Representatives, the U.S. Attorney General, local politicians, judges, physicians, brokers, lawyers, and businessmen, etc. The *New York Herald* said, "The oldest timers at fairs, shows and walking matches admitted they had never seen the like of it." Thousands more were unable to get in, for the arena simply could not hold any more people.

For tickets, the crowd paid from $1 all the way up to $25 for box seats. "Over $20,000 were taken in. When it is remembered that the President of the United States is paid at the rate of about $270 a day...the transcendent

---

[91] Sullivan at 94-95, quoting *Cincinnati Enquirer* (no date provided); *National Police Gazette*, January 2, 1883.

[92] *New York Clipper*, January 27, 1883.

[93] *New York Clipper*, February 3, 1883.

abilities of the two performers of last night can be appreciated." U.S. President Chester A. Arthur's salary was a huge $50,000 per year, a presidential salary that would not increase until 1909. The Vice-President made $10,000 per year, while U.S. Senators earned $5,000 per year.

The winner of the fight was to earn 65% of the gate, and the loser the 35% remainder, after expenses.

Mace's boosting of Slade helped make the odds for this one tight, with the betters laying $80 on Slade to $100 on Sullivan.

The ring was 24-feet-square with an 18-inch extension beyond the ropes to help prevent a pugilist from going through the ropes and onto the floor. It was on a platform in the center of the arena, raised about 4 feet from the floor. Steps led up to the top of the platform. Mace had insisted on the ring extension, as well as stronger, tighter ropes, not wanting his man to be sent through the ropes into the crowd like Mitchell.

As usual, Captain Williams and Inspector Thorne were present with a strong force of policemen. Also present in the arena were Harry Hill and Richard K. Fox.

The heat was oppressive inside, although it was cool outside. Ventilation was poor, and the densely packed mass of humanity sweltered amid the haze of smoke from countless cigars.

The preliminary bouts started just after 8 p.m., and after an hour, the main event was about to start.

Upon entering the ring, the loud applause and cheers that Sullivan and Slade received showed the spectators' excitement. It was thrilling. Sullivan wore a white shirt and pink trunks. Slade wore all white. Before the fight began, they would remove their shirts. John L. sat down with his arms outstretched upon the upper ropes. He looked at Slade like a hungry cat about to pounce on a mouse. His eyes blazened. Slade did not return the gaze.

Sullivan's superb physical development caused murmurs of admiration. "Although said to be weighing 197 pounds, he was in such perfect condition that each muscle and quick-gliding tendon stood out in bold relief upon his spotless skin." No fat could be seen. Slade, although clearly taller and heavier, lacked the champion's symmetry. "He weighed 220 pounds they said, and he looked it." Sullivan sized him up with a contemptuous smile.

Barney Aaron refereed. Parson Davies was the timekeeper. Joe Goss seconded Sullivan, and tied his gloves. Mace did not work Slade's corner, but instead a man named Harry Montague, who tied Slade's gloves. Mace sat near his corner, though.

Master of ceremonies Pop Whittaker introduced the fighters, and then told them, "I only want to impress on you two gentlemen – no wrestling, and when the referee calls upon you to break away we want you to obey the referee – if you please. That's all I have to say."

At 9:23 p.m., the fight began to a tremendous chorus of cheers, shouts, screams, and whistles.

1 - After some early feinting, Sullivan ferociously attacked with "irresistible rushes." Sully landed a heavy left hook on the side of Slade's head. They clinched and struggled. After breaking, Slade moved around, but found it difficult to hit the oncoming attacker. Several times they exchanged blows and clinched. Sullivan threw more punches than Slade and was more effective. Sullivan's succession of blows came so rapidly that Slade could parry only some of them. A Sullivan left to Slade's nose drew blood. A downward blow to Slade's neck almost brought him down. Slade backed away. Sullivan rained blows on his head. Slade took them, but then ferociously returned the attack until Sullivan clinched. Slade again attacked but Sullivan blocked and landed an uppercut to the chin that staggered Slade. Sullivan rushed again and a right under the ear and a left to the eye and nose sent Slade falling backward and down onto the floor.

Slade rose within two seconds, clinched, and then fired uppercuts which Sullivan blocked. Sullivan broke free from the clinch and rained a succession of furious blows fired from his shoulder upon Slade, running forward chasing after him while punching at the same time, ending with a left to the nose that turned Slade halfway around, and then a swinging right to the jaw that literally raised him from his feet and flung him backwards through the ropes and off the platform stage down onto the floor several feet below. Mace's efforts to prevent such an occurrence had been to no avail.

It required Slade more than 10 seconds to re-enter the ring, but no one seemed to mind, for he needed to walk around to the steps. Captain Williams and Jem Mace assisted him. Sullivan rushed at him but Slade returned the fire until Sullivan caught his head in a hold. They were ordered to break, and then the round ended. Slade's left eye was swollen.

2 - Sullivan began the round throwing with less power, but then he made a rush and drove Slade back with a "shower of sledge-hammer blows." However, Slade fought back hard and countered, landing well. They both landed some hard body shots. Slade's nose was bleeding. Sullivan made another rush, and a right and left to the neck and jaw sent Slade down.

Slade quickly rose and continued fighting. Sullivan landed several body blows. After they broke from a clinch, Sullivan attacked with two rights, a right uppercut and a right to the head that dropped Slade again.

Slade rose, and after taking a few blows, he tried to rally and fight back, giving blow for blow, landing some good ones. Then he clinched and wrestled a fair amount. Nevertheless, Sullivan kept up the attack, firing away with merciless rapidity, forcing Slade back up to the ropes, where a right under the ear dropped him again. At that point, the round ended. Slade was bloody and bruised, while Sullivan was unmarked.

The *Police Gazette* later reported that at times, Slade's seconds assisted him to his feet after being knocked down. Although technically this was a violation of the Queensberry rules, Slade's seconds were more familiar with the LPR rules, which allowed them to assist their man after a knockdown. Slade also wrestled a great deal, which was typical of an LPR-trained fighter.

3 - Sullivan's white gloves were slightly stained with blood. Slade's gloves were still white. Slade's left eye was swollen nearly shut and was purpled. Blood poured down from his bruised nose, and his lips were swollen.

Sullivan again went on the attack, firing blows as swift as bullets. Slade ran away in an attempt to escape "the succession of blows showered on him." Sullivan hurt him with a left to the body and right to the head. He again hurt him with a right to the body and right to the head. A right to either the cheek or nose turned Slade partly around. Sullivan followed with an onslaught that staggered Slade backward.

Slade reeled to the ropes, but he made a desperate dash at Sullivan and landed two heavy blows to the head, and then followed up with two more. They clinched and Slade landed on the neck.

Sullivan sprang away, but then quickly darted forward and planted two heavy lefts, one on the nose and one on the left eye, followed by a heavy right uppercut that sent Slade through the ropes again, falling heavily in a heap, although this time he did not fall off the platform. "Slade fell like an ox knocked down with a butcher's axe, and he lay bleeding from the ear, mouth and nose, beaten and helpless." He was "sprawling upon the floor, face downwards, under the ropes." Yet, Slade slowly rolled back in under the ropes, with blood pouring from his nose, and his eye almost closed.

While Sullivan had been pounding away, Police Captain Williams had mounted the stage, getting very close to stopping it, for he saw that the "game was up."

Slade got to a sitting posture, but was badly dazed. One of his seconds helped him to his feet and led him to the corner. "When lifted up and taken to his corner he was quite stupid, and being unfit to face Sullivan again, Harry Montague gave up for him, and Barney Aaron, the referee, declared Sullivan the winner of the fight amid the uproarious cheers of the crowd." Captain Williams and Inspector Thorne had entered the ring as well, and if Slade's cornermen had not stopped it, they were going to do so. Others said that Williams and Thorne were the ones who stopped the match, two minutes into the 3rd round.

The *New York-Tribune* summarized that Slade was not a good dodger and showed little skill in escaping blows. However, he stood up manfully, closed in and landed some good hard returns in response to Sullivan's tremendous pounding. But with all his strength, Slade could not hit like Sullivan. "When the champion struck the whole man seemed in the stroke."

The *New York Sun* said Slade was no match, but had put up a furious fight for 2 ½ rounds.

The *Brooklyn Daily Eagle* summarized that it was not a fight at all, but a brutal beating administered by the world's greatest pugilist. Although disguised as a "friendly set to with gloves," the "gloves are put on merely to evade the statute against pugilism."

Afterwards, the champion shook Slade's hand and said, "You're the best man I've ever tackled."

THE CHAMPION STILL VICTORIOUS.

A reporter interviewed Slade. "How do you feel?" "A little blowed and a trifle bruised but otherwise all right." "What do you think of Sullivan?" "He's a hard hitter." "Do you want to fight him again?" Slade did not answer. Slade's left eye was closed entirely, badly swollen, and blackened, and his nose and hips were bruised.

Jem Mace said he thought his pupil had stood his ground with pluck, but "his head was in the way."

Later that evening, a great crowd stood in front of the Ashland House, calling for Sullivan, who came out on the balcony and bowed. He had not the slightest scratch.

Sullivan told a reporter that Slade was a little superior to Mitchell, and far superior to Tug Wilson. Sullivan admired Slade for taking the blows that he did and still fighting back hard, although John L. said Slade never hurt him. Explaining the end, Sullivan said, "Well, I had been hitting him under the lower rib, hoping to wind him by my under-cuts, but the two blows which I gave him right on top of the nose knocked him silly, and that was the last of him."

John Boyle O'Reilly, writer for the Boston *Pilot*, assessed Sullivan's skills and ability:

> The superiority of Sullivan lies in his extraordinary nervous force and his altogether incomparable skill as a boxer.
>
> In what does his extraordinary skill consist? In hitting as straight and almost as rapid as light; in the variety and readiness of his blows; in standing firmly on his feet and driving his whole weight and nervous force at the end of his fist, - a very rare and a very high quality in a boxer; in movements as quick and purposeful as the leap of a lion. He can 'duck' lower than any feather-weight boxer in America; he can strike more heavy blows in ten seconds than any other man in a minute, and he watches his opponent with a self-possession and calculation that do not flurry with excitement, but only flame into a ravening intensity to beat him down…
>
> Other boxers begin by sparring; he begins by fighting – and he never ceases to fight. But from the first instant of the fight, Sullivan is as fierce, relentless, tireless as a cataract. … He does not waste ten seconds of the three minutes of each round.
>
> And look at the odds he offers, and offers to all the world! … Observe, he will not only defeat all comers, but he will defeat them in four rounds – in twelve minutes! …
>
> The American champion, Sullivan, has done more than attempt to defeat all pugilists…he has made a manly and most creditable effort to establish the practice not only of sparring, but of fighting with large gloves. The adoption of gloves for all contests will do more to preserve the practice of boxing than any other conceivable means. It will give pugilism new life, not only as a professional boxer's art, but as general exercise.[94]

The very next day, on August 7, 1883 in Boston, Sullivan opened up a new business, which anyone who knows anything about Sullivan's proclivities towards alcohol would not be surprised to learn was a saloon. He paid $15,000 for the building at 714 Washington Street, but invested well over $20,000 to stock and decorate it.

The crowd that came to the establishment on opening day was so huge that it took up more than a block. Foot- and mounted-police were everywhere. The sign over the door simply said, "John L. Sullivan." The champ's initials, JLS, were carved in the frosted glass border of each window and etched into each bar glass. The bar was adorned with fight pictures. Patrons wanted to drink at the champion's bar, and were hoping to shake his hand.

---

[94] *New York Times*, *New York Herald*, *New York Tribune*, *New York Sun*, August 7, 1883; *Brooklyn Daily Eagle*, August 6, 7, 1883; *National Police Gazette*, August 18, 1883; *New York Clipper*, August 11, 1883; Isenberg at 137; Sullivan at 98-99.

The Tour Of All Tours

John L. Sullivan already had established his successful business model of touring around via train, performing in controlled sparring exhibitions in various cities, and occasionally fighting seriously against anyone who accepted his offer of money if they could last 4 rounds. He was about to take his touring style to an unprecedented level.

Sullivan signed a contract with Al Smith to manage and arrange a lengthy 8-month tour across America, allowing nearly the entire country to see him in action. Spanning from 1883 to 1884, it would be the grandest and most ambitious tour ever up to that point.

The tour was announced on September 18, 1883. Sullivan would leave Boston for New York on September 26, and leave New York on the 27th. With him would be heavyweights Herbert Slade and Steve Taylor, both former opponents, and middleweights Pete McCoy and Mike Gillespie, as well as Sully's now pregnant wife Annie, master of ceremonies Frank Moran, and treasurer/accountant Jake Munzinger.

At least 136 cities and towns would be visited, many of which had never before seen live boxing. Such a tour would not only increase Sullivan's popular renown and pocketbook, but also help stimulate further interest in boxing. Hugh Coyle was in charge of advance publicity, which included newspaper advertisements and posters in whatever town was next.

Nearly every day, Sullivan would spar two or three times per exhibition, 3 or 4 rounds with each of his touring members (who also exhibited with each other as well). This helped Sully remain in shape, further sharpen and hone his skills, and demonstrate the fact that he had good defense, for few folks without solid skills could spar that much or often without being injured.

There was a definite market demand to see Sullivan. As one newspaper wrote, "Do what we will with him, man is naturally a fighting animal."[95]

The tour across America would begin in Baltimore, Maryland, and then make stops varying in duration and frequency, including Virginia, Washington D.C., Pennsylvania, Ohio, West Virginia, Kentucky, Indiana, Missouri, Illinois, Iowa, Wisconsin, Minnesota, Nebraska, Kansas, Colorado, Wyoming, Utah, Montana, Nevada, California, Oregon, Washington Territory, British Columbia, Canada, Arizona Territory, New Mexico, Texas, Louisiana, Alabama, Georgia, South Carolina, Tennessee, Arkansas, and Michigan. There also were plans for Sullivan to visit, at some future point, England, Ireland, Scotland, and possibly Paris.[96]

---

[95] *People's Advocate* (Washington D.C.), September 29, 1883.

[96] *New York Clipper*, September 22, 1883.

On September 28, 1883 in Baltimore, Maryland, at Kernan's Theatre, the tour began. 2,000 people enjoyed watching the man who had "succeeded in securing to himself the name of being invincible in a fight."

Sullivan, who claimed to weigh 222 pounds, sparred gently and prettily with Herbert Slade, who showed cleverness with counters and parries. Sullivan's "shoulder blades were worked up and down like the walking-beam of a steamboat." In the last round, when the audience urged Sullivan to knock out Slade, John L. momentarily "sailed in, delivering his blows with right and left alternately, knocking Slade back to the footlights and very nearly over them. Then he smiled and turned his back to the Maori." He only gave them a brief taste of the real thing.

The next day, on the 29th, they repeated their performance twice more in the afternoon and evening.

During the tour, only on rare occasion would someone accept the offer of $250 (and sometimes $500) to anyone who could last 4 rounds with Sullivan, so typically he worked in relatively tame fashion with his sparring mates.[97]

Some suggested that Sullivan was so popular that he could run for public office and be a viable candidate.

Sullivan said that although the prize-ring business (LPR fighting) was not doing very well, "glove contests are growing more popular, and a set-to with the mittens, no matter how lively, is not often interrupted." One news writer opined, "All decent people will be glad that prize fighting has rushed to a swift degeneration." Simultaneously, Sullivan was stimulating interest in gloved boxing exhibitions.[98]

On October 1, 1883 in Richmond, Virginia, Sullivan sparred with Steve Taylor and Herbert Slade, taking a break between the two exhibitions to allow McCoy and Gillespie to spar.

Next on their itinerary was Petersburg, Virginia on October 2, Norfolk, Virginia on the 4th, and Washington D.C. on the 6th (twice). Pennsylvania was next – Harrisburg on the 8th (Sullivan also umpired an afternoon baseball game), Reading on the 9th, Lancaster on the 10th, Pottsville on the 11th (where two of the drunken fighters and two locals got into an argument in a whorehouse), Wilkes-Barre on the 12th, Scranton on the 13th (where Sullivan refused to spar because he was shorted his $250 guarantee and the outdoor venue was very muddy, much to the chagrin of the angry patrons present who had paid 50 cents each, requiring the police to handle them), York on the 15th, and Altoona on the 16th (when Sully almost got into a fight when he was dining with Annie and overheard some folks at the next table say that they did not understand how a woman that attractive could marry a prizefighter).[99]

---

97 *Baltimore Sun, Baltimore American*, September 29, 1883.

98 *People's Advocate, Baltimore Sun,* September 29, 1883; *Baltimore American*, September 30, 1883.

99 *New York Clipper*, October 6, 20, 1883; Sullivan at 96.

On October 15, 1883, the U.S. Supreme Court declared the Civil Rights Act of 1875 unconstitutional. The Court held that the Act, which had guaranteed that everyone, regardless of race, was entitled to equal accommodations and privileges in public places such as inns, hotels, public transportation such as railroad cars, and theaters and other places of recreation, was not consistent with the U.S. Congress' powers under the 13th or 14th Amendments, and that Congress had exceeded the scope of its power. The Court said it was no infringement of those amendments to refuse to any person the equal accommodations and privileges of an inn, place of public entertainment, or the like, and to do so was not a badge of slavery or involuntary servitude implying subjugation. The U.S. Congress did not pass another civil rights law until 1957. Essentially, at that time, separation of the races was the legal and social norm, not the exception.

In his lone dissent from the majority opinion, Justice John Harlan (a Kentucky lawyer) wrote,

> It is, I submit, scarcely just to say that the colored race has been the special favorite of the laws. What the nation, through Congress, has sought to accomplish in reference to that race is, what had already been done in every state in the Union for the white race, to secure and protect rights belonging to them as freemen and citizens; nothing more. The one underlying purpose of congressional legislation has been to enable the black race to take the rank of mere citizens. The difficulty has been to compel a recognition of their legal right to take that rank, and to secure the enjoyment of privileges belonging, under the law, to them as a component part of the people for whose welfare and happiness government is ordained.

It was said that the decision would not actually affect the colored people in the South, because no one had obeyed the law there anyhow.[100]

Also in 1883, in deciding *Pace v. Alabama*, 106 U.S. 583 (1883), the U.S. Supreme Court upheld as constitutional Alabama's anti-miscegenation statute, which prohibited marriage, cohabitation and sexual relations between whites and blacks. States were within their rights to prevent sexual relations based upon race. The Court argued that it was the duty of the state to protect marriage as a public institution. The state had a duty to protect married couples against disturbances such as interracial relationships, because such relationships between whites and blacks "must naturally cause discord, shame, disruption of family circles, and estrangement," and therefore were incompatible with the family life that the state needed to protect. This interpretation of the constitution was the law for the next 81-plus years.[101]

---

[100] *Philadelphia Press*, October 16, 17, 1883. The Court's decision was not applicable to the District of Columbia, but affected all of the states.

[101] This ruling was not overturned by the Supreme Court until 1964 in *McLaughlin v. Florida* (holding that laws prohibiting interracial cohabitation of unmarried persons were

While John L. Sullivan was in Altoona on October 16, Baptist preachers approached the champ and asked if he did not see the error of his ways. Sullivan recalled,

> I listened to them, and when through I said I thought my way of robbing the people about as clever as theirs, and on the whole it didn't make much difference. They didn't bother me the balance of the time I spent in Altoona. Fanaticism prompts some men, you know, to step beyond what is right, and I looked at it in that light.[102]

On Wednesday October 17, 1883 in McKeesport, Pennsylvania, at the local opera house, Sullivan fought 27-year-old 160-pound James McCoy, the first man on this tour to accept Sullivan's challenge. One newspaper said that McCoy had 15 victories under his belt. McCoy took pride in his science and grit, and recently had defeated a local pugilist named Callahan after 9 LPR rounds. McCoy's chest was tattooed with anchors, white and blue snakes, wide-mouthed dragons, and flowers.

Because he was at least 50 pounds smaller than Sullivan, McCoy was advised to take on another member of the combination, but he wanted to win the $250 offered for lasting 4 rounds with Sullivan. McCoy said, "I have been anxious to meet Sullivan for years. I do not believe any man can knock me out in 4 rounds."

They shook hands and McCoy landed a light blow on Sullivan's mouth. John simply laughed. Sullivan then landed a right and left, neither of which appeared to be very hard, but McCoy was dropped to the stage. Before rising, he said that was enough for him. Another version said that after a "few gentle taps, and futile efforts by McCoy to protect himself, Sullivan landed a left-hander on the poor fellow's mug; the blow felled him and he refused to again face the champion. The round lasted twenty seconds."

Afterwards, Sullivan said, "I didn't want to slaughter a duck like that. … I only tapped him lightly. I would have broken his jaw had I struck hard." Nevertheless, McCoy's lower lip was cut badly.

McCoy said, "Well, I always wanted to meet Sullivan. I never thought any man could knock me out with gloves; but holy murder! I never thought any man could hit as hard as he does. … I can say what few men can, that I fought with the champion of the world."

In December 1883, McCoy would fight Pat Moran in a 1-hour 36-minute (114 rounds) LPR fight, retiring with a broken wrist. Men who could fight well against others were playthings in Sullivan's hands.[103]

The tour's next stop was Youngstown, Ohio on the 18th.

---

unconstitutional), and in 1967 in *Loving v. Virginia* (holding that laws prohibiting interracial marriage were unconstitutional).

[102] *New York Times,* October 21, 1883.

[103] *New York Clipper,* October 27, 1883; *National Police Gazette*, December 22, 1883; *Seattle Daily Post-Intelligencer*, February 5, 1884; *Daily Arkansas Gazette,* April 30, 1884, quoting the *Pittsburgh Times*; Isenberg at 149, 151; Sullivan at 104-106.

On October 19, 1883 in Allegheny City, Pennsylvania, the combination entertained 3,000 - 4,000 people who utterly packed the Coliseum with members of all classes, from bullies and toughs to lawyers and doctors. "Merchants and manufacturers worth their hundreds of thousands sat in the same row of chairs with the $7-a-week clerks." Only one woman was present – Sullivan's wife Annie.

After some preliminary exhibitions that included Mike Gillespie vs. Steve Taylor, and Herbert Slade vs. Pete McCoy, wearing yellow tights and white stockings, but bare-chested, the "champion of the world" boxed with Steve Taylor. They looked like "twin gladiators," but Sullivan was "beyond doubt one of the finest specimens of physical manhood that ever faced an audience." The crowd "howled and stamped with delight," giving John an ovation as he bowed.

During their sparring, a Sullivan punch to the neck "sounded all over the house," momentarily staggering Taylor. However, as usual, John L. backed off and worked with him.

> For the space of two minutes there was a display of science that took the crowd off its feet. As Sullivan warmed to the exercise every movement of his body developed a wonderful suppleness. He rarely let out that powerful right arm, but when he did it counted. Taylor, who is a scienced boxer and athlete, brought great skill into play, but Sullivan was more than his match.

Pete McCoy and Mike Gillespie sparred next, and then Sullivan and Slade provided the wind-up. Against Slade, Sullivan "sprang into the air like a cat" and landed a right to the cheek, and followed up with another right that staggered Slade. Twice in the round, Sullivan rushed in and beat down his guard. Slade took some blows, defended some others, and slugged back as well as he could, particularly with a quick succession of body blows, but Sullivan was superior. This was the usual pattern and style of their exhibitions, for on most dates, they just sparred with each other.[104]

The next day, on October 20, they again exhibited in Allegheny, in front of 1,000 folks in the afternoon, and 3,000 more in the evening.[105]

Sullivan said that every man should learn to box. He recognized the sport's growing popularity, although he also realized that the public generally thought poorly of pugilists.

> I am aware of the fact that they are regarded as a set of brutes and a degraded class generally. The public might be right to a certain extent, but I maintain that there are gentlemen in the profession. ... The public forget that John Morrissey [a former bareknuckle fighter] was a member of Congress. ... Why is it that people raise such a cry against boxers...when there is not a college in the country of any

[104] *Pittsburg Dispatch*, *Pittsburgh Daily Post*, October 20, 1883.
[105] *New York Clipper*, October 27, 1883.

> standing that does not encourage their students in boxing, fencing, and rowing? …
>
> Aristocratic gentlemen of Europe, and sometimes in this country, go out with a couple of friends and try to kill each other with swords or revolvers at 20 paces. Why don't they settle the question with their fists? There would be no loss of life, and it would be equally as effective in determining who is the better man. …
>
> I tell you that this science of self-defense is growing in favor. There is hardly a city or town that does not have its class of gentlemen who are under instructions. Look at the audience last night at the Coliseum. It was as orderly and intelligent an assemblage of men as I ever saw.[106]

Their itinerary listed the troupe as heading to Wheeling, West Virginia on the 22nd (crowd of 2,000), Steubenville, Ohio on the 23rd (ticket prices for better seats raised from $.50 to $1), Newark, Ohio on the 24th, Columbus on the 25th, and Dayton on the 26th and 27th.[107]

On October 28, 1883, they were in Cincinnati, Ohio, filling the house during both afternoon and evening exhibitions.[108]

On October 29, they arrived in Louisville, Kentucky. While drinking bourbon in a local bar, Sullivan spoke to a local reporter about how he dealt with fame:

> No matter where I go there is a multitude of people who seem to know me, and always a certain portion of the rabble and gutter duffers who consider it an honor to shake my hand. I am gazed at by everybody, and at first this was calculated to overawe me, but I have well gotten used to it. It is an innocent request to satisfy and I don't mind them a bit.

Sullivan said that he would fight anyone in the world who posted $10,000, but insisted that he would not fight in a bareknuckle LPR contest again. "I would not fight a ring fight and make myself amenable to the laws for a bloody $10,000. Fist-fighting days are over with me. I have introduced the new rules of the fight into this country, and I intend to stand by them." Sully said he could hit just as hard with gloves as with his bare fists.

Sullivan also said that the *Police Gazette* had "never done him justice, and that a strictly correct account of his life and battles had never been written."[109]

That evening in Louisville, as usual, after the preliminary exhibitions of Taylor-Gillespie and Slade-McCoy, Sullivan sparred Steve Taylor. Sullivan and Taylor "went to work and gave and took blows that seemed hard

---

106 *New York Times,* October 21, 1883; *Saint Paul Daily Globe,* November 25, 1883.

107 Sullivan at 96.

108 *New York Clipper,* November 17, 1883.

109 *Louisville Evening Post,* October 29, 1883.

enough to fell an ox, for three rounds and a wind-up. The crowd went wild with delight."

After an intervening exhibition, Sullivan sparred Slade for the grand wind-up, and they went at it in "good earnest, and, though there was no 'slugging,' the blows were hard enough and fast enough to satisfy any one." A few times, Sullivan, "with surprising agility, sprang three or four feet in the air, raining down terrific blows on Slade's exposed face during this short fight."[110]

That evening, Sullivan injured slightly the tendon of his right arm by landing on the elbow of one of his sparring partners.[111]

Nevertheless, the next day, on October 30, they exhibited in Indianapolis. They were in Terre Haute on October 31, Lafayette, Indiana on November 1, and then Danville, Illinois on November 2.[112]

On Saturday November 3, 1883 in East St. Louis, Sullivan fought James Miles (a.k.a. Gypsy Brady), the second man to take him on during his grand tour. The 5'7" Miles weighed only 140 pounds, but refused Sullivan manager Al Smith's offer to win $200 to box 155-pound Pete McCoy for 2 rounds. Miles insisted on fighting Sullivan, for he wanted the glory associated with having the courage to fight the champ. To make things interesting and fairer, Smith offered the Gypsy $50 if he could last just two minutes with Sullivan.

The Sullivan vs. Miles bout was the main event, coming after the usual preliminary sparring exhibitions between the combination members.

Sullivan was listed as weighing 224 pounds, standing just over 5'11", and it was "at once evident that he does not allow any superfluous flesh to accumulate on the upper portion of his body."

As soon as Miles raised his hands, Sullivan landed his first punch, a powerful left hook that sent him spinning half-way across the stage. The game Miles attacked and struck at Sullivan but John did not bother to defend, for Miles "might has well have struck the water tower, for all the effect it produced." Sullivan landed another left hook to the side of the head that knocked Miles to his knees.

The Gypsy rose and staggered, and struck out wildly, but Sullivan immediately pounded on him, and within four seconds dropped him again with a left to the mouth. Miles fell against Sullivan, grabbing his legs on the way down. The blood flowed in streams from his nose and mouth. The audience shouted for it to stop, asking Sullivan not to hit him anymore.

The police chief entered the stage, separated Miles from his grasp around Sully's legs, picked him up, and said that was enough. Miles asked the timekeeper if it had been two minutes, but it had been only twenty

---

110 *Louisville Courier-Journal,* October 30, 1883.

111 *Chicago Herald,* November 4, 1883; *National Police Gazette,* November 24, 1883.

112 *Louisville Evening Post,* October 29, 1883; Sullivan at 96; *Chicago Herald,* November 4, 1883.

seconds. Miles wanted more, and convinced the policeman to allow him to continue.

Miles lunged at Sullivan, who landed a left uppercut under the chin, knocking Miles off the stage into the left wing, where his head struck between the rounds of a ladder.

After the third knockdown, the police chief again stepped in and ordered a termination of matters. After taking a few seconds to recover, although "about half dead from the pummeling," the game Miles wanted more, and would have continued, but this time the police would not relent. The fight had lasted only 30 seconds.

Since the Miles bout was so short, Sullivan entertained the crowd further by sparring with Steve Taylor, who was called the ex-heavyweight champion. Sparring between Pete McCoy and Mike Gillespie followed, and then Sullivan sparred some more with Herbert Slade. The Maori did well, landing forcefully to the nose several times, but Sullivan was better, demonstrating "his usual style, and all the spectators left with the conviction that he was indeed, the best man in the world."

Sullivan later said that he did not hit Miles hard, although everyone else thought the blows were quite vicious.[113]

The following day, on November 4 at the Sportsman's Park in St. Louis, Missouri, Sullivan pitched 6 innings for the St. Louis Browns baseball team, but the press called him a poor ball player, for neither his hitting nor his pitching impressed anyone (0 for 4 in at-bats, giving up 8 runs as a pitcher, and committing an error), and his team lost 15-3. Yet, 4,000 to 5,000 people paid to see him play ball. The public wanted to see Sullivan, regardless of what he was doing. He earned $1,400, which was 60% of the gate.[114]

On November 5, 1883 at the People's Theater in St. Louis, the Sullivan combination sparred before a packed house that included Missouri Governor Thomas Crittenden. As usual, sandwiched between other exhibitions, the "champion of the world" sparred 4 rounds with Taylor, but only 2 rounds with Slade.

During their exhibition, Taylor fought back vigorously and landed several strong blows, but he was overmatched, even though Sullivan appeared to be holding back most of the time. Still, Sully landed some punishing blows. At the end of the 1st round, Sullivan landed a left hook to the side of Taylor's head which sent him staggering backward. "Moran ran up as Taylor took a chair and said: 'Sullivan stepped on your heel, didn't he?' 'No,' said Taylor grimly. 'He stepped on my head with his big foot.'"

Against Slade, at one point the champion garnered a round of applause "by springing to the air and coming down over Slade's guard with a hot one on the top of the head." When the curtain fell, the pleased audience rose to their feet and cheered vigorously.

---

113 *Missouri Republican* (St. Louis), November 3, 4, 1883; *St. Louis Daily Globe-Democrat*, November 4, 1883.

114 *Missouri Republican*, *St. Louis Daily Globe-Democrat*, November 5, 1883.

One local paper complimented Sullivan:

> Judging from his appearance last night it is safe to say that he is fully entitled to all that has been said of his wonderful muscular powers. He is a fine specimen of physical manhood, quick in his movements, and delivering his blows with good judgment.

Another local paper said,

> The secret of the champion's prowess was apparent. … He carries his strongly-muscled shoulders forward. The consequence is that when he delivers a blow he doesn't have to bring the upper part of the body forward in the delivery. The arm straightens out and the blow is in with a suddenness which seems paralyzing to the spectator, to say nothing of the man in front of him. There are no recoil movements in Sullivan's fighting. He stands with one foot well behind and his body pressing forward.[115]

They again sparred in St. Louis on November 6. After Taylor seemed to be groggy and unsteady on his feet as a result of the champion's blows, Sullivan took it easy and "showed a better left hand than was expected."

Sullivan and Slade engaged in rapid exchanges. John L. "proved himself a two-handed boxer…[and] essayed dodging to an unexpected extent." Although the Maori often was awkward with his footwork and position, he otherwise was clever. The locals said the exhibition was worth the price of admission.[116]

On November 7, when the troupe was about to leave St. Louis, the police arrested Sullivan and Taylor on warrants charging them with having violated the law with their sparring exhibitions on the 5th and 6th. This was ironic, given that the state governor had attended one of the exhibitions. They posted bonds for their appearance and left town. They did not show up for their scheduled November 16 hearing, and forfeited their bonds.[117]

On the 7th, the tour was in Quincy, Illinois. The tour itinerary showed them scheduled to be in Keokuk, Iowa on November 8, Burlington, Iowa on the 9th, and then the following Illinois towns: Peoria on the 10th, Galesburg the 12th, Mendota the 13th, and Streator on the 14th.[118]

From November 15 - 18, 1883, the tour was in Chicago. On Friday November 16 inside the Battery D Armory, a huge crowd of 9,000 people, about half of which was standing room, paid $.50 and $1.00 for admission. At 225 pounds, Sullivan appeared a bit fat, perhaps the result of his rumored excessive drinking.

Regarding Sullivan's clever scientific sparring with Steve Taylor, a local paper said, "There is no child's play about Sullivan's sparring. His is a sharp

---

[115] *Missouri Republican* (St. Louis), *St. Louis Daily Globe-Democrat*, November 6, 1883.
[116] *St. Louis Daily Globe-Democrat*, November 7, 1883.
[117] *New York Clipper*, November 17, 1883.
[118] Sullivan at 96.

stand-up fight, first, last, and all the time." Although pursuant to agreement there were no knockout blows, still the punishment was severe. At various times, in order to prevent Sullivan from doing too much damage, the master of ceremonies interrupted and told them to walk around for a moment.

In the 1st round, Sullivan landed a "few telegraph poles on Taylor's neck and shoulders." In the 2nd, he landed eight effective blows to four by Taylor. In the 3rd round, Sullivan staggered Taylor with two lefts to the neck. Taylor managed to counter, but Sullivan forced him to the ropes. In the 4th round, both hit hard, and Taylor rushed in several times. After a clinch, they whirled around, and John L. could have hit him when Steve momentarily was without his guard and was turned away, but Sullivan checked himself and refrained from hurting his sparring mate.

After some other exhibitions, a long and lean Hoosier from South Bend, Indiana stepped up and asked to fight Sullivan, and he was accommodated. The Hoosier advanced with a grin. Sullivan hit him lightly with a left to the nose, but even his lightest touch was like a ton, and the Hoosier went down. He rose and attempted a blow, but Sullivan immediately sent him down again. The Hoosier rose and was given time to recover. He advanced again, but was knocked out completely.

Sullivan closed the show by sparring with Slade, who tried as hard as he could, and even hit Sullivan's nose. As a result, to get payback, the champion ferociously sprang at him. "Jumping from the floor as if to leap over the Maori, he made a feint with his right, and as Slade ducked to dodge it, Sullivan's left described a half-circle and landed with the motion of an upper cut on the Maori's under jaw." The blow paralyzed Slade, and time had to be called to save him from further punishment.

In the 2nd round, Sullivan leapt into the air several times. "At each leap he would curve his arm over his opponent's head and come under with his left. He jumps viciously and hits hard. Moran called time as soon as it became evident that Sullivan's punishment of Slade was becoming too severe to be strictly hippodrome." A hippodrome was a contest wherein the fighters were working with one another in entertaining fashion but not fighting seriously. It also could be a term for a fake. Often, when Sullivan became a bit too fierce, his exhibition rounds had to be cut short to prevent him from doing too much damage.

In the 3rd round, during several exchanges on the inside, Slade mixed it up well. The round ended with Sullivan momentarily stepping away but then quickly returning, flying through the air, driving Slade to the ropes. They sparred one more round as a finale.

The combination exhibited in Chicago again on November 17. Sullivan claimed that they made between $18,000 and $19,000 in Chicago.[119]

---

119 *Chicago Herald,* November 16, 17, 1883; *New York Clipper,* November 24, 1883; Sullivan at 96, 107, 108.

At one of the Chicago performances, Charles "Parson" Davies, who had been sitting with Paddy Ryan, announced that Sullivan had offered Ryan 50% of the receipts for a gloved bout in San Francisco, or 100% of the receipts if Sullivan failed to knock him out in 4 rounds. Ryan accepted the challenge. Articles of agreement were signed the next day.

However, Ryan later backed out. It was a common occurrence throughout Sullivan's career for various fighters to agree to fight him, only to change their minds later.

Sullivan said that any story claiming that he would be giving up drinking for a year was "bosh." "I don't drink much, say five or six glasses of ale a day and a bottle for dinner, if I feel like it."[120]

According to the tour itinerary, they were in Wisconsin for a week: Racine on November 19, Milwaukee on the 20th, Fond-du-Lac on the 21st, Oshkosh on the 22nd, and Eau Claire on the 23rd.[121]

The *Eau Claire Daily Leader* said the exhibition there on November 23 was a hippodrome, for the boxers exerted themselves little and threw few hard blows. Sullivan was "as powerful as a Clydesdale, and about as graceful." A couple weeks later, the *Eau Claire News* said that Sullivan was "probably the hardest hitter in the world, though inferior to many in pugilistic science."[122]

Next up was a tour through Minnesota. They exhibited in Stillwater on November 24 before heading to St. Paul on the 25th.[123]

---

120 *National Police Gazette,* November 24, 1883; Sullivan at 110.
121 Sullivan at 96.
122 *Eau Claire Daily Leader*, November 24, 1883; *Eau Claire News*, December 8, 1883.
123 Sullivan at 96.

On Monday November 26, 1883 in St. Paul, Minnesota, Sullivan fought 6' 195-pound Morris Hefey or Hafey, a muscular stationary engineer whom the press said had a local reputation as a "vigorous and plucky man with his fists. … Hefey has some little skill, and is a powerful man among average men." Hefey had accepted Sullivan's offer of $1,000 to anyone who could stand up to him for 4 rounds without being knocked out. At that time, $1,000 was a huge amount of money.

The local *St. Paul and Minneapolis Pioneer Press* called Sullivan "Champion of the World" and "the best man with his fists on the face of the earth." "So far he has met in the prize ring, or upon the stage, fifty-two men, and all have succumbed to his wonderful strength and science as a sparer. … His style of boxing is peculiarly his own, and has not been learned by book." The *St. Paul Daily Globe* said,

> Sullivan is a man of Herculean proportions, his massive frame giving evidence of the muscular might which enables him to withstand the assaults of the most scientific pugilists, and when he chooses, to break down his opponent's guard and close the contest by dint of the crushing force of his irresistible blows. … Probably no man has yet presented himself in the prize ring in America who could withstand the impact of Sullivan's fist when it shoots out from the shoulder with the intent of doing harm.

First, Steve Taylor sparred with Mike Gillespie.

Next up was Sullivan and Hefey. John L. wore pink tights and white stockings and gaiters. He weighed 226 pounds, but the local press said he looked good and wore the weight well.

As soon as time was called, Sullivan dashed in and decked Hefey, who fell heavily against the stage. Hefey rose and advanced, and even landed on the champion's neck, but Sullivan again sprang forward and knocked Hefey down into a corner so heavily that many thought that he was hurt seriously. Hefey rose, reeled, and staggered, and was knocked down again. Sullivan had "knocked him silly."

At first it appeared as if Hefey had fallen asleep. However, he awoke, rose, and leaned weakly against the scenery. Yet, obviously he had enough, and he retired. "All of this did not occupy over fifteen or twenty seconds."

Describing the champion, the local press said,

> [Sullivan] was as swift and supple on his feet as a squirrel, striking always from the shoulder, the blades of which gyrate with a rotary movement, and at times you could hang your hat on them. His blows are always aggressive and they beat like hail on the neck of his antagonist.

Afterwards, Hefey said, "If you want to know what it is to be struck by lightning, just face Sullivan one second."

The entertainment was not over. Slade and McCoy boxed 4 rounds.

Steve Taylor boxed Professor John Donaldson, dropping the latter twice, which caused Donaldson to quit, saying that he wasn't there to slug. Allegedly, Taylor was getting revenge, either for Donaldson's alleged claim that he once had made Taylor quit, or because Donaldson had said that he was going to "do him up."

Taylor then sparred 4 rounds with Sullivan.

> Sullivan was magnificent; he tapped Taylor on the neck, the blows falling with the precision of clock-work. The latter showed great sand and took the punishment in fine shape. It was evident that Taylor is no slouch himself, but although very "gamey," he was not equal to the corkers of the wonderful man who stood before him. … At times Sullivan would change his attitude and fairly spring upon his antagonist, indicating the wonderful amount of reserved strength there is tied up in his anatomy and before which it is safe to say, no man could face and live.

Pete McCoy and Mike Gillespie sparred 4 rounds.

Winding up the exhibition, Sullivan sparred 4 rounds with the strong-looking Herbert Slade, who still sported the remnants of a black eye from his encounters with Sullivan. Although "in prowess Slade is no match for the champion," he put up a fair resistance. However, "it was a picnic for the giant and his blows fell with crushing force on Slade's neck."[124]

On November 27, 1883, they exhibited in nearby Minneapolis. "The New Zealander [Slade] was a little the worse for liquor. The exhibition was not brutal enough for one half of the audience, and there was not enough good sparring for the other half."[125]

According to the tour itinerary, they were in Winona, Minnesota on November 28, La Crosse, Wisconsin on the 29th, followed by a tour of Iowa, including McGregor on the 30th, Dubuque on December 1 and 2, and Clinton on the 3rd.[126]

On Tuesday December 4, 1883 in Davenport, Iowa, John L. Sullivan fought 35-year-old 190-pound local blacksmith/iron worker Mike Sheehan (or Shean or Shehan), supposedly the "strongest man in Iowa." Sheehan took up the offer to spar 4 rounds to win $250. Before the bout, Sheehan's wife begged Sullivan not to fight her husband, not because she feared for her husband's life, but because she feared for *Sullivan's* life! They had children, and she did not want her husband to be a murderer, for she expected him to kill John L.

1,197 men and 3 women of all classes packed the local opera house. First, Taylor sparred Gillespie. Then Sullivan took on the local man.

---

124 *Saint Paul and Minneapolis Pioneer Press*, November 24, 26, 27, 1883; *St. Paul Daily Globe*, November 25-27, 1883.

125 *Saint Paul and Minneapolis Pioneer Press*, November 28, 1883.

126 Sullivan at 96; *Eau Claire News*, December 1, 1883.

Sheehan wore pants, with his torso bare. He appeared to be a powerful man. Sullivan wore flesh-colored tights and was "stripped to the buff." Sheehan's two sons acted as his seconds. The fighters shook hands and began the contest.

The *Davenport Daily Gazette* said,

> As Shean put up his hands he seemed dazed, or stage struck. In an instant more something else struck him as with a movement inconceivably swift for so burly a man, Sullivan lengthened out like a leaping panther and smacked the blacksmith a facer, while the building shook with yells and inextinguishable laughter. Shehan evidently had enough, but was persuaded to again 'scratch,' getting another 'biff on the smeller' so sudden and solid that he stayed no longer, and hurriedly tore off the gloves after consuming exactly three seconds of John's valuable time.

The *Davenport Democrat* version was a bit more detailed:

> Sheehan put up his fists; Sullivan pushed down those fists with his right, and with his left tunked Sheehan on the right side of his nose – and the latter threw his two hands to his face and looked at Sullivan in perfect amazement! It was pitiable, but very laughable. After a little loss of time, Sheehan approached the champion again – down went his guard again, and a light blow fell upon his left cheek and turned him partly around, and quick as lightning a cuff under the left jaw fairly sent him spinning towards the rear of the stage. The $250 was no object now – and Sheehan went to pulling off his gloves and walking toward the north wings, behind which he disappeared feeling of his nose the while. Mr. Sheehan is a very powerful man…but he lacks training as a boxer. Had he got in one on Sullivan, the latter would have felt it, surely.

To provide additional entertainment, Sullivan and Steve Taylor sparred in clever fashion, doing some heavy work. "In science they were not so unequal." Slade then sparred McCoy, and then McCoy worked with Gillespie. In the finale, Sullivan sparred Slade, and "showed during several close encounters what vicious work he could do."

While Sullivan was sparring Slade, Sheehan appeared off to the side, and as soon as the crowd saw him, they began hissing him and saying, "Go back and hide yourself." Sullivan had sympathy for a man who had the courage to face him, and, not caring for the crowd's treatment of Sheehan, in his defense he turned and said to the crowd angrily, "If any of you fellows who are hollering and hissing, think it is fun, come up here and I will give you some." The crowd began hissing at Sullivan, calling him a bully. The round was ended. Many still hissed him during the 2nd round as well. When the 3rd round began, Sullivan stepped forth and said to the crowd:

> Gentlemen: I wish to say that when I made the remark I did in the other round, I didn't mean it as an insult to the whole house, I only

meant it for those that were hissing and hollering. I am no speech maker. We are traveling in the country giving exhibitions of what can be done in the art of boxing. Two of these gentlemen fought me in New York and I done 'em up – but they are my friends now and I am their friend. We do no fighting though we hit hard; we are simply giving these exhibitions that the people may see something of the art of boxing. … I challenge any man in the world to box with me, and I'll back up what I say with money – that's the kind of man I am.

Sullivan and Slade resumed sparring, and their "fearful, heavy hitting, avoiding, and close, exciting slugging, stalled the audience as if they were in church." After the bout concluded, the audience cheered wildly.

Sullivan generously gave Sheehan a gift of $100.

The exhibition had not been brutal, but "a display of the wonderful quickness of movement, litheness, nimbleness and agile activity which men can attain by training."[127]

On December 5, they exhibited in Davenport again, but only 600 people attended, which wasn't bad, but nowhere near the numbers from the previous night. The exhibitors demonstrated their "power of great endurance and most wonderful agility and quickness of movement."

A reporter asked Sullivan if the blows, which appeared tremendously powerful, hurt. He replied,

> Well…not often. Such blows would hurt any person whose training of flesh and muscle had not made him ready. … [T]hough we hit hard…we suffer no injury. … Slade got a black-eye once, and was laid up a couple of days by a body blow, since we started out, but those were accidents; … We know what we are about, what we have to endure; it keeps us in practice and in good form, besides putting money in our pockets, and we like it. Why, man…do you think if it hurt that we could endure these blows night after night? … Sometimes they sting like fury, but it doesn't last long. … But it would be terrible punishment if a novice had to take it…and that's why I just merely cuffed Sheehan last evening.[128]

They exhibited in various other Iowa cities as well, including Muscatine on December 6, Marshalltown on the 7th, Oskaloosa on the 8th, Ottumwa on the 9th and 10th, and Des Moines on the 11th (over 200 people hung around the Morgan Hotel, hoping for a glimpse of the champ).

From Iowa, they would head to Lincoln, Nebraska on the 12th and Omaha on the 13th (the sparring at Boyd's Opera House was done while an orchestra played music), before returning to Iowa on the 14th to exhibit in Council Bluffs. St. Joseph, Missouri followed on the 15th and 16th.

---

[127] *Davenport Daily Gazette, Davenport Democrat,* December 5, 1883; *National Police Gazette,* December 29, 1883, reported that the Sheehan bout lasted 1 minute 30 seconds.
[128] *Davenport Democrat,* December 6, 1883.

Next up was Kansas: Atchison on the 17th (Slade, like some of the others, was growing tired of the constant sparring and traveling, and he boxed in a lackluster fashion), Leavenworth on the 18th, Lawrence on the 19th, Topeka on the 20th (John L. and Annie were growing a bit tired of all the fanfare, and avoided the crowd at the depot), and Wyandotte on the 21st.

They visited Kansas City, Missouri on December 22. Then they headed to Colorado, visiting Central City on the 24th, and then Denver on the 25th, giving two Christmas Day performances.

Publicly, Annie always spoke well of her husband, "like a true wife," but privately she was growing weary and despondent by John's frequent alcohol splurges. The long tour was wearing on everyone.

One report claimed that while in Denver, Slade had a fight with a local celebrity in front of a saloon. The tour members were all drunk. "An officer interfered, but was soon done up. Others came to the rescue and the belligerents were all jailed." Allegedly, Sullivan tried to demand and grab a revolver from the saloon proprietor.[129]

A story that Sullivan admitted was that while in Denver on Christmas Day, he literally nearly killed Gillespie. He saw a two-barreled shotgun lying on a table. One of the hall attaches told him that it was not loaded. He pointed it at Gillespie, pulled the trigger, and nothing happened. However, Sullivan then aimed the other barrel at a table near Gillespie, pulled the second trigger, and blasted it to pieces. Had he pulled the trigger on that barrel when aiming at Gillespie, he would have killed him. Gillespie, whose left sleeve was riddled with buckshot holes, was scared out of his wits, crying, "I'm shot, I'm shot." It required an hour to convince him that he had not been shot. Sullivan later wrote, "I realized at once the danger, and never since then have I fooled with a gun."

On December 26, 1883 in Denver, Colorado, Sullivan allegedly fractured Taylor's jaw in their sparring. Taylor said that Sullivan had been unusually vigorous. Early on, a right to the jaw hurt him. Every subsequent blow hurt, and he had to retire from the sparring before it was half over. A doctor said the jaw had received a bad fracture. However, Taylor's jaw likely was misdiagnosed, because he was back sparring again in early January. Sullivan hit him so hard that it probably felt broken. Likely, the jaw swelled up, giving the impression that it was broken.[130]

From December 27 to 30, the troupe was in Leadville, Colorado. They were given a grand reception. A large banner read, "John L. Sullivan Is Leadville's Guest." The entire town was draped in bunting.[131]

One report claimed that after their Leadville exhibition on the 29th, a drunken Sullivan and Pete McCoy got into an argument. When John went to strike him, Pete picked up a chair and broke it over his head. As McCoy

---

129 *Helena Independent,* January 3, 1884.

130 *New York Clipper,* January 5, 1884.

131 Sullivan at 96, 112.

ran away, Sullivan threw a lamp at him and missed. A police marshal stepped in to stop the fray, but Sullivan told him to get out of his way or he'd knock him out. The marshal replied by drawing his revolver and saying that if John came near him, he would put a bullet through him. Sullivan finally calmed down.[132]

Another report claimed that the recent stories about Sullivan were false. In his autobiography, Sullivan said that no one ever threatened him or attempted to shoot him. He said that such stories were the result of over-zealous reporters looking for some sensational news.[133]

However, more and more, there were indications that alcohol was becoming a problem for Sullivan and his troupe. Word on the street was that Sullivan could be a mean drunk.

Allegedly, Sullivan's inebriation caused him to miss the final Leadville performance and also a scheduled January 1, 1884 exhibition in Denver.

The tour got back on track, and, according to the itinerary, they were in Cheyenne, Wyoming on January 2, 1884, then Laramie City on the 3rd, Rawlins on the 4th, Salt Lake City, Utah on the 5th and 6th, and Ogden on the 7th.

While in Montana, Sullivan told a reporter there, "Oh, the days of prize fighting are over. There never will be any more big prize fights in this country. The gentlemanly sport of sparring has supplanted it, and I think in some respects, wisely, too." A Montana writer subsequently said, "These exhibitions are not for the purpose of 'slugging,' but only to show the skill which training will give, and are consequently unobjectionable."

On January 8, 1884, when he arrived in Butte, Montana, Sullivan received a grand reception. People crowded the sidewalks in a line, and the city band played and formed a procession. The sparring troupe exhibited there the next day.

One Butte writer analyzed Sullivan's huge popularity:

> The problem of why a successful pugilist should excite in the public mind such a furor as has been created by the fistic successes of John L. Sullivan is difficult to solve, but it probably rests upon that subtle influence, which exists in every human composition to admire everything in which the mind recognizes great superiority, whether it be in the achievements of the intellect or victories of muscle. It is said that Champion Sullivan has vanquished no less than forty-five adversaries, ten of whom were recognized champions. … Wherever he has appeared the largest assembly rooms obtainable have been packed to their utmost capacity. … The champion is accompanied by ten pugilists of scarcely less renown.

On January 10 and 11, 1884, the "Champion of the World" and his combination exhibited in Helena, Montana. Admission was $2 for regular

---

132 *New York Clipper,* January 5, 1884.

133 *Butte Daily Miner,* January 5, 1884; Sullivan at 111.

seats, double the usual rate for first-class entertainments; $2.50 for reserved seats; and upper boxes were $15, while lower boxes cost $18.

On the 10th, as usual, first Steve Taylor sparred Gillespie 4 rounds. Slade then sparred McCoy.

Next, Sullivan sparred Taylor 3 rounds. Sullivan showed that he was "a model of strength and agility." "His blows...were sudden, straight from the shoulder, and quickly followed up, and fell with staggering force upon his opponent, Taylor often narrowly escaping a fall. He did fall once."

Next, McCoy and Gillespie sparred 3 rounds.

Sullivan and Slade boxed in the finale.

> This was the most animated bout of the evening, both men apparently going in for all they were worth. But Sullivan's superiority was plainly apparent. His eye was quick to detect an opening, and he let no such opportunity pass without taking advantage of it – and a blow once in was quickly followed by several others, each of them seemingly heavy enough to knock an ox down. Slade, however, stood up unflinchingly, and although not able to give his antagonist blow for blow, he got in a number of good ones.

The next evening, on the 11th in Helena, general admission was reduced to $1.50, for the previous night's fee had been a bit too expensive. The "order of business was the same as on the previous night, with perhaps a little more vim thrown into the wind-up of each encounter."

Afterwards, Sullivan said that he was 25 years and four months old, and was weighing 219 ½ pounds, ½-pound more than Slade.

Sullivan more than hinted that he was worn out from all of the boxing that he had been doing. "He is now tired of prize fighting and intends retiring from it after another year." They had been exhibiting almost every night for over three months, sometimes twice a day.[134]

On Saturday January 12, 1884, back in Butte, Montana again, a 225-pound Sullivan fought 153-pound Fred Robinson of Texas, a miner who was attempting to win $1,000 for lasting 4 rounds. An immense crowd (for that location) of 1,700 paid $2 each to see if he could do it.

Not wanting to be perceived as a bully taking advantage of a much smaller man, Sullivan announced to the audience that he had not sought the contest, but Robinson had requested it, for he wanted to win the $1,000 for lasting 4 rounds. If someone wanted to try to earn the money, Sullivan was willing to give them the opportunity.

Despite their huge weight disparity, Robinson showed a great deal of pluck, endurance, and skill, being both aggressive and defensive, showing that he had fight knowledge and experience. Regardless, Sullivan dropped him seven times in the 1st round. Yet, each time, Robinson quickly rose and

---

[134] *Helena Daily Herald,* January 8, 9, 11, 1884; *Butte Daily Miner,* January 8, 9, 1884; *Helena Daily Independent,* January 8, 11, 12, 1884.

continued fighting. At one point, Sullivan even knocked him through the ropes off the stage (practically a Sullivan signature), but Robinson quickly rose and ran up the steps, back onto the platform stage again.

In the 2nd round, despite fighting hard, Robinson once again was dropped several times. Upon the seventh knockdown of the round, Robinson again went through the ropes to the floor. He re-entered the ring and continued, but Sullivan decked him for the eighth time. Upon rising, Sullivan dropped him for the ninth time in the round. The *Butte Daily Miner* said that at this point, there was some confusion.

> Just here is where there seems to be a diversity of opinion. One party claiming that time had been called before the 'Boy' rose to his feet, and the other that it was not called until after he was knocked down the last time. … The fight, however, was awarded to Sullivan.

Despite the lack of clarity, it sounded as if Robinson had been counted out and the fight was over. The *Police Gazette* later reported, "As he was unable to stand Sullivan's batteries any longer, Sullivan was declared the winner."

Although he had been no match, everyone admired Robinson for being the only man in Montana with enough courage to face John L., and because he had fought in gallant style. Even Sullivan said that Robinson was one of the toughest men that he had met in a while.

To provide further entertainment, Sullivan still sparred Slade, and "showed his superior skill in the manly art."[135]

The combination again exhibited in Butte the following evening, on January 13, to another large crowd of 2,000 people. McCoy knocked out Dave Cusick, who retired after the 2nd round. The other sparring contests between combination members were the same as on the previous evening.[136]

The *Police Gazette* confirmed that Sullivan said that he wanted to retire. "I am going around the world now, and am prepared to meet any man living. After this trip is over I am done with the ring."[137]

According to their itinerary, they were in Salt Lake City, Utah on January 15, and then in Nevada towns such as Reno on the 17th, Carson City on the 18th and 19th, and Virginia City on the 20th.[138]

The combination then headed to California, performing in towns such as Nevada City on Monday January 21, Sacramento on the 22nd, Stockton on the 23rd, and San Jose on the 24th.

With the troupe members getting worn down from all of the constant day-after-day work, sometimes they cut the rounds short, sparred a fewer number of times, or were less enthusiastic. This caused the tour to garner

---

135 *Butte Daily Miner,* January 9, 1884, January 13, 1884; *National Police Gazette*, February 9, 1884.

136 *Butte Daily Miner,* January 13, 1884, January 15, 1884.

137 *National Police Gazette*, February 9, 1884.

138 Sullivan at 97.

some criticism from those who at times thought the sparring was too tame or too short. The other complaint was that the prices were too high. It wasn't easy to put on a rousing performance every single day. Wear and tear had an impact. Some of their sparring sessions were unsatisfactory, for the fighters mostly played defense with one another. When one spectator asked if their program was being cut too short, he was invited to "come up here and we'll make it as long as you want."[139]

Sullivan's brother Mike Sullivan, Jr. briefly joined the tour. From San Francisco, he would accompany John L.'s now 6 months pregnant wife Annie back to Boston.

On January 25, 1884, they exhibited in San Francisco, California. Between 5,000 and 7,000 people waited at the docks for their ferry to arrive. The crowd rushed over to the champion and swarmed around him, shouting themselves hoarse chanting, "Sullivan, Sullivan!" The band played "Hail to the Chief." Police were everywhere to keep order.

In the courtyard outside his hotel, 2,500 people assembled. As a result, John L. appeared at the balcony and took a bow, receiving cheers.

A black fighter named Bill Williams wanted to attempt to last 4 rounds with Sullivan to earn the $1,000 offered. When asked if he had seen the black man's challenge, Sullivan responded,

> Yes; but I have never sparred with a colored man in public and never will. However, if he or any of his friends have money and will bring five of his friends and allow me to take five of my friends into a private room I will give him all the Marquis of Queensbury he wants.

Sullivan's position garnered no criticism.

The admission prices were $2, $1.50, and $1, but ticket speculators drove up the prices to $5. The high ticket prices explained why only 3,500 attended, when the pavilion could have accommodated 6,000. Master of ceremonies Frank Moran announced that Sullivan had decided that the ticket prices would be lowered on the following evening to $1 for all seat locations, first-come first-served.

A grand jury attended the exhibition. They were present to determine whether criminal charges should be brought if the exhibition was too rough. Perhaps as a result, the sparring was fairly dull. The rounds were shortened to one-minute each. Taylor held back and played for 4 one-minute rounds with Gillespie. Slade and McCoy's lackluster 3 rounds of sparring aroused no enthusiasm from the spectators. Some locals then boxed.

By the time the world's champion was introduced to spar with Taylor, the audience had become indifferent. Sullivan mostly held back, though in brief moments he demonstrated his tremendous talent. The *San Francisco Daily Examiner* was impressed with Sullivan, saying,

---

[139] *San Francisco Daily Examiner,* January 25, 1884.

> He is as lithe as a panther, and his rush is like an avalanche. His fists flash through the air like bolts of lightning, and his every movement is the perfection of grace. The trouble was that he simply showed what he could do. His exhibition with Taylor was nothing more or less than a farce. … The disparity between the men was too great. … All that Taylor did was to try to keep out of Sullivan's way, and the latter extended his hearty sympathy by allowing him to do so. Once Sullivan struck Steve on the forehead with his right, knocking his head back, and was following it up with a blow on the jugular as the throat lay bare, when Taylor threw up his hands in a pitiful way and John's hands fell to his side. … Sullivan darted around jumped up and lunged out in splendid style, but refrained from touching Steve. As a matter of fact, Sullivan acted as though he was fighting an imaginary foe, with neither life nor substance.

The *San Francisco Chronicle* also admired Sullivan, saying,

> What was most noticeable about Sullivan's performance was the lightning quickness with which he stretched out his shapely arms at the touch of which Taylor recoiled like a rubber ball. The force with which the blows, some times re-enforced by a rush and jump, in which the whole body was thrown forward, were delivered was tremendous, and more than once Taylor, only a target, was forced to look for protection near the ropes and in the corners. Sullivan either forgot himself or his antagonist, much to the latter's damage to chest and head. They boxed three rounds, in which Sullivan fully succeeded in convincing everybody that the reports of his strength and agility have not been exaggerated.

Sullivan threw lightning-like blows that had the force of a mule-kick, driving Taylor around the ring, several times causing Taylor to raise his arms in the air to remind Sullivan to cool it and settle down.

After a couple other exhibitions, Sullivan and Slade sparred for 3 one-minute rounds. The *Examiner* said, "[Slade] could no more resist the onslaught of the champion than can the soft earth the sharp edge of the plow. He was a babe in Sullivan's hands. Although he made a show of resistance, it was evident to all observers that he is no match for the Boston boy." The *Chronicle* said of the Sullivan-Slade exhibition,

> Here again Sullivan showed how terrific is the force with which he delivers his blows, jumping forward on his right leg at the same time, apparently throwing the weight of his whole massive body into his arms. The movement is executed with lightning-like rapidity, and it certainly seems that no man can stand up against it.

Although the spectators were disappointed with the show overall, they still enjoyed seeing Sullivan, who was all that he had been represented to be.

On January 26, they again exhibited in San Francisco. Despite the reduced ticket prices, an even smaller audience of about 1,600 attended.

The exhibitions once again were too short and the audience was no more enthused than they were the previous evening. Whenever Sullivan got warmed up and became too vicious towards Taylor, in order to prevent him from doing damage, the referee/master of ceremonies called time, which made the rounds last only about 30 seconds. That caused the audience to hiss. They liked what they saw, but they wanted to see more.

Despite the rounds' short length, Taylor's mouth was bleeding and his eye was darkened. As he left the stage, Taylor said to the audience, "If any of you fellows want to see some more, get up in front of Sullivan yourselves." The audience hissed him.

A sensitive and upset Sullivan addressed the audience, saying, "Gentlemen, this hissing is all uncalled for. I am sparring in a friendly set to with Mr. Taylor. I am not obliged to kill him. If the law allowed me to knock out somebody I would be willing to accommodate any or all of you." Another quoted him as saying,

> You fellows ain't got no right to hiss. I did the best I dared. If I did all I knew these exhibitions would stop right here. Them as hissed are a lot of loafers, they are; and any man as hissed and dares say so, I'll give him a slap in the jaw. I'm sorry I can't give every gent here the pleasure of seeing me knock out someone, but there ain't no one to knock out, and the police won't allow it.

After some other exhibitions, Sullivan wound up by sparring Slade, though before he did he gave another, more conciliatory speech. Slade suffered some punishment because Sullivan was a bit upset, but also eager to please the crowd.[140]

The tour was in Oakland on January 28 and 29.

To that point, to say that Sullivan's tour had been successful financially would be an understatement. They had made between $18,000 and $19,000 in Chicago, $10,220 in Pittsburg, $5,040 in Dayton, Ohio, $4,900 in Cincinnati, $3,000 in St. Paul, and $3,007 in Minneapolis. Wherever they went, they were making good money. "It would not be an exaggerated estimate to put down the clear profits of the tour at $150,000, or about one hundred times as much as a brainy homunculus would earn in the same time."[141]

On Friday February 1, 1884, "The Champion's Triumphal Tour Across the Continent" was in Astoria, Oregon, where Sullivan fought a 300-pound Frenchman named Sylvester La Gouriff (or "Le Gowriff"), who was attempting to win $1,000 for lasting 4 rounds. Admission was $1.50.

---

140 *San Francisco Daily Examiner, San Francisco Chronicle,* January 26, 27, 1884; *New York Clipper,* February 9, 1884, quoting the *Alta-Californian.*

141 *Daily Astorian,* February 1, 1884.

Before the bout, when Sullivan was told that the Frenchman weighed 340 pounds and was bigger than the building, he replied, "The bigger he is the bigger the fall."

La Gouriff, who was a fisherman by trade, had some kind of oil rubbed all over his body, and his stomach was wrapped with four yards of blue flannel. They put on the gloves, shook hands, and began.

After La Gouriff raised his fists, Sullivan made one or two feints, and then landed a powerful left to the cheek that staggered him. La Gouriff advanced but Sullivan bounded toward him and a vicious blow "sent him sprawling on the stage."

La Gouriff rose, but Sullivan decked him for the second time with a right to the neck. La Gouriff removed his gloves, shook his head, and retired. The local *Daily Astorian* said it lasted about 30 seconds.

After the show, in the dressing room, the Frenchman told Sullivan, "I break wood and fences with my fist, but you break stone."

After stopping La Gouriff, Sullivan sparred 3 rounds with Steve Taylor.

Slade and McCoy were next, followed by Gillespie and McCoy.

The evening's final bout was between Sullivan and Slade. It was obvious that Sullivan was holding back and not trying to hurt his opponent, for every now and then when he was about to unload, he checked himself. Slade was mostly defensive. Still, the local writer admired them. "Both are heavy weights but display the most wonderful activity in ducking and dodging." Slade would be a "holy terror" to the ordinary man, but had more than met his match with Sullivan.

Sullivan received plaudits. "Whatever has been said in praise of Sullivan is not exaggerated."

> He is about the most restless piece of humanity that we ever saw in the shape of a man. His every move conveys the idea of restlessness. He strikes to count, and fights to win. He goes at his opponent with a dash, hits out right and left, recovers his guard and strikes another smashing blow, then, jumping from the ground he rushes at his antagonist and follows him up, shooting out terrific blows and recovering himself with lightning rapidity.

The local writer called the exhibition an excellent and extraordinary display of science.[142]

The tour was in Portland, Oregon from February 2 through 4, and New Tacoma, Washington Territory on the 5th.

Regarding Sullivan's career, one paper said, "Sullivan claims to have met and vanquished 45 men, but many of these do not appear in his record."

Sullivan said he was elevating the sport of boxing to unprecedented levels. Soon it no longer would "be considered a disgrace to be a boxer. … It will not be long before the best people of the country will attend boxing

---

[142] *Daily Astorian*, February 1, 2, 1884; *New York Clipper*, February 16, 1884; *National Police Gazette*, March 1, 1884, April 15, 1905; Sullivan at 114.

contests."[143] In fact, members of all classes and levels of education already were attending his bouts and exhibitions.

On Wednesday February 6, 1884 in Seattle, Washington Territory, over 2,000 people watched James Lang, a tall, strong, and well-developed man, attempt to win the $1,000 offered if he could last 4 rounds with Sullivan. As usual, Sullivan quickly knocked out his opponent. According to the *Seattle Daily Post-Intelligencer*,

> It took just a little less than seven seconds to make Mr. Lang aware of the fact that he had business elsewhere. … In that time he was knocked from side to side as if he were a child, battered to the floor twice and forced to quit. It was simply impossible to withstand the rain of blows and the force with which they were delivered.

The local writer said of Sullivan,

> He is a marvel of strength, skill and agility. If there is another man on earth who is equal, certain it is that that man has never been publicly known. He is a master in the art of boxing. The force with which he delivers a blow is simply appalling to ordinary people. … There is nothing comparable to it, unless it be those guns holding several charges, which are discharged one after another. … He is wonderfully agile, and his motions resemble those of a tiger in the act of springing on its prey. No ordinary man has any chance at all before him, and it is idle, foolish, to talk otherwise.

Next, Steve Taylor sparred Gillespie, and McCoy boxed Slade.

Then Sullivan and Taylor gave an exhibition of "stroke and parry." Although working with one another, "the quickness, force and skill with which Sullivan delivered and parried the blows of his opponent were as conspicuous as in his previous contest with the volunteer whom he 'knocked out.'"

McCoy then boxed with Gillespie.

As usual, Sullivan and Slade gave the finale.

> Here was indeed a contest of giants, and one worthy of seeing. … To either of them, however, an ordinary man is as a toy, to be tossed about at will. The rounds were sharp, fierce and exciting. Blows were given and returned of sufficient force apparently to fell an ox, and the exhibition of skill in striking and warding off blows was interesting to even the most unenthusiastic observer. The audience cheered loudly at the end of each round, and at the close retired in good order, apparently well satisfied.

The combination traveled to Victoria, British Columbia, Canada, to exhibit there on February 7 and 8. At a banquet, Sullivan got drunk, and

---

143 *Seattle Daily Post-Intelligencer,* February 5, 1884.

when the mayor asked all to rise and drink to Queen Victoria's health, Sullivan refused and allegedly said, "To hell with the Queen!" He then left. The Irish did not care for the "Famine Queen."

They returned to Seattle to exhibit there again on February 9 and 10. An immense crowd, which included prominent citizens, paid $1.50 for tickets, and they jammed the hall. Sullivan sparred with Taylor and Slade, as usual. The "marvelous exhibition" drew great applause.[144]

They were scheduled to be in Dayton, Washington on February 12, Walla Walla, Washington on the 13th, Dallas, Oregon on the 14th, and Portland, Oregon on the 15th.[145]

On February 18, 1884, the Sullivan Combination returned to San Francisco. They would remain there for a few weeks. That evening, 1,200 people attended the exhibition. Sullivan was suffering from a muscular strain in his leg, so he only sparred Taylor 3 lively one-minute rounds. Slade did not spar at all.[146]

Fed up with being pounded on by Sullivan for what he considered insufficient pay ($50 a week), Slade decided to leave the tour. On February 23 in a San Francisco saloon; a drunken and upset Sullivan found Slade and butted him in the face. Slade grabbed him, threw him to the floor, and held him there until the police arrived and took John L. back to his hotel. The tour members were known for getting into the occasional drunken bar brawl, either with each other or with various members of the public.[147]

In the meantime, Sullivan scheduled a real bout against the local Olympic Athletic Club's champion, George Robinson. The 6'1" 189-pound Robinson was a trained clever boxer and powerful man, who in early 1883 had sparred with and allegedly bested Slade. He also impressed people with his ability to raise a 100-pound dumb-bell 20 times and a 50-pound dumb-bell 58 times, and he once raised a 25-pound dumb-bell 427 times.[148]

Comparing the two fighters, the *San Francisco Examiner* called Robinson a man of muscle and nerve, who was well-trained and took care of himself.

> With Sullivan it is a different thing. He is such a prodigy in the fistic world that there seems to be no rule, whether physical or mental, that can apply to him. He is a phenomenon. He is always in fighting condition, notwithstanding his continual sprees. It is his nature to fight. His prowess has never been doubted or diminished by any one with whom he has come in contact. All have succumbed to his fearful blows and terrific 'rushes.'[149]

---

144 *Seattle Daily Post-Intelligencer,* February 10, 1884.
145 Sullivan at 97.
146 *San Francisco Daily Examiner,* February 19, 1884; *New York Clipper,* March 8, 1884.
147 *New York Clipper,* March 8, 1884.
148 *National Police Gazette,* February 10, 1883, March 15, 1884.
149 *San Francisco Daily Examiner,* March 3, 1884.

THE CAREER OF A CHAMPION.

MUSCLE AND PLUCK'S INVINCIBLE RECORD, AS ILLUSTRATED BY THE VICTORIES OF JOHN L. SULLIVAN—FIGHTING FOR GLORY AND GAIN IN MANY FIELDS, AND WINNING IN ALL.

THE CHAMPION ON HIS TRAVELS.

HOW THE WORLD OF SPORT ACKNOWLEDGES THE TRIUMPH OF A MODERN GLADIATOR AND THE BOSTON BOY KEEPS HIS HAND IN PRACTICE WITHOUT DAMAGE TO HIMSELF.

On Thursday March 6, 1884 at Mechanics' Pavilion in San Francisco, the John L. Sullivan versus George Robinson fight took place. The fight was huge, in part because 1/3 of the population was Irish-born or the children of Irish immigrants. The pavilion was jammed with 12,000 people who paid over $20,000 to witness the bout, and there were 5,000 more outside who could not get in; the arena was so packed. Some said 15,000 people were inside (although one said it was 8,000). The main floor and the galleries were filled and overflowing with dense humanity. Only about six women were present. The police struggled, both to clear a path inside the arena and to maintain order outside. In the crowd was a developing 17-year-old Olympic Club amateur named James J. Corbett, who eight years later would fight Sullivan.

Sullivan would receive 2/3 of the gate receipts and Robinson 1/3. After expenses, allegedly Sullivan earned about $10,000 and Robinson $5,000. However, reports regarding finances and financial divisions often were inaccurate, and the public at times was told one thing when the truth was another. The same is true today.

At about 8:30 p.m., the preliminary fighters approached the ring. "Gangway there; make room there for the boxers." Master of ceremonies Frank Moran introduced Mike Gillespie and Pete McCoy, who sparred. After another bout, Steve Taylor boxed Young Dutchy. Another exhibition followed.

At 9:47 p.m., Sullivan entered the ring, and the crowd honored him with a champion's greeting. A minute later, a shout went up that made the building quiver, as Robinson, the pride of San Francisco, appeared. Attendants followed, holding a bucket of water, a sponge, towel, and fan. Then came Thomas Chandler, the referee, and Misters William Muldoon and Hiram Cook, timekeepers. A band of blue-coated police, led by Captain Douglass, was on hand around the ring to keep the peace.

Some claimed that Sullivan weighed 204 pounds to Robinson's 170, but those reports likely were off by about 15 pounds, for both appeared to be much larger. Sullivan looked like a building; Robinson a greyhound. Robinson wore red tights. Sullivan wore flesh-colored tights.

They fought in either a 21-foot or 24-foot ring with two ropes, on a platform that was four-feet high off the ground.

The police refused to allow them to use 3-ounce gloves, and insisted that they fight with 8-ounce sparring gloves, considered large at the time. Just before the fight, Sullivan's friend and timekeeper, world wrestling champion William Muldoon took the platform and made a speech, saying,

> This affair tonight was intended to be a knockout contest with gloves. A little difficulty, however, has arisen today in regard to the gloves. I hold in my hand one of the three-ounce gloves that Sullivan used in his fights. … It was intended that, the same should be used here tonight, but the authorities would not allow it. … The gloves to

> be used are 8-ounce – the only ones they will be allowed to fight with. The men are going to fight on their merits, and Sullivan is going to try to knock Robinson out if he can, although it might be considered a miracle for a man to do so with these gloves.

The crowd groaned, hissed, and hooted their displeasure at the police's decision to insist on 8-ounce gloves. Today, an 8-ounce glove is the smallest size used in a boxing bout. In Sullivan's era, such gloves were perceived to be large pillows. Larger gloves diminish more of the force and offer a greater area of protection from blows. It turned out that the glove size did not matter much.

At 9:54 p.m., Sullivan and Robinson shook hands and prepared to begin the battle.

1 - When the fight began, immediately it became obvious that it was not going to be a fight at all. Sullivan led with a left that glanced off Robinson's shoulder, but he went down. Robinson rose, dodged a punch and landed a right on the nose, but then immediately went down from a Sullivan right that barely grazed his mustache. It would be not only the last blow that Robinson landed, but the last one that he threw. He was afraid to leave himself open to getting hit. Every time the champion's glove barely landed, George went down. Sometimes he even dropped down at the slightest Sullivan feint. The audience hissed and howled in disgust at Robinson's tactics, which mirrored Tug Wilson's.

The *San Francisco Chronicle* and *San Francisco Call* both said Robinson went down 9 times in the 1st round. The *San Francisco Examiner* said Robinson dropped 11 times "without receiving a blow that would have hurt a boy."

After the round was over, the referee said something to Robinson about his tactics. Sullivan seemed taken aback, and he stared at Robinson, then at the referee, and then at the audience.

2 - The *Examiner* said Robinson dropped 6 times from blows that were nothing, although the seventh knockdown was legitimate, for Sullivan knocked him off his feet with a powerful right. Robinson went down 3 more times. When he tried to drop the 10th time, Sullivan caught him with his left and held him up while he landed a right uppercut to the jaw that sent him down. Robinson only received slight punishment on the 12th and 13th times that he went down in the round.

Sullivan appealed to the referee, stretching his arms out and opening his hands. The referee cautioned Robinson to behave and follow the rules, which made it illegal to drop down just to kill time, which is what Robinson was doing. Twice more George went down to save himself from punishment and to kill the clock. Once, when Robinson was preparing to drop, Sullivan landed a good blow to the forehead. He also managed to land a solid body blow that sent Robinson doubled up under the ropes.

The *Chronicle* said that sometimes Sullivan landed a hard uppercut, but it was difficult to land solidly because Robinson was so busy going down. Robinson went down 20 times in the round. The *Call* agreed.

3 - The crowd became louder and more uncomplimentary towards their local champion and his disgraceful tactics. Robinson showed no pluck whatsoever, and kept going down incessantly. The *Examiner* said Robinson looked groggy, but only received one full blow in the face during the first 7 knockdowns of the round. Once, Sullivan held his head and hit him with an uppercut. Another time, when Robinson was falling, Sullivan fell on top of him. Robinson's claim of foul was not allowed. John L. asked Robinson to remain at ring center, but he ran away. After Robinson went down again, Sullivan pointed at him in disgust. Upon another knockdown, Sullivan danced a jig while Robinson was on the floor.

The referee again cautioned Robinson about his illegal tactics, but nevertheless, he kept dropping at the slightest provocation, and sometimes with none at all, other than he thought Sullivan was about to him.

After Robinson had fallen down 16 times in the round, Sullivan landed a "staggerer" to Robinson's neck that legitimately dropped him. Robinson rose and played his game to escape punishment. The *Chronicle* said Robinson went down 22 times in the round. The *Call* said it was 21 times.

4 - According to the *Examiner*, Robinson dropped 8 times in the round, only being hit on the third and eighth times, while the other knockdowns were from pushes or feints. The *Call* said he tumbled 12 times. The *Chronicle* said Robinson went down a total of 15 times in the round.

Referee Chandler warned Robinson not to go down without being hit, on penalty of losing the fight. However, in foul fashion, Robinson voluntarily went down 3 more times without being struck. Finally, Referee Chandler decided to stop the fight and disqualify Robinson, awarding the contest to Sullivan.

William Muldoon announced to the crowd that the referee had given the fight to Sullivan on the ground that Robinson had violated the rules by dropping to the floor without being struck. The crowd was disgusted with Robinson. The disqualification obviously was warranted.

The *Chronicle* said Robinson had dropped disgracefully 66 times in 4 rounds. The *Examiner's* account totaled about 51 knockdowns. Another paper said that Sullivan knocked down Robinson 60 times. The *Call* counted 62 tumbles. Robinson had "evidently decided that discretion was the better part of valor, and that it hurt less to tumble of his own accord than to be knocked down by Sullivan's fist."

Most called Robinson a coward. Robinson's response was that he had not contracted to knock out Sullivan, but vice versa, and he had decided to act on the defensive, for his objective was to make sure that he was not knocked out. He claimed to have drawn blood from Sullivan's nose, said that Sullivan struck him in the 1st round while he was down, and criticized

John L. as having only swinging blows. However, Robinson was branded as a coward and his reputation destroyed.[150]

The next day, Robinson and Steve Taylor got into a fight in the bar of Baldwin's Hotel, the result of Taylor firing an insulting remark at Robinson. Subsequently, for having embarrassed it, the Olympic Club expelled Robinson.

STRAIGHT HITS AND LIVELY DODGING.

HOW JOHN L. SULLIVAN DID NOT KNOCK OUT G. M. ROBINSON IN THE GREAT SET-TO AT THE PAVILION, SAN FRANCISCO, CAL., AND HOW STEVE TAYLOR DID IT AFTERWARD.

[From Sketches by Special Artists and a Photograph of Robinson Made Expressly for the "Police Gazette."]

150 *San Francisco Daily Examiner, San Francisco Chronicle, San Francisco Call*, March 7, 1884; *New York Clipper*, March 15, 1884; *National Police Gazette*, March 22, 1884, April 5, 1884.

Many years later, James J. Corbett, who had observed the Sullivan-Robinson fight, said that a prime Sullivan was a terrific hitter with both hands and was pretty quick with both his feet and hands, as fast as heavyweight champion Jack Dempsey of the 1920s. Still, Corbett also felt that Sullivan was not a highly skilled boxer, calling him a member of the "slugger class." Corbett was a slick defensive specialist.[151]

Having been in San Francisco since February 18, the tour went back on the road again, heading towards Los Angeles on March 11. Sullivan would spar with McCoy and Taylor, now that Slade had left. They would be in Los Angeles from March 12 to 17. At that time, future heavyweight champion James J. Jeffries was an eight-year-old growing up in Los Angeles. The combination performed in San Bernardino on the 18th and 19th, before heading to Tucson, in the Arizona Territory.

On March 21, 1884 in Tucson, Arizona, Sullivan's 3 rounds with Pete McCoy were timed at 1:45, 1:30, and 1:05 respectively. McCoy was an active, wiry fellow with a vigorous style. In the 1st round, Sullivan was the aggressor constantly, pushing his opponent around the ring, never standing still. In the 2nd round, Sullivan played defense as McCoy vainly tried to hit him. In the 3rd round, Pete was allowed to land a couple punches. Overall though, it had been tame and uninteresting.

After an intervening exhibition between McCoy and Gillespie, Sullivan sparred Taylor 3 short rounds that lasted only 42, 35, and 30 seconds respectively. Clearly, Sullivan was just going through the motions.

As of March 22, they were in Tombstone, Arizona. On March 23 in Tombstone, Sullivan visited five bandits in the jail who were awaiting execution. They had robbed the Bisbee copper mining company's payroll, and killed four people. One bandit told John L. that he knew a man who could beat him – the sheriff. Sullivan responded that the sheriff didn't look like a fighter. "Well, he ain't…but he'll knock five of us out in one round next Friday morning, all the same." On Friday March 28, the five bandits were executed by hanging.[152]

The tour headed to Deming, New Mexico on the 24th, and then to Texas locations such as El Paso on the 25th, Fort Worth on the 29th and 30th, Denison on the 31st, Sherman on April 1, Dallas on the 2nd, Corsicana on the 3rd, Waco on the 4th, Austin on the 5th, San Antonio on the 6th and 7th, and Houston on the 8th.[153]

On April 9 and 10, 1884, Sullivan's tour performed in Galveston, Texas. Seats sold for $1. The "respectable was largely in the majority" of those in attendance. At that time, six-year-old Jack Johnson, a future heavyweight champion, was growing up in Galveston.

On the 9th, Sullivan sparred Pete McCoy, who was called the most scientific middleweight in the world.

---

151 James J. Corbett, *The Roar of the Crowd* (N.Y.: G.P. Putnam's Sons, 1925), 115-116.
152 *Arizona Weekly Citizen,* March 22, 29, 1884.
153 Sullivan at 96-97.

> [Sullivan's] arms cut through the air with almost inconceivable rapidity in blow upon blow upon McCoy, which, though lightly dealt, resounded throughout the theater. Pete stood up gamely through his three rounds, and exhibited his science at every move.

After another exhibition, Sullivan boxed Taylor, who was taller than Sullivan and about equal in weight.[154]

On Thursday April 10, 1884 at the Tremont Opera House in Galveston, Sullivan fought Al Marx (or Marks), who said he wanted to box the champion in an attempt to win $250 if he could last 4 rounds without being knocked out. Born in Pennsylvania, Marx had resided in Kansas, but had been living in Galveston for the past year. His was a cotton screwer, packing and pressing cotton. He was 23 years old and claimed to be 6-0 in his fight career. Marx was beefy, with a chubby face, and his "generally soft look excited a spasm of sympathy."

AL. MARX,

A COWBOY OF TEXAS, WHO MADE A GOOD SHOWING WITH THE UNCONQUERABLE CHAMPION, JOHN L. SULLIVAN.

Marx began by landing a lead right to Sullivan's collarbone. Sullivan countered with a left that landed on Marx's eye and staggered him. Al recovered quickly and threw two blows that fell short, and Sullivan landed a well-directed blow that knocked him down.

Marx rose and made a rush, landing a few body shots before Sullivan sent him down again, this time with a bloody nose.

---

[154] *Galveston Daily News,* April 10, 1884.

A groggy Marx rose and rushed inside. Some infighting took place, but Sullivan drove him back until a body shot dropped him for the third time.

When Marx rose, Sullivan advanced to strike, but, "realizing the helplessness of his enemy, said: 'Do you want any more?' 'No,' was the gasping reply and this ended the bout. Time – 55 seconds."

Marx said that being hit by Sullivan was like being struck with a pile-driver incased in a football.

Sullivan said "that he was sorry for the young man and didn't want to hurt him more than he could help."

After some intervening sparring exhibitions, Sullivan and Taylor sparred in the show's finale.[155]

In late April, in an LPR bout fought with soft gloves, Al Marx would defeat Jim Trainor, an old-time prize-fighter, in 1 hour 8 minutes (66 rounds), when the fight was stopped as a result of Trainor's foul of going down to escape punishment. Al Marx could fight.[156]

The tour headed to New Orleans. On April 12, 1884, Sullivan received word that Annie had given birth to his 10-pound son, John Jr., on that day.

While in New Orleans, Sullivan said,

> Well, I have been on the road very nearly seven months. I have visited almost every State and Territory in the United States; had a good time; knocked out twelve men, including Robinson, and have cleared over $100,000. …
>
> All those announced as the 'coming men' have dropped quick enough. … I will be done with fighting in about six months. I don't believe there is anyone too anxious to meet me, but I will meet all comers within that time. … England has…sent her best men over here and I have defeated them.[157]

On April 13 and 14, 1884, Sullivan exhibited in New Orleans at the St. Charles Theatre. Audiences packed the auditorium on both days. On the 13th, first Sullivan boxed Pete McCoy.

> A man weighing 230 pounds, he moved as rapidly and was spryer on his feet than the majority of light weights. Sullivan uses both hands well and hits clean. He dodged and guarded splendidly, leaped into the air to throw all his weight into the blow. … Once Sullivan hit out and caught McCoy square in the face. McCoy was knocked about a dozen feet and narrowly escaped going over the footlights.

After another exhibition, Sullivan boxed Steve Taylor, who was nearer Sullivan's size. "The champion showed what he was capable of and

---

155 *Galveston Daily News, Daily Picayune,* April 11, 1884.

156 *Daily Picayune,* April 28, 1884; *National Police Gazette,* May 24, 1884.

157 *Daily Picayune,* April 13, 1884.

although he was bent more upon showing science than hitting hard, the crowd could judge of his capabilities."[158]

The following evening in New Orleans, a then 180-pound Mike Donovan joined the crew, replacing Slade and giving McCoy a break. Taylor would do the finale with Sullivan. First, Donovan sparred McCoy. Donovan was quick, clever, game, and a straight hitter with skill, coolness, and in-and-out two-handed fighting abilities. Two other exhibitions followed.

When Sullivan first sparred, he took on Mike Donovan. It was the third time they had met in the ring. Sullivan "moved with the easy step of a panther, and was rapid in his movements to a degree wonderful for a man of his size." Donovan showed his skill, but "Sullivan showed he had not forgotten his old trio of rushing, feinting with left and landing with right hand." The crowd applauded when John rushed and showered in several blows before Donovan could escape.

Two more exhibitions followed, and then Sullivan ended the show by sparring Taylor, who earlier had sparred Gillespie. This was more of a give-and-take affair, and as usual, Sullivan gave better than he took. Although he checked his full power, Sullivan landed several hard blows that did damage. The champion demonstrated many of his tricks, including jumping into the air and putting all his weight into the blow, throwing his hand from behind his back, ducking, and showing all elements of a champion pugilist.

Although no white fighter was willing to attempt to win the $1,000 offered to anyone who would stand up to Sullivan for 4 rounds, "Some colored giant is said to have offered his services, but Sullivan declined to fight a colored man in public."[159]

The itinerary listed the tour as scheduled to be in Mobile, Alabama on April 15, Montgomery, Alabama on the 16th, and then to the following Georgia towns – Columbus on the 17th, Macon on the 18th, and Savannah on the 19th and 20th, then on to Charleston, South Carolina on the 21st (where Sullivan was extremely drunk, and admitted it to the crowd, which was disappointed by the tameness of his sparring with McCoy and Taylor), and then on to Augusta and Atlanta, Georgia on the 22nd and 23rd (where the crowd was disappointed by a drunken Sullivan's staggering through 3 tame rounds with Taylor), Chattanooga, Tennessee on the 24th, Birmingham, Alabama on the 25th, and Nashville, Tennessee on the 26th.[160]

On April 27, 1884 in Chattanooga, Tennessee, there was a rumor that the man advertised as John L. Sullivan actually was an imposter. Acting on the bad tip, when John L. appeared on the stage, the chief of police demanded that he establish his identity, and Sullivan "raved like a mad bull and swore roundly." He called the policeman's demand an "outrage." He told the chief, "- - if you don't believe I'm Sullivan, you just send any man

---

158 *Daily Picayune,* April 14, 1884; *New York Clipper,* April 19, 1884.
159 *Daily Picayune,* April 15, 1884.
160 Sullivan at 97.

in the house on the stage and if he faces me five minutes I'll give him $1,000. … There's but one Sullivan, - -, and I'm the man."

Performing before an all-male audience, the exhibitions that evening were tame and disappointing. Audiences wanted to see the real thing. Badly needing a rest, Sullivan said that he intended to abandon the ring as soon as he reached home.[161]

The next day, on April 28, 1884, the company was in Memphis, Tennessee. The crowd of 1,000 to 1,500 people included large numbers of representative citizens, and even a few ladies. The 24-foot ring was elevated 3 feet from the floor.

First, Pete McCoy sparred Mike Donovan 4 rounds. Then Sullivan sparred Donovan for 3 or 4 rounds. Donovan did his best to land a blow, and it was obvious that Sullivan was holding back, not wanting to punish him. After another exhibition, Sullivan and Steve Taylor boxed in the most spirited contest of the evening.[162]

Commenting on the growing popularity of sports, one newspaper said,

> Within a few years the popularity of athletic sports has increased to such an extent that its influence has reached all classes of people. … There are many ways in which athletics affect the lives of young men for the better if they are inclined toward dissipation. … There is also a certain mental benefit in all athletics. … For example, when a man stands up to box he must keep a cool, clear head and his wits about him or his opponent will get the better of the game.

In an interview about his career, Sullivan said,

> I never had but one fist fight in my life…and that was with Paddy Ryan. … I sent him to grass in nine rounds, consuming 10 minutes and 23 seconds. I have had about fifty glove fights. … I claim to have worked a revolution in the public sentiment by substituting gloves for the naked fists. … What causes the early decay of so many of the champion fighters? Too much heavy drinking.[163]

On Tuesday April 29, 1884 in Hot Springs, Arkansas, Sullivan fought 6' 190-pound Dan Henry, a local Irishman who was trying to win $1,000 for lasting 4 rounds. Henry "sparred vigorously" but was "deficient as a tactician," and Sullivan quickly stopped him in the 1st round. Still, "he evinced no disposition to retire until he saw he would be badly used up. He escaped with only slight bruises."

When in Little Rock, Arkansas the next day, Sullivan was asked about the Henry bout, and he said, "Yes, I polished him off in fifteen seconds."[164]

---

161 *Daily Picayune,* April 28, 1884; Sullivan at 117.
162 *Memphis Daily Appeal,* April 29, 1884.
163 *Daily Arkansas Gazette* (Little Rock), April 29, 1884, quoting the *Pittsburg Times.*
164 *Daily Arkansas Gazette,* May 1, 1884; *National Police Gazette,* May 24, 1884; Sullivan at 118.

1 (center) – Sullivan's palace saloon, 714 Washington Street, Boston, 2 (top middle) – unviewable photo of the champion's father, 3 (left center) – Michael Sullivan, 4 (right center) – Mrs. John L. Sullivan, 5 (top left) – Sullivan's birthplace, Concord Street, Roxbury, 6 (top right) – Sullivan's parents' home, 7 (bottom left) – the champion's home, 4 Lovering Place, Boston, 8 (bottom right) – exterior of Sullivan's saloon, 9 (bottom center) – the champion at rest, 10 – Sullivan running, 11 – Early efforts with a pick and shovel, 12 – playing baseball, 13 – fighting

On April 30, Sullivan sparred in Little Rock, Arkansas. The local ad claimed that he had defeated 59 men and would spar twice at every exhibition; four rounds each with two members of the combination. Admission was $1.00.[165]

However, Mike Donovan was able to handle only 2 rounds against the 217-pound Sullivan. The local *Daily Arkansas Gazette* said, "Donovan did his best but the sledge hammer blows of the champion were too much for him, and he retired after two rounds."

Later, Sullivan sparred 3 rounds with Taylor, who held his own, but "stood no show" against Sullivan, whose "lightning blows punished his arms and head and chest. One blow struck across his arm and strained it badly." The local writer opined, "There is not probably in America today a man who can stand up against him, and no foreign importations have yet succeeded in doing so."[166]

On Thursday May 1, 1884, back in Memphis again, just two days after the Henry bout, Sullivan fought William Fleming, a bricklayer who once had fallen four stories from a scaffold but miraculously was not injured. His

[165] *Daily Arkansas Gazette* (Little Rock), April 29, 30, 1884.
[166] *Daily Arkansas Gazette*, May 1, 1884.

theory was that if he could fall that far and not be knocked out, he could take Sullivan's blows. Apparently, Fleming had prior boxing experience, because the local paper said he had "local boxing fame."

About 3,000 people, the largest local crowd in years, packed the building, paying $.50 each to watch Fleming try to win $1,000 if he could last 4 rounds.

Master of ceremonies Frank Moran introduced Fleming as an ambitious Memphis amateur boxer, and Sullivan as the world champion.

According to the local *Memphis Daily Appeal*, Sullivan rapidly advanced towards Fleming, who retreated and threw up his left arm. "Like a flash the champion tore down Fleming's guard with his left hand and struck him with the edge of his right under the left jaw. The brickmason fell like a clod, his back striking the chair in the corner, his side striking the hard pine floor with a dull thud." Just like that, in a few seconds, it was over.

The *Daily Memphis Avalanche* version said that in an instant, Sullivan hit him with a left that, although partially blocked, still staggered Fleming. With lightning rapidity, Sullivan followed with a right that caught Fleming under the left ear, dropping him as if he had been shot dead. As he fell, his shoulders struck the edge of his chair. Some thought that his spine had been broken.

A concerned Sullivan and others rushed to his aid. Fleming was completely unconscious for quite a while. They did everything they could to revive him. A pitcher of water was emptied one glass at a time into his face, head, and back. They slapped his hands, back, and chest, and also rubbed the back of his neck. Yet, Fleming would not wake up. There was some fear that he had been killed. However, eventually, after several minutes, finally he woke up. Fleming required assistance to walk away. Afterward, his jaw swelled up considerably.

In his autobiography, Sullivan said the Fleming fight lasted only 2 seconds. As the result of one punch, Fleming was out cold for 20 minutes.

When Fleming awoke, the first question he asked was, "When am I to meet Sullivan?" "You already fought him." "Did I win?"

Despite the near-death experience, the show continued. Donovan and McCoy sparred, followed by Taylor and Gillespie.

Sullivan then boxed Donovan. In the first couple of rounds, the aggressive Sullivan pressed him to the ropes. "In the third he stood while Donovan delivered four or five straight from the shoulder directly at his head, dodging as fast as they came with the greatest ease and without moving an inch out of the spot upon which he stood." Sullivan could dodge them too! To this day, his defense is underrated. At one point, Sullivan grabbed Mike's head, but Donovan hit him with two stomach blows. Before time was called, Sullivan gave him a smack on the ear.

After some other exhibitions, the final bout was between Sullivan and Taylor, "who is a splendid specimen of manhood and nearer on an equality with Sullivan than any other member of the company. Their rounds were much shorter than the others, and considerably hotter, too." They engaged in "heavy slugging," and Taylor landed a few flush blows.

In order to combat the anti-boxing arguments that the sport only attracted hooligans and would cause disorderly conduct, those newswriters who supported boxing often observed that the Sullivan combination's exhibitions were orderly and contained society's best members. Hence, the local press noted that the crowd included 300 of the city's best men, and that the affair had been orderly.[167]

A couple days after the bout, Fleming told a friend that "he did not have any idea of whipping Sullivan, but he merely wanted the glory of having stood before him." In response, the local paper said, "He got the glory and is immortal." However, he was part of a short story. "Sullivan struck Fleming and Fleming struck the floor." Hence, "nothing but a swelled head remains to tell the tale of how he got kicked by a mule." Regardless, even back then, folks knew that Sullivan was very special, and that his legend would continue on throughout history. Many just wanted to be a part of that legendary story. Sullivan was proving the fact that "muscle is still worshipped as a king."

Describing Sullivan, the *Daily Memphis Avalanche* said,

> He suggests the big Corliss engines when in action, and hardly fails to attract the admiration of even the cultured and refined. There is no doubt that if the law did not prevent prize-fighting now to a large extent…about three-fourths of the population would turn out to see it.[168]

On Friday May 2, 1884 in the Grand Opera House in Nashville, Tennessee, the day after the Fleming bout, John L. Sullivan fought a 20-year-old 150-pound local man named Enos Phillips.

The *Nashville Daily American* said that 1,400 of Nashville's best citizens attended the exhibition, and there was "an unusually small percentage from the lower strata of society."

Sullivan had been scheduled to box a 174-pound man, but, as was often the case, the day of the fight he declined to meet Sullivan.

Instead, Enos Phillips said he wanted the opportunity. He had been scheduled to meet Mike Gillespie, but once the other man dropped out, Phillips decided that he only wanted to fight Sullivan.

Sullivan's manager was concerned about their size disparity, and, fearing for his safety, wanted Phillips to meet McCoy, Gillespie, or Donovan, all of whom were within 12 or 14 pounds of his weight. However, Phillips insisted on fighting Sullivan.

---

167 *Memphis Daily Appeal,* May 2, 1884; *Daily Memphis Avalanche,* May 1, 2, 1884; Sullivan at 117.

168 *Daily Memphis Avalanche,* May 3, 1884.

The bare-chested Sullivan appeared to have some excess flesh, but nevertheless was quite active. Phillips "stood up and took his punishment heroically," and even landed a number of counterblows, which drew applause from the crowd.

> Sullivan drove Phillips into the wings three times, and he, of course, had to take a good deal of punishment. The fourth time Sullivan ran him against the back scene, where he bowed his head, and, with his nose bleeding, was receiving buffet after buffet from the champion, when Capt. Kerrigan, the Chief of Police, came from behind the scenes and led him from the stage.

The local paper said that although Sullivan evidently was striking hard and administering punishment, when the police interfered, Phillips could have continued, and had more rounds left in him. Phillips exhibited pluck "in coming to the score every time, and was still coming when the police interfered and stopped that part of the programme." However, clearly the police saw that Sullivan was pounding on him, and they wanted to prevent brutality and serious injury to the much smaller man.

Many secondary sources report this as a 4th round stoppage win for Sullivan, but it appears that this actually was a 1st round stoppage. It could have been 4 rounds if the rounds were counted in London rules fashion – beginning and ending each time Phillips was driven to the "wings," which happened thrice before the bout was stopped.

In his autobiography, Sullivan said Phillips "endured my blows for two minutes, and, although thrice driven into the wings of the stage, manfully toed the mark for the fourth round. He had been punished so severely that he was taken off the stage by force." Obviously if it only lasted a little more than two minutes, then there could not have been 4 rounds under Queensberry rules, but rather less than 1 round. Hence, it was 1 Queensberry rules round, but 4 London rules rounds.

The *Nashville Banner* gave the impression that it was only one round of boxing, referring to the "round" in the singular, saying, "The crowd cheered frequently during the round, but evidently had no sympathy for Phillips."

Summarizing, the *Banner* said Phillips had shown "bull dog courage, but in the hands of the great slugger he soon got punishment enough to last him for some time." Enos had landed a left to the champion's mouth, but it only riled Sullivan, who began fighting in earnest. He was punishing Phillips severely when the police interfered.

Following the Phillips bout, several other exhibitions took place, including Donovan-McCoy, Taylor-Gillespie, McCoy-Gillespie, Sullivan-Donovan, and Sullivan-Taylor; and all displayed "a great deal of science." "They slugged each other unmercifully, giving and receiving blows which would have killed or crippled less experienced men."[169]

---

[169] *Nashville Daily American*, *Nashville Banner*, May 3, 1884; Sullivan at 118.

Despite its immense popularity, some writers feared boxing's potentially adverse moral effect. One said, "The whole proceedings were brutal and disgusting throughout. … They tend to make sluggers and roughs of the boys who witness them. It is hoped no other performance of the kind will ever be tolerated in this city." Another said,

> Have we sunk so low in morals and respectability that the "best citizens of Nashville" turn out en masses to witness the brutal and demoralizing scenes of the prize ring – so low that the leading and representative paper of the city must needs commend and praise such things in order to gratify the tastes of its readers?

Regardless, as a result of Sullivan's magnetism and popularity, he had turned "denunciation into praise and commendation" from many of those who previously had denounced boxing.[170]

On May 3, the tour was in Louisville, Kentucky. Sullivan showed marked improvement in his sparring with Donovan, who was a "child in his hands," and he ended the successful show by sparring with Taylor, "who made a good showing with the champion, although by no means his equal." The audience left well-pleased.

Sullivan spoke of potentially going overseas to England, demonstrating that he might not be retiring after all. He said that he had earned over $100,000.[171]

They were supposed to exhibit in Cincinnati, Ohio on May 4, but the mayor refused to allow the show. Instead, Sullivan pitched in a baseball game before a crowd of 4,000 which paid 25 cents each.

They were set to be in Vincennes, Indiana on the 5th, Evansville, Indiana on the 6th, and St. Louis, Missouri on the 7th and 8th.[172]

Pete McCoy left the tour to prepare for a scheduled May 18 LPR fight against Duncan McDonald in Montana (which McCoy would win in 31 rounds).

On May 7, 1884 in St. Louis, Missouri, Sullivan sparred with a new heavyweight named Florie Barnett, who was McCoy's substitute. The typical show order would be Barnett-Donovan, Taylor-Gillespie, Sullivan-Barnett, Donovan-Gillespie, and Sullivan-Taylor. Although handicapped by superfluous flesh, the pudgy Barnett made a favorable impression with Sullivan. After the intervening exhibition, Sullivan sparred with Taylor, who was a bit under the weather. The show satisfied the crowded house.[173]

On May 8, the St. Louis police chief refused to allow a local man to fight Sullivan for the opportunity to win $1,000 if he could last 4 rounds. Sullivan offered to pay the man's expenses to travel to Illinois, where they would be

---

170 *Nashville Banner*, May 3, 1884.

171 *National Police Gazette*, May 31, 1884.

172 *Vincennes Daily Commercial*, May 6, 7, 1884; *New York Clipper*, May 10, 1884.

173 *Missouri Republican* (St. Louis), May 7, 8, 1884; Isenberg at 167.

allowed to fight the next day, if he was willing. However, the fight did not take place. Sullivan again sparred with Barnett and Taylor.[174]

The tour continued, exhibiting in places like Springfield, Illinois on May 9, Bloomington, Illinois on the 10th, and then Michigan, including Kalamazoo on the 14th, Grand Rapids on the 15th, Saginaw on the 16th, East Saginaw on May 17 and 18, Bay City on the 19th, Jackson on the 20th, and Detroit on the 21st and 22nd (the sparring was light and Sullivan was called fat as a prize hog).

On May 23, 1884, the "Sullivan's Sluggers" tour closed at Toledo, Ohio. Sullivan showed up drunk again and just went through the motions. Some reported that a drunken Sullivan hurled abusive and foul language at the hotel staff and vile and vulgar insinuations at ladies present at the local baseball stadium.

Sullivan took a train back to New York, and then on to Boston, arriving on May 26. Upon his arrival in Boston, the first place he visited was his saloon. Instantly, his presence attracted hundreds wanting to shake his hand and have a drink with the champ.

After hanging out at the bar, Sullivan went home to 4 Lovering Place, a large three-story brick house with a silver plate on the front door with the engraving, "Sullivan." There he saw his wife, and for the first time, his infant son, John Jr. His parents lived in a three-story wooden house on Parnell Street.[175]

The tour, which had spanned from late September 1883 to late May 1884, had shown Sullivan at his best and his worst. At times he was drunk, uncouth, and aggressive, being surly when inebriated, but he also could be warm, sincere, and generous. He paid off the mortgage on his parents' home, and gave monetary gifts to combination members and those who fought him. From a sporting perspective, he had impressed an entire nation with his boxing prowess. Either way, he always made good copy. Hence, he received consistent press and publicity, further boosting his fame.

The *National Police Gazette* said of Sullivan,

> To claim that John L. Sullivan is a well-formed physical specimen of a man, does not begin to express the idea. Sullivan is perfection itself, and mother nature has done tenfold more for him than he has ever done for himself, although he is perfectly cultured in his profession. He can strike out with either right or left, and knock a man down with as much ease and grace as an accomplished lady can gently and languidly handle an opera fan. No effort, no particular determination or energy does he seem to put forth in his art, but all comes as natural and easy as the balmy breezes of May.[176]

---

[174] *Missouri Republican,* May 9, 1884.
[175] Sullivan at 97, 118.
[176] *National Police Gazette,* May 24, 1884.

Anyone who ever questions Sullivan's skills should consider just how difficult it would be to spar or fight two or three times a night, nearly every night, for eight months straight, if one did not have very good defensive skills. Try it sometime, every single day, even for just a month, with light or medium intensity, and see how you feel. Keep in mind also, they weren't wearing headgear, and they were boxing with gloves that were never bigger than 8 ounces.

Overall, the national tour had been a huge financial success. One secondary source said it achieved profits of around $80,000 to $100,000. Moran estimated the profits at $110,000, after $44,000 in expenses were deducted. In his autobiography, Sullivan said the total receipts were a little over $187,000, with expenses of about $42,000, making the profits about $145,000. Some estimate that Sullivan alone earned over $80,000 as a result of the tour. Many years later, Sullivan claimed to have generated $400,000 from his exhibitions during the 1883 - 1884 winter season.

By comparison, in 1884, a well-paid university professor might make $2,500 per year. The highest paid baseball player, even as of 1887, was team captain Mike Kelly of the Boston Red Sox, who earned only $5,000 per year. The uneducated son of poor Irish immigrants was making tremendous money with his fists. As of mid-1884, John L. Sullivan was only 25 years old.

The tour had made Sullivan a huge celebrity. He had been seen by more people in the country than anyone else, including U.S. President Chester A. Arthur. Folks read about him, saw him in person, and even saw his picture in magazines and saloons. John L. Sullivan certainly was the most famous athlete, and likely the most famous person in the country.[177]

[177] *National Police Gazette*, April 15, 1905; *Louisville Courier-Journal,* December 24, 1899; Isenberg at 166-170; Sullivan at 118.

Not Yet

Although during his national tour John L. Sullivan had been discussing retirement, once the tour was over, it appeared that he was not retiring so soon after all. Once he arrived back East in late May 1884, Sullivan negotiated a potential rematch with Charlie Mitchell. Sullivan wanted the fight to be winner-take-all. On June 6, they agreed that 65% of the receipts would go to the winner and 35% to the loser. The 4-round match was set for June 30 at Madison Square Garden in New York, less than a month away. Sullivan trained in Boston with Goss and McCoy.

The Champion Home Again

The cordial reception of John L. Sullivan in New York and Boston upon his return from his Western tour

Regardless of the scheduled fight, Sullivan's penchant for drink did not diminish. Bar-hops loved him. He often bought drinks for the entire house. Sometimes they bought him drinks just to enjoy his company.

Scouting the upcoming bout, one writer said that Sullivan had "unquestionably improved to a great degree in boxing skill." Mitchell, already a scientific master, had grown larger and stronger than he was the first time they met. Tickets were selling for $2 for seats, and $20 and $25 for boxes.[178]

[178] *New York Clipper*, May 31, June 14, 28, 1884.

Four days before the fight, Sullivan was informed that the fight was off, for Mitchell had malarial fever. At that point, Sullivan went straight for the bottle, drinking heavily once again in an extended debauch. However, two days before the fight, word came that Mitchell's fever had broken and the fight was back on. Sullivan boarded the train to New York, but kept drinking brandy all the way there.

On Monday June 30, 1884, Madison Square Garden was packed with at least 5,000 spectators, including aldermen, judges, and city politicians. They watched two preliminary bouts under the glare of the electric lights.

Madison Square Garden

However, when it was time for the main event, John L. entered the ring in his street clothes. He removed his hat and fanned himself, at the same time hanging onto the ring ropes to maintain his balance. Billy O'Brien also removed his white Derby hat and said, "Gents: Mr. Sullivan is in no fit condition to spar tonight. He is sick and we will put Dominick McCaffrey in to spar Mitchell or Burke."

Then Sullivan, slurring his words, gave a speech, calling off the match and excusing himself. "Gents: I am not in fit condition to spar tonight. Some will say I'm drunk, but I'm dead sick. This (hic) is the first time that I ever disappointed anybody in New York. It'll be the last too. I never give a fake show. I hope you'll forgive me. I meant to give you a good show, but gents I'm dead sick." Boston City Councilman Tom Denny called out, "Fight anyway." Captain Williams thundered, "Sit down." Denny replied, "Well, I come from Boston to see a fight and I want one." "Put that man out," said Williams. Sullivan, grasping the ropes to steady himself, said, "It's no use, Tom. I'm dead sick and here's a doctor as says I've got the fever." He also claimed that his condition was due to lack of sleep for two days and the effect of some medicine. Dr. Brown said, "Mr. Sullivan is a very sick man. He is not in condition to spar."

Mitchell was not at his best either, having been suffering from malaria, of which he informed the crowd, although he also said that he was present and willing to spar. Graciously, he excused Sullivan. "Gentlemen, I am satisfied that Mr. Sullivan is sick, and I don't think it would be fair for me to ask him to spar. I was sick, but I came here tonight to spar. I never like to spar with sick men, and I believe Mr. Sullivan is very sick. It's no use. I don't want to spar a sick man." Naturally, the thousands of spectators were extremely perturbed. O'Brien led Sullivan from the stage.

The Great Fistic Fizzle At Madison Square Garden
Fifteen Thousand Admirers of the Manly Art Are Badly Victimized After Paying Two Dollars Each to Witness A Match Between Sullivan and Mitchell, And Go Away Disappointed Owing to the Great John L. Having Imbibed Too Much of Mumm's Extra Dry

Most everyone believed that Sullivan was dead drunk, not "dead sick." The *New York World* said that Sullivan had been drinking freely all afternoon, and on his return from a Turkish bath, he was greatly intoxicated. His condition had not improved by that evening.

> The champion was drunk; very drunk; drunk all over – and he looked it. He appeared like a man who had returned to life after having been kept forty years in a barrel of alcohol to preserve him, with the exception that he was not preserved. Notwithstanding his condition was apparent, he denied it.

Gossip in the Garden was that Sullivan had been on a prolonged spree, that he had spent nearly all of his money on liquor (despite having divided with Al Smith $125,000 in profits from the tour), and that he did not own the saloon in Boston, but ran it for a brewer on a percentage. One New Yorker said, "He is a drunkard and has killed himself with New Yorkers. He will never again draw such a house as this and people will not pay fifty cents to see him again."

Although many hoped that Sullivan had learned his lesson about drinking, "some men cannot learn. The fiasco…added to the peculiar jollities of his Western trip, proves conclusively that Sullivan has no control over his appetite for drink." If Sullivan did not control his drinking habit, it "will ere long break down his constitution and land him where he was before the set-to with Joe Goss, which may be said to have been the starting point of his unprecedentedly successful career."[179]

A month and a half later, Sullivan told a reporter, "You know as well as anybody that I was sick and unable to fight Mitchell or anybody else in

---

179 *Brooklyn Daily Eagle*, July 1, 1884; *New York World*, July 2, 1884; *New York Clipper*, July 5, 1884; *National Police Gazette*, July 12, 1884.

Madison Square Garden that night. This has been the regret of my life, but I will make amends for it before long."[180]

Sullivan later claimed that he did not prepare for the contest because he was led to believe that Captain Williams refused to allow it to take place. He also heard that Mitchell was ill and would not be able to fight him. Therefore, thinking the match was off, "I grew careless in eating and drinking, and was thrown off my guard." He was "incapacitated through sickness," although his sickness was "caused by my own fault." "I was in no condition to fight."

Sullivan also said that the fight did not sell well, and a great many of the patrons were sold counterfeit tickets, so very little money was taken in. The great number of counterfeit tickets made it impossible to return the money to the patrons. Sullivan told Al Smith to give his share to charity. Regardless, it was a huge fiasco, and a big blow to Sullivan's reputation. Many saw him as a drunkard and swindler. The fans had paid to see him fight, did not, and had lost their money.[181]

Manager Al Smith subsequently parted ways with Sullivan, saying he would not have any further dealings with him. He was fed up. He later said that Sullivan had been drinking all afternoon.

Despite the embarrassment, Sullivan's drinking did not get better. Instead, it grew worse. He spent the summer mostly intoxicated. He was not boxing, though occasionally he played baseball.

On August 13, 1884 in the New England Institute Fair Building in Boston, nearly a month and a half after the Mitchell fiasco, at a benefit tendered for local Councilman Tom Denny, the champ's friend, Sullivan performed in three 3-round sparring exhibitions; against Dominick McCaffrey, Steve Taylor, and Councilman Denny. Charlie Mitchell was among the spectators, and Sullivan asked him to spar, but Mitchell declined. The exhibition was not supposed to be serious. 4,000 people attended.

First, Sullivan boxed McCaffrey, who was introduced as the middle-weight champion. Although McCaffrey seemed afraid, he boxed well, and their 3 rounds of sparring were interesting and scientific. Sullivan mostly used his left hand, but, according to the *Boston Herald*, "Every now and then, however, John would rush in on McCaffrey like an avalanche, and, after delivering a few half length arm hits, would let the Pittsburg pugilist escape. In truth, it must be said that McCaffrey got in the most blows and showed most science." McCaffrey landed a number of lefts, and even drew some blood from John's nose. "Of course, John was at a disadvantage in not being at liberty to exercise his giant strength."

The *Boston Daily Globe* said of the McCaffrey exhibition,

> [T]he bout was in every way a friendly one, and no hard hitting was indulged in. … John evidently didn't let himself out except at

---

[180] *Boston Herald*, August 15, 1884.
[181] Sullivan at 119-120.

intervals, when with a quick shuffle of his feet, and a few rapid passes with his left he would send McCaffrey scudding across the stage in a way that would have laid him open to some pretty severe punishment had the champion the inclination to administer it. McCaffrey, however, showed himself a most clever sparrer, and kept his adversary at work all of the time.

After some other exhibitions, Sullivan boxed with Steve Taylor. Because the latter was closer in size to the world champion than was McCaffrey, "Sullivan let himself out more and did better. Two or three times he chased Steve around the ring and hammered him well." Another observer said that although he made no special exertion in his bout with Taylor, Sullivan "showed by the agility of his movements and the rapidity with which he dealt his blows that he can still lay good claim to the title of champion." However, the Taylor bout was "entirely friendly."

Following some more boxing exhibitions, Sullivan boxed beneficiary Councilman Thomas Denny, who made a creditable showing, for he had boxing experience in his younger days.

The *Boston Daily Globe* said it was the finest show of physical skill and activity that the world could afford. The fans appreciated the boxers' developed artistry. Despite the fact that he was a bit fleshy, Sullivan seemed to be in good condition.

Afterwards, in an interview, Mike Donovan spoke about Sullivan:

> "He can settle any man in the world, sure, and the bigger the man against him, the better it is for him. Let me give you a pointer. I was with him in Hot Springs when they picked a terrible big fellow for him to knock out. I felt of this fellow at the hotel, and I tell you he was something immense. He had the broadest shoulders of any man I ever saw, was as hard as iron, and weighed about 240 pounds. I told John of the kind of a fellow he had to meet. "Is he a big fellow?" says John. "You can bet," says I. "He's a stunner" "Then the bigger he is the harder he'll fall," says John. … Well, he knocked that big fellow out in just two punches. He hit him there once," and Mr. Donovan landed his left under the reporter's chin. "Then he cross-countered him and he went down. When he came to the fellow was silly. … When he was traveling he used gloves with about an ounce of hair in each of 'em. … In Memphis he knocked a big fellow out in 11 seconds. The fellow was out, didn't come to for 20 minutes. … Well, the man laid there and Sullivan rubbed him and slapped his hands, but he couldn't bring him around. You could hear people in the audience saying, "He's killed him," and it's my opinion they would have killed Sullivan if the man had died. Finally the fellow came to, and Sullivan lifted him up, but he staggered like a drunken man. … I

> tell you that Sullivan thinks no more of knocking a man out than I do of eating an apple."[182]

The Boston exhibition did not mean that Sullivan's drinking problem had subsided. Far from it. His drinking sprees were continuing, and many said that he was intoxicated even when he sparred at the benefit. Sullivan frequently stayed out until the late-night hours and came home inebriated. Supposedly, he did this several times a week.

Alcohol brought out Sullivan's vicious temper. His intoxication led to allegations of domestic violence against his wife Annie, who left with John Jr. and went to her brother's home in Centerville, Rhode Island.

On August 25, 1884 in Boston, a 164-pound Dominick McCaffrey fought 148-pound Pete McCoy. Initially it was reported that McCoy was the better fighter. He was stronger at wrestling, and threw Dominick down a number of times. However, his actions were illegal under Queensberry rules. Some initial dispatches claimed that McCoy knocked down McCaffrey twice in the 3rd round. However, subsequent reports said McCaffrey was not knocked down, but thrown down. As a result, the audience was in pandemonium, a number of them jumped onto the stage, and a melee ensued. Sullivan, who was acting as McCoy's second, knocked down a half-dozen or so McCaffrey supporters. Some claimed that Sullivan was the one who started the brawl, for he punched out a local sport who had been "chaffing" him. The police stopped the fight and the bout was declared a draw.

Some speculated that Sullivan had wanted to see McCaffrey beaten, and told McCoy to do what he did:

> Up to the time of Councilman Denny's benefit in Boston...Sullivan and McCaffrey had been warm friends; but when the latter on that occasion stopped a couple of rushes by the champion (who had again been partaking too freely of the ardent and was not in good form) and had rather the best of their set-to, Sullivan's sentiments toward the young Pennsylvanian underwent a change, and he seemed to depend on his especial favorite, McCoy, to secure for him the revenge he wanted.

Before the McCoy fight, McCaffrey had issued a challenge to any man in the country, "barring Sullivan." However, after the McCoy incident, McCaffrey issued a challenge to Sullivan to fight under LPR rules for anywhere from $1,000 to $2,500 a side. Dominick said, "As I am the only man who ever bested Mr. Sullivan, he cannot with credit to himself decline to meet me." Clearly, there was bad blood.[183]

---

182 *Boston Herald*, *Boston Daily Globe*, August 14, 1884.

183 *New York Sun*, August 26, 1884; *New York Clipper,* March 22, 1884, June 7, 1884, August 30, 1884, September 6, 20, 1884; *National Police Gazette*, September 13, 1884.

Allegedly, on August 31, a drunken Sullivan arrived in Natick, seeking his son, and struck his wife. They subsequently reconciled, but that reconciliation would last only for about four more months.

On October 13, 1884 in New York, Dominick McCaffrey won a 4-round decision over Charlie Mitchell, although some questioned the verdict. Mitchell had trained down from 184 to 158 pounds, while McCaffrey had reduced from 197 down to 164 pounds.

The 1st round was tame, with McCaffrey mostly playing defense. There were a series of clinches in which Mitchell had the advantage. The round ended with Mitchell landing a telling left to the ribs, but McCaffrey countered him on the side of the head, staggering Mitchell. "It had been a lively round, Mitchell forcing the fighting, and McCaffrey keeping away from him with the prudence of an old and wary professional. Altogether he had slightly the best of it."

The 2nd round was livelier, and each scored well, but Mitchell was more aggressive and even forced McCaffrey to the ropes, getting the best of matters. It was a Mitchell round.

The 3rd round was the same, with Mitchell the aggressor and McCaffrey clinching often. McCaffrey got the better of some long-range fighting, and landed some effective lefts to the body and face. One said a McCaffrey right staggered Mitchell, the most significant blow of the round. Another said Mitchell rushed him to the ropes and showered blows upon him. He was the much stronger man. However, McCaffrey was countering well. Overall, Mitchell seemed to have slightly the better of matters in this round.

In the 4th round, McCaffrey forced the fighting and landed a left and right that drew blood from Mitchell's eye. McCaffrey got the better of some slugging. One source said Mitchell landed more often and with the most effect, forcing matters, driving McCaffrey to the ropes. Towards the end, McCaffrey seemed weak. However, another version said that at the call of time, Mitchell was groggier.

The referee awarded McCaffrey the verdict. The *Sun* agreed with the decision. However, the *Clipper* did not, saying,

> The general belief was that a draw would be proclaimed, and with such a verdict at the termination of so even a contest, all reasonable, fair minded men would have been satisfied…but great astonishment was expressed when the announcement was made that McCaffrey had won.

Although McCaffrey had fought well, the *Clipper* opined that "it is not right that he should have honors thrust upon him to which he is not clearly entitled." Conversely, the *Sun* said the American was too much for the English champion. The *Tribune* said the decision was a surprise. Regardless, his performance against a man with a strong reputation further legitimized McCaffrey's challenge to Sullivan.[184]

---

[184] *New York Tribune, New York Sun*, October 14, 1884; *New York Clipper*, October 18, 1884.

A week later, Mitchell fought Jack Burke to a 4-round draw.

In the fall of 1884, Sullivan took on a new manager, Chicago gambler Pat Sheedy. Sheedy believed that the best way to rehabilitate Sullivan's reputation in New York was for him to fight there again. Following flooding in Ohio, Sheedy arranged for Sullivan to fight John Laflin in New York, with some of the proceeds to benefit the flood victims. Patsy Sheppard once again trained him, and Sully lost a lot of weight, some saying about 30 pounds.

In the meantime, during October, Sullivan exhibited in places such as New York; and McKeesport and Allegheny, Pennsylvania.

As the fight approached, huge crowds appeared at the Monico Villa on 146th street in Manhattan, where Sullivan was training. They wanted to see the champion. Clearly, his popularity had not waned all that much, despite the Mitchell debacle. All were willing to wager on Sullivan at any amount. Two Boston brokers offered to bet up to $20,000 that he would defeat Laflin. Nearly a hundred ladies sent cards to Sullivan's room, wanting to meet him. He politely declined.

On Monday November 10, 1884 at Madison Square Garden in New York, a 194- or 196-pound 26-year-old John L. Sullivan fought 6'2", 208- or 210-pound John Laflin. Laflin claimed to be 36 years of age, though some said he actually was 42. Back in March 1883 at Madison Square Garden, Sullivan and Laflin had sparred 3 semi-friendly rounds, and Laflin had held his own and acquitted himself well. Hence, some locals believed that he could test Sullivan, and that his previous experience in the ring with Sullivan would be valuable. However, this time it was a serious 4-round bout, and those who followed Sullivan's performances knew there was a big difference in his power and ferocity when it was a real bout as opposed to a friendly spar.

A crowd of over 5,000 was in attendance (the *World* said 7,000), including politicians, bankers, brokers, a general, a senator, a judge, and Thomas Edison. Boxing men present included Harry Hill, Billy Edwards, Charles Mitchell, Dominick McCaffrey, George Rooke, Paddy Ryan, Mike Donovan, Alf Greenfield (who was scheduled to box Sullivan the following week), Jake Kilrain, Mike Cleary, and Joe Coburn. Greenfield wore a white satin scarf, horseshoe pin, with rubies. Hill wore a black bow with a "G" in diamonds. Edison wore plain buttons. Captain Williams wore a short coat buttoned up close to his neck, with no other ornament but a long club. McCaffrey wore a plain black-and-white-striped scarf with a diamond stud. Pat Sheedy wore a very red carat and very green emerald. Inspector Thorne's eye-glasses were fastened to his coat button. Arthur Chambers wore a ten-stone scarf-pin in a scarlet scarf. Paddy Ryan wore an abundance of hair oil. Mike Donovan wore a red cravat and a gold ring.

The *Herald* reported that the fight was winner-take-all, which some said was about $7,500 or $8,000. Others said the gate receipts amounted to between $12,000 and $15,000. The air was misty from the smoke of countless cigars.

At about 10 p.m., master of ceremonies Mahoney introduced Paddy Ryan to the crowd, and he received loud cheers. Mahoney announced that Sullivan would fight Ryan again in January. The crowd cheered again. Pat Sheedy had made the match.

"Professor" Laflin entered the ring with Billy Edwards and Arthur Chambers, and he received terrific applause. Edwards had a sponge and a tin pail, while Chambers had three palm-leaf fans and a pair of snow-white boxing gloves. Laflin sat down in a corner. He wore a loose hickory shirt and white trunks. He had a bald spot on the top of his head.

"Boston Pride" Sullivan bounded through the ropes, naked to the waist. The cheering was redoubled. No Roman gladiator ever was received in the old Coliseum with more enthusiasm. Patsy Sheppard and Tom Delany followed with sponge, gloves, fans, and napkins. John sat down and put on his gloves while his seconds fanned him. Then he rested his arms on the ropes.

After removing his shirt, the *New York Clipper* said that Laflin's physique was magnificent. Conversely, it said Sullivan's reckless manner of living had left him in less than his best shape. However, the *New York Tribune* said Sullivan was in the most perfect condition he had been in ever before in New York. Laflin was taller and heavier. Sullivan's flesh looked firm and hard, while Laflin seemed a trifle paunchy, with his body too heavy for his legs. Sullivan was clean-shaven except for two slight tufts of side whisker, while Laflin had a slight curling mustache. Edwards and Chambers rubbed Laflin down.

Speaking of Sullivan, Robert Morris said to Alf Greenfield, "Look at him. He's a dandy, isn't he?" Greenfield responded, "Oh, he's all right." Harry Hill said, "Wait till you see him get to work in the third round." Greenfield replied, "Well, I want to see him work a bit, you know. That's what I'm here for." Dominick McCaffrey was there for the same reason – scouting Sullivan.

Mike McDonald refereed. Hat in hand, he introduced the fighters. Both bowed in response to the furious plaudits. McDonald announced that the bout was to be fought using Queensberry rules. Jim Wakely called time.

1 - As soon as they finished shaking hands, Laflin immediately struck Sullivan with a right to the ribs. John L. was surprised and dumfounded by his insolence, and responded like an infuriated bull. Laflin started out gamely, and they beat each other wildly about the head and neck. However, soon Laflin became overwhelmed, and he started to clinch and grab around Sullivan's neck to save himself. Sullivan tried mightily to throw him off and break free from the clinches as the referee called Laflin to break away. The champ finally freed himself and landed a terrific left that sent Laflin down into a corner and "spattered his gore onto the spectators." Laflin's face was covered with blood.

Laflin rose and clinched for dear life. Sullivan kept trying to push off and work a free hand. They grappled and tussled about. Laflin tried to hold and hit as well, with emphasis on the former. Finally, Sullivan landed a right that dropped him for the second time. The spectators were frantic.

Laflin remained on the floor and did not rise within the 10 seconds required under Queensberry rules. Both fighters' backers entered the ring. Laflin's seconds, Billy Edwards and Arthur Chambers, assisted him to his feet (illegal under Queensberry rules, but legal under LPR rules), and, 38 seconds after the knockdown, he continued fighting. Apparently Laflin was more familiar with the traditional LPR rules, not Queensberry rules. Once again, this demonstrates how boxing was in a transitional period. Sullivan made no objection, probably because he wanted to give the spectators more entertainment for their money.

The round continued. Laflin alternately grabbed and slugged in close. Sullivan dropped him anywhere from one to three more times, depending on the version. Laflin even grabbed the ropes to stop himself from going down. His nose was bleeding badly.

The *New York Clipper* said, "Laflin was down three times in the first round, and once more than thirty seconds elapsed before he rose, instead of the ten allowed by the rules under which they fought." The *New York Herald* also said there were three knockdowns in the round. The *New York Times* said Laflin had been down five times, and agreed that Laflin once had been given 30 seconds to continue. It called Laflin's grabbing tactics cowardly. The *World* confirmed that at one point, Laflin was down for 38 seconds.

2 - At the start of the round, Laflin fought hard, and they collided like locomotives, slugging in terrific fashion for 40 seconds. In between the hard blows landed, Laflin kept grabbing Sullivan around the neck, ignoring the referee's calls to break. Eventually, Sullivan landed a stiff blow to the ear, and as Laflin staggered like a drunken man, John L. decked him. Police Captain Williams rose up the platform to stop it, but the participants convinced him to allow the bout to continue.

They rushed in close and it was give and take for a while, until Laflin clinched again. As a result of all of the wrestling and Laflin's laying his weight on Sullivan while pulling on his neck, combined with John L.'s efforts to free himself from Laflin's grasp, Sullivan seemed to fatigue and slow down a bit.

At one point, Laflin swung John L. around and forced him onto the ropes, and then he landed a dozen punches as Sullivan made little to no effort to stop the blows, "and stood staring blankly at his opponent without any regard for the punishment until he got his wind."

Sullivan recovered and attacked again. At the end of the round, once again he dropped Laflin.

3 - As usual, at the start of the round, Laflin attempted to fight. They rushed at each other and punched with both hands until Sullivan landed a blow to the ear that dropped him.

Laflin rose and resumed hugging, ignoring the referee's orders and the crowd's jeers. While he was holding Sullivan's neck, a blow decked him again. Some said Sullivan threw him down.

Laflin rose and fought well in some exchanges, pressing Sullivan back to the ropes while grabbing his neck. However, Sullivan recovered his wind, rallied and landed staggering blows in succession. He pressed Laflin to the ropes, but was held. Sullivan tried to push to break free, while the holding Laflin was leaning back against the ropes and slightly over them as he was being pushed.

After breaking, Sullivan chased him around the ring and "struck the most telling blows of the night," battering Laflin with one of his famous rushes. Sullivan knocked Laflin into a corner with a left with such force that his body rebounded and his head rung on the timbers as he went down.

Laflin was out, and his seconds, Billy Edwards and Arthur Chambers, picked him up and carried/dragged him to his corner. One local paper said time had expired before they brought him back, but another said, "the last knockdown quite settling him; but he was picked up and carried to his corner before the expiration of time." Another reporter said only two minutes and five seconds had elapsed. Once again, it appears that the bout was using a hybrid of Queensberry and LPR rules. Police Captain Williams wanted to end it, but once again was convinced to allow it to continue.

4 - For a while, in close, they swung wildly and ineffectively. Laflin resumed his hugging. Eventually, Sullivan landed a right that staggered Laflin, and then, striking round-handed blows, forced Laflin into his corner. Laflin was weak and unsteady, and he received punishing blows. Finally, Sullivan knocked him down with a right.

Once again, his seconds lifted Laflin to his feet and carried him to his corner. They tried to revive him. The *New York Times* said that despite their best efforts, "his legs refused to sustain him, his arms hung limp, and his head fell back." The impression here is that Laflin was knocked out. The *New York Clipper* backed this version. It said that after being knocked down, Laflin decided "to cut it without further ado. He was assisted to his feet by his seconds…and upon getting to his corner removed the gloves, whereupon the referee awarded the victory to Sullivan." This gave the impression of an LPR retirement. The *New York World* agreed. "The Professor, after being assisted to rise, pulled off his gloves, thus giving the fight to Sullivan." The *New York Tribune* version said Police Captain Williams insisted that the men be separated. "Laflin was thoroughly winded and, as he sat in his chair panting, his backers gave the match to Sullivan, who was almost as much used up." However, the *New York Herald* said that after the knockdown, "Again Laflin was brought to his corner and his seconds tried to bring him out again. But although he arose and moved forward unsteadily at their solicitation the time had elapsed and the round was declared finished." Hence, one might glean that he was given the 30 seconds rest while the 3-minute clock was still running, which 3 minutes then elapsed. The *Police Gazette* simply said that after his seconds carried Laflin to his corner, the referee decided the bout in Sullivan's favor. The *Sun* said, "He was knocked out, and the referee gave the fight to Sullivan. He was assisted to his feet by his friends. A minute afterward he tottered to the opposite corner and feebly shook hands with his opponent." When Laflin left the ring, he leaned on his seconds.

Hence, under Queensberry rules, one could consider this either a KO1, KO3, or KO4, for in each of those rounds, Laflin was knocked down for more than 10 seconds and required assistance to rise and continue. Most accounts give the impression that Laflin either retired or was not able to continue the 4th round. Either way, Sullivan had won, and he had scored several brutal knockdowns in each round.

Afterwards, Laflin was bruised badly. As a result of their intense exertion, in their dressing rooms, both men vomited.

The *New York Herald* called it 4 unscientific rounds of hugging and slugging. Laflin's blows made little impression on Sullivan.

The *Tribune* opined that Sullivan was not in his old form, and perhaps had overtrained. Nevertheless, he had beaten Laflin badly.

In his autobiography, Sullivan said, "In spite of hugging and crawling, Laflin was knocked out."

Years later, Mike Donovan said that "Laughlin" had no nerve, for he simply jumped around and clinched. At one point, he rushed and clinched and pushed Sullivan back into the ropes, but as Sullivan rebounded, he decked Laughlin with a lightning right to the neck. Donovan said Laughlin was counted out.[185]

Once again, John L. Sullivan had proven to a large New York crowd that he was far too powerful a fighter for anyone to compete with successfully.

---

[185] *New York Tribune*, *New York Sun*, *New York Times*, *New York Herald*, November 11, 1884; *New York World*, November 12, 1884; *New York Clipper*, November 15, 1884; *National Police Gazette*, November 29, 1884; Donovan at 104.

SULLIVAN'S EASIEST KNOCK-OUT.

THE COMBAT BETWEEN THE AMERICAN CHAMPION AND PROF. LAFLIN ENDS IGNOMINIOUSLY FOR THE LATTER.

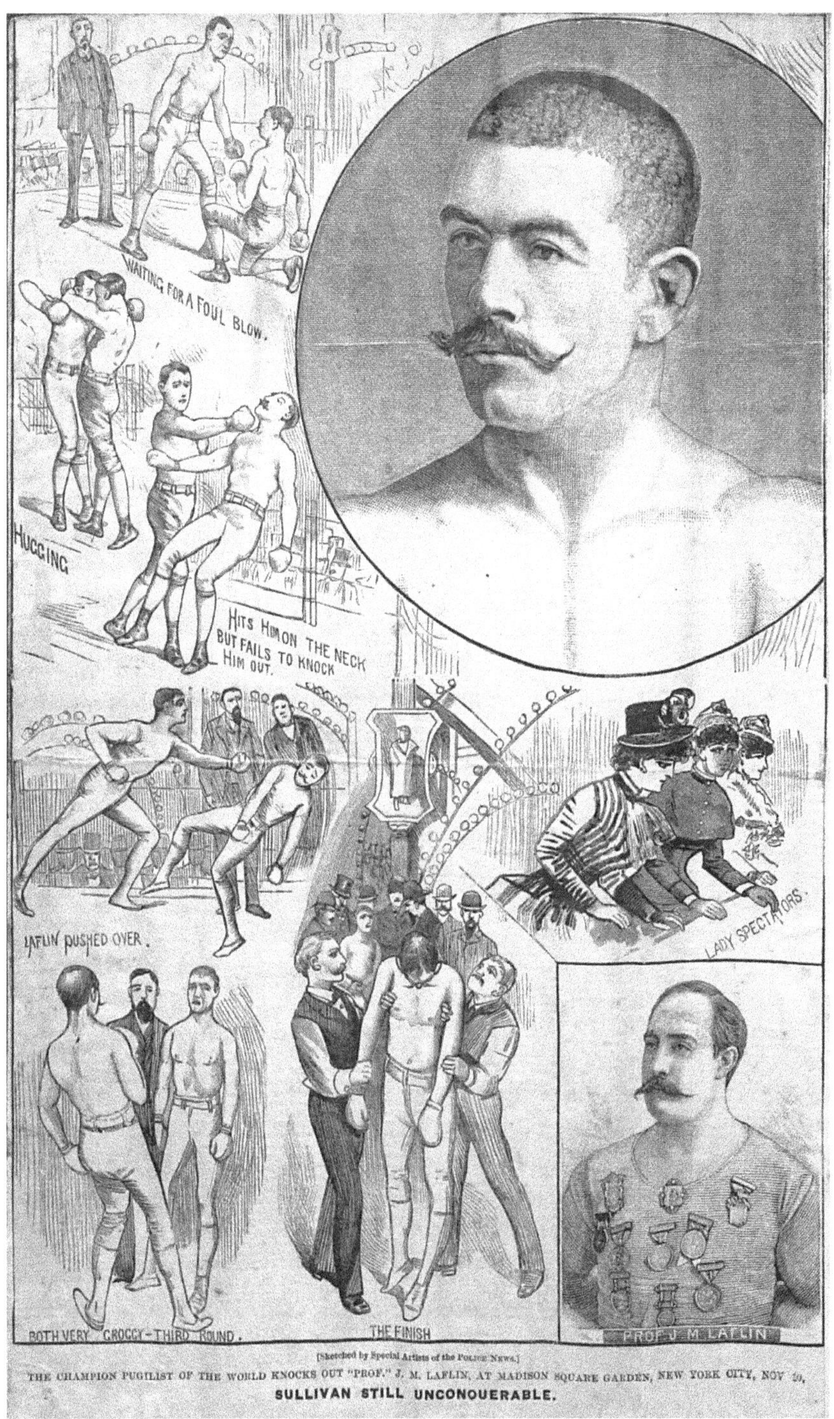

[Sketched by Special Artists of the Police News.]

THE CHAMPION PUGILIST OF THE WORLD KNOCKS OUT "PROF." J. M. LAFLIN, AT MADISON SQUARE GARDEN, NEW YORK CITY, NOV 10,

SULLIVAN STILL UNCONQUERABLE.

Alf Greenfield

Following his victory over Professor John Laflin, John L. Sullivan was scheduled to be back in the ring again in New York just one week later, this time against England's Alf Greenfield, an LPR ring veteran with a reputation for being very scientific. The 31-year-old Greenfield stood 5' 8 ¾" and weighed about 162 – 165 pounds. A few years earlier, some said that Greenfield could test Sullivan. Richard K. Fox backed Greenfield and had financed his trip to the U.S.

Greenfield's LPR bouts included a fight against Pat Perry that lasted 56 minutes before the police stopped it. Greenfield won an 1878 fight against Sam Breeze in 58 minutes. That same year, he defeated Jimmy Highland in 1 hour 15 minutes. He punished Denny Harrington over 1 hour 25 minutes, but lost on a claim that he hit Denny while he was down, which was hotly disputed. In 1880, Greenfield defeated Glasgow's James Stewart on a foul in 1 hour 20 minutes (20 rounds). In 1881, Greenfield and Tug Wilson fought 28 rounds lasting 1 hour 20 minutes (or 1 hour 45 minutes), though apparently Wilson had been considered the better man, for Greenfield's supporters entered the ring and stopped the fight, which was declared a draw. Some have said he once lost to Charlie Mitchell, possibly in a gloved contest.

In 1883, Jem Mace organized a gloved boxing tournament in England, and in the final, Greenfield won a 3-round decision over the "Irish Lad" Jack Burke. Hence, the *Police Gazette* advertised Greenfield as the English champion.[186]

[186] *National Police Gazette*, September 9, 1882, June 28, 1884, July 5, 1884; *New York Clipper*,

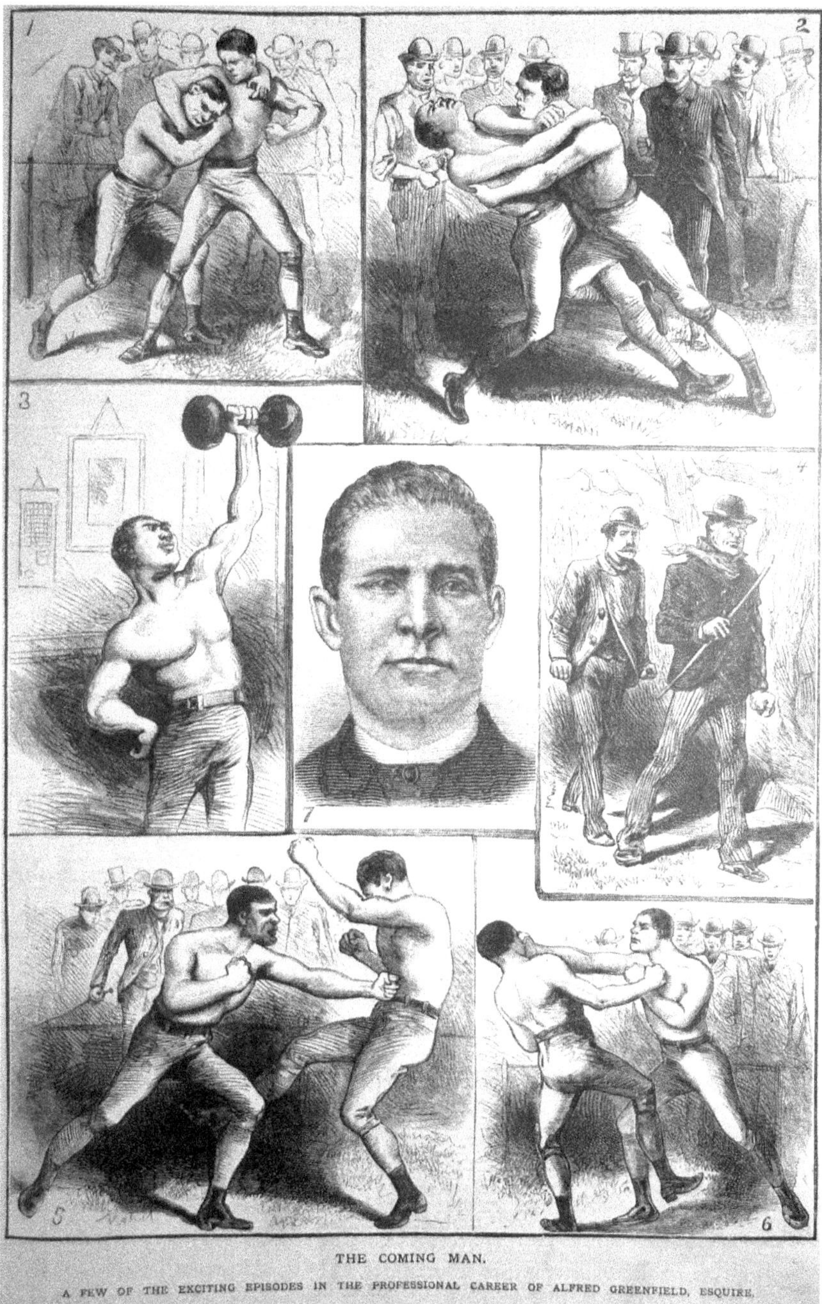

THE COMING MAN.
A FEW OF THE EXCITING EPISODES IN THE PROFESSIONAL CAREER OF ALFRED GREENFIELD, ESQUIRE.

I – He Whips Jimmy Highland. II – He Conquers the Scottish Giant With a Broken Arm. III – He "Puts up" at the Swan With Two Necks. IV – He Goes Out For a Spin With George Probert. V – He Loses a Battle to Harrington Through a Foul. VI – He Fights a Draw With Tug Wilson. VII - Himself

---

March 20, 1880, November 8, 1884.

The British Champion Comes To Try And Take the Laurels From the Yankee Boy

1 (center) – Greenfield's reception outside the *Police Gazette* office building, 2 (top left) – He is introduced at Harry Hill's, 3 (top right) – He comes down the gang-plank, 4 – words obscured, 5 (bottom right) – The sports greet him, 6 (left center) – He admires the *Police Gazette* champion belt in the *Gazette* office, 7 (right center) – The sporting editor shows him around the *Gazette* office, 8 (bottom center) – The tug-boat goes to meet him, 9 (top left) – Greenfield, 10 (top right) – Richard K. Fox, 11 (center left) – Jack Burke, 12 (center right) – Jake Kilrain, 13 (bottom left) – John L. Sullivan, 14 (bottom right) – Charlie Mitchell

The Sullivan vs. Greenfield bout was scheduled to be held on November 17, 1884. However, unfortunately, New York Mayor Franklin Edson, no fan of prizefighting, pressured the police to prevent the fight. He was cognizant of the fact that the "exhibitions" actually were real fights. Despite the fact that boxing had become very popular among all classes of society, many politicians and their constituents still were very uncomfortable with any form of fighting being legitimized. All of the press that Sullivan's fights had been receiving gave anti-boxing politicians the opportunity to get their names in the paper by opposing boxing, which satisfied a significant constituency, particularly religious folk. They were concerned that boxing bouts were taking place with much greater regularity.

Mayor Edson wrote the police board, "I believe that such exhibitions are disgraceful to the city in the higher degree, demoralizing to young men, and in their tendency leading to disrespect of law and order." Section 458 of the Penal Code made it illegal to engage in, instigate, aid, or encourage a ring or prize fight, or to send or publish a challenge or acceptance of a challenge for a fight, or to train or assist a person in training for such a fight. It was a misdemeanor punishable by up to a year in jail, a $250 fine, or both. It had been the law since 1859.

A couple days before the bout, on November 15, Police Captain Williams arrested Sullivan, Greenfield, Fox, and Sheedy on warrants secured by Police Inspector Thorne based on the latter's affidavit, signed by Judge Jake Patterson, alleging that they were proposing to violate the law against prizefighting. After their arrest, a crowd followed them all to the Jefferson Market Police Court.

The Defendants were taken to Judge Patterson's courtroom. Sullivan wore a blue peajacket, a high buttoned waistcoat, a white flannel shirt and collar tied with red cord, and a green tie. Greenfield wore a four-button cutaway coat, check suit, and dark trousers. He carried a silver-headed cane and a brown Derby hat. A diamond horseshoe sparkled in his salmon-colored tie.

Lawyer Colonel Charles Spencer appeared on behalf of the prisoners, and he cross-examined the witnesses. Col. Spencer got Inspector Thorne to admit that his affidavit in support of the warrant was based on hearsay, not personal knowledge. Col. Spencer entered into the record the papers from the January 1883 case of Mace and Slade. They were charged similarly, but the judge had discharged that case.

Sullivan was sworn in and he sat in the witness chair. He gave his name in a deep bass voice. Sullivan testified that it was his intention simply to give a scientific exhibition of the manly art of self-defense. His lawyer asked whether he had any enmity against Mr. Greenfield. "None at all." He was asked if he intended to inflict any damage. Sullivan laughed and said, "Pshaw no. We were merely going to spar scientifically, not hurt each other." He confirmed that they were not fighting for a prize. Also, the science of self-defense was something discussed in books. The clerk asked him to sign his statement, and when Sullivan hesitated, the clerk asked, "You can write, can't you?" Sullivan replied, "Just about." He signed.

A smiling Alf Greenfield, a tall, stout man, who at that time appeared to be almost as heavy as Sullivan, testified that he was born in "Hingland," and knew Mr. Sullivan "slightly." Captain Williams chimed in, "Yes, and he wants to know him better." Both Sullivan and Greenfield smiled. "Hi'ave made harrangements with 'im to give, you know, what you call a scientific hex'ibition." When asked if he had any enmity towards Sullivan, Greenfield responded, "Lud bless me, no," closing his eyes and shaking his head. "Hi don't hintend 'im hany 'arm." Sullivan grinned. Continuing, Greenfield said, "We would use the hordinary boxing glove, which, you know, his very soft, the same as amateurs use." When asked to sign his name to the typed up statement, Greenfield replied, "Beg your pardon, but you know hin hour country we don't 'ave a chance to learn; but hi can make my mark," and he put a big X at the bottom.

Patrick F. Sheedy testified that he was Sullivan's manager, not backer, and had paid between $1,700 and $1,800 in expenses for the preliminary arrangements for the bout, which was going to be only a "scientific set-to."

Colonel Spencer said that if the Justice decided to hold the men he would take the matter before the Supreme Court on a habeas corpus. Justice Patterson paroled the defendants until the 17th, by which time a decision could be made by a Supreme Court Judge.

Sullivan subsequently told reporters, "I did not make this match to knock any man out, but I should like to show the New York public that I can spar scientifically. I have no doubt Alf Greenfield means the same, and scientific points will count." Considerable money was being wagered, and Sullivan was the odds favorite at 10 to 7.

On Monday November 17, the date originally set for the bout, the parties made their arguments to New York Supreme Court Justice Barrett. Sullivan's lawyer argued that there would be no referee and no formal decision, proving that it was just an exhibition. The money was to be split 65% to Sullivan and 35% to Greenfield, not based on a winner-loser division, again bolstering the fact that it was just a friendly bout.

Judge Barrett ruled that the law would not be violated as long as they "intended to engage in a friendly sparring match not calculated to injure either party," which required that "the blows are to have no relation to the injury or exhaustion of either party." However, if "several blows are struck which are likely to cause injury or to inflame passion or the passions of the bystanders," the police could stop the bout and arrest both pugilists.[187]

On Tuesday November 18, 1884, the Sullivan-Greenfield bout took place in New York's Madison Square Garden, the fight having been delayed for a day owing to the legal proceedings. About 4,000 or 5,000 people were in attendance. The gate was hurt by the delay, the legal proceedings, and concerns that the bout would be tame as a result.

The ring consisted of eight posts, one at each corner and at each midpoint, and three ropes.

There was greater police presence at this bout than ever before on similar occasions. In appearance, Inspector Thorne was big sideways, whereas Captain Williams was big up and down, and towered over him.

Also present was Joe Coburn, Harry Hill, Billy Madden, Frank Moran, Al Smith, and Col. Charles Spencer, Sullivan's counsellor.

At 10:15 p.m., the fighters entered the ring. Sullivan was first to pierce through the gray foggy cloud of cigar smoke. He wore a short black coat that was a yard and a half wide, as well as white drawers. Jack Delay held the bottle, and Bob Smith the pail, while Patsey Sheppard was his second.

The 26-year-old Sullivan stood 5'10 ¼" and weighed an alleged 197 or 198 ½ pounds, though some thought he weighed more. Many said Sullivan looked bad. "One or two who knew him vowed he had been drinking. He certainly was not in prime condition." Others said Sullivan appeared to be in better condition than he did the previous week against Laflin. He sat on his chair as Sheppard fanned him with a big towel. His flesh was pink.

The 31-year-old Greenfield was listed as standing 5'9" and weighing 165 pounds, about 30 pounds less than Sullivan, though some thought he was closer in size to Sullivan than that. Greenfield was fine-looking, evenly built,

---

187 *New York Sun, New York Tribune,* November 16, 1884; *New York Herald,* November 18, 1884; *Daily Evening Bulletin,* November 18, 1884; Isenberg at 176-178.

shapely, and well-muscled. He crunched a little heap of rosin under the soles of his shoes. Both fighters wore white tights and stockings.

Arthur Chambers and Nobby Clark were Greenfield's seconds. Chambers manipulated Alf's gloves, kneading and pulling at them as though trying to get the padding away from the knuckles. Alf's seconds helped him get the gloves on.

Sullivan sat on his gloves, but then took the flattened gloves out from underneath and put them on. He too rubbed his feet in rosin. Sheppard pulled up his thin white drawers and affixed a new bright-green silk handkerchief around his waist.

In light of the legal proceedings and the intense police interest in the bout, in order to avoid having it be perceived as a fight, there was no referee, but rather Charles Johnston acted as the "master of ceremonies."

Johnston introduced both fighters to the crowd, which roared madly. The fighters walked to ring center, shook hands, and then returned to their corners.

1 - Both boxers began the bout holding their lefts well out in front and keeping their rights covering their ribs, sparring cautiously. Greenfield was game, not acting as if he was afraid. He fired quick blows and showed his agility, dodging Sullivan's rushes and countering. The round was competitive, with several exchanges. Sullivan was more of the aggressor, while Greenfield held his own with his counters, though his blows did not have much power. Alf circled around him. Sullivan momentarily knocked him about, crowded him to the ropes, and knocked him into the corner. Greenfield grabbed around the neck, and Sully pressed his elbow into his face. After that, Alf did not care to get too close to Sullivan again.

Overall, other than a few brief moments, the round had nothing of the "fast and furious order." Sullivan was just getting started. Still, the spectators gasped at the mere sight of some of his trip-hammer strokes. Greenfield was breathing rapidly at the end, while Sullivan was as calm as a judge on the bench.

For the most part, Sullivan had held back, not using his famous rushes or hurricane style. Therefore, the quick, well-scienced Greenfield did well. Although he landed more often, it was on the retreat, and his blows did not seem to make any impression on the champion. Still, he smiled at Sullivan when the champ's blows missed, something no one else had done to the champion. In the corner, Sullivan's seconds waived the big palm-leaf fans in his face, and also rubbed him.

2 - Sullivan became much more aggressive. He had woken up, and was anxious to crowd into Greenfield. He half ran and half leaped at his foe with a wicked look in his eyes. He fired off sledge-hammer blows, but Greenfield returned fire, landing some clean punches, though they lacked Sully's steam, and then he retreated. A few times when John drew close, Greenfield held, including around the neck, which drew hisses from the crowd. Johnston cautioned him not to use such tactics.

Greenfield kept moving around in a circle. Sullivan again lunged in with rights and lefts, one of which cut Greenfield's forehead just over the left eye. John L. was doing "terrific execution." Others said it was unclear whether the cut came from a blow or an accidental head butt when Alf grabbed Sullivan around the neck and pulled him in. The blood flowed and dripped over Greenfield's shirt. Sullivan showed blood behind his own ear, either from being cut there, or from Greenfield's blood dripping on him in the clinches. Johnston shouted, "Let go! Let go!" The spectators called out the same, for Greenfield kept holding on.

According to the *Clipper*, Sullivan again rushed him to the ropes and landed both hands in quick succession. Greenfield again grabbed around the neck. At that point, Captain Williams entered the ring and stopped the contest.

The *Times'* version said that Sullivan had "rained a series of tremendous blows upon his opponent and battered down his guard. In another moment Greenfield would have been numbered with the victims of Sullivan who have gone before, when Capt. Williams suddenly pushed between them."

The *Herald* said it would "have proved a very spirited round had not there been official interference." It described the conclusion:

> While Sullivan was thumping his antagonist on the ropes, right and left, and it looked as if the stranger was getting side winders, crushers and slashers in such quick succession that it would go hard with him, though he was fighting back with courageous recklessness, the law stepped in, and the fight was at an end before the three minutes had expired.

The round had lasted only 2 minutes 15 seconds.

The *Sun* version said that Sullivan had forced him to the ropes and punched him viciously. A stream of blood was on Greenfield's forehead and a little streak of blood over the right eye. "It looked as though the champion had everything his own way, and was going to demolish him." The spectators cheered. Captain Williams stepped between them, put his hands on their shoulders, and told them that they were under arrest.

The *New York Tribune's* account said Sullivan was rapidly worsting the Englishman, who clinched. At that point, Captain Williams was on the stage and then led them to their corners. Superintendent Walling had followed Judge Barrett's advice and had the fighters arrested as soon as he saw that the law was being violated.

The master of ceremonies announced to the audience that the police had stopped the exhibition and placed both pugilists under arrest, that Sullivan was the winner and had the best of it, sparring the most scientifically, while Greenfield had disobeyed orders, kept clinching, and would not break when told to do so.

The crowd moaned, groaned, hooted, hissed, and booed the police's actions, yelling, "Shame!" "Oh, let them go on."

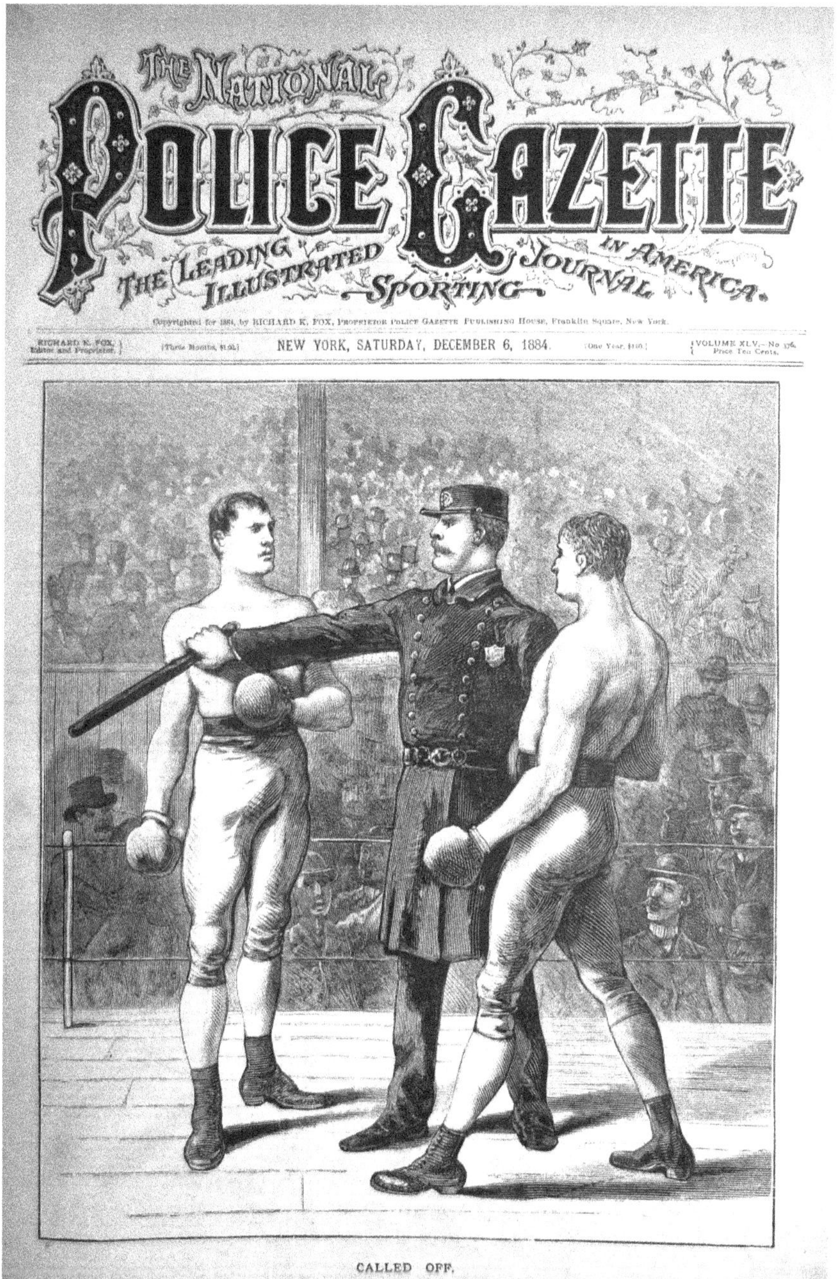

THE NATIONAL POLICE GAZETTE

THE LEADING ILLUSTRATED SPORTING JOURNAL IN AMERICA.

Copyrighted for 1884, by RICHARD K. FOX, PROPRIETOR POLICE GAZETTE PUBLISHING HOUSE, Franklin Square, New York.

RICHARD K. FOX, Editor and Proprietor. | (Three Months, $1.00) | NEW YORK, SATURDAY, DECEMBER 6, 1884. | (One Year, $4.00) | VOLUME XLV.—No. 376. Price Ten Cents.

CALLED OFF.

CAPTAIN WILLIAMS INTERPOSES THE SCEPTRE OF THE LAW BETWEEN SULLIVAN AND GREENFIELD AND KNOCKS THEM BOTH OUT OF MADISON SQUARE GARDEN.

Of the decision, the *Clipper* opined that its basis was "presumably because of Greenfield's persistence in hugging, and his tardiness in 'breaking' when ordered. On the score of points, it might have been decided a draw." The *Times* believed the decision was justified because Greenfield was about to get knocked out at the time of the stoppage. The *Sun* summarized that although Greenfield was the best man who ever faced Sullivan, it looked as if he was going to be whipped when the law stepped in and stopped it.

The local press opined that the 1st round had been a scientific exhibition, but the 2nd round was a slugging match in violation of the law.

Afterwards, Sullivan said that he never was in better condition and had not even begun to fight when the bout was stopped. "I can lick that fellow in two rounds." Captain Williams, who was in the dressing room with Sullivan, said, "Come, John, hurry up." Sully responded, "Wait, Cap, till I get some brandy." The brandy was rubbed on a small cut in the champ's scalp, the result of contact with Greenfield's forehead.

Greenfield's deep cut was on his forehead, just under the part in his hair and reaching to a point between his eyebrows. He also had a small bulge under his right eye, and his left ear was swollen. The cut kept bleeding. Asked what he thought of Sullivan, Greenfield replied, "Oh, 'e's a big, 'andy, strong chap, and I'd like ter to meet 'im again."

Years later, Mike Donovan said that a Sullivan right sent Greenfield spinning across the ring, and when he went in to finish, Alf held on for dear life. The police thought there was danger of a knockout, so they stopped it. "It was a lucky thing for Greenfield that the police interfered."

In his autobiography, Sullivan said, "I had Greenfield at my mercy."

The crowd of thousands jeered and hurled epithets at the police as they took the gladiators out of the building and walked them to the police station. The fans were upset that their entertainment had been terminated prematurely, and perturbed by the pugilists' arrest. The crowd followed them to the 30th Street Police Station. 500 men gathered in front of the doors, yelling and howling. A dozen policemen were sent out to protect the police station doors.

George W. Walling was listed as the complainant. At the police station, Sullivan, who chewed on a toothpick, said he was married, could read and write, and gave his occupation as liquor dealer.

Greenfield also said he was married, age 31, born in Northampton, England, was "a beer 'ouse keeper," and could not read and write. Looking disgusted with matters, he said, "It's an 'ell of a fuss fur nothing, yer know."

Either Harry Hill or Billy Bennett, who was a liquor dealer and ex-Alderman, posted bail for Sullivan, while Richard K. Fox did the same for Greenfield.

When a reporter asked what he thought of the turn of events, Sullivan responded, "What - - do you think I think?" Naturally, he was quite upset.[188]

It appeared that boxing was dead in New York, for the authorities were clamping down on real fights. The irony was that Sullivan had fought in New York several times, in fights that were even more brutal, which were attended by politicians, police, local dignitaries, and members of all classes, including bankers, brokers, lawyers, wealthy businessmen, and the like.

While out on bail, Sullivan's drinking continued. His conduct became so bad that on or about December 6, 1884, his wife Annie finally left him for good, taking with her their infant son John Jr. and heading to Providence, Rhode Island. From that point on, they were husband and wife in name only.

On Tuesday December 16, 1884 in New York, about a month after their bout, the Sullivan-Greenfield prizefighting criminal trial began. Sullivan wore his dark blue pea-jacket, blue pants, and a high silk hat. A gold chain hung from his waistcoat. Greenfield smiled at him, but Sullivan seemed surly and just nodded. Sully was represented by his lawyer Peter Mitchell. William F. Howe represented Greenfield. District Attorney Peter B. Olney, as well as his corps of assistants, represented the State of New York. Harry Hill sat next to Greenfield, with 6 to 8 feet of heavy gold chain around his neck. He looked solemn. Also present was Richard K. Fox.

While waiting for his case to be called, Sullivan said,

> If they don't treat me right this time, I won't run any risks, and they'll never get me again. What, am I going to sacrifice my peace and be dragged around like this, to make a few dollars? I guess not. And just because my head struck against Greenfield's and cut it.

In the courtroom were Captain Williams, who had arrested him, Superintendent Walling, who made the charge, and Inspector Thorne. Williams carried the gloves, which were wrapped in brown paper.

After a couple of hours, the case finally was called. "Hear ye, hear ye, hear ye." The jury selection began. Accepted as jurors were Felix Cohen, a bookkeeper in a liquor store, who did not know Sullivan or anything about athletics, Thomas R. Bronson, a drug merchant who knew about Roman gladiators, David Kirsch, a lace merchant who was opposed to the class of men Sullivan belonged to, but thought he could be fair, James D. Spraker, a broker and ship handler who had attended exhibitions at Madison Square Garden, John Graham, builder, Joseph Swan, silk goods, Lippman Toplitz, millinery and straw goods, Julius Friend, lace merchant, Ludwig Schwabacher, metal broker, Silas H. Rushton, bookkeeper, John G. Gnadt, machinist, and Henry A. Barclay. One of the prospective jurors who had

---

[188] *New York Sun, New York Tribune, New York Herald, New York Times*, November 19, 1884; *New York Clipper*, November 29, 1884; Donovan at 106; Sullivan at 126.

been excused, Alfred H. Thorp, was an architect who said, "I don't object to boxing, but I haven't much of an opinion of Mr. Sullivan or of his past acts." After two and a half hours, the jury selection was complete.

The next day, on December 17 in Judge Barrett's courtroom, the testimony began. This time Sullivan wore bright purple trousers. Greenfield wore a blue broadcloth.

The first witness was Superintendent Walling. He described the fight. There was a platform erected in the middle of the Garden with ropes stretched around it. The pugilists entered the ring dressed in tights and belts. A man named Johnston said they were going to fight under Marquis of Queensberry rules. He called "time" and "break." In the 2nd round, Greenfield feinted and then seized Sullivan around the neck. The master of ceremonies called "break," but Greenfield did not break. He held on. (At this point, laughter was heard in the courtroom.) The master of ceremonies then sternly ordered "break" three times, and said to Greenfield, "If you don't break, I'll decide against you." Blows followed, and soon blood was over Greenfield's eye. At that point, Walling ordered Captain Williams to arrest them. It was Walling's opinion that they had fought hard. He ordered their arrest when he saw Greenfield bleeding from his forehead, hanging onto Sullivan's neck.

Captain Williams produced the white gloves, each one smeared with blood. Walling testified that when Sullivan put on the gloves he pressed them on the back of his hand. "I think Mr. Sullivan wanted to harden the gloves."

On cross-examination, Superintendent Walling admitted that he had never seen a genuine prize fight. He admitted that there was very little blood on the gloves, and that just as much blood might come from a little boy's nose bleed. Judge Barrett refused to allow the lawyer to elicit testimony regarding the character of the crowd, because it was irrelevant. Walling also admitted that he had told Police Commissioner Matthews that the 1st round was "all right" and that Sullivan "could have knocked Greenfield out if he had wanted to." Hence, Sullivan had shown restraint. Continuing, Walling said, "In fact, I have said a hundred times that Sullivan could knock out anybody he wanted to. No one can beat him."

Next to testify was Captain Williams, who, as required, took the oath and kissed the Bible. He said the platform was 4 feet 6 inches high and 30-feet square. Stakes 5-feet high supported two ropes which were 2 ½ feet apart, and ran all around the platform. He said he only arrested the men because the Superintendent ordered him to do so. He did not think there was anything brutal about the bout. "I didn't see any great severity about the blows." The punches were of ordinary sparring force. Between rounds, each drank some water. The 2nd round mostly consisted of considerable hugging and clinching initiated by Greenfield, until blood became visible on Greenfield's face. "Then, Superintendent Walling said to me, 'This has gone far enough, Captain, you must arrest these people.' I did so."

LAW AND SPARRING.

SCENES IN AND AROUND THE SUPREME COURT ROOM BEFORE, DURING AND AFTER THE PROCEEDINGS IN THE CELEBRATED SULLIVAN-GREENFIELD CASE.

Captain Williams further testified that he had been president of the Police Athletic Club for 18 months, and nearly everyone there sparred, including himself, sometimes with Captain Clinchy. He often had seen blood flow during set-tos. The blood drawn from Greenfield was not significant, and only accidental, as the result of a collision of their heads. The police often used gloves smaller than the ones that Sullivan and Greenfield had used. Before the contest, the referee had announced that they would box for scientific points, and that was what they had done. Williams admitted that he had never seen a real prize-fight.

Sullivan looked pleased by the testimony, and sporting men in general brightened up.

The portly Inspector Thorne testified that he thought about the same as Captain Williams, except that Sullivan did hit a few "short-hand blows" while they were clinched. He demonstrated on the district attorney, grabbing around his neck and throwing mock punches with his right. He too admitted that he had never seen an actual prize-fight.

The jury was given the blood-stained boxing gloves to examine, and one juror even tried them on.

Captain Clinchy, a man with rosy cheeks and a broad chest, testified that he thought the hitting was not very hard. "I didn't see any hard blows struck. The men were smiling at each other. There was no knock down." When Greenfield grabbed, Sullivan "remained passive." The captain boxed himself, and liked it.

Police Surgeon Cook described the cut on Greenfield's face.

Less than pleased, the prosecution rested, and there was a recess.

The defense called Harry Hill. Large quantities of very thick gold chain leaked from all parts of his waistcoat, and the diamonds in his shirt blazed. He was shocked by the charges against his friends. He saw the fight, and said they could not have been less ferocious.

Professor James O'Neil said he instructed the men on the rules at the Racquet Club. The gloves were ordinary gloves, the same he used to teach his pupils, and the hitting done had not amounted to anything.

Billy Edwards testified that the gloves were slightly larger than ordinary gloves. The hitting was not hard, and it was a very tame affair. He had taken part in affairs that were not so tame, and bareknuckle too.

Edward Plummer did not care to say whether he had been the timekeeper, but did testify that the blows were very light.

Walter de Baun, an ex-amateur champion, testified the same.

Alfred Greenfield testified next. He wore a cutaway coat, and a big gold serpent was twisted four times around his left little finger. His tone was that of disgust by the proceedings. He said it was only an exhibition to please the public. They fought under no particular rules, but he did not want to hurt Sullivan any more than Sullivan wanted to hurt him. In England, he taught boxing, and he treated Sullivan the same as he treated any of his gentlemanly pupils. They were boxing for points. "'E as gits the most points 'as the honor of being the best man." Explaining the end, he said, "The way we came to clinch, is this. 'E's a good judge of the bizness, and when I tried to 'it 'im 'e ducked 'is 'ed, and my arm slipped round 'is neck." His injury was caused by the accidental collision of Sullivan's head with his eye. Greenfield said they did the exhibition just to make a little money. "I 'ad no ill feeling, and 'e had no ill feeling. We do it in England all the time, but of course I don't know whether it's allowed 'ere or not." He had nothing but "brotherly love" for Sullivan.

Sullivan took the stand next. His tread shook the room. His testimony came in a bass growl.

> I'm a married man, with a wife and child. I'm in the saloon business. This man Greenfield came across, and it was arranged we should have a friendly set to when we got Judge Barrett's decision. I was arrested and taken before Justice Patterson and all over. At last we got Judge Barrett's decision and prepared to stick by it. Before I went on the stage Captain Williams says to me: "You mustn't have any hard sparring; it won't do." There wasn't any. I didn't receive any blows from Greenfield that hurt me at all. There was no knockouts, or anything, and so you may be sure I didn't try to hurt him.

Sullivan put on a glove and said, "This is the way I hit," and he aimed a gentle blow in the air. Everyone gazed admiringly at the demonstration. He said he might have hit much harder blows had he so desired.

When asked, "Were your passions aroused at any time?," Sullivan responded, "Naw, none of them. I never did such a thing in my life. I shake hands friendly before I begin. They shake hands before prize fights too, but this was all friendship." He said he struck Greenfield's eye by chance when he was ducking.

In their closing arguments, the Defendants' lawyers expressed a hope that the jury would not send two such harmless young men to the penitentiary.

In a mere eight minutes, the jury returned with "not guilty" verdicts. Sullivan grinned. Greenfield retained his mild air of disapproval of the entire affair.

The next day, the State moved to dismiss the cases against Fox and his editor William Harding for aiding and abetting the fight.[189]

Unfortunately, increasingly, police and political pressure would hover over and influence many subsequent Sullivan bouts. The general public accepted boxing long before the politicians and legal authorities would.

Back in Boston, Sullivan's drinking continued for two straight weeks.

On or about December 28, Sullivan hired out some horses and a double sleigh. He and a few friends went to Yeaton's saloon. There, Sullivan insulted a waiter girl, who gave him a sharp retort. Allegedly, the slugger

---

[189] *Brooklyn Daily Eagle*, *New York Sun*, *New York Tribune*, December 17, 18, 1884; Isenberg at 178-181; Sullivan at 126.

then struck her a brutal blow in the face. The police asserted that she was not hurt seriously, but the common report was that she was knocked insensible to the floor and that Sullivan kicked her as she lay prostrate.

When he left, Sullivan struck one of the horses with a sledgehammer blow on the side of the head and began kicking it. A policeman arrived and ordered him to desist, but the champion threatened to treat him in the same way. The policeman left him alone, for Sullivan was with a party of sluggers.

Sullivan jumped on the sleigh and attempted to drive it down the street, but the horses were frantic and Sullivan too drunk to control them. The team overturned the sleigh, and the drunken Sullivan clung to the reins and was dragged at a breakneck pace 600 feet through the mud and slush with the sleigh on top of him. Eventually the team was stopped and Sullivan was pulled out. Amazingly, he was not injured. Any ordinary man would have been killed.

Although the girl whom he assaulted refused to make a complaint against him, there was some discussion about prosecuting him for cruelty to the horse.[190]

Sullivan subsequently claimed that he merely tapped the waiter-girl with wet driving gloves, and left the place on good terms. Regardless of the truth, eventually he settled out of court with the waitress.

However, the Society for the Prevention of Cruelty to Animals was granted a warrant for Sullivan's arrest. He would face trial for that offense in late January 1885.

Following the incidents of December 28, Sullivan traveled to Brooklyn, New York, where, at the Academy of Music on New Year's Eve and twice on January 1, 1885, he sparred Mike Donovan in a mild but scientific set-to in the concert scene during performances of a play called *The Lottery of Life.*

On Monday January 12, 1885 in the hall of the Institute Building in Boston, John L. Sullivan and Alf Greenfield boxed in another scheduled 4-round sparring match. Sullivan was called the "champion of the world," while Greenfield was billed as "the champion of England."

According to the local press, Sullivan's reputation and conduct outside the ring had impacted adversely his popularity to some degree. "There was a time when Sullivan could pack the largest building in the city with men from every walk of life, and reap a pecuniary benefit of thousands of dollars, for a few minutes of not very exhaustive labor. That time has gone by." Only about 2,000 people attended, still very good numbers, but modest by Sullivan's previous tremendous local standards. "The blue blood element was far less noticeable than usual."

Perhaps affecting attendance even more than Sullivan's outside-the-ring conduct was the fact that even up until the day it was held, there was doubt about whether the bout would be allowed. Like New York, there were signs in Boston that the legal authorities would be clamping down on boxing. It

[190] *New York Sun*, December 31, 1884.

took a while for the license to be granted, but finally on the day of the fight, by a narrow 7 to 5 vote, the Board of Alderman granted the license. Hence, there was not a great deal of prior notice to the fans that the bout would be allowed to take place. Usually that hurt attendance.

Regarding the champion's condition that day, local Police Captain Twombly said, "Sullivan is all right (in regard to intoxication), but he has shamefully abused himself, and it shows." Sullivan was extremely fleshy, with an inflated stomach. Although perhaps not drunk on this day, the common belief was that he usually was under the influence of intoxicants, which left his body looking fat and flabby.

ALF. GREENFIELD.

Sullivan wore white tights and a pink shirt. Greenfield was bare-chested. The difference in their musculature and weight was clear, with Sullivan obviously the larger man.

Unfortunately, before the fight, Police Captain Twombly told Sullivan that he and Greenfield could punch as hard as they wanted to, just as long as "there was no knocking out." The captain confirmed, "I told them I would arrest both of them if they exceeded the bounds of my restrictions." Sullivan shook his hand and said, "Captain, I'll do just as you say." Hence, once again, Sullivan's performance against Greenfield would be limited by his fear of being arrested. He could not land any knockout blows or try to finish him if he hurt him.

1 - Sullivan was the aggressor and forced the fight, doing most of the leading. He landed a number of head-jarring blows and had the best of it. "Sullivan had it all his own way, striking hard and getting few and light returns." Greenfield threw back only occasionally, and often resorted to clinching when Sullivan drew near.

2 - Sullivan used his rushes to force Greenfield back to a corner, stake, or the ropes, and when he was there, Sullivan pounded on him. Greenfield began hugging, and the crowd began hissing. At one point, Greenfield

ducked a right, but not far enough, for it caught him on the ear and dropped him.

Greenfield rose and leaned against the ropes, but Sullivan stood at ring center and ignored the crowd's pleadings to finish him off. He had the law to worry about. Clearly, Sully backed off and was carrying him. After they resumed, Greenfield clinched often, which brought hisses from the crowd.

3 - The "world's champion struck England's champion three terrific blows on the side of the head to start off with, and before he could recover from this attack he brought his right glove full on the neck, and Greenfield went full length upon the floor - a half knockdown."

Greenfield rose and held on in order to survive. His holding and moving tactics helped him survive. The attacking Sullivan rushed in, "holding out his dangerous left arm like a ramrod, smiting him fiercely on the face. In the rapid in-fighting which ensued, Greenfield was knocked down and through the ropes in Sullivan's corner."

When Greenfield rose, he ran away, which brought hisses from the crowd. Sullivan caught up to him and hammered away. In return, Greenfield landed a hard left, his best punch of the fight, but an unfazed Sullivan forced him into a corner and staggered Greenfield with a blow to the neck.

4 - Greenfield mostly danced and moved about the ring to survive, but still, "Sullivan hit him just about as he pleased." Greenfield landed a right and left, "but he might just as well have hit the side of a house, for Sullivan did not budge."

The crowd hissed Greenfield's tactics of sprinting around the ring. At one point, he "came to a sudden stop as the result of a right and a left blow from Sullivan, and many thought he was asking him to hit a little lighter. From this some got an idea that the whole thing was arranged between the men." In his autobiography, Sullivan confirmed, "Greenfield repeatedly asked me to let up on him, which I did." Of course, he had to, for if he won via knockout, he would see the inside of a jail cell. It appears that the crowd and even some newsmen did not know about law enforcement's edict that no knocking out would be allowed.

Subsequently, Sullivan fought Greenfield to the ropes and landed three moderately hard blows. The Englishman ran away and time was called.

The referee declared Sullivan the winner. Sullivan earned 65% of the receipts, while Greenfield earned 35%.

The local press said that although the fight had its moments and Sullivan clearly proved his superiority, showing that he was more scientific, skillful, and powerful, overall the rematch was fairly tame. The aggressive Sullivan did almost all of the leading, and forced the fighting throughout, while Greenfield only threw back occasionally, and often resorted to clinching or moving. The 3rd round was the most exciting round, "and that is not saying much." Sullivan was far superior despite the fact that his condition did not appear to be the best. "No one in the hall held any other opinion but that Sullivan could easily have settled Greenfield." John L. could have knocked him out, but instead carried him.

Afterwards, Greenfield said that no one knew as much about fighting as Sullivan, and no one hit as hard. Greenfield asked the crowd to excuse his hugging and running, for a man had to show generalship against Sullivan. There was no other way to fight him. Regardless, he admitted that Sullivan had shut him off.

Sullivan said, "I have treated Greenfield with respect, and if I was allowed to go on - but for the order of the captain - I would have done better work."

The fight had been tame owing to Greenfield's tactics of hugging and running, and because Sullivan showed restraint, holding back at times so as not to score a knockout and invoke the wrath of the police.[191]

On Monday January 19, 1885 at Madison Square Garden in New York, just one week after his rematch with Greenfield, Sullivan fought a rematch with Paddy Ryan, this time wearing four-ounce gloves fighting under Queensberry rules.

One might wonder why his manager Pat Sheedy would schedule or keep the date for another bout in New York, given what had happened there recently. Several factors may explain the decision. First of all, New York was the most populous state in the nation, which could mean a greater number of ticket sales. Second, because Sullivan had been acquitted by a jury, that emboldened him to believe that in the future, the authorities might leave them alone. Finally, New York had elected a new mayor, William Grace, and they believed that he might be more lenient than the prior mayor. Grace was a native of Ireland and the first Irish Catholic mayor of New York, and Sullivan was an American Irish Catholic hero.

However, it turned out that Mayor Grace did not want to be perceived as showing favoritism towards a champion with Irish ancestry. The day before the fight, the Mayor said, "[P]rize fighting cannot be conducted with impunity in this city so long as I am Mayor." Pursuant to his orders, the police told the boxers that any slugging would force them to interfere. Captain Williams said, "If the men get to fighting I shall arrest them. I will not permit any knocking out business." Hence, once again, Sullivan's hands would have to be tied to some degree.

Paddy Ryan said of Sullivan's natural power, "His stroke is like a kick from a mule. When he hit me on the neck under the left ear, at Mississippi City, I never knew what struck me."

Less than pleased by the police testimony during the Sullivan-Greenfield trial, the District Attorney sent two of his subordinates to attend the exhibition to gather evidence.

---

[191] *Boston Herald*, *Boston Daily Globe*, *New York Sun*, January 13, 1885; Sullivan at 126.

Showing his bias, local Judge Gavan Duffy, to whom Sheedy had sent complimentary tickets, announced his opinion that the local authorities should prevent the fight. The judge said that if requested, he would grant a warrant for the arrest of the pugilists, "On the grounds that a breach of the peace has been arranged for; on the ground that for the time being Madison Square Garden will be transformed into a disorderly house, in which will be gathered thieves and other disreputable characters." Given the judge's position, it becomes clearer why so many newsmen often mentioned the fact that many of society's most reputable members attended Sullivan bouts, and that the exhibitions were orderly. Despite what the judge said, boxing had a fan base across the class spectrum, and such exhibitions did not necessarily or always cause breaches of the peace. However, boxing still had a reputation to the contrary, which it needed to combat and refute.

Some reporters said Sullivan weighed about 220 pounds or more, but Sullivan claimed to be weighing 213 pounds. Ryan allegedly had reduced his weight from 225 down to 195 pounds. Neither man stepped on the scales.[192]

The *New York Herald* and *New York Sun* said a huge crowd of 10,000 was present. The *New York Clipper* said that 6,000 people attended the match, while the *New York Tribune* said 7,000 or 8,000 were in the arena. The seats sold for $1 and $2. Boxes were $10.

Some spectators wore sealskin coats. Others wore diamonds. Present in the crowd were Pat Sheedy, Ex-Senator Roscoe Conkling, Richard K. Fox, John Flood, Billy Madden, Harry Hill, James Wakely, John Wood, Denny Costigan, Professor Miller, Charley Mitchell, Alf Greenfield, Mike Cleary, Professor Laflin, Billy Edwards, Joe Coburn, and Captain James C. Daly. Pat Sheedy had offered 3 to 1 odds to those who were willing to wager on Ryan.

As usual, the police force was well represented. Captain "Clubber" Williams, with new gold stripes on his cuffs, was on hand, ready to club order into those who might be disorderly. Inspector Thorne was there as well.

The first preliminary was Pete McCoy and Mike Gillespie, who sparred 3 rounds. Next, two Japanese wrestlers exhibited their skills in a wrestling match, and then they put on the gloves and sparred.

After several other preliminary bouts, at 10:15 p.m., Sullivan walked towards the ring. "Here he comes," some cried. He wore a pale pink silk shirt that revealed his naked arms, white tights/trunks, and blue-green stockings that ran down to his black leather shoes. He also wore a short pea-jacket. He received cheers, and sat down in his corner. Tom Delay and Dan Murphy rubbed and fanned him.

Ryan followed, and he appeared to be in better condition than the champion. He did not have the excess fat around his waist that Sullivan did.

---

192 *New York Sun,* January 17, 1885; *Brooklyn Daily Eagle, Boston Daily Globe,* January 19, 1885.

He wore bright green stockings, and was naked above the waist. The yell that greeted him was nearly as loud as the one that Sullivan received. Both men removed their jackets, revealing what they wore underneath.

The *Herald* said, "The weights given out were 197 for Ryan, who looked much bigger despite the vast amount of work he had done, and 212 pounds for Sullivan, who did not look that weight." The *Clipper* said Sullivan looked fat. The *Tribune* said that despite recent stories of Sullivan's dissipation, he seemed to be in at least as good condition as when he last appeared in New York. Ryan seemed a trifle too fleshy to be prime, but looked fine, about 13 pounds more than when they first fought. Sullivan was more than 35 pounds larger than when they first fought. Their faithful esquires fanned them.

Both Captain Williams and Inspector Thorne spoke with the fighters, who nodded at them. During the bout, these two policemen would stand just outside the ropes. The gloves were put on and tied. Williams examined the gloves to make sure they were soft enough. Master of ceremonies John Scanlan introduced the boxers, and then called time to start the bout.

1 - A moment was consumed engaging in preliminary sparring. Ryan looked determined, while Sullivan, mindful of what the police had told him, started with a smile and lightly threw a gentle blow at Ryan's chest that fell short. Ryan landed a light left to Sullivan's stomach and fired a right that missed.

They danced around, smiling. Still smiling, Sullivan led, and although it was a gentle punch for him, it landed full on Ryan's neck and slightly staggered him. In response, Ryan landed a hard right to the jaw that made a loud sound and removed Sullivan's smile. Sullivan's face grew ugly and his eyes blazed with fury. Sullivan then made one of his mad rushes and planted a right on the side of the head, which Ryan countered with a left to the ribs. Newsmen differed in their accounts regarding what happened next:

New York Sun: Close together, for three seconds they fired thundering blows. Ryan landed on the face and neck, but Sullivan seemed to mind the punches "no more than a puff of wind." John L. did not attempt to defend, but showered blows to Ryan's chest and ribs with savage ferocity. "Just as it seemed that Ryan must go down under the terrible punishment, a portly form was seen climbing through the ropes, and Inspector Thorne's arm and club were stretched between the men." However, the boxers ignored him, continuing to fight savagely up close.

Then Captain Williams entered the ring as well, and he said, "John," and told him that he had to stop. Sullivan stepped back, and the two fighters glared at one another. Williams marched Sullivan to his corner and pulled off his gloves. Thorne did the same for Ryan.

New York Tribune: After Ryan landed a solid right, Sullivan became furious and fired off a series of short right and left blows. Ryan fought coolly, firing back with much effect. As Sullivan tried to duck a right the punch caught him on the neck. Ryan followed with several short blows to the face and clinched. Sullivan freed himself, but Inspector Thorne stepped between them and ordered them to their corners.

Summarizing, the *New York Times* reported that Sullivan began with "a little gentle sparring," as he "had taken a lesson from his last experience in Madison-Square Garden, and evidently intended to do no heavy hitting." However, Ryan attacked and landed two heavy blows. As a result, Sullivan "threw discretion to the wind," attacked, and in "a second he had broken down Ryan's guard, and in another second it would have been all up with the Trojan. But Inspector Thorne had carefully watched the fight, and he crawled under the ropes when the first heavy blow was struck." The police terminated the bout.

The *New York Herald* summary said Ryan landed a number of good punches. In a clinch, Ryan held Sullivan's head and hit him twice to the ribs. From the outside, Ryan countered some blows, and also got the best of some inside exchanges. After another clinch, Inspector Thorne jumped on the stage and stopped the fight. Both men went to their corners thinking that the fight would be resumed, but the inspector would not yield.

The *New York Clipper*'s fight description said they made a few exchanges and there was a clinch. Each put in some heavy shots at close range, in the midst of which Inspector Thorne and Captain Williams, "seeing that the blood of the boxers was up," stepped in and ended it.

The *Times* said the boxing had lasted only 1 minute 8 seconds. The 1st round barely had gotten underway when the police stopped it. The *Sun* said that except for the preliminary back-and-forth sparring, the fight was over after just 10 seconds of real red-hot fighting. The *Tribune* said barely a minute had been consumed. The *Herald* said, "The total time of fighting was 90 ¼ seconds." The *Clipper* said barely 30 seconds had elapsed when the police stopped it.

The crowd had been excited by the boxers' burst of energy, and so when it was stopped, the disappointed fans were indignant at the police, firing off a storm of groans, hisses, howls, and roars that continued for several minutes. However, the police refused to allow the bout to continue. Some feared a riot, but Sullivan stepped forward and waved his hand to his friends, who cheered for him. Ryan then did the same, and he too received cheers.

The referee declared that it was no fight, so all bets were off.

There was a wide divergence of opinion regarding the relative merits of the combatants up to the point in time the bout was stopped, as well as a divergence of opinion regarding what the ultimate outcome would have been had it continued. Some said Sullivan had the best of matters and would have won, while others declared that Ryan had been superior and would have been the victor. Some said Sullivan was just getting started and had been holding back. And other observers said matters remained unclear, for too little time had elapsed for either man to have established an advantage. The *Tribune* said, "Save in the case of confirmed Sullivanites, there were no two opinions as to the merits of the fight. There was not a sporting man present but was convinced that Ryan would have outmatched his man had the rounds been fought out." Some said if Ryan had fought like that a few years earlier, he would have defeated Sullivan. The *Herald* reported, "The referee said he considered it no fight, but the popular verdict was that Ryan had the call. No arrests were made." The *Brooklyn Daily Eagle* reported that the fight was stopped when Sullivan was getting the worst of it, and as a result, many now believed that Ryan was his equal, and that a third match between them would be arranged. However, the *Times* and *Sun* both thought that Ryan would have been knocked out. The *Clipper* offered a middle-of-the-road opinion, saying, "The encounter was too brief to be regarded as having the slightest bearing on the question as to the present relative merits of the men. So far as it progressed neither had a whit the better of the other." In truth, the result was inconclusive, owing to the bout's very short duration. There had not been sufficient fighting to determine the outcome. Either way, the official referee verdict, and properly so, was a no contest. The police had warned them not to slug, and they had, so the police stopped it.

Afterwards, Sullivan said,

> I want this to come off somewhere else, and that soon. I am satisfied I can whip Ryan, though he is the best man I have ever tackled. I can't say he is a better man than he was at Mississippi City, but even if he is, so am I. I was only a boy then and relied entirely on my heavy hitting. Now I consider myself the best boxer that can be found and you can bet I can hit as hard as ever. I could have whipped him tonight, I think. I want to meet him again, and I also want to meet Dominick McCaffrey. Then I am through.

Ryan was fresh and smiling, as usual, and said,

> When I got that heavy blow in on Sullivan I could not help thinking of my old mother, and I tell you the thought gave me renewed determination. I had made up my mind to give Sullivan as good as he sent, and not stand up to be hammered without returning the blows. I am a large man, and he can't drive me about the stage, and his rushes lost their effect. Sullivan has never been met by a man, except myself, who fought back, and if the police had not interfered I should have surprised Sullivan still more. I don't like to put it stronger or brag much. We will come together again where the police won't stop it, and I don't think he will stop me. I always had confidence in my own ability to whip Sullivan, and from tonight's experience my faith is still stronger.

Pat Sheedy offered to back Sullivan against Ryan again for $5,000 or more. The gate receipts amounted to nearly $11,000.

Sullivan claimed that he gave Ryan one-half of the profits as a favor, for Paddy had been in dire financial straits. His Chicago saloon had burned down, he had no job, and he was trying to support his 80-year-old mother and his own family. The way the fight had been made was that Ryan had come to Sullivan and asked him to give him a fight so he could earn some money.[193]

The Meeting of the Giants

A Very Interesting Match Between Paddy Ryan and John L. Sullivan Interrupted by the Police

Although this time the police did not arrest the fighters, and no trial would be held, the message sent was clear – the legal authorities were not going to allow any more real fights. Simply by stopping the fight quickly, the impact would be made. Fans would not pay to see another fight that would be stopped just as soon as it started. New York was dead to Sullivan.

Sadly enough, that same day in Boston, the Board of Aldermen voted that no licenses for sparring matches would be issued except by unanimous consent, which would be rare. Hence, his own hometown of Boston would be closed to Sullivan as well. Except for mild exhibitions, never again would Sullivan fight a real fight in either New York or Boston. That had a big financial impact, because both cities had huge populations.

Sullivan returned to Boston and resumed his drinking habits. Two days after the Ryan fight, he was driving his carriage down Beacon Street, when the team of horses bolted. Sully lost control and was thrown from the

---

193 *New York Times, New York Herald, New York Sun, New York Tribune,* January 20, 1885; *New York Clipper,* January 24, 1885; *Boston Daily Globe*, January 19, 1885; Isenberg at 182-183; Sullivan at 126-127.

carriage, striking his head, which was badly gashed. The carriage was smashed.

Allegedly, the next day, at the bar of the Delmonico Exchange, a drunken Sullivan got into a row, butting a young man in the head. He then turned on a bystander who had reproached him and knocked him out cold. The bartender drew a revolver on Sullivan before eight officers subdued the champion. No charges were filed.

In late January 1885, Sullivan was in court for his charge of having abused a horse on December 28. Witnesses testified that Sullivan kicked a horse three times in the ribs and struck it several times with his fist. Sullivan's lawyer argued that there had been no abuse, for the horse was a runaway and a bucker. Sullivan was found guilty of fast driving and unnecessary cruelty in beating a horse. He was fined $100 plus court costs, which came to a total of $115.07.

Sullivan signed for a June bout with Paddy Ryan to be held in Wyoming, although the fight there never materialized.

On February 24, 1885, Annie Bates Bailey Sullivan filed a petition for divorce from John L. Sullivan in Massachusetts, alleging her grounds to be John L.'s cruel and abusive treatment and gross and confirmed habits of intoxication. Through her attorneys, she requested that his property be attached for $20,000 for support of herself and their son John, Jr. A judge entered a restraining order against Sullivan, pending trial. Sullivan contested the divorce, which is something one could do back then.

On March 24, Sullivan's friend Joe Goss died of Bright's disease of the kidneys and liver. He passed away in his room above his Boston saloon, the Saracen's Head. The press said the disease was alcohol-related. He was 47 years old.

On April 2, 1885 in Philadelphia, two and a half months after the Ryan bout, a 210-pound Sullivan was supposed to fight 163-pound Dominick McCaffrey. However, a judge issued a warrant for their arrest, charging them with conspiring to create a breach of the peace. Both Sullivan and McCaffrey were arrested. They tried to do the usual convincing of the local judge that they were not going to hurt one another, but the judge wasn't buying it. Each had to post $5,000 bonds for trial, and $5,000 more agreeing to keep the peace, which bonds would be forfeited if they fought, which was more than what the ticket sales likely would generate, so it did not make sense to fight.[194]

The McCaffrey fight would have to wait, and be held elsewhere. Ticket receipts had to be refunded to purchasers. Despite its popularity, once again boxing had run up against a legal barrier, in the third major city within just a few months. The anti-boxing sentiment was on the rise with those in power.[195]

---

[194] *New York Tribune, New York Sun*, April 3, 1885.
[195] *Brooklyn Daily Eagle*, April 2, 1885; *New York Clipper*, April 11, 1885.

Soon thereafter, Sullivan and Pat Sheedy severed their relationship. Sullivan said the reason was financial – his manager wanted too much money. Sheedy said the hostile and aggressive Sullivan would wind up dying with his boots on. However, they later would reconcile.

On May 27, 1885, the Sullivan divorce trial began. It was the sensational event of the day, and attracted a great deal of attention. Both parties laid it all out there. John L. wore a clerical Prince Albert coat and a shiny new silk hat. His moustache and hair had grown out to a fashionable length. He paid no attention to his wife, who was a fine-appearing woman. Annie Sullivan wore a close-fitting black dress, valuable solitaire diamonds in her ears, yellow silk gloves, and a black half-veil shading her eyes. She was a brunette, and had a nice physique.

Annie testified that Sullivan was abusive, addicted to the excessive use of liquor, and had beaten her on several occasions. She claimed to have been faithful, but said her husband had not been. She said that on August 31, 1884 at her brother's home in Natick, John L. knocked her down senseless in a drunken rage in front of his brother Mike and an outsider named Matilda Adams (who later testified and corroborated her story). He left such a bad mark on her face that she used paint to hide it. She said he also had beaten her at their home at Lovering Place. During the 1883-1884 national tour, in a drawing-room car, he threw a glass at her, and in Montana, he kicked her and threw objects at her in the presence of Pete McCoy and Frank Moran. She claimed that in Leadville, he had hit her even though she was pregnant, driving her out of their hotel with a pitcher. Herbert Slade had to protect her from her drunken husband, who had threatened to kill her. The attacks always occurred when he was under the influence of liquor. When he was sober, they got along well. She had left him several times, but returned on his promise to cease drinking. When he was drunk, she did not dispute him, for she feared for her life. She finally left him on December 6, 1884.

On cross-examination, Annie denied that she ever drank herself or that she ever threw missiles at her husband. Annie refused to say whether she had lived with John L. before marriage. Sullivan's lawyer's questions implied that she knew about his habits and tendencies before they married, having lived with him for quite some time, so she knew what to expect. She admitted that she had been married before, to a man named Bailey, and she was a widow. She could not swear that she had informed Sullivan of her previous marriage. She was 28 years old at present. She declined to say how much money she had when her first husband had died. She denied that she ever knew a Zack Hollingsworth or that she ever received money from him to pay for her house. She admitted that John L. gave her lots of money and always was generous. Sullivan's lawyer also implied that her associates were women of ill repute. Before the cross-examination was complete, Mrs. Sullivan became faint, and was excused until the next morning.

During the testimony, John L. rarely glanced at his wife. He sat next to his lawyer and stroked his moustache or chewed on a toothpick.

Annie's brother, Henry Bates, testified to having helped put John to bed when he was drunk.

> I have seen him kick Mrs. Sullivan while she was taking off his boots. One day in October Sullivan came home cross. Mrs. Sullivan was combing her hair. He got mad with her without any reason that I know of, and swore at her so badly that she went into the sleeping room and began to cry. He asked her to come out, but she didn't and he went in and grabbed her by the hair and pulled her out.

On cross-examination it was revealed that when Henry was unemployed, Sullivan had supported him for four months, allowed him to live with them, and he gave Henry gifts of clothing.

Annie's brother William also testified on her behalf.

John L. Sullivan testified that he first met his future wife Annie in April 1882, just after his fight with Ryan. He met her in Boston on Shawmut avenue. A man named Albert Stickney introduced them.

> From what he had said to me, I told him to introduce me to her. After I was introduced I got in the back with her and we went to the Hawthorne. We stopped there about three-quarters of an hour and drank sherry together. … Three days later we went to the Hawthorne again and drank together, stayed three hours and she acted as my wife for the first time on that occasion. I lived with her a year and two weeks before we were married. I married her for religious purposes, after I had been very sick. A priest came to see me and I told him I was married. Afterward I denied it to a second priest. I married her the next Sunday, on May 1, 1883. I am a Catholic and she is a Protestant.
>
> I was in the habit of giving exhibitions both before and after my marriage, and my wife has attended all of these but one in Washington, where I would not let her go.
>
> I am in the habit of drinking, and was so before marriage. I am not near so bad now as I was then. Mrs. Sullivan drank with me, and she did not object to me drinking or going on these tours. … She used to drink in my company. … She always drank wine, beer, or whiskey with me. She could drink as well as I could.
>
> I never was drunk in my life. I have been full, but I could always get home without assistance. It is necessary for men in my business to be in good training, and they cannot if they drink to excess. … I have been intoxicated, but I never was drunk. I don't drink to excess, but in this business a man must drink, so many people ask him.

> It is not true that I was ever unfit for a match through my intoxication, although the papers said so. … When I disappointed the public in New York I was seriously sick, and the doctor advised me not to appear. I have his bill here for $58.
>
> I was in the habit of getting home around 3 or 4 o'clock in the morning – hardly before 1 o'clock. I did not get home any earlier before marriage.
>
> I never kicked my wife in my life. I have kicked men, but not since I have been a professional man.
>
> When my wife went away she was vexed because I stayed out on a Sunday night and when I went to Natick I asked her why she left me. She said the child could not live in the city, so she had taken it there. … She said the child was sick, and I went down with my brother. I went to the room where my wife was, a bedroom. She stood at the door, and I said: "I want to see the child." She replied: "You cannot." I pushed her on one side, and she fell down. Then I went to the bed and took the child up. I did not hit her. She fell down and said I was going to kill the child. I never painted her face at all, and know nothing about her eye being black. As she fell down she struck her face against the bedstead and it was swollen.
>
> I had words with her once about a man named Hollingsworth. While I was away once I heard she had written to him asking for $1,000. I was giving her all the money she needed, $3,000 or $4,000 at a time. She said she knew Hollingsworth before she knew me.
>
> We had some words about her relatives. I told her I didn't mind supporting two or three of her relatives, but I did not propose to support the whole state of Rhode Island. [This created a general laugh, and even the judge smiled.]

Sullivan swore that he had never struck his wife, or thrown a glass at her as she claimed. She had thrown bottles and books at him. He also testified that she was in the habit of drinking whenever he did. She often drank with him, taking beer, wine, whiskey, or rum punches. He had not seen her since December 6, 1884. Sullivan further said that his wife was a jealous woman who constantly accused him of cheating. He claimed that she had never told him about her previous marriage.

On cross-examination, Sullivan admitted that he had been fined for abusing a horse.

> The horse overturned the sleigh and I hit him a slug on the jaw. I didn't knock him down. I don't think I could knock a horse down. I have a little respect for my hands. I might have been a little excited then. I had been drinking, but not to excess. I was under the influence of drink, but not drunk. I could always write my name and attend to my own business. I never was helped up stairs in my life.

> My wife says I was drunk the whole year of my trip, but I couldn't have been very drunk, as I sparred nearly every night for eight months, knocked fifty people out and brought back $100,000.

John's brother Mike Sullivan testified that he had never seen his brother strike Annie. Rather, he had seen Annie hurl bottles at John. Annie was fond of brandy punches and wine.

Frank Moran said the Sullivans were a loving couple during the big tour.

Sullivan's sister Ann also supported her brother with her testimony.

Hack driver Albert Stickney, who had introduced Annie and John, stated that after they were married, he had taken Annie riding several times with a Zack Hollingsworth, hinting that there was something more to the relationship than mere friendship.

The Sullivan's housekeeper, Annie Durgin, testified that Annie Sullivan was in the habit of having liquor brought in by the caseload, and drank much of it. However, she also testified that after Annie left her husband in December, John L. was visited by a woman named Lottie Boswell, who went into the bedroom with him. When she left, she took with her a large roll of bills.

In delivering his opinion denying the divorce petition, Judge Allen said that by her actions, Annie had condoned Sullivan's acts. Regarding his drunkenness, the court held that while he undoubtedly drank to excess, his habit could not be called gross and confirmed. Annie had failed to sustain her burden to show that the habit had been contracted after marriage. She knew that he was a drinker going in, and she drank with him. He had been generous to her. "The judge remarked that had the case been one of an innocent girl the circumstances would have been different, but the libellant was a woman of mature age who had sought Sullivan, and knowing what he was had lived with him before marrying." The judge found that she had failed to sustain her burden of proof that he was cruel to her.[196]

Regardless of the ruling, never again would the Sullivans live together. They remained permanently separated. Although John L. gave her the Lovering House, Annie lived in Rhode Island with John, Jr., and rented out the Boston residence, until later selling it. John L. temporarily moved to 7 Carver street, and then in the fall of 1885, he purchased 26 Sawyer Street, a nine-room house near his parents' Parnell Street address. Eventually, he gave the house to his parents, but they just rented it out.

On Saturday June 13, 1885 in Chicago, just two weeks after his divorce trial had ended, 26-year-old John L. Sullivan was back in the ring to fight again, this time against 23-year-old Jack Burke, an experienced fighter known as "The Irish Lad." It was five months after Sully's last fight - the no contest against Ryan.

---

[196] *Salt Lake Evening Democrat*, May 28, 1885; *Daily Evening Bulletin*, May 30, 1885; *Rock Island Argus*, May 29, 1885; *New York Sun*, May 28, 29, 1885; Isenberg at 185.

The 170-pound 5'8 ½" Burke was born in Ireland, but raised in England. Some said that Burke was Jewish, but had changed his name in order to escape prejudice and obtain fights. He had his first fight at age 15, and won an amateur middleweight tournament. In 1881, he fought Charley Mitchell to a bareknuckle LPR 1-hour 47-minute 25-round draw, with darkness ending the contest. Burke lost an 1883 3-round decision to Alf Greenfield, but disputed it, claiming that many spectators disagreed with the decision.

Jack Burke

On October 6, 1884, Burke got the better of Steve Taylor in an exhibition, knocking him down in the 1st round. In late October 1884, Burke fought Charley Mitchell again, in a competitive gloved 4-round battle that resulted in another draw. A third bout between them in November 1884 resulted in an 8-round draw. Burke also fought a December 1884 5-round draw with Jake Kilrain.

In February and March 1885, Burke won 5-round decisions over Captain James Dalton and Alf Greenfield. The Chicago locals had seen Burke defeat the respected Greenfield on March 2, 1885, so they were excited to see him go against Sullivan. Burke may also have defeated Greenfield in 7 or 8 rounds in 1885, likely in late March. Clearly, Jack Burke was a very experienced, capable, and worthy opponent. He had proven himself to be equal to Mitchell and better than Greenfield.[197]

The fight was held outdoors in front of the grandstand of the Chicago Driving Park. The Stars-and-Stripes and the Union-Jack flags floated side-

[197] *National Police Gazette*, June 28, July 5, November 8, 1884, December 4, 1886; *New York Clipper*, October 11, 1884, March 7, 1885.; *San Francisco Daily Examiner*, July 25, 1887; *Boston Daily Globe*, March 11, 1888; Donovan at 102; Boxrec.com.

by-side over the grand-stand. 10,000 to 12,000 people were in attendance, including women. The crowd was peaceful and orderly, and no arrests were made. Hundreds of police officers and Pinkerton detectives were in attendance.

At 6:11 p.m., John L. entered through the clubhouse's arched gateway. As he walked 200 yards down the track to the ring, a 20-piece brass band played "See the Conquering Hero Comes." The crowd stood up as they watched him approach along with Nobby Clark and Patsy Sheppard.

A couple minutes later, Burke approached, accompanied by Parson Davies, Tom Chandler, and Ned Mallory. He too received an ovation.

Estimates for Sullivan's weight ranged from 210-215 pounds to 230-237 pounds. Newsmen said that as a result of his excessive drinking, Sullivan was fat, with a big paunch. He appeared to be untrained and in poor condition. John L. denied a story that he had been drunk while in Philadelphia, but several reports indicated that he had been on a spree while there. Some said that on the afternoon of the fight, Sullivan had to be aroused from a drunken sleep. Sullivan also had two large boils on the back of his neck. Some said the boils had been removed, and pieces of black court-plaster covered the sore areas. In his autobiography, Sullivan admitted that he never trained a day for the fight. Conversely, at 170 pounds, Burke looked hard and firm, like a race horse.[198]

[198] *Chicago Daily News,* June 12, 1885; *Chicago Herald,* June 13, 1885; *Philadelphia Inquirer,* June

Sullivan was dressed in white tights, with a sleeveless flesh-colored silk shirt. Burke was stripped to the waist, with white tights and green socks and belt.

Sullivan would earn 65% to Burke's 35% of the receipts.

The fight was scheduled for 5 rounds. They wore 4-ounce gloves, which Police Lieutenants Ward and Shea examined and approved. Ring veteran Sherman Thurston refereed. Parson Davies acted as the master of ceremonies. The fight started at 6:23 p.m.

1 - Burke began by dodging blows. They mixed it up until there was a clinch. They fought on the inside. Sullivan continually swung his right. The *Chicago Tribune* said Burke went down "by the overpowering force of the big fellow's onslaught." The *Chicago Herald* version said Sullivan knocked Burke down, "not however, so much by the hit as because Jack was off his balance when it came."

Burke rose and continued. He landed some counters, but received some blows on his back, which showed their marks. Burke attacked Sullivan's ribs. After a clinch, he attacked again, but according to the *Chicago Tribune*, Sullivan rushed and sent him down with a right to the left shoulder.

2 - Burke was smiling, but Sullivan jarred him with a jolt to the back of the neck. Burke continually played defense, and occasionally countered Sullivan's blows with a left to the face or ribs. Several times, Sullivan pushed him to the ropes and hurled him to the stage. The round ended with some cautious sparring, with no one hurt. Burke made up for his lack of weight with speed, dexterity, science, and nerve.

3 - Burke continued playing defense. Sullivan kept forcing him to the ropes and down to the stage. However, Burke remained clear-headed and fresh compared to Sullivan, who was doing all of the hard work. Burke landed a left to the chin, causing an angered Sullivan to make one of his famous rushes. They exchanged blows, and after successfully eluding Sullivan's right, Burke clinched.

Some said the police influenced Sullivan's performance. According to the *National Police Gazette*, in this round, Sullivan became a bit too ferocious, and a policeman warned him. The *Brooklyn Daily Eagle* confirmed that when Sullivan scowled and his eyes flashed, Police Lieutenant Ward "shook his cane over the ropes and said warningly, 'John!' Sullivan retreated and the round ended." Hence, once again, Sullivan had to walk a fine line and hold back in order to keep in the good graces of the law and not have his bouts stopped or find himself arrested.

4 - Sullivan rushed Burke into a corner, but Jack held. Sullivan threw Burke across the ring. Burke responded by attacking, twice striking Sullivan with his left to the face. Sullivan rushed in and decked Burke with a body blow, sweeping him down to the stage with a crash.

15, 1885, said Sullivan weighed 237 pounds.

Burke rose and Sullivan quickly rushed in again, sending in rights to the side and back that again sent him to the floor. Both times that he had gone down, Sullivan's sheer momentum and weight mixed with the punches had carried Burke off his feet. The *Chicago Herald* said,

> Sullivan bore him down simply by superior weight and heavier hitting, but he had not punished Burke very severely. By mistake time was called and the men took their seats nearly a minute before the round was over, but they went together again in heavy short arm work, in which Jack got the worst of it, although he took his punishment gamely. Sullivan forced the fighting over into Burke's corner, fighting him onto the ropes, and Jack dropped once or twice to avoid punishment.

Although the *Herald* called the act of terminating the round early a mistake, often a master of ceremonies intentionally called time early in order to prevent Sullivan from scoring a knockout, giving his opponent time to recover. This might have been done owing to legal considerations.

5 - Sullivan went at him with a fierce rush that sent Burke down.

After Burke rose, Sullivan attacked ferociously, leading with his right and pressing Burke to the ropes, sending in right and left "for all he was worth." The *Herald* said Burke fought back hard, but "had to drop to avoid the punishment." The *Tribune's* account differed, saying that Burke did not go down to avoid punishment, but rather Sullivan's swarming arms and shoulders sent him down. The referee told Sullivan to get back to his corner, but he did not obey.

Burke rose with a quick spring to avoid Sullivan's rush. The *Tribune* said that five times total in the round, Sullivan's rushes and swarming arms sent Burke to the floor. Conversely, when Burke landed, it was like hitting a brick wall.

The round and battle ended with the men clinched. Neither of them was used up, but "Sullivan had done the better fighting and the referee awarded him the match."

The *Chicago Tribune* said that Sullivan was not as good as he was two years ago, but "despite the abuses to which he has subjected himself, he is still head and shoulders above any pugilist in the ring today." Despite the impact of excessive drinking upon his body, John L. still could overpower and defeat his opponents. However, Burke had proved himself "worthy of his past record. … [H]e made a creditable showing…a fight which in point of skill and courage showed him the champion's equal at every point."

The *New York Clipper* reported, "It is manifest that Sullivan made no serious attempt to knock Burke out, being content to demonstrate his superiority as a fighter." The *Sun* said, "It was plain from the beginning of the fight that Burke was no match for Sullivan, and this in spite of the manner in which the champion is abusing his magnificent constitution." Most non-local sources confirmed that Burke was dropped multiple times in the last two rounds, and also that he went down to avoid punishment. The decision for Sullivan received cheers.[199]

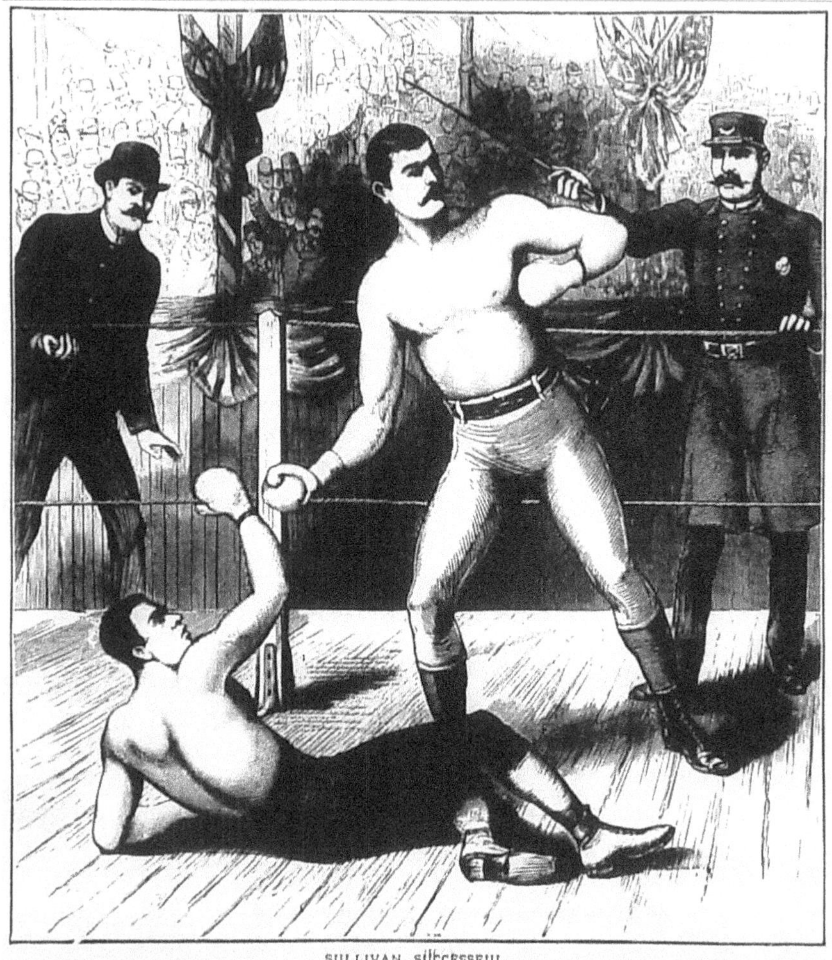

SULLIVAN SUCCESSFUL.
THE GALLANT BUT UNEQUAL CONTEST BETWEEN JOHN L. SULLIVAN AND IRISH BURKE IN CHICAGO, ILLS.

In his autobiography, Sullivan said that despite the fact that he did no training for the fight, "Burke was but a mere boy in my hands."

Years later, Mike Donovan said, "Burke did the sprinting act. … He was a clever fellow on his legs, and his skillful sprinting and ducking saved him. He certainly could not have lasted another round. … [Sullivan] would have put Burke out in a round had he been in shape."[200]

Two weeks later, Jack Burke fought Charlie Mitchell to a 6-round draw.

Present at the Sullivan-Burke fight was Dominick McCaffrey's manager Billy O'Brien, who issued a challenge to Sullivan, saying, "McCaffrey's the

---

199 *Chicago Tribune*, *Chicago Herald*, *New York Sun*, *Brooklyn Daily Eagle*, *Salt Lake Herald*, *Boston Herald*, June 14, 1885; *National Police Gazette*, June 27, 1885; *New York Clipper*, June 20, 1885.
200 Sullivan at 127; Donovan at 102.

only man Sullivan's afraid of. … He saw McCaffrey knock Jack Stewart out in thirty seconds." Sullivan accepted the challenge.[201]

In June 1885 in New York City, Sullivan posed for photographic portraits at John Wood's Broadway gallery. The photos became immediate best-sellers, appearing on cards and above bars for years to come.

Also in June, Sullivan posed successfully at Boston's Howard Athenaeum as a living statue, the Fighting Gladiator. It was relatively easy money. Folks liked to look at him, and were willing to pay to do so.

The financial success of his photos and posing caused the Lester and Allen's minstrel show to offer Sullivan a lucrative contract to pose on stage for about five months on their tour during the late '85 to '86 season. In July, Sullivan signed the contract. He would be paid $500 a week just to pose on stage. However, in the meantime, he had another fight scheduled.

On Saturday August 29, 1885 in Cincinnati, Ohio, two and a half months after the Burke fight, 26-year-old John L. Sullivan fought Pittsburgh's 21-year-old (nearly 22) Dominick McCaffrey. Dominick stood nearly 5'10" and weighed in the range of 165 - 178 pounds. Known as a scientific boxer, McCaffrey had fought Mike Cleary to a 5-round draw. In 1884, he won a 5-round decision over Jack Walsh. McCaffrey had knocked out Canadian champion and former Sullivan opponent Jack Stewart in 30 seconds. A 162-pound McCaffrey gave an exhibition with 223-pound John Flood and appeared to have the better of it.

Sullivan and McCaffrey had sparred 3 rounds one year prior, in early August 1884, and Mac showed his superior science, though Sullivan was holding back. McCaffrey used his performance against the champ to boost his reputation. Later that month, John L. witnessed his friend and sparring partner Pete McCoy fight

Dominick McCaffrey

[201] *Chicago Herald*, June 14, 1885.

the 164-pound McCaffrey in a contest that was declared a draw when McCoy fought in a foul manner by throwing down McCaffrey, and Sullivan and members of the crowd engaged in a fistfight. Sullivan made it clear that he did not think all that much of McCaffrey. Since then, McCaffrey had been challenging Sullivan.[202]

In October 1884, McCaffrey defeated Charlie Mitchell, "champion of England," via a 4-round decision.

Philadelphia legal authorities had prevented a scheduled April 1885 fight between Sullivan and McCaffrey.

A couple of weeks before the bout, a *Brooklyn Daily Eagle* article about the upcoming Sullivan-McCaffrey fight, entitled "To Fight Six Rounds," reported, "Six rounds, Marquis of Queensberry rules are to be fought." A week before the fight, the *New York Clipper* also reported that they were to fight 6 rounds, Queensberry rules.[203]

On August 23, the local *Cincinnati Evening Post* reported that a telegram from the champion confirmed that the contest would be fought with four-ounce gloves, "six rounds, Marquis of Queensberry rules, 'or to a finish.'" Apparently, negotiations as to the terms of the bout were ongoing, and likely what Sullivan meant was that he was agreeable to a fight of either 6 rounds, or one to the finish. Or he meant 6 rounds or less, if someone was knocked out. A report out of Pittsburg from McCaffrey stated that they would fight to the finish.

However, subsequent discussion of the fight gave the impression that it was scheduled to be a 6 rounder, for a gentleman named John F. Kennedy was willing to wager that Dominick would last the full 6 rounds. He laughed at the claim that Sullivan would knock him out in the 1st round with one punch.[204]

Three days before the fight, on August 26, the local *Cincinnati Commercial Gazette* advertised in a big headline, "SULLIVAN AND McCAFFREY WILL FIGHT SIX ROUNDS." Queensberry rules would govern; once a man had his knees off the ground "he is up, and, being up, may be struck by the contending pugilist, who may stand over him till he rises or attempts to do so." Commands to break were to be obeyed instantly. They would fight in a 24-foot ring, with three-ounce or lighter gloves.[205]

William Muldoon gave his pre-fight analysis:

> [McCaffrey] will fight Sullivan cleverly, adopting the keeping away from him as his tactics, and thus possibly staying with him throughout the six rounds. But I think that Sullivan, without a day's training, can lick any pugilist living, if Sullivan is in good health and not drinking. … I have never yet seen his face flushed by a blow

---

[202] *National Police Gazette*, March 1, 1884, August 16, 1884, September 13, 20, 27, 1884, October 24, 1885, December 4, 1886; *Cincinnati Commercial Gazette*, August 29, 1885.

[203] *Brooklyn Daily Eagle*, August 13, 1885; *New York Clipper*, August 22, 1885.

[204] *Cincinnati Evening Post*, August 25, 1885.

[205] *Cincinnati Commercial Gazette*, August 26, 1885.

> from the best of them, and he has never received a black eye or bloody nose. … Sullivan's advantages are many: His activity --- that of a light weight, his strength – greater than that of any pugilist who ever lived, and his wonderful reach.[206]

However, a passenger on a train upon which Sullivan was traveling claimed that Sullivan had been drinking all night and was thoroughly intoxicated. Yet, other reports said the champ was sober upon his arrival in Cincinnati from his training quarters in Maine. Sullivan was the 5 to 3 favorite.

Unfortunately, as all too often was the case with recent Sullivan bouts, the legal authorities made an effort either to prevent or limit the fight. The local Law and Order League tried to stop the fight, and sought to have Sullivan arrested.

On August 27, upon his arrival, the Cincinnati police arrested Sullivan and took him before a local judge. Sullivan pledged that there would not be a prizefight, but only a three-ounce gloved boxing match. Nevertheless, the judge required that a $1,000 bond be posted.

The day of the contest, on August 29, 1885, John L. "signed a bond in the sum of $1,000 by which Sullivan is bound not to engage in any fight or contention, commonly called a prize fight. … This, it is maintained, does not include a glove contest or a sparring exhibition." Being required to sign such a bond was a sign that the police would be hovering over and potentially influencing the fight, just as they had with other recent Sullivan bouts. Once again, legal authorities were seeking to prevent brutality and limit Sullivan's slugging. Of course, such legal interest meant that there was no way it could be a fight to the finish. Perhaps such talk is in part what got the authorities involved. Legally, it only could be a "sparring match."[207]

A couple weeks before the fight, McCaffrey said he would weigh about 178 pounds when he entered the ring against Sullivan. The local *Cincinnati Commercial Gazette* reported that Sullivan was not in fighting trim, weighing 230 pounds. He was not going to make much of an effort to lose the weight, because he felt that he would "do up" McCaffrey without trouble. A week before the fight, a non-local source listed McCaffrey as standing 5'8½" or 5'9" and weighing 165 pounds to Sullivan's 235 pounds.[208]

Yet, as of August 25, the *Cincinnati Evening Post* said that Sullivan had been training hard and had worked off most of his superfluous flesh. As of the 27th, Sullivan claimed to be weighing 208 pounds. On August 28, the *Commercial Gazette* also reported that Sullivan had managed to lose a considerable amount of flesh, though his weight still was several pounds

---

206 *Cincinnati Evening Post,* August 27, 1885.

207 *Cincinnati Evening Post,* August 27, 28, 1885; *Brooklyn Daily Eagle*, August 29, 1885.

208 *Cincinnati Commercial Gazette,* August 17, 23, 24, 1885; *Brooklyn Daily Eagle*, August 16, 1885.

over his usual. Sullivan felt confident though, saying that he could whip McCaffrey as he pleased.

The day before the bout, McCaffrey sparred with Dennis Kelleher. Afterwards, McCaffrey said that he would enter the ring at about 167 pounds.

The *Cincinnati Enquirer's* day-after-the-fight report listed Sullivan as 210 pounds to McCaffrey's 165 pounds. Since no weigh-ins were required for heavyweight bouts, no one knows for sure what they weighed.

With a $1,000 bond on the line, as well as the threat of arrest, John L. was much less likely to attempt to score a knockout. Hence, one local reporter asked the question, "Will they fight, spar, hippodrome or have a glove contest, or will the authorities interfere?" The local sheriff said he would allow only a sparring match, and that he and his officers would be present to prevent any brutalizing contest.

Originally, ticket prices were $3, $2, and $1. However, on the day of the fight, after half an hour of morning sales, the ticket prices jumped to $6. Eventually, ticket brokers were asking for $20 for a first-class front seat.

At 3:05 p.m. on the day of the fight, it was announced that a change was made to the terms, and the fight was "to be fought to a finish if not settled in six rounds." However, ten minutes later, at 3:15 p.m., the sheriff contradicted that report, saying that he would maintain order and only allow a contest in strict accordance with the law. That meant there was no way he would allow a fight to the finish. Perhaps the false announcement regarding a fight to the finish was an attempt to further stimulate ticket sales.

Thousands of fight fans approached the big and beautiful Chester Park, the fight site, an amusement park which sometimes hosted Red Stockings baseball games as well as horse races. The *Enquirer* said 15,000 people "of every element of society," including women, witnessed the contest. It was one of Sullivan's biggest ticket-selling fights, so whatever hype and marketing had been conducted, it had worked. Beer, ginger ale, and sandwiches were sold. A group of Pittsburgh ironworkers, many of whom were sporting pistols, gathered near the ring to support their hero, McCaffrey.

Some said John L. earned at least $5,680, while others said he earned $8,500, or about 60% of the gross receipts. In his autobiography, Sullivan claimed that he made about $5,200. Someone's accounting seemed incorrect. Either he was not being paid what he was owed, or fewer tickets had been sold than what was represented, or the overhead was great.

Sullivan said George Campbell had arranged the match. Campbell told Sullivan that McCaffrey wanted a $1,000 guarantee before he would fight him. Sullivan replied, "I will meet McCaffrey under one condition only; that is, that the winner of the contest is to receive all the money." Sullivan would earn 60% of the gate receipts, guaranteed, while Campbell would earn 40% of the receipts for managing and running the show, and he likely guaranteed McCaffrey the $1,000 out of his share.

Well after 5 p.m., the fighters entered the arena. Both pugilists wore sleeveless shirts, flesh-colored tights and hose, and rubber-soled shoes.

Sullivan was announced as the champion of the world. A local *Commercial Gazette* writer asserted that Sullivan's only correct title was champion of America, though noting that he practically and frequently was called champion of the world. Of course, the writer did not say who the champion was, if not Sullivan.

The fight began at 5:45 p.m. Toledo's William Tate refereed.

1 - Sullivan began aggressively, but Dominick ducked and clinched and hit John in the face. The *Evening Post* said Sullivan attacked and landed a terrific body blow that sent McCaffrey to the ropes and down onto his knees, although Mac landed a punch on the way down. The *Enquirer* version of the knockdown said Sullivan rushed at him, but "while McCaffrey avoided being hit by anything but half-arm blows, he was borne down in the north-east corner."

McCaffrey rose and clinched. Sullivan again struck McCaffrey, who fell against the ropes and clinched. Sullivan continued his rushing tactics but could not land cleanly. He forced McCaffrey to the ropes, but Mac landed a punch to the head. Sullivan was not deterred.

McCaffrey again fell to his knees along the ropes, but rose and clinched. After escaping, McCaffrey led and landed a punch on Sullivan, which according to the *Enquirer* was "the first clean blow of the round."

2 - Dominick began the round eluding blows and crowding into Sullivan. John L. pushed McCaffrey to the ropes, but Dominick escaped by using a left to the face. When Sullivan rushed, McCaffrey utilized clinching tactics to neutralize him. Hence, McCaffrey "got off with very little punishment." Dominick then landed "two stingers with his left full in Sullivan's face," which apparently hit the nose. Between clinches, they continued to exchange blows, to the enthusiastic cheers of the crowd. The *Evening Post* said, "Honors so far are easy."

3 - Sullivan "led and caught McCaffrey, who fell to his knees." Overall though, Dominick's defense was holding up.

Sullivan seemed confused by McCaffrey's defensive tactics. John L. slowed down and grew more cautious, asking McCaffrey, "Why don't you ever force the fighting?" Dominick responded, "Aren't you the one who was going to knock me out in two punches? Why don't you knock me out?" McCaffrey continued eluding Sullivan's blows.

Eventually, the champ got to the inside again. "Sullivan's dexter mauler played on the neck and face of his antagonist." McCaffrey returned fire and hit him in the ribs. A right to the back of John's neck injured Dominick's hand and rendered it useless.

According to the *Enquirer*, in close, Sullivan landed "several half-arm blows on his face and neck" and "McCaffrey was again forced down on the ropes. He arose and resumed the battle." The *Evening Post* version said

Sullivan ducked a blow and landed a straight counter right to the face that floored McCaffrey. After he rose, John L. fought McCaffrey to the ropes.

4 - The first two minutes of the round were occupied by Dominick's ducking and hugging Sullivan around the neck, with only inside short-arm blows landing. While clinched, Sullivan forced McCaffrey through the ropes. After another clinch, McCaffrey led and struck Sullivan with a stinger on the jaw. McCaffrey kept clinching to avoid Sullivan's blows.

According to the *Enquirer*, in a breakaway, Sullivan "landed a good blow on the forehead and scored a clean knock-down." The *Evening Post* version said, "It was apparent that Sullivan would win. Sullivan hit McCaffrey two terrible blows on the jaw and forehead, knocking him to his knees."

McCaffrey rose, and Sullivan's rush sent him to the ropes. A right under McCaffrey's eye drew blood.

5 - As usual, immediately after punching, McCaffrey would clinch so as to prevent Sullivan's returns. Such tactics angered Sullivan. A Sullivan straight right drew some blood from McCaffrey.

According to the *Evening Post*, Sullivan "reached him with his left, and McCaffrey went to his knees, but reached Sullivan as he went down. McCaffrey is a little groggy." The *Enquirer* version said, "Sullivan rushed and swung his right and drove the Pittsburger before him, and the latter went down on a push."

At this point, there was some confusion. According to the *Enquirer*,

> This was a short round, one minute and forty-five seconds being occupied, owing to a mistake of the referee in permitting the men to go to their corners after a fall. McCaffrey was on the floor seven seconds. Dan Murphy, in his anxiety to have Sullivan win, called out time. Mr. Donohue denied time was up, and cried for the men to resume fighting, but Referee Tait, in the confusion that prevailed, ordered the men to their corners.

At the same time, there was a fight in the crowd.

As a result of the confusion and the early termination of the round, an extra round wound up being fought, which may have been perceived as either a completion of the 5th round or a make-up for the lost time. Or they just might have lost track. It might have been that the round was terminated erroneously in LPR fashion, after a knockdown, giving McCaffrey extra recovery time. Clearly, this was not the original intention of the parties.

6 - At the start of the round, McCaffrey, "though badly punished, came pluckily to the front," landing a left to Sullivan's face. Sullivan seemed tired, but McCaffrey still waited for him to lead. Both were wary and playing for wind, taking a break in this round. Although both were cautious, Sullivan remained the aggressor, while McCaffrey played defense and tried to counter. Sullivan tried to draw him into a lead by using feints, but without any success.

7 - The round began like the previous one. Each time that Sullivan attacked, McCaffrey was able to avoid the blows. Sullivan forced the fighting and managed to corner McCaffrey until he was held. Throughout the round, they alternated between exchanging blows and clinching. Sullivan remained the aggressor. In one clinch, both went to the floor, with Sullivan on top.

After time was called to end the last round, McCaffrey offered to continue, to fight to a finish, but Sullivan did not reply. According to the *Evening Post*, "The decision of the referee could not be heard, some claiming a draw, others a decision in favor of Sullivan. The referee declared Sullivan the winner."

Then, McCaffrey's brother got into a fight with one of Sullivan's representatives, Arthur Chambers. McCaffrey's brother drew a revolver, but John L. and Dominick broke up the melee.

Still To The Fore
John L. Sullivan Has a Little Harmless Fun With Dominick McCaffrey

The local papers offered their post-fight analysis. The *Cincinnati Evening Post* said that Sullivan won the hardest battle of his life, although its bout description gave the impression that Sullivan clearly was the better man. It said that 7 plucky rounds were fought. The local *Commercial Gazette* agreed.

The *Cincinnati Enquirer* was the lone dissenter, criticizing Sullivan's performance and lauding McCaffrey, feeling that the latter had won or at least earned a draw. "The referee declared at the end of the seventh round, for, by some mistake, there was an extra round, 'Sullivan has the best of it,' yet the vast audience that saw the rounds from first to last considered it a draw." This writer minimized Sullivan's good points and maximized the description of McCaffrey's positive work. "McCaffrey can claim the honor of giving Sullivan the hardest tussle of his life. … [A]t the end of seven good rounds, he was on hand smiling and serene, anxious for more of the medicine, while Sullivan was only too glad to quit." Although the *Enquirer* granted that the referee awarded Sullivan the decision, declaring him the winner and "still the champion of the world,"

> [T]here are very few persons who do not condemn the decision as outrageous. At best the fight should have been declared a draw, as McCaffrey made equally as good a showing as his opponent. In fact, most people are of the opinion that he had the best of it. In the whole seven rounds of fighting Sullivan never landed a clean blow at long range, while McCaffrey planted his hands right in the champion's face no less than five times.

Of course, this writer overlooked the fact that Sullivan had done most of the work, was the aggressor, had scored all of the knockdowns (in rounds 1, 3, 4, and 5), and that McCaffrey had played defense and clinched a great deal.

McCaffrey was described as a "wiry, active, agile fellow, who jumped round and round like a cat." The local writer praised his clever dodging and generalship. This writer criticized the referee for failing to declare a foul when Sullivan hit McCaffrey several times while he was down after a fall.

Clearly, the underdog, smaller McCaffrey "had the sympathy of the crowd," and the sympathy of this writer. They appreciated his defense and ability to last the distance. Yet, the fight description gave the impression that McCaffrey mostly fought to survive, only landed the occasional blow, and was down on his knees a number of times.

Many patrons did not realize that the referee had decided the fight on the merits, with points taken into consideration. They believed that the fight was to be decided on another basis:

> There as elsewhere the mistaken idea prevailed that Sullivan was compelled to knock McCaffrey out, and as that was not done, there was considerable comment. Most of the spectators of the contest did not know that it was decided on its merits, the best points made being taken into consideration.

Many incorrectly believed that under the terms of the contest, Sullivan was obligated to knock out McCaffrey. The mistaken belief that it was not a points contest, but rather that McCaffrey's goal was to survive the distance, may account for the crowd's sympathy and impression that McCaffrey had won or at least earned a draw by lasting.

Apparently adding to the confusion was the fact that the referee later hedged regarding whether he had rendered a decision. He claimed that he had not awarded Sullivan the decision, but merely had said that Sullivan had the best of the fight. "This is curious speech to come from a referee who decided a fight." Perhaps he became hesitant when he heard the rumors that Sullivan was required to knock out McCaffrey. However, such rumors had to be incorrect, because the police had forbidden such a contest.

Afterwards, Sullivan said, "It is a matter of impossibility to fight a man who is continually either running away from you or hugging you like a child would its mother. I am not a sprint-runner."

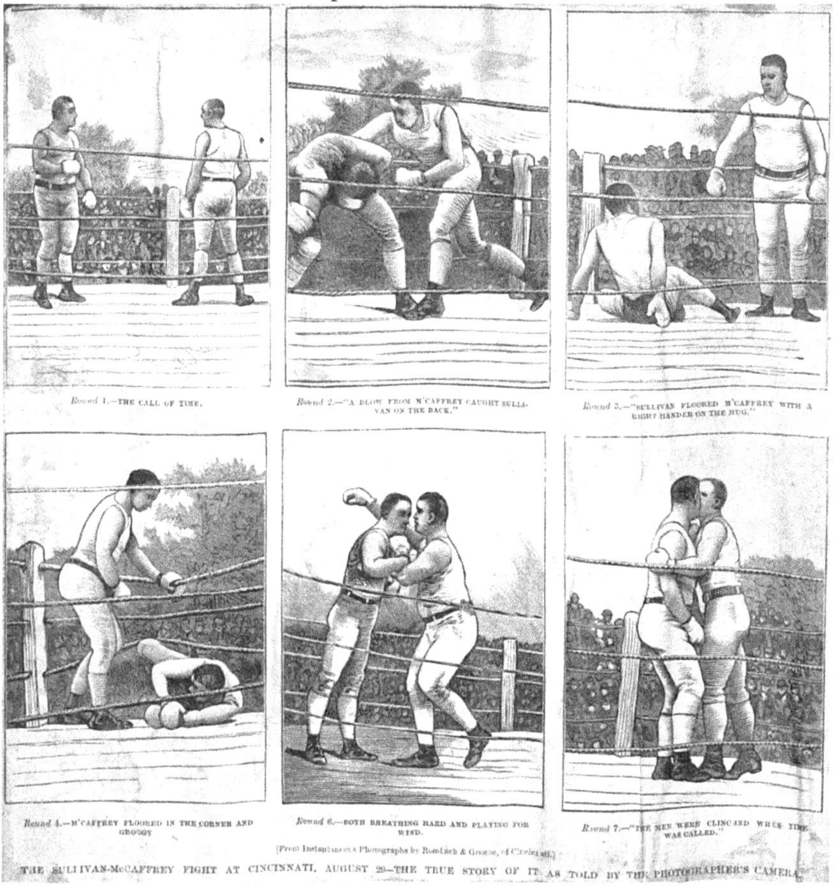

Round 1.—THE CALL OF TIME.

Round 2.—"A BLOW FROM M'CAFFREY CAUGHT SULLIVAN ON THE BACK."

Round 3.—"SULLIVAN FLOORED M'CAFFREY WITH A RIGHT HANDER ON THE MUG."

Round 4.—M'CAFFREY FLOORED IN THE CORNER AND GROGGY

Round 6.—BOTH BREATHING HARD AND PLAYING FOR WIND.

Round 7.—"THE MEN WERE CLINCHED WHEN TIME WAS CALLED."

(From Instantaneous Photographs by Rombach & Groene, of Cincinnati.)

THE SULLIVAN-McCAFFREY FIGHT AT CINCINNATI, AUGUST 29—THE TRUE STORY OF IT AS TOLD BY THE PHOTOGRAPHER'S CAMERA.

While examining the cut on his face, McCaffrey said, "He did have me down; that's so, but he didn't knock me down. It was his brute strength, not his science. … He is the stronger man, of course, but if I didn't show more science in the contest I will never spar again." Later that evening, McCaffrey said,

> Who did the cleverest work? Why, I tell you, young man, there was never such clever dodging done in a ring as I did today. … I stopped him every time. He stopped me, too, I'll admit, and did it very cleverly. Often, I couldn't get at him when I wanted to, but he never got at me once.

Dominick also discussed the post-fight melee:

> McCaffrey emphatically denied the report that his brother had pulled a revolver on Arthur Chambers, claiming it was a stranger who raised the rumpus, and that he (McCaffrey) took the revolver away from him. The Pittsburg boy showed no marks of the encounter, save a slight scratch on the right cheek, where the skin was broken by one of Sullivan's vicious upper cuts.

McCaffrey believed that he deserved to win the match, and claimed that he could knock out Sullivan with bare knuckles.

Regarding the contest's terms, McCaffrey's trainer said, "The conditions were that if Sullivan did not whip McCaffrey in six rounds the fight was to go on to a finish. Mac was ready and anxious to go on, and if he is not entitled to the entire gate receipts, he is at least entitled to one-half." Since often the division of the gate gave the larger share to the winner, the decision had a major financial impact on the McCaffrey side. Typically, in the event of a draw, the receipts were split evenly. Hence, they were arguing that Mac should have received no worse than a draw. They were making whatever argument they could in order to bolster a claim for a greater share of the profits, or to further hype their man.

However, there has been some indication that that the pay was set in advance, regardless of result. Either way, the referee had made his decision. Furthermore, if it was a fight to the finish, the terms would have been just that, a fight to the finish, without any reference to the number of rounds, so McCaffrey's trainer's argument regarding the terms did not make sense. Plus, the law would not allow such a fight, given their arrest, bonds posted, and police presence. Like a lot of boxing people, McCaffrey's trainer was trying to create a controversy where there was none.

One of Sullivan's backers rhetorically asked, "Who won the fight? Sullivan, of course. Why, in the third round, McCaffrey's brother had to pick him up off the ropes. The fight should have been given to us then and there, but the referee ordered the men to their corners. A minute and forty seconds had been lost."

From his hometown of Toledo, Ohio, Referee Tate gave a statement. "He says that the match was a regular farce, and that as Sullivan displayed the most science, and that as McCaffrey did nothing but dodge to escape punishment, he based his decision on each man's individual merits." In another report from Toledo,

> [The referee] says that Sullivan had the best of the fight from the beginning; that Sullivan had the opportunity to knock out McCaffrey, but for some reason did not take advantage of it; does not know whether Sullivan agreed to knock McCaffrey out in six rounds or not; if that was the agreement he did not do it; his decision is in favor of Sullivan; a clever big man can do a clever little man every time; the decision was on the merits of the fighting.

The referee's opinion that Sullivan could have knocked out McCaffrey was interesting. One has to wonder whether Sullivan was not able to do so because of his poor condition, or because of McCaffrey's survival tactics, or because he was holding back, fearful of what the law might do to him if he scored a knockout. There could be financial and legal consequences to a knockout – his $1,000 bond might be forfeited, and he might have been arrested. However, initially Sullivan did not claim to be holding back, but rather that McCaffrey's ducking, running, grabbing, and falling tactics enabled him to last the distance.

In his autobiography, Sullivan claimed that McCaffrey's friends, who were connected with certain local sporting newspapers [likely the *Cincinnati Enquirer*], had gone to Billy Tate's home in Toledo, attempting to bribe him with money to withdraw his decision, but he refused to do so.

The *Cincinnati Commercial Gazette* said the average citizen could not decide whether the match was a genuine scientific contest or a farce. "He is sure it wasn't one of those 'slugging matches' he has read about." This supports the claim that the bout was tame, McCaffrey only fought to survive, and that Sullivan did not or could not make much of an effort to stop him.

This writer criticized McCaffrey's use of clinching and other purely defensive tactics as a way to avoid blows and neutralize and survive, rather than to win:

> A clinch stops the fisticuffs, and the referee orders them to part. Thus a clinch may be practiced as a dodge to escape blows. This was McCaffrey's great tactics. …
>
> McCaffrey's play was to keep out of the way of blows, and by dodging to keep through six rounds with out getting knocked out. … McCaffrey's tactics were to evade, dodge back, duck his head, dodge forward into Sullivan's arms, and dodge down to his knees. He played this game with expertness and activity; but this was not fighting. …
>
> On the other hand, the beholder could not tell for certain whether Sullivan was doing his best to knock out McCaffrey. As it looked, there were many times when if he had followed up quickly he could have finished the other one. And his antagonist's blows seemed unable to get in with any force on Sullivan.

McCaffrey had engaged in what the *Commercial Gazette* previously had called "the eternal dodging and monkeying of the old ring." This author said that the fight had not been brutal, but "gentle enough for an entertainment for a peace society convention."

Ultimately, this writer complimented this new limited form of fighting, where fists were muffled by mittens, where there was no wrestling, throwing and falling upon, or holding the head with one arm and punching it with the other, and where a clinch was followed by a break. This form of fighting had brought about a revival of the ring, where police protected rather than prevented bouts. "Convenient places and police regulations have enabled men of wealth and high social and political station to attend these displays." Hence, this writer wondered why the legal authorities made such a fuss over it all.[209]

Although 7 rounds were fought, clearly the extra round was the result of a mistake rather than the agreement of the boxers. Although later accounts say the controversy occurred in the 3rd round, the local round-by-round accounts indicated that the 5th round was terminated early. Having them go to their corners after a fall was consistent with London rules, causing only half of the round to be fought, giving Dominick extra recovery time. Possibly, the resumption of fighting was perceived as and considered by the officials to be a continuation and completion of the 5th round, rather than as an additional round. Or perhaps that short round is why they fought an extra make-up round. Regardless, because of this mistake, extra fighting resulted, likely either to make up for the short round or because in the confusion the timekeeper lost track, but it clearly was not what was intended. Many called it a 6-round bout even after it was over.

There was some discussion regarding what the terms of the fight were. A New York correspondent reported that the original proposed agreement was for 6 rounds, or to a finish, scientific points to be considered, with the winner to take the gate receipts. Allegedly, Sullivan objected to the clause stating that scientific points were to count, and so it was removed. However, the referee had not seen the agreement. When he entered the ring for the fight, he "merely stated that it was for a six-round glove contest for the championship of the world." No one said otherwise at that time.

When asked for his decision, the referee said, "I decide that all through the contest Sullivan has had the best of it; and besides that, on one or two occasions, when McCaffrey went down, he struck Sullivan on the leg." The referee received some criticism for his statement that McCaffrey had fouled, because no claim of foul had been made, and at the time, the referee did not call attention to any foul. Thus, the fight had to be decided on scientific points, the very thing to which Sullivan allegedly had not agreed.

> The generally understood conditions were that Sullivan was to knock McCaffrey out in six rounds, if not sooner, the latter clause being expressed by the words 'or to a finish.' The whole matter of conditions is in a muddle, no two persons understanding them in the same way.

Clearly, the alleged terms were confusing. Consistent with what many in the crowd had believed, this newsman understood the phrase '6 rounds, or to a finish' to mean that Sullivan had to knock him out in 6 rounds or less.

---

[209] *Cincinnati Evening Post,* August 25, 28, 29, 31, 1885. *Cincinnati Commercial Gazette,* August 26, 28, 29, 31, 1885; *Cincinnati Enquirer,* August 30, 1885; *Philadelphia Press,* August 29, 1885; Sullivan at 128.

Naturally, McCaffrey and his supporters were eager to foster a controversy in an attempt to boost him.

Some believed that the terms meant that if the two continued to fight after 6 rounds, the bout would not terminate until someone was knocked out. Others felt the terms meant that the fight would be 6 rounds, or less if someone was knocked out before the end of 6 rounds – hence, 6 rounds or to a finish. Some believed it was a fight to the finish. Still others believed it simply was a 6-round bout. Yet others interpreted '6 rounds, or to a finish' to mean that Sullivan was willing to do a fight of either 6 rounds, or one to a finish, and ultimately a 6-round fight was agreed upon. The local pre-fight reports leading up to the contest all simply said that the bout was scheduled for 6 rounds.

Less than a week later, the *Cincinnati Enquirer* published the articles of agreement, which were signed on July 31, 1885, one month before the fight. They simply stated that it was to be a "six round glove contest, Marquis of Queensberry rules to govern." Nothing was mentioned about a finish fight, or about Sullivan being required to knock out McCaffrey. All of the speculation had been just that – rank speculation. Any talk about a clause "or to a finish" had to do with contract negotiations and proposed clauses.

This newswriter claimed that Sullivan had objected to a clause stating that scientific points were to count. McCaffrey's manager claimed that the referee would have decided it a draw had he reviewed the terms before the bout. However, the contract terms did not say that Sullivan was required to score a knockout to win, nor did it say that scientific points would not count. The contract was silent as to the decision-making criteria.

The terms also said that three-ounce gloves were to be used, though this newspaper claimed that one-ounce gloves actually were used.

The contract further said that the winner was to receive 60% of the gross receipts. Clearly, the contract contemplated that there was to be a winner, though it did not specifically state what the criteria was for a winner to be determined. However, if it was a 6-round Queensberry rules bout, the natural way to determine the winner of a contest that went the distance was to decide based on scientific points.[210]

Certainly, out of legal necessity, the fight had to be one in which scientific points would count. Given the fact that Sullivan was arrested and had to sign a bond agreeing not to engage in a prizefight, and also, given his argument to the judge that it merely was going to be a scientific exhibition, it is understandable why the referee would consider it a scientific points bout.

Sullivan issued a challenge to McCaffrey to fight to a finish within three weeks. "A private meeting is suggested, as it would be almost impossible to carry a public fight through in any State without official interference." Given that it would be impossible to host a finish fight without official

---

210 *Cincinnati Enquirer*, September 4, 1885.

interference, certainly the police would not have allowed them to fight to a finish when they had fought.[211]

Some of the eventual controversy may have been generated either by Sullivan haters, McCaffrey supporters, or unscrupulous newsmen who either had biases, had been bought, or sought to sell more newspapers by fostering controversy.

On the East Coast, the *New York Times* called the fight "tame and bloodless" and "little more than a clever sparring match of six rounds with three-ounce gloves." The crowd was disappointed by the lack of slugging. At the end of the fight, McCaffrey was in better condition than Sullivan. However, Sullivan likely was more fatigued because he had done most of the work.

The referee's decision was in Sullivan's favor because he had forced the fighting and scored the most points. The only criticism of the decision was that "it has been the understanding all along that if McCaffrey was not knocked out in six rounds he was to be considered the winner." Hence, the *Times* was fostering the incorrect belief about the terms.

The *Times* also published a more local August 30 report out of Toledo, Ohio indicating that when the referee was questioned regarding his decision, he stated that he had made no decision.

> He thinks Sullivan had the best of the fight so far as fighting points were concerned, but if the Boston boy was to knock out McCaffrey in six rounds he failed, as the Pittsburg lad came up smilingly every round. He has not seen the agreement as yet under which they fought, and cannot, in consequence, render a decision.

Hence, if there was any uncertainty, it only was regarding whether Sullivan was supposed to knock him out.

The *Times* also reported that after McCaffrey had "heard the referee's decision he fired up, and demanded that the fight go on to a finish, but Sullivan's friends paid no attention to him." Thus, it appears that McCaffrey asked for the fight to continue only after the decision already had been rendered. Of course, the official terms and the law would not have allowed the bout to continue even had Sullivan been willing.

McCaffrey's proposition for a second fight, one to the finish, to take place within the next three months, was countered by Sullivan with different monetary terms, and for the fight to take place within three weeks. "This proposition has been sent to McCaffrey and has not yet been heard from."[212]

The *National Police Gazette* published several accounts. Allegedly, after the bout concluded,

---

[211] *Cincinnati Commercial Gazette,* August 31, 1885.
[212] *New York Times*, August 30, 31, 1885.

> McCaffrey then went over to Sullivan, both shook hands and the referee gave his decision, which was that Sullivan was the winner, but no one heard it. … The referee said, but in a tone to be heard only by those nearest the platform: "I decide that all through the contest Mr. Sullivan has had the best of it. Besides that on one or two occasions when McCaffrey went down he struck Sullivan on the leg."

Its description of the bout certainly gave the impression that Sullivan was the better man. Ultimately, McCaffrey mostly had fought to survive, utilizing Tug Wilson tactics, dodging and eluding, clinching, slipping and falling, and his blows had little to no effect. The exhibition was called poor. McCaffrey had landed about as much as Sullivan, but his lighter weight and inferior force made him appear weak and ineffective.

McCaffrey also was alleged to have said after the fight, "We fought 7 rounds, and at the end of the seventh round I says to Sullivan and his seconds: 'Here, now we're here let's fight to a finish.' 'No,' says Sullivan, 'this match was for 6 rounds, and we've fought 'em.' Now what could be fairer than my proposition?" Even if there was an extra round fought, clearly Sullivan correctly believed that it was supposed to be a fixed-duration 6-round bout. And with the law having been involved in the proceedings, there is no way the police were going to allow a finish fight. Hence, McCaffrey's proposal was not genuine because it was impossible.

It also was said, "McCaffrey claimed he injured his right hand during the contest. He claimed the referee should have decided the affair a draw. … Sullivan will not accept McCaffrey's challenge to fight with bare knuckles to a finish within three months because he is under engagement with a minstrel troupe."

Ultimately, the general impression is that both men understood that the fight was over and that McCaffrey, although not entirely satisfied, understood that he had lost, and wanted another chance.[213]

The *Police Gazette* subsequently reported that the referee had re-affirmed his decision for Sullivan, stating that because the authorities had forbidden a knockout or slugging, therefore it was understood that it merely was a boxing exhibition, and hence, he decided the bout on points.[214] Of course, if the authorities had forbidden a knockout, under those circumstances the fight could not be continued and fought to a finish, nor could Sullivan be expected to knock him out without being subject to arrest and bond forfeiture. Thus, it had to be only a 6-round points bout.

Other national post-fight reports suggested that Sullivan was more cautious in the bout because he had signed the bond, and because the sheriff had been present and instructed them to behave.[215]

---

[213] *National Police Gazette*, September 12, 1885.

[214] *National Police Gazette*, September 19, 1885.

[215] *Boston Daily Globe*, August 30, 1885, August 31, 1885; *Boston Herald*, August 30, 1885; *National Police Gazette*, September 12, 1885.

However, some of Sullivan's comments indicated that he was trying to knock out McCaffrey, and he even claimed to have done so. In one interview, Sullivan alleged that McCaffrey was knocked out in the 2nd and 3rd rounds, and was down for over a minute. He also claimed that Dominick's cornermen illegally assisted him to his feet in the 3rd round. Sullivan claimed to have in his possession six photographs of the fight, three of which showed Mac lying down in a heap looking as if he was knocked out.

Yet, the *New York Times* quoted Sullivan as providing an excuse for why he failed to knock him out, saying, "How could I knock a man out…who kept running away from me?" There was "little doubt that Sullivan wanted to administer a good punishment to his adversary." Either way, Sullivan did not claim to be holding back.

Some reports indicated that Sullivan was declared the winner in part on account of fouls, McCaffrey possibly having kicked, punched, or grabbed Sullivan's legs. The referee may have alluded to McCaffrey's fouls in order to justify his decision further. Sullivan claimed that McCaffrey illegally tried to throw him several times by grabbing him around the legs.

Sullivan also alleged that McCaffrey's brother pulled a gun and told him that if he hit his brother Dominick, that he would blow Sullivan's brains out. In his autobiography, Sullivan claimed that in the 3rd round, McCaffrey's brother came onto the stage, pulled a revolver, and used a lot of epithets, saying, "If you hit my brother again I will kill you." Several spectators grabbed McCaffrey's brother and pulled him off of the stage.

Sullivan claimed that the referee did not award him the fight at the time of the various fouls because he was afraid of the howling pro-McCaffrey mob, most of whom had revolvers. John L. believed that the referee was frightened and reluctant to disqualify Dominick, despite the rule violations. This might explain why the referee made a points decision, but referenced the rule violations by Dominick as part of his justification, even though McCaffrey had not been disqualified.[216]

What is odd about all of the claimed shenanigans is that the sheriff was present with law enforcement, so one has to wonder how all of this happened right in front of them without any repercussions. Perhaps they simply felt outnumbered, or did not notice, or did not care. Some said there were as many as 500 gun-toating McCaffrey fans present.

The two never fought again. A year and a half later, in 1887, 175-pound Patsy Farrell twice decked 170-pound McCaffrey in the 2nd round, and the police stopped the contest. McCaffrey had dropped Farrell once in both the 1st and 2nd rounds before getting caught and badly hurt himself.[217]

Word was that after the Sullivan-McCaffrey fight, Sullivan had gotten drunk, and had remained drunk.

---

[216] *National Police Gazette*, September 19, 1885; *Cincinnati Enquirer*, September 4, 1885; Sullivan at 128.

[217] *New York Sun*, March 9, 1887; *National Police Gazette*, March 19, 1887.

A Change of Pace

Following the late August 1885 McCaffrey bout, John L. Sullivan started a phase in his career in which he fought less often, in part owing to all of the legal impediments that he encountered, but also in part due to the fact that he could earn money in other ways.

Sullivan said that he was tired of chasing men around the ring, and was considering retiring. He had been floating the idea of retirement for the past year or so. Perhaps he was a bit weary of fighting, having been boxing and exhibiting regularly for the past five years. He also was frustrated with the legal obstacles that he kept running up against. Eventually, he tried to make arrangements for some bouts, but legal authorities and politicians kept stifling his efforts.

On September 13, 1885 in Cleveland, Ohio, about 4,000 spectators were in Brooklyn Park to see John L. Sullivan pitch in a baseball game for the Forest Citys against the Sanduskys. He lost 2 to 0.

As he was leaving the grounds, a police officer arrested Sullivan on a warrant for violating the Sunday law by playing baseball. He had violated the "sacred day of rest." So much for separation of church and state. The warrant was sworn out at the request of John D. Rockefeller of the Standard Oil Company, representing the Law and Order League. No other player was arrested, so obviously it was harassment of a famous athlete. Apparently it was wicked for pugilists to play ball on a Sunday, but not for anyone else. Sullivan pled guilty and was sentenced to a fine of $1 plus court costs, which amounted to $15.90.[218]

Back in Boston, after his sister's child died, Sullivan attended the wake. It was reported that he had been drunk ever since. Rum had gotten the best of him. It was knocking him out – something no person could do. At a recent sparring exhibition he was so drunk that he was unfit to appear, but did so nevertheless.

Allegedly, Sullivan spent his money as fast as he made it, and had little left. He gave much of it away to friends and family. When he paid bills, he never asked for change. Word also was that Sullivan once again had been pitched from a buggy.[219]

In July 1885, Sullivan had signed an exclusive contract with the Lester and Allen's minstrel show for 21 weeks (five months), set to start in late September, doing statuary acting at a salary of $500 per week. All he had to do was pose on stage as statues of ancient and modern gladiators, all to soft music and various lighting. Sullivan's fame and aura was such a great lure

[218] *Memphis Daily Appeal*, September 15, 1885.
[219] *Daily Honolulu Press*, September 18, 1885.

that people would pay just to see him. He could make money without training or fighting. During this time, his boxing career would be on hiatus.

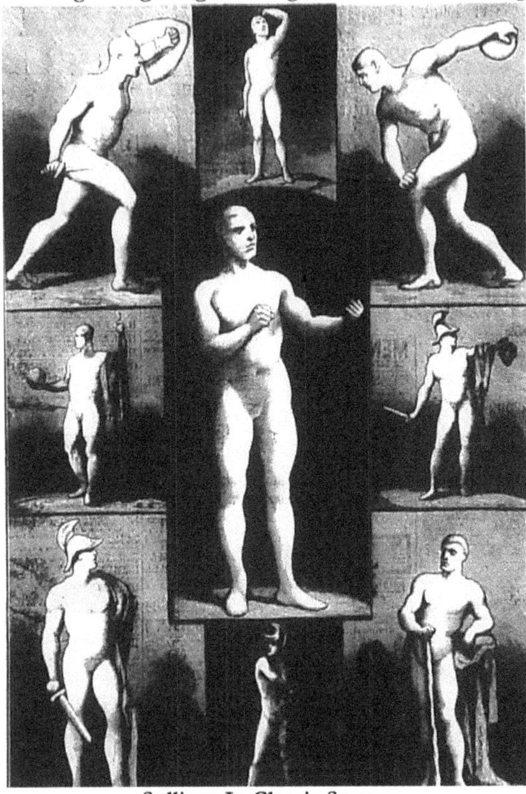

Sullivan In Classic Statues
A New And Artistic Business For Finely Formed Pugilists

On or about September 20, 1885, Sullivan started traveling with the minstrel show. He continued his lucrative model statuary business until May 1886, closing in Chicago. The show did consistently solid business. Ladies especially seemed interested, despite the fact that Sullivan weighed well over 230 pounds. Fearing his drunkenness, the company had gotten Sullivan to agree that if he failed to appear for a scheduled performance, he would forfeit $700.[220]

Around this time, Sullivan was dating a woman named Annie Livingston, a serio-comic singer who performed with the Davene combination. Some even claimed that he married her, had a ceremony, gave her a ring, and started calling her his wife. Technically, he still was married to Annie Bates Bailey, the woman whom he had refused to divorce. Livingston was just his mistress. Livingston was married as well, separated from her husband Frank Anderson since 1884. They had a daughter who lived with his parents. Livingston was her stage name. Her maiden name was Anna Nailor. She had sued for divorce, but her petition was denied. Few realized that Annie Livingston was a different woman from Annie Bailey, particularly since Livingston typically would be introduced as and called Sullivan's wife, and they had the same first name.[221]

On December 10, 1885 in Olean, New York, Sullivan and muscular world champion wrestler William Muldoon, who had joined the posing crew, as well as his brother Martin Muldoon, were arrested and charged with assault upon two men. At the trial, no evidence was produced

---

220 *Referee* (Sydney), October 26, 1892; Isenberg at 191; Sullivan at 130.
221 *Wahpeton Times*, December 10, 1885; *National Police Gazette*, December 17, 1887.

implicating Sullivan in the fracas, so he was acquitted and discharged. William Muldoon pled guilty and was fined $50. His brother was fined $10.[222]

William Muldoon

During his modeling tour, while in New York, Sullivan reconciled with his old manager, Billy Madden.

On January 3, 1886 in New York, a 13-year-old newsboy named Tommy Lee alleged that Sullivan assaulted him by hitting him in the upper lip. When Tommy approached and asked him if he wanted a newspaper, Sullivan turned around, and, in raising his umbrella, struck him in the mouth, forcing his front teeth through his upper lip. Others said a drunken Sullivan intentionally struck him a savage blow in the mouth with a heavy silver-handled umbrella. Allegedly, Madden gave the boy a dollar and asked him not to speak of the incident, saying, "My friend is a little drunk." Some said it was accidental, while others said it was an intentional act. Before the warrant could be served, Sullivan took a train out of town.[223]

After the statuary tour concluded in May 1886, Sullivan arranged an 8-round rematch with Charlie Mitchell to be held on June 14, 1886 at the Le Grand skating rink in Chicago, under Pat Sheedy's management, with the winner to earn 75% and the loser 25% of the proceeds.

Sullivan also scheduled a friendly bout with the Nonpareil, middleweight champion Jack Dempsey, set to be held on May 31, 1886 in Chicago.[224]

However, the local Chicago Citizens Association appealed to Mayor Harrison to stop boxing in the town, and he acquiesced to their wishes. On May 22, the police chief refused to grant permits for any boxing contests. "The authorities announce that no more boxing or sparring exhibitions will be permitted in public." No explanation was given, but evidently it was the outcome of the letter to the Mayor from the Citizens' Association. Yet again, another major city had barred boxing, which derailed scheduled Sullivan bouts.[225]

---

222 *New York Sun*, December 11, 1885; *Evening Star*, December 14, 1885.

223 *Omaha Daily Bee*, January 6, 1886; *Daily Evening Bulletin*, January 7, 1886.

224 *New York Sun*, May 3, 1886; *St. Paul Daily Globe*, May 17, 1886.

225 *Omaha Daily Bee*, May 21, 1886; *New York Sun*, May 23, 1886.

The Mitchell fight was rescheduled for July 4, 1886, oddly enough at the Polo Grounds in New York, a state that was no friend to boxing.

Sullivan became a partner with William Bennett in a New York saloon business. He had sold his share of the Washington Street saloon in Boston to his brother.[226]

On or about June 25, 1886 in Boston, an intoxicated Sullivan got into another saloon fight with a gambler named Michael Meehan, badly beating him until other patrons pulled Sullivan off of him. Meehan swore out a warrant for assault and battery, but Sullivan left town for New York before it could be served.[227]

Frank Herald

Unfortunately, New York Mayor William Grace refused to grant a license, preventing Sullivan from fighting there, which was no surprise given his previous stance against boxing. On July 2, the Mitchell fight was declared off.[228]

Sheedy next tried to arrange a fight with the up-and-coming Frank Herald (known as the "Nicetown Slasher" or "Nicetown Pet") in a fight to be held in New Jersey in August, but the police refused to allow the bout. Attempts were made to reschedule it for late August in Brooklyn, but once again the authorities interfered.

Herald left for Pittsburgh, and then outraged Sullivan by suggesting that the champion had been the cause of the fight's

---

226 Sullivan at 130; Isenberg at 195-196.

227 *St. Paul Daily Globe*, June 26, 1886.

228 *New York Sun*, *New York Tribune*, July 2, 1886; *Lancaster Daily Intelligencer*, July 3, 1886.

derailment. As a result, Sullivan followed Herald to Pittsburgh, informing him that he was willing to fight him anywhere, including in his home state of Pennsylvania. A match was arranged for Allegheny City, across the river from Pittsburgh.

On September 18, 1886 in the Coliseum in Allegheny City, Pennsylvania, a 210-pound John L. Sullivan took on 5'10 ½" 187-pound Frank Herald. Called the "new wonder" and the "coming champion," the powerful Herald had a number of good victories, including KO22 "Sparrow" Golden, KO2 Bill Gabig, KO1 Dennis Doyle, KO1 Jim Cannon, and KO1 Mike Conley, the huge, highly-touted "Ithaca Giant." Sullivan had not fought in over a year.[229]

Mike Conley, the Ithaca Giant, whom Frank Herald stopped in 1 round

As usual, at first the local authorities wanted to prevent the fight. Eventually, Mayor James Wyman agreed to license the bout with the agreement that there was to be no slugging or knocking out. Once again, the law was interfering with and limiting the sport.

Furthermore, in order to exclude "the tough element," it was agreed that the admission prices would be set at $2 minimum for the promenade, $3 for a regular seat, and $5 for the best locations, which about a quarter of those in attendance paid. The local *Pittsburg Dispatch* said 3,000 people attended the contest.

Although the police were told that it merely was going to be a scientific sparring exhibition for points, "the old gag, which the officials of New York, Jersey City and Brooklyn declined to swallow – being, in all probability, the nearest correct," they were suspicious that those involved with the contest simply had given lip service and just told the authorities what they needed to hear in order to hold the show. "Private talk among the people directly interested showed conclusively that the contest was to be nothing short of a real fight."[230]

The bout was scheduled for 6 rounds, for a stipulated percentage of the admission receipts.

---

229 *National Police Gazette*, July 10, 1886, August 28, 1886; *Pittsburg Dispatch*, September 16, 1886.

230 *Philadelphia Press*, September 18, 1886; *Pittsburg Dispatch*, September 16, 1886; *New York Clipper*, September 25, 1886.

The day before the fight, the *Pittsburg Dispatch* reported that Herald was weighing 186 pounds. Sullivan said that he had not touched a drop of liquor in eleven weeks, and felt well. The local newspaper's day-after-the-fight report said that Sullivan tipped the beam at 210 pounds, with Herald at 187. Some claimed that Sullivan was only 205, while others said he was 220.[231]

Sullivan entered the ring first, wearing white trunks, light blue stockings, and the national colors for his belt. The auburn-haired Herald wore drab tights and a blue belt. Reports of the glove size varied, with claims of 2, 3, and 4 ounces. Either way, the gloves, though soft, were very thin and small.

1 - Both started cautiously. Sullivan feinted and smiled. He positioned his right arm across his breast and held his left well out in front. The champ was the aggressor, while Herald, "lithe and active as a cat," moved and danced around to remain at a safe distance, showing his agility.

Herald moved around the ring until eventually Sullivan made a rush at him and landed a right to the stomach. Herald countered to the chest, but received a right on the nose that "sent him flying half across the ring."

Herald then stood his ground and fought hard, exchanging blows with Sullivan, but his punches had little effect. A succession of clinches followed. In general, for the remainder of the round, when Sullivan rushed, Herald clinched.

During one of the many clinches, Sullivan pushed Herald over the ropes. The referee ordered them to break, but the fighters, whose blood was up, did not listen. Finally, their attendants had to pry them apart and force them into their chairs. This caused the round to end slightly early. Only 2 ¾ minutes had elapsed. Herald was bleeding slightly from his nose.

The *Clipper* said, "The round might be called a succession of clinches and breaks, and neither man could do much execution."

2 - They started the round cautiously, although it was the calm before the storm. At first, Sullivan followed him and feinted, looking for an opening on the moving Herald. Eventually Herald attacked, but Sullivan held him on the inside, and then let go and landed multiple rights to Frank's head.

Herald got away, and then came back and landed a good right under the eye, which was the only clean blow that he landed. Excited by the good hard punch, Herald followed up and attacked. A stunned Sullivan "seemed staggered for an instant, and was apparently too surprised to do more than protect himself from the blows that Herald was showering on his guard."

However, Sullivan gathered himself and then decked Herald with a huge uppercut under the chin. Frank quickly rose and clinched. "The fight had become a mere rough-and-tumble." Amidst it all, some said Herald slipped and fell down, while others said Sullivan decked him again. At that point, Chief of Police Murphy and his officers rushed in and "with difficulty separated the men." Both fighters were anxious to continue, but the police refused to allow them to do so.

---

[231] *Pittsburg Dispatch*, September 17, 19, 1886.

The *Pittsburg Dispatch* version of the end said that Herald missed his right and was countered by a right and left that dropped him. He quickly rose and Sullivan struck him with a right to the jugular, lifting him off his feet onto his back.

The police began mounting the stage. Herald rose and Sullivan hit him with a left to the ribs before Herald clinched. The police chief then stepped between them and announced that it must stop.

The *Philadelphia Press* and *New York Clipper* version of the end said,

> Sullivan smashed him straight on the mouth with such force that he fell to the floor like a log. His head struck the boards with such force that the sound echoed through the building. The police at once rushed into the ring and declared that the fight must end. Both fighters desired a resumption, but the Chief said he was satisfied that Herald would be either seriously injured or killed if the fight continued.

Herald had been dropped "by one of the most terrific blows that ever came from a man's shoulder. The blow seemed almost fatal. So much so that the police, numbering about eight, rushed on the platform and stopped the fight."

Another non-local dispatch reported,

> Herald's blows did not affect Sullivan in the least, except to make him angry, while it was only a question of time when Herald would be stopped, and might be badly injured in addition. This was so evident to the police that the contest was ended when Herald was knocked down in the second round by an upper-cut.

After the fight was over, Sullivan dashed at a reporter who was acting as Herald's timekeeper. The reporter reached for his revolver, but the police disarmed him and Sullivan was forced back to his chair.

Sullivan later asked the police chief, "What did you stop us for? … I just wanted to get another good square crack at that fellow Herald, and I would have paralyzed him." The chief responded, "I know that…and that is just why I stepped in between you at that juncture."

Herald was credited as being a better man than McCaffrey and putting up a better showing. Although he moved and played defense, he also came to fight. He did some good in-fighting and showed no fear.

Upset by the stoppage, the crowd howled and yelled in disgust at the police's actions.

The referee announced that Sullivan was the winner. "I give the fight to Sullivan…as he manifestly had the best of it up to the time of the interruption by the police."

Herald's backers were upset by the decision, given that their man was ready and willing to continue at the time of the police stoppage. Some writers agreed that there should not have been a decision under the circumstances.

However, the *Clipper* revealed that the referee had based "his decision on the clause in the agreement providing that, in case of police interference, the man who had the better of the encounter should be declared the victor." Hence, before the fight, the parties had anticipated such a scenario, and had agreed to a decision on points based upon the work done up until any police stoppage.

Despite Sullivan's year of inactivity, he still was a tremendous fighter. Afterwards, he gave a speech that demonstrated his conceit. "I have had clearly the best of the fight as you have seen and as the referee has decided. I will say that it is no shame to Herald to be defeated by a pugilist of my ability. … I remain your kind and sincere friend, John L. Sullivan."

THE PUGILISTIC CHAMPION MEETS HIS FIRST EQUAL.

The *National Police Gazette* reported that Herald, of Nicetown, covered the Keystone State with glory by bravely challenging the world-famous Sullivan.

When later asked what he thought of Herald, Sullivan said, "Why, he is like all of the rest of them, no good. … I had figured on going easy in the first round in order that he might think he was a fighter. … He said I tried to throw him over the ropes. Why, he is a chump."

Sullivan offered some insight regarding his methods and strategies. When asked why he did not knock out Herald the first time that he had him in a corner, Sullivan responded,

> Why, there's no use in hitting a man when you first chase him into a corner. He is always dead wary to get out, and the chances are you won't find him, while if you let him out he will think you are getting tired or afraid and the next time he gets there why he will be off his guard, and you can punch him. People may say what they please about fighting, but I tell you that a good fighter is a man who uses his brains. He has to know what he is doing and how to do it.

> My objective point in hitting is the corner of a man's shoulder, and if he ducks his head he is bound to get it in the neck. A man will break his dukes if he goes hitting at his antagonist's skull.

Some believed that Sullivan, in part, won his fights through fear, for his opponents were intimidated by his power. They rarely performed nearly as well against him as they did with others. "Sullivan frightens his man every time. They lose their nerve the moment they face him." Another said, "They all know that if John gets in a blow they are virtually done for. This makes them nervous and they lose their heads." Fighters were well aware of Sullivan's awesome punching power. The knowledge that he only needed to land one good blow to daze them made them get tight and tense, which nerves adversely affected their performance.

The receipts from the Herald fight were an alleged $5,000, of which Sullivan took 20%. Others said $8,000 or $2,300 was earned. Gate receipt numbers and fighters' earnings are among the mysteries of boxing. It often depends upon who does the accounting or reporting, and what their incentives are.[232]

Nearly three weeks later, on October 7, 1886, Joe Lannon knocked out Frank Herald in the 6th round. Eventually, Lannon would become a Sullivan sparring partner. In November 1886 in Baltimore, 180-pound Jake Kilrain would knock out 176-pound Frank Herald in the 1st round.[233]

---

[232] *Pittsburg Dispatch,* September 19, 20, 1886; *Pittsburgh Daily Post,* September 20, 1886; *Philadelphia Press,* September 19, 1886; *Philadelphia Inquirer,* September 20, 1886; *New York Clipper,* September 25, 1886, October 16, 1886; *National Police Gazette*, October 2, 1886; *Denver Daily News,* September 20, 1886.

[233] *Salt Lake Herald, Sacramento Daily Record-Union,* November 9, 1886.

A Familiar Pattern

Prior to the Herald fight, Pat Sheedy had arranged for another Sullivan tour with a sparring combination of fellow fighters. This time it would not be as long or at such a breakneck pace, but nevertheless, it would follow substantially the formula that had earned Sullivan a lot of money. The touring combination included Steve Taylor, George La Blanche (the "Marine"), Jimmy Carroll, Patsy Kerrigan, and others. They would spar with Sullivan and with each other, giving exhibitions in various Midwest cities before heading to San Francisco.[234]

The reason the tour would head West to San Francisco is that Sheedy also had arranged for a third bout with Paddy Ryan, a scheduled 6 rounds to be held in San Francisco in November 1886. The winner would take 75% and the loser 25% of the receipts. The idea was that the tour would enable Sullivan to spar and prepare while earning money at the same time. After the Ryan fight, the tour would continue on. This was a pattern that worked for Sullivan – make money exhibiting, which got him in shape, make money fighting, and then make more money exhibiting again.

They would open in late October in Racine, Wisconsin. Stops would include Milwaukee, Wisconsin; Stillwater, St. Paul, and Minneapolis, Minnesota; as well as Tacoma, Washington; Victoria, Canada; Butte, Montana; and Leadville, Denver, Colorado Springs, and Georgetown, Colorado; as well as many other towns.

On October 25, Sullivan also signed to fight an early 1887 6-round bout against the heavyweight champion of the Northwest, Patsy Cardiff, who was a "strong, hard-fisted young fellow, with good staying powers and hard-hitting propensities." Cardiff weighed over 200 pounds, but expected to reduce to 185 for the contest. He would train under John Donaldson's tutelage. He did not want to fight right away, but wanted sufficient time to train so he could be at his best. Cardiff said,

> I suppose I might go up and make a sprinting match out of it, or lie down and take my ten seconds whenever Sullivan struck at me, as some of these duffers have done, but I won't do that. … I don't expect to be able to best the big fellow, but I don't think he can knock me out in six rounds. … I guarantee that I'll be able to give John L. something to do. I don't mean to play the baby act, but will stand up to my work like a man.[235]

[234] Sullivan at 131.
[235] *St. Paul Daily Globe*, October 26, 1886.

That evening, October 25, 1886 in Racine, Wisconsin, the combination tour began. $1,000 was being offered to anyone who could stand up before Sullivan for 4 rounds.

Sullivan had been in Chicago the past week. Traveling with him were George La Blanche (the "Marine"), Steve Taylor, Jimmy Carroll, Dan Murphy, Jim McKeown, Pete McCoy, and George Weir, known as the "Spider."

William Gleason, who was helping to manage the tour, said their schedule included shows in St. Paul, Duluth, Minneapolis, Des Moines, and Omaha. Then they would head to San Francisco for the Ryan fight on November 13. Gleason claimed that Sullivan had not drank a drop in five months.[236]

On October 27 in Winona, Minnesota, the Sullivan combination gave a sparring exhibition at the Grand opera house before a large audience. A man who witnessed the bouts said of Sullivan: "He is really quite a clever fellow, and looks as powerful as an ox."

Seats for the upcoming St. Paul and Minneapolis shows would be $1, $.75, and $.50. Sullivan would appear twice each evening.[237]

On October 28, 1886 in New York, the dedication ceremony for the Statue of Liberty, a gift from France, took place. It had required ten years to design, construct, transport, and reassemble.

Unfortunately, also on October 28, in North Centerville, Rhode Island, John L. Sullivan's 2-year-old infant son John Jr. died of diphtheria. At that time, no vaccine had been developed for the disease. Sullivan did not attend his son's funeral, nor did he suspend the tour. He boxed in La Crosse, Wisconsin that evening.

In an interview she gave a year later, Sullivan's wife Annie Bates Bailey Sullivan alleged that when she asked him to pay for a headstone, John L. wrote her back and said that he would not pay a cent unless she came back to live with him. She refused. "He knew I wouldn't do that." Annie said, "He has plenty of money to spend on wine and on other women, but he can't provide a stone for his own child's grave."

Annie further said that she was Sullivan's wife, not the woman with whom he was traveling and calling wife. Regarding their history, Annie said,

> I used to think how grand it must be [to be his wife], but when I found out what a drunken brute he was I realized my fate. … [W]henever he got drunk, and that was nearly all the time, I had to look out for myself. I thought things would be different when the baby came, but he was just as bad as ever. … He thought the world of the baby, and even when he was drunk, he made no attempt to hurt him. But when he was drunk he didn't know what he did, and I was afraid he would kill the baby when he was hitting me. I lived with

236 *Minneapolis Tribune, St. Paul Daily Globe*, October 25, 1886.
237 *St. Paul Daily Globe*, October 28, 29, 1886.

him as long as I could, but when I found that my life was in danger I left him, and came here to my brother's, bringing baby with me.[238]

George LaBlanche

On October 29, the Sullivan combination performed in Stillwater, Minnesota to a good house. Each set-to between combination members lasted 3 rounds. First, George La Blanche (who earlier that year suffered his first loss, a LKOby13 to world middleweight champion Jack Dempsey in a very good fight) sparred heavyweight Tom Hinch. Following this exhibition was Jimmy Carroll - Steve Taylor, Sullivan - Hinch, Carroll - La Blanche, and finally Sullivan - Taylor.

One report said that Sullivan was in excellent condition at 231 ½ pounds. No one was willing to stand before him for 4 rounds.[239]

On October 30, 1886, the combination performed at the Exposition rink in St. Paul, Minnesota. One local newspaper said that judging by the reception; Sullivan was the most popular man in Minnesota. The audience numbered over 4,000 people, filling every chair in the rink. "Never in the history of Northwestern sport has a larger crowd gathered to see any pugilistic contest." Others said the Sullivan-Sheedy pugilistic combination drew between 3,000 and 4,000 people.

Sheedy was the master of ceremonies. First, 165-pound Illinois champion Thomas Hinch and 200-pound Steve Taylor sparred 4 rounds. Next, the 5'7" 165-pound LaBlanche undertook to knock out 140-pound local amateur Octavius Blandoin, and did so in the 1st round with a punch to the jugular. LaBlanche then sparred 3 rattling rounds with the smaller Jimmy Carroll, New England's middleweight champion.

Con Cotter, who agreed to box Sullivan, did not show up. All too often, it was like that. Men would agree to box him, but then get cold feet.

Instead, Sullivan, "the champion of all champions," sparred tamely with Hinch, content just to demonstrate his defense.

> [Sullivan's] cleverness was the feature of this contest. … [T]he only work Hinch could do was to attempt to hit the champion. In this he was entirely unsuccessful and the man who has never had a blackened eye or scratched body from fighting easily managed to keep Hinch at a distance.

---

238 *National Police Gazette*, December 17, 1887.

239 *Minneapolis Tribune*, *St. Paul and Minneapolis Pioneer Press,* October 30, 1886; *New York Clipper*, November 6, 1886. La Blanche would go on to score an 1889 KO32 over Jack Dempsey in a non-title bout rematch.

Following this, Taylor sparred Carroll 4 slow rounds, and Hinch sparred 3 even rounds with Jack Keefe.

Sullivan and Taylor closed the show with 3 rounds of sparring. This time, Sullivan was more aggressive, and his "celebrated rushes were gently illustrated, as were those wicked lefts which have been known to crack a two-inch plank."

The local newspapers generally said that the exhibitions were tame and disappointing, failing to satisfy the crowd.[240]

On November 2, they exhibited in Minneapolis. Jack Keefe had said that he was willing to attempt to last 4 rounds with Sullivan, but as the local newspaper predicted, Keefe was a no-show. The exhibitions were called tame hippodromes.[241]

On Thursday November 4, 1886 in Omaha, Nebraska, the Sullivan combination exhibited in the exposition building.

Dan Murphy was listed as the combination treasurer. Dr. Crawford was listed as Sullivan's physician and trainer.

That day, Sullivan and his "wife" were assigned a room. Sullivan was wearing a dark Prince Albert coat with light trousers and patent-leather pointed shoes.

Discussing the upcoming Ryan fight, Sullivan said that the receipts would be split 75/25% based on winner/loser, and it would be a 6-round contest with soft gloves. Speaking of Ryan, Sullivan said, "Well, he is a clever fellow and all that, but I don't think he is in any better condition than he was when I met him the first time. I propose to show him what I can do, and I shall be very much surprised if he shows up at the end of the third round."

When asked whether he might meet Jem Smith, the current English champion, Sullivan said it was by no means certain that they would fight.

> Smith, in my opinion, is a big bag of wind. We've tried to get him over here to make a match, but he won't come. So as soon as we are through with the show business, Sheedy and I will go to England to see if we can't arrange a match with him. What do I think of his chances? They are about even with those of Ryan.

Sheedy said Sullivan never was in such good condition, and had not touched a drop of alcohol in six months. He was weighing 230 ½ pounds and stood 5'10 ½" tall. His fighting weight was 220, though he could train down to 210. Despite his weight, "he is just as quick as lightning. The man don't live today that can best him."[242]

In early November, the weekly *New York Clipper* reported that the Sullivan combination's Western tour had not been creating the expected

---

240 *Minneapolis Tribune*, *St. Paul and Minneapolis Pioneer Press*, *St. Paul Daily Globe*, October 31, 1886.

241 *St. Paul and Minneapolis Pioneer Press*, October 31,1886, November 1, 3, 1886.

242 *Omaha Daily Bee*, November 5, 1886.

furor, owing to the absence of local men willing to take on Sullivan. Hence, combination members just sparred with each other in tame fashion.[243]

Describing Sullivan, respected fighter Billy Edwards observed that John L. allowed one arm to hang almost limp just in front of him, with the other slightly bent, in order to stay relaxed and avoid muscle tension, which prevented "weariness to the muscles and leaves them free for action on the instant." Edwards spoke of what it took to make a great fighter, noting that Sullivan had all of those qualities:

> Given pluck, and the science that comes of good training, and a light man may often clean out a big one. You know, as a rule, big men are slower than little ones. A quick man, of medium build, is really the most dangerous kind of a fighter. Sullivan is not only big and strong but wonderfully quick, and there lies his power; it is a very unusual combination. In fact, Sullivan has all the attributes of a great fighter. … Yes, I think much of him as a fighter, for he is scientific as well as powerful.[244]

Paddy Ryan was prepared to give the champion a hard struggle, and said that Sullivan would find himself in front of a different man. "I underrated Sullivan when we first met, but this time I will size him up for all that he is worth."[245]

On November 10, Sullivan arrived in San Francisco for the Ryan fight, scheduled to be held in three days. 400 people gathered at the ferry-landing to greet him. He appeared to weigh 20 pounds more than he did the last time he had been in town. He was with Pat Sheedy, Steve Taylor, and George LaBlanche. He stayed at the Grand Hotel.

In an interview, Sullivan said, "I tell you that of all the men I ever met Ryan stood up the best. … He did not show any disposition to hug the floor and waste time, but stood up and gave me the best he had till I knocked him out fair and square, and he lay down in his corner insensible."

The blue-eyed Sheedy, whose shoulders were as broad as the champion's, said, "John is better now than he ever was. He weighed 245 pounds when he met Burke, and will scale just 210 pounds when he meets Ryan. … John has left the bottle alone for a long time."

Police Chief Crowley said the fighters had obtained a permit from the mayor for the boxing exhibition, so it would be allowed. Hence, it would be the first Sullivan fight in two years that would not have to endure police limitations and interference.[246]

Nevertheless, the San Francisco Society for the Suppression of Vice attempted to stop the fight, writing an appeal to Mayor Washington Bartlett, urging him to withdraw the license granted for the contest. They

---

[243] *New York Clipper,* November 6, 1886.
[244] *San Francisco Evening Post,* November 6, 1886.
[245] *San Francisco Call,* November 9, 1886.
[246] *San Francisco Evening Post,* November 10, 1886.

said the bout would cause social demoralization, contribute to the town's evil reputation, and would adversely affect young men by glorifying mere brute strength, brutalizing the minds of all who witness such contests. However, the mayor declined to revoke the license.

The night before the fight, every seat had been sold.[247]

Paddy Ryan

On Saturday November 13, 1886 in San Francisco, inside Mechanics' Pavilion, just under two months after the Herald fight, for the third time, 28-year-old John L. Sullivan fought 33-year-old Paddy Ryan. Their first fight was fought in February 1882 under LPR rules, which Sullivan won in 9 rounds totaling about 11 minutes. Their January 1885 Queensberry rules rematch had been entertaining for the short time it lasted, but the police stopped it prematurely in the 1st round, just when the fight really was heating up. Many said that Ryan was doing well. Hence, the third bout would settle matters definitively, once and for all.

In order to give those who attended a local benefit for the Charleston earthquake sufferers time to reach the Pavilion, the fight would start after 11 p.m.

Pat Sheedy predicted that the fight would not last 15 minutes. He said that Sullivan intended to knock out Ryan so suddenly that he would not give the police any chance to interfere.

A massive crowd waited outside. As early as 7 p.m., when the pavilion doors were opened, the eager and impatient crowd rushed in, trying to get the best seats. Many were crushed badly.

---

[247] *San Francisco Call,* November 13, 1886.

About 8,000 or 9,000 spectators (another said more than 6,500), which included only about six to eight women, paid for tickets priced at $2.50, $2.00, $1.50, and $1.00. Sheedy estimated that the receipts would reach $12,000. Others said the total gate was $10,030, or between $10,000 and $10,500.

The aisles and galleries were utterly packed. Every class of the city's citizens was represented, including bankers, merchants, lawyers, brokers, prominent society men, fighters, car conductors, and laborers, all jumbled into one great sweltering mass of humanity. There even were students from Berkeley, "whose bloodthirstiness is in inverse ratio to their strength and courage."

Police Captain Douglass and his men forced their way to the ring platform and stationed themselves every two feet around the base of the 24-foot ring.

Just after 8:40 p.m., after the impatient crowd started hooting and whistling, master of ceremonies Billy Jordan appeared. He received applause, and then he announced the preliminary exhibitions. Pat Sheedy, Sullivan's manager, also tried to make a speech, but there was so much noise that his remarks were totally inaudible to anyone other than those at ringside.

The several preliminaries included bouts between LaBlanche and Carroll and one between Con Riordan and Steve Taylor that was in Taylor's favor. Years later, future champion Bob Fitzsimmons would kill Riordan in a sparring session.

Once the preliminaries concluded, there was a long wait. After a while, the impatient spectators started to whistle and groan. Just after 10:30 p.m., Billy Jordan did his best to keep them quiet, telling them that the next bout would be the gladiators. The band played a few airs. Eventually, the crowd grew impatient again. Jordan told them that the principals would arrive in five minutes. Every five minutes, he kept saying the same thing, until his old story drew cries of "chestnuts."

At 11:14 p.m., the stars made their appearances. Accompanied by his seconds, Tom Barry and John Carr, Paddy Ryan arrived first, shouldering his way through the dense throng and climbing up the platform stairs.

Ryan removed his coat and the huge crowd loudly cheered him. He wore crimson-colored leg tights, supported around the waist with a black band. The *San Francisco Call* said, "He looked the picture of health and condition." His muscles stood out. However, the *San Francisco Evening Post* disagreed. It said Ryan "came into the ring with a heavy dewlap of loose flesh depending from his neck to his waist, and huge rolls of loose flesh on his back told of flabby muscles." Ryan sat down in the corner that he selected.

Sullivan followed, to deafening applause that seemed to shake the building. He was accompanied by LaBlanche, Taylor, and Carroll. The *Call* said, "Sullivan did not look in anything like as good condition as Ryan. … [H]e looked fleshy and rather untrained." Another newspaper agreed that

Sullivan appeared "a trifle too fleshy." Sullivan kept drinking water, from the time he entered the ring to the time the fight started.

The champion wore white trunks, green stockings, and a green waistbelt.

Both likely weighed in the ballpark of 220 pounds or more. However, they were announced as 215 pounds for Sullivan and 210 pounds for Ryan. They fought with four-ounce gloves.

Captain Hiram Cook refereed. Daniel Murphy kept time for Sullivan, while Charles or George Smith did the same for Ryan. The principals and seconds shook hands and the bout began at 11:18 p.m.

1 - They shook hands and sparred for five seconds, feinting and feeling for an opening. Suddenly Ryan fired a right to Sullivan's cheek. Cries of "Good for Paddy!" were heard. Another version said Ryan fired a left and right, but Sullivan stepped back and stopped both blows very easily. Old sports stared in disbelief at seeing Sullivan playing defense. Ryan again took the lead and attacked. They fought savagely on the inside, with the aggressive Ryan leading throughout. However, no real damage ensued. Ryan grazed John's chin with a left, and a right glanced off his side. Sullivan countered with a left stab on the chin. Ryan kept attacking. Paddy landed another right to the cheek, but fell short with a follow-up stomach blow. Most of his blows missed, for Sullivan gave ground, parried, or stopped him with his left jab. They clinched, and the referee broke them. Ryan kept rushing and firing. Sullivan was cool and taking matters easily. He kept stopping Ryan's blows. Ryan fired off looping right hands that came down towards the neck. He also launched rights to the ribs. John L. only smiled and moved back out of danger.

One observer said the fighting was so intense, and at such a fast pace, that Ryan began to show some signs of fatigue. The alert Sullivan took advantage of this and rushed at Ryan, who cleverly evaded blows and clinched to stop his attack. They exchanged some sharp short-range punches, but without any damage of note.

Another version said that towards the end of the round, the aggressive Ryan threw "some heavy sledge-hammer blows that reached his opponent's face," while Sullivan mostly used his left and only delivered a few hard blows.

There were several perspectives about this round. One said the round had consisted of fierce slugging. Another said that very little slugging had been done. Although Ryan tried to force matters and had landed the most blows, they had little effect. Sullivan appeared to be feeling him out. Regarding their condition, one said that Ryan was looking quite confident, while Sullivan was puffing. Still others said it was Ryan who was doing the most work, and hence showed the most fatigue.

2 - Ryan again started as the aggressor and continued forcing the fighting, landing to both the body and head, though without much apparent effect, either because some of his power had left him as a result of fatigue, or

because Sullivan was giving ground so the blows did not land with much force.

Either because he noticed Ryan slow down, or because someone in the crowd called to him, "Oh, hit him, John," Sullivan "commenced work" and began leading and forcing the fight more. Ryan's counters were ineffective.

Another version said Ryan landed a heavy right to the neck, which riled Sullivan, who rushed at him. Sharp exchanges ensued. Ryan landed a right, but Sullivan responded with a left and right to the jaw, rattling Ryan.

Sullivan followed up and decked Ryan, one report saying it was with a body blow, another saying it was a "terrific short-arm blow on the chin," likely a right, while another said Sullivan avoided an attempted body blow and dropped Ryan with a straight right to the forehead. Yet another version said Ryan started to deliver a blow as he was coming forward but Sullivan caught him with a half-arm punch to the chin that half-knocked and half-pushed him to the ground. The crowd cheered loudly. Sullivan walked towards his corner.

Paddy quickly rose in less than five seconds and attacked again. Sullivan rushed in at him as well and they slugged it out. However, Ryan tired a bit, his blows lost some of their force, and Paddy clinched to avoid punishment and save himself.

Ryan's left glove came off. The extra time required to put it back on and readjust it aided his recovery and survival. However, it also helped the winded Sullivan, who smiled and seemed willing to allow Ryan to take all the time he needed to put it back on again.

Soon after resuming, Sullivan again ferociously attacked and decked Ryan, either with blows to the head and body, or a right and/or a left to the head, drawing blood from Ryan's mouth. Each local version told it differently.

The distressed Ryan rose, rushed in and clinched around Sullivan's neck to survive. After breaking, Sullivan had the best of the exchanges that followed, and Ryan again clinched. Paddy would punch and clinch.

Sullivan was having his way with him. One reporter believed that John L. even held him up a couple of times, and moved away to give Paddy a chance to steady himself before striking again. Another said Ryan was game and courageous, while Sullivan was out of wind, happy to kill time.

Ryan's glove again came off, and time was taken putting it back on.

Sullivan rushed in and slugged him hard. The rattled Ryan responded and slugged back heavily, driving Sullivan backwards to the ropes, where they clinched. After breaking, Ryan rushed in again, but Sullivan decked Ryan once more, with either a blow to the forehead, or a right and left to the neck, or a severe punch to the ribs and a clean smash in the face.

Ryan rose to his feet just as the bell rang. It was clear that his chances for victory had evaporated. He was very shaky, and seemingly a beaten man. He had been knocked down three times in the round.

3 - Having better wind, Sullivan forced matters, landing a heavy left and right on the neck. However, the plucky Ryan slugged it out with him. Both men showed signs of punishment.

Sullivan fought him all over the platform and into a corner, where Sullivan landed a terrific right that came upward from his side in a slightly curved swing, landing to the jaw or neck under the left ear, sending Ryan spinning to the ropes and down in a heap, partially through them. The blow had the force of a club, and the sound of the crunch of flesh and leather was heard all over the hall.

With some difficulty, the badly rattled Ryan struggled and staggered to his feet. Several reports said that Ryan led with a left to the face that Sullivan blocked in pretty fashion. Sullivan then so violently landed his well-directed right to the jaw that it sent Ryan "down as if shot out of a cannon. It was a knock-out of the cleanest kind. Ryan laid on the floor utterly unable to move."

The *Examiner's* version of this final knockdown said that Sullivan "struck out like a battering ram, showering blows upon the defenseless face of his opponent and the latter again fell through the ropes with a crash, bleeding from the mouth." The *Evening Post* agreed. "Sullivan leaped on him and showered blows on his face and breast so fast that no eye could count them. He literally buffeted him to the ground, and Ryan went down bleeding from the face, an unconscious heap."

The police entered the ring, but they were too late, for there was nothing for them to do. Paddy was out cold.

After the count was concluded, Sullivan approached Ryan, waved off the seconds and time-keepers, knelt down, lifted up the unconscious warrior, and carried him to his chair in his corner. Ryan's head was limp and his eyes glassy. Sully and all of the seconds worked on the unconscious Ryan, trying to restore him. He was out, and even rubbing did not revive him for quite a while.

Everyone wanted to shake hands with Sullivan; even the police officers present. The crowd quickly dispersed, amid shouts for Sullivan. Ryan received accolades for his gameness. Pat Sheedy complimented Ryan for his courage. Everyone agreed that he had done his best.

The *San Francisco Chronicle* said that Sullivan had knocked out Ryan with ease. The champ seemed to be a "giant toying with a child." Others said it was a short but sharp fight. Sullivan had paralyzed the game but overmatched Ryan, who had been down five times.

The *San Francisco Evening Post* harshly criticized Sullivan's physical appearance, although it still acknowledged his superiority over every fighter in the world, regardless. It said that unless Sullivan took better care of himself and got into top condition, eventually he would be an ex-champion. It admitted that such was a stale prophecy, for every writer in the country had been making the same prediction for the past several years. Nevertheless,

> Sullivan is going down hill physically, and the first time he faces a really good man he is likely to be caught napping. Probably the really good man does not exist now, but he will be heard of before long. … Age, ease and luxurious living have put a goodly paunch on Sullivan. His limbs have grown to a mighty size, and, while his strength is so great that he can carry his thirty odd superfluous pounds of flesh with ease and gracefully, they form a fearful handicap. … Every time Sullivan makes a match we hear stories of his careful training, and on Saturday it was announced that he entered the ring at the moderate weight of 210 pounds. He looked to be at least 20 pounds heavier, and probably was. … Sullivan is still a wonderful man, however, and Ryan has no more business with him than a club-armed savage has with a Gatling battery. …
>
> Ryan is simply a big man, and rather a clever one, but Sullivan is unique. His strength is even proportionately greater than his size; his skill greater than either.

The day after the fight, Paddy Ryan offered his thoughts:

> Well, Sullivan is the king of fighters, and whenever he hits a man the recipient of the blow is not very liable to soon forget its effects. … I faced the champion of the world like a man. I did not flinch from his terrible blows, although John administered to me some very hard ones, I can assure you. The blow I received that felled me the first time I was knocked down was heavy enough to knock out most any man, but, as you know, I came up again to meet another and still heavier blow from that great right hand of his. The last blow that John gave me with his right on the left ear was one of the heaviest blows that I ever got. I went down and out, and although I was knocked out fair and square, I would have faced my opponent again if I was able to do so. When Sullivan ever hits a man a full blow with his right, there is not much danger of the recipient coming up for another.[248]

The day after the fight, Sullivan was paid handsomely to umpire a baseball game in Alameda, near Oakland. However, his appearance excited the 15,000 spectators so much that the management feared the game would be interfered with by the enthusiastic spectators forcing their way upon the diamond. Hence, they decided that he would not umpire after all. Sullivan occasionally enjoyed being involved in baseball games in some way. It was fun for him, and he earned money doing it.

---

[248] *San Francisco Examiner*, *San Francisco Chronicle*, *San Francisco Call*, *Los Angeles Herald*, *Rocky Mountain News*, *Helena Independent*, November 14, 1886; *San Francisco Evening Post*, November 15, 1886; *Sacramento Daily Record-Union*, November 15, 16, 1886; *Desert Evening News*, November 15, 1886; *National Police Gazette*, November 27, 1886.

ONE MORE FOR THE CHAMPION.

SCENES AND INCIDENTS OF THE RECENT GREAT GLOVE FIGHT BETWEEN JOHN L. SULLIVAN AND PADDY RYAN AT THE PAVILION, SAN FRANCISCO, CAL.

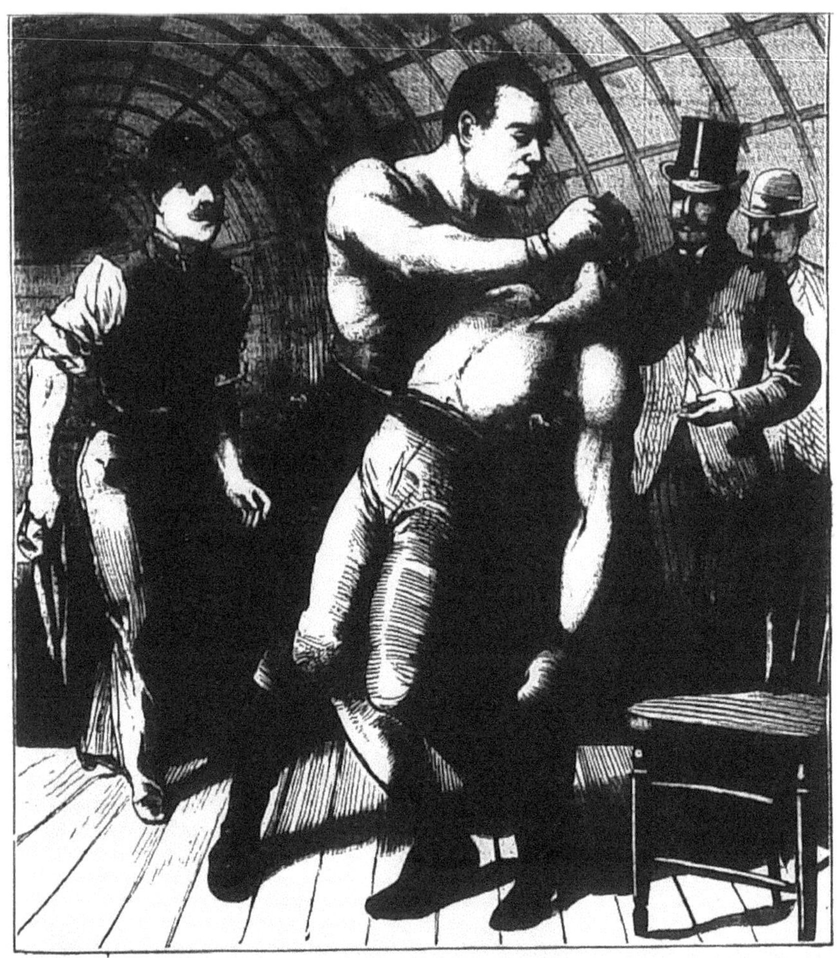

A MAGNANIMOUS CHAMPION.

AFTER KNOCKING OUT PADDY RYAN IN THE THIRD ROUND, AT THE PAVILION, SAN FRANCISCO, JOHN L. SULLIVAN CARRIES HIM TO THE CORNER AND SPONGES OFF HIS BATTERED BROW.

Following his victory over Paddy Ryan, Sullivan repeated the same pattern of touring and exhibiting leading up to a fight. His combination of sparrers made money giving exhibitions in various towns, leading up to the scheduled fight with Patsy Cardiff.

On November 27, 1886 at the Turn Verein Hall in Los Angeles, exhibitions included Le Blanche – Riordan, Carroll - Taylor, and then Sullivan – Conrad in a 4-round set-to. Carroll – Le Blanche followed, and then 4 rounds of Sullivan – Taylor.

The impressed *Los Angeles Herald* wrote that the 28-year-old Sullivan weighed 215 pounds and was in perfect condition, healthy and vigorous:

> He is by all odds the most powerful man of this age, and probably has never had a superior in physical development in any age. He is as round in the trunk as a tree. The muscular development of the shoulders, arms and chest is a wonder. The whole body is of the

most symmetrical make. His head is well poised on a very firmly rounded neck rising from colossal shoulders. Such a perfect shoulder blade is rarely seen in a human body. The lower part of the trunk fits perfectly with the giant shoulders above, and the legs are very powerful and shapely, terminating in a pair of comparatively small feet. He is as quick as a flash of lightning, and as nimble as a deer. He springs from the floor like a cat, and strikes like a catapult. His arms are long, shapely, powerfully muscular. He holds the left mauler – and his hands are large – hanging loosely by his side while sparring, and hurls it with telling effect at his antagonist with the speed of a cannon ball. Scarcely has the left fallen like a sledge hammer, on the chest or proboscis of the victim, when the right strikes like a thunderbolt on the head or body of the half dazed unfortunate. Even in sparring he hit at Taylor, who stopped the blow with his own hand, but even through the big gloves his hand was half broken. One has but to look at Sullivan to see that no living man can stand before his terrific blows for a fight to the finish.

Sullivan was scheduled to head back north to Sacramento, Woodland, and San Francisco again, then Victoria, Canada (although ultimately he was denied the permit to spar there), Portland, Oregon, and then East. His manager Pat Sheedy, a pleasant gentleman, also had scheduled Sullivan to tour England and France.[249]

On November 29 at the Metropolitan in Sacramento, they exhibited to a small house. John L. boxed a man named Conrad of San Francisco in a tame manner. He later boxed 3 rounds with Steve Taylor.

The legal authorities in Seattle refused to allow Sullivan to exhibit there.

On or about December 11 or 12 they exhibited in Vancouver, Canada to a crowded house that paid $1 each. Law enforcement did not interfere, despite the fact that "the law on the subject is clearly against everything of the kind."[250]

From the 18th to the 21st, the combination exhibited in Butte, Montana at the Opera House. A Montana paper said the combination had gone through Montana during the course of a week, including Helena, earning about $11,000.[251]

Sullivan was advertised to exhibit in Salt Lake City on December 22 at the Walker Opera House.

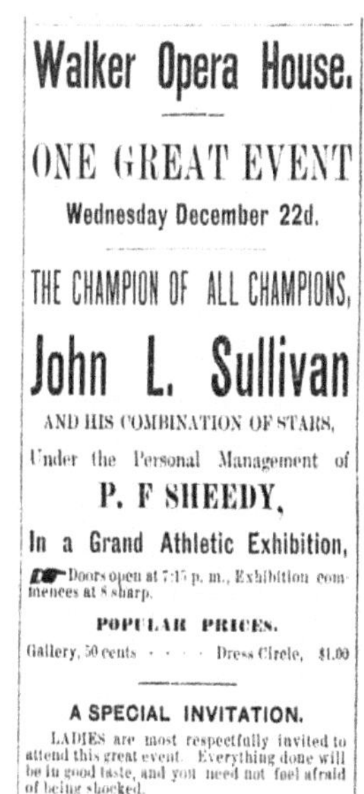

Walker Opera House.
ONE GREAT EVENT
Wednesday December 22d.
THE CHAMPION OF ALL CHAMPIONS,
John L. Sullivan
AND HIS COMBINATION OF STARS,
Under the Personal Management of
P. F SHEEDY,
In a Grand Athletic Exhibition,
Doors open at 7:15 p. m., Exhibition commences at 8 sharp.
POPULAR PRICES.
Gallery, 50 cents - - - - Dress Circle, $1.00
A SPECIAL INVITATION.
LADIES are most respectfully invited to attend this great event. Everything done will be in good taste, and you need not feel afraid of being shocked.

249 *Los Angeles Daily Herald*, November 28, 1886.
250 *Sacramento Daily Record-Union*, November 30, December 13, 1886.
251 *Butte Semi-Weekly Miner*, December 11, 18, 22, 1886. *New North-West.*, December 24, 1886. *Great Falls Tribune.*, December 18, 1886.

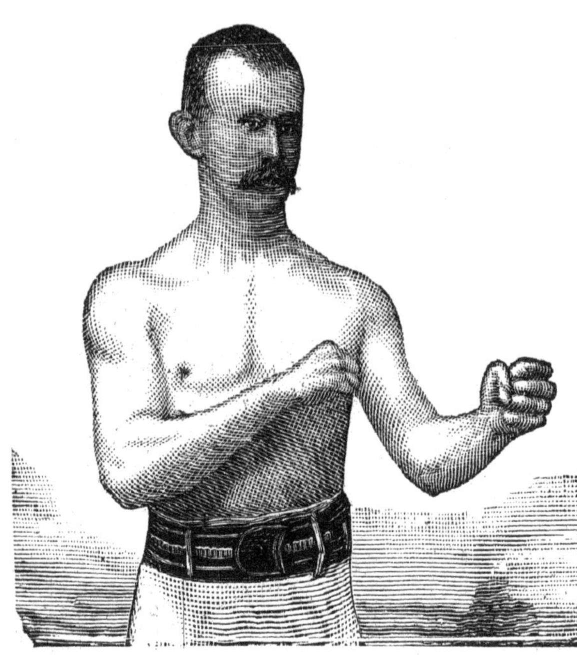
DUNCAN McDONALD.

At that time, the Sullivan combination consisted of Steve Taylor and Northwest champion Duncan McDonald (both of whom would spar with the champion), George La Blanche, lightweight champion James Carroll, and Boston's Daniel Murphy and James McKeon or McKean.

In his May 1884 bout against Pete McCoy, the 6' 174-pound McDonald broke his right hand in the 3rd round, but continued to fight for 2 hours 15 minutes before suffering defeat in the 31st round.[252]

In July 1886, McDonald fought a 6-round draw against a young, promising amateur named James J. Corbett. Many suspected that although he and Corbett boxed in an entertaining bout, really it was a friendly arrangement/hippodrome. McDonald was a skilled veteran who knew how to work with someone. McDonald and Corbett might have been sparring partners who traveled around giving exhibitions, earning money.

In August 1886, McDonald fought former Sullivan challenger and sparring partner Herbert "The Maori" Slade, dropping Slade in the 3rd round before winning an 8-round decision. On September 18, 1886, the same day that Sullivan defeated Frank Herald, in their rematch, McDonald knocked out Slade in the 9th round. Hence, Duncan McDonald was no slouch of a sparring partner for the champion.[253]

Sullivan had upcoming bouts scheduled with Patsy Cardiff, Pat Killen (a well-known entertaining puncher), John Burns, and James Flood, all set to be held in January and February 1887.

Of the December 22, 1886 exhibition in Salt Lake, a crowded gallery and well-filled parquette greeted the combination. La Blanche boxed Duncan McDonald, Jimmy Carroll boxed local lightweight William Shields,

---

[252] *New York Clipper,* May 24, 1884. Some say it was the 34th round. *Denver Daily News,* December 29, 1886.

[253] *National Police Gazette,* November 15, 1884, October 16, 1886; *Salt Lake Daily Tribune,* August 29, 1886.

and then John L. Sullivan, "the champion of champions," boxed Duncan McDonald in give-and-take fashion. Sully appeared to be in good condition. After intervening exhibitions, including Carroll – La Blanche, Sullivan boxed 3 rounds with Taylor.[254]

On December 24 and 25, 1886 in Leadville, Colorado, the combination performed to a packed theater. "This combination has more genuine representatives of the fistic art than any ever organized." While there, Sullivan donated $200 to a priest.[255]

Despite Sullivan's reputation for being a phenomenal puncher, his boxing skills also found appreciation. One expert writer for the *Chicago Herald* wrote:

> You have heard of hundreds of men, when speaking of Sullivan, say, "He wins by brute strength," and I have seldom seen a man who advanced the truth, which is that Sullivan is as clever as any man. His unquestioned ability as to being the hardest hitter ever seen has caused the overlooking of the fact that his blow is always planted where it will do the most good, either upon the jaw or jugular - again, it is certain that could an adversary so land his blow, Sullivan would fall as quickly as another, and yet having knocked out about sixty men, he has never been harmed.
>
> The truth is that Sullivan is a careful, scientific fighter. …
>
> Do I think his equal as a pugilist ever trod the earth? Certainly not. …
>
> Even in imagination the ancients never conceived such a hitter as Sullivan.[256]

On December 27, 1886, the combination exhibited to a crowded house in Colorado Springs. First, McDonald sparred John Davis for 4 rounds. Set-tos between Walker and Carroll, and Taylor and Le Blanche followed. "The event of the evening then took place, being a purely scientific match between John L. Sullivan and Duncan A. McDonald."

The local press called it a highly satisfactory exhibition. "The champion was in fine form, and he delighted the large audience with his exhibition of scientific sparring." One newspaper said that Sullivan's sparring was part of a joint engagement with a Presbyterian pastor. "The one lectured on physical science, the other illustrated it, and both won applause."[257]

On December 28, 1886, they exhibited in Denver. The 1,000 chairs were taken, plus another 300 folks filled the standing room and beyond. Like the prior evening, the first 4-round exhibition was between John or Jack Davis and Duncan McDonald. Next was Jimmy Carroll - Dave Walker, then La

---

[254] *Salt Lake Evening Democrat*, December 17, 1886; *Salt Lake Herald*, December 19, 23, 1886.
[255] *Denver Tribune-Republican*, December 26, 28, 1886; *Omaha Daily Bee*, January 8, 1887.
[256] *Denver Daily News*, December 27, 1886, quoting a *Chicago Herald* writer.
[257] *Denver Daily News*, *Denver Tribune-Republican*, December 28, 29, 1886.

Blanche - Nathan Brambley, Davis – Walker, and Carroll - La Blanche. "Le Blanche is without doubt the best sparer, barring Sullivan, that has visited Denver." Then, according to the *Denver Daily News*,

> [T]he champion of the champions came on, and sparred four of his peculiar rounds with McDonald, who does excellent work both in stopping and leading considering the fact that Sullivan is in front of him, liable at any time to expend a portion of his surplus strength. Sullivan's method of sparring is beyond criticism. It is the basis of the modern school, and to its system of throwing the weight with the leads and follows is due the terrible execution with soft gloves that has become more or less common in Sullivan's time. Sullivan looks a great deal better than he did three years ago when he appeared at the Exposition building with McCoy, Taylor and Slade.[258]

The *Denver Tribune-Republican* said of the 4-round McDonald - Sullivan exhibition:

> The two men went at each other as if their lives were at stake. It was give and take, McDonald standing up to his work bravely. Sullivan showed one point of his science by quick movements of his head, completely eluding, on such occasions, the heavy blows which were aimed by McDonald. Sullivan showed his quickness and alertness. … The bout was roundly applauded. Sullivan's weight is 226 pounds, and he is the pink of condition. His physical appearance is that of "The Champion of Champions."

Although the spectators were pleased with the show, those who knew something of the game realized that the sparrers generally had engaged in "make believe slugging matches" and "sham rough encounters." They were working with each other and putting on a good show. Steve Taylor did not spar, owing to the fact that he had suffered a sprained elbow.

The following evening, on the 29th, they exhibited in Denver again. La Blanche knocked out Pacific-slope Greco-Roman wrestling champion Professor Smith in the 1st round. McDonald then sparred with La Blanche, "and it was the prettiest exhibition of sparring ever witnessed in Denver. The men proved to be very evenly matched."

Sullivan sparred with McDonald, and later Taylor, the latter bout constituting the wind-up, which was "brief but interesting." "Sullivan gave a number of his famous 'rushes.'"[259]

On December 30, the combination exhibited in Georgetown, Colorado. The exhibitions included bouts between Duncan McDonald and George LaBlanche, as well as Steve Taylor and Jim Carroll. Sullivan then faced McDonald, and "those who have any knowledge of the art could readily see the superiority of the 'big one,' yet the Butte City man is quite an adept."

---

258 *Denver Daily News*, December 29, 1886.
259 *Denver Tribune-Republican*, December 29, 30, 1886.

LaBlanche and Carroll sparred next. The final bout was between Sullivan and Taylor. "Many good points were observed but the cleverness with which the champion ducks his head, thus escaping many a well directed blow, was admired by all. His antagonist stood but a poor show with him."[260]

On January 1, 1887, the combination again performed in Denver, to a packed house that was even more crowded than on the two previous occasions there. The "loud applause which greeted the 'champion of champions' shows to what extent admiration can be carried even for a prize fighter." As usual, Sullivan sparred with McDonald and Taylor.

The tour was heading east, with potential stops in Central and Cheyenne, Topeka, and the river towns.[261]

Supposedly, at least 615 gloved boxing contests had occurred during 1886.[262]

Despite gloved boxing's vastly growing popularity, the *National Police Gazette* still did not entirely appreciate Queensberry rules boxing, and still maintained that LPR fights were the real deal and true test of a champion.

> Thirteen years ago pugilists fought with bare knuckles and London prize ring rules for the championship, and there was no limit to the number of rounds. Nowadays they fight a stipulated number of rounds with pillows and rules made for convenience, which do not prove who possesses courage and stamina, and yet they style themselves as champions.[263]

A Denver writer observed a shift in boxing's style:

> The modern prize fight is a knock-out. It used to be that men would fight one hundred rounds with bare knuckles, while now it is the rule to knock a man out with gloves in a few rounds. It is not that men have less endurance than formerly, for it is not now a question of endurance. The secret is a blow from the shoulder on the side of the neck. Such a blow, fairly planted, knocks a man out. In the modern prize-fight it is a question of skill in getting in this blow. Occasionally two men are so equally matched as to skill that neither can get in this blow until either is too weak to make it effective. In such a fight we have the old contest of endurance.[264]

John L. Sullivan offered some of his thoughts on boxing as well:

> The essentials of a thoroughly good fighter are pluck, skill, endurance and a good head on his shoulders. A man fights with his head almost as much as he does with his fist. He must know where to send his

260 *Colorado Miner* (Georgetown), January 1, 1887.

261 *Denver Tribune-Republican,* December 26, 28, 1886, January 2, 1887.

262 *San Francisco Examiner,* July 18, 1887.

263 *National Police Gazette,* January 8, 1887.

264 *Denver Republican,* January 1, 1887.

blows so they may do the most good. He must economize his strength and not score a hit just for the sake of scoring it.

> I endeavor to hit my man above the heart, or under the chin, or behind the ear. A man wears out pretty soon if one can keep hammering away in the region of the heart; a blow under the chin or behind the ear will knock out a man quicker than a hundred blows on the cheek or any other portion of the face. …
>
> I can tell pretty well when my man is giving in. I watch his eyes, and I know at once when the punishment is beginning to tell on him. And when I talk to a man before I stand up before him at all, I can make up my mind whether he is a fighter or not. There is more intelligence required in this business than outsiders give us credit for.
>
> I do not train. I know better than to waste my vitality in training. I lie in bed until 10 o'clock in the morning, read all the papers, smoke a cigar, take a cup of black coffee, then get up and have my bath and breakfast. Now, when I meet a man that I think is going to give me some trouble, I will train, but I have not met that man yet.

All of the sparring and exhibiting he did kept Sullivan in good form.

Sullivan didn't always knock out his opponents as quickly as he could. He said that sometimes, in order to give the public a good show, he carried his foe. One time, he allowed his opponent to hammer away at him for a couple of rounds. After the 2nd round concluded, John L. told his second to call out to him about 30 seconds before the conclusion of the next round. During the 3rd round, John once again allowed his foe punch away, and the audience cheered, thinking that the challenger was doing well,

> [B]ut at that close range his blows hurt me about as much as you could by fibbing me on the top of the head with a soft glove. There I lay, as snug as you please, taking a great deal of amusement out of the enthusiasm of the audience. Presently my second, who had kept his eyes upon his watch, called out "John," and then I stepped back and landed my young man one under the ear, and that was the last of him.[265]

On January 7, 1887, the Sullivan combination performed to an immense crowd in Kansas City, Missouri.[266]

On January 11, they exhibited at the Exposition building in Omaha, Nebraska. In an interview with a local reporter on the 10th, Sullivan said,

> My weight at present is 230 pounds, which is considerably more than I ought to weigh to be in good fighting condition. I can easily bring myself down to 195 pounds, which is about my proper fighting

---

[265] *National Police Gazette,* January 15, 1887; *Denver Daily News,* January 3, 1887; *St. Paul Daily Globe,* January 17, 1887.

[266] *National Police Gazette,* January 22, 1887. On the 8th, they were in in West Kansas, MO.

weight. I never felt better in my life so far as general health is concerned.

The Cardiff fight was a week away.

Sullivan said that it looked as if the hard-punching Pat Killen was backing out of their scheduled match. John L. was willing to meet Jem Smith in Europe. He did not think Smith was any better than Greenfield, who fought Smith for 1 hour 40 minutes.[267]

THE GREAT

Sullivan-Cardiff

6 ROUND GLOVE CONTEST 6

WASHINGTON RINK, MINNEAPOLIS,

Tuesday Evening, Jan, 18.

Secure reserved seats in Minneapolis at Nicollet house news stand; St. Paul, at Billy Twombly's, on Third street.

Admission $1, Reserved seats $2.

ACCOMMODATION FOR 12,000 PEOPLE.

After his Nebraska exhibition, Sullivan headed to Minnesota for the fight with Patsy Cardiff, the Peoria Giant. Despite Cardiff's reputation for being a strong fighter, Pat Sheedy was so confident that Sullivan would stop him that he had booked Sullivan to exhibit the following night in Fargo. Regardless of result, Cardiff would earn 25% of the gate, or he could take $1,200 guaranteed up front.[268]

On January 16, the "Lord High Executioner" Sullivan arrived in Minneapolis. The champion's brother Mike Sullivan was with him. All day long, the Nicollet house rotunda was filled with people anxious to see the champion. Everyone was asking, "Where's Sullivan?" However, the champ remained in his room until after supper. He wore his Prince Albert coat and a Derby hat. He was slightly unshaven, and seemed to want to be left alone. However, a crowd instantly surrounded him.

When asked what he thought of Cardiff, Sullivan replied, "Don't know anything about him. I never saw him spar – suppose he's a pretty good man from what they say. I'll do with him what I do with the rest of 'em – knock him out as soon as I can. I don't know anything about Killen. Ask Sheedy."

Sheedy said that Pat Killen had shown the white feather. He had signed articles for a 4-round meeting, but was afraid, and therefore was attempting to re-negotiate the contract.

Allegedly, Cardiff was in very good shape, weighing about 180 pounds. He said, "All I have to say is that I am going to do the best I can. I am not going to sprint, either, but hope to keep out of the way of Sullivan's sockers. I hope to make a good showing, and expect to stay."

---

[267] *Omaha Daily Bee*, January 11, 1887.
[268] *St. Paul Daily Globe*, January 15, 1887.

Patsy Cardiff

The talk of the town was how long Cardiff would last. Most said 3 - 5 rounds, while his ardent admirers insisted that he would stand for the full 6 rounds. The police were insisting upon larger-than-usual 6-ounce gloves.

Although the preliminary bouts would start at about 8 p.m., the main fight would not take place until 10 p.m., in order to accommodate those arriving from St. Paul by train. For the preliminary, Sullivan's combination of sparrers - Taylor, McDonald, La Blanche, and Carroll were scheduled to spar with each other and with local boxers.[269]

The local Minneapolis native Cardiff had between 20 and 30 contests of experience, plus multiple exhibitions, which included several meaningful victories such as: 1885 KO9 and/or KO4 over 175-pound Billy Wilson (a black fighter who held an 1885 KO1 over the highly touted 210 - 220-pound Mervine Thompson), and victories over former Sullivan foes Captain James Dalton (1884 W4), Professor John Donaldson (1885 W4), and George Rooke (1886 W6). The *Police Gazette* called him a "wonderful pugilist."

In June 1886, Cardiff fought Charley Mitchell to a 5-round draw, scoring a knockdown of Mitchell in the process. A few weeks later, Cardiff again defeated Billy Wilson, this time the contest ending after the 7th round concluded. About ten of Cardiff's fights had been held in the St. Paul/Minneapolis area, where he lived, so the locals were quite familiar with him.[270]

---

[269] *St. Paul Daily Globe*, January 15 – 18, 1887.

[270] *Minneapolis Tribune*, January 19, 1887; *National Police Gazette*, July 14, 1888; *Chicago Herald*, June 15, 1885; *St. Paul Daily Globe*, June 26, 1886; Cyberboxingzone.com.

When the Sullivan fight was made in late October, Cardiff then said that "though I may not whip Sullivan I'll give him a hard fight and it will be the best match ever seen in this city."[271]

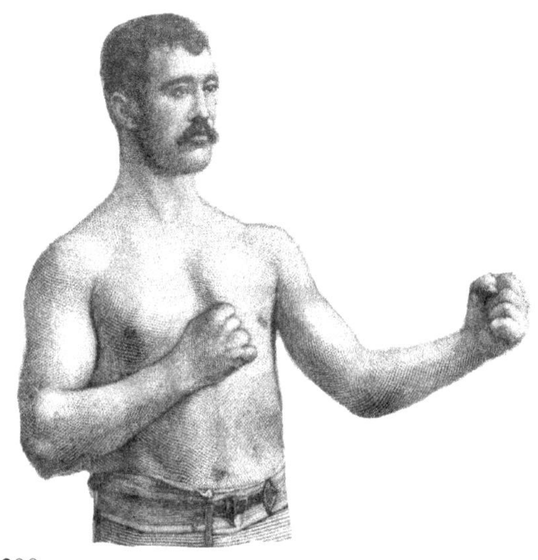

On Tuesday January 18, 1887 in Minneapolis, upon the stage of the Washington Rink, John L. Sullivan fought Patsy Cardiff in a scheduled 6-round bout.

The local *Minneapolis Tribune* listed the 28-year-old Sullivan as weighing 211 pounds, though others said he was closer to 229 or 230 pounds. The 24-year-old Cardiff was listed as 5'10" and 185 pounds, having worked down from 200.

About 8,000 people were in attendance inside the immensely large rink. The crowd was the "largest audience ever seen under a roof in Minneapolis." The stage was placed at the further end of the rink so as to give the purchasers of reserved seats the best views. On the stage was a 20-foot ring. The 2,000 chairs around the stage were filled. The galleries contained about 3,000 spectators. The balance of the audience remained standing. The box office receipts amounted to at least $10,000.

The cosmopolitan audience waited for the main event in an atmosphere that was fairly blue with tobacco smoke. All stations of life were represented - lawyers, merchants, professional men, as well as toughs and bums all jumbled together in "one great crazy patch of humanity." Minnesota's Lieutenant Governor C. A. Gilman, as well as Minneapolis Mayor A. A. Ames were both present. Folks from nearby states were in attendance as well. They had come from the Dakota Territory, Iowa, Wisconsin, and Chicago.

The preliminary began at 8:30 p.m. Pat Sheedy acted as the master of ceremonies. He requested that the smoking cease. He explained that the local boxers had gone on strike. "They wanted 50% of the receipts, like Killen." McDonald and LaBlanche sparred 4 rounds.

A crash was heard, followed by a rush of people. A fence that had been built across the center of the hall to divide the folks who had paid $2 for reserved seats from those who paid $1 general admission had fallen. The immense pressure of over 2,000 people was more than it could stand.

[271] *Minneapolis Tribune,* October 26, 1886.

Sheedy announced that the intruders must retire and return to their allotted area or there would be no boxing.

Eventually, Steve Taylor boxed Jimmy Carroll, and then Billy Wisdom boxed Billy Phalen, followed by Carroll - LaBlanche and Taylor - McDonald.

A wait of nearly an hour ensued before the main event. Sheedy announced that the same 5 ½-ounce gloves that had been used throughout the evening would be in service for the big fight. Sheedy also announced that local Minneapolis referee Pat Sullivan would officiate.

At 10:30 p.m., John L. Sullivan appeared, attended by Taylor and LaBlanche. The applause that greeted him was light compared with that which the local man Cardiff received a few minutes later. He was attended by John Donaldson and Jerry Murphy. After the usual preliminaries and shaking of hands they faced one another.

1 - At first, Cardiff seemed nervous and a bit panicked. After sparring lightly for an opening, Sullivan made a rush that carried Cardiff to the ropes. After breaking, Sullivan landed a blow to the neck. Cardiff responded by taking the initiative, landing three punches on Sullivan's face. The local favorite's exhibition of pluck created a great deal of enthusiasm. Cardiff avoided Sullivan's following onslaught by ducking. In his next rush, Sullivan landed on Cardiff's neck. The men sparred cautiously, and a Sullivan feint caused Cardiff to make "a rather absurd effort to get away." They came to a clinch and time was called.

2 - Sullivan fired a lead, but Cardiff ducked and the blow landed on the top of his head. Cardiff rushed the champion and pushed him to the ropes, where he landed a couple of telling blows to the side of John L.'s face.

The balance of the round was uneventful, for very little was done. There was some ineffective short-arm work. The *St. Paul Daily Globe* opined that Sullivan appeared to be waiting for Cardiff to throw and leave himself open, but the cautious Cardiff was not willing to take any chances. The *Minneapolis Tribune* agreed that not much occurred in the round, though the slight advantage seemed to be with Cardiff. Neither man had thrown many blows.

3 - Sullivan was leading with his right, while Cardiff was dodging and clinching. After Sullivan again led with his right, Cardiff rallied and landed on the champion's jaw, but then ran away. Sparring at a safe distance followed.

The crowd began to hiss the lack of action. Sullivan finally made a dive at Cardiff, who sprang away across the stage. After more cautious sparring, Cardiff rushed Sullivan to the ropes and landed a right. A clinch followed, when time was called.

4 - Both men were very cautious. Not much happened in the round. They walked around each other, but did not fire or exchange blows of any significance. The audience hissed and groaned at the tame bout.

5 - Sullivan started with an ineffective blow on Cardiff's neck. Sullivan again led and Cardiff dodged and blocked a blow on his shoulder. The balance of the round was spent in "pedestrian exercise." Nothing significant occurred.

Cardiff seemed anxious and nervous about the possibility of a Sullivan rush, so he kept away and did not do much. Sullivan seemed inclined to take things easy and not attack. The vast audience was hissing. At the close of the round, the crowd was yelling, "Hippodrome," implying that it was a fake or a friendly bout.

6 - Cardiff led with a rush, pushed Sullivan against the ropes, and landed two body blows. Sullivan responded with a rush, but Cardiff mostly avoided him. Sullivan landed a round-arm blow on Cardiff's neck, but Patsy took it well.

Thereafter, little to no effective work was done by either man. It seemed that Cardiff was eager for the bell to ring and for the bout to end without his being knocked out. After a clinch, time was called.

Once the bout was over, the audience cried, "Hippodrome!" They also yelled for a decision in Cardiff's favor. It was a boisterous scene.

Pat Sheedy claimed and indicated by his motions that Sullivan's left arm had been broken, but this claim was received by a cry of derision from those who believed the bout had been a fake.

Finally, quiet was restored, and Referee Pat Sullivan declared that his decision was that the fight was a draw. The audience expressed its dissatisfaction with his decision, feeling that their local man had won. They dispersed in bad humor. Later, an effort was made to induce the referee to change his decision, but he refused.

The *Minneapolis Tribune* said there had been little fighting done in the very tame bout, particularly after the 3rd round, although overall, Cardiff did most of the work.

The *St. Paul Daily Globe* called the fight a "great fizzle" that disgusted the crowd of 8,000, for there was almost no slugging whatsoever. The spectators considered it to be a disappointing hippodrome. Hardly a dozen good blows were exchanged.

Sullivan said that in the 1st round, he rushed and delivered a swinging left which Cardiff ducked, and his forearm had landed on the top of Patsy's head, causing his arm to fracture. That explained why he had fought the way he did. Sullivan was in considerable pain. "I have spoiled many a bloke, but I never hurt myself like this before. Once I smashed my right, but it didn't amount to anything." In another report, John said that as he threw a left uppercut, Cardiff ducked and his forehead struck Sullivan's forearm. Yet, few believed the announcement about his arm.

However, two reputable local Minneapolis physicians, Doctors F. E. Towers and Thomas F. Quinby, M.D., confirmed that the injury was genuine. They explained that the main larger bone, or radius, in Sullivan's left arm was broken midway between the wrist and elbow, caused by a misdirected blow. "Sullivan did not even wince, but stood up for the remaining five rounds, although he did not once use his left." The break was noticed easily, for the arm was quite swollen, and the grating of the bones when it was being set was quite audible. Sullivan was in excruciating pain. The arm was placed in two splints.

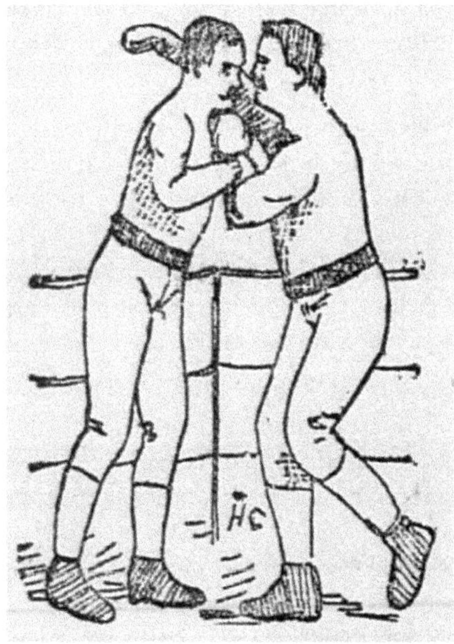

Regarding the decision, the *St. Paul Daily Globe* opined that Cardiff had done the greater part of the fighting, although that was not saying much. Its writer believed that had Cardiff been aware of what had happened to Sullivan's arm, he might have taken more chances and won. As it was, Cardiff fought cautiously from start to finish, anticipating that if he took any chances, he might receive a knockout blow. Regardless, the writer also said that Cardiff had done most of the fighting, rushed the champ against the ropes several times, drew the first blood, and on the merits, was entitled to the decision. However, this writer also opined that referee Pat Sullivan probably intended to be fair with his decision.

The *Minneapolis Tribune* opined, "The fact that Sullivan broke his arm…made the fight, the little there was, entirely Cardiff's, and it ought to have been given him." Cardiff had done "surprising work," a few times momentarily getting Sullivan to the ropes (in the 1st, 2nd, and 6th rounds). However, overall, the fight was dull, with Cardiff for the most part keeping away, concerned about taking too many chances, while Sullivan did not do much owing to his badly crippled left arm. The bout's overall tameness explained why the referee declared it a draw.

THAT HISTORIC FIGHT

AT MINNEAPOLIS, MINN., IN WHICH PATSY CARDIFF GOT HOME TWICE ON JOHN L. SULLIVAN BEFORE THE HITHERTO ALL-CONQUERING CHAMPION BROKE THE BONE OF HIS LEFT WRIST.

Regardless of the decision, the split of the receipts was set by contract ahead of time, regardless of result, which was 25% to Cardiff and 75% to Sullivan. The formal articles of agreement had been signed back on November 2.

Later that evening, at his place of business on Second Avenue South, Cardiff received congratulations. He kicked considerably about the decision, but the *St. Paul Daily Globe* opined that evidently he was satisfied with escaping a knockout. The only regret Cardiff expressed was that he had not known that Sullivan's arm was broken. If he had known, he might have taken more chances and made it impossible for the referee to take the fight from him. Essentially, Sullivan had been able to mask his injury sufficiently to fool Cardiff, who, had he figured it out, might have been more aggressive, taken more chances, and thrown more punches. He remained cautious, fearing what Sullivan might do.

A non-local newspaper reported that unaware of the injury, Cardiff did not seize his opportunity, and later "said he expected to be knocked out, and he acted with great caution, knowing Sullivan was only awaiting one good effective blow."

Naturally, any potential match with Killen had to be canceled, although it was not certain that Killen wanted to fight Sullivan anyhow. Pat initially had agreed to fight him, but had changed his mind, insisting upon 50% of the gate receipts.

The local doctors said it would require at least two months for Sullivan's arm to heal fully.[272]

Why did so many believe the bout was a hippodrome and not genuine, and not believe Sullivan's injury claim? The *Saint Paul and Minneapolis Pioneer Press* explained that even before the fight, there was some rumor and suspicion of a side agreement that Sullivan would carry him. That suspicion appeared to be confirmed by the bout's tameness. (Hence, the spectators were disinclined to believe the real facts.)

> Everyone looks upon the affair as savoring of a hippodrome. As a prominent sporting man said yesterday:
>
> "I'll wager a nice little pile that Cardiff is not knocked out. A man who would not meet Mitchell on the square certainly will not go before Sullivan unless there is some sort of an arrangement made before hand. You will find that either Sullivan has put up a forfeit that he will not knock Cardiff out, or else the latter has an understanding with the police whereby they will insist upon the largest kind of gloves being worn, and also interfere and stop the fight the moment Cardiff is getting the worst of it."[273]

Bolstering this argument was the fact that Sullivan would not have to try his best to knock out Cardiff, because he was guaranteed 75% of the receipts regardless of result.

---

[272] *Minneapolis Tribune*, January 17, 19, 1887; *St. Paul Daily Globe*, January 19, 1887; *National Police Gazette*, January 29, February 12, 1887; *Helena Independent*, January 19, 20, 1887.
[273] *Saint Paul and Minneapolis Pioneer Press*, January 19, 1887.

A day later, in irresponsible yellow journalism fashion, the *Saint Paul and Minneapolis Pioneer Press* said, "The Whole Affair Has the Appearance of Being an Out-and-Out Hippodrome." This writer believed that the dull bout's tameness was proof that it was a fixed fight in which both fighters had agreed to work with each other and do little. Nevertheless, this newspaper criticized the referee's draw decision:

> His decision should have been in favor of the Northwest champion, for Cardiff did more of the fighting, thrice rushing the champion to the ropes, and getting in three clean blows to Sullivan's one. In the fourth round not a single lead was made, and in the fifth there was but one exchange of blows, neither landing squarely. After the close of the sixth round Sullivan's manager announced that the champion had broken his left hand early in the fight, and as a consequence, was compelled to let up. The crowd did not believe this, and every one cried hippodrome.

Despite the fact that the local doctors confirmed that Sullivan had broken his left radius bone, nevertheless, this local writer still believed and fostered the idea that there was an arrangement between the fighters.

> Even with his left hand helpless Sullivan could have taken all the fight out of Cardiff had he felt so inclined. The fact that Cardiff made such a good fight is evidence that there was some sort of an arrangement made before he went on the stage. No one for a moment supposed that he would go at the champion the way he did, unless he knew he would not be hurt.

The next day, this newspaper said many still questioned the genuineness of Sullivan's break, and also questioned the decision. "The opinion was quite common that the referee should have given Cardiff the fight." Cardiff wanted to meet Sullivan again in a fight to the finish.[274]

The local weekly *Irish Standard* reported that Sullivan's arm was broken in the 2nd round. "The fight was decided a draw, although the general opinion is that Patsey had the best of it."[275]

Cardiff had not impressed Sullivan. A week after the fight, John L. said of Patsy, "He ran about the ring like a sucker and a coward, and failed to notice that something wrong had happened to me."[276]

Cardiff subsequently was quoted as saying, "Had I known…that Sullivan had broken his arm, I think that today I would be the recognized champion of the world; for I would have gone at him and forced the fighting until I should have put him to sleep."[277]

---

[274] *Saint Paul and* Minneapolis *Pioneer Press,* January 20, 1887.
[275] *Irish Standard,* January 22, 1887.
[276] *Minneapolis Tribune,* January 25, 1887.
[277] *Referee* (Sydney), June 16, 1887.

Several years later, in 1891, when discussing the Sullivan fight, Cardiff said, "I knew that the left was gone, but I thought a good deal of my jaw when he began poking that right at me, and am well satisfied that I got off so easy."

In 1909, Mike Donovan wrote that Cardiff "was very clever, but lacked nerve. He did nothing but clinch, clinch. … He was a good runner and sprinted all through the bout."[278]

There was some discussion of a potential rematch, but it never materialized. On August 5, 1887 in Minneapolis, Cardiff fought Pat Killen to a 10-round draw. The following year, in late June 1888, the 186-pound Killen knocked out 180-pound Cardiff in the 4th round.[279]

The Sullivan combination continued on, exhibiting along the Red River Valley, in Fargo and Grand Forks, in the Dakota Territory, and then up to Winnipeg, Manitoba, although Sullivan only appeared in street clothes and acted as the master of ceremonies, much to the spectators' chagrin. They wanted to see him box.

His left arm still bothering him, about two weeks later, Sullivan returned to Minneapolis to have the doctors examine it again, and they placed the arm in felt splints.

Sullivan then traveled to Chicago, and from there to New York. His arm was still hurting, so he had Dr. Louis Sayers examine the arm. Sayers said the break had been set improperly and was healing incorrectly. Sayers had his two sons hold Sullivan's arm, and then, holding his hand, Sayers pulled and re-broke the arm. He then re-set the arm and locked it in place with a plaster of Paris cast, which Sullivan would wear for the next five weeks.

JOE LANNON.

In March 1887, the cast was removed from Sullivan's arm.[280]

On March 28, 1887 in Hoboken, New Jersey, Sullivan performed in two 4-round exhibitions, one with Joe Lannon, and the other with Steve Taylor. Lannon had scored an October 1886 KO6 over Frank Herald, although on March 8, 1887, Jake Kilrain stopped Lannon in the 11th

278 *San Francisco Examiner*, December 28, 1891; Donovan at 108.

279 *Minneapolis Tribune*, January 25, 1887; *National Police Gazette*, July 14, 1888; *St. Paul Daily Globe*, August 6, 1887, June 27, 1888.

280 *National Police Gazette*, February 12, March 28, 1887; Sullivan at 132-133.

round. Kilrain also held a November 1886 KO1 victory over Herald.

Before the sparring began, Sullivan gave a speech, asking the spectators in advance to excuse his performance, because he was nursing his recovering left arm. The sparring was friendly and tame, and John used his left infrequently. Still, at one point, Sullivan told Lannon, "Let her go, Joe, don't be afraid." In the 4th round, Sullivan let himself out a little, landing some stinging rib shots.

After a couple of other exhibitions, Sullivan sparred Taylor, once again mostly keeping his left in reserve. Sullivan "was badly winded, and showed that he was greatly out of training." However, his right remained quite powerful, and one of them crashed across Taylor's face, causing him to reel and stagger off the stage. Sullivan said, "That was a little harder than I intended."

This exhibition was just the start of an Eastern tour with Lannon, Taylor, LaBlanche, Carroll, and McKeon. On March 30, they were in Philadelphia; and on the 31st in Norristown. On April 1, they exhibited in Baltimore, Maryland. On the 3rd, they were in Lancaster, Pennsylvania.[281]

On April 4 in Washington D.C., Sullivan and his combination visited the White House, and John L. met and shook hands with U.S. President Grover Cleveland.

Other cities visited over the next five months (or scheduled to be visited) by the exhibition tour included Harrisburg, Wilkes-Barre, and Connellsville, PA; Youngstown, OH; Wheeling, WV, Columbus and Cincinnati, OH; Evansville, IN; Kalamazoo, Bay City, and Saginaw, MI; Cleveland and Akron, OH; Buffalo and Amsterdam, NY; New Haven and Hartford, CT; Holyoke, Boston, and Brockton, MA; Hartford, CT; and Boston again.

The tour encountered some political/legal difficulties along the way, which limited the number of cities in which they could perform. The mayors of Pittsburgh, Allegheny City, and Erie, Pennsylvania refused to issue the combination licenses, as did the authorities in Springfield, Ohio; Syracuse and Rochester, New York; and New Haven, Connecticut. Some politicians and even members of the press argued that boxing exhibitions were indecent and demoralizing. They were determined to impose their beliefs on others.

---

[281] *National Police Gazette*, April 16, 1887; *Referee* (Sydney), June 16, 1887.

A Title Dispute

On May 7, 1887, Jake Kilrain (whose original name was John Joseph Killion or Killian), backed by Richard K. Fox's *National Police Gazette*, challenged John L. Sullivan to fight for the championship, depositing a $1,000 forfeit with the *New York Clipper.*

Given that he still was touring the East, and because he still was recuperating from his arm injury, Sullivan did not accept Kilrain's challenge.

Kilrain then claimed the championship by default, and of course, Fox's *Police Gazette* recognized his claim. Contrary to popular belief, title disputes have existed since modern boxing's inception.

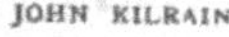
JOHN KILRAIN.

JAKE KILRAIN.

Like Sullivan, Kilrain was the son of Irish immigrants. He was four months younger than Sullivan. Originally, he was a top amateur sculler/oarsman before he took up boxing. Apparently, the 5'10 ½" 180-pound Kilrain and Sullivan had sparred 3 or 4 rounds back in 1880, and Jake received "some hard punishment." They again boxed in an 1882 benefit at Revere Hall in South Boston, when Sullivan agreed to go easy. Sullivan said they met again about two years later at a benefit in Monument Hall, Charlestown. "Godfrey was to have sparred with me, but he wanted too much money, so Kilrain was selected to take his place. Before Kilrain would put on the gloves he made me promise that I would not punish him hard." An 1884 *National Police Gazette* article confirmed that Kilrain "has had several friendly set-tos with John L. Sullivan."

Kilrain held victories over Jem Driscoll, Dan Dwyer, and Dennis Roach, and a KO1 over Harry Allen.

In 1883, Kilrain bested Pete McCoy at a Sullivan benefit.

That same year, Kilrain stopped top American black fighter George Godfrey in the 3rd round of a scheduled 6-round bout.

On March 26, 1884, Kilrain fought Charley Mitchell to a competitive 4-round draw. The *National Police Gazette* then opined that although Jake had acquitted himself well, and it felt that with further development he could be a champion, "at present he is no match for either Sullivan or Mitchell." The *New York Clipper* said that Kilrain performed well against Mitchell, was the aggressor, did most of the fighting, and landed more blows, but Mitchell's punches were more effective.

At that time, Kilrain was "willing to fight any man in the world, barring Sullivan." However, over the next couple of years, Kilrain continued to develop into a fine fighter.

In May 1884, Kilrain scored a KO3 over William Sheriff (bout stopped by the police). Kilrain fought Mike Cleary to a 4-round draw, though the spectators believed that Jake was the better man.

In December 1884, Kilrain fought a 5-round draw against Jack Burke, although once again many said that Kilrain was the better fighter. In late 1884, Kilrain's financier said that he would back Jake against any man in the world, except for Sullivan.

Kilrain scored a KO2 over 200-pound Jerry Murphy.

In 1885, Kilrain scored a KO3 over Jem McGlynn.

In 1886, Kilrain won an 8-round decision over Jack Ashton (who had 15 victories), scored a November KO1 over recent Sullivan title challenger Frank Herald (bout stopped by police after Herald down and hurt), and a

KO2 against Joe Godfrey (different from George). He also won some miscellaneous 4-round bouts, including KO4 Tom Kelley and W4 Denny Killeen, who was decked 15 times.

On March 8, 1887, Kilrain knocked out Joe Lannon in 11 rounds. Lannon had stopped Frank Herald in the 6th round. Kilrain's victory over Lannon convinced the *Police Gazette* that Kilrain had what it took to defeat Sullivan, so it backed his challenge for the championship.[282]

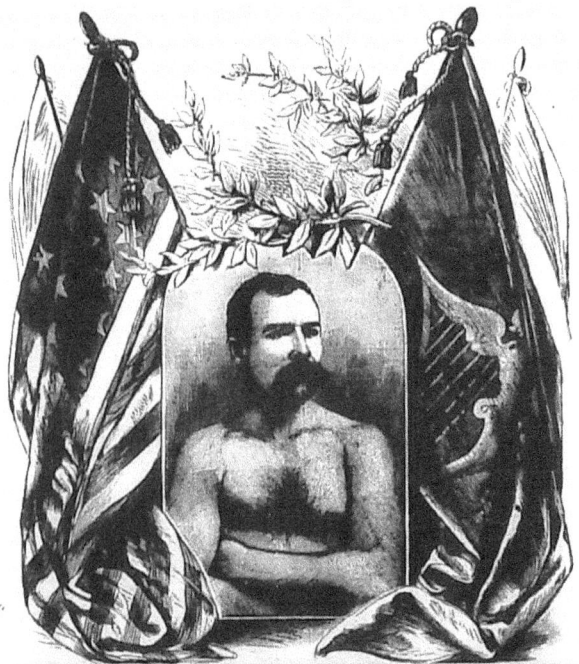

JAKE KILRAIN.

"The modest yet courageous gladiator who took from John L. Sullivan the title and office of champion of the world."

Sullivan's failure to accept Kilrain's challenge only served to boost Kilrain and further market him. Some believed that because he failed to accept the challenge, Sullivan forfeited his title. In June 1887, the *New York Clipper* (which held the forfeit money posted by Kilrain) wrote, "John L. Sullivan having, for some reasons which cannot have any weight in sporting law and usage, declined to accept the challenge regularly issued by Jake Kilrain, the title of champion-pugilist of America…is forfeited to the challenger." Hence, both the *Clipper* and the *Police Gazette* boosted Kilrain as the new champion.[283]

---

[282] *National Police Gazette,* March 29, 1884, April 12, 1884, July 12, 1884, November 15, 1884, November 27, 1886, November 5, 1887; *New York Clipper,* April 5, 1884, May 17, 1884; *Daily Alta California,* December 31, 1888; *Evening World, Boston Daily Globe, San Francisco Daily Examiner,* July 8, 1889. Kilrain and Godfrey met again many years later, in 1891, and Kilrain scored a 44th round knockout.

[283] *New York Clipper,* June 11, 1887.

On June 4, 1887 inside Kernan's Monumental Theatre in Baltimore, *National Police Gazette* editor William Harding presented Kilrain with the *Police Gazette* diamond championship belt.

When asked what he thought about Kilrain receiving the championship belt, a nonplussed Sullivan called the belt a "dog collar." Nevertheless, on a consistent basis, Fox would continue to promote Kilrain as the champion.

On June 7, 1887, Sullivan's combination of sparrers exhibited in Boston. Sully boxed with Lannon and Taylor. He again boxed with them on June 9 in Brockton, Massachusetts. The tour continued.

On July 4, 1887 in Hartford, Connecticut, after umpiring a baseball game there, Sullivan sparred with Lannon. That was the final exhibition of his current tour.[284]

The general public and most of the world did not necessarily recognize Jake Kilrain's claim to the title. In Australia, the *Referee* wrote,

> As soon as the unprecedented bruiser John L. Sullivan broke his arm a new aspirant for the boxing championship instantly arose. ... In America, Fox seems to be the despot of sport. ... [T]he despot decided that in spite of everything, Kilrain was to be champion. ... This was harmless ambition, and no doubt Sullivan smilingly calculated at the time what a deal of cheap advertising the new aspirant was getting, and what a big house there would be when they met.[285]

Fox matched Kilrain to meet England's Jem Smith for the world championship in a traditional LPR bout to be held in Europe. In 1886, Smith had fought Alf Greenfield to a 13-round LPR draw, when the fight was terminated by Greenfield's fans breaking into the ring. Most considered Smith to have had the best of matters.

Speaking about the scheduled Smith - Kilrain championship fight, Sullivan said, "[I]t is a big advertising scheme by a certain very foxy newspaper manager. Pugilists in general take no stock in it, and I hear it seldom discussed among those with whom I associate. Championships won by wind are frail honors."[286]

Perhaps to counter what the *Police Gazette* had done with Kilrain, on August 8, 1887 in Boston at the Boston Theater, 3,000 people watched Sullivan receive the most costly championship belt ever made. Pat Sheedy had managed to raise donations from Bostonians who were perturbed by the fact that Kilrain had a belt. They wanted to bestow an even more gaudy and impressive belt upon Sullivan. It was valued at about $8,000, four times the annual wage of a skilled laborer, or thirty times the average yearly income of a local citizen. The belt contained a centerplate of a large shield made of solid 14-carat gold. The shield was surrounded by six flags, two

---

[284] Sullivan at 133.

[285] *Referee*, August 4, 1887.

[286] *San Francisco Daily Examiner*, August 8, 1887.

each for America, Ireland, and England. At the top of the shield was a solid gold American eagle with its wings spread. The smaller panels, four on each side (symbolic for the eight stakes of a prize ring), bore images of Sullivan in ring costume, photos of Sheedy and Sullivan, Irish symbols such as the harp, shamrock, and flag, and the American shield and Stars and Stripes flag. The panels were checkered with diamonds. Inscribed on the main shield in block letters was, "Presented to the Champion of Champions, John L. Sullivan, by the Citizens of Boston, July 4, 1887." Sullivan's name was encrusted with about 256 diamonds. Above his name was a three-carat diamond. Other smaller stones surrounded the shield. The belt was almost four feet long and weighed about 30 pounds. No doubt, John L. Sullivan was the people's champion.

Present were Sullivan's father and Mayor Hugh O'Brien. A poem entitled "Our John" was read. To accept the belt, as the band played "Hail to the Chief," Sullivan stepped forward with Sheedy and Councilman William Benjamin Franklin Whall. John L. received a huge ovation. Speeches were given, and then the belt was placed around Sullivan's waist. Sullivan confirmed his love for Boston and his pals. "I remain, as ever, your devoted friend, John L. Sullivan."

Then he sparred 3 rounds each with Mike Donovan and Steve Taylor. The benefit generated about $4,000 for Sullivan, in addition to the belt.[287]

Later that year, Mike Donovan spoke about Sullivan and offered his observations of him from their August sparring. Donovan told a reporter that Sullivan had "wonderfully improved in science of late."

> He told me to hit him as hard as I could, and I gave him two or three right-hand swipes on the jaw that ought to have felled a bull, but they never fazed him. He holds his hands higher and better than he did, and he is the cleverest big man the ring ever saw. He ducked away from several blows with a quickness that astonished me. He can stand off ten feet and fiddle in a way that disconcerts you and breaks your guard. Then he comes at you like a battering-ram, you get it on the jaw and down you go. You can't help it.[288]

In late August, Donovan discussed Sullivan's personality and early career, of which he had intimate knowledge:

---

[287] *St. Paul Daily Globe*, *New York Sun*, August 9, 1887; *New York Clipper*, August 13, 1887; *Referee* (Sydney), October 26, 1892; Sullivan at 133 claimed the belt was worth $8,000.
[288] *San Francisco Chronicle*, September 26, 1887.

I don't believe that any man in this world has been more extensively lied about than John L. Sullivan. I travelled in John's company for a long time, and I was with him constantly, and, while I don't mean to set him up as a Chesterfield or the paragon of politeness, I will say that he is one of the best natured and most amiable of men. The papers have published so many wild and fantastic stories about him that people have an idea that Sullivan is a sort of unnatural monster that goes around raising rows from one end of the country to the other, is always surly and ugly, and lacks the elements that makes our men popular. I have known Sullivan longer than any of the rest of them, and when I speak of him I speak by the card.

Long before he ever fought Flood, or before even sporting men had heard his name, I knew him in Boston. He did not look big or strong then. … He wanted to put on the gloves with me one night in a theatre where I was playing an engagement. Nobody knew him and everybody knew me. I looked him over, and as he seemed to be very much in earnest, and had the right spirit in him, I told him to come around at 8 o'clock and I would give him a set-to. He came, and he had evidently made up his mind to do me. He did not know much about fighting then, but he came about as near using yours truly up as any man that ever lived. … He had the same terrific hitting power then as he has now. We left our corners and I led out on him. The next thing I knew I got a terrific clip on the top of the head that knocked me backward as though I had been hit with a slingshot. I lay on the stage for a minute trying to realize what had hit me. I was groggy then, and seized Sullivan's legs to steady myself and slowly got to my feet. I saw in an instant that I must pull myself together, because there was a raw man in front of me who had nothing to lose and everything to gain, while I had a life's reputation at stake. I saw that if Sullivan did me in that round it would fix his position at once, and undo all that I had been at so much pains to accomplish. I thought this out as well as I could with the terrible humming at my head, and then they called time, and we came together again. I was knocked down twice in that round. Then I knew I had got to fight as I had never fought before to get out with a whole skin. The next three rounds we went at it hammer and tongs. Sullivan had very little science at that time and that is what saved me. But it was the closest call that a man ever had in this business. It was only by the utmost skill, by dodging and feinting continually, that I escaped his terrific sledgehammer blows, and so I managed to last out the five rounds and save my reputation. I went outside and told some friends of mine that Sullivan was the greatest fighter in the world at that time. They laughed at me, but they believe it now.

Donovan said that Sullivan had improved his skill over time, and now was a clever scientific fighter and a shrewd man.

Donovan also said that Sullivan did not have an ugly temper. If he had been drinking or was up late the night before, he was crusty and sullen, as anyone would be. But the newspaper stories of his being snappish, brutal, and ugly were all nonsense.

When folks would rush to the platform at train stations, wanting to see Sullivan,

> Al Smith and myself or somebody would be very likely to ask Sullivan to go out on the platform and show himself to the crowd, and he always did it, lounging about in a good-natured way, while they cheered him and stared at him to their hearts' content. It was pure good nature on his part, because he is not a man who cares to show off at all.

In Memphis, Sullivan was scheduled to go up against a big and powerful local champion with a fair knowledge of boxing and lots of grit. He attacked, and Sullivan quickly decked him twice. The fellow laid on the stage like a log. "I thought the man had been killed. He lay as dead as a stone, and the 5,000 citizens of Memphis…were as quiet as so many graven images." Donovan doused the man with water from a pail. A concerned Sullivan took the fighter in his arms as if he were a baby. Finally, the man's eyes slightly opened, and Sullivan carried him in his arms down the steps and took him to the dressing room. Halfway there, the crowd cheered Sullivan so loudly that it almost lifted the building's roof. [This likely was the William Fleming fight.]

> They were going to kill Sullivan when he struck the blow that knocked out their pride and champion, but when they saw how tenderly he cared for the vanquished man they almost made a god of him. … You can't tell me that a man has got no tact who will turn a crowd of 5,000 enemies into as many warm admirers as he did that day by a little stroke of humanity and tact.[289]

[289] *Omaha Daily Bee*, August 23, 1887.

The United Kingdom

In late 1887, recognized by the *Police Gazette* and the *New York Clipper* as the American champion, Jake Kilrain traveled to Great Britain to give exhibitions there with his trainer Charlie Mitchell, before fighting then English champion Jem Smith in a world heavyweight championship fight under LPR rules.

OUR CHAMPION AND HIS VICTORIES.

Jake Kilrain, the Brave Boy From Baltimore, Who Will Represent America In The Great International Battle With Jem Smith of England, and Some of the Historic Contests in Which He First Came Into Victorious Prominence

In late August 1887, John L. Sullivan and manager Pat Sheedy split, the result of both financial and personal reasons. Sullivan felt shortchanged in the payment he was receiving, and did not care for Sheedy's ordering him around and making himself the star of the show. Sheedy was fed up with Sullivan's drinking. Apparently, during the second half of August, Sullivan and his pals had been having a "high time" at Nantasket beach.[290]

In October, Sullivan hired Harry Phillips to manage his planned European tour through England, Ireland, Scotland, and Wales. Interestingly enough, the timing coincided with the Smith – Kilrain fight, also scheduled to be held in Europe. Not only was the tour scheduled for money-making purposes, but also to allow Europeans to compare Sullivan with Kilrain and Smith, so they could see who the real champion was.

On October 27, 1887 at 8 a.m. in Boston, Sullivan set sail on the steamer *Cephalonia*, heading to Liverpool, England to start his long

290 *St. Paul Daily Globe*, September 3, 1887.

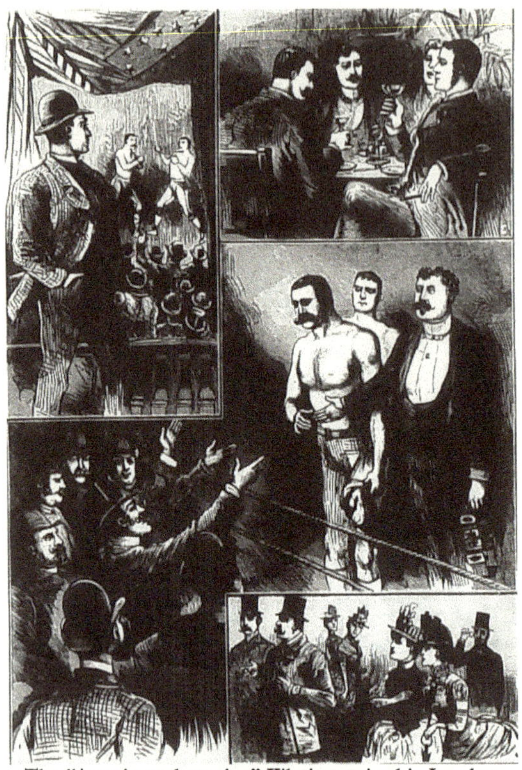

The "American champion" Kilrain received in London, the English capital, with all the honors of a king

contemplated European tour. "The pomp and circumstance attending the great pugilist's departure were simply stupendous." Bands played tunes such as "Wearing of the Green" and "Hail to the Chief." Sullivan shook hands with his admirers. Present were John L.'s father Michael, mother Catherine, brother Michael, and the champ's sister Annie Lennon (her married name). John L.'s father said, "John may be a bit wild at times, but he has ever been a good boy to me and his mother." With the champ on the voyage would be sparring partner Jack Ashton (who had lost a close 1886 8-round decision to Kilrain), John Barnett, and Harry Phillips, as well as John L.'s "wife" Annie (Livingston).

Sullivan said that while in Europe, he wanted to fight Charley Mitchell "and shut him up," as well as Kilrain or Jem Smith.[291]

On November 5, 1887, Sullivan arrived at Queenstown in the British Isles, before heading to Liverpool, arriving there on the 6th. He was met by prominent members of the sporting fraternity, including Alf Greenfield. Thousands cheered him. He stayed at the Grand Hotel.

Once he arrived in London on November 7, Sullivan made a brief speech to the crowd of about 5,000 which greeted him at the train station. "Gentlemen, I'm very thankful to you all, and on Wednesday I hope you'll all come and see the best exhibition you ever saw in your lives. I am yours truly, John L. Sullivan." He then was taken to the Salisbury Hotel. Huge crowds followed him wherever he went. The Pelican Club made him an honorary member.

Sullivan was scheduled to meet with Charlie Mitchell to arrange a match. John L. said he intended to return to the U.S. as champion or die.[292]

---

[291] *New York World*, October 27, 1887; *New York Sun*, October 28, 1887; *New York Clipper*, November 5, 1887.

[292] *New York Sun*, November 8, 1887; Sullivan at 135-136.

Although Sullivan had brought with him the championship belt recently endowed upon him, because the customs officers wanted to impose an import duty of 120 pounds, or $600, Sullivan left the belt in the Queen's bonded warehouse, where it would remain until he set sail to return to America. Interestingly enough, Kilrain's belt, given to him by Richard K. Fox, only received a tax of 7 pounds 7 shillings.

On November 9, 1887 inside St. James Hall in London, Sullivan gave his first public exhibition in England. The 1,800 in attendance included many noblemen, all of whom paid double the usual prices for Sullivan's exhibitions. England's champion Jem Smith was present, and he introduced Sullivan, who received tremendous applause. John L. thanked the audience and said he hoped to fight and defeat Smith, but also that he hoped the best man may win. He further wished Smith success in his go with Kilrain, which was scheduled to be held in December. Smith said that he would do his best to defeat both Kilrain and Sullivan.

Bare-chested with pink silk tights and a silk American flag wrapped around his waist as a belt, a 222- or 230-pound Sullivan sparred 4 rounds with heavyweight Jack Ashton. In the 1st round, they went at it hammer and tongs, and John L.'s rushes delighted the audience. "That Ashton stood up under such hurricane blows proves that he is a tough one." Sully banged him about the stage. The 2nd and 3rd rounds were spirited as well. "Several times Sullivan said to Ashton, 'Don't be afraid, give it to me,' and Ashton complied to the best of his ability, but he was scarcely more than a child in the bean-eater's hands." After the 3rd round, they shook hands, and it appeared to be over, but the audience begged for another round, and the pugilists granted their wish, boxing a hotly contested 4th round.

Jack Ashton

It was said that Jem Smith smiled when he had seen Kilrain spar, but he did not smile when he watched Sullivan. Afterwards, Smith said, "Well, he's a big 'un and a good 'un."

Every impartial judge was convinced that "Sullivan is what Americans know he is, the man appointed by nature to knock his fellows out." The English were impressed. "Exclamations of amazement at Sullivan's agility, considering his weight and condition and hard work of the previous rounds, were heard on every side." A club member said, "Sullivan, why he's a cat and a locomotive combined."[293]

Sullivan quoted a next-day local newspaper as saying that Ashton was about the same stature as himself, though lighter.

> While both men were remarkably quick and agile, the rapidity and springiness of Sullivan's movements created the deepest impression, and evoked universal admiration. It can readily be understood, even by those who saw no more than last night's exhibition, why few of the American champion's antagonists have been able to keep the field after the third or fourth round. Once an opportunity occurs he delivers a perfect bombardment of blows with a speed which the eye can scarcely follow. In attack he seems literally to throw himself upon an opponent with puzzling and disconcerting suddenness and impetuosity.[294]

Sullivan was scheduled to tour England, with appearances in Birmingham on November 12 and 14, Sheffield on the 17th, Wolverhampton on the 18th, Leicester on the 19th and 21st, Bolton on the 22nd, Manchester on the 23rd, Leeds on the 24th, and then a twelve-night engagement in London. Each time he would box Jack Ashton, unless some local boxers could be found willing or able to box him. In his autobiography, Sullivan said that he also exhibited in Liverpool, Newcastle-on-Tyne, Nottingham, Derby, Preston, and Oldham.[295]

On November 12 in Birmingham, England, between 8,000 and 9,000 spectators attended the Sullivan combination exhibition show. First, John L. sparred the clever boxer Ashton, who "was let off lightly." The wind-up was between Sullivan and former opponent Alf Greenfield. During their 3 rounds of sparring, Sullivan "used his left with good effect, and made one or two of his hurricane rushes. The set-to was generally of a light, but scientific character, Greenfield making a very creditable display."

John L. said that the two Birmingham exhibitions had brought together 19,000 people total. A writer for the *Birmingham Gazette* said,

> Kilrain and Mitchell have been completely snuffed out by the arrival in Birmingham of John L. Sullivan. The name of Sullivan has been a household word in the mouths of pugilists on both sides of the Atlantic for years. It is small wonder, then, that his admirers – and they are many – should give him a welcome scarcely accorded to a royal prince. Sullivan is certainly a superior class of pugilist.

Wherever he appeared, Sullivan was received warmly by large crowds.

---

293 *New York Tribune*, *New York Sun*, November 10, 1887; *New York Clipper*, November 19, 1887.

294 Sullivan at 137.

295 *New York Clipper*, November 19, 1887; Sullivan at 137-138.

In Wolverhampton, Sullivan's "brilliant display of science and his finely built form" in sparring against Ashton was "greatly admired." "His quickness in attack and marvelous defense was the subject of admiration, and the way in which he delivered his blows was watched with the greatest interest." Their scientific exhibition brought forth great applause.[296]

After his Nottingham exhibition, Sullivan visited Cardiff, Wales. While there, someone asked him, "You don't attach much value to the diamond belt in the possession of Kilrain?" Sullivan replied, "No, it is only a dog-collar. As I said before, its real value is only about thirty pounds, and if I win it I intend to offer it for competition among the New York boot-blacks."[297]

In late November, Sullivan returned to London to exhibit there.

On November 29, 1887, Sullivan and Charley Mitchell signed an agreement to fight with bare knuckles for $2,500 a side. Sullivan wanted the ring limited to 16 feet, but Mitchell insisted on the regulation LPR rules 24-foot ring. "Mitchell taunted Sullivan repeatedly, one remark so incensing the American that he proposed that they settle the matter by a fight on the spot, but wiser counsels prevailed." Mitchell was a talker.

Sullivan said Mitchell disputed and negotiated every article, which caused the transaction to take several hours. When Mitchell entered the room, he told his friends, "Now boys, I have got him." When Mitchell insisted on the larger-sized ring, Phillips said, "You are not signing for a foot-race, Mitchell." Sullivan added, "And I am not a sprinter." However, eventually Sullivan gave in. John L. later wrote, "During the whole two hours, Mitchell had been taunting me in the most outrageous manner. Finally he called me a dirty rogue." That was when Sully sprang to his feet and offered to fight him that day, calling Mitchell a "young whelp."[298]

One has to wonder why Sullivan agreed to an LPR fight. Clearly, with the Kilrain – Smith LPR fight on the horizon, billed as a true championship

---

[296] *New York Clipper,* December 3, 1887, quoting *London Sportsman*, *Birmingham Gazette*, and *Sporting Life*; Sullivan at 138.
[297] Sullivan at 139.
[298] Sullivan at 150.

fight, Sullivan sought to counteract that bout with an LPR championship fight of his own. Sullivan was not one to allow others to outdo him. Hence, once again the purists had induced him to engage in an LPR fight.

In the meantime, in the U.S., the *National Police Gazette* continued hyping the Jake Kilrain – Jem Smith championship fight. "America's real and indisputable champion" Kilrain was visiting various towns throughout Great Britain, giving exhibitions with Charlie Mitchell, and training for the big fight. Hence, the Brits were able to see Kilrain, Sullivan, and Mitchell.

HOW THE AMERICAN CHAMPION IS MADE READY FOR THE GREAT INTERNATIONAL BATTLE.

On December 5, 1887, Sullivan began the second week of his London engagement at the Royal Aquarium. The admission prices were doubled, but nevertheless the house was full. "His performances during the preceding week yielded a profit of over $500 per night."

Sullivan was scheduled to be giving almost daily exhibitions. His plan was to continue exhibiting until late January, when he would go into training for the Mitchell fight.[299]

On December 8, 1887 at the London Royal Aquarium, Sullivan and Ashton gave their regular exhibition, but then afterwards they gave a separate, private exhibition at the Pelican Club, of which the champion had been made an honorary member. At that exhibition, a letter from the Captain of the Scots Guards was read, inviting Sullivan to breakfast the next morning to meet the Prince of Wales, "who has repeatedly expressed the desire to make your personal acquaintance."

Sullivan meets the Prince of Wales

On December 9, 1887 at the London Fencing Club, at a private exhibition, Sullivan first met and spoke with, and then later changed clothes and sparred for His Royal Highness, Edward, the Prince of Wales, heir to the throne, as well as various noblemen, including Lord Randolph Churchill, father of future prime-minister Winston Churchill.

First, the heavily muscled Jem Smith sparred Alf Greenfield, showing power, accuracy, and aggression, demonstrating his superiority over Greenfield, making a great impression. (The earlier proposal to have Smith spar Sullivan was vetoed when Sullivan refused to take it easy on him, saying, "If Smith gets up before me, I'll knock the head off him if I can.") Then Sullivan, announced as the champion of the world, sparred Ashton.

The Prince was "duly impressed by the massiveness of the Bostonian, his skillful and powerful boxing, and the wonderful agility displayed by him." He led the applause, and was seconded heartily. The Prince said, "He is the quickest big man I ever saw." "I never saw anything like him in the world. He's a marvel of a man, altogether out of the ordinary run."

---

299 *New York Clipper*, December 10, 1887.

When asked what would happen if John L. met Jem Smith, the Prince said, "Sullivan has the weight, the height, the reach, and undoubted pluck. How can anybody compete with him?" Harry Phillips injected, "That put together generally wins the fight, does not it?" The Prince replied, "Well, of course I am an Englishman and want Smith to win. That is, of course, officially I disapprove of prize-fighting entirely, and would be grieved if it came off in the United Kingdom." Sir William Cumming said, "I should expect Sullivan, with those awful blows, to knock Smith out in the first three rounds." Jack Ashton said that Sullivan would knock out Smith with ease, particularly since Smith seemed to be game and wiling to mix it up, something that would prove fatal when fighting Sullivan. "Smith is a good young fellow and strong and lively, but he'll only want to rush at Sullivan like that once. That'll be enough. John will land him on the jaw. He'll make him turn a somersault, and there'll be no more fight that day."

When asked what he thought of the Prince, Sullivan said, "He is a nice, sociable fellow, with splendid manners; he is a splendid good all-round man. He is the sort of man you like to meet anywhere, at any time." Sullivan and the Prince got along very well. John L. told the prince to "look me up" if he ever came to Boston, and he would show him around.[300]

On December 11, 1887, Sullivan arrived in Dublin, Ireland. The Irish-American Sullivan said that 15,000 people gathered at the steamboat landing for his reception. They cheered and called his name, and two brass bands played music, including "See the Conquering Hero Comes!" and "The Wearing of the Green." They followed him to his hotel. From the Grosvenor Hotel veranda, Sullivan said to the crowd, "I thank you for your kindness to me this evening. As a descendant of Erin's Isle, I will endeavor always to prove myself worthy of your attention and to uphold the honor of my father's native land." The Irish adored him.

Over the course of the next week in Ireland, Sullivan would exhibit with Ashton. On the 12th in Dublin, Sullivan refereed amateur bouts before sparring 4 rounds with Ashton.

Sullivan also received enthusiastic receptions in Waterford, Cork, Limerick, Dublin again (at Leinster Hall), and Belfast, Richard K. Fox's birthplace. Sullivan said that he earned more money in one week in Ireland than he did in six weeks in England.[301]

24-year-old Jem Smith stood 5'8 ½" and weighed around 182 pounds trained, or 212 pounds untrained. Supposedly, Smith was undefeated since beginning his career in 1881. Amongst his many victories, in 1883, Smith defeated Bill Davis in 1 hour. In 1884, Smith defeated Harry Arnold in a hard-glove fight in 55 minutes (14 rounds), and Woolf Bendoff in 48 minutes (12 rounds). In 1885, Smith quickly knocked out Jack Davis, who did not wake up for two hours.

---

300 *New York Sun*, December 10, 1887; *New York Clipper*, December 17, 1887; Sullivan at 144.
301 Sullivan at 146-148.

Jake Kilrain Provides A Little Innocent Amusement For Some Of His Lady Callers
He Puts On the Gloves With Charlie Mitchell, His Second and Trainer, and To the Great Delight of the Spectators Gives Him A Good Rattling

As the Two Champions Will Appear In the Great International Fight
Jake Kilrain, the American Hero, and Jem Smith, the Heavy-Weight Pugilist of England, Who Will Battle For Richard K. Fox's Magnificent "Police Gazette" Diamond Belt, $10,000 in Gold and The Championship of the World

In February 1886, in a fight for the English championship, Smith got the better of Alf Greenfield over 1 hour 8 minutes. However, when Greenfield's supporters saw defeat looming large, they broke into the ring, causing the bout to be declared a draw, although Greenfield was "carried senseless from the ring."[302]

[302] *National Police Gazette*, March 6, 1886; *Referee* (Sydney), December 18, 1889.

As a result of his performance against Greenfield, there was some discussion regarding a potential Smith vs. Sullivan match. Sullivan said if Smith wanted to win the world's championship, he needed to come to America to fight him, but it appeared that Smith either was unwilling or unable to travel to the U.S.[303]

On Monday December 19, 1887 on the Isle des Souverains in the River Seine, France, Jake Kilrain fought English champion Jem Smith in a bareknuckle LPR fight. The 184-pound Kilrain (who ordinarily weighed about 210 pounds) proved his skill, conditioning, and toughness by fighting the 180-pound Smith in a marathon 2-hour 30-minute 106-round bareknuckle fight that ended in a draw due to darkness. Observers agreed that Kilrain had the best of the contest. Primarily, it was a wrestling match, with the rounds often terminating as a result of the combatants throwing each other down. However, Kilrain won nearly every fall, and also scored multiple knockdowns as the result of punches. He had punished Smith. Charley Mitchell, Pony Moore, and Ned Donnelly seconded Kilrain.[304]

OUR CHAMPION DOWNED THE BRITON EVERY TIME.

Jake Kilrain, the Police Gazette's Great Champion, Throws Jem Smith Every Time They Wrestled In the International Fight, To the Surprise Of Those Who Witnessed the American's Wonderful Skill

The *National Police Gazette* treated the draw like a de facto victory for Kilrain, for most everyone considered Kilrain to have been the superior pugilist. The *National Police Gazette* continued hyping a potential Kilrain - Sullivan match, calling Kilrain the real world champion and the man with

303 *Brooklyn Daily Eagle*, March 14, 1886.
304 *National Police Gazette*, January 21, 1888.

the skill, size, strength, endurance, and toughness necessary to defeat Sullivan. His performance against Smith only served to convince Richard K. Fox further that he was the man to beat Sullivan. Fox said he would back Kilrain for up to $10,000.[305]

JAKE KILRAIN TOO MUCH FOR JEM SMITH.

THE REAL CHAMPION OF THE WORLD.

JAKE KILRAIN, AMERICA'S PEERLESS REPRESENTATIVE, WHO WAS ONLY PREVENTED BY DARKNESS FROM KNOCKING OUT JEM SMITH OF ENGLAND IN THE GREAT INTERNATIONAL FIGHT.

305 *New York Sun*, December 20, 1887.

JEM SMITH YIELDS THE HONOR TO JAKE KILRAIN.

THE NATIONAL POLICE GAZETTE

THE WORLD'S CHAMPION

THE LEADING ILLUSTRATED SPORTING JOURNAL IN AMERICA.

Copyrighted for 1888 by RICHARD K. FOX, Proprietor POLICE GAZETTE PUBLISHING HOUSE, Franklin Square, New York.

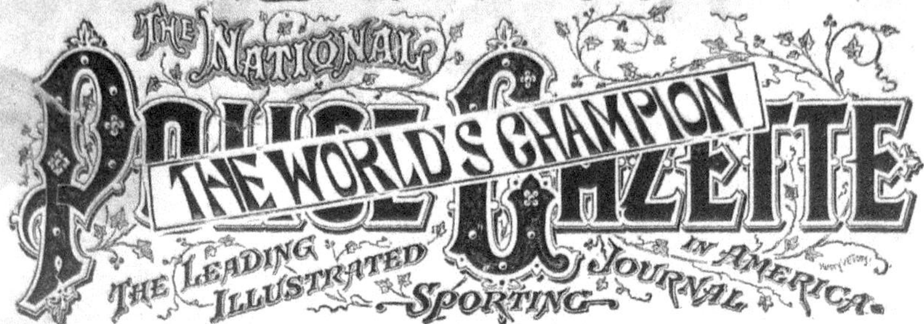

RICHARD K. FOX, Editor and Proprietor. | NEW YORK, SATURDAY, JANUARY 7, 1888. | VOLUME LI.—No. 538. Price Ten Cents.

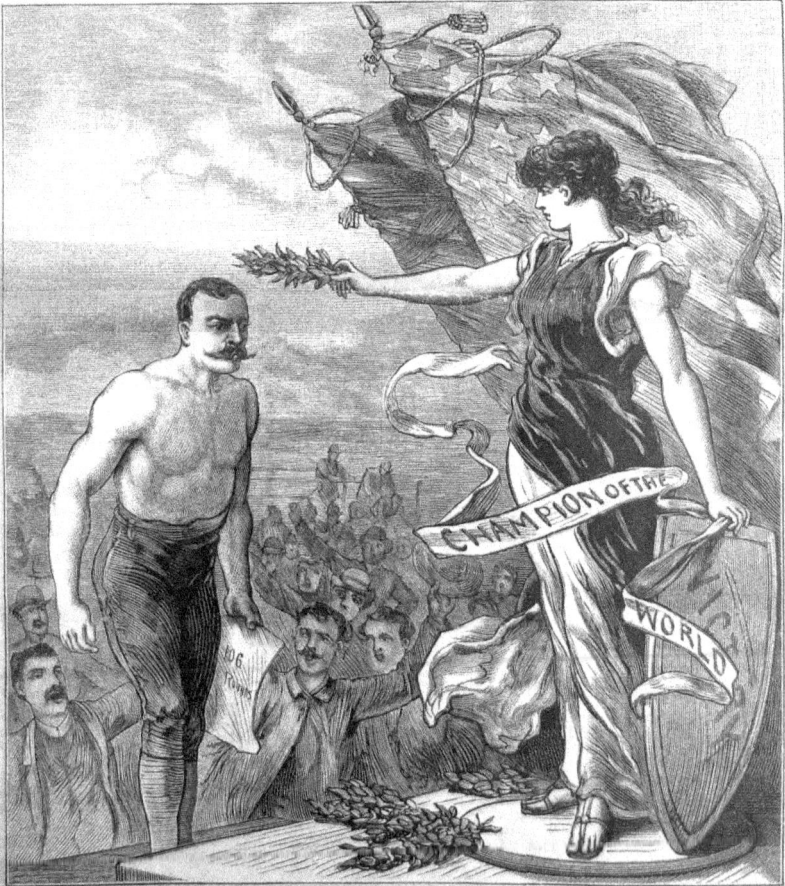

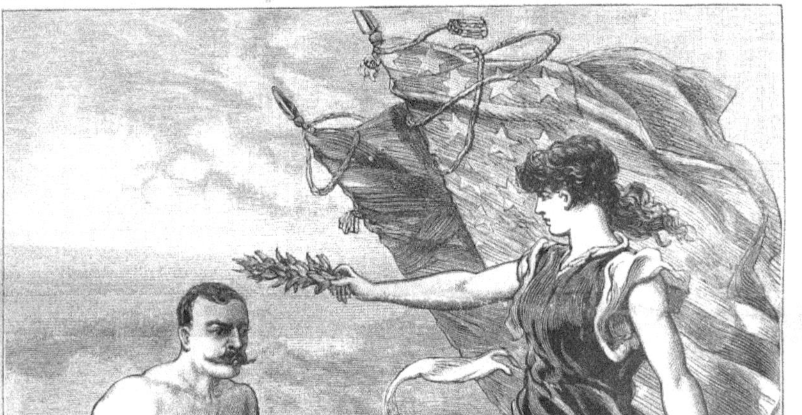

HAIL TO THE VICTOR.

COLUMBIA CROWNS THE MODEST BROW OF THE GLADIATOR WHO BRINGS HER BACK THE CHAMPIONSHIP OF THE WORLD.

KILRAIN HAD MUCH THE BEST OF IT.

The Wonderful American Champion Outfights Jem Smith, England's Best Man, 106 Terrific Rounds on the Island of St. Pierre, River Seine, France, Until Darkness Compels the Referee to Make the Battle a Draw

THE GLADIATOR AND HIS TROPHY.

The World's Champion Is A Victor In Another Kind Of Contest
Jake Kilrain, America's Peerless Gladiator, Beats His Late Antagonist, Jem Smith, At A Game of Billiards In the Palatial Home of "Pony" Moore

Kilrain's Christmas Gift
The Valorous Champion of the World Receives a Cablegram from Richard K. Fox, Presenting Him with Six Thousand Dollars, as a Tribute to His Courage

ONE RING FIGHT WON'T DO.

JOHN BULL TO BLUFFER SULLIVAN—"SEE HERE, IF YOU'RE A CHAMPION YOU MUST HAVE A GO ONCE IN A WHILE IN THE REGULAR OLD RING STYLE. THIS GLOVE BUSINESS WON'T WORK OVER HERE, SO COME OFF."

In the meantime, John L. Sullivan's exhibition tour was continuing. In Scotland, he visited Glasgow, Dundee, Aberdeen, and Edinburgh. While in Edinburgh, Sullivan said, "My desire is to fight Kilrain. I whipped him once and can do it again, and well they know it." Sullivan's manager Phillips offered to back Sullivan against either Kilrain or Smith.[306]

On Thursday January 5, 1888, the Sullivan combination appeared in Cardiff, Wales. Sullivan sparred with Ashton, and also had a set-to with a local boxer named William Samuells. Sullivan "toyed with him during the first two rounds." The crowd cheered the local man, thinking that he was doing well, on the merits. However, it soon became clear that Sullivan had been carrying Samuells. In the 3rd round,

> [Sullivan] let himself out just once, but the blow he planted on Mr. Samuells' caput proved sufficient to lay him flat and knock all the fight out of him. When he rose from the floor…the local boxer stepped to the front of the stage and acknowledged that he was no sort of a match for Sullivan, whom he was convinced had simply been playing with him before putting the right mauley where it would do the most good.[307]

On January 10, 1888 in Portsmouth, England, Sullivan's successful exhibition tour came to a close. John L. claimed to have boxed in 51 exhibitions during his tour, and to have cleared 5,000 pounds.[308]

At that point, Sullivan would go into training for the Mitchell fight.[309]

---

[306] *New York Sun*, December 21, 1887; *Brooklyn Daily Eagle*, December 23, 1887.
[307] *New York Clipper*, January 14, 1888.
[308] Sullivan at 138, 148.
[309] On January 31, 1888 in Jersey City, world middleweight champion Jack Dempsey, the "Nonpareil," won a 10-round decision over Dominick McCaffrey.

Bareknuckle Again

In January 1888, John L. Sullivan began formal training for his bareknuckle London Prize Ring Rules fight with Charley Mitchell, scheduled to be held in early March 1888.

In his fights, Mitchell always had shown skill, speed, power, and footwork. In 1883, although Sullivan had knocked down and badly hurt Mitchell, stopping him in 3 rounds under Queensberry rules, Mitchell had scored a flash knockdown, the only time that Sullivan ever had been down. In 1884, Mitchell fought Jake Kilrain to a 4-round draw. An 1884 rematch with Sullivan was scheduled, but John L. had shown up drunk, or ill, and called off the match. That same year, Mitchell lost a close and disputed 4-round decision to Dominick McCaffrey. He ended the year by boxing Jack Burke to a 4-round draw.

In 1885, Mitchell was defeating Mike Cleary when the police stopped it in the 4th round, causing the bout to be declared a draw. Mitchell then fought 6- and 10-round draws with Burke. In May and July 1886, authorities in Chicago and New York prevented attempts at a rematch with Sullivan. Mitchell then fought a 5-round draw with Patsy Cardiff. Mitchell had fought various other bouts, and had boxed in several exhibitions with Jem Smith and Jake Kilrain.[310]

Mitchell was in good shape already. He had sparred and trained with Kilrain, helping to prepare Jake for the Smith fight. Kilrain would return the favor by assisting Mitchell in his preparations for Sullivan. Mitchell trained at the St. Mildred Hotel at Westgate-on-Sea, 60 miles from London.

Sullivan was fairly fit as well, given his daily sparring exhibitions with Jack Ashton. However, he needed to reduce his weight in order to be as efficient as possible for a fight to the finish, and to get into good enough shape to be able to fight for a potentially unlimited duration. He trained at Bull's Royal Adelaide Hotel in Windsor. Every day he walked and/or ran either 6 or 13 miles, shadow boxed with dumbbells, and punched the bags.

While he was training for Mitchell, Sullivan also tried to arrange a bout with Jem Smith, offering to fight either bareknuckle or in a 6-round gloved bout in which Sullivan would forfeit 200 pounds to Smith if he failed to knock him out. His offers were refused. Sullivan said, "Any of the offers I have advanced to Smith are open to Kilrain. Can any man living make more sacrifices or concessions than I have? Surely Smith must come to the front or wilt like a wet rag."[311]

---

310 *Boston Daily Globe*, March 11, 1888.
311 *New York Clipper*, February 4, 1888.

Charley Mitchell, The Champion English Boxer
Has A Rattling Bout With Jake Kilrain, the Gentlemanly American Champion, While Training For His Fight With Boston's Pride, John L. Sullivan

GETTING IN SHAPE FOR HIS CONTEST WITH MITCHELL.

In late February, it was reported that Sullivan was weighing 206 pounds. "It is pretty generally known that when Sullivan arrived here last November he scaled, stripped, 238 pounds, and was very 'beefy.'" Sullivan's diligent training for the Mitchell fight had removed the excess flesh. He was taking 3-hour walks and running 3 or 4 miles, in addition to his other work.[312]

---

312 *New York Clipper*, February 25, 1888.

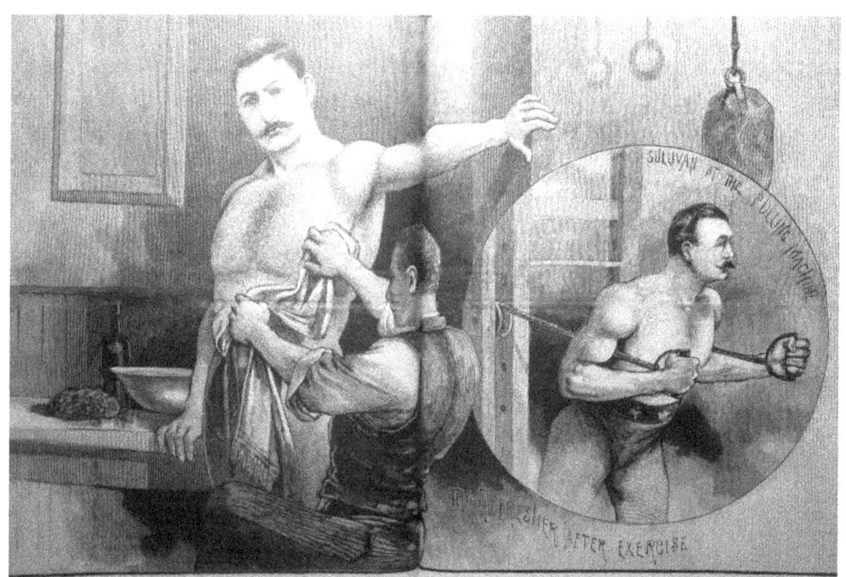

The Giant Pugilist Makes Ready For the Great Fight

The Renowned John L. Sullivan's Final Preparation for His Lively Encounter With Charley Mitchell, the Plucky Englishman and Hard Hitter

THE QUEEN ADMIRES THE BOSTON BOY.

THE BIG AMERICAN BOXER FIGURES IN A NOTABLE INCIDENT IN WINDSOR PARK, ENGLAND.

On March 2, Mitchell was arrested and taken before an English magistrate. The authorities were concerned that the fight might take place on English soil. Mitchell swore that he would not disturb the peace in England, and posted a required 200-pound guarantee bond.

Actually, secretly, Mitchell had won a coin flip and set March 10 in France as the final date and location of the fight.

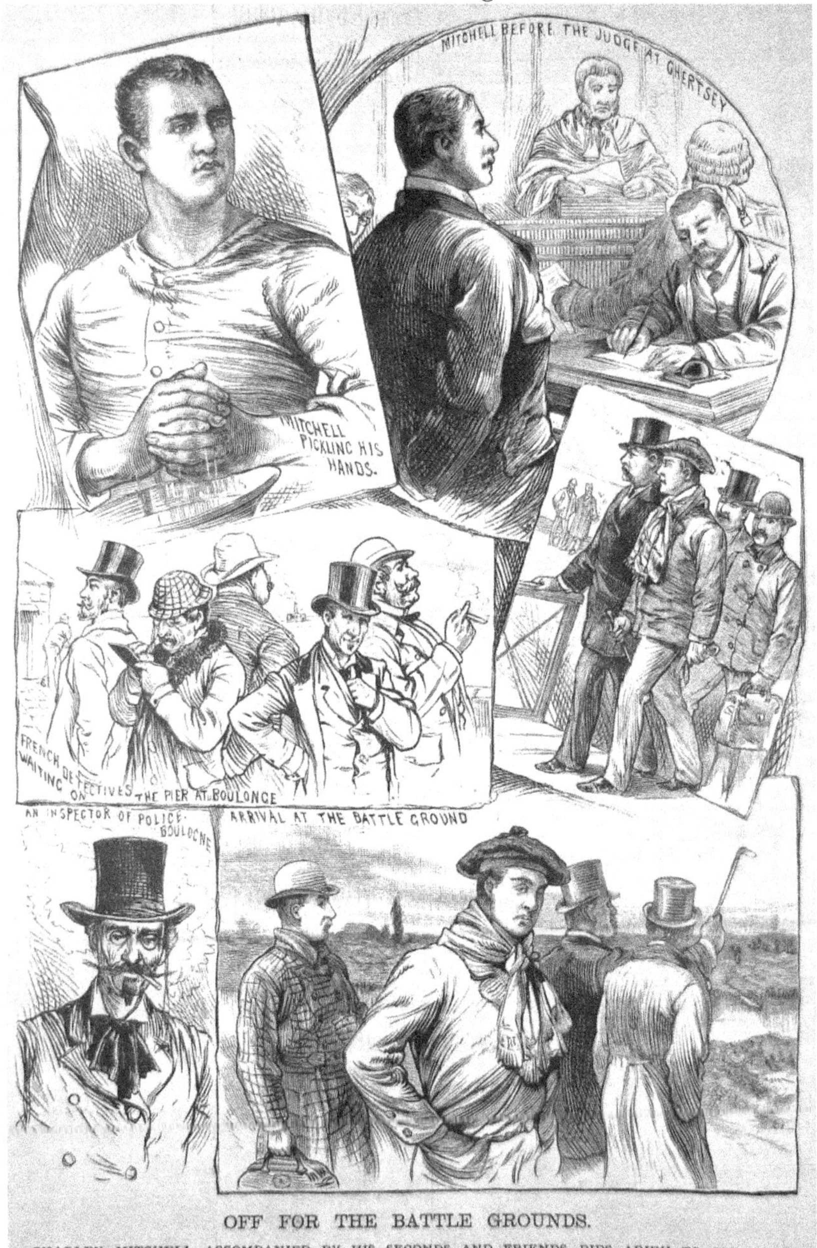

OFF FOR THE BATTLE GROUNDS.

CHARLEY MITCHELL, ACCOMPANIED BY HIS SECONDS AND FRIENDS, BIDS ADIEU TO OLD ENGLAND AND STARTS FOR THE SCENE OF THE GREAT INTERNATIONAL PRIZE RING FIGHT BETWEEN HIM AND AMERICA'S WORLD RENOWNED PUGILIST, JOHN L. SULLIVAN.

On Saturday March 10, 1888, in Apremont, France, over one year after his last defense - against Patsy Cardiff, John L. Sullivan fought a rematch with England's Charles Mitchell, this time under bareknuckle London Prize Ring Rules. It was Sullivan's first bareknuckle fight since his February 1882 contest against Paddy Ryan, six years prior. Sullivan fought the man he called the "bombastic sprinter boxer" for a purse of 500 pounds, or $5,000.

This time, they would fight with their bare hands, the ring would be larger, on turf, and the rounds would end as soon as a fighter went down. Instead of having to rise within 10 seconds unassisted, a knocked down fighter would have 30 seconds for his handlers to assist and revive him, and then another 8 seconds to resume fighting. The fight was to the finish, meaning that they would fight until someone could no longer continue, or a draw or a foul was declared. Hence, there would be no decision on points.

The *New York Herald*, *New York Sun*, and *Referee* had reporters with the fighters.

The night before the fight, the two combatants and their friends slept at Amiens, France.

Early in the morning on the 10th, the fighters and their associates had breakfast, and then at 6 or 6:30 a.m. they left to take a train from Amiens to Creil, about a mile from Chantilly. Actually, in order to deceive the police, they purchased tickets to Paris. However, they all exited the train at Creil, a little town 15 miles from Paris. The precise fight location was kept a secret as long as possible.

The *Herald* said that during their journey on the train, both of the fighters were relaxed, as if they were headed to a picnic. Mitchell laughed and bantered with his father-in-law, Pony Moore. He said, "I expect to show that the American is not such a wonder as the Americans think him to be." Jake Kilrain was quiet and self-contained. Jack Baldock, Mitchell's other second, spoke cheerily. He hinted that their strategy was to weary Sullivan as much as possible. The *Sun* said that before the fight, Mitchell did not deny that he was anxious only to make such a showing as would help his reputation. The feeling was that he did not really believe that he had much of a chance at victory. Nevertheless, Mitchell appeared cheerful, while Sullivan looked serious and determined. On the way to the fight grounds, a confident Sullivan said, "You won't have travelled far before my hands will have spoiled another face."

With Sullivan were his attendants – Jack Ashton, Edward Holske, Jack Barnett, and Sam Blakelock. Around their necks, Sullivan's friends wore his colors – an American flag with an eagle, shamrock, and the harps of Erin.

After the 2-hour train ride, they arrived at Creil. Mitchell, who had won the toss to decide the specific location, which had to be within 1,000 miles of London, had been unable to find a suitable location where there was no danger of interference from the gendarmes. However, Johnny Gideon of the *Sportsman* (who also was a Paris bookmaker) and two of Sullivan's friends had helped find a good fight location – Apremont, which was a few miles from Creil and about a mile from Chantilly.

There was some difficulty in obtaining a sufficient number of carriages at Creil, and several spectators had to walk. Eventually, eight carriages were secured and took most everyone from the train station to Apremont, where the fight would be decided, which was halfway on the road to Chantilly.

The ring had been pitched on Baron Rothschild's grounds at Apremont, behind the stables which faced the Baron's private race course. From either side they were excluded from view by bushes and trees. Hence, the shelter would allow the fight to proceed without interference. Outside the ring, an old church tower and the clock of Creil could be seen. Another writer said the ring was pitched on the edge of a wood at the back of one of the outbuildings on Rothschild's beautiful training grounds. Baron Alphonse Rothschild was the head of a great French banking family.

There was good turf, but the ring location was a little too much in a hollow. Another writer said the ring was pitched on well-rolled clay. Yet another said the ring was pitched on grass.

The ropes and stakes made the ring 24-feet-square, favorable to Mitchell, who was known as a defensive mover, bobber, and dodger.

The morning featured sunshine and warmth, but there were ominous clouds looming above.

At 12:25 p.m., after throwing his hat into the ring, an old prize-fighting custom, Sullivan entered the ring. Five minutes later, at 12:30 p.m., Mitchell followed. Sully wore his Stars-and-Stripes silk handkerchief, on the left hand corner of which was an Irish harp. He sported ornamented green socks. Both fighters wore warm wool drawers/trunks. Mitchell also wore a large fighting plaster of the old pattern. Sullivan declined to wear one.

Mitchell was 26 years old to Sullivan's 29 years of age.

Reported weights vary, ranging from 162, 166 – 168, or 170 - 185 pounds for Mitchell, and 200, 204, or 215 pounds for Sullivan. One observer said it looked as if Sullivan would have been better off to have lost a stone more of weight (14 pounds). Conversely, others believed that Sullivan appeared over-trained. "He is quite too fine; In getting down his weight Sullivan has sacrificed strength." His appearance was a bit drawn. On the contrary, Mitchell appeared to be in the pink of form.

B. J. Angle refereed. He was a stock broker, a member of the London Stock Exchange, and a well-known amateur boxer. He began nervously toying with his watch chain.

Sullivan offered to bet 500 pounds on himself against 200 pounds. There was no response. Sullivan challenged Jinks, a man who had bet on and backed Mitchell, to accept the wager. Jinks said he had wagered enough already. Eventually, when Harry Phillips offered 3 to 1 odds, he got some of Mitchell's supporters to place bets.

Mitchell won the toss for corners, and he took the one with his back to the sun, which was disappearing under threatening clouds. Sullivan had to face the wind and sun. Sullivan looked spiteful, while Mitchell was laughing.

41 people were present. George MacDonald and Jack Ashton seconded Sullivan, while Baldock and Kilrain seconded Mitchell. Jack or John Barnett umpired for Sullivan. Mitchell's umpire was Charley Rowell.

The principals and seconds shook hands and the fight began either at 12:47, 12:52, or 12:55 p.m., depending on which source one believes.

1 - The round started in silent intense excitement. Mitchell began entirely on the defensive, dancing about. Although advancing, Sullivan showed caution. After thirty seconds of sparring, Sullivan led but Mitchell dodged, landed a left on the chin, and then ducked.

Mitchell tried to draw a lead by using his left, so that he could counter, but Sullivan was too artful, and several times beautifully stopped Charlie's lefts. Sullivan landed a left on the cheek and a right on top of Mitchell's head. John L. also landed a heavy blow to the left jaw that made an ominous sound. Mitchell staggered just a bit, but almost immediately responded with a rapid but light left to the body.

Mitchell keenly maintained his guard and moved around, while Sullivan clearly was seeking an opportunity to lunge. It quickly became obvious that Sullivan was nettled by Mitchell's defensive tactics.

Describing the end of the round, the *Herald* said Sullivan made a mad rush and landed a tremendous right to the head, knocking Mitchell down. The *Sun* said Sullivan aimed a body blow but stopped short and then let go with both hands to the head and knocked Mitchell down. However, the *Referee* said Sullivan finally cornered Mitchell, who went down to avoid punishment. Another version said Mitchell was knocked down 7 minutes 7 seconds into the bout.

The *Herald* said half of the spectators expected the fight to be over. To the surprise of all, Mitchell picked himself up from the ground and walked back to his corner. Already, hard bruises were apparent. Conversely, the *Sun* said Baldock and Kilrain carried Mitchell to his corner. Sullivan walked.

In his corner during the rest period, Sullivan looked at Mitchell like a roused lion that seemed to be thinking, "You are plucky to stand that."

2 - Mitchell seemed just a trifle dazed. There was a lot of maneuvering and sparring at a distance for an opening, sandwiched between recorded blows. Mitchell led on the eye and eluded a return, but Sullivan landed his left on the cheek and closed in. They clinched, then separated without any wrestling. They sparred and closed in again, and once again separated without blows. Sullivan rushed him into a corner, and Mitchell dodged about.

The *Herald* said Sullivan made another rush and landed a ponderous right to the head that decked Mitchell. This time, Mitchell's seconds picked him up and attended to him. Yet, Mitchell seemed fine. The *Sun* said Sullivan ended the round by knocking Mitchell down with a blow on the left eye, which caused it to puff, though it grew no worse. The *Referee* said Sullivan rushed in and landed a right to the head that scored the first knockdown. One version said the round lasted only 50 seconds.

In his corner, Sullivan seemed sullen while his seconds whispered to him, and he shook his head.

3 - An alert Mitchell seemed fresh and springy, but the right side of his face was beginning to swell. He moved all about the large ring, much to Sullivan's disgust. John L. asked him not to run around so much. Mitchell landed a left to the belly and closed in. They broke away and Mitchell landed his left on the mouth, but received a right in return.

The *Herald* said that after about a minute, Sullivan made a mad rush and again knocked Mitchell down to the ground, as he had done in the prior two rounds. The *Referee* said Sullivan rushed, and his left to the temple and right to the jaw sent Mitchell down. The round lasted 3 minutes 20 seconds.

4 - Mitchell came up with a lump on his temple. He again moved about with the speed of a bantamweight. Sullivan looked chagrined, which appearance only increased as Charlie continually utilized his defensive tactics, dodging about. Mitchell led with his left on the belly. A lengthy period of long-range sparring followed. Mitchell frequently led for the body, but Sullivan stopped his punches. Sullivan tried his right and rushed. They clinched, but drew away without wrestling. Mitchell landed two punches to the chest. Sullivan, who was waiting, rushed again, but Mitchell cleverly slipped away.

The *Herald* said Mitchell went down as he was dodging, apparently without being hit by a blow. Essentially he dropped down in order to avoid punishment. Conversely, the *Referee* said the round ended in a fast rally, with Sullivan landing a right to the left eye that sent Mitchell down.

The *Herald* said they retired to their corners, without any effective work having been done in the round. The referee quietly addressed Mitchell's umpire, cautioning him against the illegal trick of dropping without exchanging blows.

5 - Sullivan forced the fighting. In a fast rally, Mitchell clinched. They separated. The *Herald* said Mitchell partially managed to avoid a powerful Sullivan right lunge with an ingenious drop down to the ground. The *Referee* said Sullivan decked Mitchell with a right. This was a short round

6 - Up to this point, Sullivan clearly was winning the fight. The *Herald* writer noted that Sullivan slowed down in this round, and concluded that he seemed slightly winded. However, after the fight, Sullivan claimed to have injured his right hand or arm in the 5th round.

Mitchell opened with three lefts on the body. He also landed two good blows to Sullivan's face. Mitchell got the worst of an exchange, but stopped a heavy right to the body. Nevertheless, Sullivan decked him with a blow to the cheek.

The *Sun* said the first several rounds of the fight were similar, but with variations. Pity for Mitchell was universal. He appeared pale and worried, and much smaller. Yet, he was plucky, which won him admiration.

7 - Mitchell tapped and stung Sullivan, who seemed to show signs of fatigue. Perhaps he was just conserving his energy. Conversely, Mitchell seemed fresh and jolly. Mitchell led with the left at the belly.

The *Herald* said that after Mitchell's nails scratched Sullivan's face and drew just a little blood, he claimed, "First blood." Everyone laughed. Mitchell said he had a bet that he would win first blood. Sullivan told him he could have the betting point.

In a rally, Mitchell rushed in to clinch and in pushing, he forced Sullivan backwards and down, with Mitchell falling on top of him. Sullivan always walked to his corner, but usually Mitchell's seconds carried him.

8 - The *Referee* said Mitchell claimed first blood in this round. Mitchell landed several times on the belly and avoided Sully's tremendous right. After heavy exchanges, Mitchell landed a hot one on the right eye and got down to the ground to avoid punishment. The referee did not allow the claim of foul. However, it appeared that in order to avoid blows, Mitchell intentionally fell and went down without being struck, which technically was illegal. The round had lasted only a minute.

The *Herald* said that Mitchell's tactics had become clear. For round after round, he retreated and dodged, sparred, and then dropped down to avoid getting hit. The contest became monotonous and tedious. Feeling that he should be disqualified, an American bystander said that if the referee had been American he would have done more than just caution Mitchell for his dropping-down tactics.

One report said that Mitchell's rights had made Sullivan's mouth and left ear bleed and swell. Sullivan's right eye was damaged partially as well.

9 - Sullivan landed a right on the neck. After a rally, Mitchell's left landed on the mouth, and then he landed on the ear. Sullivan twice landed with his left on the ear and temple.

Mitchell went down from a right on the arm. Sullivan's friends claimed a foul, saying that Mitchell was going down to avoid punishment. He was guilty, but Sullivan did not press the point. The referee warned Mitchell. Others said Mitchell went down from an openhanded right to the ribs or back.

The *Referee* claimed that during this round, a fearful rainstorm started. The temperature plummeted. However, the *Herald* said the rain started several rounds later.

10 - Mitchell had a lump on his left temple. Sullivan's right eye was bad. During this round, Mitchell's spikes cut Sullivan's boot and stabbed his foot. Sullivan viciously rushed, and Mitchell got down to save himself. Others said Mitchell went down from a slap on the back.

11 - Mitchell twice landed on the body with his left. Sullivan attacked, worked him into a corner, and Mitchell went down to avoid punishment. The *Referee* said the ground was slippery from the rain, which Mitchell could use as his excuse. The round only lasted about 50 seconds. Others said

Mitchell went down from a punch to the eye. As Mitchell was carried to his corner, he said, "Well, I think I shall begin to fight now."

12 - Unlike the *Referee*, the *Herald* said the raindrops started falling at the start of the 12th round. The wind also was rising. The wind blew into Sullivan's face in his corner, which clearly annoyed him. With the wind at his back, Mitchell was less bothered.

The *Referee* said both were still fresh. Sullivan was savage. Mitchell repeatedly slipped as Sullivan's rushes bore him down. After Mitchell fell without receiving a blow, a claim of foul was made, but Mitchell rose and continued. Sullivan made a vicious rush and once again Mitchell fell without receiving a blow, likely to avoid punishment. However, the claim of foul was not allowed. Mitchell was laughing, cool, and confident.

The *Herald* said that as the raindrops grew larger and fell faster, Sullivan began to shiver slightly in his corner. Both were quite wet.

Adding to Sullivan's frustration and disappointment, the rain softened the turf, which made it more difficult for him to get a good grip with his feet to rush in with momentum. Sullivan's greater weight made his movement more difficult. The smaller Mitchell minded the disadvantages less. The muddy ground was further trodden and damaged by the six spikes of their shoes, particularly by the foxy Mitchell's running about. The turf became marshy and miry, and the footing oozy and insecure.

The *Herald* writer said a description of the rounds thereafter would be as tedious to read as they were to see.

13 - Sullivan landed a left on the body. He waited for a while as Mitchell retreated and moved about. Finally, a Sullivan right on the neck sent Mitchell down.

14 - The rain was heavy. Under the circumstances, they killed time for a minute. Sullivan looked serious, while Mitchell laughed. There was a harmless rush and some exchanges made. Mitchell received a blow on the mouth which drew blood. Sullivan received one on the temple.

One source said Sullivan sent Mitchell down with his right on the ear. Another said Mitchell led with a left but a counter right to the chest dropped him.

15 - Mitchell did most of the work, but went down to avoid punishment. One writer said that Sullivan could have won the battle on a foul, had he wanted. But he did not want to win that way. Others said the referee was not inclined to award the victory on a technicality.

Another version said the round concluded with an awful right to the temple that sent Mitchell down like a shot. He was almost knocked senseless.

The *Referee* said the storm was so bad from rounds 9 to 15 that sometimes everyone retired to a nearby shed to take shelter. In one round, which lasted 25 minutes, Mitchell received several nasty blows on the temple. However, Sullivan was tiring, shivering visibly, and his teeth were chattering. Regardless, Mitchell mostly was on the retreat throughout, loath to take chances.

After the 15th round, the storm subsided and the sun came out again, at least for a short period of time, and Sullivan seemed to recover.

16 - At times, Sullivan made tremendous rushes, trying to finish him, but Mitchell's agility stood him in good stead and he cleverly got out of the way. Most of the time, Charley fought on the retreat. There were some slight exchanges.

Sullivan landed a right and Mitchell went down. The round lasted 2 minutes 50 seconds.

Conversely, the *Sun* said that at the start of the round, Mitchell had an enormous bump on the side of his head, and was too shaky to have withstood or escaped Sullivan had he rushed in his old way. However, Sullivan let the chance go and fought patiently and methodically.

17 - Mitchell was shaky, and a mere ten seconds into the round, Sullivan floored him with a left to either the chest or stomach.

18 - After slight exchanges, Mitchell quickly went down again. Another version said a counter to the jaw sent Mitchell down only 33 seconds into the round. Yet another said Sullivan dropped him with a blow to the top of the head.

19 - Mitchell was a bit on Queer Street, but nevertheless was game and active. In a rally, Sullivan dropped him with a right to the temple. Nevertheless, Mitchell rose and continued. Both were busy with lefts on each other's bodies. Mitchell spiked Sullivan's shin. Sullivan made a desperate rush, and Mitchell went down to avoid him.

The *Sun* said that rounds 17 through 19 featured a succession of rapid knockdowns, but Sullivan's blows did not have all of his power behind them, and Mitchell kept coming up again.

20 - Some brisk exchanges ended with Mitchell going down, one saying it was from a stomach blow.

During the contest, a handful of Frenchmen had gathered and watched the fight from a distant pavilion. Although they watched most intently, they also expressed unmitigated horror and disgust at the proceedings.

After 20 rounds, three men in uniforms approached. "Gendarmes!" was called out. However, it turned out that they were game keepers. They joined their fellow Frenchmen in watching the contest.

21 - The heavy rain returned. Mitchell landed a hard right, but Sullivan twice landed on the ribs. In a rush and rally, Mitchell went down, one source saying it was from a left to the body. The round lasted 3 minutes 15 seconds.

22 - Mitchell was "cheeky." Sullivan landed a left on the chest and right on the neck. Mitchell cleverly slipped the next attempt, but finally Sullivan

landed a blow on the eye and Mitchell went down. Another version said he went down from a right on the neck.

Sullivan's teeth began chattering and his bare skin turned blue with cold.

23 - The ground was dreadfully slippery. Sullivan was breathing hard, while Mitchell's condition had improved. Still, Sullivan fought him down; one source saying that a left to the neck did the job.

The rain was coming down in torrents. Sullivan clearly was disturbed by it. His mouth and eyes were swelling.

24 - This was a long round. Mitchell twice landed on the mouth, but Sullivan finally landed a heavy right thump on the neck that sent him down.

25 - Mitchell had the best of the fighting, scoring on the body. Sullivan threw a right but Mitchell went down in order to avoid it.

26 - Mitchell twice landed on the left eye and ear. Sullivan landed on the lump on Mitchell's forehead. Mitchell then went down to avoid punishment. Some said the sun came out again.

27 - Sullivan drove Mitchell about the ring and used his left well in exchanges. After some heavy fighting, Mitchell went down to avoid blows.

28 - Sullivan cleverly forced Mitchell to prolong a fierce rally. Charlie lightly landed his right on the ear, but then either was sent down or slipped and fell down.

Another source said Sullivan's bare hands were in bad condition. For the past four rounds, Mitchell often was "fibbing and getting away," while Sullivan usually was "rushing and getting well stopped."

29 - Mitchell started showing fatigue. Sullivan also seemed to be suffering for breath. His face looked blue, like someone with malaria. Their seconds started encouraging them, which each evidently needed. Mitchell continued pursuing his wearying tactics. As a celebrated general once said, "It's splendid, but it's not war." Observers said his tactics were ingenious, but not fighting. One source said Mitchell fell to end the round, which lasted either 4 minutes 15 seconds or nearly 6 minutes.

30 - Although the rain had subsided during the last four rounds, once again, the rain fell heavily, coming down in sheets. Word spread that Sullivan's right hand was gone. After exchanging blows, Mitchell threw himself down. "Mitchell ended the round when it suited him by stopping a well-meant lead and getting down." One source said the round lasted 2.5 minutes, while another said it was 6 minutes 50 seconds.

31 - This was a very long round, lasting 21 minutes. The hard rain made it difficult to do much. There were several exchanges, until finally, in a clinch, Mitchell bore Sullivan to the ropes and pushed him down. This was one of the few times in the contest that Sullivan went down.

32 - This was another long round. Sullivan drove Mitchell around the ring until the latter clinched. Mitchell kept rushing away. Sullivan could not get in a hit. John L.'s teeth were chattering, for he was chilled completely by the pelting rain, and seemed to be in a bad state. He took to standing in the middle of the ring while Mitchell walked around the ring's edge. At long last they decided to end the round voluntarily, and went to their corners without a blow having been landed. The round had lasted either 21 minutes 45 seconds, or 25 minutes, terminating with no punishment done.

In his corner, Sullivan showed signs of ague, the effect of the cold rain on his body. He shook until his star-spangled handkerchief seemed to be waiving. Mitchell had the shivers too, but not as pronounced.

33 - After a series of exchanges, Sullivan drove Mitchell around the ring until the latter fell. The round was just short of 5 minutes.

34 - It was obvious that Sullivan's hands were in very bad shape, and he was tired from chasing Mitchell around the ring. In between light exchanges, a great deal of time was spent walking around the ring. The 14-minute round ended with Mitchell slipping down in a clinch.

35 - The rounds had become farcical. Although Sullivan seemed to get his second wind, the 15-minute round was scientific but without effect. Mitchell went down in an exchange.

One observer said that Sullivan seemed unsteady, but the ground was so bad and slippery that Mitchell couldn't do much either.

36 - Mitchell attacked, landing to the body, and then he wrestled and threw Sullivan down.

37 - The ground was in a terrible state. Frequently, Mitchell slipped down on his hands, but he rose quickly. He seemed fresher and more confident than ever. He landed some punches and walked about, having the best of matters. Sullivan was tired and could not land. However, he still had danger in his fists, so Mitchell remained cautious and did not push the fighting. Charley was always on the alert, ready to move away. It was no use to chase after him, for he was too agile.

The fight had lasted a total of 2 ½ hours. Someone made a reference to the Smith – Kilrain draw. This caused some tittering, but John L. looked serious and would not reply.

Eventually, Sullivan drove Mitchell to the ropes and down. The round lasted about 3 minutes.

38 - Sullivan was vicious, but could not land a significant blow. Mitchell ended the round by falling comfortably.

The *Referee* summarized that from rounds 16 through 39, they often separated from clinches in a polite manner. Mitchell once twisted Sullivan onto the ropes and sought to cross-buttock him. However, neither seemed inclined to wrestle to end the rounds. Much talking was done, usually followed by a smack and a rush, with Mitchell usually getting away laughing.

Sullivan acknowledged some of Mitchell's hits, saying things like, "That's a good one, Charley." Sully's right eye was in mourning, his lips were swelling, and his nose and lips trickled carmine. Yet, he refused to have his moustache removed. Mitchell's temple had a big red lump. From rounds 29 through 39, Mitchell gained some advantage, but not significant enough to get anyone excited.

39 - This was another very long round. Various sources clocked it at 30 minutes, 31 minutes 49 seconds, 35 minutes, and 38 ½ minutes. The *Sun* said the round was a farce. The *Referee* said the round was exceptionally tedious. Mitchell frequently walked around the ring. Sullivan stood still and said, "Now then, let's have a round." Four times they briefly retired to their corners to have the clay removed from their boots and get refreshed, until one would challenge the other to continue. They feinted and sparred ineffectively. It had become obvious that neither one could stop the other. Sullivan was wholly unable to get in a good blow, and Mitchell could not finish Sullivan except by taking enough time to wear him out completely. The *Herald* said the spectators began to murmur and audibly express their desire for a draw. One said, "This is simply becoming a danse de pugilistique." A spectator mentioned that the fight had lasted over three hours. The boredom continued.

Finally, the parties agreed to call it a draw and end the contest. The *Herald* said that at the end of the round, it was about 4:15 p.m. The sky was black from the clouds and nightfall was approaching. There was a consultation between the umpires and the referees. Baldock, for Mitchell, and Phillips, for Sullivan, agreed to a draw. The two pugilists shook hands, carriages were called, and they headed back to Paris.

Unlike the *Herald*, the *Sun* said at least two hours of daylight remained. Its version said Mitchell's friends proposed to make it a draw. Sullivan accepted, though Phillips bitterly opposed the decision.

The *Referee* said a draw had been suggested earlier, but declined, but then after 4 p.m., all of those present got impatient, for the finish still seemed to be at least two hours off. Mitchell said, "Well, let's shake hands or fight on as John likes." Baldock then moved in and joined their hands, Sullivan nothing loath, for both were tired.

Another version said,

> Mitchell was understood to express some impatience, and Ashton, who was standing near him, at once chimed in with, "If you don't like it why don't you agree to a draw." Mitchell still sparring, "I'll draw if John likes…What did you say, John? Shall it be a draw?" Sullivan replied, "I don't mind," whereupon Baldock said, "Then shake hands; it's a draw."

The *Sun* said the fight had lasted 3 hours 11 minutes. The *Referee* said the fight had lasted 3 hours 10 minutes 55 seconds.

Those Left-Handers of Nimble Charley Were Perfect Stunners
The Plucky English Champion Boxer, in the Great International Prize Fight Between Him and Big John L., the Boston Slugger, Draws First Blood

Both men received a great ovation from those present. Still, John's side looked glum. He had never before been so done up. Mitchell was like a cricket. He had shown his cleverness. Pony Moore, Mitchell's father-in-law, was wild with delight. When the draw was declared he threw his arms around Mitchell's neck and kissed him. He held up a bottle of brandy that he had been hugging to his vest and he danced about in triumph. He even affectionately embraced Sullivan.

Sullivan's body was bruised, and his right eye and mouth were punished. His right hand was gone. Mitchell's right eye and temple received the most damage. His body was quite bruised, and his left eye was closing.

Another *Referee* version said Mitchell's left eye was almost closed and the parts above it were very swollen. His body had several marks. Despite having scored all of the knockdowns and almost all of the throw-downs, Sullivan looked worse. His right eye was almost closed, and the left wasn't far behind. His left ear was cut and the lobe was swollen, with the blood oozing from the inside. Blood trickled from his nose and lips.

Afterwards, Sullivan and Kilrain also shook hands, and some applause followed.

Summarizing, the *New York Herald*, which had a correspondent on scene, said the first half of the fight was good. The second half still featured some fierce hitting, but the waits in between exchanges were absurdly long. The rain rendered the battleground a mere marsh, which did not suit Sullivan. Calling the fight Sullivan's Waterloo, this writer opined that Sullivan's reputation as a terror had taken a hit. The 39-round draw was treated as a practical defeat for Sullivan because he had failed to stop Mitchell. Of course, Mitchell had adopted Tug Wilson tactics, which he used to tire out his man. Sullivan's blows could knock him down, but not out.

The *Referee* said that Mitchell had "played a splendid 'get away' game," working the London rules system very well.

The *New York Sun*, which also had a reporter on scene, called the fight a triumph for Mitchell. He tired out the champion and caused the fight to end in a draw. Sullivan tried to knock him out, but his blows lacked force. Out of more than a hundred wild rushes that Sullivan made, any one of which would have resulted in a knockout in Madison Square Garden, not a half dozen resulted in anything. Mitchell was knocked down 15 times, but came up smiling every time. Mitchell claimed first blood. The champion was numbed by the cold. He lost his wind chasing the little Englishman around the ring. It was a complete surprise to everyone, including the fighters. Despite his banged-up eyes and swollen temples, Mitchell was all smiles. He showed skill and pluck.

Sullivan's tactics were to wait for a chance to land his right. Mitchell's tactics were to keep away, dodge blows, and land on the body. Mitchell's clear strategy was to tire out Sullivan. He kept up his running, though fighting pluckily. These were wise tactics. Sullivan's efforts were desperate and vain. He exhausted himself both by trying to hit Mitchell and by waiting so much.

This writer also opined that Sullivan's reputation had been injured by the result, which in part was due to Sullivan's "folly in altering his style of fighting, replacing with caution and diplomacy the daring slugging tactics which made him always victor in the first few rounds."

The *Sun's* analysis failed to recognize that a fighter had to pace himself in a fight to the finish, or else he might be left spent of energy. Regardless, this author opined that Sullivan's caution played into Mitchell's hands. This writer believed that twice in the fight Sullivan could have won by using his old tactics of pressing his man, but he did not do so, fearing that he would leave himself open or fatigued, so he was not willing to take the same risks that he usually did. The writer harshly said it was like a bull imitating a fox. Towards the end, neither man had enough energy to finish the other.

In general, the rounds were brought to an end by the punishment Sullivan inflicted or by Mitchell's falls in running away. Sullivan knocked him down again and again, no less than 15 times, but Mitchell showed a wonderful ability to recover after the 30 seconds rest and continue. Each time he was being carried off in his seconds' arms, he would turn his bruised face and say, "Not yet. You haven't whipped me yet."

Sullivan went to the ground only twice on his hands, but fell backward once through slipping and another time in wrestling.

During the fight, a half-dozen fouls were claimed on Sullivan's behalf, when Mitchell went down without being hit, but Sully invariably declared that he did not make money that way, and withdrew the claim made for him.

Sam Blakelock, the tough little English fighter, attended to Sullivan and acted as his chair. He literally got on his hands and knees, crouching down humbly in the mud, and allowed Sullivan to sit on him between rounds. Blakelock had bet all of his savings that Sullivan would win within half an hour. He was broken-hearted.

The *Sun* claimed that Kilrain had smiled at and taunted Sullivan during the fight.

At one point, after Mitchell had just escaped being knocked out, the grey-haired Jack Baldock implored Mitchell, "Think of the kids, Charlie, dear little kids, calling of you at home and counting on you for bread. Think what their feelings will be if you don't knock the ear off him and knock it off him again." Sometimes Baldock would recite bits of poetry or song to encourage him. Other times he would pour forth volleys of vile profanity. At intervals, he threatened immediate chastisement to anyone near the ring who had a word to say for Sullivan. He offered to bet sums he had never seen at ridiculous odds. He was a real enthusiast.

After the first few rounds, Jinks, the American gambler who had money wagered on Mitchell, but had declined additional wagers before the fight, started offering bets.

This writer opined that despite the disappointment, Sullivan still was the great Sullivan, even though his reputation had decreased. Mitchell had shown great improvement. He was plucky and game. He was smiling afterwards, despite being hammered and showing bumps and bruises on his face.

The writer further opined that Mitchell's smaller size gave him quickness on the retreat, which was a disadvantage to Sullivan. "There is no possible doubt that had Smith, Kilrain, or any man of about his own size and quickness of motion been in the ring Sullivan would have beaten him quickly and with ease." Sullivan would have landed more often on bigger men. But he could not chase a smaller man around a huge 24-foot ring. Plus, being smaller made Mitchell more efficient. This is one case in which smaller size, particularly in a fight to the finish, where footwork and condition meant so much, actually helped Mitchell.

Another *Sun* report said many were surprised that Sullivan was not whipped, given how long the battle had lasted. They thought that if the fight had lasted a significant period of time, the advantage would be with Mitchell, who would wear him out and then finish him.

Analysis and discussion about the fight proliferated and reverberated throughout the world. Everyone had their spin and perspective on matters.

Some said that so many lengthy bouts that terminated in draws would ruin prizefighting. Smith-Kilrain had concluded similarly.

George Cunningham, ex-lightweight champion, said, "We didn't have no draws in my time. We fought till we couldn't see and then we went on fighting without seein'. The only way as Mitchell could stand up agin John L. was on account of that twenty-four foot ring. John couldn't hit him because he kept a running out."

Many were disappointed that Sullivan had failed to knock him out. It was a curious thing to find so many Englishmen dissatisfied to hear that their own countryman had managed to survive. Most were surprised and flabbergasted by the result.

Many believed the news was incorrect, or that the fight had been a fake. They couldn't believe that Sullivan had failed to put him out. Of course, they were wrong.

Billy Edwards said he had expected Mitchell to last no more than 20 minutes, and therefore it was a virtual victory for Mitchell.

Mike Donovan said, "Some people think that prize fighting is the same as glove fighting, but there's a big difference between them." He had thought that Mitchell would give Sullivan a good hard fight.

Ex-champion Tom Allen said, "Gloves are one thing and the bare fists another."

One man said he was glad that some of the "conceit" was taken out of the great big "duffer" Sullivan. This feeling was echoed by some of those who wanted to see Sullivan taken down a peg. However, this man also said, "I'll bet even that Mitchell's legs and not his arms pulled him through."

Others said Mitchell was a better runner and sprinter than Sullivan, and John L. simply could not catch up with him.

Many opined that Sullivan had been living too high, that the result was a virtual defeat, and that it would be a long time before he could recover his lost prestige. Some said he had seen his best days.

Richard K. Fox said,

> It is just as I thought. Sullivan was overconfident and did not half train, while Mitchell never lost an opportunity to get himself in thorough condition. … Sullivan has been drinking hard for several years, and has undermined his constitution to an alarming extent. No man can expect to drink almost continuously and not injure his health. I tell you John L. Sullivan is not the man he once was.

Fox's editor William Harding said,

> While in Europe I met both Mitchell and Sullivan frequently. The former took most excellent care of himself, refusing all invitations to drink and going to bed early every night. Sullivan, on the contrary, did about as he pleased; drinking wine and dining with the big guns and acting as though it was mere child's play for him to fight. … Sullivan's day for posing as a gladiator has gone by. He is no longer the great man he once was, nor never will be again.

He said that Kilrain would whip Sullivan. "Of course he can, and that will doubtless be the next great sensation in pugilistic circles."

John L.'s estranged wife Annie, upon hearing of the news, said, "I am glad of it. I wish Mitchell had killed him. … Mitchell is a dodger and kept him at bay until he lost his wind. Then my brave John L. was winded and helpless. He is a greatly overrated man. … He will die a beggar, as he deserves to do, for his ill treatment of me."

Bostonians were shocked. They said the reports were fakes and lies, or that Sullivan must have been drunk, or badly seconded, etc. They were upset by the result.

Mike Sullivan, the champ's own brother, blamed Annie Livingston. "She is playing him for a fool, and he has completely lost his head for her. Poor John! I am sorry for him. He has brought disgrace upon himself and upon his family."

Jim Keenan hoped that the fight had taught Sullivan a lesson. His success made him think he could whip anyone without an effort, but the fight had shown him otherwise.

One of his former backers said that Sullivan should have insisted on a 16-foot ring. "As it was, Mitchell dodged around and played 'possum until John was winded."

Tom Early said, "It is a Tug Wilson show over again. Mitchell just dodged and fell down to save himself. It is a shame."

Colonel George Eland said, "I feel like committing suicide. It is wrong – all wrong." Most were feeling sorry for Sullivan, and thought he had been misused.

Frank Glover noted that the LPR rules were against Sullivan. Still, if Mitchell had gone so far as to tire out the big man, it was surprising that he did not continue the fight and try to finish him off. Hence, his performance was not as good as some might think, nor Sullivan's as bad.

Most sporting men believed there was more running than hitting in the contest. The fight proved that Mitchell was a better sprinter than the big fellow. Mitchell kept him chasing him inside the big ring. Others said Sullivan was not a stayer, that if he did not stop his man in 4 or 5 rounds, he was done. Mitchell was too cunning for him. Yet, Mitchell had not stopped Sullivan either.

Responding to those who said Sullivan must have carried him, Arthur Chambers said, "No money in the world could induce Sullivan to throw a fight. If Sullivan was in condition I don't think any man in the world could whip him." Chambers figured that if Sullivan could not whip Mitchell in a half hour that Mitchell would whip him. He was surprised that Sullivan had stayed so long.

Tom Kelly said, "I have said all along that Mitchell would go to running and get Sullivan weak. … A twenty-four foot ring is a hard place to corner a clever man in, and everybody knows that Mitchell is cleverer."

The *New York Times* reported that the whole fight favored Sullivan. Sullivan dropped Mitchell with rights to the head to end the 1st through 3rd rounds. Mitchell moved about the large 24-foot ring to survive. In the 6th, Charley dropped to avoid a right hand and was cautioned against breaking the rules. Eventually, Sullivan grew fatigued from chasing him around the huge ring, and the rain and muddy turf did not help matters, slowing up John. The 32nd round lasted 27 minutes, as the rain was "falling in torrents." The 39th round lasted 30 minutes. Both were weak and fatigued and their blows had lost their steam. Because it was clear that "no definite result was likely to be reached," it was suggested and agreed that the bout be declared a draw, after 3 hours 11 minutes. Mitchell had a lump on his jaw, his left eye was banged up, and his body was bruised.

The *National Police Gazette* reported that Mitchell tried to move for the first 3 rounds but was knocked down to end each, coming up for the 4th with a lump on his left temple. A right to Mitchell's eye ended the 4th. He dropped from a right in the 5th and a blow to the cheek in the 6th. Sullivan fell in the 7th, with Mitchell on top of him. Usually, Charley was carried to his corner, but Sullivan walked. A Mitchell left in the 8th drew first blood from Sullivan's nose. After landing a right to John's eye, Mitchell went down to avoid retaliation. A right to the arm dropped Charley in the 9th. Sullivan's eye was looking bad by the 10th. Mitchell went down that round amidst a Sullivan rush, and he did the same in the 11th. He clearly fell without a blow in the 12th, the claim of foul being disallowed, for Charley had some excuse because the muddy ground was slippery. A right to the neck dropped Mitchell in the 13th. Mitchell was laughing in the 14th, but a right to his mouth drew blood, and a right to the ear dropped him. Charley again went down to avoid punishment in the 15th. From the 16th round to the end, they would talk to each other and then punch, and then Mitchell would run away or go down. Sullivan's right eye was bad; his lips were swelling and nose bleeding, while Mitchell's temple had a big lump.

The *San Francisco Chronicle* said Mitchell's agility had saved him from defeat. He fought with skill and cunning, going to the ground whenever the slightest push would justify it. The champion's right arm began to puff up in about the 12th round, when the sleet began to fall, and it was not used very often. The rain continued until the 32nd round. It was very cold and the grounds were in terrible condition, resembling a pigsty. "Mitchell's blows were quick, but puny as a baby's, while Sullivan stalked around, a mere shadow of what he was. … The secret is now in every one's mouth that Sullivan's fighting days are finished."

The *New York World* said "the tactics of Mitchell were those of a man half afraid to stand up and do battle honestly. Mitchell did all he could to have the fight made a matter of wind. He played a waiting game, and, like 'Tug' Wilson…did his best to 'stand up' against Sullivan by going to grass at every opportunity."

The day ended more dramatically than it began. After the fight was over, driving single-file in five separate carriage cabs, the fight party had gotten about a mile from the battlefield, heading to Creil, where they had left their baggage. A man on horseback rode towards them. He wore an odd cap and a cloak, beneath which there was something red, which made him appear to be a French officer. The fight group kept riding on. Suddenly, the gendarme rode up to the cab and ordered them to stop. The officer drew his sabre, and they had to obey him. The *Herald* reporter exclaimed, "Nabbed, by Jove!" Up to ten other gendarmes eventually rode up from different directions. One of them said, "If any one tries to get out he'll be shot."

Nevertheless, William Raymond, an American sporting man, bolted for the woods. The gendarme gave chase and fired a warning shot in the air, and then aimed at the runner and shot but missed. Raymond disappeared into the woods. Baldock had started to run, but found a gendarme pointing a gun at his head. He removed his hat, bowed, and returned to the carriage, exclaiming that he only meant to have a look at the country, and did not intend to leave his new friends. The others were sobered by the shot and did not run. "Well, lads, it's no use fighting, we're collared." One report said Raymond later returned and surrendered.

The police arrested everyone, including the *Herald* and *Sun* reporters. They had to follow the officers to Senlis, ten kilometers away. It was pouring rain. They had not eaten since morning. It took almost an hour to reach the town. The fight party numbered about 30 men.

They arrived in Senlis at about 6 p.m. They all were brought into a detention room and told to wait. One member of the group said, "I'd give a couple of hundred to be out of this." Another said, "I'll think myself lucky if we get off with a month." A brigadier came in, looking for the principals in the contest. Seeing Mitchell with a very black eye and Sullivan with his lip all cut about, the officer knew they were them. He marched them upstairs to the magistrate, in the big hall of the Sous Prefecture. Then they were brought down again, each handcuffed to a gendarme.

Taken In By Gendarmes
The Sullivan-Mitchell Party On Their Way To Senlis In the Custody Of French Police

The officers wrote down the names and addresses of the seconds. They all were questioned, one by one. They denied that there had been a prize fight. "Prize fight? Lord bless you, no! Only a wrestling match. What was I doing there? Why, I ran against the gentlemen quite by accident in the train. Any betting! Certainly not, no betting." Pony Moore claimed that he was a comedian and impresario in search of artists. They all showed return tickets as evidence of their intention to leave France in peace.

One of them distracted the attention of a gendarme as they were being marched upstairs, and Jake Kilrain slipped away and escaped.

After they had been half-starved and badgered to death, the magistrate decided to let everyone go, except for the fighters. Their trainers and seconds, George McDonald and Sam Blakelock, were released on a promise to appear at 9 a.m. on Sunday morning. Most of the fight party returned to Paris by train. Sullivan and Mitchell remained in jail at Senlis. "Mitchell and Sullivan are in the lockup still, and when they will get out Heaven only knows."

The walls of the dungeon jail cell were made of stone. Water ran down from them. The only accommodations were army blankets spread on plank beds. At first, applications for rugs and fur coats were denied.

At midnight, the *Sun* correspondent arrived at the jail with a doctor, whose services proved to be sadly needed. Both men were in a sad plight. This reporter said they were in separate cells, cold and damp, without food or coverings to their beds.

Upon seeing them, the French doctor threw his hands toward heaven and vowed that the men had been trying to murder one another.

Mitchell was the worse off. His head was covered with bumps, and his discolored face was a mass of knobs and bruises. His knees bore several contusions from the repeated falls. He fell more than 40 times during the fight. There was a sinking in among the ribs, toward the lower part of his back. The doctor declared that this indicated an awful blow had landed and broken something inside. The doctor reported that Mitchell's left eye was discolored, and he had a nasty swelling on his left temple.

Sullivan showed why he had failed to knock out Mitchell. His right hand was swollen to twice its natural size, and the left was in bad condition as well. The doctor said a tendon had been strained, torn, or badly damaged. He said the arm needed to be lanced and carefully tended. Otherwise, Sullivan was not damaged beyond a swollen lip.

The doctor induced the authorities to provide plenty of covers, though fire could not be procured. He also gave them food from a hotel.

The fighters would see the judge again at 9 a.m.

After spending the night in jail, the next morning, on March 11, the boxers were brought in front of the magistrate at Senlis. One reporter said that Sullivan's eyes were both swollen and discolored, his lips were cut and puffed up in a way that disfigured him, and his left ear was swollen and smeared with blood, the effect of a counter from Mitchell in the 15th round.

Mitchell only had one good eye with which to see. His left eye was puffed out in a most extravagant way, and united many colors. His ears were fine, but the rest of his head was battered completely. His scalp had lumps all over. His left temple carried a lump on the angle of the eye and literally was bigger than a hen's egg. That was the result of a blow received in the 14th round that was nearly a knockout. The reporter opined that had the fight been under the Marquis of Queensberry rules, Sullivan would have won at that time.

Both men's hands were in a poor state. Mitchell's left was a complete wreck. After the 20th round, all of his lefts were ineffective. Both were pitifully stiff and scarcely able to move. Mitchell was pulled over to one side like a man paralyzed, due to the internal injuries that literally had caved in his back.

A lawyer had been hired to represent the fighters. A young Englishman did the translations from French to English for the fighters. At 10 a.m., the lawyer persuaded the judge to allow Sullivan and Mitchell to sign a bond of 1,000 francs bail for their release. The magistrate evidently was moved by their physical condition, and expressed regret that the law made it necessary to lock them up all night in such a state of physical dilapidation.

After their release, the two fighters had breakfast at the Hotel du Grand Cerf. They sat at two tables, which included Sullivan, Phillips, Holske, Kilrain, and Barnett at one, while Pony Moore, Mitchell, Charlie Rowell, and Ned Donnelly were at another.

One reporter said the swelling in John L.'s right hand that started in the 4th round when he dropped Mitchell like a felled ox, narrowly missing the point of the jaw, had nearly disappeared. Another version said it was in the 4th round that Sullivan landed his right on the point of Mitchell's elbow, straining his right tendon, disabling it. He practically fought with one arm after that. Mitchell had lost the use of his left soon thereafter. When it was even money on Mitchell, Charlie landed a left on Sullivan's elbow, injuring his left arm. Hence, it was a one-handed affair on both sides.

This reporter said Mitchell only had a mouse over his left eye. Sullivan did not have any marks, though his upper lip was still swollen by the "frequent but feeble visitations of Mitchell."

Sullivan was "as gay as a lark during breakfast, singing matches from comic songs." He said he would never again enter the "ring." In the future, he only would engage in boxing competitions and glove fights.

Perhaps fearing that they might flee, the magistrate judge showed up and said he had decided to increase their bail. They had to put up an additional bond of 3,000 francs, making it 4,000 francs total, or $800, for their appearances the next morning. Phillips and Moore again had to pay up for their fighters.

The judge's suspicions proved to be correct. They all headed to Paris on a train. Sullivan briefly turned up at a bar in the Rue Scribe. Instead of remaining in France for the trial, at 7:45 p.m. that evening, they left on a ship to London.[313]

In London, contrary to general reports, Sullivan's face showed little if any sign of punishment. However, he moved his right arm awkwardly, and evidently it was hurt. He arrived in Liverpool from London. He had a sparring engagement there that week, but he would not be able to fulfill it, given the state of his arm.

Sullivan went straight to the home of his friend Arthur Magnus and went to bed. Some said that Sullivan was miserable.

Sullivan derived comfort from the fact that everyone praised the fair and honorable manner in which he fought. The *London Sporting Life* said, "We never saw a man fight fairer than Sullivan did. Even when he was unintentionally spiked he only asked Mitchell to be more careful."

Sullivan attributed the prolongation of the affair and the draw to Mitchell's tactics and tumbling powers, the horrid weather, and the disablement of his right early in the fight. The rules also helped Mitchell, who could rest and recover for 30 seconds each time that he was decked or dropped down to avoid blows. That made it difficult to finish him off.

One reporter said that even those notoriously hostile towards Sullivan had little to shout about other than the fact that Mitchell succeeded in avoiding being knocked out. The enthusiasm over his feat cooled down considerably when it became generally known by what tactics his survival was achieved.

---

313 *New York Herald*, March 11, 12, 1888; *New York Sun*, March 11, 12, 1888; *New York Times*, *Boston Herald*, *Boston Daily Globe*, *San Francisco Chronicle*, March 11, 1888; *San Francisco Examiner*, March 12, 1888; *New York World*, March 14, 1888; *National Police Gazette*, March 24, 1888; *Referee* (Sydney), April 19, 1888, quoting *Sporting Life*, an English paper.

As of March 13, the right side of Sullivan's face was a rich chrome yellow, but his eyes were fine, and there was only a very slight swelling of his lips. His right fist was still swollen, and his arm was bandaged under his shirt. He actually attributed his facial blemishes to the fact that he was locked up in a wet, dirty cell, without the chance to take his customary hot bath after the fight. He attributed his failure to stop Mitchell chiefly upon the injury sustained in the 5th round. He was prepared for the dodging tactics, and felt that he could have overcome them had his best wing not been damaged.

Sullivan denied that he was retiring or that he no longer was the same man. He said he would meet anyone with standing to challenge him. He was willing to rematch Mitchell, although he understood that Charlie intended to retire.

Sullivan said he was perfectly satisfied to make the fight a draw, for there was no use in continuing, although he asked for and would have liked a couple more rounds. Everyone seemed anxious to make it a draw, especially the Mitchell party, who proposed it. Sullivan agreed to the draw because he was fighting one-handed. They might have gone on all night, because Mitchell's blows had little effect on him and could not possibly have knocked him out.

Arthur Magnus said he still had full confidence in and admiration for Sullivan. He said Mitchell's escape was due to the accident to Sullivan's right. He was willing to match them for 5,000 pounds a side in a 16-foot ring, and would bet an additional 1,000 pounds that Sullivan would dispose of him within 40 minutes.[314]

In late March, the *San Francisco Chronicle* said,

> Sullivan has taught us afresh that physical vigor cannot be preserved by burning the candle at both ends. After years of dissipation, Sullivan pretended to reform, and then we were told that he was as good a man as he ever was. The student of physiology knew better. A man cannot trifle with his body. … He abused his system in every way. … The moral is that men who would retain their physical or mental powers must lead regular lives. If they indulge to excess the shadow of decay will early fall upon them.[315]

In April, a month after the fight, Sullivan said,

> I never claimed to run as fast as Charley Mitchell, and the Chantilly fight was a sprinting match throughout.
>
> I would have won anyhow had not my arm been hurt in the fourth round, but among the circumstances which militated against me are the unfairness of the referee, Mitchell's foul play in spiking me at every opportunity…the partiality of the timekeeper, an Englishman,

---

[314] *New York Sun*, March 13, 14, 1888.

[315] *San Francisco Chronicle*, March 26, 1888.

who timed the intervals between the rounds from Mitchell's reaching his corner, and not from where he fell; I also charge him with having lengthened each rest interval from twenty-five all the way up to seventy and eighty seconds, and, lastly, the rainstorm, which blew straight into my corner…with such violence, in fact, as to knock out even several men who were not fighting.[316]

Sullivan also said,

I won the fight with Mitchell forty times on fouls. But the referee would not allow my claims. … [Mitchell] wanted 30 seconds time allowed from the moment he got to his corner after a knockdown, and I allowed him that. For the first five rounds of the battle I hit him almost when and where I wanted to. In the first round he undertook to hit me with his left hand, but I gave him my elbow and it smashed his hand almost into halves. He never had a strong left hand, and that smash made it very weak. When I got through with the fight all I had was a black eye. That was done after my right arm was injured in the fifth round.

At first, when Mitchell fell without a blow my second claimed a foul each time. Referee Angle would not allow it. When I saw there was no use of claiming fouls I told my second to keep quiet. … Somehow I always hit him in the upper part of the head, and that part of his head was swelled to almost twice its normal size before the draw was declared.[317]

In his autobiography, Sullivan said,

I wanted to fight this sprinter in a sixteen-foot ring, knowing well that his tactics in a twenty-four-foot ring would be to run around or to lie down, which he did at every opportunity afforded him in the fight. I wished to prevent this cowardly and unfair business. … In this fight with Mitchell I was fouled a number of times by being spiked repeatedly by Mitchell. Of this the referees seemed to take no notice. …

In the fifth round, when I was swinging the right, I caught Mitchell at the back of the head and severely bruised the muscles of the right arm. Still Mitchell seemed afraid to stand up to the fight. In the tenth round, when he was continuing his tactics, I said in disgust, "Oh, don't run around the ring."

"First blood" to Mitchell was claimed in round eight, to which I replied, "You can have it." He said, "Well, there is nothing in it but to decide a bet."

---

316 *San Francisco Chronicle,* April 9, 1888.
317 *New York Sun,* April 25, 1888.

> Running and dropping was his game. … Once he dropped without a blow and received a caution, and after this he went down a number of times for a mere tap.
>
> Had I desired to practice the tricks of the London prize-ring rules I had good opportunities to do so by giving my weight to Mitchell; but I tried my best to avoid falling on him. Mitchell adopted a saving game throughout. …
>
> [W]hen he went into the ring he did not go to win my five hundred pounds, but to save his own, which, thanks to the big ring, the weather and my accident, he succeeded in doing.
>
> In this fight I was unfortunately in the worst corner where the rain beat incessantly in my face and body, causing me to become chilled, and I refused numerous times to partake of any brandy which my seconds insisted upon my taking.

He also said that Mitchell's "whole game was to avoid me, not to fight me."

Regarding the end, Sullivan said that Mitchell's second, Jack Baldock stepped into the ring and said, "Shake hands and call it a draw." Sullivan replied, "Let us fight a couple more rounds." But everyone then said, "No." So they agreed and retired from the ring.

They were locked up from 7 p.m. until 1 p.m. Sunday. They all sat down to breakfast. The party included Harry Phillips, Jake Barnett, Edward Holske, William O'Brien, Pony Moore, Jake Baldock, Kilrain, Mitchell, and Sullivan. When the officials came to suspect their intentions, they increased the bonds from $800 to $1,600 each.

They went from Senlis to Paris, then by way of Calais to England. He took the boat at Calais to Dover, and arrived in London the following morning.

Sullivan went to Liverpool and stopped at the home of his friend Arthur Magnus, who had witnessed the fight.

Sullivan was tried in absentia and sentenced to three days in jail and a 2,000 francs fine.

Magnus told a reporter,

> Yes, the fight, as you say, was a walking tournament the greater part of the time. Mitchell did not face Sullivan as he ought to have done. He danced continually around the ring. … In the fifth round Sullivan disabled his hand with a blow at Mitchell's head. … So I leave you to judge what a mishap it was to Sullivan to be compelled to fight practically with one arm.
>
> Could Mitchell have tired out his opponent with his tactics? I honestly believe he couldn't. His blows were not strong enough to tire any one out, and even in his disabled state Sullivan could have kept it up as long as Mitchell.

Although ultimately the fight resulted in a draw, John L. Sullivan had proven that he could endure a lengthy battle. Fighting for three hours in the cold windy rain with bare hurt hands, in a large muddy ring, and shivering badly, is a valiant feat for any fighter.

Charlie Mitchell took a beating and went down either from knockdowns, as a result of slipping down, as a result of intentionally going down from light blows so he could get a rest and recovery period, or because he voluntarily went down to save himself from blows. Sullivan never was knocked down, although he slipped and was wrestled down a few times. But by far, the vast majority of round-ending falls were the result of Mitchell being sent down.

Ultimately, the truth is that the very large ring, the muddy conditions, the cold rain that left Sullivan trembling, the damage to his hands, particularly his right, from landing without gloves in cold conditions, combined with Mitchell's tactics of moving and dropping, along with the long rests after falls and knockdowns, all combined to make the bout a lengthy war of attrition.

Technically, it was a violation of the London Prize Ring Rules to go down voluntarily in order to get a rest or avoid punishment, and was grounds for disqualification. However, the actual rule left some room for interpretation, stating,

> It shall be a fair 'stand up fight,' and if either man shall willfully throw himself down without receiving a blow, whether blows shall have previously been exchanged or not, he shall be deemed to have lost the battle; but this rule shall not apply to a man who in a close slips down from the grasp of his opponent to avoid punishment, or from obvious accident or weakness.[318]

Clearly, Mitchell often violated the spirit of the rule. The LPR rules and the tactics that could be employed help explain why so many LPR fights lasted so long. This fight was a perfect illustration of the LPR system's limitations.

Mitchell mostly fought to survive. He utilized guerilla tactics, scoring occasionally and moving a great deal, hoping that Sullivan eventually would wear himself out or that his eyes would close. Although his survival tactics worked to prevent Sullivan from stopping him, ultimately they were not effective at stopping Sullivan.

Some used the fight result as a way to criticize Sullivan. They said that it was a sign that he was slipping. They compared this result with the 1883 gloved fight result when Mitchell was stopped in 3 rounds. However, their analysis overlooked the different rules and conditions.

The *Sun* had criticized Sullivan for not attacking ferociously enough. However, in a fight to the finish, if a fighter did not pace himself, and failed to finish off his opponent, he could have been left so drained that it would be he who was knocked out. Consider also the fact that even when Sullivan

---

318 Sullivan at 187-188.

did attack ferociously, often Mitchell either would run away or drop down, nullifying Sullivan's efforts and rendering the expenditure of energy futile. Finally, without gloves, in cold conditions, hand injuries were more likely to occur, as was the case here. Especially in a bareknuckle bout, one had to be more careful about where one threw and landed. Punching hard to the skull with one's bare hands often can damage the hands as much as or more than the receiver's head. All of these factors in part explain why Sullivan preferred gloved Queensberry rules, wherein a fallen fighter only had 10 seconds to rise and continue again after knockdowns.

The Title Dispute Continues: Hype, Debauchery, Illness, and the Color Line

On April 12, 1888, John L. Sullivan took the steamship *Catalonia* from England to Boston, arriving back in the U.S. on April 24. His friends came to the harbor to welcome him home, and gave him a grand ovation. A band played "Johnny Comes Marching Home" and "Auld Lang Syne."[319]

Welcoming The Champion Pugilist
Exciting Scene In Boston Harbor On the Arrival of the Steamship Catalonia With John L. Sullivan, Boston's Pride, and His Party On Board

Supposedly, during the return trip, Sullivan had resumed his drinking ways, engaging in a spree. As usual, John L. was a violent drunk, having run-ins with various fellow passengers, crew members, and even his drinking buddy and girlfriend Ann Livingston. Many alleged tales circulated: A steward defended himself by breaking a soda siphon bottle over John L.'s head. A chief engineer threatened to spray him with a hot water hose. Sullivan struck a storekeeper in the back. He bloodied a fellow passenger who accidentally stepped on his toes. The captain threatened to put him in irons. Sullivan and Livingston threw things at one another, including glasses and shoes. Allegedly, Sullivan told a clergyman's wife that he would swipe her brats out of existence if she didn't keep them out of his way. How many

[319] Sullivan at 149-154, 178; *New York World*, April 24, 1888.

of these stories were true, or just exaggerations or inventions, is not clear. However, what is clear is that Sullivan had a reputation for being a mean drunk, merited or not.

Upon his return, John L. said his right hand and arm were improving, but he would have to be careful for some time to come. Sullivan said he was in the best possible condition when he entered the ring with Mitchell; his trainer George McDonald having done a good job. Sullivan said he had been taking the best care of himself. He wanted to meet either Mitchell, Kilrain, or Smith in a 16-foot ring for $10,000 a side.

Sullivan said that both Mitchell and Kilrain had declined to meet him in 8-round glove contests. He even offered to give them the entire receipts if he failed to knock them out. Most believed that Mitchell would retire and rest on the laurels he had gained in their fight, and that no amount of money would induce him to fight again. He could earn in exhibitions.[320]

On May 2, Ed Holske, who had been there in the Sullivan camp, discussed the Sullivan-Mitchell fight, as well as how it ended. He said,

> I wish to state that to my mind any man, however good he may be, will find it next to impossible, when he has been attacked with the shakes and is minus the use of the arm with which he does most of his execution, to score a victory over a man who, under other conditions, is inferior to him.

Holske said the result was no disgrace to Sullivan.

Holske claimed that Mitchell landed far more blows than Sullivan did: 122 to 74, while each landed once or twice during the thirty-two exchanges. Sullivan scored the knockdowns, in part because Mitchell would go down from light blows. Mitchell wrestled Sullivan down in the 6th and 36th rounds. Holske disputed that Mitchell scored first blood early in the fight. He said it was in the 25th round that he actually drew blood. However, he also said that a good umpire could have gotten Sullivan the fight in the 8th, 11th, and 24th rounds, because Mitchell went down without receiving a blow, which was a foul warranting disqualification.

Interestingly, Holske also claimed that in about the 20th round, he asked Carney to ask the Mitchell party members if they would agree to a draw. However, at that time, they would not. He then asked Carney to offer money. When there was no acceptance, Sullivan's backers kept increasing the amount offered. He claimed that Phillips and Probert got involved as well. Eventually, Baldock agreed. However, no one noticed the deal made. "The whole transaction was done so quickly and cleverly that it failed to arouse suspicion."

In response, Harry Phillips, Sullivan's manager, said there was no truth to Holske's accusations that the Mitchell side was paid off to agree to a draw. "Why, if there had been any job of that kind suggested, Mitchell would have kicked, and the fact that he says he is satisfied with the result of

---

[320] *New York Sun*, April 25, 1888.

the battle shows that he was not sold out." Phillips said Baldock's character was unimpeachable, for he was one of the most prominent sporting men in England. Phillips denied giving Holske any money to buy the fight.[321]

However, Frank Beckwith, a friend of Harry Phillips, also claimed that Phillips bribed Mitchell's second, Baldock, with 250 pounds to agree to a draw, for Phillips believed that Sullivan was a whipped man. Regardless, Sullivan was in no way cognizant of or part of the deal.

Holske and Beckwith's claims were at odds with all of the accounts of those reporters who were present at the fight. Possibly the reporters did not notice the dealings, if any, before the draw was declared. It is possible that Sullivan's financial backers, fearing the potential loss of their money, overreacted and made the offers, even though it was not necessary. The way the fight came to an end certainly gave the impression that neither fighter was able to stop the other, the fight had become exceedingly dull and dreary, and everyone was content with a draw at that point. Both Sullivan and Mitchell seemed perfectly content to end the fight.[322]

The *New York Sun* reported that while in England, Harry Phillips had paid all of Frank Beckwith's bills. He had paid for his boat ticket, hotel stays, champagne, etc. It said "Beckwith" was not his real name. He was known in Montreal as Detective Wilson, though his real name was Frank Hayner. Several years prior, private detective Fahey and policemen Burean and Naegele were arrested for the robbery of the Grand Trunk Railroad. The arrest was brought about by Wilson/Beckwith, who claimed to have been in with them and learned all of their secrets. He was the principal witness. At the trial, it was revealed that the robbery plans were laid out at the residence of Harry Phillips. Phillips was not in Canada at the time the arrests were made. Phillips subsequently took Wilson/Beckwith with him to England. Fahey was convicted and sentenced to 14 years imprisonment. The trial of the other two was scheduled to be held in a few weeks.

When Phillips and Beckwith/Wilson met in a newspaper office, Phillips said, "You are a dirty loafer and sponge. I have fed and clothed you for a long time. I have a good mind to have you arrested as a blackmailer." Beckwith calmly responded, "You dare not, for I would have you locked up at the same time. I was going to Montreal tonight, but I will stay in Boston for a day or two longer, so that you can have me arrested. You talk about paying my board; what did you get for it?" Phillips replied, "I did it for the sake of my friends and not for myself. I have got letters in my pocket which would send you to prison." Beckwith's answer: "And I have documents in my pocket which would put you behind the bars to keep Fahey company for fourteen years."[323]

Throughout the rest of 1888, the *National Police Gazette* continually hyped Jake Kilrain as the man best entitled to the heavyweight

---

321 *Evening World*, May 3, 1888.

322 *Evening World*, May 10, 1885.

323 *New York Sun*, May 14, 1888.

championship title and to uphold America's honor. It criticized Sullivan's draw performance against Mitchell (even though Kilrain had only drawn against Jem Smith). It also implied that Sullivan was a sell-out, given the claims that the Mitchell party had been bribed to accept a draw (even though no one claimed that Sullivan had anything to do with it). A potential Kilrain – Sullivan fight was being built up. Kilrain would not return to the U.S. until late August.

Columbia, Liberty's Fair Goddess, Honors Our Champion Jake
She Considers the Boston Boy, Who So Badly Failed To Whip England's Champion Boxer, Unworthy To Hold and Defend the Stars and Stripes

The Spectre Of The Banquet
A Vision Of Kilrain's Manly Form Rises Up, Warning John L., Boston's Strong Boy, That He Has Been Weighed In the Pugilistic Scale And Found Wanting

Kilrain Is The Champion
All the Great Pugilists of the World Acknowledge It, And Many Pay Him Well-Deserved Homage By Challenging Him to Meet Them In the Fistic Arena

In early May at the Boston Music Hall, Sullivan acted as master of ceremonies at a benefit given to Joe Lannon.

On May 15, 1888 in Boston, two months after the Mitchell fight, 3,000 people attended a benefit tendered to Sullivan.

The master of ceremonies asked if George Godfrey, the colored pugilist, was in the hall. Godfrey announced that he was. The master of ceremonies then said that he was announcing on behalf of Sullivan that he would give Godfrey money to stand before him in a 3- or 4-round glove contest that evening. Godfrey said that he had not come prepared for a bout, but just was there as a spectator. "They advertised that I had been offered a sum of money to appear here tonight and spar Mr. Sullivan. They did not come near me. … If Mr. Sullivan had come to me personally and asked me to spar with him, I would have been happy to do so for nothing."

When Sullivan appeared, John L. said that he had not authorized the statement, and it must have been issued by his former manager Phillips. However, although the statement had not been made with his knowledge or consent, he was willing to spar Godfrey at that time, and would give him a fair sum. "I am here to spar Mr. Godfrey, if he is ready to spar me, as he has often stated, and I will spar him as the master of ceremonies has just told you." Godfrey replied that he would have to do so at another time, as he had not come prepared to spar with anyone. Godfrey said he would box Sullivan in the future for any amount of money named by the latter or for the gate receipts.

At that point, Sullivan troupe members George La Blanche and Jack Ashton took turns challenging Godfrey to box anywhere, anytime. Godfrey responded that he had offered $1,000 to fight Ashton the previous year. The crowd's hissing response drowned out Godfrey's voice. George insisted, "I am black, but I have a right to my say." Ashton replied, but it could not be heard. Eventually the master of ceremonies broke up the argument and they left the stage.[324]

George Godfrey

35-year-old George Godfrey began boxing in about 1879, weighed about 170 pounds, and stood 5'10 ¼". Back on September 21, 1880, Sullivan had been matched to box Godfrey, but just before they were about to start the fight, the police prevented the contest.

John L. Sullivan refereed a match for the colored heavyweight championship between Godfrey and Professor Hadley in February 1883, which Godfrey won by 6th round knockout.

Sullivan said that in 1883 at a benefit in Charleston, "Godfrey was to have sparred with me, but he wanted too much money, so Kilrain was selected to take his place."

Jake Kilrain fought Godfrey in 1883, stopping him in the 3rd round. Kilrain said that he "hit the darky so hard that he quit in the third round."

Godfrey had the better of an 1886 6-round bout with Joe Lannon, but, according to the Sydney *Referee*, the white referee called it a draw owing to racial favoritism. Kilrain subsequently scored a KO11 over Lannon.[325]

---

[324] In November 1889, Godfrey would score a KO14 over Ashton.

[325] *Boston Daily Globe*, September 22, 1880; *National Police Gazette,* March 17, 1883, November 15, 1884, November 5, 1887, June 3, 1905; *Daily Alta California,* December 31, 1888; Cyberboxingzone.com; *Ring*, June 1926, page 9; *Referee* (Sydney), September 26, 1888, April

This benefit was one of the few times in his career that Sullivan expressed a willingness to box a black fighter. Usually Sullivan drew the color line.

Instead, Sullivan and Ashton sparred in a scientific manner. They went right to work in fast give-and-take fashion, although no powerful blows were exchanged. The spectators enjoyed the 4 rounds.

> On all sides people might be heard commenting on Sullivan's remarkable dexterity and cleverness. His movements betokened a light-weight boxer, rather than a man of his actual division. ... John L. took matters with a coolness that seemed positively marvelous, and the admiration of his old time admirers was increased a hundredfold.[326]

After the show, Godfrey said he wanted to fight Sullivan for a purse within four or eight months of signing articles. He was as confident now as he was back in 1880, when the police prevented their intended glove fight to the finish. "At that time he had no objection to my color, so that should be no obstacle."[327]

The *Sun* reported that the rupture between Sullivan and Phillips was complete. At the benefit, Sullivan had told the crowd that he didn't realize a cent on the show because Phillips had gobbled up the entire receipts. That gave the wrong impression. The truth was that Phillips simply was paid back what he was owed. Sullivan subsequently admitted that he owed Phillips about $1,800. John had told him to square himself with the proceeds of the benefit. Phillips said that Sullivan was a drunk. John L. was seeking new management.[328]

On June 4, 1888 in New York at the Academy of Music, at another testimonial benefit for Sullivan, the champion sparred with Mike Donovan and Jack Ashton in tame and short set-tos that were "devoid of excitement." Only about 500 people attended. Sullivan was very fat, projecting a paunch, and appeared to weigh 260 pounds. He was not the Sullivan of old. He had no wind, and his sparring partners landed whenever and wherever they liked. "It was apparent that his day as a great fighter is over." Increasingly, the press was perceiving Sullivan as a has-been who was past-it.[329]

Sullivan had accepted an engagement to travel with John Dorris' circus, wherein he would give exhibitions with Jack Ashton during the spring/summer tour. He began in mid-to-late June.

27, 1892; Burns, William. *Incidents in the Life of John L. Sullivan and Other Famous People of Fifty Years Ago*. 1928, at 31.

326 *Boston Herald*, May 16, 1888; *New York Clipper*, May 26, 1888.

327 *New York Sun*, May 15, 1888.

328 *New York Sun*, May 17, 1888.

329 *Evening World*, June 5, 1888; *New York Clipper*, June 9, 1888.

On July 6 in Norwich, Connecticut, after their performance, several athletes and employees of the circus sought out the sheriff to serve an attachment on Sullivan's and Dorris' property, claiming arrears in salaries. When Sheriff Joab Rogers appeared, he warned John L. not to move the property. However, after some discussion, allegedly Sullivan reached for the 180-pound sheriff, grabbed him by the coat collar, and with one hand forced him down to the grass. Rogers called for his arrest, but no one present made the attempt. Ultimately, the proprietors effected an arrangement with their employees and the show left the city.[330]

As of July 21, Sullivan had taken over the management and control of the circus. However, the lack of financial success caused it to disband a week later on July 28 in Boston, with most of the employees not having been paid for two weeks.[331]

Sullivan sojourned at Nantasket Beach for a while. Eventually he went to Boston Harbor, spending some time at Crescent Beach. During this time, he drank continuously. Unable to endure his drunken rages, Annie Livingston briefly left him (although she soon would return).

On August 11, 1888 in Brighton, Massachusetts, a drunken Sullivan was returning from the Beacon Park races, near Boston, when he drove his team of horses into a passing carriage. He was arrested for public drunkenness. He was bailed out, but the next morning failed to show up to court, being too ill to get out of bed. They needed to wait for him to sober up.

On August 22, 1888 at the Clarendon House at Nantasket Beach, John L. Sullivan was shot by the proprietor, Dan Murphy. Murphy, who claimed to be an expert rifle shot, asked Sullivan to hold a silver quarter between his thumb and fore-finger, and he would shoot it out. Foolishly, Sullivan complied, and Murphy fired and missed, tearing off some flesh on Sullivan's thumb and finger. Sullivan truly had a dangerous combination of a fighter's courage and lack of judgment.[332]

At that time, another contender was on the rise, a black man named Peter Jackson. Jackson stood 6'1 ½", and in his prime usually fought between 190 and 210 pounds. He was born in 1861 in St. Croix, British West Indies, but moved to Australia. Training at Larry Foley's famous gymnasium, Jackson began fighting in 1882. He became famous for his quick left-right combinations to the body and head, good uppercut, defensive skills, and endurance. Although not a big puncher, usually he cautiously and methodically broke down his opponents.

Because boxing was legal in Australia, Jackson obtained plenty of experience. His only loss came early in his career, in July 1884 when fellow Australian 165-pound 32-year-old Bill Farnan knocked him out in the 3rd

---

330 *Omaha Daily Bee*, July 7, 1888.

331 *St. Paul Daily Globe*, July 24, 29, 1888.

332 *Sacramento Daily Record-Union*, August 23, 1888.

round of a Queensberry rules bout. Jackson had dropped Farnan in the 1st round with a punch to the jaw followed by one to the ribs. He again dropped him with a punch to the neck. However, in the 2nd round, the durable Farnan attacked, staggering Jackson with a body shot. Farnan grabbed Jackson, and hit him "hard between wind and water, the effects being instantaneously shown by the darky seeming to double up." In the 3rd round, Farnan punished Jackson with body shots until he fought him down and out along the ropes. Farnan was then called the "antipodean Sullivan."[333]

Peter Jackson

Despite the loss, Jackson continued to improve. Two months later, in September 1884, Farnan and Jackson fought to a 6-round draw in a bout stopped by the police when spectators entered the ring in protest of Farnan's rough tactics. One reporter wrote, "That Jackson ought to win there can be no two opinions, as Farnan has no science…and is evidently a bit of a glutton in the way of taking his gruel – a quality which the darkey evidently does not possess, being liable to get out of order about the stomach."[334]

When discussing Farnan as a possible opponent for Sullivan, the *Sydney Bulletin* said,

> Farnan may be a good rough-and-tumble fighter among his own set, but it makes us shudder when we picture him before Sullivan – or even facing our own Larry Foley. … As a matter of fact, *Farnan has no science*, and when he fought Jackson in Sydney – we did not see the Melbourne affair – the darky was all over him in the first round; but Jackson was very wild, and struck half his blows with open hands, and appeared afraid of his man. Should Farnan and Foley meet, we shall not be surprised if Farnan does not show for a second round.[335]

---

333 *Australian Sportsman,* June 25, 1884; *National Police Gazette,* August 30, 1884; *New York Clipper,* September 27, 1884, quoting *Australian Sportsman.*

334 *New York Clipper,* November 15, 1884, quoting *Sydney Bulletin,* October 4, 1884.

335 *New York Clipper,* January 17, 1885, quoting *Sydney Bulletin.*

Jackson continued boxing and exhibiting quite often, developing his skills. In March 1886, Jackson knocked out Mick Dooley in the 3rd round.

On September 25, 1886, in a gloved Queensberry rules fight to the finish, a mature Jackson won the Australian heavyweight championship with a KO30 over Tom Lees. Lees had twice knocked out Bill Farnan, in 12 and 4 rounds respectively in 1885 and 1886. Jackson proved that he had the skill, strength, and stamina required to win fights to the finish.[336]

Due to its legality, boxing was proliferating in Australia, and several top fighters emerged, including: Peter Jackson, Bob Fitzsimmons, Jim Hall, and Frank Slavin, amongst others. Most had been groomed at Larry Foley's boxing academy, where weekly gloved boxing bouts took place. Despite its popularity in Australia, there was more money to be earned in America. Hence, eventually most top Australian fighters sought to fight abroad.

In late April 1888, Peter Jackson set sail for San Francisco, in the U.S.A. The first time Americans saw the 200-pound Jackson in the ring was in June 1888 in San Francisco, in 4 rounds of sparring against 165-pound Con Riordan, a boxing teacher at the Golden Gate Club. Observers were impressed with Jackson. He was quick on his feet, clever at ducking, accurate with his punches, throwing them straight from the shoulder without swinging, and he was good at getting in and out. Jackson's counterpunches swelled Riordan's lip.

---

336 *San Francisco Daily Examiner*, December 29, 1888; *Australian Sporting Celebrities* (Melbourne: A.H. Massina & Co., 1887), 64; Boxrec.com.

The local *San Francisco Daily Examiner* quoted admiring spectators as saying, "Fear alone…will prevent Sullivan from meeting him. … The white fighters will draw the color line tighter than ever, now."[337]

The *National Police Gazette* noted that Sullivan had refused to fight George Godfrey on the ground that he would not fight a colored man. It took the opportunity to criticize Sullivan and report that its champion, Jake Kilrain, "did not run behind the door and peep through a crack when Godfrey wanted to meet him and arrange a match."[338]

Speaking of Godfrey, the *San Francisco Examiner* noted that "those who are recognized as the champions do not care particularly to face him, not because he has not backing enough, but because he is a man of color." Later in 1888, it was said that Godfrey had "repeatedly challenged John L. Sullivan and other claimants to the championship, but never got a battle."[339]

Jake Kilrain said, "It is not customary in this country for white men to fight colored men for the championship, but I will fight any man."[340] Yet, during the time that Kilrain called himself the champion, he made no matches with any black fighters, including Godfrey, whom he had defeated several years prior.

Some viewed the color line as a legitimate and acceptable barrier to competition between whites and blacks. Others saw it as a mere excuse to mask cowardice.

When trying to foster a fight between Peter Jackson and California champion Joe McAuliffe, the *San Francisco Daily Examiner* said that in America, "competition is free to all." Although some believed that McAuliffe's position in drawing the color line was un-American, others felt that he would "degrade himself by fighting the dusky Australian." A judge said, "I consider if any pugilist objects to meeting him it will be merely a subterfuge and a virtual acknowledgment that the Australian is a better man, whom the other is afraid to fight." A policeman noted, "The only case I know of…in which the color line was utilized is in connection with the colored pugilist Jackson. … I suppose the excuse is as good as another to avoid a dangerous man." The color line was "a remnant of the feeling that once existed between master and slave."[341]

In late June 1888 in San Francisco, Jackson and top local Jewish pro Joe Choynski, known as the cleverest local pugilist, boxed 4 rounds. Jackson once again demonstrated his ability, although the 160-165-pound Choynski's quick work forced Jackson to make some effort.[342]

The *San Francisco Daily Examiner* wrote:

---

337 *San Francisco Daily Examiner*, June 5, 1888. Jackson said that Riordan was the first boxer that he sparred with in America. *Referee* (Sydney), April 20, 1892.

338 *National Police Gazette*, June 9, 1888.

339 *San Francisco Daily Examiner*, August 25, 1888, December 28, 1888.

340 *National Police Gazette*, January 19, 1889.

341 *San Francisco Daily Examiner*, June 12, 1888.

342 *San Francisco Daily Examiner*, June 27, 1888.

> At no time in the history of pugilism have affairs looked so bright as they do now. The presence of Peter Jackson, the Australian champion, who asks for nothing better than to meet America's best man, has done a great deal to bring about this state of affairs. The only drawback to the situation is the perceptible reluctance of the State's heavy-weight champion [Joe McAuliffe] to meet Jackson, putting his refusal under the ridiculous head of drawing the color line.[343]

The Australians took note of the fact that the San Francisco newspapers were unanimous in declaring Jackson the cleverest sparrer that had been seen on the coast. "[H]is quickness in ducking away and coming up at beautiful hitting distance instantly behind or beside his opponent is noted...one of Jackson's best points." An Englishman told an Australian reporter, "Well, I consider he's the cleverest man I ever saw. I did not always say so to you, because you and all Australians are so mad about your nigger: but now he's gone I tell you. If he's as game as he's clever there is none can beat him."

Australians criticized the American color line:

> The painful part of all this is that the Americans make his colour a bar to fighting him, a thing that should never have obtained in any country, least of all in the land whose sons actually went to war with their own brothers for the emancipation of these very negroes, whose descendants they now refuse to box with, eat with, or sit beside. Then there is another feature, and that is that in manner, deportment, and decency of living Peter Jackson is to Sullivan and a lot more like him as a schoolgirl is to a slum virago. ... It is only these windbags, these men who don't want to meet men who mean real fight, that raise this black shield between them and the chance of defeat at the hands of a coloured antagonist.[344]

On August 24, 1888 in San Francisco at the California Athletic Club, Peter Jackson fought the best American black, Boston's George Godfrey, in a gloved Queensberry rules fight to the finish for the colored championship. Only club members could attend, which incentivized and stimulated membership, and "there was not a single absentee" from the fight. At that time, there was a loophole in California's anti-boxing laws that allowed boxing bouts as long as they were held at athletic clubs before club members.

From the beginning, it was obvious that Jackson was the better man, though Godfrey "fought hard, gamely and took the severest ring punishment. How he managed to stand up under Jackson's left and right handers over the heart is almost beyond comprehension."

---

343 *San Francisco Daily Examiner*, July 2, 1888.

344 *Referee* (Sydney), August 2, 1888.

In the 2nd round, Jackson blocked a Godfrey right and then countered with a left to the chin that dropped George. Godfrey rose and continued fighting hard, but Jackson was much better at hitting and not being hit.

In the 4th round, a Jackson right to the body caused a thud that "sounded like that of a baseball bat fetching a side of beef." Yet, the game Godfrey could take it, and he fought back, staggering Jackson with a right. Jackson retreated, but caught Godfrey with a left, "drawing a copious rivulet of the crimson from Godfrey's left eye."

In the 5th round, Jackson again hurt Godfrey, but Godfrey continued absorbing punishment and fighting back, landing some solid blows of his own and occasionally putting Jackson on the defensive.

In the 9th round, Jackson asked Godfrey, "Do you want me to kill you?" He was suggesting that Godfrey should retire. However, the game Godfrey refused, and kept coming on, so Jackson paced himself and gradually broke him down over many rounds, striking the head and body.

In the 16th round, Godfrey started clinching more.

In the 19th round, Jackson attacked with both hands. After striking him with multiple lefts to the stomach, Godfrey, still standing, said, "I give in," and retired. "It was a wonder he held out as long as he did."

Afterwards, Godfrey said, "I don't know if anybody else can lick Jackson, but I know that I can't. He is a very hard man for anyone to reach, and the person that can beat him has not many equals." The *Examiner* said,

> Jackson's fighting qualities astonished many of those present, while a few were disappointed with his hitting powers. … Jackson struck at and hit one of the hardest men in the world, one whose powers of endurance are acknowledged by all as superior to those of almost any other fighter. If Jackson's well-directed blows did fail to knock out Godfrey, it was not that they were so weak, but that Godfrey's endurance was so great.[345]

On August 25, 1888, Jake Kilrain returned to the U.S. When asked why Mitchell had not accompanied him, Kilrain said that Charlie had encountered legal troubles. A constable who believed that he was going to fight arrested and charged Mitchell with inciting a breach of the peace. Mitchell merely had stepped into a ring, and had no intention of fighting.

Of Sullivan, Kilrain said, "He treated me very badly. A dozen times he spoke from stages where he sparred and said that he hoped Jem Smith would whip me." When Sullivan spoke with Kilrain, he denied making such statements, but Kilrain believed that he was a liar, and "I'll tell him so, too."

Kilrain was headed home to see his wife and kids. In general, the *Police Gazette* and other newspapers painted Kilrain as a good guy and a modest moral family man, overtly contrasting him with Sullivan, who often was depicted as a violent drunk, braggart, and adulterer. The *Police Gazette* also

---

345 *San Francisco Daily Examiner*, August 25-27, 1888.

said that Charlie Mitchell had lowered Sullivan's colors and made him take a back seat in pugilism. It called Kilrain the real champion.[346]

JAKE KILRAIN, THE CHAMPION, LIONIZED.

THE FAMOUS AMERICAN PUGILIST IS MET BY A CROWD OF ENTHUSIASTIC SPORTING MEN ON HIS ARRIVAL FROM ENGLAND PER STEAMSHIP ETRURIA.

JAKE KILRAIN'S PUGILISTIC AND ATHLETIC TRIUMPHS.

SOME NOTABLE EVENTS IN THE CAREER OF THE FAMOUS FIGHTER WHO HOLDS THE "POLICE GAZETTE" DIAMOND BELT, REPRESENTING THE WORLD'S CHAMPIONSHIP.

346 *New York Sun*, August 27, 1888; *National Police Gazette*, September 1, 1888.

The sensational news of the day was the story of a serial killer of women in the Whitechapel district of London, England. Eventually known as "Jack the Ripper," his signature methods included deep throat slashes and removal of his victims' internal organs. The Ripper remained a mystery.

Sometime during late August or early September 1888, during his time at Crescent Beach in Boston Harbor, John L. Sullivan became very ill. John L. later wrote, "I had typhoid fever, gastric fever, inflammation of the bowels, heart trouble, and liver complaint all combined." As a result, he remained in bed for several weeks.

During his illness, in early September, Sullivan swore off drinking. "Sullivan has been a sick man. For some time before he stopped drinking his stomach would not fulfill its functions. This was a state of affairs he had never experienced before."

As of September 17, Sullivan still was "dangerously ill with gastric fever at the home of a friend at Crescent Beach." Three physicians all confirmed that he was very ill, and said it would be another two weeks at least before he could go out. Sullivan said, "I'd give a million dollars if I could get out of this and be in New York." He had lost 20 pounds already. His stomach could not stand a substantial meal. "I'm all right. I'll be around in a week or two, and then I'll call down some of these fellows who have been making talk about fighting for big money and the championship, which they'll never be able to earn."[347]

As of September 19, Sullivan had not improved. Family members and his spiritual advisor were with him. He was very emaciated and weak. He was not able to keep anything in his stomach. Dispelling rumors that he had died, his physician, Dr. Bush, said, "He will not die. He is a very sick man, but two weeks of good care will put him on his feet again. It is a severe case of gastric fever, attended by throat difficulty."[348]

As of September 20, the *Evening World* reported that Sullivan was near death's door and had taken a turn for the worse. He laid tossing and moaning in pain in his bed. His hands and feet were cold. Annie Livingston was there nursing him. His mother had tears in her eyes. His father came that evening as well.

Two priests cleared the room and met with him privately. When asked who the woman was, Sullivan eventually admitted that Livingston was his mistress. The priests said, "You must send her away." John L. replied, "I cannot and will not." They pleaded with him, but it was no use. "Annie Livingston has been a true friend to me in time of trouble; she has stuck to me when others who were nearer gave me the cold shoulder; she has nursed me kindly the last three weeks, and I don't propose to go back on her now."

---

[347] *Evening World*, September 17, 1888; *New York Sun*, September 18, 1888; Sullivan at 154-155.

[348] *Sacramento Daily Record-Union*, September 20, 1888.

Despite the poor report, his physician said that Sullivan was getting better, for he was retaining some food and not having diarrhea quite as much.

The next day, it was reported that Sullivan was gaining in strength. The physicians believed that he had passed the critical stage of his illness.

Yet, on the 22nd, word was that he had suffered a relapse. His nurse said that Sullivan was more feverish than he was the previous day. "His temperature at one time was as high as 102 ½. His pulse was also very high, and the general symptoms were somewhat alarming."

The relapse alarmed his friends. As of September 25, he had shown no improvement. His very concerned doctor prescribed some quinine. His pulse was about 100.

However, the next day, on the 26th, it was said that his pulse had dropped to 93, and he was improving.[349]

As of October 8, his doctor said Sullivan was doing well, and would be in prime condition and ready to fight by the following May.[350]

In his autobiography, Sullivan claimed that during his illness, twice the doctors gave up on him, believing that he was going to die.

Sullivan said he did not emerge from bed until Monday, October 15, 1888, the day he turned 30 years old. From his illness, he contracted what the doctor termed incipient paralysis, being unable to use his legs without the assistance of crutches, which he had to use for the next six weeks.[351]

Mike Donovan confirmed that for a while, Sullivan was not expected to live. "When he recovered he was only a shadow of his former self."[352]

The illness had weakened Sullivan. Few expected him to recover as well as eventually he did, although most expected it to mean that he never would be the same again. After all, many were saying that he was past his prime even before the illness. Most figured that his body finally was giving out after years of abuse. Even by as late as 1900, the average life expectancy for a male was only about 48 years.

Sullivan said that he would recover fully, and when he did, he would be ready to make a fight.

In late 1888, Charlie Mitchell had arrived in the U.S., and he and Kilrain gave exhibitions together. Kilrain was introduced as the champion of the world. Some cheered and some hissed. Sometimes the gallery crowd would chant, "Sullivan! Sullivan! Sullivan!"[353]

On November 24, Sullivan said he would give Mitchell $1,500 if he could stand up for 8 rounds against him under Queensberry rules. Sully said

---

349 *Evening World*, September 20, 25, 26, 1888; *New York Sun*, September 22, 23, 26, 1888.

350 *Sun*, October 8, 1888.

351 *San Francisco Daily Examiner*, July 8, 1889; *Referee* (Sydney), October 26, 1892; Sullivan at 154-155.

352 Donovan at 110.

353 *New York Sun*, November 21, 1888.

that despite his recent illness, he would be willing to fight Mitchell over that distance in five weeks' time.[354]

In late November, there were rumors that Sullivan and Kilrain were in negotiations for a fight.

On December 1, Sullivan arrived in New York with Jack Barnett and Jack Hayes. He said that either Mitchell or Kilrain had to fight him or go to the rear of pugilism. If a match was not made, it would not be his fault. Sullivan said he would fight for $10,000 or as much more as they could raise, the fight to be held in six months. He did not think Mitchell would fight, for he was shrewd and would take no chances. Charlie was in the U.S. to make easy money, not to fight. "Kilrain is more likely to accept a challenge than Mitchell." Regarding his health, Sully said, "Well, I am not as good yet as I was. It takes time to recover when a fellow is run down, you know. I am improving rapidly, and my friends need not worry about me. I will be all right again soon." He was weighing about 210 pounds.[355]

Arthur T. Lumley of the *Illustrated News* said that Sullivan would issue a challenge to Kilrain to fight under LPR rules within 100 miles of New Orleans for a $10,000 purse. Richard K. Fox said that he would put up all the money necessary to make the fight.

On December 7, 1888, Sullivan made an official challenge to fight either Kilrain or Mitchell for $10,000 per side under LPR rules. He deposited a $5,000 forfeit with the *Clipper.*

Kilrain said, "I am delighted to hear that he has put up a deposit, and all that now alarms me is that he will back out again, like the last bluff he made. … I am ready and anxious to settle the thing once and for all." Jake was confident that Fox would back him. Things were looking up. The boxing world eagerly anticipated that the big fight soon would be signed.[356]

As of December 20, Sullivan wrote the editor of the *Herald* that it was about time that the wily Fox should cover his deposit at the *Clipper* office and not have the public become disgusted with his efforts to find some loophole through which to crawl out of the match with his "dog-collar braggart." "Now, Mr. Richard Fox, do show yourself a man of something more than long-winded courage. You have been trying to gull the public into the belief that you would spend $10,000 to see me whipped. You have not succeeded yet." Sullivan questioned Fox's earnestness, saying that "battles cannot be fought on wind alone." Fox needed something more than "printers' ink, pink paper, and meaningless mouthings."[357]

The next morning, Sullivan's $5,000 forfeit was covered by William Harding, Fox's sporting editor, on behalf of Kilrain. Kilrain wrote that he was ready to fight for $10,000 a side and the "*Police Gazette* diamond belt,

---

[354] *Evening World*, November 24, 1888.

[355] *Evening World*, December 1, 1888.

[356] *Evening World*, December 4, 7, 8, 1888.

[357] *New York Sun*, December 21, 1888.

which represents the championship of the world." Kilrain signed "Champion of the World" under his name.[358]

In late December 1888, Peter Jackson had his second fight in the U.S. Although California champion Joe McAuliffe initially had drawn the color line, the *San Francisco Examiner* "pointed out to him the nonsensical position," and, realizing that if he did not face Jackson "it would be considered a palpable sign of weakness," McAuliffe agreed to fight him, a decision that "was hailed with delight by every lover of sport."[359]

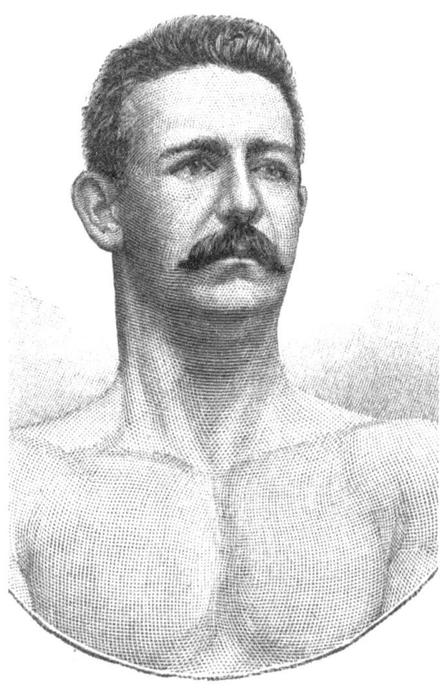

JOE McAULIFFE.

McAuliffe had several important victories, including: 1887 KO44 Mike Brennan and KO3 Paddy Ryan; and 1888 KO49 Frank Glover and KO2 Mike Conley, the Ithaca Giant.[360]

On December 28, 1888 in San Francisco, 27-year-old 204-pound Peter Jackson fought 24-year-old 219-pound Joe McAuliffe in a Queensberry rules fight to the finish. The 6'3" McAuliffe was the betting favorite.

Throughout the bout, the quicker and more skilled Jackson inflicted punishment and was able to avoid McAuliffe's harder blows. The *Examiner* said McAuliffe had a bright moment in the 10th round, landing a powerful right to the back of the head that sent Jackson to the floor. However, the *Chronicle* said Jackson's foot slipped, and as he clinched, McAuliffe threw a punch and Peter rolled to the floor. Although it was not a true knockdown, the crowd roared anyway. The *Examiner* said Jackson recovered and landed a body shot and uppercut, but McAuliffe once again hit him with a powerful right, making Jackson more cautious.

In the 15th round, Jackson hit McAuliffe often, with every type of blow.

In the 16th round, "Jackson still did the rushing, but he was always careful not to take chances against Joe's right."

In the 18th round, McAuliffe suffered a beating. After an exchange, McAuliffe went down to his knees near the ropes. Jackson's body shots had weakened him, and at that point, McAuliffe seemed near defeat.

358 *Evening World*, December 22, 1888.

359 *San Francisco Daily Examiner*, August 26, 1888.

360 *San Francisco Daily Examiner*, December 24, 1888, December 28, 1888; *San Francisco Chronicle*, December 29, 1888.

In the 19th round, Jackson dropped McAuliffe with a body shot. After McAuliffe rose, Jackson continued punishing him with blows to the head and body.

In subsequent rounds, Jackson methodically broke him down with a consistent pounding to the body and head.

In the 24th round, Jackson knocked McAuliffe down and out with a straight right to the nose. It appeared as if Jackson "had almost knocked the life out of him. His eyes seemed almost closed, his nose was fearfully swollen, and his body was covered with great red blotches which marked where every blow had landed."

SPORTING SURPRISES WEST AND EAST.
PETER JACKSON'S TRIUMPH OVER JOE McAULIFFE AT SAN FRANCISCO, CAL., AND THE UNPROVOKED ASSAULT ON CHARLEY MITCHELL, THE ENGLISH BOXER, AT CLEVELAND, OHIO.

The *San Francisco Examiner*'s report was entitled, "The Color Line…Peter Jackson Knocks Champion Joe McAuliffe Under It." Jackson was both a better boxer and fighter, for he was "too skillful, too quick, too scienced, too much of a general, and 'our big Joe' bit the dust." Jackson had demonstrated "extraordinary skill in keeping away from McAuliffe's crushing right and never planting a blow when he would risk getting one in return." He could duck faster than McAuliffe could strike. He had "chopped him to pieces in as masterly a manner as was ever witnessed in the history of the squared circle. … Jackson is a short-odds horse in the race for the world's laurels of modern fistiana. He has earned the chance, and earned it well."

Afterwards, McAuliffe said, "I had no idea of going down, but my legs sunk under me, and that's all there was to it. I didn't know I had been knocked out until my seconds had helped me to my corner." In sportsmanlike fashion, McAuliffe graciously said, "Peter Jackson is the best boxer I ever knew, and those who say that he can't hit hard ought to let him try it on them. They'd soon learn their mistake. He is quick and smart as a man can be, and in addition to his skill he is a nice, gentlemanly fellow."

San Francisco's black population rejoiced:

> The colored population of San Francisco have not had such a jubilee since Mr. Lincoln signed the Emancipation proclamation. … Every one of them had money on Jackson, but deeper even than the pleasure of winning was their joy at the victory of race. … Every one that had bet jingled coin in his pocket, and for once was disposed to dispute the superiority of any other race than his own.

Boxing had symbolic power. For many, that symbolism carried potential racial and political implications.

Jackson was willing and anxious to meet Sullivan or any other top contender, including Jake Kilrain, believing that he could defeat anyone. "No man can hurt me." "If they draw the color line on me I will claim the championship anyhow. That is a 'chestnut.' They cannot avoid meeting me by such a plea." However, Sullivan's backers said that he "had long ago declined to meet any colored man in the ring, or any man who stands up with a colored fighter."

Some lamented that Jackson's victory would hurt the sport. "Many regret that Jackson won, on the ground that no first-class Eastern pugilist will care to fight a colored man, and they think it will have a tendency to lessen the regard of outsiders for boxing if a black man demands the championship."[361]

The president of the California Athletic Club, which backed Jackson and hosted his fights, expressed his opposition to the color line being drawn by Sullivan and others:

> It sounds strange to me that John L. Sullivan has drawn the line. It is a well-known fact that at his benefit in Boston he challenged George Godfrey, the colored man, to go him four rounds there and then. Godfrey did not see where the money would come in as Sullivan proposed to do the business 'for fun,' so he refused. I have heard it stated, too, that when Sullivan was here some years ago he accepted quite a large sum of money and promised to spar Bill Williams, a colored man, six rounds at the Pavilion. The only reason he did not do it was that his manager could not get a license.

Another boxing club delegate said of Jackson,

> He has fought his way to the front honestly and fairly, and his color must be lost sight of by those who would lay claim to championship honors. Kilrain, Sullivan, and others cannot afford to draw the color line under the circumstances. It would lay them directly open to the

[361] *San Francisco Daily Examiner*, December 28-30, 1888; *San Francisco Chronicle*, December 29, 1888.

charge of cowardice. I do not think the color line, which the war effaced, will stand between Jackson and the championship.[362]

Some wondered just how staunch or consistent Sullivan's beliefs regarding the color line really were. Apparently, for nine years, black pugilist Billy Wilson had been a member of a sculling crew in which Sullivan was a double stroke.[363]

Sullivan was "on record that he was once stripped to meet George Godfrey in Boston, when at the last moment the police interfered."[364]

Once, Sullivan and Godfrey were set to spar at a benefit (supposedly in 1883), but it didn't happen because Godfrey wanted to be paid, and Sullivan wanted him to box at his benefit for free. Godfrey said,

> I am fighting for a living just the same as Sullivan is. … I was asked to box with him at that benefit of his in Boston, and I replied that I would do so if paid for it. … I made a very business-like proposition to Sullivan afterwards when I told him that I was going to take a benefit, and that I would give him 50 percent of the receipts if he would come and box with me. I didn't want him to box for nothing as he did me.[365]

In 1883, Sullivan had fought Herbert "the Maori" Slade, who was a "half breed Maori," for he was half white and half Pacific Islander. Slade had been a member of Sullivan's tour.

Before meeting Slade in 1883, Sullivan drew the color line on American black C. A. C. Smith. In early 1884, Sullivan said that he never would box a colored man in public, but would box Bill Williams in a private room. In April 1884, while in New Orleans, Sullivan confirmed that that he would not meet a colored man in public.[366]

Yet, in May 1888, Sullivan was willing to box Godfrey in public, when the master of ceremonies asked them to box. At that time, it was the unprepared Godfrey who declined the meeting, offering to fight at a later date.[367]

In early 1889, Sullivan would referee a mixed-race contest between Joe Lannon and George Godfrey, declaring it a draw after 15 rounds.[368]

The newspapers recognized that Sullivan "has declared many times that he will not fight a man of black color. Should he meet and best Kilrain,

---

362 *San Francisco Daily Examiner*, December 31, 1888.

363 *San Francisco Daily Examiner*, July 30, 1889.

364 *Referee* (Sydney), September 26, 1888, April 27, 1892; *Police Gazette,* June 3, 1905; Cyberboxingzone.com; *Ring*, June 1926, page 9; Burns at 31.

365 *San Francisco Chronicle*, July 30, 1888; *Daily Alta California,* December 31, 1888.

366 *National Police Gazette*; August 4, 1883; *San Francisco Daily Examiner,* January 26, 1884; *Daily Picayune,* April 15, 1884.

367 *New York Clipper,* May 26, 1888; *Boston Herald*, May 16, 1888.

368 *National Police Gazette*, February 23, 1889.

however, he may be forced into a fight with the Australian to save his title of champion of the world."[369]

Although Sullivan's position was consistent with the era's social norms, boxing precedent was against his attitude. In 1810 in England, then champion Tom Cribb fought and defeated Tom Molineaux, a former slave from Virginia. Also, the "whole history of warfare shows that it admits of no color line." The British had fought black men, and fought side by side with them. Colored troops fought in the U.S. Civil War. The *New York Sun* wrote,

> It is all well enough for a great man like Sullivan to refuse the overtures of second or third-rate men, like Prof. Hadley or Prof. Godfrey, or that tall and sable Canadian, Prof. Smith, who figured in the Northwest a few years ago, or the Black Diamond of this neighborhood. But against a palpably good one, like Jackson, the only thing that can protect Mr. Sullivan's reputation is his own science. He cannot confront the Australian with a theory.[370]

Regardless of the color line and the rising Peter Jackson, Sullivan had a much bigger fight on his mind. The huge Kilrain bout, which had been building for well over a year, was on the horizon.

[369] *Evening World*, January 1, 1889.
[370] *New York Sun*, January 2, 1889.

Settling All Doubts

On January 7, 1889 in Toronto, Ontario, Canada, articles of agreement were signed for an LPR fight between John L. Sullivan and Jake Kilrain to occur on Monday July 8, 1889 within 200 miles of New Orleans. The fight would start between 8 a.m. and 12 p.m. The purse would be $10,000 per side and the championship belt, winner take all. The final deposit of $5,000 would be made on April 8. The ring would be 24-feet square. The parties would split the cost of building the ring and ropes. They could have three spikes in their shoes, no greater than 3/8 of an inch each. Sullivan was present along with Charley Johnston and W. H. Germane. Representing Kilrain were *Police Gazette* editor William E. Harding and Parson Davies.[371]

KILRAIN AND SULLIVAN TO FIGHT
THE NATIONAL
POLICE GAZETTE
ARTICLES SIGNED IN TORONTO
THE
ILLUSTRATED
SPORTING
JOURNAL
IN AMERICA
NEW YORK, SATURDAY, JANUARY 19, 1889.

NO BLUFF THIS TIME.
SULLIVAN SIGNING ARTICLES WITH KILRAIN'S REPRESENTATIVES AT TORONTO, TO FIGHT FOR

Although he preferred gloved contests, clearly Sullivan felt that he still had something to prove, particularly given his unsatisfactory result in the Mitchell contest, and the fact that for years the *Police Gazette* and others had been claiming that a fighter was not a real champion unless he defended the crown in an LPR fight. The old system still had its allure and prestige. The fact that the *Police Gazette* had been touting Kilrain as the true LPR champion likely had something to do with it as well. Plus, the money was right.

---

[371] *Evening World*, January 7, 1889; *San Francisco Daily Examiner*, December 24, 1888; *Boston Daily Globe*, July 8, 1889; *Referee* (Sydney), October 26, 1892; Isenberg at 263.

[Next week's issue will contain an elegant full page handsomely embellished portrait of John L. Sullivan.]

CHAMPION JAKE KILRAIN,

WHO IS MATCHED TO MEET JOHN L. SULLIVAN FOR $20,000 AND THE POLICE GAZETTE DIAMOND BELT REPRESENTING THE CHAMPIONSHIP OF THE WORLD.

JOHN L. SULLIVAN,

"BOSTON'S PRIDE," WHO IS TO FIGHT CHAMPION JAKE KILRAIN FOR $20,000, THE POLICE GAZETTE DIAMOND BELT AND THE CHAMPIONSHIP OF THE WORLD.

Immediately the likely fight-result debate began. John L.'s financial backer Jimmy Wakely said, "If I did not think Sullivan superior in every way to Kilrain I would not risk a dollar on him." His other backer, Charley Johnston, said Kilrain would be knocked stiff, for John was the better man beyond question.

Billy Edwards did not think Sullivan was or would be the same man again after his illness. "Kilrain is a very good man and ought to win, now that Sullivan is not the Sullivan of old."

William Ottman, an old-time amateur middleweight said Sullivan had the best record and had done what no other man could do.

Barney Aaron, ex-lightweight champion, said it would be a very hard battle, for even at his best Sullivan would have no walkover with Kilrain.

Richard K. Fox said, "Sullivan was a great man in his day, but you must remember that his day has passed away."[372]

Those who had seen Kilrain fight Jem Smith in England believed that Kilrain would defeat Sullivan. The *London Sporting Life* wrote,

> There is not one impartial man in this city who believes that Sullivan has a three to one chance in a prize ring encounter with Kilrain. … Nearly all the sporting men at the clubs were of the opinion that Kilrain will win, and they think Sullivan is aware he has no chance.[373]

A New York correspondent of the *London Sporting Life* reported that despite his claims of sobriety, Sullivan had been on another wild drinking spree in January.

This writer also criticized Sullivan's drawing of the color line:

> His flat refusal to meet Peter Jackson, on the thin excuse of his objection to fight a coloured man, was already sapping his new found popularity. … Sullivan has already put himself on record as refusing to meet a negro, and he now says that under no consideration will he meet Jackson. Many sporting men construe this as an acknowledgement of Jackson's great fighting powers. … Would it not be a curious thing if Sullivan was whipped by a nigger, and a British subject at that?[374]

On January 24, it was reported that a week prior, Annie Livingston gave John L. a black eye that was still present. He was in Behan's saloon on Harrison avenue. His friends were trying to get him to go to another establishment, where he could be kept from whiskey, but he would not heed their advice. They went and got Annie Livingston, and she came. "John, come with me. You are not doing right." He sneered at her and turned to the bar for more drink. Then she grabbed his coat lapels and said, "John, if you ever cared for me, I want you to listen to my advice and leave

---

372 *Evening World*, January 10, 1889.

373 *Brooklyn Daily Eagle*, December 9, 1888, quoting *London Sporting Life*.

374 *Referee* (Sydney), February 27, 1889, quoting *London Sporting Life*.

the place with me at once." He replied, "Leave go." She tried to pull him towards the door, and then he became savage and made a motion as if to strike her. Quick as a flash she fired a right into his right eye. "He has taught her how to spar, and she knows more than a good many noted sports do about the art of self-defense." Sullivan fell back against the bar. She held her ground. "She has a temper when aroused, second not even to Sullivan." The giant looked surprised as he gazed at her. Then he started laughing and shook her hand. "You have done what no man here could have done." He ordered another round of drinks. A few minutes later he left with her.[375]

Sullivan was drinking, smoking cigars, his weight was climbing, and his training almost nonexistent.

Regardless, a confident admirer wrote a poem about Sullivan: "He is a man you can defy, and he will whip Kilrain by and by. Hush, big baby, don't you cry. You will know who is champion by and by."

In March, Sullivan said his weight was up to 232 pounds. He said Frank Moran would train him.[376]

Sullivan said that in general, the press greatly exaggerated his drinking habits.

> I'm not nearly so black as I'm painted. Of course, I go on a spree now and then, but who doesn't? No notice is taken of others, while if I take a drink of lemon soda it is telegraphed all over the country that Sullivan's on a 'bender.' But I don't really mind what the papers do say about me. The impression gets abroad that I'm a devil of a fellow, and only it makes people more curious to see me.[377]

Sullivan was laughing all the way to the bank, so to speak. He was well aware of the marketing value that the adverse press had, even if it wasn't always true.

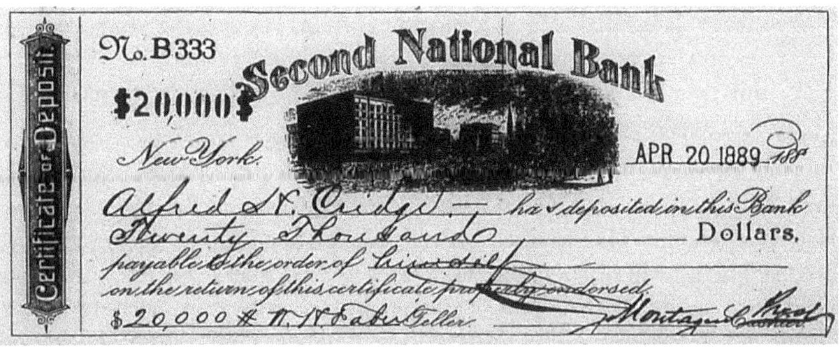

Certificate of Deposit.

No. B333

$20,000

Second National Bank

New York. APR 20 1889

Alfred N. Cridge has deposited in this Bank Twenty Thousand Dollars, payable to the order of himself on the return of this certificate properly endorsed.

$20,000

Deposit of the $20,000 with stakeholder Al Cridge

---

[375] *Evening World*, January 24, 1889.

[376] *Evening World*, March 11, 15, 1889.

[377] *Evening World*, March 26, 1889.

KILRAIN AND SULLIVAN.

GOOD AND EVIL AS TYPIFIED AND CONTRASTED IN THE LIVES AND HABITS OF TWO FAMOUS AMERICAN PUGILISTS, THE BOSTON BOY AND OUR CHAMPION JAKE.

On April 24, 1889 in Brooklyn, New York, Sullivan sparred with Jack Ashton. The champ looked soft and fat, not as if he was preparing for a fight to the finish. Although the crowd paid $1 and $1.50 to witness the exhibition, the rounds only lasted 30 seconds and the boxing was light and not particularly interesting.

John L. seems to be quick with his hands and to get home on the neck with considerable precision and force. He is not himself at all, though, and those who knew him when he was downing everybody with the greatest ease remarked the difference. However, allowance must be made for his recent sickness.[378]

Another reporter said that although Sullivan made a clever display, he was not as agile as he was before his illness. However, he still was able to more than hold his own with Jack Ashton, who had conquered Joe Lannon, and his exhibition of skill and quickness evoked applause.[379]

On April 26, 1889 in San Francisco, 200-pound Peter Jackson fought 185-pound Patsy Cardiff, who had fought Charley Mitchell to an 1885 5-round draw and had fought Sullivan to an 1887 6-round draw. Cardiff also had an 1885 and 1886 KO9 and KO7 over Bill Wilson, a black fighter. In 1887, Cardiff drew with Pat Killen over 10 rounds. However, in 1888, Killen stopped Cardiff in the 4th round. Killen also had an 1886 KO4 over Mervine Thompson, a 210-220-pound black fighter, and an 1887 KO2 over Duncan McDonald. In September 1889, Joe McAuliffe, whom Jackson had defeated, would stop Killen in the 7th round.

1 - Cardiff fouled Jackson, grabbing around the legs, pushing him over the ropes, and head butting him. A Cardiff counter to Jackson's nose brought first blood.

2 - The round was tame and cautious.

3 - Cardiff clinched around the waist and tried to throw Jackson down or break his back. They both did some effective infighting.

4 - Jackson began finding the mark, hitting Cardiff with his left to the face and avoiding most counters.

5 - Cardiff's left cheek was bleeding and his eye puffed. Once again, he grabbed Peter's legs. Cardiff landed a good counter that momentarily staggered Jackson. He then tried to push Peter over the ropes. They exchanged often, but Jackson landed more blows.

6 - While grabbing around his waist, Cardiff attempted to knee Jackson in the stomach. Cardiff also hit with an open hand.

A Jackson right under the ear dropped Cardiff. He rose and Jackson again hurt him with a hard left on the nose.

7 - Jackson hit Cardiff's nose often.

8 - Jackson punished Cardiff. He landed a telling smash on Patsy's gory lips, and Cardiff tottered. Jackson followed up with a right smash under the ear on the jaw and Cardiff went down to the floor.

---

378 *Brooklyn Daily Eagle,* April 25, 1889.
379 *New York Clipper,* May 4, 1889.

Cardiff rose and hugged and tried to grab Peter's leg. Jackson punched him to the ropes. While pounding on him there, Peter asked, "Do you give up?" Patsy refused, and continued to take a beating.

Between rounds, Cardiff's cornerman illegally rubbed resin on Patsy's gloves, but the referee discovered it and forced them to remove the substance prior to the start of the next round.

9 - Cardiff appeared to be near the end of his rope. He seemed out of it. He turned to his second, as if asking him to stop it. Jackson kept jabbing him. Cardiff did catch him with one good right that caused Peter to back off for a while and be more cautious. However, eventually, Jackson forced Cardiff to the ropes again. At the bell, Patsy was almost out. Jackson seemed to pity him.

10 - Jackson landed hard lefts and rights to Cardiff's jaw, sending him back to the ropes. Patsy held onto the ropes. Jackson stopped momentarily and asked Patsy if he wished to give in, but he refused. Jackson continued pounding on him. Rights and lefts sent Cardiff back into his corner against the ropes, dropping his hands. Patsy turned his back and bent over the ropes.

Cardiff's cornerman urged him to continue to fight, but he said, "I can't fight." Jackson paused, waiting for him to raise his hands in the ready position, but he did not. Seeing that his man was done for, his second retired Cardiff by throwing up the sponge. The referee stepped in and raised Jackson's hand, looking at Cardiff and saying, "Out."

The *San Francisco Chronicle* said that from the start, Jackson was superior in every way, hitting the body and head with both hands. Although Cardiff occasionally landed a good counterpunch, Jackson smiled throughout, and the only mark he had at the end of the fight was a small lump on his forehead where he was head butted in the 1st round.

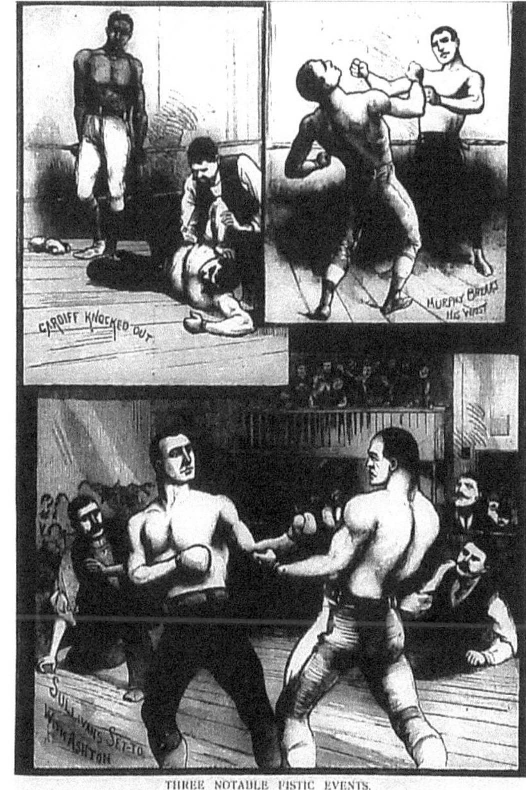

THREE NOTABLE FISTIC EVENTS.
THE SULLIVAN-ASHTON SPARRING MATCH IN BROOKLYN; JACKSON-CARDIFF FIGHT IN SAN FRANCISCO, AND THE McCARTHY-MURPHY MILL IN BOSTON.

The *San Francisco Examiner* was more critical of Jackson, saying that although he was a clever boxer, he lacked finishing power, depending on defeating his opponent "by jabbing him into insensibility and not by a clean knock-out." Hence, it called him overrated. Regardless of the criticism, this writer still said, "Jackson displayed his wonderful quickness and ability to dodge at short range. He had decidedly the best of the slugging."[380]

Other than Sullivan and Kilrain, Peter Jackson clearly was the next best heavyweight. His manager believed that Jackson could defeat both Sullivan and Kilrain, saying that the only man who could whip Jackson was the Sullivan of old.

In May, it was reported that Sullivan soon would buckle down to serious training for the Kilrain fight. On May 4, he said that he was smoking his last cigar, and would start training in earnest on Monday May 6. He was weighing in the neighborhood of 230 pounds.[381]

On May 6, 1889 in Tarrytown, New York, Sullivan and Ashton gave a sparring exhibition. Afterwards, there was a fight on a train between railroad detectives, train men, and a gang of toughs who had attended the exhibition. Sullivan and Ashton were on the train, along with 300 of the spectators. The conductor asked for tickets. William Doris, a local fighter, claimed that he already had given him his ticket. The conductor reported him to the railroad detectives. When one informed Doris that he had to pay, Doris became abusive and threatened to do up the detective. They wound up grappling. Fifty of Doris' friends rushed to his rescue. Trainmen and detectives rushed in as well, and succeeded in beating back the crowd with their clubs. In the midst of it all, Sullivan rescued one of the detectives. He told the crowd that if any fighting was to be done, he would do it. He said that he would not allow anyone to interfere with the officers' discharge of their duties. Eventually, Doris was taken off the train and locked up. He was sentenced to six months in the penitentiary. He had served several terms already, having been discharged only three weeks prior.[382]

Initially, it was reported that Sullivan's training quarters would be on the Coney Island Boulevard, a mile from the ocean.

However, Sullivan's backers believed that he needed a more secluded training site, away from temptations. The metropolis was a climate which was "not healthy enough for a man so easily led from the paths of sobriety." They had real money on the line, and, fearing the loss of their money, they hired former wrestling champion William Muldoon, a stern disciplinarian, to train John L. on his farm in Belfast, New York.

Sullivan arrived at Muldoon's farm on Saturday May 11, about two months from the fight.

---

380 *San Francisco Chronicle*, April 27, 1889; *San Francisco Daily Examiner*, April 26, 27, 1889; *National Police Gazette*, May 11, 1889.

381 *Evening World*, May 1, 1889; *Sun*, May 5, 1889.

382 *Sun*, May 8, 1889.

JOHN L. SULLIVAN. JAKE KILRAIN.

THE TWENTY-THOUSAND-DOLLAR PUGILISTS

JAKE KILRAIN AND JOHN L. SULLIVAN WHO ARE TO DO BATTLE FOR A FORTUNE NEAR NEW ORLEANS ON JULY EIGHTH

FAC-SIMILE OF THE FAMOUS POLICE GAZETTE TROPHY OF THE HEAVY-WEIGHT CHAMPIONSHIP

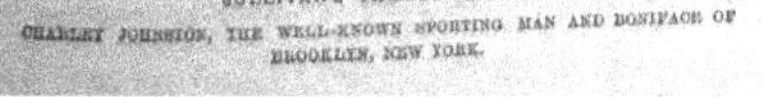

SULLIVAN'S FAMOUS BACKER.

CHARLEY JOHNSTON, THE WELL-KNOWN SPORTING MAN AND BONIFACE OF BROOKLYN, NEW YORK.

THE MAN WHO HOLDS THE MONEY.

MR. "AL" CRIDGE, THE WELL-KNOWN BOOKMAKER, WHO HAS CHARGE OF THE $20,000 KILRAIN-SULLIVAN STAKES.

Every day before breakfast, Sullivan walked a mile to the farm, he would milk the cows, return one mile, and then eat wheat, oatmeal, milk, and raw eggs. The rest of the morning was taken up wrestling, pounding the bag, and boxing. Muldoon was working on Sullivan's wrestling skills, which could prove invaluable in an LPR bout, which allowed wrestling above the waist. Sullivan also was taking a 12-mile daily run, chopping trees, and working the plow. He was weighing 225 pounds, and expected to reduce to 210 pounds. Assisting Muldoon was J. W. Barnett. Mike Cleary was his sparring partner.[383]

It also was reported that Sullivan's training included wrestling and sparring, hitting the punching bags, shadow boxing with 4-pound weights, jumping rope, throwing a 10-pound ball, swimming, running, and taking long walks that lasted 1 to 3 hours.

AT JOHN L'S TRAINING GROUND.
HOW THE BIG FELLOW IS WORKING OFF HIS SUPERFLUOUS FLESH AND STRENGTHENING HIS MUSCLES AT WRESTLER MULDOON'S FARM, BELFAST, N. Y.

Analyzing the upcoming fight, the *New York Sun* wrote:

> There never was a fighter like John L. Sullivan, and there never was a fighter who had his opportunities. In the plenitude of his powers no man could successfully resist him. Not long ago Peter Jackson, the colored Australian boxer, was talking to Pat Sheedy about him, when he remarked: "From all accounts he must have been the high daddy of all fighters. He went against everybody and nobody had the ghost of a show with him." …
>
> He is now backed against Jake Kilrain for the largest stake ever posted for a ring contest, and despite the fact that the agreed-on day of battle is not two months off, he went on a rousing spree, which,

[383] *Sun*, May 10, 15, 1889; *New York Clipper*, May 18, 1889.

fortunately for him, was nipped in its bud. Then his backers, after sending him away from temptations to Billy Muldoon's farm, met in consultation to devise ways and means to keep him sober and to bring him to the scratch in a fit condition to do battle with any show of success. They resolve that it will not do to leave him unguarded day or night, asleep or awake, and they send him a retinue of trainers such as, in numbers and ability, no fighter since Goliath's time ever had. …

His intimates admit with sorrow that his legs do not grow strong as rapidly as they expected. He is to fight under London ring rules, and he can't wrestle a little bit. Purely a Queensberry fighter, he has never thought it worth his while to acquire an intimate knowledge of cross-buttocks, grapevine twists, or inside clicks, and now Billy Muldoon is to try and teach him in a few weeks what men who have a natural aptitude for wrestling find it difficult to acquire in years. …

His best friends admit now that his chances of success with Kilrain are none of the best. They confess that in their opinion Sullivan cannot stand a long fight. …

He must whip Kilrain off the reel or he will not whip him at all. Jake is not as quick on his feet as Charley Mitchell, but he is far from being a slow coach. If Sullivan cannot hit Jake good and hard at the very outset of the contest he is a goner. Jake is a very clever wrestler… .

If he is able to land with anything like his old-time severity on Jake's jaw, neck or stomach, the contest will be as short and sweet as a donkey's trot. Kilrain is banking a good deal on Sullivan's inability to get into condition. … He may attempt to imitate Mitchell's tactics and make a waiting fight of it, but no man that ever lived can evade Sullivan if he is well and strong on his legs. He is the quickest big man that ever fought in the ring, and when he once gets an opponent on the run, that is the end of that man's chances. Mind, that is when he is well and strong.[384]

The *Evening World* marveled at the confidence the general public had in Sullivan, calling it remarkable considering how much he had done to shatter their faith. Many wealthy gentlemen were so confident in him that they offered to put up enormous wagers.[385]

Starting the last week of May, Sullivan and Muldoon gave wrestling exhibitions for more than a week, at locations such as Detroit, Cincinnati (27 minutes of wrestling on May 28 – Sullivan won six falls out of 10), Philadelphia, New Jersey, and New York. At each show, they attracted full

---

[384] *Sun*, May 19, 1889.
[385] *Evening World*, May 25, 1889.

houses. Mike Cleary was sparring with John as well. Kilrain had Charley Mitchell as his trainer.

On Decoration Day, May 30, Sullivan and Muldoon wrestled at the Gloucester ball grounds on the Jersey shore, three miles south of Philadelphia. A crowd of 1,000 or 1,500 were in attendance. Sullivan wore black tights. Muldoon's tights were lavender. Sullivan threw Muldoon over his hip onto his hands and knees. Next, Muldoon grasped Sullivan around the waist and threw him down to the carpet on his side. Then Sullivan got a hold on Muldoon and forced his shoulders to the carpet and was awarded the first fall after two minutes.

A great deal of strength was exhibited in the 2nd bout. They kept trying to pick each other up and throw the other to the ground on his back. At one point, Sullivan fell upon Muldoon so hard that the spectators thought he had driven him into the ground. However, when Sullivan was thrown he went down on the carpet hard, like a log. Muldoon finally landed him on his shoulders in three minutes. Sullivan was puffing hard.

In the third bout, Muldoon grabbed Sullivan's head and shook it viciously. When he broke free, John's face and ears were very red. After Sully had tripped him and thrown him on his side, Muldoon rose, grasped Sullivan in his arms, lifted him from his feet and threw him with great force upon his back heavily enough to shake the earth. Sullivan rose and drew his right arm as if to deliver a punch, but he checked himself.

In the evening, Sullivan and Mike Cleary gave a lively 3-round exhibition of boxing for 500 or 600 people.[386]

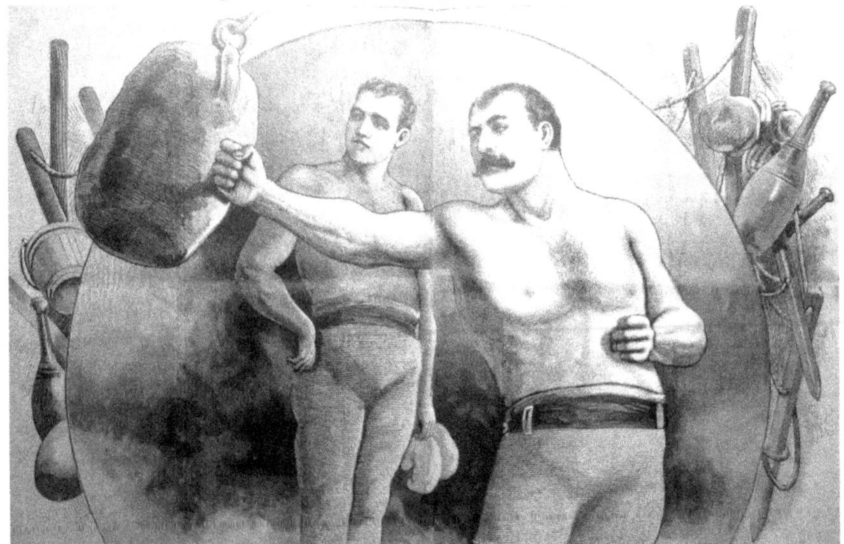

The Police Gazette Champion In Training
Jake Kilrain Working Off Superfluous Flesh By Biffing the Bag In His Training Quarters While Charley Mitchell Keeps Tally

---

386 *Pittsburg Dispatch*, *Omaha Daily Bee*, May 29, 1889; *Evening World*, May 31, 1889; *Sun*, June 2, 1889; *New York Clipper*, June 8, 1889.

Word was that Kilrain's mother had died. Sullivan expressed his sympathy, saying he felt sorry for Jake. "A fellow can have as many wives as he wants, but no one can fill the place of his mother. Whatever else people may say about me, nobody can truthfully say I have ever neglected my parents."[387]

Sullivan told a lady reporter, Nellie Bly, about his training regimen. He woke up at about 6 a.m., got rubbed down, and then he and Muldoon walked and ran a mile or a mile-and-a-half and back. He took a warm shower bath and had a rub-down with a mixture of ammonia, camphor and alcohol. He wore heavy clothes. "When I came here I weighed 237 pounds; now I weigh 218 pounds, and before I leave I will weigh 195."

He ate oatmeal for breakfast, meat and bread for dinner, cold meat and stale bread for supper, without any sweets or potatoes. He had not smoked any cigars while there. Occasionally Muldoon allowed him a glass of ale.

Sullivan said he would rather fight twelve dozen times than train, but it had to be done.

After breakfast he ran and/or walked for 10 or 12 miles, doing it in 2 hours. Upon his return, he was rubbed down again. Then he had dinner. In the afternoon, he punched the bag, hit the Rugby football, which was suspended from the ceiling, threw a football, swung Indian clubs and dumbbells, worked with the chest expander fastened to the wall, and other various exercises until supper.

When asked if he liked fighting, Sullivan replied, "I don't. I did once, or rather, I was fond of traveling about and the excitement of crowds, but this is my last fight. … I am tired and want to settle down; I am getting old." John L. had turned 30 the previous October. He wanted to travel for a year giving sparring exhibitions and then settle down and become a hotel proprietor. He said that he had made between $500,000 and $600,000 in boxing, including $125,000 from September 1883 to May 1884.

In the ring, he wore knee breeches, stockings and shoes, but no shirt.

The lady reporter remarked that his hands seemed relatively small to have recorded so many knockouts. The only difference from an ordinary hand was their thickness. Sullivan told her to feel his arm. Bly wrote, "I tried to feel the muscle; it was like a rock. With both hands I tried to span it, but couldn't."

Sullivan said he hardened his hands and face with a mixture of rock salt, white wine, vinegar, and other ingredients.

When asked whether he hated to hit a man or felt sorry about it, he said, "I don't think about it. I never feel sorry until the fight is over." When asked how he felt when hit, Sullivan said, "I only want a chance to hit back."

Muldoon told her, "I don't make any money by this. … I am anxious to see Sullivan do justice to himself in his coming fight. … Sullivan is the most

---

[387] *Salt Lake Herald*, May 30, 1889.

obedient man you ever saw. He hasn't asked to drink or smoke since he came here."

Sullivan told Bly, "You are the first woman who ever interviewed me. I have given you more than ever I gave any reporter in my life. They generally manufacture things and credit them to me, although some are mighty good fellows."[388]

On June 5, 1889 on a barge anchored off Dillon's Point, opposite Benicia, in the Carquinez Straits, California, 22-year-old 180-pound James J. Corbett knocked out 20-year-old 172-pound Joe Choynski in the 27th round of their Queensberry rules fight to the finish.

As of June, Sullivan was looking a good deal lighter than he was a couple weeks prior. Billy Muldoon said, "I have never seen a man work harder or more faithfully than he has done. … So far he has behaved himself to my perfect satisfaction."

Charley Johnston said he believed that fit and well, Sullivan could whip Kilrain. Victory in this fight meant a great deal. "If he wins, he is a made man, and he can retire on his laurels for life."

According to Sullivan, during the training camp, he only had one "little misunderstanding" with Muldoon, but after a day they buried the hatchet. Some have said that was an understatement, for the truth was that Sullivan resented Muldoon's strict training regimen. Sullivan might have snuck off one night to drink, which led to an argument with Muldoon.

A month before the fight, the *San Francisco Evening Post* said the general belief was that Sullivan would lose. Billy Edwards said,

> I had a look at Sullivan last Friday, and assuredly he is not the man he was. … He and Kilrain are of the same age, but one has taken good care of himself and the other hasn't. If they had met five years ago Kilrain would have stood no show. … [Kilrain] never does anything for show. He's all business in the ring. … He is a two hander and a jabber from way back. Besides that he's got a right that is able to put Sullivan or anybody else to sleep. He's as good a general, too, as ever put up his hands. … If there is a meeting it will surprise me if Sullivan wins.[389]

However, many were just as sure that Sullivan would win. George LaBlanche picked Sullivan. Jimmy Carroll said, "With Sullivan's wonderful hitting powers and his great cleverness he ought certainly to win." Jack Dempsey said Kilrain would provide little more than a pleasant sparring bout before getting knocked out.

William Muldoon said that Sullivan was working hard.[390]

---

388 *Salt Lake Herald,* May 28, 1889.

389 *San Francisco Evening Post,* June 10, 1889.

390 *San Francisco Chronicle,* June 10, 1889.

Mr. Al Cridge of the bookmaking firm of Cridge & Murray was holding the stakes, the largest ever. Betting on the result was heavy throughout the country. Even non-sporting folks were wagering, including women, who had caught the fever. Despite his recent serious illness, Sullivan was the favorite with the majority. In New York, he was the 5 to 4 favorite.

The *Evening World* said, "The great John L. is, without doubt, the most popular pugilist that ever lived." Since defeating Ryan seven years ago, his every move had been chronicled in print and telegraphed throughout the country. He was the "pugilistic marvel of the age. He has received an amount of adulation and flattery without precedent in the annals of the ring, such, indeed, as has never been bestowed on any other fighter."

On June 13, 1889 at Madison Square Garden, Kilrain and Mitchell sparred as part of an exhibition benefit show for the Johnstown flood sufferers. Kilrain was in fine condition. His legs were muscular, strong, and well-developed. He was introduced as the "champion of the world," and the announcement was met with a blend of cheers and hisses. "At the conclusion of the bout the opinion was almost unanimous that Sullivan will have to be himself on the day of the fight if he wants to win."[391]

KILRAIN SPARS FOR SWEET CHARITY'S SAKE.
THE POLICE GAZETTE CHAMPION COMES TO THE FRONT FOR THE BENEFIT OF THE JOHNSTOWN SUFFERERS AT MADISON SQUARE GARDEN.

On June 18, Sullivan, Muldoon, and a young Buffalo lawyer named Martin Laux were bathing in the Genesee River. Laux became seized with cramps and was swept over a mill-dam and drowned.[392]

The *Evening World* said that Sullivan's years of dissipation had lost him some supporters, while Kilrain's good care of himself had won him friends.

---

[391] *Evening World, Sun,* June 14, 1889.
[392] *Evening World,* June 19, 1889.

Sullivan had indulged in excesses painful to his admirers and injurious to himself. Still, plenty said that Sullivan was a phenomenal talent who defied the laws of nature, and his size, strength, speed, and skill would overcome it all.

Dan Daly said Sullivan was a wonder, and in condition, no fighter had any show with him. Another man said that the talk of Sullivan having only brute strength was all bosh, for he had as much science as anyone, and a rush which no one else had. Bob Farrell said if Kilrain tried to fight Sullivan he had no chance. The only way to whip him would be to outgeneral him.

Kilrain Wrestling with Mitchell.

Tom Kelly, who had seconded Paddy Ryan, said that Jem Smith was better than Mitchell, Kilrain was better than Smith, and Sullivan only drew with Mitchell. Therefore it stood to reason that Kilrain would win. Kilrain had proven his condition in the 106-round draw with Jem Smith, having administered a beating to Smith. Some noted that Kilrain had seen Sullivan against Mitchell, so that knowledge would help him. Plus Mitchell was a great teacher and sparring partner for Kilrain, and Mike Donovan, who the Kilrain team had hired to help him, was as knowledgeable and skillful as any.

Tom Allen said Kilrain would win, for Sullivan was greatly overestimated. He was a knockout artist with gloves, but there was a big difference between Queensberry rules boxing and "real fighting." "Kilrain is a very clever fighter, well up in the London prize ring rules, and he will whip Sullivan."

It was only Sullivan's third bareknuckle prizefight, although he had other LPR fights with gloves. He actually had more experience than Kilrain, in both gloved and ungloved contests, something which many overlooked.

Kilrain was the betting favorite in Chicago. They too said that Sullivan was a sparrer and not a fighter. Hugh McManus said, "Sullivan is not the man he used to be, and it is a question whether he ever was the man Kilrain is." Many said dissipation had broken Sullivan down. "No man can drink and carouse as Sullivan has done and retain his strength and condition. It is against the rules of nature, and any man who does it invariably fails." Parson Davies picked Kilrain, for he was a naturally good fighter, and his training had been most rigorous. Otto Floto said, "During all the time John has been pouring liquor down his throat Kilrain has been rapidly improving, and to my judgment he will win the fight."

However, Ed McAvoy said, "Kilrain can't lick the big man. Sullivan is rapidly getting into his old-time form, and when in that condition you know he is invincible."[393]

The Big Fellows In Training At Their Respective Quarters

What Jake Kilrain and John L. Sullivan Have Been Doing To Get Themselves In Trim For the Coming Fight Near New Orleans On July 8

Mike Cleary, John L. Sullivan, Dan Daly

[393] *Evening World*, June 29, 1889.

The *New York Evening World* took postal-card votes from the public on the fight. Despite tight odds amongst the gamblers, the general public picked Sullivan to win. On the first count, it received 219 votes for Sullivan, 34 for Kilrain, and 8 for a draw. Some predicted the authorities would prevent the contest. One man predicted that the fight would not take place, for the principals could make more money by never meeting. However, "If it does take place Kilrain is a sure winner." Another said Sullivan would win if he could stay away from whiskey. Ned Graham wrote, "As paradoxical as it may seem, if Kilrain stands up he won't stand up!"[394]

As of the second day of voting, it was 986 Sullivan, 181 Kilrain, 17 draw, and 8 fizzle, meaning the fight would not happen. One man predicting a Kilrain victory gave his reasons - chastity, mentality, sobriety, meekness, Christian character, and his exalted calling. Eventually, the vote got up to 2,419 Sullivan, 648 Kilrain, 37 draw, and 33 fizzle.

PARTING WITH HIS WIFE AND CHILDREN.
JAKE KILRAIN'S DEPARTURE FROM HIS HOME IN BALTIMORE FOR THE FIELD OF BATTLE.

On July 1, Sullivan started his journey southwest from Belfast, New York. On July 3, Sullivan left Cincinnati, while Kilrain left Baltimore, both taking trains towards New Orleans. Jake said, "I'll do my best to win." Despite his humble statement, "The confident way in which he put it, however, led everyone to know what he really meant."[395]

As usual with LPR prizefights, the legal authorities sought to get involved and prevent the contest. The governors of Mississippi, Louisiana, Alabama, Texas, and Arkansas, not knowing the exact fight location, but knowing that the fight was supposed to take place within 200 miles of New

394 *Evening World*, July 2, 1889.
395 *World*, July 3, 6, 1889.

Orleans, all issued edicts that the fight would not be allowed to occur in their states. Jumping on the bandwagon, even Nebraska's governor pledged to stop the fight.

As a result of fear of official interference, the fight location had to be kept a secret until the last moment. Naturally, that could hurt attendance. Still, so many folks wanted to see the fight, and were willing to pay good money to do so, that a very good gate was reasonably assured. Regardless of the potential attendance, there was big money to be made on the stakes and wagers. Plus, the fighters had earned money in exhibitions leading up to the contest.

Back in February 1882, the Sullivan-Ryan LPR prizefight had taken place in Mississippi, against the will of Mississippi Governor Robert Lowry, who was unsuccessful in his attempt to prevent the fight. A month after that fight, on March 7, 1882, the Mississippi state legislature passed a law making prize-fighting a misdemeanor punishable by up to a year in jail and/or a $500 - $1,000 fine.

Still the governor, Lowry issued an order to all state officers to prevent the Kilrain–Sullivan fight. He was willing to use the state militia if necessary. It is somewhat ironic that he was willing to use violence to prevent consensual sporting violence. Alabama and Louisiana granted Governor Lowry permission to allow troops from his state militia to pass through their states if necessary in order to stop the fight or arrest the combatants. Lowry offered a $500 reward for the arrest of Sullivan and Kilrain; $250 each.

Louisiana Governor Francis Nicholls also proclaimed that the fight was forbidden in his state, and the state militia would be used to stop it.

> The Governor's proclamation is severely criticized in certain quarters. … During the riots in Lafayette, Iberia and Gretna he was called upon for assistance, but in each case responded that it was the Sheriff's duty to preserve the peace, and he would only interfere when the Sheriff's power had been overthrown. The Gretna riot was hatching for three days within two miles of the Governor's residence, yet he issued no proclamation and made no offer to assist the Sheriff.[396]

Although Louisiana's militia had been called upon to stop the fight, the fact that one of its members had been mentioned as a possible referee made some wonder how vigilant they would be. Many of the militia's members admired the fighters, and probably wanted to see the fight. One militia member allegedly was a manager of a rail line which had signed a contract to supply special trains to the fight location.

In order to avoid potential arrest en route to New Orleans, Sullivan took a special train from Alabama that went straight through Mississippi without stopping. He arrived in New Orleans on July 4, and stayed at a

[396] *New York World*, July 3, 1889.

private boardinghouse. He worked out at the Young Men's Gymnastic Club, which eventually became the New Orleans Athletic Club.

Former gunfighter and Kansas sheriff Bat Masterson was hired to be Kilrain's bodyguard.

Five days before the fight, allegedly Kilrain was weighing 185-188 pounds. Some said he was closer to 195. He walked 20 miles, hit the punching bag for two hours, and did other exercises.

A few days before the bout, John L. did two hours of work in the morning, and two more in the evening. He tossed the medicine ball, skipped rope for 20 minutes, did calisthenics with light dumbbells, and punched the bag.

Like Kilrain, Sullivan had removed all of his superfluous flesh. Two days before the fight, Muldoon said that Sullivan was weighing 203 pounds and would weigh 205 in the ring.

Muldoon said that both Sullivan and Kilrain would wear a protective plaster reaching just above the waist and around the body, protecting the loins. Apparently, the rules did not prevent such a thing. It was made of buckskin and lined with pitch pine. It was the era's version of today's protective cup.[397]

The general public talked about nothing else but the fight. The contest had been building for quite some time, with the *National Police Gazette* billing Kilrain as the real champion since 1887. Although most everyone knew that Sullivan was the true champion, the title dispute made the fight more intriguing. It was *the* big fight of the era, the one that every fight fan wanted to happen. Every era has such a fight. Both men were undefeated. Wealthy gamblers and backers were confident enough that they were willing to risk huge money on Kilrain, so the fight had the aura of danger for Sullivan. It was supposed to be a true test, and possibly more.

Tickets were being sold for the very high prices of $10 and $15 apiece.

Noting the huge popularity of Sullivan and Kilrain, and boxing in general, the New Orleans *Times-Democrat* said,

> There must be something esthetic in a contest that involves human muscle directed by fistic science. It cannot be that ten millions of people in the United States are today devouring with avidity the least details of the coming mill, if there be not in such a struggle something that appeals to other than our brutish instincts. Candor compels us to say that many of our educated and refined people are excited over the event. … The brutality in man's nature gives no adequate explanation, for men who are not brutal are eager to witness

[397] *Times-Democrat*, July 3-6, 1889; *Daily Picayune*, July 7, 1889.

> the fray. … There is in us all an unconscious worship of physical perfection in the human form. … To this admiration…is added the peculiar pleasure felt at any exhibition of scientific skill. … The well-directed blow, the parry, the swift counter blow – this is not brutality; it is skill. We instinctively admire it in every other sphere – why not in the realm of prize fighting?[398]

Fans debated who would win. Some were impressed by Kilrain's performance against Smith, and believed that Sullivan's recent typhoid and gastric fever would leave him at less than his best. Paddy Ryan picked Sullivan, saying that when fit; no living man could defeat him. "You might as well try to make an impression on a lamppost with your fist as on Sullivan's face or body." Another said, "Science will not avail much against such blows as Sullivan will deal out."[399]

The *Los Angeles Herald* called it the great sporting event of the age. By July 7, 800 tickets for seats around the ring had been sold. Speculators were getting from $25 up to $40 for tickets. One estimated that the gate receipts would total $30,000. The profits would be split 60% to the winner and 40% to the loser. Railroad fare to the fight was $2.

The day before the fight, Muldoon gave Sullivan a shave. At 3:15 p.m., Sullivan, Muldoon, Cleary, and Dan Murphy were driven to the New Orleans depot, where they quietly embarked for the secret battleground.

When he and Mitchell left for the train, Kilrain smiled and said, "Good-bye, boys, I will be back with you in a short time and I'll bring you good news." The confident Mitchell said, "If Sullivan don't lick him in ten minutes, he won't do it in a month."

Kilrain and Sullivan were in separate coaches. The train departed at 4 p.m. They arrived at the battleground at 6 p.m.

The 50-member Louisiana Field Artillery received orders from Governor Nicholls to be ready with their rifles. Members of the National Guard were used as well, making a force of 100. The governor thought the fight might take place at Honey Island. Some believed it might occur at Bay St. Louis, Mississippi. Supposedly, the governors had every station on the railroad lines crossing the border from Louisiana to Mississippi guarded by militia members, under instructions to arrest the principals.

By 11 p.m., sales of tickets had amounted to $25,000. With the $20,000 stakes, it was the most money on the line in the history of the ring.

Some word leaked out that the fight might take place at Richburg, in Marion County, Mississippi. The governor wired Sheriff Cazenure at Nicholson to use all lawful power to keep the trains with the fighters on them out of Mississippi.[400]

---

398 *Times-Democrat*, July 7, 1889.

399 *Times-Democrat*, July 3-8, 1889.

400 *Los Angeles Daily Herald*, July 8, 1889.

In an abundance of caution, the fighters had gone to the fight site ahead of the spectators on a special train that would not stop at any station, lest they might be arrested by police or bounty hunters. They ignored anyone who ordered them to stop.

The 3,000 spectators had to take a special train to the fight site, leaving at midnight. The Louisiana Attorney General and the New Orleans chief of police rode on one of the trains to ensure that the fight would not take place in Louisiana. However, most believed that they wanted to see the fight, which explains why they did not return even after the train crossed into Mississippi.

At 2 a.m. on the morning of July 8, 1889, it was learned that the fight would take place that day in Richburg, Mississippi, about 7 miles from Hattiesburg, and 103 miles from New Orleans.

Richburg essentially was Charles W. Rich's estate. It also was known as Rich's Mills. Rich had allowed the combatants to use his property for the fight. He was a wealthy owner of 30,000 acres of pine-land and a sawmill. The lumber town, with a population of about 900, contained the sawmill, a school, a church, and a general store. Years later, in 1901, Rich would become the mayor of Hattiesburg.

The day before the fight, on the 7th, Rich hired laborers, both black and white, to pitch the 24-foot ring. They drove eight 8-foot ash stakes into the ground. They linked the stakes with manila ropes. They also built a scaffolding for plank bleachers.

Kilrain spent the night in Rich's beautiful residence. Sullivan's quarters, about 200 feet away, were not quite as nice.[401]

---

401 *Times-Democrat, Pittsburg Dispatch*, July 8, 1889; *New York World*, July 10, 1889.

I – Leaving the Train for the Fight. II – West End Hotel, Kilrain's Headquarters. III – Farm House Near Scene of Battle. IV – Train Crossing Long Bridge At Lake Pontchartrain On Its Way To the Fight. V. Where the Ring Was Pitched.

On Monday July 8, 1889 in Richburg, Mississippi, the John L. Sullivan vs. Jake Kilrain London Prize Ring Rules world heavyweight championship fight took place. Both men were 30 years old and stood 5'10 ½ ".

Approximately 3,000 spectators attended the fight. Only men were present.

The winner's share represented the greatest single payday ever for a pugilist up to that point. It was estimated that after expenses, the winner would clear about $22,000. Another report said the stakes and gate money combined totaled $50,000. Given that tickets sold for $10 and $15, approximately $30,000 is a fair estimate for the gate alone, which would be split 60% to the winner and 40% to the loser. Plus the winning side would earn $10,000 in wagers.

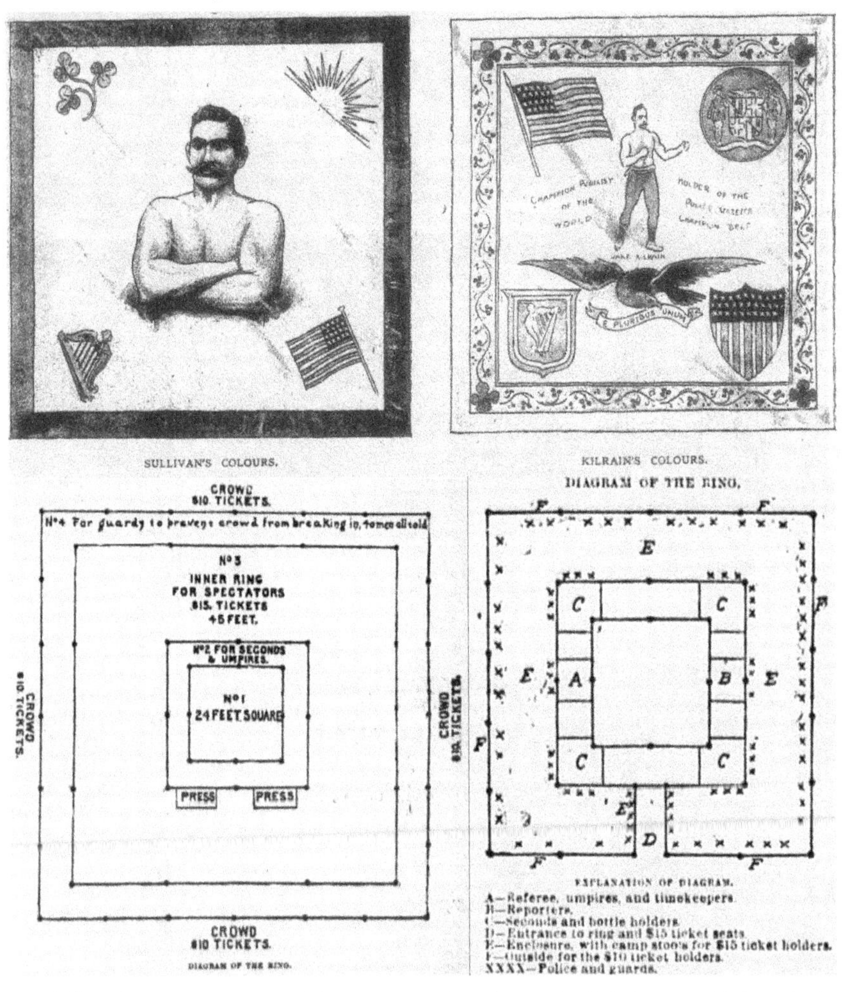

SULLIVAN'S COLOURS.

KILRAIN'S COLOURS.

DIAGRAM OF THE RING.

DIAGRAM OF THE RING.

The thermometer on this very hot day showed 108 degrees Fahrenheit. Try fighting outdoors in the South in July sometime. The *Daily Picayune* said it was so hot that many observers suffered badly and almost fainted. Eventually, the sun would render the fighters' skin red from sunburn.[402]

---

402 *Brooklyn Daily Eagle*, July 8, 1889; *Daily Picayune*, *San Francisco Examiner*, July 10, 1889.

At 9:50 a.m., the fighters' representatives appeared. Mike Donovan, Pony Moore, and Johnny Murphy, Kilrain's seconds, all armed with fans, pushed and elbowed their way through the mob around the ring. Then came Bud Renaud, Frank Stevenson, Bat Masterson and Denny Butler.

Following them were those on the Sullivan side, including Leonard Tracey, Philip Lynch, Dan Murphy, Mike Cleary, Tom Costello, and William Muldoon.

Cleary and Donovan tossed for corners. On Kilrain's behalf, Mike Donovan won the toss and selected the northeast corner, putting the sun at their back. Muldoon was forced to take the southwest corner for Sullivan.

Local Sheriff Cowart and his men showed up, and initially the sheriff said that no fight could take place. However, the managers and participants managed to convince him otherwise.

> [A friend of the sluggers] politely met the sheriff and posse at the ring side, showed them all possible attention and courteously escorted them inside the ring. The sheriff entered his protest against the fight, and, with his deputies retired to a choice spot, specially set aside for them, witnessed the brutal exhibition.

Four days after the fight, William Muldoon admitted that he had bribed the sheriff.

> I walked up to him and put $250 in his hand. "Here, says I, is $250 and Duffy will give you as much more." He hadn't more than felt the money till he sang out: "Well, gentlemen, I am powerless to stop you, because I've only got six men and you 3,000," and on he sneaked.

Bud Renaud stepped to the center of the ring, raised his hand for silence, and announced that the county sheriff had commanded peace, but had retired, saying that he was unable to cope with 3,000 men singlehanded and he didn't think he could stop the fight. He had thought so but had changed his mind. A reporter opined, "Strange, wasn't it?" The announcement was greeted with uproarious cheers.

Sullivan's flag, brought from Boston, was placed in his corner amidst great enthusiasm.

At 9:55 a.m., the sun went behind a cloud. Kilrain appeared, accompanied by Donovan and Mitchell, who had gone back to meet him. He was greeted with applause from thousands of throats that were roaring like wild bulls, but maintained a serious air. He wore black tights, white socks, and black shoes. The Baltimorean followed the time-honored custom of "shying his castor over the ropes." He took a seat in his corner. Some thought the unshaven Kilrain looked as though he might be just a trifle overtrained.

When the Big Fellow, Muldoon, and Cleary, all cleanly shaven, entered the ring, the cheers were deafening. Sullivan wore green tights, white socks, and black shoes. He seemed perfectly at ease. He was enveloped from head to foot in a Turkish bath-rug, fashioned into the shape of a coat. He too tossed his hat into the ring and entered. He threw aside his covering and presented the perfect picture of the ideal fighter. Although still a trifle fat, he looked like a Hercules. He seemed to be walking on springs, and was not the flabby Sullivan familiar to so many of late. He appeared to be the Boston strong boy of old.

Jake Kilrain

Sullivan's plaster reached several inches above his waist. Kilrain's plaster was not as large and mostly covered his back.

According to the New Orleans *Times-Democrat*, Jake's friends said he weighed 195 pounds. Sullivan had been weighing around 205 pounds, though some said he had gained a couple pounds of weight in the days leading up to the fight. This writer opined:

> Sullivan was by far the heavier man and so pronounced is this impression that it is difficult to believe that the big fellow's weight was accurately stated in the figures given out concerning it. … Had it been stated that Sullivan weighed 217 pounds and Kilrain 197 the statement would have gained ready credence.

According to the New Orleans *Daily Picayune*, Sullivan claimed to weigh 207 pounds. Mitchell said that Kilrain weighed 195 pounds, although at another time he said he weighed 190. As usual for a heavyweight contest, no official weigh-ins were required.[403]

Mitchell examined the spikes on Sullivan's shoes. Cleary did the same with Kilrain.

After some debate and haggling, both sides agreed that John Fitzpatrick of New Orleans would referee. Fitzpatrick was a popular politician who in 1892 would become mayor of New Orleans. Initially, Fitzpatrick had been a spectator. When neither side could agree on a referee, he was asked to do

---

[403] *Daily Picayune,* July 10, 1889.

the honors. Although known as an honest man, Fitzpatrick admitted, "I am not very conversant with the rules. This will be a fair contest of the merits of the two men and I will do the best I can." He decided that the 30 seconds rest time between rounds would commence from the time a man went down. The fighters then would have 8 seconds to resume fighting.

Police Gazette sporting editor William Harding stepped up to Kilrain and put $1,000 in his hands, telling him that Mr. Fox had sent the money for him to bet Sullivan. Kilrain went over to Sullivan and offered to bet him the $1,000, which John L. and his backer Charles Johnston immediately accepted. The money was deposited in the referee's hands.

JAKE BETS ONE THOUSAND DOLLARS.
AFTER THE TWO PUGILISTS ENTER THE RING THE BALTIMORE BOY BACKS HIMSELF.

Present at the fight were Billy Madden, Pony Moore, Al Cridge, Harry Hill, Dominick McCaffrey, Billy Edwards, Billy O'Brien, and Billy McCoy.

The principals and seconds advanced to ring center and shook hands. The seconds retired to their positions just outside the ring. Sullivan wore a confident smile, while Kilrain appeared serious.

At 10:15 a.m., referee John Fitzpatrick made the call of "Time!" and the fight for the undisputed world's heavyweight championship began:

1 - Both fighters carried their lefts low and only moderately extended. Jake held his right loosely across his chest with the forearm extended upward. John held the forearm tightly against his chest in a nearly horizontal position, looking anxious to lead or counter.

Both fighters fired lead lefts that missed, Sullivan ducking his head down and off to the right to elude Kilrain's jab, and then firing a right that missed. Kilrain quickly rushed in and clinched, grabbed him by the neck, and used a hip-lock to throw Sullivan across his hip and down to the ground, with Kilrain landing on top of him in the process.

Estimates of the round length varied from 5 seconds, 12 seconds, and no more than 30 seconds. Sullivan seemed surprised at how quickly Kilrain had thrown him.

2 - Although smiling, Sullivan started the round with a slight bruise on his back from the fall that had ended the 1st round.

Kilrain landed a light left to the body and received a light blow in return. Sullivan grabbed Kilrain by the waist and hit him in the ribs. Jake cleverly jumped out of the way of the next punch.

Kilrain rushed in and they wrestled. They broke free and exchanged some blows. Eventually, Sullivan clinched, cross-buttocked his man and threw Kilrain down, landing on top of him. Another said it was a dog fall and they landed side-by-side. The local New Orleans papers said the round lasted either 1 ½ or 2 minutes.

3 - Kilrain landed a hard right to the neck, but Sullivan landed his own right to the neck that slightly staggered Kilrain. Jake stepped away but then came in with a left on the face and right to the body. They clinched. Sullivan hit the body. Jake twice hit below the belt, and the second time it appeared deliberate. Some said Kilrain landed a half-dozen low blows in the round, which brought hisses and cries of "foul" from the crowd. Sullivan landed his big right to the ribs twice in succession. Kilrain clinched and swung his right on the neck.

In the clinches, they engaged in vigorous infighting. Both landed to the ribs with such force that the sound of the blows could be heard around the ring. Sullivan's fists seemed to bury themselves in Jake's side, a sight that was "absolutely sickening." John L. also landed strong blows to the heart, or just under it. Some of the punches made Kilrain turn pale. Jake got away and moved around the ring.

When they came together again, they wrestled, and Kilrain threw Sullivan down heavily, although both went down.

The *Daily Picayune* clocked the round at 5 minutes 30 seconds, while the *Times-Democrat* timed it at 3 minutes.

The *Times-Democrat* said it was a terrific round. Despite the fact that Kilrain landed a number of heavy blows and had the best of the fall, Sullivan's rights to the ribs and heart did more damage. The body punishment that Kilrain received in this round seemed to weaken him.

4 - Sullivan smiled a savage sneer and "glared with the baleful gleam that has disconcerted so many opponents in the past." Whenever he feinted, Kilrain would jump away. Sullivan's smile exuded self-confidence. Kilrain ran in and clinched, struggled for a moment, and then broke away. Jake

smiled back. They conversed a bit during the round. Jake landed a jab to the stomach. After some misses and wrestling by both, Kilrain twice landed rights to the ear. He also landed a right and a left to the body. He moved about the ring, eluding Sullivan, and twice landed lightly on the body again. Sullivan shook his head and raised his hand with a deprecating gesture.

Someone in the crowd, encouraged by Kilrain's performance thus far, offered to bet on him. Sullivan heard it and said to his backer, "There's a bet for you, Johnston." Jake leaped backward and walked around. Sullivan lost his temper and said, "Why don't you fight?" Charley Mitchell coached Kilrain and said, "Go in Jack: you know he can't hurt you." Sullivan replied to Mitchell, "I wish it was you I had in here, you sucker." Every now and then Mitchell would make some remark calculated to exasperate the big fellow.

Sullivan landed a light left to the nose that drew just a slight speck of blood. After wrestling for a moment, they engaged in fierce and rapid exchanges, both landing a number of shots to the body and head. Kilrain landed a blow to the neck hard enough to knock out an ordinary man, but Sullivan laughed contemptuously and danced backwards to avoid the follow-up.

They sparred, evaded, and clinched for a bit. Eventually, Sullivan rushed in with his head lowered, and Kilrain jumped to the side, caught and grabbed his neck under his arm, twisted it and threw him down on his back, although Kilrain went down as well. The round was either 2 ½ or 3 minutes. Sullivan's seconds rushed in to pick him up, but he majestically waved them off, saying, "Don't carry me."

Unlike Kilrain, who sat between rounds, Sullivan preferred to stand. "What is the use of sitting down? I have to get up again."

5 - As Sullivan came forward looking fierce, Kilrain seemed distressed. Sullivan stalked Kilrain, who walked around in a circle as the crowd jeered.

After several rapid exchanges, Sullivan landed a vicious uppercut to the eye, momentarily staggering Kilrain, who clinched and wrestled. After further fighting, Kilrain landed an effective right to the ribs around the heart, which seemed to hurt Sullivan. Finally, Sullivan landed a solid left to the jaw, Kilrain clinched, and in the wrestling that followed, both fell, with Sullivan underneath. Kilrain seemed to be the better wrestler. The round lasted 2 minutes.

6 - When Sullivan led for the ribs, Kilrain cross-countered on the ear with such force that blood started streaming from John's ear down his neck. Kilrain had scored first blood, one of the betting points, and his claim was allowed. Sullivan grinned savagely.

Jake led for the stomach and landed, but the aroused Sullivan paid it no mind and immediately cross-countered with a powerful right to the neck, dropping Kilrain to the grass limp and half-senseless, the first knockdown of the fight. The crowd cheered the result of another betting point. The round had lasted 1 minute.

7 - Sullivan rushed in but Kilrain stepped aside, grabbed him by the neck and twisted. Sullivan grabbed back and they wrestled. According to the *Daily Picayune*, eventually Sullivan released his hold and was about to strike Kilrain, but Jake went down to avoid punishment. The *Times-Democrat* version said Jake's hold slipped from the perspiration and he went down. His seconds carried him to his corner. The *Picayune* clocked the round at 2 ½ minutes, while the *Times-Democrat* said it lasted only 20 seconds.

8 - Kilrain's right eye was discolored badly. He danced away from Sullivan, laughing. Some spectators called Jake a cur.

It became evident that Kilrain had abandoned his plan to be aggressive and fight, and instead was trying to save himself, adopting Mitchell's tactics of delay, constantly moving and walking around the ring, trying to extend the fight's length.

Several times Sullivan taunted him and asked why he didn't fight. "Come here and fight." "Take your punishment like a man." "You're the champion, you know. Come, prove your title." "Stand up and fight like a man. I'm not a sprinter; I'm a fighter." Sullivan did not want to use up his energy chasing after him in the 24-foot ring.

During the round, a section of seats came down, but the fighters paid it no mind.

Eventually, Kilrain stepped in and landed a left under Sullivan's right eye, opening up a gaping cut and drawing blood, which flowed freely. At this point, Sullivan was cut on the ear and under the eye.

Kilrain closed in and clinched. The *Picayune* said Kilrain back-heeled and threw Sullivan to the ground, but the *Times-Democrat* said Sullivan threw Kilrain down. Perhaps they both went down and it was unclear as to who threw whom. Time: 1 ½ minutes.

9 - Kilrain was aggressive again and rushed in. A Sullivan right counter to Jake's left ear caused blood to flow. Kilrain clinched and looked weak, and Sullivan pushed him off. Another Sullivan right to the neck dazed him. Sullivan followed up and Kilrain moved about.

Sullivan rallied and landed a right to the pit of the stomach that dropped Kilrain, doubled up on the turf. Kilrain was in distress and his body showed signs of the punishment, revealing a deep hue. The *Picayune* said the round lasted only about 15 seconds, although others said it was about 30 seconds. The *Times-Democrat* said it looked as if Kilrain would be done for pretty soon.

10 - Sullivan feinted his left, and when the weak Kilrain tried to stagger out of the way, Sullivan quickly sprang forward and landed a crushing right to Kilrain's cheek or the side of his head that dropped him "as though stricken with a pole-ax." Time: 10 seconds.

11 - After the 30 seconds rest, when Kilrain was slow to come to the scratch within the 8 seconds required, the referee warned him. Kilrain staggered to the scratch. He was too weak to avoid Sullivan's rush.

Eventually, after several short exchanges, according to the *Times-Democrat*, Sullivan knocked him down with a crushing left to the neck. The *Picayune* said a right to the jaw sent Kilrain down. "Kilrain was carried to his corner as if he weighed a ton. His flesh was quivering and he showed signs of distress. Time: 1 ½ minutes."

12 - Sullivan landed several uppercuts. Kilrain landed a solid blow to the eye. A Sullivan right to the heart caused Kilrain to fall forward in an attempt

to clinch, grabbing John's neck. The *Times-Democrat* said Sullivan fought him down with repeated rights and lefts to the neck and ear. The *Daily Picayune* differed, saying Sullivan got Jake in a neck hold and threw him down, falling heavily upon him. Time: 1 ½ minutes.

13 - Kilrain showed some pluck, but his blows were so weak that Sullivan did not even bother to parry them, preferring to counter. Kilrain's ribs, ear, and neck were damaged. The *Times-Democrat* said Sullivan fought Kilrain down, and Jake's seconds carried him to his corner. The *Picayune* version of the end said Kilrain clinched to avoid punishment, but Sullivan pushed him and Jake fell down. Time: 1 minute.

14 - Both came up smiling, but Kilrain's seemed forced. As Jake walked around the ring and cleverly avoided punishment, Sullivan looked at him with scorn.

The *Times-Democrat* said that in a clinch, Sullivan slipped and went down, his back striking against one of the ring posts as he fell. However, the *Picayune* differed, saying that that after some feints, Sullivan made a rush and landed to the head with both hands, knocking Kilrain down. Time: 1 minute.

15 - Sullivan carried his left low. His wrist looked swollen. He wore a grim smile, but Kilrain seemed somewhat recovered. During some rapid exchanges, an uppercut to Kilrain's nose brought blood, but Jake countered with a heavy punch to the stomach.

Kilrain stepped on Sullivan's left foot and the spikes gashed his foot. Jake claimed that it was an accident. Sullivan asked him to be more careful.

Kilrain began moving around more and kept well away from Sullivan. Whenever Sullivan came within rushing distance, Kilrain walked or ran away. In response, the crowd shouted and called out, "You cur!" "This isn't a foot race." "Make him fight!" Sullivan taunted him, saying, "You are a champion, eh…a champion of what?" Several minutes elapsed.

Eventually, Kilrain stepped forward and fought again. Sullivan got the best of the infighting.

Finally, Sullivan landed a hard right to the ear or neck, and then followed up with a left to the ribs and Kilrain fell, John going down with him and falling on Jake with his knees.

Clocked at 7 minutes, this was the longest round of the fight.

16 - Twice Kilrain clearly fouled Sullivan by hitting him low. When Kilrain moved and generally kept away, the crowd jeered at him. Occasionally Kilrain would land a good punch to the head or body, but then he would go on a long walk. His strategy was to keep away and punch once in a while.

Eventually, Sullivan punished Kilrain's body and forced matters, despite Kilrain's counters. Sullivan got Kilrain into a corner, where he landed a blow to the right ear that knocked Kilrain down. Time: 4 minutes.

17 - Mike Cleary asked the referee to examine Kilrain's hands. As Kilrain was coming to the scratch, the referee accused him of having rosin on his hands. Kilrain denied having rosin on his hands, saying that if something was there that looked like rosin, likely it was due to coming into contact with the plaster that Sullivan wore over his stomach. Nevertheless, Jake went back and washed his hands, but then he accused Sullivan of having rosin on his hands. Sullivan also washed his hands.

During the round, Kilrain landed a stinging right to the eye. According to the *Times-Democrat*, in the follow-up exchanges, Sullivan fought him down to the ground. However, the *Daily Picayune* differed, saying that in a clinch, Kilrain tried to throw Sullivan, but instead Sullivan threw him down and fell on top of him. Time: 4 minutes.

In its description of the round, the *Boston Herald* said Sullivan landed body shots to the ribs, "the sound of the blows being like a smith's anvil under the hammer. Kilrain got in a stiff one under John's left eye in the closing moments, cutting a deep gash and starting the blood. In a wrestle Kilrain back-heeled John, and fell on him."

In the corner, Cleary sucked the blood out of Sullivan's eye.

18 - The cut under Sullivan's left eye was bleeding. Blood also could be seen coming from his left foot, where he had been spiked. Sullivan followed Kilrain around the ring, and, after Sullivan landed a relatively light right to the chest, Kilrain went down, obviously so that he could avoid further punishment and get a rest. Time: 1 minute.

19 - Sullivan asked Kilrain, "What's the matter with you? Do you want to wrestle, fight, or race?" Sullivan landed a right to the ribs and then held Kilrain up to keep him from falling. Later, Kilrain ducked a right, but in doing so went down to one knee. Another version said that in order to avoid punishment, he dropped down without being hit.

Sullivan complained to the referee, but Kilrain quickly rose and continued. Sullivan landed two body shots and a blow to the neck and Kilrain went down again. Time: 3 minutes.

20 - Sullivan landed a blow to the stomach that staggered Kilrain. The *Times-Democrat* said Kilrain punched back but fell from the force of his own blow. The *Daily Picayune* said Sullivan landed a light right to the body and Kilrain fell. Sullivan called the referee's attention to Kilrain's survival tactics and asked him to make Kilrain fight. Time: 30 seconds.

21 - The left side of Kilrain's body was horribly discolored. Kilrain seemed groggy, especially after Sullivan landed a right to his nose. The *Times-Democrat* said that on the inside, Sullivan landed his left and right on the neck and ribs and Kilrain fell to the ground with a groan. However, the *Picayune* said Jake fell down from a mere push. Time: 15 seconds.

The *Times-Democrat* said that from the 18th to the 21st rounds, Sullivan had the best of it, fighting Kilrain down in each round.

According to the *Boston Herald*, for the last several rounds, very little action had taken place. Kilrain would go down from light blows, or sometimes without being struck at all, in addition to the occasional wrestle down.

22 - Soon after the round began, a Sullivan right to the ribs either knocked Kilrain down or Kilrain dropped to escape further punishment. Sullivan protested, saying that he had not landed: "Never touched him." Even if he had, clearly he did not think the blow was powerful enough for Kilrain to drop legitimately. He thought Jake was using stall tactics. Time: 15 seconds.

Sullivan's rib shots had been particularly effective throughout the contest. The left side of Kilrain's body was very inflamed, and he clearly was distressed by the body punishment.

23 - Sullivan dug both hands into Kilrain's ribs. Kilrain was targeting Sullivan's damaged eye, trying to close it. According to the *Picayune*, "As usual, at the slightest push Kilrain went to grass, and, in exasperation, Sullivan jumped on him with both knees, striking him in the head. It was a foul, but was not allowed. Time: 1 minute and 45 seconds."

The *Times-Democrat* version said that after receiving blows to the heart, Kilrain tried to clinch, but Sullivan grabbed his waist, threw Jake down, and dropped down on him with his whole weight, both knees landing on Kilrain's neck and head. Another source said Kilrain claimed Sullivan punched him in the stomach with his elbow as they fell.

Kilrain's seconds excitedly claimed that the fight should be awarded to them on a foul, but the referee disallowed the claim. One accused the referee, "You have money on the fight." Referee Fitzpatrick responded, "You are a liar."

24 - Kilrain continued walking away from Sullivan, and the crowd jeered Jake's tactics. According to the *Picayune*, in avoiding one of Kilrain's blows,

Sullivan slipped to one knee, and Kilrain taunted him, saying, "You are pursuing my tactics." Time: 2 minutes.

The *Times-Democrat* version completely differed, saying that Sullivan landed a blow to the ear that staggered Kilrain. As John followed up, Kilrain lifted up his right hand to block a Sullivan punch and fell down, partly from the force of stopping the blow, and partly from weakness. Another source said Kilrain went down from a blow to his elbow, which hurt John's hand.

25 - The *Picayune* said that although Sullivan's blow to Kilrain's neck only glanced off, nevertheless Kilrain went down. Time: 30 seconds. The *Times-Democrat* said Sullivan landed a sharp punch to the ribs and followed with a rally that sent Kilrain down.

For the first time in the fight, Sullivan sat down in his corner.

Several sources said Kilrain's nose was swelling, the body blows were sapping his strength, and his left side below the heart was as "red as scarlet from the repeated visitations."

26 - Blood streamed from Kilrain's ear. They wrestled until Kilrain gained the fall over Sullivan by using a back-heel/cross buttock to throw Sullivan down. Time: 1 ½ minutes.

The *Times-Democrat* said that the 24th, 25th, and 26th rounds were decidedly in Sullivan's favor, although Kilrain threw him down in the 26th round.

27 - This round was more action-packed. At one point, they gave and took powerful blows for about 20 seconds, until Sullivan landed a left to the neck, a right to the breast, and a right to the left ear or jaw and Kilrain went down (or was pushed down). Time: 3 minutes.

Sullivan's left eye was puffy and swelling, and there was a little mouse under his right eye.

28 - Kilrain kept firing punches towards Sullivan's eyes, some of which landed and hurt. The *Times-Democrat* said Sullivan landed a punch to the damaged ribs which doubled up Kilrain. John L. followed up with a savage uppercut to the eye that dropped Kilrain.

The *Picayune* version said Sullivan landed a right to the body and Jake dropped to avoid further punishment. Time: 2 minutes.

29 - The *Picayune* said Sullivan landed a right to the breast, and as Kilrain attempted to clinch, Sullivan knocked him down with a left on the jaw. Time: 1 minute.

The *Times-Democrat* version said Kilrain tried to close in, but Sullivan stepped aside and hit him on the shoulder, and then, pushing him off at arm's length, dropped Kilrain with a right to the neck.

30 - The *Times-Democrat* said the round was very short. Kilrain tried to close in, but Sullivan pushed him and Jake fell. The *Picayune* version said that

after Kilrain walked around stalling for time, Sullivan rushed at him, but Kilrain dropped to escape punishment. Time: 1 minute.

According to the *Herald*, the referee finally warned Kilrain not to fall without receiving a blow, on penalty of losing. However, in subsequent rounds, Kilrain often would fall from light blows, and sometimes, he would fall even when he wasn't hit at all.

31 - Sullivan hit Kilrain's damaged eye. Kilrain landed a nice counter right to Sully's left eye. Sullivan landed a left to the mouth, twice struck the damaged ribs, and Kilrain went down. Time: 1 ½ minutes.

32 - In a clinch, Kilrain pushed Sullivan's head back with his open hand. Sullivan said, "Don't put your fingers in my eyes, you bloody coward." Jake walked around the ring. Sullivan became so angry that he said, "You are a scoundrel and a cur."

The *Times-Democrat* said Sullivan landed a left and right to the ribs, knocking Kilrain down. However, the *Picayune* said Sullivan landed a right to the ribs and followed with a rush, under which Jake dropped to avoid punishment. Time: 1 minute.

33 - A left uppercut to the nose sent Kilrain down. Time: 1 minute. Kilrain's nose was bleeding.

34 - This was a short but intense slugging round. Kilrain took the initiative, landing a solid blow to the breast, but Sullivan laughed and said, "I'm not hurt." They exchanged several punches. Sullivan's body blows were terrific. Sullivan rushed in and landed a right to the nose and left uppercut to the ribs and Kilrain went down. Time: 45 seconds.

35 - Kilrain clinched and wrestled, but Sullivan threw Jake down and fell on his abdomen with his entire weight and rolled over him. Time: 2 minutes.

36 - Kilrain walked around for a while. Sullivan asked him, "Why can't you fight like a man?" Eventually, Sullivan hit him in the chest with both hands

and Kilrain went down. From the ground, Kilrain kicked Sullivan. John L. turned to the referee and asked, "What do you think of that?" Time: 3 ½ minutes.

37 - Kilrain mostly avoided Sullivan. John L. folded his arms, waiting for Kilrain to come to the scratch and fight. The crowd jeered and hissed. Kilrain would strike a blow and then move away. Nevertheless, a number of blows were exchanged.

Sullivan landed to the stomach and Jake countered to John's right eye. In the rally that followed, Sullivan countered and Kilrain went down, some saying that he fell before the blow even landed, which caused the crowd to jeer at Kilrain. They thought he either was going down intentionally from light blows, or without being hit at all. They did not appreciate his hit and move and drop strategy. Time: 2 minutes 20 seconds, or 4 ½ minutes.

38 - Kilrain walked around, but Sullivan refused to follow, standing in the center of the ring. The crowd called upon Kilrain to fight. Sullivan complained to the referee, who told Kilrain, "You must fight." The crowd yelled, "Fight, fight."

After a while, Kilrain engaged in some exchanges. Sullivan knocked him down with an open-handed blow to the face. Time: 4 ½ minutes.

To this point, the fight had lasted 1 hour 22 minutes.

39 - Kilrain continued moving about. Eventually, Sullivan landed a left to the ribs and Kilrain blocked a follow-up blow with his hand and fell. The crowd cried, "Foul!" Sullivan's second claimed a foul for Kilrain's going down without punishment, but it was not allowed. Time: 3 minutes.

According to the *New York Tribune*, after the 27th round, the "next twelve rounds were but a repetition of the former ones, Sullivan getting the best of them all, landed several heavy blows on Kilrain's side, the latter falling regularly to avoid punishment." Kilrain continued going down from slight taps or from fear of being hit.

40 - Kilrain again engaged in his usual tactics of moving around the ring. Eventually, after Sullivan hit him with a left to the ear, Kilrain dropped down to escape punishment. Time: 2 ½ minutes.

41 - Sullivan landed a right to the body and to the chest, and also an uppercut. The *Times-Democrat* said that after receiving a right to the ribs, Kilrain staggered and fell just in time to escape another blow. The *Picayune* said that when they tried to clinch, Kilrain fell. Time: 1 minute.

From the 39th through 41st rounds, when Kilrain went down without being struck, or it appeared that Kilrain went down voluntarily instead of as a result of the force and impact of the blow, the spectators howled, "Foul!"

42 - Kilrain rallied and landed some good straight blows to the head and body. He also landed some uppercuts. Sullivan wrestled with him, getting Kilrain in a neck hold and nearly twisting his head off, until he threw

Kilrain down and fell on top of him, one source saying with his knee to his neck. Another said Sullivan sat on his head. Mitchell claimed foul, but the referee said they must fight on. Time: 2 ½ minutes.

43 - Sullivan continued landing telling rights. He easily stopped Kilrain's blows or pushed him away. In a clinch, they hit each other with uppercuts. Sullivan laughed. Kilrain went down from a light right to the back of the neck that landed as Jake was ducking to avoid the blow. Time: 1 ½ minutes.

The *Times-Democrat* said that from the 27th to the 43rd rounds, "Kilrain was playing a waiting game, much to the disgust of the crowd." He would walk and move about the ring, generally avoiding Sullivan and killing time. "The referee also objected to Kilrain's tactics. During all this dodging and dancing around, however, Kilrain had managed to land again and again on Sullivan's stomach."

44 - Sullivan came to the scratch and began vomiting. Mike Donovan urged Kilrain to attack, but he did not. Jake responded, "No, I won't, Mike; no I won't. John, I won't hit you while you are vomiting. I don't want to hit you while you're in that condition. Will you give up?" Sullivan responded, "Give it up! You're crazy. I've got you whipped." Another version said Kilrain asked him to call it a draw. "Will you draw the fight?" Sullivan replied, "No, you loafer. We'll fight it out. Come on, I'm ready."

Having concluded his vomiting, Sullivan appeared fresher and stronger and fought even harder. Conversely, Kilrain gradually grew weaker. The round ended when Sullivan landed blows to the midsection and ribs - right, left, and right, and Jake went down. Time: 1 ½ minutes.

45 - Despite the advanced stage of the fight, Sullivan still exhibited good defense. "Sullivan got out of the way of Kilrain's blows as cleverly as if the fight had just commenced." He hit Kilrain with rights to the ribs and jaw.

Kilrain once again fell without punishment, and once again Sullivan jumped through the air and dropped down on Kilrain's neck and head with either his knees or feet. Jake's seconds claimed a foul, but as usual, the referee did not allow it. Time: 1 ½ minutes.

To that point, the length of the fight, the heat, and the body punishment were all wearing on Kilrain, who appeared to be weakening.

46 - Sullivan had the best of a rapid exchange of blows, pounding on Kilrain's ribs. After John L. landed a right to the nose, Jake either slipped or intentionally fell down in an attempt to avoid the follow-up. Time: 1 minute.

47 - Sullivan got the best of a rally, landing both hands to the jaw, causing Kilrain to clinch. Sullivan then threw Kilrain and fell upon his neck and rolled over on him. Time: 1 minute.

48 - After a short rally, Kilrain rushed in but fell from a mere shove. Time: 30 seconds.

49 - Kilrain led to the stomach but was knocked down with a cross counter to the jaw or a right to the chest. Time: 30 seconds.

50 - The *Times-Democrat* said that after Sullivan staggered him, in trying to escape, Kilrain stumbled and fell rather suspiciously. According to the *Picayune* version, when Sullivan cornered him, Kilrain dropped without being hit. The referee did not recognize the claim of foul. Time: 2 minutes.

51 - The *Times-Democrat* said Sullivan struck Jake with an open-handed blow on the jaw and Kilrain went down. The *Picayun*e said Sullivan landed a right to the ribs, and just as Sullivan was about to repeat the blow, Kilrain fell. Time: 2 minutes.

52 - The *Times-Democrat* said Sullivan drove Kilrain to the ropes and fought him down. The *Picayun*e said Sullivan landed on the ear and Kilrain went through the ropes to escape punishment. Time: 30 seconds.

53 - With blood flowing from his mouth, Kilrain kept away. Sullivan followed and laughed at him. When Sullivan closed in and was about to hit him, Kilrain fell, and Sullivan dropped down on top of him. Time: 3 minutes.

54 - Sullivan grabbed and twisted Kilrain's neck and then threw him down, landing on top of him, some saying on his neck. Time: 1 minute.

The *New York Tribune* said Kilrain gradually was growing weaker, and increasingly the crowd was becoming discontented with his tactics of retreating and falling from slight blows. This continued, with Sullivan occasionally falling on top of him in the process.

55 - Kilrain walked and ran away, ignoring the crowd's jeers. He even leaned on the ropes for support. Sullivan folded his arms and stood laughing derisively at him. Eventually, the referee told Jake that he had to fight. Kilrain landed two rights to the neck, causing a slight cut which bled. Sullivan landed a light blow to the nose in return, and Jake dropped, grabbing John's legs as he went down. A foul was claimed but not allowed. Another version said Sullivan fought him down in a clinch. Time: 2 ½ minutes.

56 - In dodging a right, Kilrain fell or dropped down to escape punishment. Time: 1 ½ minutes.

57 - Kilrain missed a right to the body and either fell from the force of his own lunge or went down as a result of a light tap on the face. Time: 2 minutes.

58 - The *Times-Democrat* said Kilrain grabbed Sullivan's neck, but his arm slipped over his head and he went to the ground. The *Picayune* said that in a clinch, Sullivan threw and fell on top of Kilrain. Time: 30 seconds.

59 - In a rally, when Sullivan grabbed him with his right, Kilrain fell down rather suspiciously before John L. could do anything. Time: 1 minute.

60 - The *Times-Democrat* said Sullivan knocked Kilrain down with a right to the ribs. The *Picayune* said Sullivan feinted and Kilrain fell without being hit. Time: 2 minutes.

61 - The *Times-Democrat* said Kilrain went down in a rally. The *Picayune* said Kilrain rushed in, and when Sullivan dodged to avoid the clinch, he fell to his knees, the first time in a long time that the round ended as a result of Sullivan going down. Kilrain's supporters jeered at John, who then apologized. Time: 10 seconds.

62 - Sullivan hit the ribs and chased him around the ring until Kilrain fell to escape being hit, or he went down from a slight tap to the ear. Time: 1 ½ minutes.

They had been fighting for 2 hours.

63 - Kilrain walked around for a while. One source said a right to the ribs dropped Kilrain, but another said Sullivan feinted and Kilrain dropped without a blow. The crowd jeered. Time: 3 minutes 15 seconds.

64 - Kilrain went down from a mere tap in a scramble. Cries of foul were heard, but disallowed. Time: 2 ¾ minutes.

65 - Kilrain killed time. Sullivan accused him of cowardice. The *Times-Democrat* version said Sullivan pushed him down. Fearing that John L. would jump on him again, Jake put up his leg and spiked Sullivan's thigh. Sullivan turned to the referee and asked, "How is that?"

However, the *Picayune* version said Sullivan landed both hands to the face and Jake went down. Time: 30 seconds.

At this point, no one would bet against Sullivan, even when Charley Johnston offered 10 to 1 odds to Kilrain's backers ($500 to $50).

66 - The *Times-Democrat* said Kilrain looked dazed and helpless. He tried to hit the stomach, but Sullivan knocked him down with a swinging right. The *Picayune* said Kilrain fell from a light punch. Time: 30 seconds.

67 - Kilrain did not toe the line on time, and several times he had to be called upon to rise. During the round, Sullivan finally cornered him, and in rapid succession landed two body shots to the breast and ribs and a right to the face that sent Kilrain falling under the ropes. Time: 1 ½ minutes.

Knocked Him clean through the Ropes.

68 - Sullivan hit the ribs and face and knocked him down with a vicious uppercut. Time: 1 ½ minutes.

69 - The *Times-Democrat* said a right and left to the ear and jaw sent Kilrain down, while the *Picayune* said Sullivan landed a right to the body and Kilrain dropped to avoid further punishment. Time: 30 seconds.

70 - Sullivan landed a blow to the

ribs and Kilrain "slipped" to one knee to escape further blows. Time: 30 seconds.

71 - At one point, Sullivan held Kilrain up to keep him from falling. After cornering Kilrain, Sullivan landed a right to the neck or ear and Jake dropped to one knee. Sullivan saw that the end was near. Time: 1 ½ minutes.

72 - Kilrain went down either from a shove, an open-handed blow, or a push on the chin. While on the ground, Kilrain tried to spike Sullivan. John L. asked the referee, "What do you think of that?" Time: 30 seconds.

Kilrain was very weak and groggy. The *Picayune* said, "The fight was virtually over. What with the heat of the sun, in which he had been for two hours, the punishment he received and the evident superiority of his opponent it was simply a matter of a few more rounds when nature would get the better of Kilrain's stubborn courage."

73 - Sullivan decked Kilrain with a right to the ribs. Time: 1 minute.

74 - Kilrain walked around for a while until either he fell, or a slight right or slap to the neck dropped him. Time: 1 minute.

75 - Kilrain staggered out of his corner and wandered about in a dazed condition along the ropes. Sullivan went after him and fired a moderate right to the chest that knocked him down. Another version said the blow did not land, but Kilrain fell in stopping it. "The referee warned him against going down without punishment. It was not Kilrain's fault. He could not stand up anymore."

Mitchell ran over to Sullivan's corner and asked if he would consent to a draw. Sullivan replied, "I came here to whip Kilrain, and I'm going to do it or die in the ring. I want no draws or compromises." Mitchell then asked John L. if he would give Jake a $1,000 present if he gave up. Sullivan said, "Yes, that would be all right," but his backer refused, saying, "No, we won't." Sullivan replied, "That settles it then; we'll fight." Mitchell was about to negotiate further, but Mike Donovan threw up the sponge, retiring Kilrain. Jake objected. Mitchell initially disputed the propriety of this action, because Kilrain was willing to continue. However, Donovan said, "I do not wish to be a party to a murder." After some discussion, the sponge once again was thrown up, this time with Mitchell consenting. John L. Sullivan was declared the winner and undisputed world heavyweight champion.

The *Daily Picayune* at one point said the fight had lasted 2 hours 13 minutes, but at another time said it lasted 2 hours 16 minutes 23 seconds. The *Times-Democrat* said it lasted 2 hours 15 minutes, "counting the close of the seventy-fifth round as the end of the fight, though as a matter of fact the decision of the Kilrain party to abandon it was not satisfactorily demonstrated until about three minutes later." Hence, some reported the fight as lasting 2 hours 18 minutes. The *Picayune* was based in New Orleans, a mere 105 miles away from Richburg, and claimed to have had bulletins before any other newspaper.

The *Picayune* reported that Sullivan had won $22,000 plus his share of the gate receipts. Of course, he would have to split it with his financial backers, which included Jim Wakely, Charles Johnston, and *New York Illustrated News* owner Arthur Lumley. In reality, Sullivan and his backers had won $10,000 in prize money (they had put up the other half) plus 60% of the gate receipts (or about $18,000 of the $30,000), plus whatever they earned in side-wagers, including the $1,000 wager with Fox, less expenses.

Afterwards, Mike Donovan said,

> I threw up the sponge because I saw that there was no chance of continuing the fight without endangering our man's life. … Kilrain was game to the last, but I believed him to be in danger of sunstroke and, besides, the blow over his heart, which Sullivan landed, bid fair to the serious in its effects. … I do not consider that Sullivan was ever in his life the man he is now.

Years later, Donovan said that he wanted to retire Kilrain in the 50th round, because he knew that Jake had no chance and might be killed, but Mitchell would not allow it. Kilrain was so weak that he was falling from exhaustion.

Unlike those who felt that alcohol during the fight was of no help, Donovan said, "Kilrain could never have gone through this fight without whiskey, of which he drank over a quart between the rounds." Apparently, whiskey helped dull the pain.

Donovan said that Sullivan dropped Kilrain with a right to the body to end the 75th round. Jake was carried to the corner, clearly all gone, causing Donovan to decide to stop it. "I will not be a party to manslaughter." As he threw up the sponge, he saw Mitchell in Sullivan's corner. He later learned about Charley's attempted negotiations.[404]

Summarizing the fight from the 45th round on, the *Times-Democrat* said that Sullivan knocked Kilrain down several times, and often a push would provide the latter with an excuse to fall down. On two occasions, Jake fell suspiciously. The punishment to the ribs and heart, combined with the day's heat and the bout's length, had taken Kilrain's strength.[405]

---

404 Donovan at 125-128.

405 *Daily Picayune*, July 9, 1889; *Times-Democrat*, July 9, 10, 1889; *Boston Herald*, *Boston Daily*

The *Brooklyn Daily Eagle* reported that Sullivan had a broken finger and a painful foot from being spiked. Despite no agreement having been made, afterwards, Sullivan decided to give Kilrain $1,000 for his suffering and efforts.[406]

The *Daily Picayune* said that Kilrain wept at his defeat. He was crushed psychologically and physically. His body was badly bruised and his head showed the punishment. His mouth was swollen badly, a bleeding cut disfigured his upper and lower lips, his left eye was puffed and swollen, and his left ear was cut and swollen.

Although the crowd had often jeered his tactics during the fight, afterwards the spectators felt sympathetic towards Kilrain and collected $500 for his relief.[407]

William Muldoon said that Sullivan's only injuries were a black eye, cut ear, slightly swollen face, and hurt wrists and hands.

The local paper reported that Sullivan's foot was gashed from Kilrain's spikes. One eye was a little bruised, and the other one had a small cut over the eye and another one on the cheek below. His side was a little bruised. The following day's report said that both of John's hands were puffed badly and his left wrist very swollen. Both fighters were sunburned.

Sullivan had been the aggressor throughout, mostly attacking the body. This helped to preserve his hands. Sullivan's body shots, which sounded like "a smith's anvil under the hammer," wore down Kilrain. At first, Kilrain was aggressive. However, he quickly realized that he could not defeat Sullivan in this manner, so he became much more defensive. He tried to extend the fight as much as he could, hitting, moving, wrestling, and dropping, killing time, hoping that Sullivan would tire. He used tactics similar to those used by his trainer Charley Mitchell. At times he fell down when hit lightly, and at other times fell when not even struck at all, causing cries of "foul" from the Sullivan side and jeers from the crowd. Sometimes Sullivan fell on or pounced on top of Kilrain's body. Although Jake occasionally landed some good punches, perhaps hoping to close John's eye, he was too afraid to do much more, moving about so much that at times the referee had to tell him to fight. The rounds typically did not last over a minute, and often were much shorter. Sullivan had the best of it throughout, although it was a hard-fought battle.

The *New York Tribune* concluded, "At no time, excepting when Sullivan's stomach gave evidence of weakness, was there a doubt as to the final result of the fight."

The *New York Times* and others reported that the 3rd round body punishment "was said to have done more than anything else to decide the battle." Even the *Picayune* agreed that "Sullivan hit Kilrain a blow in the

---

Globe, *New York Daily Tribune*, *New York Times*, July 9, 1889; *National Police Gazette*, July 20, 27, 1889.

406 *Brooklyn Daily Eagle,* July 9, 1889.

407 *Daily Picayune*, July 9, 10, 1889, July 24, 1889.

short ribs in the third round which settled the contest." Most sources indicated that after suffering body punishment in the 3rd round, Kilrain was not the same.[408]

Because interest in the fight was so great, and because the fight concluded before 1 p.m., several newspapers scrambled to be first to have day-of-the-fight reports, but their accuracy was questioned. Some were wildly wrong, saying that Sullivan won in 8 or 9 rounds, that Kilrain had won, or that Sullivan had broken Kilrain's jaw in the 3rd round. One report said that Sullivan had won in the 72nd round, being only slightly wrong.[409]

The *Times-Democrat* commented,

> The Northern evening papers…are models of inaccuracy. … It seemed to be fashionable last Monday to send off bogus news, and such was the anxiety of the papers to give something that they gladly accepted anything they came across, whether they believed it or not. They waited impatiently for some information from New Orleans, and when they could get nothing, apparently invented it. We mention this fact, because journalism of this kind seems to be coming into favor in America. It is the duty of the press to expose and crush it at the very start. …
>
> The press has not the same time as the historian to examine facts, and is therefore liable to err sometimes, but to invent news or publish news which it knows to be false, is a degradation which cannot be tolerated. … Let it be understood that the public can credit the newspapers. If it ever gets to doubting them, journalism has a dark future ahead.

Initially, Sullivan kept away from reporters, saying that many of them had little regard for the truth. He acknowledged that he had fouled Kilrain, but said he did not do so until after Jake had fouled him. He could have been awarded the fight many times on fouls, but was glad to have proven that he was a finish fighter. He said that he had whipped Kilrain 11 years ago and knew how to fight him. He also said that the blows to the stomach are what did in Kilrain.

Regarding his vomiting in the 44th round, John L. said that his seconds gave him a drink of whiskey, and it did not mix well with the tea that he was given. He felt stronger after vomiting.

Of Kilrain, Sullivan said, "Jake is a good fighter, and he gave me a better fight than I ever got before." He also said that Kilrain had given him more punishment than any other man. "Of course, he hardly fought fairly, going down, as you know he did, numbers of times without a blow. Still, he took by far more punishment than I believed he would."

---

408 *Daily Picayune*, *Boston Herald*, July 10, 1889; *Boston Daily Globe*, July 9, 1889.

409 *Brooklyn Daily Eagle*, July 8, 1889.

Later that month, Sullivan said, "I knew after two or three rounds I was the sole master of the situation. … If Kilrain had stood up and fought like a man, I think I could have whipped him in about eight rounds."

Trainer Muldoon agreed that Kilrain was not in the fight after the 6th round, and, although game, he was outclassed.[410]

Sullivan refused to accept Richard Fox's *Police Gazette* championship belt, "feeling that it is not necessary in establishing the fact that he is the champion pugilist."[411] He had called it a dog collar. Sullivan was not the first nor was he the last champion to believe that title belts did not make the champion. He had proven himself inside the ring.

Sullivan said that he was going to retire, would never enter the "ring" again, and that others could fight for the *Police Gazette* belt. He noted that no one that Fox had backed had been able to defeat him. Another report said that Sullivan never again would fight bare knuckled, but only with gloves under Queensberry rules.

THE TERRIFIC BATTLE OF THE GIANTS
JAKE KILRAIN AND JOHN L. SULLIVAN FIGHTING FOR THE $20,000 STAKES, THE "POLICE GAZETTE" CHAMPION BELT AND THE CHAMPIONSHIP OF THE WORLD
AT RICHBURG, MISS., JULY 8, 1889.

Sullivan's performance in the Kilrain fight garnered tremendous praise and accolades. The *Daily Picayune* said that Sullivan "was as cautious as any prize ring tactician who ever lived. He made no wild rushes, did not lay himself open to injury, and made every blow count." It opined that "Sullivan, when in condition, is an enormous ox who cannot be hurt." One man commented that if John L. had used his rushing tactics he would have been defeated, but he fought a cool, scientific fight; not a slugging match. The *Daily Picayune* summarized,

---

[410] *Times-Democrat,* July 9, 11, 1889; *Brooklyn Daily Eagle,* July 9, 1889; *Boston Herald,* July 30, 1889.

[411] *Boston Daily Globe,* July 9, 1889.

> Kilrain was crafty and cool…wrestled nicely for two rounds and kept warily out of the way after Sullivan's body blows had reduced his wrestling chances, got in some good hits until he found Sullivan imperious and himself growing weaker constantly, and then devoted himself to getting hurt as little as possible, getting all the rest he could, and staying in the ring as long as possible. In short, Kilrain is a general and a clever fighter, but was only a chopping block for Sullivan. … Pony Moore poured brandy down his throat after each round, and it is doubtful if this did him good.[412]

Sullivan had proven his patience, poise, and science. The *Times-Democrat* said, "From first to last Sullivan never lost control of his temper more than momentarily, and cool, calculating judgment never for one instant forsook him." His opponent was a worthy foe. Kilrain was powerful, a hard hitter, and a clever general, but, despite his shiftiness, "Sullivan proved equally cunning, and until he had found his opponent so completely worn out as to be unable to administer a dangerous blow he never afforded him an opportunity of landing one. … John L. Sullivan has proved himself a marvelously scientific boxer." One writer also noted that Sullivan was careful to strike the neck and body, so as not to injure his hands to a great extent.

Sullivan also had proven his endurance. "After the thirtieth round those who counted on the Bostonian's lack of endurance began to look blank and blue. After the middle of the fight the victory of the champion was foreordained." For most of his career, Sullivan had stopped his opponents quickly. This time, he had proven that he could break down a good man over a lengthy period of time as well. No longer would his ability to win a long fight be questioned.

Muldoon was complimented for allowing Sullivan to add seven pounds of weight before the fight in order to combat the fact that he would lose weight during the contest as a result of the heat. The added weight helped his strength and vitality.

At times, both fighters committed fouls. Sullivan would drop down on top of Kilrain in the falls. Kilrain went down without being hit. The referee refused to disqualify either one. Although criticized for not being well-versed in the London rules, the referee was fair. He overlooked both of their fouls.

Joe Coburn said that Sullivan had proven himself to be "a perfect wonder" and the greatest fighter in the world, even though he "did not think Sullivan was as good a man today as he had seen him in other years, but was satisfied that he would never be asked into the arena again." He was impressed. "Were I called on to fight Sullivan…I would say, 'Sullivan, take the money; I don't want it: it belongs to you.'"

[412] *Daily Picayune, Times-Democrat,* July 10, 1889.

Coburn calculated that Sullivan's share of the proceeds would come to $20,000.[413]

Former fighter Tom Allen, who had predicted a Kilrain victory, was impressed, and had changed his mind about Sullivan (whom he thought weighed about 220 pounds).

> He must have the constitution of ten mules, for in spite of the heat, which was simply terrific, his flesh suffered but little, his wind the best I ever saw, and he did not blow much at any time. He did not seem to care any more for Kilrain than an ordinary man would for a child. He did not sit down ten times during the entire fight and laughed at Kilrain's efforts to hit him. … I don't think Kilrain could have whipped him with a ball bat.

Referee John Fitzpatrick observed that Kilrain was game but overmatched on this extremely hot day. Kilrain spiked Sullivan many times, but he could not determine if it was intentional. Of Sullivan, he said, "[He] is simply a wonder. … I do not think we'll ever see his like again."

Sullivan's trainer, William Muldoon, said,

> I don't think a man was ever born who could have whipped Sullivan yesterday. … I have always been anxious to prove to the public that he is a natural born fighter and could fight a long and scientific battle if necessary. … I consider Kilrain the greatest heavyweight fighter outside of Sullivan.

One reporter said of Sullivan, "Even his most sanguine advocates could not believe before the battle that his staying qualities were such as he showed them to be."[414]

Dominick McCaffrey said, "Sullivan, in my opinion, won this fight through punching him over the heart." He said that Sullivan was a hard hitter and a wonderfully clever stopper for a big man. He rushed and forced the fighting the whole way. He could not land effectively to the head, so he focused on the body. Dominick confessed that he had thought that Kilrain would win and was the far better man. However, Jake had taken a terrible licking and was outclassed. Donovan would have stopped it far sooner, but Mitchell would not allow it. "I personally heard Mitchell say to Donovan that Jake would die before he would give up." Both men had fouled. Sullivan fell on Kilrain's face, neck and breast with his knees. Kilrain hit below the belt and went down several times without a blow. Hence, McCaffrey thought the referee was fair. They were about equal in wrestling, though Sullivan was more defensive with his wrestling skills. "I always contended that any man Sullivan could hit he could beat. … [for] there is

---

413 *Times-Democrat,* July 9 - 11, 1889; *Brooklyn Daily Eagle,* July 9, 1889.

414 *Times-Democrat,* July 11, 1889; *San Francisco Examiner*, July 10, 29, 1889; *Brooklyn Daily Eagle,* July 9, 1889.

no man living can stand his blows." Dominick said if Sullivan fought Mitchell again, he would bet on Sullivan.

Everyone agreed that Sullivan had proven his science, endurance, strength, and toughness.

Even Richard K. Fox had to tip his hat to Sullivan. Fox allegedly had lost over $25,000 as a result of the stakes, wagers, and expenses he had posted for the fight. Of course, he would make it back and then some with magazine sales.

Fox said that he never had any doubt that Kilrain would win, because Jake was intelligent and strong, had endurance, took care of himself, and knew about Sullivan's tactics. Conversely, Fox believed that Sullivan was a short rounds fighter who never took care of himself and would wear himself out. "By this fight Sullivan has proved that he is a first-class pugilist in every respect. He is a stayer as well as a slugger." He admitted that Kilrain got the worst of it from start to finish.

Lem Fulda, President of the California Athletic Club, said,

> The best way to be a fighter is to be born a fighter, and Sullivan was born that way. … Kilrain was whipped because Sullivan hurt him and he could not hurt Sullivan. … He can strike harder blows and more of them, he can stand more fatigue and more punishment, his blows are too powerful to be stopped, and his strength too great to be weakened, and he is so much the physical superior of any other man in the ring that a few touches of science more or less make no difference.

Interest in the fight was tremendous. "Not since the days of the war were the people of New York city so absorbed in any one event as in the great fight. The interest was intense and universal. It was extraordinary and unprecedented. Nothing else was talked about." This was the era's big fight.

This fight further cemented Sullivan's legendary status. Because most of his bouts were short, either because John L. knocked them out quickly, or because they were scheduled for a limited duration owing to legal constraints, Sullivan had not often had to demonstrate that his style, skill, and talent would prove effective in a lengthy bout. Some old-school purists who believed in the traditional LPR system still doubted him, particularly in light of his LPR performance against Mitchell (despite the fact that Sullivan was the one who scored most all of the falls and all of the knockdowns).

Against Kilrain, the man advertised as the true LPR champion, Americans had witnessed Sullivan demonstrate his determination and stamina in a lengthy, over two-hour fight to the finish, in a winning effort against another large, strong, well-conditioned, and well-respected fighter, under the broiling hot sun with bare hands and legal wrestling.

An editorial to the *Times-Democrat* said, "It is not likely that anybody will want to meet the big Boston Slugger very soon. Just now he is the most famous person in the country, and now more highly valued than ever will be the privilege of 'shaking the hand that Sullivan shook.'"[415]

Most every good judge of fighting who saw the fight said that an in-shape Sullivan was invincible. John Boyle O'Reilly said of Sullivan, "His equal as a boxer never entered the ring in ancient or modern times." The *Sun* said that even the ancient Greeks never approached Sullivan in terms of size and strength. "If Hercules himself were no bigger and brawnier than the old sculptors made him, the Sullivan of today could pick him up and break him in two across the knee like a stick."

The *Wheeling Daily Intelligencer* said Kilrain was game and a good fighter, but no match for Sullivan. He was whipped honorably, with no cause to be ashamed. Kilrain would be the favorite to defeat any other man but Sullivan. Kilrain won first blood and the first fall, but Sullivan won the first knockdown. The result was a disappointment to many whose sympathies were with Kilrain "because of Sullivan's well-known personal character."[416]

That evening, Kilrain allegedly weighed 183 pounds, having lost 12 pounds or more from the grueling lengthy fight under the broiling sun.

The *New York World* reported, "No previous prize-fight in this country has ever created such a widespread interest." Even President Benjamin Harrison was making inquiries regarding the fight's result.

During the fight, shouts loud enough to penetrate all the pine woods in Marion County were continuous. Although Sullivan's backers were in the

[415] *San Francisco Examiner*, *Times-Democrat* (New Orleans), July 10, 1889; *Boston Daily Globe*, July 9, 1889.

[416] *Wheeling Daily Intelligencer*, July 9, 1889.

majority, Kilrain was not neglected, and his generalship gained him many admirers.

Kilrain keenly felt the defeat and was very morose. He said a blow over the heart did the business. Weeping, he said, "I had him beaten." He claimed to have had Sullivan "done up" twice, but was unable to take advantage. He said that he had not been trained properly. In contradictory fashion, he also said he punched Sullivan several times, but he didn't seem to hurt him. He thought something must have been done to him, implying that he was drugged. He didn't have the necessary strength. He could stand any amount of punishment, but couldn't inflict any. He could see that his blows were not hurting Sullivan. He also complained about the manner in which Sullivan had jumped upon him deliberately with both feet while he was down. In other interviews, Kilrain claimed it was the sun and heat that defeated him more than anything.

The *World* opined that the London rules greatly increased Kilrain's chances of success, given that he was shifty on his feet and a good wrestler. Plus the long rests between falls allowed him to recover well. With Queensberry rules, there would have been no wrestling, and Kilrain only would have had 10 seconds to continue after knockdowns. Ultimately, Kilrain found himself growing weaker, while Sullivan's strength did not diminish. For more than 30 rounds it was a foot-race, with Sullivan chasing, growling, swearing, and begging him to stand and fight. Jake believed it was his only chance to wear down the big man. He played a waiting game, going down to avoid punishment, or as a result of sledgehammer blows. However, his chance to win never came. Kilrain expended his own strength wrestling and moving. Sullivan knew enough of the wrestling art to fall without being hurt. Also, Sullivan's legs did not give out as expected.

Many of Kilrain's friends believed that Mitchell had deserted him, failing to encourage him or give him good enough advice when he saw the contest was going against Kilrain.

Supposedly, Sullivan dislocated a knuckle on the first finger of the left hand in about the 7th round, and broke one finger on either hand during the fight.

Afterwards, Sullivan said he would never enter the ring again under any consideration. He had done his share of slugging and wanted no more of it. "He certainly did not intend to fight the California negro for the simple reason that he considered it entirely too degrading for a white man to place himself on an equality with a negro." Sullivan once again made it clear that he was drawing the color line.

The question was whether he ever again would fight anyone, regardless of color. It was not clear whether Sullivan was retiring, or simply meant that he would never again fight in an LPR prizefight. However, some quoted him as saying, "But I'll never fight again." "Anybody who wants the championship now can come to me and I'll give it to 'em." Regardless, in the hearts and minds of the general public, Sullivan was the champion until someone defeated him, now more than ever, given his victory over Kilrain.

Boston was wild with joy, as were all those who had wagered on Sullivan. The champion was called a lion among men.

> Henceforward John can have anything he wants. He can be an Alderman, or, for that matter, if he moved into the right district, he can go in the Governor's Council. Boston is proud of him – proud to the verge of insanity – the more because of the doubt which forced itself into so many minds whether he could get into condition for another finish fight.[417]

After the fight, the spectators had taken everything that was part of the ring, and every article surrounding the ring. They later sold the various items and parts for good money. Sullivan's hat sold for $50. The buckets sold for $25. Splinters from the ring posts went for $5 apiece. Even sponges and towels had disappeared. Louisville's fire chief took Sullivan's drinking can, and refused to sell it for any amount of money.

Fearing possible arrest, everyone took the train back to New Orleans as quickly as they could. Before the train left, someone who heard another train in the distance gave the alarm, saying that the militia was coming. Sullivan jumped through the train window and ran into a thicket. However, some friends told him it was a false alarm, so he returned and they went on their way. The train opened up to full throttle and did not stop for the waiting squadron of soldiers.

Sullivan said he bore no marks other than a little scratch under his right eye, and a small sore on one side of his lip. His hands were swollen to three times their natural size.

In New Orleans, he had supper consisting of chicken, cold meats, and Bass's ale. He remained awake celebrating with his friends until 1 a.m.[418]

---

[417] *New York World, Boston Herald, San Francisco Examiner,* July 10, 1889.

[418] *New York Sun, New York Evening World,* July 9, 1889; Sullivan at 161.

The Fight After the Fight

Although John L. Sullivan and Jake Kilrain had fought each other for over two hours, they were about to encounter an even tougher and more brutal opponent: the law. They would have to combat the legal and political authorities who hated London Prize Ring Rules fights. Upset that the fight had taken place in his state, Mississippi Governor Robert Lowry was determined to have the participants arrested and tried for engaging in or aiding and abetting an illegal prizefight. He quickly secured warrants for the arrest of the known participants.

Although a significant percentage of the population supported prizefighting, there also was a very strong anti-boxing voting contingent, which often found support from politicians. An editorial writer for Jackson, Mississippi's *Clarion-Ledger* wrote,

> [I]n defiance of civilization and decency, these 'sluggers'...by the aid of railroad officials, the Western Union Telegraph Company, civil officials and sympathizers of the ring, defied the law of the State. ... [T]he sheriff could have stopped the fight if he had made the slightest attempt. ... The law approved in 1882, passed just after the Sullivan-Ryan fight, should also be amended as to make prize-fighting a felony, with increased penalty, as it is in a majority of the States. ... [E]very effort will be made to return them that they may answer for the great outrage and crime committed on the soil of Mississippi.[419]

Having heard that warrants for their arrest had been issued, and that a sheriff was looking for them, Sullivan and Kilrain left New Orleans. Some said Kilrain headed to Virginia. Others said he went to Ohio. Sullivan and crew took a train heading to Alabama, and then to Nashville.

Three days after the fight, on July 11, 1889, Sullivan's train arrived in Nashville, Tennessee. Mississippi Governor Lowry had telegraphed the Nashville chief of police, offering to pay him $1,000 to deliver Sullivan and his fighting party.

As soon as the train stopped in Nashville, chief of police Clack and members of his force boarded the train. The chief found Sullivan, Muldoon, and Charley Johnston, his backer. The big fellow was asleep. The chief asked them their names. Johnston said, "Lynch," and Muldoon said, "Robertson." The chief said, "Gentlemen, I'm sorry to disturb you, but I am the chief of police for Nashville and you must go with me." Johnston asked, "On what charge?" "I have authority for the arrest of your party and you must go with me." "I will not go without a warrant. You must show

[419] *Clarion-Ledger*, July 11, 1889.

your authority. I am a citizen of New York and a tax payer, and I stand on my rights as an American citizen." Except for swollen hands, Sullivan did not look like he recently had been engaged in a prize fight. The chief told his friends that they must wake him, but they declined to do so. The chief shook him slightly. Sullivan woke up. The chief said, "You need to come with me." Sullivan replied, "I will not." The chief said he meant business and intended to arrest John L. Sullivan. Sullivan said to Muldoon, "Well, what are we going to do about it?" Muldoon replied, "Of course we won't be arrested unless they show us a warrant." John L. said, "Then I won't go. You can't arrest me, my name is not Sullivan." The crowd outside began cheering.

The officers took hold of Sullivan. He called upon his friends to help, but they told him that he was dealing with the chief of police, and advised him not to hit the officers. "No, I will not hit anybody; but I be – if I will go." The chief grabbed him by the collar and a struggle ensued. Some of the officers drew their pistols. Others drew their clubs. Three or four men grabbed Sullivan. John L. jerked and pulled and tried to push them off. The police chief stuck a pistol in his face and said, "If you strike, I will kill you." The champ said, "Give me a show. I won't hurt you, but I won't go with you." Eventually, while being held by several officers, one slipped nippers on one of John L.'s wrists, and then the other. Finally, Sullivan gave in. Johnston was handcuffed as well. They were taken off the train. Both Sullivan and Johnston spent the night in a jail cell.

JOHN L. SULLIVAN COLLARED.
CAPTURED BY NASHVILLE, TENN., OFFICIALS ON AN ORDER FROM GOVERNOR LOWRY OF MISSISSIPPI, AND TAKEN FROM THE CARS TO THE LOCK-UP BY CHIEF OF POLICE CLACK.

Muldoon narrowly escaped arrest. He later explained,

They were about to place me under arrest when I said to them: "What do you mean? I am no prize fighter. Do I look like one? I am a gentleman, and it is your duty to protect me and not to offer me an insult." They at once abandoned me and devoted their efforts to securing the Big Fellow and Johnston.

Attorneys were hired immediately, and they applied for a writ of habeas corpus, requesting the prisoners' release, arguing that prizefighting was a misdemeanor in Mississippi, not a felony, and therefore it was not an extraditable offense. Hence, they had been arrested without any process known to law, held without any charge against them in the state of Tennessee, and therefore not subject to legal restraint.

Judge McAlister agreed, ruling that holding Sullivan would be arbitrary, for the officers had arrested him without warrant or authority of law, given that misdemeanor offenses were not extraditable. He ordered them released. The immense crowd outside the courtroom applauded the decision. The fight crew boarded a train and headed east.

Allegedly, Muldoon, not shy about admitting to a bribe, said that both the Nashville lawyer and the judge had been paid $500 each. Sullivan denied bribing the judge, and said that malicious newspapers falsely made the claim. However, he did say that his legal and other expenses amounted to $4,500, a hefty sum.[420]

Regardless of his release, Governor Lowry remained vigilant. He would seek the arrest of the pugilists wherever they might go. Many reporters and politicians supported him. Some analysis hinted at or revealed the existing regional tensions between the North and the South, or tried to tap into and foster such acrimony. The *Clarion-Ledger* wrote, "What mattered it that the encounter was forbidden by special act of the Legislature? What cared the first citizen of classic Boston that the Governor of a Southern commonwealth had issued a proclamation forbidding the proposed outrage upon society, decency, law and order?" Although, "Generally speaking, the newspapers of the country, both North and South, have spoken fairly of Gov. Lowry in his efforts," nevertheless, it was noted that the *Chicago Tribune* had said,

> They taught the arrogant Mississippian that the North is still in the saddle, and that Northern men, when it pleases them, will invade his State and set all its laws at defiance. They are not to be bulldozed. They are not to be scared away like colored citizens. It is a pity, that the black voters of Mississippi have not the nerve and manhood of the men who took possession of the State this week. … It might be a fine scheme for the colored men to hire Sullivan and a few of his companions to look after their interests at the next election.

---

[420] *Pittsburg Dispatch*, July 12, 1889; *Brooklyn Daily Eagle*, July 11, 1889; *Times-Democrat*, July 12, 13, 1889.

The southern paper took offense. "If he thinks the sluggers can do so much bulldozing, why not get up a car-load of fellow-toughs around Chicago and come down here and just wipe us off the face of the earth?" However, other Chicago newspapers supported the South in this case. The *Chicago Inter-Ocean* said, "It is only unfortunate that the law would not hold him and return him to the tender mercies of Mississippi, whose law he violated."[421]

Fearing arrest, Charlie Mitchell and Mike Donovan fled to Canada to protect themselves.[422]

Sullivan traveled to Chicago, where he remained for a week, drinking.

On July 14 at Curtis's saloon in Chicago, Peter Jackson and Sailor Brown, a white man whom Jackson had knocked out in the 4th round in Chicago on July 11, entered the bar. Sullivan and Brown had words. Allegedly Sullivan criticized Brown for lowering himself by "fighting with a nigger." Another version said Brown and Sullivan got into a debate about something, Brown called Sullivan a liar, and John L. proceeded to punch and knock him down. Professor Mike Conley, the Ithaca Giant, tried to intervene, but Sullivan knocked him down as well. Yet another report said that no violence occurred, but after Sullivan issued his criticism, Brown reached for his revolver, but his friends hustled him out of the saloon. The next day, Brown denied that Sullivan struck him or that Sullivan was drunk. The accuracy of news reports were as varied then as they are today.[423]

Allegedly, William Muldoon gave an interview in which he said of Sullivan, "He is as thorough-paced a loafer as I ever had anything to do with. All these stories about his great love for his parents and his generosity are the veriest bosh. A more unappreciative fellow I never saw, and now that it appears to be useless to induce him to behave himself, the sooner the truth is told about him the better." After the fight, a telegram had arrived informing Sullivan that his mother was very ill and he should return home. He seemed indifferent, and Johnston told him that he should be ashamed of himself: "Your poor old mother is lying sick, and you don't seem to care a cent. Why can't you be a man?" Continuing, Muldoon said,

> Sullivan is a man with the lowest kind of tastes. It was difficult to prevent him from gratifying his low desires. That he is giving full play to them now is clear from the character of the neighborhood which he is frequenting in Chicago. As for rum, why he loves it. He is a stubborn brute, and it is a mighty hard thing to compel him to do anything that he doesn't want to do. This talk about his being tempted to drink by friends is bosh. He drinks in order to satisfy a craving for liquor, and not because he is a good fellow. …

421 *Clarion-Ledger*, July 18, 1889.
422 *Times-Democrat*, July 20, 1889.
423 *Alexandria Gazette*, July 15, 1889; *Salt Lake Herald*, July 16, 1889.

> When he came to me his stomach was so weak that it could retain only the lightest kind of food…and his flesh was as soft and flabby as a baby's. He looked like a man who would not live three months.[424]

The next day, Muldoon claimed that the articles printing his alleged words were unjust and untrue, and written by a malicious individual trying to create trouble between them.

> I have always been and still am his friend. Our close companionship while training has only strengthened our friendship. A few unpleasant things occurred during our training, but they were made right at the time and forgiven and forgotten. We parted the best of friends, and we entertain today the warmest friendship for each other. I know that he entertains the deepest love for his parents, brother, and sister. He is kind hearted and generous to a fault. I am positive that he fully appreciates what has been done for him by his backers and trainers.

Some believed that Muldoon simply had cooled off and regretted his hot words. Others believed that his prior quotes were fabrications.[425]

Sullivan next traveled to Brooklyn, New York, where Charles Johnston resided. He then went to New York City. On July 23, stakeholder Al Cridge turned over to Sullivan $20,000 and the diamond championship belt. Sullivan gave the "dog collar" to Johnston for safe-keeping. Much of the money would have to be returned to his backers. The *Illustrated News* had contributed $5,000, Charley Johnston $2,500, and Jim Wakely $2,500.[426]

Unfortunately, unbeknownst to Sullivan, New York Governor David Hill granted a requisition warrant for Sullivan's return to Mississippi.

On July 31, 1889 in New York, Inspector Thomas Byrnes arrested Sullivan. The judge refused him bail. Therefore, John L. consented to his return to Mississippi so that he could obtain bail once there. The next morning, on August 1, law enforcement officials accompanied him on a train back to Mississippi.

Upon reaching Jackson, Mississippi three days later, on August 4, Sullivan "was treated more like a conquering hero than a common criminal. The President of the United States would have attracted less attention than this man Sullivan." At first, the local sheriff allowed him to stay at a hotel – the Edwards House. However, Governor Lowry heard about it and ordered the sheriff to place Sullivan in jail. Hence, Sullivan was taken to the jail. The kind sheriff allowed John L. free access to the jailyard, "where I could walk around and smoke."

Apparently, at some point, Colonel Jones Hammonton (or Hamilton) interceded and convinced the powers that be to allow Sullivan to return to the Edwards House.

---

424 *New York Sun*, July 16, 1889.
425 *New York Sun*, July 17, 1889; *Indianapolis Journal*, July 18, 1889.
426 *New York Sun*, July 24, 1889.

Sullivan's lawyers filed a writ of habeas corpus, demanding that he be taken to the county where the alleged crime had been committed. The judge agreed, and Sullivan was brought to Meriden, and then on to Purvis, Mississippi, the county of the offense.

JOHN L. SULLIVAN IN QUOD.
ARRESTED IN NEW YORK, ARRAIGNED IN COURT, AND TAKEN TO MISSISSIPPI BY DETECTIVE CHILDS—SCENES AND INCIDENTS ATTENDING THE ARREST.

Sullivan posted a $2,000 bond guaranteeing his appearance at trial and was released. He had to remain in Purvis until his trial.[427]

On August 15, 1889 in Purvis, Sullivan was tried for violating Mississippi's anti-prize-fight law. District attorney James Neville said, "Stand up, John L. Sullivan." He did, and looked straight at the attorney as he read the indictment. "What say you, John L. Sullivan, guilty or not guilty." "Not guilty," he replied with emphasis, in a clear voice. The trial then began.

The first witness was Major W. W. Robinson, a deputy sheriff who went to Richburg on July 8. He gave a detailed description of the ring being pitched in the early morning hours, before daylight, and he also described the fight. Neville asked, "Did they hit each other?" "Hit? Look at Sullivan's eye." Laughter was heard. He also said he saw Sullivan jump on Kilrain with his knees.

The next morning, on August 16, the jury found John L. Sullivan guilty of the crime of prizefighting.

On August 17, Sullivan was sentenced. Multiple petitions were read requesting only a fine, including one signed by all of the members of the grand jury that indicted him, and all but one of the trial jurors, as well as the

---

[427] *Times-Democrat*, August 1, 1889; *Clarion-Ledger*, August 8, 1889.

sheriff, the clerk, and other officers of the court, and also merchants and farmers in the vicinity. Sullivan's lawyer said that 91% of the state believed that a fine alone was sufficient. Sullivan appealed for clemency as well. "No doubt I have done something wrong, but as my counsel told you, I was ignorant of the law. … I am your humble servant, John L. Sullivan."

Nevertheless, after a long silent pause was taken to read the petitions, Judge Terrell (or S. H. Terral) asked Sullivan to stand up, which he did, and then the judge said,

> Gentlemen, passing sentence always has been of considerable trouble and concern to me, even in small cases, except where the law has one absolute punishment. It seems to me that this prize fight at Richburg, of which you stand convicted, was a gross affront to the laws of the State, where the authorities personally forbade it. It seems to have been accomplished with systematic arrangement and in the presence of invited thousands. It seems on the part of all connected with it to have been studied disregard and contempt for law. They came from and through many States whose authority and civilization deterred them from any attempt at such public lawless conduct within their limits, and they chose the State of Mississippi as the only fit ground for such a combat, indicating their utter contempt for the sentiments of her people and the laws of her statute books.
>
> The sentence of the law is that as the punishment for the offence for which you stand convicted, you shall suffer imprisonment for twelve months in the county jail.

Sullivan gloomily took his seat.

Referee John Fitzpatrick, who earlier had plead guilty, also was sentenced. "Mr. Fitzpatrick, in view of all that has been said in your behalf, and which I am disposed to believe is true, you appear to be a gentleman who was only present at the fight as a spectator, and one who did not intend to violate the law. In view of this, I sentence you to pay a fine of $200."

The champ was allowed to remain free on a $1,000 bond pending an appeal. He returned to Boston and immediately began a drinking spree.[428]

The grand jury did not indict Charles Rich or the railroad officials involved. On August 22, Bud Renaud was found guilty of participating in a prize fight and sentenced to a $500 fine.[429]

In the meantime, on August 14, Kilrain had been taken into custody in Baltimore and had posted bail. A detective sent by Governor Lowry arrived to take him back to Mississippi. Some thought that after hearing about Sullivan's sentence that Jake might jump bail, but he did not. He was

---

428 *Clarion-Ledger*, *Newberry Herald and News*, August 22, 1889; *Brooklyn Daily Eagle*, March 18, 1890.

429 *Fort Worth Daily Gazette*, August 21, 23, 1889.

brought to Mississippi, and then released on bail pending his trial in December.[430]

On August 30, 1889 at her residence on Parnell street, Roxbury, Sullivan's mother Catherine Sullivan died from water on the heart. She was 52 years old. Allegedly she had been ill and bed-ridden for the past two years, although some said she had been in poor health for the last 15 years.

Sullivan said that during the next year, while awaiting the result of his appeal, mostly he was idle, save for some short friendly exhibitions.

On September 7, 1889, the champion attended a benefit in his honor at the New York Academy of Music. His appearance brought forth several minutes of tumultuous applause. John L. said, "Ladies and gentlemen - I do not know what to say to you. I am at present suffering from a sad affliction – the loss of my mother, but I wish to thank the New York public for their kindness to me. They always have been kind to me and I never shall forget it. I beg to remain your humble servant."

Sullivan sparred 3 rounds with Mike Cleary. "Sullivan never appeared to better advantage in a scientific set-to. He looked well physically, and he was quite as quick upon his feet and with his head and hands as upon any previous occasion."[431]

That same day, Sullivan announced his intention to become a Democratic Congressman should he be offered the nomination. Former fighter John Morrissey had been elected to the U.S. House of Representatives in 1866.[432]

When asked if elected, what his policy would be regarding the present race troubles in the South, Sullivan replied,

> When it comes to floggin' men at night, whether they're black or white, I'm against it. See? I'd like to go down there on a committee. I'd stop all such foul work. I will not go into a ring with a negro, but, by Jupiter, I wouldn't stand by and see another white man lick him without reason. No, sir-e-e! It appears to me that a negro is at home in the South.[433]

Ultimately, however, Sullivan did not run for office.

Even if Sullivan had to return to Mississippi to serve his sentence, it was reported that Charles Rich, the fight's host, also was the county contractor for county prisoners. He would have charge of Sullivan, "and, you may be assured, will treat him kindly." Apparently, the county had a prison contract system whereby someone could purchase the services of a prisoner, and that prisoner could reside at the home of the man who purchased his services. Hence, Rich could buy Sullivan's services and allow him to remain at his home for the one year. Although no one wants their

---

430 *Clarion-Ledger*, August 29, 1889.

431 *New York Clipper*, September 14, 1889.

432 *Helena Independent*, *St. Paul Daily Globe*, September 8, 1889.

433 *Evening World*, September 9, 1889.

liberty restrained for a year, at least Sullivan's stay would be relatively comfortable.[434]

Australians criticized Sullivan's drawing of the color line on their champion Peter Jackson. The Sydney *Referee* wrote,

> There can be nothing more false than the idea that sneaking behind the colour-line will protect a white man from the charge of cowardice in refusing to meet a black, or enable him to hold fictitious honours. No man can call himself or be called champion while he refuses to meet and fight a black challenger.... There is no doubt but that this colour line has to go. It is against all manliness and courtesy – a fungus growth of an effete generation of self-styled champions; and the false security of these colour-line drawers has got to have the bottom knocked out of it, and that very shortly.[435]

Despite some fair-minded sportsmen and members of the press arguing that no color line existed or should exist in pugilism, Sullivan's position was consistent with the era's majority view. The fact was that separation of the races was the norm. Color prejudice was rampant. The *Times-Democrat* said, "When the negro race is left to itself it relapses into that state of barbarism in which it originally existed." The *Houston Free South* said, "[T]he young negroes – who are termed 'coons' and never knew what slavery was, are a nuisance – a curse to the South." The *Williamsburg Journal* said, "It is the fixed policy of the Republican Administration to 'draw the line,' to establish a white-man's Republican Party in the South, and thus leave the colored man out in the 'cold.'"[436]

The *Times-Democrat* alleged that color prejudice actually was stronger in the North, but hypocrisy attempted to conceal it. Noted was the fact that Northerners were upset that some blacks had been recruited in the South as postmasters. Northern merchants would not hire blacks as clerks or salespersons, no matter how deserving. White Northern mechanics refused to work with negroes, and would not work under a negro foreman, even though such sometimes occurred in the South. In New Jersey, blacks were not allowed to bathe in the ocean at the same time as whites. The newspaper asked the North,

> Does not a colored servant cook your meal, another wait on your table, another shave your face...? Well, then, I am unable to see why it is that if you can take your breakfast from black hands, you can't

---

[434] *Evening World*, September 9, 1889; *Clarion-Ledger*, September 29, 1889. The 13th Amendment technically allows slavery or involuntary servitude as punishment for a crime: "Neither slavery nor involuntary servitude, except as a punishment for crime whereof the party shall have been duly convicted, shall exist within the United States, or any place subject to their jurisdiction."

[435] *Referee* (Sydney), September 11, 1889.

[436] *Times-Democrat,* July 1889; *Clarion-Ledger*, July 18, 1889, quoting *Houston Free South* and *Williamsburg Journal.*

> also take your letters and newspapers from the hands of negro postmasters....
>
> There is nothing extraordinary about this particular manifestation of the color prejudice. There are other exhibitions of the same feeling, in the North as well as in the South, which are even more remarkable….
>
> While such things are true at the North, it is arrant hypocrisy for Northerners to prate about the "insane prejudice" of Southerners against the negro. The truth is that this color prejudice is entertained by most white people – by a great many who concede that it seems unreasonable, and yet who confess that they cannot get over it….
>
> We must remember that it is only about thirty years since Abraham Lincoln, in his famous joint debate with Douglas, in answering on the 18th of September, 1858, the question whether he was "really in favor of producing a perfect equality between the negroes and white people," replied:
>
> "I am not, nor ever have been, in favor of bringing about in any way the social and political equality of the white and black races. I am not, nor ever have been, in favor of making voters or jurors of negroes, nor of qualifying them to hold office, nor to intermarry with white people; and I will say in addition to this that there is a physical difference between the white and black races which I believe will forever forbid the two races living together on terms of social and political equality."[437]

Sullivan's heavy drinking continued, and it caused him to fail to appear at several scheduled events, including a benefit in his honor scheduled to be held on September 23 in Brooklyn.

On September 26 in Fishkill, New York, Sullivan began a scheduled brief sparring tour under the management of his brother Michael Sullivan as well as John Barnett. Sullivan sparred with Liney Tracy and 3 rounds with Mike Cleary. They next headed to Syracuse.[438]

John L.'s drinking caused him to miss several tour dates.

On October 15, Sullivan said he would fight again, but wanted only Queensberry rules bouts with gloves. He was willing to fight Jem Smith or Charley Mitchell, or anyone else if there was enough money in it.[439]

On October 26, 1889, Sullivan had been drinking and bar hopping with Tommy Kelly and Tommy Shea, the latter recently having served a 3-year sentence for highway robbery. They headed to a barber shop, where Sullivan and Shea got into an argument. Shea was trying to provoke him, insulting John L. However, the champion did not bite. The drunken Shea

---

437 *Times-Democrat*, July 22, 1889.
438 *Pittsburgh Dispatch*, September 27, 1889.
439 *Pittsburg Dispatch*, October 16, 1889.

turned his attention and insults upon Kelly, who seized a razor and slashed Shea under the left jaw. Shea spent several weeks in a hospital recovering.[440]

William Muldoon again insisted that he and Sullivan were just as good friends as ever, and stories to the contrary were false.

On November 7, 1889 in Boston, George Godfrey scored a KO14 over Jack Ashton.

On November 10, 1889 in London, in a Queensberry rules contest, Australian champion 192-pound Peter Jackson fought English champion 182-pound Jem Smith. In the 1st round, they engaged in heavy exchanges. In the 2nd round, Jackson forced the fighting and knocked the English champion all over the ring. Jem was dazed. However, Smith got inside, wrestled, and illegally threw Jackson to the floor in LPR style. He then asked for the fight to resume with bare knuckles. The police stopped the fight and the referee awarded the contest to Jackson via disqualification. "Smith was beaten at all points."[441]

The Australian press continued criticizing Sullivan for his refusal to meet Jackson.

> [S]o long as he raises that false, unmanly, disgraceful side issue as to color, and refuses to meet the only man on earth whom good judges consider likely to defeat him, Peter Jackson to wit, the world will not accord him champion honors. No man can be champion of the world while he allows the challenge of any other man in that world, whatever his creed or color, to pass unheeded.[442]

Perhaps in response to some of the pressure from the press, Sullivan said he would be willing to fight Jackson if the California Club offered a $25,000 purse. There also were discussions of him fighting either Frank Slavin or Dominick McCaffrey. However, most doubted his sincerity on the topic of Jackson, given his previous strong statements that he would not fight a black man (and that was not the term he used).

California Club President Lem Fulda received a message from Sullivan backer Captain Cook, who said, "Sullivan says white men $10,000 apiece, colored men double price."

Jackson's manager Parson Davies did not believe Sullivan wanted to fight Jackson, or that he would do so. "I can scarcely believe that Sullivan really wants to challenge Jackson, as the 'big fellow' has always said he would never fight a nigger. He has drawn the color line so closely before that I hardly believe he has chopped it off now."[443]

---

440 *Pittsburg Dispatch*, October 27, 1889.

441 *Sacramento Daily Record-Union, New York Times*, November 11, 1889; *San Francisco Examiner*, December 2, 1889.

442 *Referee* (Sydney), November 20, 1889.

443 *Evening Star, Alexandria Gazette,* November 13, 1889; *Salt Lake Herald*, November 15, 1889; *Los Angeles Herald*, November 16, 1889.

Former Sullivan manager Pat Sheedy said that when in condition, Sullivan could defeat any many alive or who ever lived, and that included Peter Jackson. "I saw Jackson fight, and I think pretty well of him, but of course I don't class him as Sullivan's peer."[444]

Sullivan explained why he might consider Jackson. "I once said that I would never fight a colored man; but they seem to think that Jackson is a world-beater, and I am anxious to show them just where he belongs." He said he would do it for a minimum of $20,000.[445]

Allegedly, a rich white widow wanted to marry Peter Jackson. The *San Francisco Examiner* said, "Of course a marriage between a white woman and a negro, even though it be a champion pugilist, would be unlawful, but they could get around this either by going three miles out at sea…or going to some foreign country." However, "even these evasions and delays will not be necessary, for it is stated that the would-be bride herself has a strain of negro blood in her veins."[446]

Regardless of the potential color-line impediment, given that Sullivan said that he might cross the line for sufficient financial inducements, discussion of a potential Sullivan – Jackson contest continued. An expert sized up the match:

> The Sullivan that Peter Jackson is to meet is only the remnants of a great man. In his day he was the greatest glove-fighter the world ever saw. He is the man that popularized glove-fighting in the United States. … For a big man he is a marvel for activity and precision in delivering a blow. He swings the right across about as quick as most men can shove out the left hand. For four rounds he will pound a man about, regardless of size, same as he would handle a sand-bag or punching ball. The left does but little execution, and for that reason he depends solely upon the deadly right. Some pugilists say that cleverness would pull a man through, and avoid the rushes that Sullivan makes, but that is a great mistake. No man can stand up under his hurricane work with the big gloves on, and the bigger the man the poorer his chances are of giving him a stand-off. The only man to defeat Sullivan is one after the Mitchell order, and even then it is odds on John L. It won't be much to Jackson's credit to defeat Sullivan as he is now, because the great slugger is past his prime. … I must say, however, that people who have seen the Australian darkey admit that for four or six rounds his chances of defeating John L. are slim, but if he can by good fortune survive for that length of time he would be afforded an excellent opening of gaining the day.[447]

[444] *New York Sun,* November 20, 1889.

[445] *Evening World,* November 21, 1889.

[446] *San Francisco Examiner,* December 2, 1889.

[447] *Referee* (Sydney), December 4, 1889.

Jem Mace called Jackson a wonder, but said that if Sullivan was in proper condition, he probably would defeat Jackson in a fight to the finish. However, "he will hardly ever get in first-class fix again. He don't like work, you know."

A wealthy gambler who backed Jackson for $1,500 against Smith said that Sullivan could lick Jackson without a doubt. Jack Harper, one of Jem Smith's seconds, believed that Smith would defeat Jackson in the old style. He also picked Sullivan to defeat the colored man.[448]

On December 14, 1889 in Purvis, Mississippi, Jake Kilrain stood trial on charges of engaging in a prizefight and committing an assault. The jury acquitted Kilrain of the prize-fight charge, but found him guilty of assault. He was sentenced to two months in jail and a $200 fine. Kilrain posted $1,000 bail for his release pending appeal.[449]

In mid-December, Sullivan began a sparring engagement with Joe Lannon in New York at the Miner's theatre. Starting on the 16th, Lannon and Sullivan boxed 3 short rounds. In his speech before the sparring began, Sullivan said, "Ladies and gentlemen, I feel very grateful for your kindness in coming here tonight and giving me this applause, and I will try always to deserve your appreciation." He once again received applause.

However, the affair was a bit too tame for the audience. Lannon did almost all of the leading, and landed some blows, but as a rule Sullivan stopped or dodged most of them. In the last round, Sullivan stood still and allowed Lannon to thump his face several times. Then he made a quick feint and Lannon ran away. Sullivan walked off the stage laughing.

Sullivan said he would not finalize a match with Jackson or anyone else until "I get my head out of the lion's mouth," meaning his legal troubles in Mississippi. He thought there was a strong likelihood that he would have to serve his sentence in Mississippi, which would render him inactive for another year. He seemed resigned to the probability that he was going to have to serve his sentence, and did not want to train and prepare for a fight that likely would not be allowed to take place, or could not owing to his incarceration.

Sullivan said he had never seen Jackson box, but heard that he was clever. If he was to fight him, it would have to be for big money.

> I admit having said…that I was willing to meet Jackson for a suitable purse and stake. … Everybody knows perfectly well that I will meet Jackson, Kilrain or any other man living who can get sufficient backing. … Next year I shall be ready to talk business with Kilrain, Jackson, or Slavin.[450]

---

[448] *Sun,* December 1, 1889.

[449] *San Francisco Examiner, St. Paul Daily Globe,* December 15, 1889.

[450] *Evening World,* December 16, 1889; *Sun, San Francisco Examiner,* December 17, 1889.

Frank Slavin was another emerging contender from Australia. The 6' 188-pound Slavin's record included: 1887 KO10 Mick Dooley, KO9 Martin "Buffalo" Costello, and KO2 Bill Farnan (the only man to hold a victory over Jackson); 1888 KO1 Dooley; and 1889 KO3 Jack Burke (who in 1885 went the 5-round distance with Sullivan and in 1887 boxed Jim Corbett to an 8-round draw).

Frank Slavin

On December 23, 1889 in Bruges, Belgium, Frank Slavin fought Jem Smith to a 14-round 22-minute bareknuckle LPR draw that was declared a draw only on a technicality - because the referee stopped it owing to Smith's fans interfering with the fight. However, Slavin clearly had been the better man. Thereafter, Slavin was acknowledged as the English champion. He challenged Sullivan to fight for up to $5,000 a side within six months.[451]

Sullivan replied that although he was willing to fight anybody, it had to be for a purse large enough to make it worth his while. He also said that he had enough of the law, and when a contest took place, it had to be under the auspices of a responsible club, like the California Athletic Club, using Queensberry rules. He wanted a legal fight without interference or impediments.[452]

On December 24, 1889 in Ireland, Peter Jackson stopped Peter Maher in 2 or 3 rounds.[453]

In January, the Southern *Clarion-Ledger*, responding to U.S. President Benjamin Harrison's criticism of the South's treatment of blacks, defended,

---

[451] *San Francisco Examiner*, *Sun*, December 24, 1889; *National Police Gazette*, January 4, 1890.
[452] *Evening World*, December 27, 1889.
[453] *London Sportsman*, December 26, 1889.

> There were no Southern men engaged in the slave trade and no Southern men having slave ships. … I can point out to him and his Northern allies crimes that they have committed against the negro very lately much greater than selling him into slavery – if conspiring against his life is worse.[454]

Men who had faced Sullivan said that when in the heat of battle, he had a most awful expression on his face, one that could intimidate even stout hearts. Paddy Ryan said that Sullivan had the expression of a murderer.

On January 17, Charley Johnston returned the "dog collar" championship belt to the *Police Gazette*.[455]

On January 29, 1890 in Boston, Sullivan was present to watch Peter Jackson give a 4-round sparring exhibition with Jack Ashton.

> The Australian made an exceedingly favorable impression. His agility was a surprise to all, and the skillful manner in which he eluded Ashton's leads was warmly applauded. Of course neither man let himself out, but it was very easy to see that Ashton stood as much show against the Australian as a mouse would have in the paws of a cat. Sullivan closely watched every move of Jackson's.[456]

In February 1890 in Hoboken, New Jersey, Jackson and Sullivan were both in town to give separate sparring exhibitions during the same week at the same place, but on different nights. In one of those exhibitions, on February 7, 1890 in front of a packed house, Sullivan boxed Joe Lannon 3 rounds. Although they did not engage in rough work, the spectators applauded and were satisfied.

Sullivan again sparred Lannon in Hoboken on February 12, boxing 3 rounds that had enough life to evoke applause.

Again on the 13th, a crowd of nearly 1,000 paid $.75 or $1 to see Sullivan and Lannon spar 3 rounds. Peter Jackson was in the audience.

Admirers of Sullivan said that he exhibited remarkable cleverness in his theatrical bouts with Lannon, and was as light and active on his feet as ever. Even those who did not like him "praise the form he keeps himself in." Sullivan was scheduled to exhibit in Troy as well.

That same week in Hoboken, Jackson sparred with Billy Elluger and Jack Ashton. Sullivan saw Jackson spar with Ashton and said that Peter was a very clever boxer.[457]

On February 17, 1890 in New Orleans, 183-pound James J. Corbett clearly won a 6-round decision over 205-pound Jake Kilrain. Although Louisiana law technically made boxing illegal, because the sport was so

---

454 *Clarion-Ledger*, January 9, 1890.

455 *Sun*, January 7, 18, 1890.

456 *Referee*, March 12, 1890.

457 *San Francisco Examiner*, February 8, 1890; *Brooklyn Daily Eagle*, February 10, 1890; *Evening World*, February 14, 1890; *New York Clipper*, February 15, 22, 1890; *Referee* (Sydney), April 16, 1890.

popular, the law was not often enforced when it came to gloved Queensberry rules bouts.

Kilrain said that Corbett was clever, but not powerful. Superior reach allowed Corbett to touch him and score. Jake had trouble landing effective blows on the quick, shifty, agile, defensive-minded fighter. Kilrain complained that the referee did not allow infighting, which helped Corbett. Still, Corbett had hit hard enough to blacken both of Kilrain's eyes, puff up his entire face, and cut him. Kilrain wanted a rematch in a longer fight.[458]

James J. Corbett

John L. Sullivan commented,

> I know this man Corbett, and I don't think for a minute that he can whip Kilrain, Queensberry rules, with small gloves. Kilrain has been having a good time lately and was out of condition. There was no in-fighting allowed, and Corbett, having a longer reach, got in some hits and got away. He is a clever fellow, no doubt, but if there is anybody in any part of the country who thinks that Corbett can stay ten rounds with Kilrain with two-ounce gloves, why, I've got $5,000 which I will bet against $4,000 that he can't.[459]

---

[458] *Times-Democrat, Daily Picayune*, February 18, 1890.

[459] *San Francisco Chronicle,* March 3, 1890.

William Muldoon, who had trained and cornered Kilrain for the Corbett bout, and who had trained Sullivan to his victory over Kilrain, offered his thoughts on the upcoming man.

> Corbett was away the superior of Kilrain the night they fought, he says, and he calls the Californian a second Jack Dempsey. Corbett has as much generalship and cleverness as a heavy-weight as Dempsey has as a middle-weight. When time was called he jumped for Kilrain, and was on top of him almost before he could get out of his corner. Kilrain only hit Corbett one square blow in the six rounds. When asked what he thought of Corbett's chances against Sullivan Mr. Muldoon said that Corbett was not such a hard hitter as he ought to be to fight Sullivan. The trouble with Sullivan would be that he could not hit Corbett. The Californian was twice as clever as Kilrain, he thought, and is just the man to whip Jackson.[460]

In Australia, the *Referee* continued calling Sullivan a coward, and offered a theory as to why he was giving the illusion of moving away from his color-line stance:

> From all appearances John L. Sullivan is bluffing most pronouncedly in his pretended negotiations for a fight with Peter Jackson. He was on bed rock, when in desperation, and seeing plainly that unless he came down off his cowardly color line pedestal, Jackson would be hailed Champion of the World, he suddenly coiled up the line and announced his willingness to meet the Australian Champion for a purse, if any club would give one. The California Club at once sprang into the breach and offered 15,000 dol. or 3000 pounds, for the two to fight for. Seeing that there was an absolute danger that he would actually be matched with and have to fight the Australian champion-extinguisher, Sullivan then changed front, and with his usual braggadocio and insulting manner and language announced that he would fight any white man the club chose to match against him for 10,000 dol., or 2000 pounds, but he wanted double for niggers. …
>
> Now we are told that Sullivan has again raised his demand, and wants 25,000 dol. … All this means one little word – bluff! Sullivan is frightened to death at the idea of meeting our long-armed, lithe-limbed champion, and will resort to any means, however despicable, to avoid a meeting with the man he dreads. Having withdrawn his old safeguard, the color line, he falls back on quibbling for a stake that is simply ridiculous as a means of getting out of a fight altogether. … [H]e knows perfectly well that by imposing such prohibitory stakes he evades all possibility of a meeting. … Hence Sullivan is safe, and can still boast himself champion while resorting to a mean subterfuge to avoid risking his hide and his title. The whole Press of America is

[460] *San Francisco Chronicle,* March 17, 1890.

against Sullivan and his cowardly and unmanly objection to fighting colored men.[461]

However, the savvy Sullivan believed that a big fight was worth $25,000, and eventually he would be proven correct.

On March 5, 1890, Sullivan entered Mike Kelly's saloon just before the bar was about to close. He was "maudlin drunk." His hair was disheveled. "The champion at once began to amuse himself at the expense of those present. He had a slap for this one, a mild punch for that, a playful dig in the ribs for the next one, and would fall over another, accompanying his antics by insulting language." One man paid him no attention. Sullivan came over, sat down, and looked at him and said, "I am John L. Sullivan and I can whip any man in the world!" He asked the young man, "Do you know who I am?" "No, I don't know who you are and I don't care to." "Well, I am Sullivan and can kill you with one blow." The man replied that he did not care and would not allow anyone to insult him. Sullivan jumped up to his feet but the young man rose as well and immediately fired a right with terrible force to the champion's mouth. Sullivan reeled and staggered and fell over two chairs. The young man fled. Sullivan rose in an ugly mood, but the man was gone. His friends led the inebriated John L. out.[462]

One reporter who spoke with Sullivan in early March 1890 said, "Reading between the lines of his conversation I am satisfied that he is thoroughly tired of the ring."[463]

On March 8, 1890 in Providence, George Godfrey scored a KO16 over Patsy Cardiff.

On March 14, 1890, one month after Corbett had boxed Kilrain there, New Orleans passed an ordinance officially legalizing boxing. Gloved Queensberry rules bouts would be allowed in athletic clubs as long as no liquor was served, no boxing took place on Sunday, the club donated $50 to charity, and $500 was posted before each contest.[464]

On March 17, 1890, good news emerged out of Jackson, Mississippi. The Mississippi Supreme Court overturned Sullivan's prize-fight conviction on a technicality. The indictment was squashed as being defective in its averments. The indictment failed to allege that the fight had been held in public or that Kilrain had fought Sullivan – only that Sullivan had fought Kilrain. However, such allegations were required under the 1882 prizefighting statute. Bud Renaud's appeal was decided similarly.

The ruling did not mean that Sullivan was out of the woods. The case was remanded to the Marion County Court. If it so chose, the State could

---

461 *Referee* (Sydney), March 6, 1890.
462 *Omaha Daily Bee*, March 6, 1890.
463 *New York Sun*, March 9, 1890.
464 William H. Adams, "New Orleans as the National Center of Boxing," *Louisiana Historical Quarterly* 39 (1956).

re-indict Sullivan properly, re-try him, and, if found guilty, once again he could receive the same jail sentence.

Nevertheless, Sullivan was happy. He said, "I shall never fight again under the London rules, and I will only engage in one more glove contest, and that will probably be either with Jackson or Slavin, and the athletic club where the fight takes place will have to put up $25,000. I haven't come down one penny in my price and don't intend to."[465]

Unfortunately for Jake Kilrain, the technicality that caused a reversal in Sullivan's case did not help his cause, because he had not been convicted of prizefighting, but assault. He lost his appeal and his conviction stood.

Determined to keep him out of jail, Charles Rich purchased Kilrain's services under the prison contract system, and Jake spent his two-month sentence as a "laborer" for Rich. In reality, Kilrain was Rich's honored guest for a couple months. "Rich is one of the wealthiest, most popular and influential young men in Marion county, and when he undertakes to do a thing, he usually succeeds." The amount of money he paid was kept confidential, but Rich had been quoted as saying that he would keep Kilrain out of jail even if it cost him $1,000.[466]

Also on March 17, 1890, Jim Corbett arrived in New York. He sparred with 42-year-old Mike Donovan, the New York Athletic Club's boxing instructor. Donovan told the newspapers,

> I regard Corbett as the cleverest big man I ever sparred with, and I have no hesitation in saying that he is the coming champion. When I boxed Sullivan at the Howard Athenaeum in Boston in February, 1880, he was practically unknown to the pugilistic world. I said then that Sullivan was the coming champion. … Corbett today is the man that Sullivan was ten years ago, and now it is his turn, and I regard him, as I said before, as the future champion.[467]

In April, Corbett said he would be willing to box Sullivan 4 rounds for a $1,000 purse.

> In Corbett, however, Sullivan will find a man fully as agile and clever as Charley Mitchell. Corbett will not stand till he is knocked down by one of the big fellow's rushes, but will be all over the ring in a round and boxing on the retreat. … Of course there is the possibility that Sullivan may put him out with one of his famous punches, but it is only a possibility and too remote to be likely to happen in four rounds with Sullivan in very poor fix for any kind of a fight.[468]

---

465 *Evening World*, March 17, 1890; *Brooklyn Daily Eagle, Los Angeles Daily Herald*, March 18, 1890; *Omaha Daily Bee*, March 19, 1890.

466 *San Francisco Examiner*, December 15, 1889; *Clarion-Ledger*, March 27, 1890; Isenberg at 278-279.

467 *Referee*, March 19, 1890.

468 *New York Clipper*, April 12, 1890; *San Francisco Chronicle*, April 7, 1890.

On April 14, 1890 in Brooklyn, James J. Corbett stopped Dominick McCaffrey in the 4th round. An observer of Corbett's performance said,

> His left flies out like a piston rod. His deliveries are fine, quick and straight…his stoppings are excellent, and his flank movements, with his long strides and perfect poise and balance, are marvelously agile for a man weighing 185 to 190 pounds. McCaffrey was fought out practically in four minutes from the first call of time … McCaffrey seemed blown and amazed at a very early stage of affairs. When he failed to land, as he usually did, he lurched in for a clinch. Corbett threw him from him quite handily, I thought, but in the operation he had a way of roughing him over the face with the glove that was quite of the English fighters' variety. … Corbett was smiling, fresh as a daisy, strong and springy. … I should not want the contract of finding a Queensberry rule glove fighter to whip him. His demonstration of outclassing McCaffrey was far more complete than Sullivan's. … Make no mistake of counting upon Corbett as easy game for any holder of the much coveted fistic championship of the world. He is in the programme with any fighter living to give him an argument.[469]

Apparently, San Francisco's California Athletic Club had offered a $20,000 purse for a Sullivan - Jackson fight. Engaging a writer in discussion, Corbett predicted that John L. would not take the fight, saying,

> "Sullivan will not fight." "Nonsense," Said I, "Sullivan has declared that he will fight for $20,000." That sum having been subscribed by the athletic club, he will fight Jackson for it. "May be," said Mr. Corbett, "but I don't believe it. Sullivan dare not train down to fighting condition now. If he were to train down as a man ought to for a fight it would kill him. He has indulged in all sorts of excesses and has tried his constitution to its uttermost. He has broken his health by these practices, and now he cannot quit drinking, try as he may. The result is that his whole physical being is laid under tribute, and he will find himself woefully lacking in physical responsiveness when he tries to train down to fighting trim.
>
> Why, when he fought Kilrain he was far from being in prime condition. He wore a plaster on his chest and stomach, and was generally in bad shape. Had he been in condition he should have won that fight in twenty rounds. I think there are several men who can whip Sullivan now, but I don't think Sullivan will fight unless he becomes very hard up. However, if he fights Jackson I will stand to go broke on Jackson's winning. I have seen Jackson in all his fights and

469 *Referee,* August 5, 1891; *San Francisco Chronicle*, April 28, 1890.

boxing bouts in San Francisco, and if he fights Sullivan I think he'll whip him. But I stick to my belief that Sullivan will not fight."[470]

Corbett favored Jackson against Sullivan, for he was fully aware of the fact that Sullivan was on the decline.

> Sullivan I don't think will ever fight Jackson to a finish, for I don't believe that he can stand the training for such a fight. He realizes this fact himself, and is taking no care of himself. In my opinion he will never be the Sullivan of the past. … The man is but human, and can't stand all excesses.
>
> Peter on the other hand, takes all possible care of himself. … In science the Australian, in my opinion, is superior to Sullivan, but then I am only one man, and don't wish at this early date to set myself up as a critic.[471]

Corbett believed that "as far as finish fights are concerned Sullivan's career is at an end." His insights came less than one year after the Sullivan-Kilrain fight.

A writer echoed Corbett's sentiments, saying,

> This man Sullivan is beyond redemption. He has been drunk night and day for months, and he is now only a shadow of his former self. I cannot see how he ever can be got to fight again, besides he has a particular dislike to fighting colored men, which he expresses when drunk as well as sober.[472]

Phil Dwyer said he would back Corbett against Sullivan for any amount up to $50,000. "You may not know it…but that man Corbett, in my opinion, outranks them all, and I took the pains to tell him so when he was here [in New York]. … I think Sullivan is retrograding sadly, and do not believe he will ever meet Jackson or any other first-rater."[473]

Sullivan said he could not do anything about the proposed Jackson fight or any other potential bout until his legal issues in Mississippi were settled. He was scheduled to be there on June 23.[474]

Many said that Sullivan was afraid of Jackson. Others said he really was not interested in fighting again at all, for he loathed the thought of abstaining from alcohol and doing all of the necessary training required for a big fight, for it would take a great deal of training to lose all of the fat he had gained. He could make easy money in light sparring exhibitions, so the incentive to fight was low. They believed that the only way that he would fight again would be if his short friendly exhibitions ceased making money, he was broke, and he needed, wanted, and was offered one last big payday.

---

470 *San Francisco Chronicle*, April 24, 1890.
471 *Referee*, June 25, 1890.
472 *San Francisco Morning Call*, May 11, 1890.
473 *San Francisco Chronicle*, April 27, 28, 1890; May 5, 12, 1890.
474 *Evening World*, April 24, 1890.

In early May 1890, Sullivan signed with Duncan B. Harrison to spar with Joe Lannon during each performance of a melodramatic play called *The Paymaster.* He would be paid $1,000 a week for six weeks. The show began on or about May 13.[475]

BROOKLYN AMUSEMENTS.
NOVELTY THEATRE | So. 4th & Driggs, Brooklyn, E. D.
Matinees Tuesday, Wednesday, Friday & Saturday.
The superb military melodrama THE PAYMASTER
Introducing, in connection with the play,
THE WORLD'S CHAMPION JOHN L. SULLIVAN
Who will spar four rounds with
JOE LANNON
at every performance during the week.

On May 19, 1890 in Chicago, 195-pound Peter Jackson fought 175-pound Denver Ed Smith in a 5-round bout with 4-ounce gloves. Jackson forced the fight throughout, while Smith alternated between defensive and aggressive tactics. Although Smith drew first blood in the 1st round with a right to the mouth, Jackson attacked and scored a knockdown, and Smith clinched and went down twice more to avoid punishment. Both landed well in the 2nd round, though Jackson again twice decked Smith with his right. Smith continued fighting hard. In the 3rd round, Smith clinched and dropped down. In the 4th round, Smith landed quite often. In the 5th round, Jackson tried to finish him, but could not land a telling blow. At the bell, Jackson was declared the winner on points. Both men had landed well during the contest, in give-and-take fashion, and afterwards their faces were swollen and marked up.

The local *Chicago Tribune* was critical of Jackson, saying that although the decision in his favor was justified,

> [T]he fight has proven that Sullivan is a better man than the Australian black. Jackson lacks two requisites necessary for a first-class man - the quality to finish and to follow up an advantage. Smith seemed able to hit him when and where he pleased, and showed that a good man can always find Jackson's face. Smith's blows lacked force. Jackson showed no ability that would stop the famous rushes of Sullivan.[476]

Eventually, Denver Ed Smith would win several important battles and become a top contender.

That same week in May in New York, Sullivan and Joe Lannon were sparring as part of *The Paymaster.* "The fistic gladiators appear attired in regulation evening dress, instead of ring costume." Despite the playful and friendly nature of their exhibitions, they received nightly ovations.[477]

On June 22, 1890, Sullivan arrived in Purvis, Mississippi. A grand jury found a fresh prizefighting indictment against Sullivan. Muldoon, Cleary, and Donovan also arrived, facing aiding and abetting charges.

---

475 Sullivan at 166; *Evening World,* May 10, 1890.

476 *Chicago Tribune, San Francisco Examiner, Evening Bulletin,* May 20, 1890.

477 *New York Clipper,* May 24, 31, 1890.

On June 24, 1890, Sullivan once again went before Judge Terrell (or Terral). District Attorney James H. Neville commanded Sullivan to stand up, which he did, and then the attorney read the indictment and asked, "What say you, John L. Sullivan, are you guilty or not guilty?" Sullivan responded, "Guilty." He then turned towards the judge and said, "If your honor please, may I address the court?" "The court would be pleased to hear from you, Mr. Sullivan." Sullivan then proceeded to say,

> In entering the plea of guilty, I do so with a humbleness of heart, and ask for the leniency of the court. I realize the fact that I have done wrong and violated the laws of Mississippi, but I assure your honor that it was unintentional on my part, and it will never occur again.
>
> Since the beginning of this trouble I have suffered awful punishments, which have told upon me severely, and I beseech the court to be as light as possible in this unfortunate affair. I remain your obedient servant, John L. Sullivan.

Sullivan's lawyer, ex-Mississippi Attorney General Thomas Ford, also addressed the court. He noted that Sullivan was compelled to either forfeit a large sum of money for nonappearance at the fight and be branded a coward, or violate the law and fight. He recognized that was not a legal argument, but one of human nature. He mentioned Sullivan's ill-health and the death of his mother. He also said a dear relative's life was hanging by a thread. He concluded, "To err is human; to forgive divine." Sullivan had tears running down his cheeks during his attorney's remarks, and he hid his face in a handkerchief.

For several minutes, there was a death-like silence in the courtroom. Judge Terrell arose and commanded Sullivan to stand, which he did.

> Mr. Sullivan, I am truly sorry that you are in such a bad predicament. In fact, I am sorry to see any human being step from the path of righteousness and commit an evil deed; but I am confronted by the will of the people – the law that protects society – and I am compelled to enforce it. I extend to you my heartfelt sympathy in your bereavement, something which every man has to bear, and I truly hope that you will reform and become a better man.
>
> In obedience to my own convictions and those of the leading citizens, I impose upon you a fine of $500, upon the payment of which into the county treasury the sheriff will release you from custody.

This time, Sullivan had escaped with just a $500 fine, and he would not be imprisoned. He paid the fine immediately and left the state. His legal troubles finally were over.[478]

---

[478] *Roanoke Times*, June 25, 1890; *Clarion-Ledger*, June 26, 1890; *New York Clipper*, July 5, 1890; *Seattle Post-Intelligencer*, July 1, 1890;.

Muldoon, Cleary, and Donovan all plead guilty to aiding and abetting a prizefight. The court fined Muldoon $250, and Cleary and Donovan $100 each.

At that time, it was announced that starting in August, Sullivan would be the lead in a play written for him by Duncan B. Harrison called *Honest Hearts and Willing Hands*. Hence, it was clear that Sullivan was more interested in getting paid to act and spar lightly than to fight. It would be the first time that an athlete would take on a starring role in a play, as opposed to just a bit part or supporting role. This meant that Sullivan essentially would be retired or semi-retired from fighting. He could get paid well, and not have to train, get hit, or fear arrest.

Sullivan's desire to move away from fighting made economic sense. John L. said that his legal bills, fines, and other expenses related to the Kilrain prizefighting case had totaled $18,675.[479]

The Kilrain fight and its legal and financial fallout illustrated why LPR prize-fighting was not worth it, and had come to its end. It no longer made any sense. A fighter had to do a lot of training, suffer punishment in a long fight, and then have to fear imprisonment, fines, and lawyer fees that would eat up the profits. As Sullivan said,

> [B]reaking these particular laws has been very expensive to me, for in all the fights that I have been in under the London Prize-Ring rules, I have not only lost money, but have also had the care and worriment incidental to arrests, trials, and penalties. It has always cost me more money to get out of my fights under those rules than I have ever gained from them.

Sullivan contrasted an LPR fight with a Queensberry rules contest, which "usually takes place in a hall of some description under police supervision, and the price of admission is put purposely high so as to exclude the rowdy element." Sullivan also preferred Queensberry rules bouts because he believed that the LPR rules did not allow for a legitimate, quick, or entertaining determination of the better fighter.

> Under the Marquis of Queensbury rules no clinching is allowed, no wrestling, and the superiority of the contestants is judged by the actions of their hands. … Under the London Prize-Ring rules…[c]ontests last too long to demonstrate which is the superior man, and the length of time occupied does not depend on the superiority of the man as a fighter or boxer, but the contemptible trickery possessed. … Gentlemen and business men of all vocations cannot afford to give up the time to witness fighting under the London Prize-Ring rules, for the reason that it takes too long. … The London Prize-Ring rules allow too much lee-way for the rowdy element to indulge in their practices. Such mean tricks as spiking,

---

[479] Sullivan at 167.

> biting, gouging, concealing snuff in one's mouth to blind an opponent; strangling, butting with the head, falling down without being struck; scratching with nails; kicking; falling on an antagonist with the knees; the using of stones or resin, and the hundred other tricks that are impossible under the Marquis of Queensberry rules.[480]

Bareknuckle boxing had existed in modern times for over 170 years, at least since James Figg in 1719, though it likely existed before that. It had extended from Jack Broughton and his rules in 1743 to the London Prize Ring Rules in 1838, all the way to July 8, 1889. The Sullivan-Kilrain fight would be the last world heavyweight championship contest fought under the London Prize Ring Rules. It was the end of an era.

Of course, Sullivan occasionally had legal difficulties with Queensberry rules contests as well, though not to the same extent as with the London rules. Still, he had to deal with the law, arrests, and trials under both systems. He would not have such concerns with an acting career.

---

[480] Sullivan at 182-184.

Continuing Championship Hiatus and Contender Emergence

Members of the California Club had seen the overweight John L. Sullivan in the East performing in *The Paymaster*, which contained a tame and short sparring exhibition with Joe Lannon. They did "not express themselves as highly pleased with the champion's appearance. They found Sullivan giving boxing exhibitions in a swallow-tail coat with Joe Lannon, and they appear to think that this style of contest is about all that the eminent Boston slogger will be ever again good for."[481]

One year after Sullivan-Kilrain, in late July 1890, there was further talk of a potential Sullivan-Corbett match-up. Phil Dwyer was willing to back Corbett for $20,000 against Sullivan, while Charles Johnston was willing to back Sullivan for the same amount against Corbett. However, Sullivan was tired of the game and not really interested in fighting any time soon.

> The big fellow does not mind fighting, for he feels that he is the superior without doubt of any man in a twenty-four foot ring. It is the severe sacrifice that he has to make while training that sickens him. "Just think of throwing two good months of your life away to train for one fight," said the champion recently.[482]

The opening of *Honest Hearts and Willing Hands* was delayed from mid-August to September 1 so that Sullivan could continue to practice and learn his lines.

On Monday September 1, 1890 at Niblo's in New York City, John L. Sullivan began his acting career as the dramatic star in the play that Duncan B. Harrison wrote for him entitled *Honest Hearts and Willing Hands*. The audience, which included adoring women, enjoyed it. The first reviews of Sullivan's acting and the play were good. The play would tour the country. Acting had become his profession.[483]

On September 7, 1890 in Boston, John L. Sullivan's 65-year-old father died of typhoid pneumonia. Sullivan was in New York, appearing on the stage at Niblo's Gardens. His father Mike often

NIBLO'S.
MATINEE
TO-MORROW,
JOHN
L.
SULLIVAN,
DUNCAN
B.
HARRISON,
AND
AN EXCELLENT
CAST.
MATINEES
WED. AND SAT.
HONEST
HEARTS AND
WILLING
HANDS.

[481] *San Francisco Chronicle*, July 8, 1890.

[482] *San Francisco Chronicle*, July 21, 1890.

[483] *Referee* (Sydney), October 22, 1890, October 26, 1892.; Sullivan at 167; *Evening World*, June 25, August 30, September 2, 1890.

had been referred to affectionately and humorously as "the only man who ever whipped Sullivan."[484]

Despite the big victory over Kilrain, the past year had been difficult for Sullivan. He had lost both of his parents, he had been chased, arrested, and tried, suffered the loss of money associated with his legal troubles, and he often had been drinking too much. Yet, he seemed content with his new money-making profession.

On September 27, 1890 in London, Australia's Frank Slavin scored a KO2 over Joe McAuliffe. The victory was significant, for after McAuliffe's 1888 LKOby24 loss to Peter Jackson, he subsequently had come back with a May 1889 KO8 Tom Lees (against whom Jackson scored an 1886 KO30) and September 1889 KO7 over the hard-punching Pat Killen (who had an 1887 KO2 Duncan McDonald and June 1888 KO5 Patsy Cardiff). Slavin's quick victory over a tough and well-respected big man further highlighted Slavin's merit.[485]

Seeing that no bout with Sullivan was likely to materialize anytime soon, back in August, Peter Jackson had returned to Australia. He gave regular exhibitions there.

On October 20, 1890 in Melbourne, Australia, Peter Jackson, "colored champion pugilist of the world," fought Australia's Joe Goddard in a scheduled 8-round bout. Goddard had such victories as 1889 KO11 Owen Sullivan and KO4 Jim Fogarty; and 1890 KO21 Mick Dooley. He usually weighed around 186 pounds.

The Sydney *Referee* said that Goddard was a vicious, aggressive, strong rusher who maintained a fast pace. He more than compensated for his relative lack of skill with "boundless energy, pluck, dash, and devil." He was "a modern Hercules, and planks his faith upon his grit and staying powers. ... [H]e is the most perfectly trained man in the world." The Goddard-Jackson fight turned out to be a grueling battle.

1 - Jackson landed several straight punches, but they only served to awaken the slumbering demon Goddard, who charged to the inside, smashing in lefts and rights to the body and head, causing Jackson to reel away, staggered and shaken. He collected himself, dodged and landed left jabs, but Goddard beat down his guard, and with his whirlwind of blows once again momentarily had Jackson in trouble. Peter kept smashing him in the mouth with his left, but he could not beat him back. It "was quite evident that the white man held his own, and many people were inclined to think he had a bit the best of the three minutes."

2 - Goddard "bounded across the stage like a lion." Jackson landed a solid right. After a clinch, they exchanged blow for blow to the body and head and it seemed as if one or the other would be knocked out. They slowed

[484] *Evening World*, September 8, 1890.
[485] *Minneapolis Tribune*, May 3, 1891.

momentarily before Goddard attacked again, "and in spite of Peter's great swiftness of foot he bore down on him…and another frantic, desperate, savage rally followed, in which Joe more than held his own until the cry of corners sent them apart."

3 - Goddard again dashed at Jackson. Peter landed a hard right and countered strongly. After a rally, "Jackson came away like an electric eel, and drove a superb left on the front of the chin, bringing Joe to the boards as if he had been kicked by an elephant."

Despite the knockdown, Goddard rose and sprang at Jackson and beat him back. "Joe held his own, fighting grimly, desperately, fiercely, as if the very pride of race and color had entered into his heart." However, "Suddenly Peter saw an opening, and shooting his right clean across he dropped his determined foe once more to the boards."

Goddard "rose and sprang at his man and drove him over the ring by sheer vim and pluck. Peter smashed him over the eye with the left and made it get on the bulge, but Joe smiled sardonically and went for more."

4 - They again fought fiercely. A flush left on the chin dropped Goddard for the third time in the bout.

Nevertheless, Goddard rose and continued setting the pace. Peter cleverly dodged and landed his jab as Joe pressed in. "Over and over again he flung himself full upon Pete and took his gruel like a white man, never flinching, never quailing, game, grim and almost reckless he fought as no man had ever been seen to fight in the Southern Hemisphere before." The crowd cheered vigorously. Despite suffering an apparent pounding, the local newspaper said, "Goddard went to his corner with a decided lead."

5 - Goddard kept attacking, but Jackson drove him back with long heavy lefts to the face. Still, Joe gave him no rest. "All through the three minutes he was rushing and pounding, and it took Pete all he knew to keep his end up under the cyclonic pressure." An American source said they both went down at the same time in this round, but the local primary source did not mention this.

6 - Both were a bit weary, but Goddard kept plugging away and had Jackson mostly on the defensive. "Jackson did mighty little besides dodge out of danger, for now it was a case of the huntsman hunted, for the knocker-out was in danger of being sent down."

7 - Jackson began aggressively and landed a strong left. However, Goddard then "punched him from one end of the ring to the other, Pete seeming fairly paralyzed by the tornado." It appeared that Jackson was weakening. "For a spell it looked as if Joe was going to win. Pete fell, but got up again quickly, and then the tongues of the throng were let loose." They fought "like dervishes, until the struggling, seething mass of humanity formed a sight such as one might hope to see in hell when it's nigh boiling point, but Peter was equal to the occasion."

8 - They were cautious for the first part of the final round, but then they went at each other hard for about sixty seconds, each trying to knock out the other. "Peter weakened, and Joe drove him all over the place. Hurling himself bodily on the great African boxer he sent him reeling from him like a child, and at the call of time it looked as if Pete had met his Waterloo."

One judge scored it for Goddard, one had it for Jackson, and the tiebreaking referee decided to call it a draw.

The local report said, "The fight was a grim one, but nearly all present agreed that Goddard had the best of it." Regardless of this opinion, the bout description gives the impression that a draw was appropriate. Some might say that Jackson deserved the win given that he was the one who had scored the clean knockdowns.

Nevertheless, the press said that Goddard had "established a claim to be considered a phenomenon in his own style, and it looks as if that wicked natural style of his will carry him right into the front ranks of the very best fighters the world possesses."[486]

The Goddard contest made some wonder whether Jackson could handle Sullivan, who was much bigger, stronger, and more talented and experienced than Goddard. Frank Slavin had demonstrated more firepower than Jackson. This made many experts view Slavin as Sullivan's next legitimate challenger. Of course, the counterargument is that Jackson had shown the ability to compete well in a rough fight with a strong, tough, well-conditioned rushing fighter. Also, Slavin had ducked Jackson while they both were living in Australia.

San Francisco reported that Jackson narrowly escaped defeat, for the plucky Goddard had outfought him. Although Goddard only weighed 182 pounds to Jackson's 197, he was the stronger man of the two. Jackson said, "I was far from well and hardly able to fight a round. It was fortunate for me the matter resulted as it did, considering the condition I was in." The *San Francisco Chronicle* opined,

> When he boxed Ed Smith in Chicago he floored the Denver man early in the battle, but Smith stuck to his work and improved toward the finish. On these public performances Jackson would have no show whatever with men of Sullivan's or Slavin's class as glove boxers, for both are knockers out who would make short work of him on the first symptom of fatigue. … Jackson claims…that he was not in proper condition. … He made a similar claim when he met Smith. This, however, is no excuse for an aspiring champion. … If he neglects his preparation…that is his fault. …
>
> The fact of the matter is that Jackson is not the most rugged type of boxers by any means. … [E]asy living tells quickly upon him. His

486 *Referee* (Sydney), October 22, 1890; *National Police Gazette*, December 6, 1890, December 13, 1890.

> successes in Europe and America changed him from a simple slogger into an athletic dude with a taste for good dinners, good clothes, fast horses and other rapid amusements. … [A]thletic abilities once impaired are not easily regained.[487]

The Goddard fight hurt Jackson's image a bit. Perception grew worse for Jackson when later there was discussion of a rematch between the two in a fight to the finish, but Jackson instead left Australia and returned to America, which some took as a sign of fear or weakness.[488]

Slavin wanted to fight Sullivan for a side-bet of $10,000 per side, but Sullivan wanted more money before he was going to train for a fight.

On November 3, 1890, James J. Corbett wrote Frank Slavin a letter challenging him:

> A few weeks ago I read in the daily papers a telegram…in which you speak very disparagingly of John L. Sullivan. … Mr. Sullivan has proved himself the greatest fighter that ever stepped within a ring, and you certainly presume considerable when you attempt to criticize his achievements. … And, after expressing yourself quite freely regarding him, your insinuations are directed toward American fighters in general. Now, my dear sir, there's one American who has not accomplished one-half as much as Mr. Sullivan, but who deems it a pleasure to accord you a meeting.

Corbett admitted that Slavin was a hard hitter, but did not believe that Frank's victory over McAuliffe meant that he was invincible. Apparently, Jim wanted to take one big leap into top contender status by defeating a highly regarded man. The *Chronicle* wrote,

> Corbett has always maintained that he could defeat McAuliffe. If Slavin goes on with his match with Jackson Corbett will meet the winner. The young Californian has evidently made up his mind to fly at the biggest pugilistic game in the world. … He is certainly as clever as the best of them, and the only question is whether he is strong enough to cope with a man like Slavin. He should be, however, for he is a bigger man every way than the determined Australian.[489]

On November 22, Sullivan was in Taunton, Massachusetts with his show. During the afternoon, allegedly a drunken Sullivan kicked Duncan Harrison in the back, injuring him so that he could not appear at the evening performance. That evening, after the performance, Sullivan "celebrated in his usual manner," drinking heavily, and he fell out of a window of the City Hotel, nearly breaking his neck.[490]

---

487 *San Francisco Chronicle,* November 23, 24, 1890.
488 *San Francisco Chronicle,* December 29, 1890.
489 *San Francisco Chronicle,* November 3, 1890.
490 *Pittsburg Dispatch,* November 23, 1890.

On November 25, 1890 in Hoboken, New Jersey, George Godfrey scored a KO23 over Denver Ed Smith.

On December 6, 1890, Sullivan's friend Joe Coburn died of consumption at age 55.

In December 1890, the *Referee* criticized Sullivan for continuing to claim the status of heavyweight champion even though he was not accepting legitimate challenges from fighters such as Slavin.

> Sullivan still clings to the title of Champion of the World, and that sign is attached to his name on the advertising bills of the theatrical Company that he is traveling with. …
>
> Slavin probably would not be so eager to meet John L. Sullivan if the latter would drop the title of Champion of the World, which everyone who is conversant with prize-ring ethics, rules…is well aware that Sullivan has no right to the claim. …
>
> According to the rules governing the Championship a Champion holds that title as long as he accepts all *bona-fide* challenges and defends it against all-comers. When a champion fails to carry out this programme he ceases to be looked upon as a champion. …
>
> Sullivan has no excuse to offer for his failure to pick up the gauntlet Slavin throws at his feet, except that he claims that he is an actor.

Yet, this same author did not believe that Sullivan's inaction was a result of fear, still favoring John L. in a potential match with Slavin.

> Sullivan has the youth, height, weight, courage and the battering abilities, and by combining agility and muscle with common sense and good judgment, he should be able to prove that he is still a champion, no matter how great a pugilist Slavin may be.[491]

As it had done with Kilrain, in late December, the *National Police Gazette* awarded Slavin its championship belt and called him the Champion of the World. The general public still considered Sullivan to be the champion, and would unless or until he was defeated. Sullivan did not care what the *Gazette* said, once again talking as if he was retired, at least for the time being.

> I have retired from the prize-ring for the present. … Whatever fighting I may do hereafter will be as a sort of recreation. My business is acting. …
>
> Whether I meet Slavin or not, no man will ever dare to accuse me of cowardice. If our business continues to be as good as it has thus far, my bit this season will amount to 25,000 dollars, and it's a whole lot better to make money this way than to get it as I did in Mississippi. I

[491] *Referee* (Sydney), December 17, 1890.

had to spend all the money I made out of the Kilrain fight in getting myself free.[492]

Sullivan was earning relatively easy money as an actor. He didn't have to train, and he could eat and drink all he wanted. He was reaping the rewards of the fame he had worked so hard to earn.

One newspaper in describing Sullivan's life said that he woke up after noon, drank champagne before breakfast, smoked 25-cent cigars, and threw $50 bills away. He rode in a coach, grew fat, weighing around 250 pounds, and received mash letters of praise and admiration from women by the dozen. Women asked for his photograph and autograph. Many begged for an introduction. He refused most requests. He was earning about $2,500 a week, more than most earned in a year. He lived extravagantly and literally threw money away, spending it as fast as he earned it. He could be extremely generous and kind-hearted, but he also could be a bully and a tyrant. Between acts of his play he drank one or two bottles of Bass ale. He occasionally sung songs. He liked to tease and joke with other actors. He said he would like to engage in at least one more finish battle before retiring permanently.

> Wherever Sullivan goes he is the center of attraction. … The secret of his prominence is the fact that even in this age, when brains are superior to muscle, there is still enough of the old animal instinct left in humanity to admire the physically perfect, and Sullivan is popularly supposed to be the physical superior of any man in the world. This is the reason people flock in crowds to see him "act." They don't care a picayune for his acting. They want to see a curiosity - the man able to "lick" any other man in the world.[493]

On December 29, 1890, James J. Corbett signed a contract to fight Peter Jackson at the California Athletic Club on May 21, 1891 in a Queensberry rules fight to the finish for a $10,000 purse, to be divided $8,500 to the winner and $1,500 to the loser. The excitement and anticipation was immediate. "This is unquestionably the greatest match ever made in the heavy-weight class, as the two men are known the world over as the most skillful boxers that the ring has ever produced."[494]

On January 8, 1891 in Milwaukee, Sullivan allegedly punched a reporter named Ed Dillon. Sullivan later said that he only pushed Dillon with the back of his hand.

At hotels, Sullivan registered himself and a woman whom he called his "wife."[495]

On January 10, Duncan Harrison signed contracts with the MacMahon Brothers of Her Majesty's Opera House in Melbourne for a tour of

---

492 *Referee* (Sydney), December 24, 1890.
493 *St. Paul Daily Globe*, December 26, 1890.
494 *San Francisco Chronicle*, December 29, 30, 1890.
495 *Indianapolis Journal*, January 9, 1891.

Australia. Sullivan and the play would leave San Francisco in June and open in Melbourne in July.[496]

On January 14, 1891 in New Orleans, 150 ½-pound Bob Fitzsimmons won the world middleweight championship by knocking out 147 ½-pound Jack Dempsey, the Nonpareil, in the 13th round. Sullivan was broken-hearted, for he liked Dempsey and had bet several hundreds of dollars on him.

On January 18, 1891 in Chicago at a local theater, Sullivan met Corbett for the first time. Afterwards, Corbett said,

> I always had an idea that Sullivan was the most maligned man in public life, and now I believe it. … Sullivan is champion of the world, and an American likewise. His record ought to protect him from the attacks of such men as Slavin. If that fellow wants to fight why don't he fight me: I'm nearer his class than Sullivan is. I posted $1,000 with a challenge to him, yet he did not accept it. I am convinced that Slavin is a blatant blowhard, who would rather talk than fight, and who takes advantage of Sullivan's engagement to get in his licks.[497]

Another man said that Sullivan was "the most misrepresented and maligned man in the whole business. I don't set him up for an angel; he is not built that way. But there is more of the human in him than he is accredited with."[498]

Sullivan said that once his theatrical engagement was concluded, he would be willing to talk about making a fight. He believed that in the meantime, the top contenders should all fight each other so that one could emerge as best entitled to a title fight, and then he would fight that man.

On January 24, the Cincinnati Order of the Elks suspended Sullivan as unworthy to associate with gentlemen, for his conduct had brought shame and discredit upon the order. He was expelled shortly thereafter.

Sullivan said he no longer had any interest in becoming a member of Congress. Why? "There is only $5,000 a year in the job, and that wouldn't buy my cigars."[499]

On February 12, while in Wilkes-Barre, Pennsylvania with his play, Sullivan said that the next time he entered the ring the monetary consideration had to be very large. "I am making plenty of money now, and making it without much effort, too. I would be a fool if I gave up my present position to go into training to fight for a small purse."[500]

Allegedly, on February 25, 1891, a 135-pound man named Townsend, a train-hand on the Georgia railroad, knocked out Sullivan, who was howling

---

[496] *Pittsburg Dispatch*, January 11, 1891.
[497] *Seattle Post-Intelligencer*, January 19, 1891.
[498] *Anaconda Standard*, January 19, 1891.
[499] *St. Paul Daily Globe*, January 25, 1891; *Seattle Post-Intelligencer*, January 26, 1891.
[500] *Pittsburg Dispatch*, February 13, 1891.

drunk and in a bad humor. Sullivan had used foul language towards him. Afterwards, John L. had a black eye.

Apparently Sullivan had been drinking considerably while in Georgia, including in Macon, where he appeared on stage in a very inebriated condition. Backstage, a black scene shifter failed to move as quickly as Sullivan thought he should, so John L. allegedly fired three shots from his pistol. In response, the property man threw several spittoons at his head. Regardless of Sullivan's conduct, he was a curiosity, so his drunkenness did not hurt ticket sales.[501]

On March 13, 1891 in San Francisco, Jake Kilrain scored a Queensberry rules KO44 over George Godfrey. This was significant, given that Godfrey had recent victories over Jack Ashton, Patsy Cardiff, and Denver Ed Smith.

At a meeting of the Newark Elks, who were considering expulsion of the champion, Duncan Harrison defended Sullivan, saying that reports of his bad conduct were false newspaper fabrications. The charges were that he had kicked Harrison in the back, knocked down a newspaper reporter, assaulted a hotel bellboy, and acted in an unbecoming manner. Harrison told them, "As a matter of fact, the reports about Sullivan's assaults on me and the bellboy were pure fabrications. As to the assault on the reporter there was no violence. The reporter was in a great hurry late at night to get an interview, and he forced his way into Sullivan's room. Sullivan took him by the shoulder and led him out."[502]

In April, Harrison said, "Sullivan, as his friends know, is as modest a fellow as you would want to see when sober, but when intoxicated, of course, you can't hold him."

On April 27, 1891 in St. Louis, Australian heavyweight Frank Slavin, who recently had arrived in the U.S., asked Sullivan whether he would consider a match. Sullivan said that he had a contract for another year to appear on the stage, and therefore no longer was in the ring. More and more, it was looking as if Sullivan had bid goodbye to the ring forever, or for the very least yet another year.[503]

On May 21, 1891 at San Francisco's California Athletic Club, 24-year-old 185-pound James J. Corbett took on 29-year-old 198-pound Peter Jackson in a scheduled fight to the finish using Queensberry rules and 5-ounce gloves.[504]

Corbett and Jackson engaged in "as clever an exhibition of boxing by two big men as ever took place in the ring." Their boxing was scientific and

---

[501] *Seattle Post-Intelligencer*, February 26, 1891; *Daily Tobacco Leaf-Chronicle*, *Alexandria Gazette*, February 27, 1891.

[502] *Evening World*, March 18, 1891.

[503] *Sun*, April 19,1891; *Evening World*, *San Francisco Examiner*, April 28, 1891.

[504] *San Francisco Examiner*, May 21, 1891; *San Francisco Chronicle*, May 22, 1891, May 23, 1891; *Daily Alta California*, *Minneapolis Tribune*, May 22, 1891; Corbett at 126 and 132-133.

graceful. Early in the contest, Jackson was more of the aggressor, setting the pace, although both feinted a great deal, and both could slide forward and back. Corbett was as nimble on his feet as a fawn, gracefully moving about on the retreat, but was good at quickly stepping in and firing a blow and then clinching. He also was good at dodging counters. Both exhibited remarkable science, though there was little heavy hitting, given their defensive cleverness. Jackson was cool, cautious, and systematic, slowly crowding and sliding forward, while Corbett demonstrated extraordinary quickness of hands and feet. They both occasionally landed a solid blow to the body or head, but the fierce exchanges were infrequent and usually short lived, given their defensive skill. They both knew how to move, duck, and clinch. Also, they had to pace themselves, given that it was a fight to the finish.

In the 9th round, some blood trickled from Jackson's lips. He kept boring in on Corbett. By the 14th round, Corbett's right eye was swelling a bit. In the 16th round, Corbett fought Jackson into a corner. However, Jackson landed a blow to the mouth that caused Corbett to spit blood.

The 17th round was vicious, both landing solidly to the head and body, with Jackson having a bit the best of it. In the 18th round, Corbett landed a solid left to the chin that momentarily staggered Jackson.

From the 18th to 28th rounds the fighting was relatively tame, save for a few occasional moments. In the 22nd round, a lump could be seen rising from Jackson's forehead. Corbett's upper lip was swelling. In the 28th round, they punched and clinched often.

In the 29th round, Corbett showed that he could fight as well as box cleverly. Up to that point, Jackson was the aggressor and Corbett more defensive-minded. However, Corbett suddenly forced matters and landed several furious blows to the body and head. Jackson was in distress.

In the 30th round, Corbett again went at Jackson hard and had him hurt, particularly from body blows. However, both were too tired to do decisive work, and the round ended tamely.

In the 31st round, Corbett went at him wickedly again and landed a solid right that staggered Jackson. However, Peter rallied and attacked again. Corbett then turned matters around and hit harder and faster. Jim had the upper hand.

However, thereafter, the fight slowed down badly. Both men appeared to be winded. The fight became very tame, with mostly long-range sparring, both resting, throwing and landing few blows.

In the 41st round, Jackson picked up the pace again, landing some solid blows, but Corbett rallied and fought back well.

Once again, the fight returned to dreary cautiousness, neither fighter inclined to take risks. If Jackson led to the head, Corbett would counter to the body, and then Peter would become respectful again. Once in a while, one would pick it up and test the other momentarily, sometimes landing a solid blow, but the other would respond, and then the fight settled back down to tiresome careful sparring again.

In the 57th round, the crowd started hissing and loudly demanding that the fighters wind it up or call it a draw. However, little happened, giving the impression that neither wanted to take risks. Some spectators left, some fell asleep, and some made sarcastic remarks.

Before the 61st round, Jackson proposed a draw. Referee Hiram Cook, the club directors, and the pugilists held a consultation at ringside. Corbett objected to a draw, so Jackson replied that he would continue to stay with him then. They boxed the 61st round, but it was no more lively. Neither fighter wanted to take the risk of fatiguing himself further. After the walk-around round concluded, the referee announced that it was evident that it could not go on as it was and come to a satisfactory conclusion. No further fighting was likely to occur. Therefore, "as it has come to an unsatisfactory conclusion I declare it no contest." Although Jackson seemed pleased that it was over, the upset Corbett vehemently objected to the forced conclusion.

They had fought 61 rounds over the course of 4 hours. A fight that began around 9:30 p.m. did not end until 1:45 a.m. Obviously it had been a contest. Since it was a fight to the finish, the club directors and the referee argued that it was the fighters' duty to try to stop their opponent. Since neither seemed willing or able to do so at that point, and the fight had become exceedingly slow, it was ruled a no contest. In truth, it was and should have been declared a draw. But by calling it a no contest, the club avoided having to pay the fighters the full amount promised. Instead of paying them $5,000 each (splitting the $10,000 purse), as would be customary in the event of a draw, the club eventually paid each fighter $2,500. Corbett said he never again would fight at the California Club.

Corbett agreed that the first 30 rounds had tired them out. "I was the short-end man…and it was Jackson's place to whip me if he could. … I hit him every time he hit me. I was not going to take chances by forcing the fight in the condition we were in. I had my friends to look after."

Both fighters had distinguished themselves as skillful boxers, many saying Corbett even more so. The *Examiner* said Corbett's boxing was brilliant. "It was a beautiful show of what men can do in the way of avoiding blows." The *Chronicle* said both were clever and cautious, exhibiting consummate skill. In the 30th and 31st rounds, Corbett almost slugged him out, but thereafter, the fight became wearisome. The *San Francisco Evening Post* said the contest mostly resembled a battle for points.

> Corbett developed a rare degree of cleverness, but his talent certainly favors the avoiding of blows more than the delivering of them. His ducking from Jackson's straight handers was simply phenomenal, and the way he managed to throw his shoulders against the colored pugilist's stomach in ducking proves that Jim knows some of the most effective tricks of the trade. Jim, further, is about the shiftiest man on his feet that ever graced the California Club's ring, and in the one or two fierce rallies that marked the go he did the more effective work. After the twenty-ninth round the aspect of the match would

have warranted odds of two to one being laid on Corbett's chances; but the lead he gained was only a flash in the pan, and thereafter the mill degenerated into a contest of condition. …

In the early rounds of the fight it looked as if Corbett had made up his mind to employ questionable tactics. He squeezed Jackson around the neck with his left arm, and seemed loath on several occasions to let go until the referee entered the ring and made him break away. Finding, however, as the contest wore on that he could hold his own, Jim discarded the practice, and the remainder of the match was marked by the fairest kind of fighting on the parts of both men.

Corbett certainly surprised those who thought he would become rattled. His demeanor throughout was that of a veteran ringster, and the cool methodical manner he acted in the couple of brisk spells of fighting wherein he had the advantage led his backers to think that he would keep his head and follow the lead he had gained, but at no stage after the thirtieth round did Jim prove dangerous enough to cause any commotion in the Jackson camp. The manner in which Corbett died away in his fighting after the middle of the contest led many to believe that he intended wearing Jackson out thoroughly and then going at him, and when the fiftieth round came along and Jim did not increase his pace it became whispered about that he had hurt his hands severely punching Peter's head.

Jackson certainly did the bulk of the forcing in the last half of the contest, but he failed to either corner Corbett or induce him to mix things for any length of time. That Peter was tired was extremely palpable. His legs dragged and he frequently dropped his hands to his side as if to rest his arms. Corbett did not seem nearly so weary. He hopped around in lively fashion and seemed but little distressed, and the only conclusion the onlookers could arrive at were that either his hands were disabled or he was fighting under instructions and biding the time when the dusky pugilist should give evidence of being thoroughly tired out before sailing in to finish him.

In comparing the methods of the two men the general opinion seemed to be that Corbett had the call in cleverness. He was certainly more rapid in his movements, whether delivering blows, hopping back or ducking, but if the question of superiority were to be decided by points it would require nice discrimination to determine which man scored the most. …

The opinion was freely expressed last night that even now John L. could make mincemeat of both Jackson and Corbett, while it was thought that in the Boston Boy's palmy days neither of last night's principals would have stood the ghost of a show with him. …

Corbett gained great praise for his coolness and ringmanship, while it was considered that he lacks punishing power. His supporters were dissatisfied that he did not force matters after the thirtieth round, as they consider he was stronger than Peter and must have won. As regards the cleverness of the men, the idea prevailed that Corbett had the call.[505]

California Club President Lem Fulda, who had sponsored most of Jackson's fights in the U.S., although criticizing Corbett's clinching, as well as the throwing of his shoulder into Jackson's body, nevertheless admitted Corbett's ability:

> Corbett did very clever work, which entitles him to great praise and established the fact that he was able to dispute the title of premier boxer of the world with all. His skill is phenomenal and unquestionable. In point of the number of blows landed I think he scored the most, generally counters, but there are other conditions necessary to make a champion pugilist besides mere landing of blows – namely, effectiveness. … [T]he aggressive or attack was confined almost entirely to Mr. Jackson…and in a competition for points would have entitled Jackson to considerable allowance, but if for points both men might have boxed differently. … Granting that during a match honors are even, the one on the aggressive would be declared the victor. Be this as it may, there is nothing compulsory upon the part of either competitor as to the method to be pursued, either aggressive or defensive, in a professional match, unless for points, and cuts no figure in this particular case.[506]

Another old follower of fighters was not quite as high on Corbett, indicating both his strengths and weaknesses:

> I saw the Jackson-Corbett contest. … But the fight I saw is not the one I see reported in San Francisco daily newspapers or in the Associated Press. … The contest was a very clever one for about thirty rounds, or, in other words, while Jackson continued to fight Corbett. When Jackson ceased chasing the Californian the fighting ceased. I can explain Corbett's handling of himself upon no theory except that he went into the ring not to whip Jackson but to keep from getting whipped, and he was both clever and strong enough to accomplish his purpose. Jackson saw that after 30 rounds of trying it was useless to chase Corbett further. … Corbett is strong and wonderfully shifty. He is a very hard man to land on, and a most puzzling man to get to when he takes the notion not to fight. He

[505] *San Francisco Examiner, San Francisco Chronicle, Daily Alta California, San Francisco Evening Post,* May 22, 1891. For more on this fight, see *In the Ring With James J. Corbett* by Adam J. Pollack.

[506] *San Francisco Chronicle,* June 15, 1891.

> cannot punch as hard, however, as many of the middle-weights do. … My estimate of Corbett is that it will take a thoroughly good one in good shape to lick him, and that at the same time a thoroughly good one in good shape will not be licked by him.[507]

Regardless of the ultimate result and analysis, Jim Corbett had fought the most feared and respected contender in the world on at least even terms for over four hours. Hence, Corbett's reputation and stock skyrocketed.

A reporter claimed that allegedly, on May 28 in Jackson's saloon in San Francisco, Sullivan and Jackson nearly came to blows. Sullivan gave his views as to why Corbett "should have licked the negro." Jackson heard his uncomplimentary talk, and said, "See here, young man, you don't know what you're talking about. You're talking through your hat." Sullivan replied, "Who are you talking to? I don't stand such language from your kind of people." Jackson repeated the same remark. Sullivan whipped off his coat and Jackson began to do the same when friends interfered and hauled the enraged men apart. It is unclear whether the story is true, and there are some indications that the incident was newspaper fabrication.[508]

In mid-1891, the *Referee* reported that Sullivan had retired from the ring. "The next battle will decide the championship. … It lies between Slavin, Jackson, and Corbett."[509]

On June 16, 1891 in Hoboken, New Jersey, Frank Slavin knocked out Jake Kilrain in the 9th round, scoring several knockdowns in the 3rd and 4th rounds, and again in the 9th round, after which Kilrain retired. Kilrain was coming off his March 1891 KO44 over top American black George Godfrey.

On Wednesday June 24, 1891 at the Grand Opera House in San Francisco, just one month after the Corbett-Jackson fight, James J. Corbett and John L. Sullivan sparred in an exhibition.

A couple days beforehand, it was said, "Among boxers Sullivan's fighting days are considered over. It is not believed he will ever again enter the ring for championship honors. … Jim is expected to outspar him very handily." Another said, "There is no doubt but what Corbett is cleverer than Sullivan, and in a setto with the big fellow he can make a pretty showing, but it is a question whether there would be much gayety left in him after Sullivan had landed a time or two." Still, Sullivan was very fat and out of shape, so it was not likely that he was going to do very much. "If Sullivan is feeling at all mellow it is expected that he will freely express himself regarding 'niggers,' newspapers and heavy weight bruisers and wind up the recitation by proclaiming, 'I can lick 'em all.'"[510]

---

507 *Referee,* August 5, 1891.

508 *New York Sun,* May 29, 1891.

509 *Referee* (Sydney), June 3, 1891, quoting *The San Francisco Daily Report.*

510 *San Francisco Chronicle,* June 22, 1891; *San Francisco Evening Post,* June 24, 1891.

The house was packed. Sullivan was big, coarse, and bloated, with a paunch like an inflated balloon. He looked like a 240-pound barrel without legs. He stepped forward, elegantly attired in a suit, and made a short speech:

> Ladies and gen'lmen, I t'ank you fur yer appresheation. Dere's been a good eal o' talk about me lately an' I want to say that I sent a telegram East t other day. Wen I retire from de ring I want Mr. Corbett to succeed me. I'll meet Slavin wen I come back from Australia in September. I never challenge any one, but I'll be with him if he wants to meet me in a ten-round go.

Others quoted Sullivan as informing the crowd that after his return from Australia, in September 1892 he would demonstrate to the world who was the better man, he or Slavin. "I have never challenged a man in my life, but I will be at liberty when I again put foot on American soil to talk business to Slavin or any other man."

Corbett then addressed the audience, paying a glowing tribute to Sullivan as an actor.

The pre-exhibition analysis turned out to be irrelevant. Sullivan insisted that they wear formal dress suits, for he did not want it to be serious. In fact, it was even less serious than that. The boxers wore large gloves and their dinner outfits, pants, shirtsleeves, collars and neckties, to the surprise of the spectators. All that was absent were their coats and vests.

The crowd was shocked. Furthermore, the boxers only "sparred" 3 friendly rounds of about 10 seconds each, though it might have been slightly longer. The *Chronicle* said they barely ruffled each other's hair, for they mostly slapped and landed light blows. It was a "love fest." The *San Francisco Evening Post* said Sullivan and Corbett acted like they were platonic lovers stuck on one another.

Sullivan was very fat, "and it was with much difficulty that he managed to remain on deck even during the brief ten seconds." The *San Francisco Call* said Corbett showed compassion, and allowed several opportunities to land uppercuts to pass. Sullivan occasionally landed his fists on Jim's neck in a clumsy manner, and Jim would smile as he replied by planting his glove lazily on the big fellow's nose. The *San Francisco Evening Post* said they simply made a few harmless passes at each other. "Neither one landed a blow that would have brushed off a fly."

Having expected more, the disappointed paying spectators hissed, hooted, and yelled from the gallery, "Get in and mix up a bit." Sullivan's manager, "Tuffy" Barnett, informed the crowd that the pugilists were the best of friends and did not propose to punish each other.

The last round was just a little bit spirited, but neither one delivered a blow forcible enough to dent the big pillows.

Most called it a swindle and a fake. The crowd had had paid $2 and $3 to see the real thing. "When the performance ended a more disgusted audience never left a house of amusement than that which walked out of the Opera House to meditate upon how badly they had been swindled."

Sullivan did not look good at all. His body was so huge, "It would take at least twelve months of careful living and hard training to bring him into anything like the form of a champion fighter in first-class condition on entering the ring." The *Call* opined that he had to be ruined internally, for no man could get into top form after so many years of debauchery. "He was unquestionably a great man in his day, but you can take it for granted that Sullivan will never fight again and the announcement he has made as to a fight with Slavin on his return may be summed up as a mere advertisement."[511]

Following their exhibition, Sullivan continued his patented drinking spree.

> John Lawrence Sullivan…seems to be working on the idea that he has a contract to drink all the whisky, beer, wine, gin and rum in the country. During the past few days he has been endeavoring to get away with this end of his job, but he has been knocked out, and if he ever again gets sober, he will realize that, although he has the drinking capacity of an army, there is more fire water in this little town than he can swallow.

Sullivan had been "beastly drunk" and stayed out all night until the following day, not passing out until noon. This was typical for him. "On his theatrical tours Sullivan is generally kept in such a condition as to admit of his performing by allowing him to soak himself with whisky at night after the performance is over. He sleeps next day until it is almost time to appear again before the curtain."[512]

Many continued to question whether Sullivan wanted to enter the ring ever again. It appeared that he was more interested in easy money in the theater and drinking to excess. He always was an alcoholic, but he seemed to be degenerating. John L. said that he would be willing to meet Frank Slavin in September 1892, but most questioned his sincerity.

> It now transpires that he wishes to put the battle off until about 1909, and it is extremely doubtful whether he is not simply working for an advertisement without having the least idea of ever again entering the ring. …
>
> During the course of his sojourn here of over a month he hardly drew a sober breath. The time was spent in a long, uninterrupted debauch.[513]

On June 26, 1891, two days after the Corbett "exhibition," John "Lush" Sullivan boarded an Australian steamer called the *Mariposa*, heading towards

---

511 *San Francisco Chronicle, San Francisco Call, San Francisco Evening Post,* June 25, 1891.
512 *San Francisco Evening Post,* June 26, 1891.
513 *San Francisco Evening Post,* June 27, 1891.

Australia with his play. When he was boarding the boat, a sport wished him well and asked, "You don't fear sickness, I s'pose?" "John Lush" replied: "Feared nothing in my life, young fellow, be it on land or water, see. … Nothing can stop me, d'ye understand? I met Professor Rum and had a tough fight with him, but I did him, see, and bet yer boots I'll do him again. My name is Sullivan."

At that point, Tuffy Barnett introduced Sullivan to Peter Jackson, apparently for the first time. "Allow me to introduce you to Mr. Jackson, John." Sullivan looked Jackson square in the face and said, "Glad to see you, but I can lick anything on earth, black, brown, white or yellow. See?" Jackson paused for a few seconds, and replied, "I am willing to have you try anytime, Mr. Sullivan." Sullivan then said, "Well, then, you go and dig up ten or twenty thousand dollars, and I'll give you a rally when I come back from your country." "All right, I will have the money when you return, and I hope that your trip across the ocean will be pleasant and profitable." "Thank ye."

However, another reporter said that when Sullivan was asked about Jackson, he said, "He is a nigger, and that settles it with me. God did not intend him to be as good as a white man or he would have changed his color, see?"

Just before Sullivan set sail, he sent a message to James Wakely. "My statement is authentic. Will meet Slavin in September, '92 for biggest purse and $10,000 a side. Tell Charley Johnston."[514]

After six days at sea, Sullivan visited Honolulu, in the Kingdom of Hawaii, and gave an exhibition there with Jack Ashton, his regular sparring partner. While there, he met Queen Isabelle, King Kalakaua's sister, who called on him at the hotel.

The ship stopped off at Tintula to deliver the mail, and then the Samoa Islands. The natives there called Sullivan "Great Chief" in their language.

They briefly stopped at Auckland, New Zealand, before landing at Sydney, New South Wales, Australia on July 20, 1891. Sullivan was with Duncan Harrison, Frank Moran, and Jack Ashton, as well as a woman listed as Mrs. J. L. Sullivan, but she was neither his wife Annie nor his on-again off-again mistress Annie Livingston.

While in Sydney, Sullivan said, "I may fight again, and I may not." It all depended upon whether he was "offered sufficient inducement to again put on the gloves when I return to America." In the meantime, he was making easy money, so he had no need or desire to stop and train for a fight. "But, as I said before; I'm doing splendidly at the business I'm in now, and as men fight for money it'll have to be made well worth my while to throw over an easy and lucrative living to go in for such a tough job as fighting." He had not fought in two years.[515]

---

[514] *San Francisco Examiner*, *San Francisco Chronicle*, *San Francisco Call*, June 27, 1891.
[515] *Referee* (Sydney), July 22, 29, 1891; Sullivan at 173.

Joe Goddard challenged Sullivan to a fight, but Sullivan declined. He was there just as an actor.

On July 30, 1891 in Sydney, *Honest Hearts and Willing Hands*, which contained a 3-round sparring exhibition with Jack Ashton, opened at Her Majesty's Opera House. For the next three months, until October 1891, Sullivan performed in the play throughout Australia.

By seeing Sullivan for the first time, Australians realized just how talented he was. In his boxing with Ashton, Sullivan was looking quick and strong despite being fat and out of shape. The impressed Sydney *Referee* said,

> [A]nd though not in any sort of condition…he has enough of his old vitality left in him to show what a marvelous man he has been, and still would be if he would deny himself some of the luxuries of life and get into something like shape. He is remarkably quick upon his feet for so big a man, and shoots out his left hand as cleverly and as neatly as a youngster, whilst his heavy right arm, of which we have heard so much, comes across like a mule kick. Considering the pace the man has lived for the last seven years, he is a marvel, and must have been blessed with a constitution like a horse.[516]

After the two-week Sydney engagement concluded, the *Referee* wrote, "He gave us a taste of his capabilities as a pugilist whilst here with Jack Ashton, and I for one consider him a fistic phenomenon and I do not think the man breathes who can make a certainty of downing him." That included even Australia's own Frank Slavin.

> [O]ur great athlete, with his big, game heart, powerful frame, unbounded confidence, quickness, strength and wonderful hitting power, will need to have every muscle braced, every nerve strained, for in this American giant he will meet such a man as the world only breeds once or twice in a century.[517]

The Sullivan show went to Melbourne, opening there on August 15. While there, the champ met various political dignitaries.

After three weeks in Melbourne, the show also stopped in places like Ballarat, Bendigo, Adelaide, Cathlenain, Maryboro, and Stahl.[518]

Although Sullivan claimed that he would fight again, it probably wasn't going to be against Peter Jackson. The *Referee* reported,

> John L. Sullivan, although he once stripped to fight George Godfrey in Boston, and once signed an agreement to fight Peter Jackson at the California Athletic Club if the club would offer a 20,000 dol. purse, made the following statement: "I vowed before the public years ago that I would never fight a colored man, because I thought, and still think, that a white man is lowering himself too much when he faces a

[516] *Referee* (Sydney), August 5, 1891.
[517] *Referee* (Sydney), August 12, 1891.
[518] Sullivan at 174.

> nigger. Why, God had a view in making them black, and I earnestly believe it was because they were always doomed to be our inferiors. Leaving this aside, if I ever lower myself so much as to step into the ring with this man Jackson, his aspirations will be cut short.'[519]

Joe Choynski, who was in Australia, told the press that Sullivan was the king of the ring and could defeat Goddard, Jackson, Slavin, or anyone else. "I don't think the man ever put on a glove who could have a look in it with him when he's well, and you can take what I'm telling you for Gospel, and good Gospel at that."

When asked by Smiler, the well-known Australian sportswriter, whether Sullivan could land his right swing on a big shifty fellow with a good jab like Jackson, Choynski responded,

> You have never seen Sully fight, Smiler. His right arm don't do any swinging; it comes across like a flash of lightning with a jerk, and if he misses he's so quick you can't get your head out of range before it's back ready for another shot at your jaw, and how it does fly, ping, ping. I think he'll land on Jackson right enough if he meets him. ...
>
> People in this country don't understand the color line, and therefore they can't grip Sullivan's prejudice against Jackson properly, but you may rest easy that John is afraid of no man breathing. Personally, I wish he would fight Jackson, for I know how long the fight would last, and who would win it.

Choynski had seen Jackson fight, and had sparred with him, so he had a basis for his opinion. Although Choynski did not draw the color line, he understood Sullivan's position and did not believe it was due to fear.

Choynski also had an informed opinion about Joe Goddard, because he had fought him twice. In both February and July 1891, Goddard had scored 4th round knockout victories over Choynski. Both fights were brutal wars, and both Choynski and Goddard had managed to hurt and deck one another several times. Choynski complimented Goddard as a good fighter, but also said,

> I don't think he'd have a ghost of a show with Sullivan. You see, it's this way. Sullivan is quicker than I am, and he hits with terrible power. If I'd a tenth of Sullivan's force I'd have beaten Goddard both times I fought him, but I hadn't it. Now, it's easy to figure it out. I think, honestly, that John would smash him down with very little trouble.[520]

In late September, the *Referee* wrote, "I always held the opinion that Slavin was a world-whipper for certain until I saw John L. Sullivan spar."[521]

---

519 *Referee* (Sydney), September 9, 1891.
520 *Referee* (Sydney), September 23, 1891.
521 *Referee* (Sydney), September 30, 1891.

On October 2, 1891 in Melbourne, Joe Goddard won an 8-round decision over Sullivan's sparring mate Jack Ashton. Sullivan seconded Ashton.

On October 5, 1891, their two months of Australian performances having concluded, Sullivan, Ashton, and crew, as well as Joe Choynski, left Australia on the *Alameda*. On October 29, they arrived in San Francisco.[522]

Once back home, Sullivan said that although after the Kilrain fight he had made up his mind never again to enter the prize ring with bare knuckles, he was willing to fight one last time in a gloved contest, against Slavin or anyone else if the financial inducements were sufficient. He claimed to have stopped drinking. He was weighing 245 pounds. "I've come home to fight my last battle. … I'll reduce the size of this Australian's head, or rather I hope I'll swell it, and then I'll retire, for I am getting on in years." Sullivan had just turned 33 years old.

However, Sullivan was not overly eager to fight again or to start training any time soon, because as soon as he returned to the United States, he signed up for another theatrical engagement. John L. said that the engagement would end in June 1892, which he claimed would give him enough time to train and prepare for a fight with Slavin in September or October 1892. That did not sound like a great deal of preparation time for a man who had not fought since July 1889. He also said that after his next fight he never would fight again.

Regardless of his plans, there were reports that Slavin and Jackson had agreed to fight each other in London, at the National Sporting Club in May or June 1892.[523]

The *New York Clipper* wrote,

> As regards Sullivan's previously expressed determination never to fight a colored man, we are of the opinion that he has since become convinced that persistence in his unjustifiable attempt to create a color line in P.R. matters would only make him appear ridiculous, besides casting a reflection on his courage, and for that reason we are satisfied that he will readily consent to meet Jackson in case the latter bests Slavin.[524]

On November 25, 1891 in San Francisco at the Wigwam, 2,500 spectators paid $1 each to watch Sullivan spar Paddy Ryan 3 short but lively rounds at a benefit held for Ryan. Sullivan was fat, about 250 pounds, but looked relatively thin compared to the even more portly Ryan. Still, they demonstrated great spirit. "Considering his lack of condition Sullivan showed wonderful quickness and hustled around his opponent like a

---

522 *Referee* (Sydney), October 7, 1891; *Pittsburg Dispatch*, October 30, 1891.

523 *Pittsburg Dispatch*, *Seattle Post-Intelligencer*, October 30, 1891; *Referee* November 4, 18, 1891; *Clarion-Ledger*, November 19, 1891.

524 *New York Clipper*, November 28, 1891.

middleweight." Given his obesity, Sullivan astonished those present with his quick and spirited manner.

Sullivan's manager Jack Barnett said the reports about Sullivan having no intention to fight anyone were erroneous. He said Sullivan had $1,000 posted with a New York newspaper since June 1891, and that neither Slavin nor his backers had covered it.

Sullivan offered his thoughts on training and learning how to box. "The fact is I never had a trainer in my life dictate to me. If a man can't train himself no one in the world can do it for him." "No man can train a fighter unless the latter is willing."[525]

> No 'professor' or master of sparring can ever claim me as a pupil of theirs. What I know about boxing I picked up from time to time by hard experiences and intelligent observation. I belong to no school of boxers, and have copied no special master's style, and I always fight according to my own judgment. I have always considered it very necessary that a young man, in order to become an accomplished boxer, should have brains as well as muscle. I never knew a thick-headed fellow yet to become skillful in the manly art. A good boxer must be clear and cool-headed, quick to decide, with a keen perception, always able to size up his man at all stages of the game, and know exactly what he's doing, even if he's punched into a dazed condition. …
>
> The first thing a 'professor' will teach a pupil is to stand in position. He will show him how to turn his toes out, spread his feet so many inches apart, and will try and convince the young man that his style and position is really the only correct one in the world. Now I consider this is all simple rot. My advice is to stand in whatever way is best suited to your purpose – whichever way you can hit your opponent the straightest and hardest blow and avoid a return by getting away quickly. … So with boxing, the position that suits you best is certainly the proper one for you to assume. …
>
> Learn to strike straight and clean; swinging blows nearly always leave an opening for your opponent. It is always well to do your leading with the left, reserving your right for a good opening. Wherever you hit your man with one hand let the other fist land in the same spot if possible. …
>
> Always watch your opponent. … Just as soon as you see him about to lead, shoot your left into his face, and the force of his coming towards you will increase your blows considerably.[526]

[525] *San Francisco Chronicle*, *San Francisco Call*, November 26, 1891.
[526] *Referee* (Sydney), December 23, 1891.

ONE WEEK ONLY!
—THE WORLD'S CHAMPION—
JOHN L.
SULLIVAN!
AND THE EARNEST ACTOR,
DUNCAN B.
HARRISON!
In the Successful Comedy Drama,
HONEST HEARTS
...AND...
WILLING HANDS!
SEE THE GREAT GLOVE CONTEST.
JOHN L. VS. JACK
SULLLIVAN ASHTON
Matinees Wednesday and Saturday.

Starting on Monday November 30 at San Francisco's Bush-street theater, Sullivan performed in *Honest Hearts and Willing Hands* for one week.

At his performance on December 1, Sullivan obviously was "in a beastly state of intoxication." Usually, Sullivan would sober up before the performances.[527]

On December 9 in Los Angeles at the Wyatt theater, Sullivan began performances of his play there.

While in Los Angeles, Sullivan started performing in a new play that Duncan Harrison had written, called *Broderick Agra*. The following week, they performed the play in San Francisco. As usual, he sparred 3 rounds with Jack Ashton.

December 20, 1891 was the final performance of *Broderick Agra* in San Francisco. That day, in the boxing scene, instead of sparring with his usual sparring partner Jack Ashton, Sullivan boxed a 3-round exhibition with Joe Choynski, whom Corbett had stopped in 1889 in the 27th round.

Choynski was quite "willing" and made "earnest attacks." John L. showed his defensive skills and landed speedy counters. They struck at one another freely. In the 3rd round, they mixed it up in a "business-like" manner, although Sullivan seemed "inclined to be gracious." However, the pace appeared to be telling on John.

One of Sullivan's backers, Jim Wakely, said,

> I like John very much, and I believe that he could whip any man living if he would take care of himself. From what I have heard about him for the past few months, however, I am convinced that he has set his mind on going to the dogs as fast as he can. … There is not the slightest doubt in my mind but that he can whip any man on earth if he will only let alcoholic stimulants alone. … He appears to think that he can thrash anybody, and he continues to try and drink all the liquor there is in every town he visits. Sullivan could beat Slavin in two rounds if he could get into condition. If he goes on at this rate, however, I would not bet a cent on him. I have heard promises to quit drinking so often that I am tired of it.[528]

[527] *Call*, December 2, 1891.
[528] *San Francisco Examiner*, December 21, 1891.

Allegedly, at some point Sullivan had said that he could "do Corbett in a punch." Corbett later replied to the assertion,

> While I have great respect for Sullivan on account of his record, I have no hesitancy in saying that he is considered a good old has-been. The night we boxed he weighed 265 lb. He was remarkably active, however, and surprised everybody in the house.[529]

Sullivan was performing in Sacramento during the holiday week. Sometimes he performed in one play, and sometimes he performed in the other.

Word was that Sullivan and Barnett had split.

Sullivan continued with his ongoing theatrical career, touring the country. In early January he was in Seattle. Places visited included British Columbia and Manitoba. In February they were in Wichita, Kansas, Omaha, Nebraska, and St. Paul, Minnesota, amongst several other places.

On March 2, 1892 in New Orleans, in a heavyweight fight, Bob Fitzsimmons stopped Peter Maher in the 12th round.

On March 5, 1892, John L. Sullivan issued a public challenge:

> To the public in general and Frank P. Slavin, Charles Mitchell and James Corbett in particular:-
>
> On the 25th day of August, 1890, I formed a partnership with Duncan B. Harrison and entered the theatrical profession. …
>
> Ever since the existence of the contract…this country has been overrun with a lot of foreign fighters and also American aspirants for fistic fame and championship honors who have endeavored to seek notoriety and American dollars by challenging me to fight, knowing full well that my hands were tied by contract and honor. … But now my turn has come; our season ends about June 4 and we do not resume again until September 12. This gives me over three months' time to prepare.
>
> I hereby challenge any and all of the bluffers who have been trying to make capital at my expense to fight me either the last week in August, this year, or the first week in September, this year, at the Olympic Club, New Orleans, La., for a purse of $25,000 and an outside bet of $10,000, the winner of the fight to take the entire purse. I insist upon the bet of $10,000 to show that they mean business, $2,500 to be put up inside thirty days, another $2,500 by May 1, and the entire $10,000 and as much more as they will bet to be placed by June 15. … First come first served.
>
> I give precedence in this challenge to Frank P. Slavin, of Australia, as he and his backers have done the greatest amount of blowing. My

[529] *Referee,* December 23, 1891, quoting the Boston *Police News.*

second preference is the bombastic sprinter, Charles Mitchell, of England, whom I would rather whip than any man in the world. My third preference is James Corbett, of California, who has achieved his share of bombast. But in this challenge I include all fighters, first come first served - who are white. I will not fight a negro. I never have; I never shall.

I prefer this challenge should be accepted by some of the foreigners…as I would rather whip them than any of my own countrymen.

The Marquis of Queensberry rules must govern this contest, as I want fighting, and not foot racing, and I intend to keep the championship of the world where it belongs – in the land of the free and the home of the brave.[530]

The $25,000 purse which Sullivan demanded in order to fight was astronomical for the time. Previously he had endured criticism for demanding so much money, such a demand being perceived as his way of pricing himself out of the market so as to avoid having to fight. However, the New Orleans Olympic Athletic Club was willing to meet his demands.

The $10,000 winner-take-all side-bet he demanded also was huge. That meant that whoever fought him would have to garner sufficient confidence for his backers to be willing to risk that type of money on their man. John L. wanted the "bluffers" to put their money where their mouths were. A challenger and his backers had to be so confident that they were willing to come away with nothing if they lost, and to lose a whole lot of money in the process. Sullivan's winner-take-all proposition demonstrated his own tremendous confidence.

James J. Corbett immediately said that he was pleased that Sullivan had challenged him, for he wanted to fight for the championship. "He says, first come, first served. Now I'll jump right in and put up the money." Jim was upset that John had classed him with bluffers. He had not previously challenged Sullivan, "because he said he was out of the ring," and because he did not want people to think he was a bluffer like Mitchell and Slavin, who had not accepted Corbett's challenges. Jim said that he would be ready to fight whenever Sullivan wanted. "I can meet him at 190 pounds, and can, I think, train down and get into condition much quicker than he can."[531]

William A. Brady, Corbett's manager, quickly deposited $1,000 in forfeit money on behalf of Corbett. Corbett wrote Sullivan, "You challenged me and classed me among the 'bombastic members of our profession.' I now respectfully ask you to stand by your defiance. You said first come, first served. My money is up; therefore I am entitled to first chance." Sullivan

---

530 *Philadelphia Press*, *Philadelphia Inquirer*, *Brooklyn Daily Eagle*, March 6, 1892; *New York Clipper*, March 12, 1892; *Referee*, April 20, 1892; Corbett at 164-166.

531 *Philadelphia Inquirer*, March 6, 1892; *New York Clipper*, March 12, 1892; James J. Corbett, *The Roar of the Crowd* (N.Y.: G.P. Putnam's Sons, 1925), 164-165.

immediately wrote his backer to cover Corbett's forfeit, and said that the fight would take place in late August or early September.[532]

Jackson and Slavin already were matched to fight, but even if Jackson won, it would not matter to Sullivan. His public challenge specifically excluded black fighters. Once again, he had drawn the color line.

Sullivan's refusal was ironic, given that he was famous for saying, "I can lick any son of a bitch in the world." He meant only whites, just as the United States Constitution meant only whites when it asserted that "all men are created equal." In fact, it was a fundamental belief that all men were not created equal. As the *Clarion-Ledger* wrote, "The declaration in the Declaration of Independence of the United States, that all men are created equal is false, utterly false in every particular."[533]

At the end of the day, Sullivan was not willing to subvert the racial caste system. Merely providing a black man the opportunity, regardless of whether or not he could win, would be offensive to that hierarchy. However, by taking on Corbett, the man who had equaled Jackson over 61 rounds, Sullivan proved that he wasn't merely looking for an easy fight, and that fear of Jackson was not why he drew the color line.

Although there were critics of Sullivan's avoidance of Jackson, many actually praised him for it, particularly in the South, in New Orleans, where gloved Queensberry-rules fights to the finish had been legalized. One wrote, "I think that the fact that he has faithfully kept his word by not fighting a colored man makes him deserving of much admiration."[534]

In 1892, there were a U.S. national record 161 black lynchings (since record-keeping began in 1882).[535]

On March 15, 1892, formal articles of agreement for a fight between Corbett and Sullivan were signed by their representatives, for a fight at the New Orleans Olympic Club to be held on September 7, in a Queensberry rules fight to the finish, for a $25,000 purse and a $20,000 side bet ($10,000 per side). Despite his reservations about John L.'s drinking, once again James Wakely backed Sullivan.

Allegedly, Sullivan said,

> Corbett is a great big stiff. If I fight him it will be just like walking out and picking up that $30,000. When I sparred for his benefit in San Francisco he came into my room and begged me not to hit him hard. Then when we got into the ring he ran away from me. It is not Corbett, however, who is doing all this talking. It's his backers. If I

---

532 *Brooklyn Daily Eagle*, March 9, 1892.

533 *Clarion-Ledger*, January 9, 1890.

534 *Daily Picayune*, September 4, 1892.

535 Robert L. Zangrando, *About Lynching*, excerpt from article in *The Reader's Companion to American History*, Editors Eric Foner and John A. Garraty. Houghton Mifflin Co., 1991.

> ever get him between the ropes, I will slam it into him so hard the ring will not be big enough to hold him.[536]

Bob Fitzsimmons said that fit and well, Sullivan ought to defeat Corbett. However, it was not clear whether Sullivan would get into proper shape.

> It seems to me, from what I have heard of Sullivan, that he will not do his work like a man who is going to meet a good and clever boxer. It may be that Sullivan will underestimate Corbett. If he does that, and will not train, he will be beaten, for Corbett is a remarkably clever man, and can hit a hard blow. Sullivan has no 'cinch' with him at any stage of the game.

Even Jimmy Carroll said that at 3 to 1 odds, he would bet on the underdog Corbett. Although Sullivan was a wonder, Corbett was fast, shifty, and had underrated power.[537]

Corbett told the press his feelings regarding the match.

> I think that I can defeat him; I always thought that I could. Ever since we boxed a friendly bout together in San Francisco I have had my mind made up that I could whip him. I think he will prove an easier man for me than either Slavin or Jackson would. I don't wish to appear boastful. I want the title of champion, but don't think that I will gain anything by whipping Sullivan. The majority will say it was not Sullivan but the wreck of the champion that I met.[538]

In the meantime, Sullivan's theatrical company continued touring, in places like Philadelphia and Brooklyn, not closing until June 4, 1892 in Boston.[539]

---

[536] *Evening World*, March 15, 1892.
[537] *New York Sun*, March 23, 1892.
[538] *New York Sun*, March 15, 1892.
[539] Sullivan at 176.

One Last Defense

By being the first to jump in and accept John L. Sullivan's offer, James J. Corbett had secured the championship match. His backers were confident enough in Jim such that they were willing to put up and risk big money on him. The fight was for a massive purse of $25,000 and a side bet of $10,000 each, the winner to take all of the money. It was "the largest sum ever fought for in the history of pugilism."[540]

Men like Mitchell and Slavin had "failed to show the color of their money." Slavin said that he already was matched to fight Jackson. However, there had been indications even back in January that he could not obtain sufficient financial backing for a Sullivan match. Despite all of the previous talk, the reality was that Slavin's backers were confident enough to risk their money on Frank against anyone *but* Sullivan.

Not willing to post the large side-bet or to agree to a winner-take-all fight, Charlie Mitchell had attempted to negotiate. Sullivan had insisted "that Mitchell prove the sincerity of his professed belief that he can master him by backing up his braggadocio with a stake the loss of which would break his heart." Mitchell had twice failed to defeat Sullivan, so he was not about to agree to such terms. Only Corbett had "acted in a business like, straightforward manner," immediately posting a deposit.[541]

Corbett and his backers were smart and confident enough to take the risk. They knew that Corbett could earn huge money if he won, plus he could earn good money in exhibitions leading up to the fight, given that the public would be curious to see the man matched to fight for the championship. The calculated risk was worth it.

Immediately after the Sullivan-Corbett match was made, analysis and perspectives proliferated, for it became the all-absorbing topic. The *New York Clipper* said, "Sullivan will, of course, be the general favorite, but the Californian has impressed many shrewd judges very favorably." Mike Donovan thought it was a smart move on Corbett's part, given Sullivan's deterioration. He said that he told Corbett that Sullivan "is so slow he can't get out of his own way. His stomach muscles are all gone, and he is flabby. You can lick him in a punch." Regardless, according to Corbett, Sullivan was so popular with the masses that many Irish-American citizens hated Irish-American Corbett merely because he had the "insolence" to fight their hero. They were Sullivan fans and believers to the end.[542]

One of Sullivan's financial backers, Charley Johnston, said,

---

[540] *New York Sun,* April 4, 1892.

[541] *New York Sun,* January 5, 1892; *New York Clipper,* January 9, March 19, 1892.

[542] *New York Clipper,* March 19, 1892; Donovan at 164; Corbett at 171.

> Sullivan is perfectly confident. … He is not drinking at all now, and weighs about 250 pounds, and will take off at least thirty or forty pounds by six weeks of hard work. … I still believe John L. Sullivan to be the hardest puncher in the game. Corbett is young and ambitious, but it will take all of his vitality to withstand a few of the blows that I am sure Sullivan will land, and yet I regard Corbett as the best man of the lot, as Slavin would be an easier mark than the Californian.[543]

The general feeling was that Sullivan would win if he was in proper shape. Mose Gunst said,

> Everybody that I talked with is of the opinion that Sullivan will win. … Jim cannot punch hard enough or long enough to put him out. Corbett has a chance, but a poor one, of making a draw as he did when he met Peter Jackson. As all know, he is very clever and shifty on his feet and may manage to keep away from John, but the big fellow is apt to land on him, and if he does the battle will end in short order.[544]

FOR THE HEAVY-WEIGHT CHAMPIONSHIP OF THE WORLD.
John Lawrence Sullivan, the Champion, and James J. Corbett, the Adonis of the Fistic Arena, Who Are to Battle September 7th Next For a Purse and Stakes of $45,000 and the Big Fellow's Title.

Reproduced from the original held by the Department of Special Collections of the Hesburgh Libraries of the University of Notre Dame.

Corbett had been giving boxing exhibitions, and he continued doing so across the country, earning plenty of money. Everyone wanted to see the man who had equaled Jackson and now was matched to fight Sullivan.

---

543 *New York Sun,* April 4, 1892.

544 *San Francisco Chronicle,* April 4, 1892.

Spectators who saw Corbett box Jim Daly 3 rounds in Providence, Rhode Island on April 4, 1892 were impressed with Corbett's pretty display of skillful scientific boxing. Corbett demonstrated "remarkable speed in leading, countering, guarding, ducking and getting out of his adversary's reach on leads and rushes. Corbett's lightning like movements astonished the spectators."[545]

On April 8, 1892 in Buffalo, the "California Wonder" Corbett sparred 3 rounds with Daly that left a favorable impression.

> In action he is quick on his feet, very shifty, and one of the most scientific and cleverest boxers that ever stepped into the ring. ... Corbett demonstrated his ability to guard admirably, duck cleverly, get away in good style, and do quick and active execution with his "dukes." He strides round the ring like a giant.

Another local paper noted Corbett's strengths, but still felt that he could not defeat John L.:

> Nobody can question his cleverness. He displayed science last night seldom seen in a ring. He is shifty, quick as a cat, jumps like a lightweight, ducks cleverly, but would never impress an audience as a man likely to defeat Sullivan.

Afterwards, a humble Corbett gave a speech and said, "The man I am going up against is the best that has ever lived. I don't know as I will win, but I will be in the ring September 7, and if I am defeated will go the way of many other good men."[546]

On April 9 in New York, Corbett sparred 3 "lively" rounds with Professor Mike Donovan at his benefit. "Their cleverness called out round after round of applause, and was the windup of the finest boxing benefit entertainment ever given in this city."[547]

A lot of the pre-fight analysis of the upcoming title bout focused on Sullivan's weight and his ability to get into proper condition. Since his July 8, 1889 title defense against Jake Kilrain, the semi-retired Sullivan had been inactive for three years, not engaging in any serious bouts, boxing only in short exhibitions with men like Mike Cleary, Joe Lannon, and Jack Ashton. These exhibitions usually were part of plays and therefore very friendly, often with short rounds. His profession had been acting. During much of that time, Sullivan's excessive drinking and eating had caused his weight to balloon up to well over 250 pounds. As of April 11, Sullivan was said to be weighing a quite large 242 pounds.

In assessing the match-up, Joe Choynski said, "Corbett is a great fighter, and he has improved and grown larger since I fought him. If Sullivan is in shape he will win." However, Sullivan's former trainer, William Muldoon,

---

545 *Providence Journal,* April 5, 1892.

546 *Buffalo Courier, Buffalo Evening News,* April 9, 1892.

547 *New York Herald,* April 10, 1892; *New York Clipper,* April 10, 16, 1892.

"says that he doubts Sullivan's ability to get into the pink of condition, and he must do so to whip Corbett, as the latter is a far better man than Kilrain." Parson Davies said,

> I believe the Californian will worry the big fellow a good deal. … Corbett will set a merry pace for John and it will be a long fight. It may result in a draw. If Sullivan goes into the ring in any sort of condition he ought to win, but it's a dollar to a dime that he won't be in shape. Corbett is a strong, active fellow, as clever as any man who ever donned the gloves, and if his heart is right, there will be some fun in the arena.[548]

Corbett's manager William Brady said that Sullivan was overconfident as a result of his long string of victories.

In April, Corbett said of the fight and his chances,

> I have sparred with Sullivan. I know him and respect his ability as a fighter; but I think my chances are good. The Eastern papers say I am too small. I shall weigh 190 pounds, stripped, when I step into the ring. Mitchell, McCaffrey and Jack Burke were middle weights and they gave Sullivan the hardest fights he ever had. When Sullivan was 23 years old and weighed 188 pounds he knocked out Paddy Ryan in eight rounds. Was he too small? … I am quicker, cleverer and have a larger reach than John L. He may be able to strike a harder blow but I have faith in my ability to avoid his knock-out punches.

Jim said that he would go into serious training in early June under the tutelage of Bill Delaney, who had trained him for the Jackson and Choynski fights. He said that he would train up in weight rather than down.[549]

On April 13, 1892, spectators in Rochester, New York watched Corbett and Daly spar. "Many passes, leads, counters, dodges, upper and under cuts and body blows were illustrated in a clever manner." That said, the general impression was that Corbett was "entirely outclassed by the great John" and "he has undertaken a contract that he cannot carry out."[550]

Bob Fitzsimmons said that a Corbett victory was not out of the question. Sullivan admitted that he had weighed 276 pounds upon his return from Australia, and was 245 as of April. Sully also admitted that he still drank "at least five bottles of ale a day," claiming, "That much won't hurt me." Sullivan reasoned that he had defeated Kilrain after getting out of a sick bed. Despite three years of relative inactivity and a great deal of hard drinking, Sullivan seemed overconfident. "Of course I will win easily. … I look on that purse…as very easy money."[551]

---

548 *San Francisco Chronicle,* April 11, 1892.

549 *Rochester Democrat and Chronicle,* April 13, 1892.

550 *Rochester Union and Advertiser,* April 9, 14, 1892.

551 *Chicago Daily News,* April 18, 1892.

During April, the confident Sullivan claimed that he had stopped drinking and would begin serious training about June 30. That would leave him only two months to overcome three years of less than serious work. "I will not work as hard or walk as much as I did for Kilrain. Rope-skipping, football playing, tossing a ten-pound ball, and fighting the bag will cover my work. Of course I'll win, and easily." He still was touring with his play.[552]

On April 23, 1892 in Chicago, at 190 pounds, Corbett looked solid and "hard as nails," not carrying any superfluous flesh. In his sparring with Daly, he demonstrated his shiftiness and cleverness with hands, head, and feet. "It occurred to seasoned judges who had not previously been so impressed that he can keep Sullivan guessing and that it will bother the big fellow a whole lot to hit him." Jim was scheduled to commence serious training on June 10.[553]

Sullivan arrived in Chicago on April 24, 1892, still touring with his play. He said, "I am going up against a hot game…and so, for that matter, is Corbett. Of course, I expect to win." Sullivan said that he was weighing 248 pounds, and claimed to have not touched a drop of liquor in three months, contradicting reports that he was still drinking.[554]

Many believed the fight would be lengthy, owing to Corbett's style.

> Corbett's supporters, and he has a good number of them, rely upon their old belief that if Jim can't lick the man in front of him the man will never be able to lick Jim. This argument is based upon Corbett's cleverness on his feet. … Corbett's supporters build to a great extent on the supposition that Sullivan can never be got into condition.[555]

In early May, Sullivan and Duncan Harrison had a falling out. Nevertheless, the tour of the two plays continued.

Apparently Sullivan was working his way into some sort of shape. He appeared in Philadelphia in early May 1892, performing in *Honest Hearts and Willing Hands*. It was said that a month ago he was weighing 257 pounds, but had dropped down to 240.[556]

Sullivan said he planned to train for the upcoming fight in New York. Although he was big, he was carrying the weight well.

A report of the May 16 performance of the play in Brooklyn said,

> [John was] quick and active throughout, and, of course, hit Ashton almost when and where he pleased. And he landed some very hard blows, too. The general opinion of the audience seemed to be that Sullivan would defeat Corbett easily and showed the champion to be the same old favorite.[557]

---

552 *Chicago Tribune*, April 19, 1892.

553 *Chicago Times*, *Chicago Tribune*, April 24, 1892; *Chicago Herald*, April 20, 23, 1892.

554 *Chicago Herald*, April 25, 1892.

555 *Referee*, April 27, 1892, from a San Francisco report.

556 *Philadelphia Inquirer*, May 8, 1892.

557 *New York Herald*, May 17, 1892; *New York Sun*, May 16, 1892.

On May 16, 1892 at Coney Island, New York, George Godfrey stopped Joe Lannon, who retired after the 4th round.

Many felt that Corbett had no chance with Sullivan, even Corbett's hometown San Francisco newspapers. The *Chronicle* said, "Though Corbett may use up every inch of the twenty-four foot ring in keeping away from Sullivan until the latter becomes tired, it is doubtful if there are enough inches for him to skip about in." Its writer also opined that Jim did not have enough force in his punches to do Sullivan any harm.[558]

At that time, Sullivan was working on his autobiography, set to be released that year, before the Corbett fight.[559]

On May 30, 1892 in London, England, at the National Sporting Club, Peter Jackson fought Frank Slavin for the heavyweight championship of England and Australia. Some, like the *Referee* in Australia, billed the bout as being for the world's championship.[560] The *National Police Gazette* previously had named Slavin as its champion back in 1890, when Sullivan had failed to accept his challenges.

Slavin was so well thought of such that he "was looked upon as a sure winner" against Jackson. Slavin's excellent performances against Bill Farnan, Jack Burke, Jem Smith, Joe McAuliffe, and Jake Kilrain made him the 2 to 1 betting favorite. He had demonstrated solid conditioning and very good power. However, one expert said,

> With the exception of Sullivan, I regard Jackson as the greatest fighter in the world. The big fellow [Sullivan], however, is the best man of them all. ... Jackson...is too clever a man for Slavin, and will not let him reach him. ... Jackson is not a rusher or quick fighter. He is like Jack Dempsey, and finishes his men slowly.[561]

A year earlier, a San Francisco reporter gave a similar assessment, saying,

> The general opinion is that Slavin would find it exceedingly difficult to land on Jackson, and that the colored man would cut him to ribbons, as he is not, like Corbett, a fighter who avoids punishment.
>
> Slavin is a one-blow puncher...and mind what I tell you, as soon as he comes in front of a man who can guard his body the Australian will not be in it. Slavin's punch is a heavy right-hand drive on the ribs. He depends on landing that blow in order to win. Either Jackson or Corbett could avoid the delivery, and either of the two would give him a very lively mill.[562]

The Jackson-Slavin bout was scheduled for 20 rounds with 4-ounce gloves in a 20-square-foot ring, for a purse to be divided 1,750 pounds to

---

558 *San Francisco Chronicle,* May 20, 1892.
559 *New York Sun*, May 27, 1892.
560 *Referee,* July 13, 1892.
561 *Referee,* April 20, 1892.
562 *San Francisco Evening Post,* June 27, 1891.

the winner and 250 pounds to the loser (approximately $8,750/$1,250). Jackson weighed 192 - 196 pounds to Slavin's 185 - 188 pounds. One of Jackson's seconds was Joe Choynski, his sparring partner.

In the 1st round, Jackson kept his long left constantly in Slavin's face, although not with much force.

In the 2nd round, Slavin attacked viciously, but Jackson kept him off with his left and was able to neutralize him on the inside. Peter fired his left and right in succession to Slavin's body.

In the 3rd round, Frank's eye began closing.

In the 4th and 5th rounds, Slavin kept boring in, but could not land his right on Jackson. The pace was very fast, but Jackson usually had the best of the exchanges.

In the 6th round, Slavin cornered Peter and landed two strong punches to the ribs, but Jackson got out of the corner and landed a left.

As of the 7th round, Slavin's eye was nearly closed from the repeated lefts.

In the 8th and 9th rounds, Jackson continued pounding on him with both hands, even though Slavin kept firing away and trying hard, occasionally landing a good punch.

In the 10th round, a right to the throat sent Slavin to the ropes. Jackson attacked with both hands, dazing him. Peter fought Slavin "all around the ring and succeeded in knocking him out in the first two minutes of the round." Jackson had displayed "wonderful science," though Slavin's "sudden collapse in the tenth round was an utter surprise to the majority of the spectators, who had thought that Jackson could win only by points."

> [Slavin], as he lay helpless and disfigured on the floor of the stage, appeared to be almost dead. … He lay motionless on the hard boards, with his eyes tightly closed, his face badly swollen and discolored, and his body covered with the blood which flowed from the cuts caused by the sledge-hammer blows dealt by Jackson.[563]

Jackson's performance against Slavin served to boost Jim Corbett's stock. More gamblers were considering a wager on the underdog Corbett.

Upon hearing of the result, John L. Sullivan allegedly said, "Any white man who fights with a nigger ought to be whipped." However, Sullivan admitted that he had wanted Slavin to win, for business reasons. "I have known all along that Slavin would be dead easy picking for me and so have all the genuine sporting men in this country. For that reason Slavin could not get any backing to go against me."[564]

On June 1 in Cambridge, Dr. Sargent weighed Sullivan at 235 pounds.[565]

---

[563] *New York Times*, May 31, 1892; Harold Furniss, editor, *Famous Fights, Police Budget Edition*, Volume 7, No. 91 (London: Frank Shaw, publisher, 1901-1904), 194-200.

[564] *Evening World*, May 31, 1892.

[565] *New York Sun*, June 3, 1892.

On June 6 in New York, Dr. Gibbs examined Corbett and said that he stood 6'1 ½" and weighed 195 pounds. His trainer Bill Delaney said that they would leave New York on the 13th to set up formal training quarters in Asbury Park, New Jersey.

For his training, Delaney said that Corbett would take an 8-mile morning walk. In the afternoon he would walk about 15 miles, and also do some running. He would punch the bag, skip rope, and play handball. Later, he would engage in wrestling and neck pulling. He also would box with Jim Daly. "I predict that Jim will be as perfect a conditioned man as ever stepped into a ring. He must be, for he is going to meet the best man that the world so far has produced."[566]

Jim Corbett had proven his condition and ability to avoid being hurt in the Jackson bout. If he could last 4 hours with Peter Jackson, then he had a good chance to do so with a less than active and aging Sullivan. Some felt that he would fight for a draw. Corbett had the style to frustrate an aggressive fighter like Sullivan if John wasn't sharp. A Corbett supporter said,

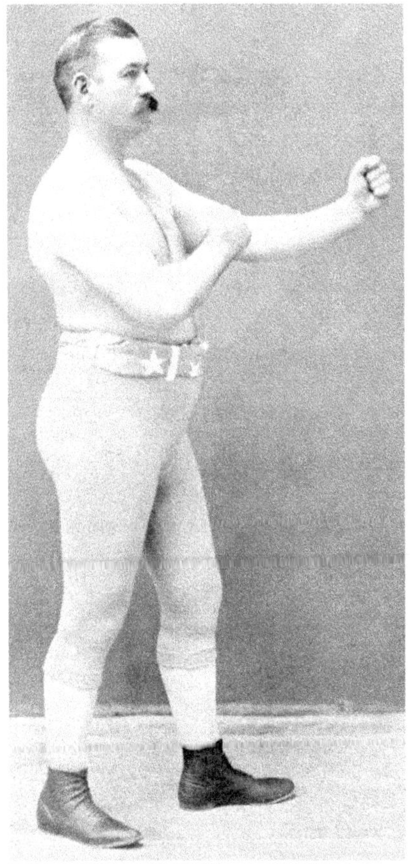

> A clever man like Corbett, with a good left hand will find Sullivan's frontispiece a very open mark if he rushes from the word go, as has been his habit in all his glove fighting. … Take a quick pair of legs playing shy of that right of John L., keeping him fighting wind and jabbing into his mug with a well-aimed left-hand as he charges forward, and it will be a new experience to him.[567]

Sullivan's theatrical season ended in early June. However, he did not go into serious training until late June/early July, which would leave him only two months to prepare.

On June 22, Sullivan arrived in New York from Boston. He admitted to having had a few glasses of wine in Boston, but insisted that he was not drunk. Yet, immediately above his left eye was a deep cut, and on his nose was a bruise. Sullivan claimed the injuries were the result of

566 *New York Clipper*, June 11, 1892; *New York Sun*, June 7, 9, 1892.
567 *Referee*, July 13, 1892, quoting a *Boston Police News* report.

falling out of bed the previous morning at his sister's house.[568]

Sullivan left for his training quarters, which were near the old Indian settlement among the Shinnecock Hills of Long Island. He stayed at the Canoe Place Inn.[569]

By late July, Sullivan was weighing 221 pounds.

Some said that although Sullivan was the greatest fighter of his day, his time had passed, he would meet his master in science, and even if he could be gotten into shape, he would not be able to hit Corbett.

Trainer Phil Casey said Sullivan had not done any boxing in training. The only boxing he did was hitting the swinging ball. Everything else was general conditioning work.

In his autobiography, Sullivan described his training. He went for a long 12- to 14-mile walk, running the last mile. He swam for 10 minutes. Over the course of 1.5 to 2 hours, he hit the football, threw a 10-pound ball at a distance of 15 or 20 feet away from his trainers, shadow-boxed with dumbbells that weighed 2 or 4 pounds, and jumped rope. He also played handball and punched the striking bag. He avoided smoking and drinking, except a bit of ale during dinner. He also drank no coffee during training.

Sparring was limited. "I do not box or spar much while in training; that I do not consider necessary. I consider punching the bag from twenty to thirty minutes as fast as I can possibly do it, the very best exercise for improving or exercising my hitting powers." He liked to punch the bag, which was attached to a rope, in all directions so he would have to chase it, the same as he would an opponent. He was training for two months, feeling that more than that would leave him overworked and stale.[570]

In other news, on August 4, 1892, Abby and Andrew Borden were murdered at their home in Fall River, Massachusetts. They were hacked to death either with a hatchet or an axe. The prime suspect was their daughter Lizzie Borden, whose trial would become sensational news.

As of August 13, Dr. Sargent said that Sullivan was weighing 216 pounds. His waist had reduced from 42 inches in early June to 38 inches.

In early August, John McVey, the heavyweight wrestler, was added to Corbett's training camp.

On August 19 at Asbury Park, New Jersey, Corbett "wrestled, pushed, pulled, clinched, and broke away from big McVey for a half hour, and then went in for the punching bag." Jim also did some running sprints. Daly said that Corbett was in perfect shape.[571]

On August 20 in Newark, New Jersey, Corbett engaged in Greco-Roman wrestling with McVey (or McVeigh), who weighed 235 pounds to Corbett's 188 pounds. Despite the size disparity, Corbett displayed his

---

568 *Sun*, June 23, 1892.

569 *Evening World*, July 1, 1892; *Sun*, July 4, 1892.

570 *Brooklyn Daily Eagle*, July 20, 1892; *New York Clipper*, July 23, 1892; *Sun*, August 1, 1892; Sullivan at 193-199.

571 *New York Clipper*, July 30, 1892, August 13, 20, 1892; *New York Sun*, August 20, 1892.

strength, "literally dragging the burly McVeigh all over the stage. In spite of his great exertion, Corbett was not even winded" at the end of six minutes. Corbett also boxed Jim Daly for 3 rounds, putting on a "rattling good bout." Corbett fired in straight lefts and rights, as well as uppercuts, with "dash and brilliancy," and did some "phenomenal ducking from Daly's right-hand swings." The bout was "as pretty a one as ever was seen, and fairly electrified the vast audience." The next day, Corbett said that he was weighing 191 pounds and would not enter the ring against Sullivan weighing less than 188 pounds.[572]

Jake Kilrain, who had fought both, picked Sullivan. Kilrain said that Corbett did not like infighting and winced from his body blows. Kilrain conceded that Corbett was a clever boxer with a good reach, but felt that he lacked power.

> Corbett's hands are liable to go back on him. He hits with his hand open. In sparring with Corbett I found there was no steam to his blows. He would touch me and get away, but, while it looked pretty, there was no damage done.

Kilrain felt that Sullivan knew just as much about the game as Corbett.

> Now, as to Sullivan. In the first place he is a heavy, powerful man, very light on his feet. He is a good two handed fighter with an extra good right. Sullivan's weight and strength give him good advantage. If a man meets him he will drive him back, and by the time he is settled Sullivan is on top of him and pounds him down. That was the way he wore me down in our fight. … Do I think Sullivan is game and will stand punishment? I believe he is as game as a pebble. I know I hit him some punches that would have knocked out a dozen ordinary men, and he didn't mind them at all. … In any sort of fair condition I expect to see Sullivan win easy.[573]

However, there were those who picked Corbett, especially the ones who saw him against Jackson, or who recalled how Sullivan had difficulties stopping scientific men smaller than Jim.[574]

Some reported that as of late August 1892, Sullivan was weighing 206 or 210 pounds. They wondered whether losing so much weight in such a short period of time might have an adverse effect.

On August 29 at New York's Madison Square Garden, Corbett gave three separate training exhibitions throughout the day. He "exhibited remarkable skill and agility, and his feats of strength and endurance aroused the enthusiasm of the large crowd present." At around noon, Jim worked with pulleys, played hand-ball, and punched the bag, which was a leather fighting ball that hung from the ceiling. Spectators were impressed. "Why, they said

---

[572] *New York Sun*, *San Francisco Chronicle*, August 21, 22, 1892.
[573] *San Francisco Examiner*, August 15, 1892; *Brooklyn Daily Eagle*, August 23, 1892.
[574] *Daily Picayune*, August 31, 1892.

this young fellow couldn't hit hard. If he ever hits Sullivan that hard he'll settle him."

After lunch, at around 2 p.m., Corbett worked the pulleys for 20 minutes, threw the 8-pound medicine ball with Delaney and Daly, and then wrestled with 220-pound McVey, engaging in "pushing, hauling and neck-squeezing." "Corbett exhibited great strength and soon had McVey puffing and blowing hard, while this violent work did not even start the perspiration on Corbett – proof positive of his condition." Jim then played hand-ball with John Lawler. Following that, he punched the bag for 20 minutes, "in a manner that drew out frequent bursts of applause. He astounded the spectators, not only by the rapidity of his blows, but also by their force. His right-handers were terrific." Another said, "His wonderful agility and his hard, clean hits elicited great applause." Corbett then ran around a track for 10 minutes.

That evening, spectators watched Corbett spar 3 rounds with McVey and 3 rounds with Daly. The audience was excited by the clever manner in which Corbett ducked and got away. When Jim sparred Daly, he had the latter's nose bleeding, and Daly was very tired at the end of the 3rd round. "The audience shouted words of encouragement and hailed him as the coming champion of the world." Jim went through his long list of exercises that day "without being the slightest bit winded, and never did a man put in a harder day's work."[575]

Another report of the exhibition that evening said,

---

[575] *National Police Gazette*, September 17, 1891; *New York Clipper*, September 3, 1892; *Newark Evening News*, *New York Sun*, August 30, 1892.

> The swings and straight leads that Daly makes showed the Sullivan men, who were there in great force, how quick Corbett could duck or jump out of harms' way if necessary. Several men were outspoken in their opinion as they left the garden that the champion would have to fight the battle of his life on September 7 to defeat Corbett.[576]

Corbett said he intended to enter the ring at his present weight, which was 187 pounds.

When Sullivan arrived in New York that same day, the crowd was huge. Sullivan's backer said, "The President of the United States would not attract that much attention from the general public."

In Brooklyn, Sullivan and Jack Ashton sparred 3 short rounds, none of which lasted more than a minute. Although they were lively and Sullivan "hit left and right with great force," as well as demonstrated "a good deal of his oldtime speed," at the end of the 3rd, "the big fellow was breathing a little more rapidly than was desirable." And this was only after three total minutes of boxing.

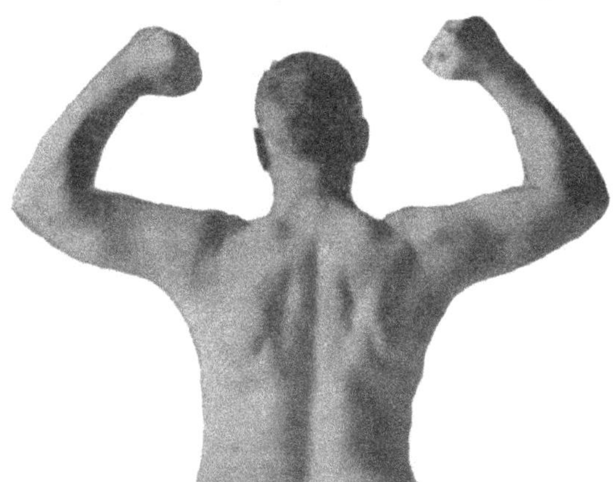

Another report said the "big fellow was undeniably fat and his stomach protruded." Sullivan claimed to weigh 204 pounds, but he didn't look it. A spectator commented, "I'll bet it's nearer 240 than 204." Another observer confirmed that John L. had rolls of superabundant flesh, and noted that the crowd "had their doubts as to his ability to stand a long fight. He looked too fat to retain his wind during a siege of violent exercise." This was about a week before the fight.[577]

On or about August 29, Sullivan's autobiography, *The Life and Reminiscences of a 19th Century Gladiator*, was published. In that book, speaking of his upcoming fight with Corbett, Sullivan said,

> Ever since I was matched against Jim Corbett various alleged authorities throughout the country have been predicting my fistic downfall on the ground that I could never get well enough to fight again with the old-time vim which has marked all of my struggles in the ring.[578]

---

576 *Birmingham Age-Herald*, September 1, 1892.

577 *Newark Evening News*, August 30, 1892; *New York Sun*, August 28, 30, 1892; *Birmingham Age-Herald*, September 1, 1892; *New York Clipper*, September 3, 1892; *Times-Democrat*, September 3, 1892, from an Asbury Park dispatch.

578 John L. Sullivan, *I can lick any sonofabitch in the house!* (Carson City: Proteus Publishing Co.,

Naturally, he disagreed.

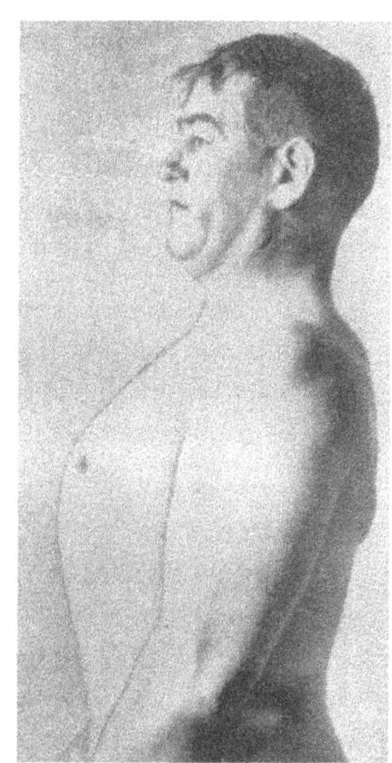

Corbett's manager William Brady said that after seeing Sullivan, he was more confident than ever, feeling that John looked fat and was breathing heavily and irregularly. He said that Jim was in excellent shape at 190 pounds, was as hard as a rock, and could undergo vigorous exercise without being winded at all. Although he admitted that Jim was not the puncher that Sullivan was, he could hit hard enough to jar a man, quickly recover his defense, and could take advantage of an opponent in a dazed condition. "Corbett is one of the shrewdest generals who ever stepped into the ring, and has the rare knack of sizing up an opponent's tactics in a few seconds."

Sullivan's former theatrical manager, Duncan Harrison, predicted that Corbett would win. He denounced Sullivan as a drunkard. He said that he had witnessed Corbett make a "monkey" out of Kilrain, and felt that Jim was shiftier and more scientific than Sullivan. He also noted that Jim "has not had to train down and tear his system to pieces by the severity of training to the extent that Sullivan has." Corbett, already in good shape, easily was able to improve his condition.

> Sullivan, on the other hand, has dissipated to a fearful extent. I do not know of anyone who has gone to the awful extremes that he has indulged in. Why, from my own experience, covering two years and three months, I tell the truth when I state that he scarcely ever drew a sober breath. I have frequently seen him drunk for five and six weeks at a time. … On the conclusion of our season, on the 4th day o' last June, he weighed 261 pounds. It is stated that he now weighs 208 pounds, a difference of fifty three pounds. Of course that amount of reduction can't help but weaken any man. … He has been on two big sprees since he commenced training, one of them lasting a week.
>
> It is claimed Corbett cannot stand Sullivan's rushes. Mark my word, if Sullivan rushes Corbett to any extent Mr. Corbett will have him at his mercy and jab him at will. It is also stated that Corbett cannot punish. I know to the contrary. No man has improved more in this respect than Corbett and, again mark my words, he will surprise you all by his execution in this respect.[579]

1979) 201, a reprint of the 1892 Sullivan autobiography *Life and Reminiscences of a Nineteenth Century Gladiator.*

[579] *Times-Democrat,* September 1, 4, 1892.

Another expert agreed that he liked Corbett's appearance better than Sullivan's. "It appears to me like pitting a good three–year old against a handicapper that has had his day. All good men, as well as good horses, meet their Waterloo, and I think Sullivan's time has come."[580]

There were those who said that Sullivan was looking to be in fine form and his strength enormous. However, many felt that it was an illusion and that Sully was a mere shell of himself. One gambler said,

> His feet are still troubling him, and his fat condition…will make a long and winning fight impossible for him. I believe that, although he looks outwardly as strong as an ox, his powers of endurance have been undermined by his excesses of recent years.[581]

Sullivan's lengthy 15- to 20-mile daily walks to lose weight had left his feet badly blistered.

115-pound bantamweight Dan Egan, known as the "Montana Kid," said that Corbett would win because he was "the cleverest big man with the gloves in the world." He had boxed Corbett at the California Athletic Club about six years ago. "Corbett broke that nose and I had to have the bone taken out. He can hit hard."

Even Sullivan's own trainer, Phil Casey, admitted, "Sullivan had not done a hard day's work before in nearly three years." Still, he said that John had worked hard in training, with steadfast purpose.

Peter Jackson believed that Corbett would keep Sullivan busy for a long time, and had a "splendid chance" of winning.[582]

Regardless, those picking Corbett were in the minority. Despite his relative inactivity for years, weight gain, and drinking, most experts and gamblers still actually backed Sullivan to defeat Corbett. It was a reflection of how phenomenal Sullivan's reputation had been over the past decade. After all, no one had been able to defeat him. He had overcome drinking and dissipation and even disease in 1889 when he defeated Kilrain, proving wrong all those who then predicted that he could not win. They had learned their lesson, and would not bet against him again. His legendary status made him a 3-1 favorite against Corbett.[583]

Joe Lannon, who had boxed in exhibitions with both, said that Sullivan hit him harder in practice than Corbett did when Jim *tried* to knock him out. He also said that Sullivan was as clever as Jim was. Furthermore, when Corbett was hit hard, "he forgets himself and goes all to pieces. I have been with him, and I know what I speak of."[584]

---

580 *San Francisco Examiner,* September 3, 1892.

581 *Times-Democrat,* September 2, 1892.

582 *Times-Democrat,* September 4, 1892; *Newark Evening News, New York Herald,* September 3, 1892; *San Francisco Chronicle,* September 5, 1892.

583 Corbett at 186.

584 *San Francisco Chronicle, Times-Democrat,* September 5, 1892.

One writer said that Corbett was "one of the most scientific boxers in the business, and is as shifty as they are made and very quick on his feet." However, "it must be borne in mind that John L. knows something of the art himself, and is one of the quickest big men in the ring on his feet."[585]

In assessing the two, one expert who on September 1 had observed both in training said,

> [Corbett] is easier, quicker, and more graceful, landing his volleys of blows with more accuracy of hand and eye. He shows less fatigue than Sullivan after a half hour's bout with the leather, his breathing being noticeably lighter. When Sullivan attacks the bag he uses great swinging blows, with an occasional quick, terrific upper cut that makes a spectator shiver. It takes a glace only to convince one that he is stronger than Corbett. The thunder of the leather as it batters the boards above is eloquent evidence that the champion's right arm has not its peer in the world. There is a marked difference between the force of Sullivan's right and that of his left, due probably to the fact that his left arm was once badly broken. Corbett's arms are equally powerful, and he depends on his left, with its superior reach, to stop Sullivan rushes. His success or failure in this will go far to determine his success or failure to win the battle.[586]

Another assessment said,

> There is naturally a great deal of discussion as to whether Corbett's youth will stand off Sullivan's great rushes and terrific blows. Sullivan's supporters think the fight will be a short one, and the followers of Corbett say that it will be a long one, as Corbett will not stay and mix it up with the champion during the early rounds, but will rather try to tire the big fellow and then defeat him at his leisure, all of which is beautiful in theory but extremely difficult in practice.
>
> Bat Masterson…is a Corbett man. … Bat said, among other things: "Sullivan is growing older, and Corbett is hardly in his prime, but you must admit that he is a great young one. I've bet $250 on Jim … I think it will be a long, weary fight. If Sullivan thinks Corbett will stand and let him rush he will be greatly mistaken, because I happen to know that he won't."[587]

Five days before the fight, on September 2 in Asbury Park, Corbett's training once again was vigorous. In the morning, Jim hit the punching bag. In the afternoon, he spent 25 minutes on the pulley weights. He then won three games of handball. Subsequently, he wrestled 40 minutes with Daly and McVey, and then sparred McVey for over 30 minutes, until John finally gave in. McVey "was ringing wet with perspiration, while Corbett felt and

[585] Sullivan at 208.
[586] *Times-Democrat,* September 4, 1892.
[587] *New York Sun,* September 5, 1892.

looked as cool as an icicle." Despite his excellent condition and appearance, the bettors still mostly backed Sullivan, placing wagers on him at 100 to 70 and 100 to 60 odds.[588]

Corbett took a train heading to New Orleans, the fight site. On the morning of September 4, just three days before the championship bout, Corbett was in Greensboro, North Carolina. After departing from there, in the baggage car, Jim threw the medicine ball with Jim Daly and Dennis Dillon. Later that morning, Corbett and Joe Choynski exercised together for more than twenty minutes. "Choynski congratulated Corbett on his appearance, and gave the opinion that Sullivan would have a hard fight."

The train also stopped that day in Charlotte, North Carolina. Jim jogged a mile and a half. He punched the bag for 30 to 40 minutes, and finished the day by sparring Daly for 40 minutes and then wrestling with him for another 20 minutes. Daly was unable to hit him, and Corbett's feints kept him guessing. Corbett "finished fresh, and every one pronounced his condition superb." "Corbett showed no symptoms of fatigue. He certainly possesses remarkable lungs." In the evening, he went for a 5-mile stroll and practiced some maneuvers with Mike Donovan.[589]

On September 4, Sullivan arrived in New Orleans. A local writer said John L. appeared to be in grand form, and the stories of his being too fat were untrue. He hit a punching ball for 28 minutes, and then spoke to Bob Fitzsimmons for two minutes before skipping rope for six minutes. He seemed to be in good condition. After the workout concluded, he was weighed at 214 pounds. Sullivan said that he did not enjoy training and this would be his last fight, regardless of the outcome.

Two days before the fight, on September 5 in New Orleans, Sullivan punched the bag for 36 minutes and skipped the rope over 700 times, but did not seem fatigued. Before exercising, he weighed 217 pounds. However, one newspaper said that rolls of fat were still there.

On that date, Corbett worked out in Spartanburg, South Carolina. He punched the bag, wrestled and sparred Daly, and tossed the medicine ball.[590]

In the days leading up to the fight, Corbett made it known that he would insist on Sullivan showing bare flesh from the navel up. Jim claimed that Sullivan bandaged up his stomach with heavy plasters for protection. Jim's trainer said, "This is to be a fight between men and not a trial of skill between upholsterers. … If it is allowed he might just as well come in the ring wearing a baseball mask." Quite a few boxers today who wear those huge protectors above their hipline and navel should be reminded of this, as well as referees and athletic commissioners.

---

[588] *Asbury Park Daily Press, New York Herald,* September 3, 1892.

[589] *Birmingham Age-Herald, New York Herald, Times-Democrat, New York Sun,* September 5, 1892.

[590] *Times-Democrat,* September 5, 1892; *Birmingham Age-Herald, New York Herald,* September 6, 1892.

Sullivan's people responded that he did not intend to wear such protection. He would wear only his green trunks held up by a silk American flag.[591]

The day before the fight, on September 6, Corbett threw the six-pound medicine ball around for half an hour and skipped rope. Jim said that Sullivan was a 4-round knockout artist, that after the 6th round, he would have things his own way. Jim said he stood 6'1 ½" and would enter the ring weighing about 190 pounds.

Sullivan hit the punching ball for 25 minutes, firing left jabs and "chop-like blows. His right was used for short, quick swings, which seemed to tear into the leather-covered ball with force enough to break the rope." "In dodging and side stepping the champion was exceptionally clever." He then jumped rope over 700 times. Later in the day, he went through this exercise once again, and then took a swim with Bob Fitzsimmons.[592] This seemed to be an excessive amount of work to be doing the day before a fight, but Sullivan had his own ideas about how to train.

The Corbett-Sullivan fight was part of a Carnival of Champions series of three fights hosted by the Olympic Club that week. On September 5, world lightweight champion Jack McAuliffe knocked out Billy Myer in the 15th round. On September 6, world featherweight champion George Dixon, the first and only black man to have won a world championship to that point, knocked out Jack Skelly in the 8th round.

It was reported that blacks were so triumphant at Dixon's victory that,

> [T]hey are loudly proclaiming the superiority of their race, to the great scandal of the whites, who declare that they should not be encouraged to entertain even feelings of equality, much less of superiority. The Olympic Club management have about decided not to hold any more colored contests.

The *New York Herald* said that the making of a mixed-race bout had caused "sharp criticism and much indignation." Such contests, particularly in the South, could only "arouse a bitter feeling between the races which will lead to bloody affrays."[593]

The *Times-Democrat* wrote that it had been a serious mistake to match a white and black, one that it hoped would not be repeated. It noted that although there had been fair play, "it was a disagreeable duty to all Southern men present."

> It was a mistake to match a negro and a white man, a mistake to bring the races together on any terms of equality, even in the prize ring…for, among the ignorant negroes the idea has naturally been created that it was a test of the strength and fighting powers of

---

591 *San Francisco Chronicle*, September 6, 1892; *New York Herald*, September 7, 1892; *Boston Daily Globe*, July 8, 1889.

592 *Times-Democrat*, September 7, 1892.

593 *New York Herald*, September 8, 1892.

Caucasian and African. … [T]he colored population of this city…because of [Dixon's] victory…are far more confident than they ever were before of the equality of the races, and disposed to claim more for themselves than we intend to concede. … We of the South who know the fallacy and danger of this doctrine of race equality, who are opposed to placing the negro on any terms of equality, who have insisted on a separation of the races in church, hotel, car, saloon and theatre; who believe that the law ought to step in and forever forbid the idea of equality by making marriages between them illegal, are heartily opposed to any arrangement encouraging this equality, which give negroes false ideas and dangerous beliefs. … Some may argue that there is no race question in the prize ring. We think differently. …

> Mr. John L. Sullivan has set a good example in this matter. … [H]e has persistently refused to meet a negro in the ring. No one can believe that he has done this for any other reasons than his confidence that such contests place the races more or less on terms of equality.[594]

Clearly, many believed that boxing had symbolic social and racial value. William Muldoon, Sullivan's former trainer said, "There should be colored champions and white champions, and I would like to see the line drawn once and for all."[595]

---

[594] *Times-Democrat,* September 8, 1892.
[595] *National Police Gazette,* September 24, 1892.

Seats for Corbett-Sullivan were being sold for $15 and $10 for box seats, $7.50 for reserved, and $5 for gallery chairs. It was estimated that the gate receipts would be in the neighborhood of $60,000 to $70,000.[596]

On Wednesday September 7, 1892, at the Olympic Club in New Orleans, Louisiana, a 26-year-old James J. Corbett took on the 33-year-old (one month shy of 34) heavyweight champion, John L. Sullivan. The bout was fought under the Marquis of Queensberry rules using 5-ounce gloves, and was scheduled as a fight to the finish.

At 7 p.m., two hours before the fight, the building doors were opened. The blue-coated police were present to maintain order.

At 8:15 p.m., Sullivan arrived at the Olympic and was shown to his dressing room. He looked strong and walked with a jaunty air.

At 8:24 p.m., it had begun to rain, and folks were raising their umbrellas. Earlier, the management had the tarpaulin roof over the arena removed, allowing a cool breeze to sweep through the building.

THE OLYMPIC ATHLETIC CLUB BUILDING, NEW ORLEANS, LA.

At least 7,000 spectators were present at that time.

At 8:30 p.m., Corbett arrived and went to his dressing room. He did not seem nervous. He moved with a light step and had a smile on his face.

By 8:36 p.m., the shower had passed by.

At 8:41 p.m., the club secretary entered the ring with a box containing gloves and a pair of scales. Police Captain Barrett ensured that the gloves weighed 5 ounces. Sullivan's ring chair was taller than Corbett's. The special chair was furnished at his request. The official club timekeeper, R. M. Frank, took his seat and tested the electric bell.

At 8:45 p.m., Sullivan's representatives lost the toss for corners, and had to take the one that was considered unlucky, for Dempsey, Maher, Myer, and Skelly all had lost in that corner.

According to Corbett's autobiography, at Corbett's insistence, Sullivan entered the ring first. On fight-night, he told John L. that he was willing to

596 *Omaha World Herald*, September 7, 1892.

wait all night unless Sullivan went in first. This enraged Sullivan, but he acquiesced and entered first to a huge ovation.

Corbett tried to convince Sullivan that he was not concerned about him, bowing and waving to the crowd, smiling and laughing all the time. When the referee gave instructions, Corbett would not meet Sullivan's stare, but instead asked the referee about the rules and what would be allowed. After this discussion, he then turned to John L. and aggressively met his stare, which seemed to startle and surprise Sullivan. Corbett then turned his back and said, "Let her go!"[597]

According to the primary sources, at 8:52 p.m., Sullivan entered the ring first, closely followed by Corbett. Both were greeted with tremendous applause. Sullivan wore short green trunks with a belt made of the Olympic Club's colors. His socks and fighting boots were black. With him were Phil Casey, Joe Lannon, Jack McAuliffe, Charlie Johnston, and Frank Moran (who acted as Sullivan's timekeeper).

One report said Corbett wore light greenish brown trunks, green socks, and black boxing boots. Another said Jim wore nothing but a "rubber jack strap." The brown five-ounce gloves were put on in the ring.

Corbett's seconds were Billy Delaney, Jim Daly, and John Donaldson, and even Mike Donovan was in his corner as his bottleholder. Bat Masterson served as Corbett's timekeeper.

Jim looked pale, but wore a smile. Sullivan "looked as unconcerned as though about to eat his dinner."

The local New Orleans *Times-Democrat* said the announced weights were Sullivan 212, Corbett 189. The *Birmingham Age* echoed those weights. The *Times* and *Sun* both said that Sullivan weighed 212 pounds to Corbett's 187 pounds, their weights as taken and announced before they stepped into the ring. The *Chronicle* said Corbett looked 195 and that Sullivan was 212. The local *Picayune* said that Sullivan was 212 to Corbett's 178 pounds, although this contradicted all of the recent news reports that said Corbett intended to enter the ring in the high 180s. The *Times-Democrat* said that Corbett weighed 178 *after* the fight. Others said he was 190 before the fight and 185 afterwards. The *Referee*, an Australian paper, reported that Corbett was 188 to Sullivan's 216 pounds. Some said that Corbett's manager claimed that he was 178 or 180 pounds in order to get even better odds. The writer for the *Omaha World-Herald*, who was at ringside, said that both men appeared to be in perfect condition, though Corbett's appearance was "magnificent."

Reports of crowd-size ranged anywhere from 7,000 to 9,000 to 11,500 spectators. The crowd contained everything from "the millionaire banker to the street fakir. Politicians, lawyers, merchants, gamblers, newspaper reporters and pugilists elbowed each other." Bob Fitzsimmons was present.

Corbett was a 4 to 1 underdog, but eventually closed to 3 to 1 in the poolrooms. Betting was prohibited in the arena. Despite the lopsided odds

[597] Corbett at 193-196.

in favor of Sullivan, "those who looked purely at form failed to see why the 'big man' should be selected as the infallible winner." According to his autobiography, Corbett was confident that he could go for a long time, and that "no man who has lived the life that Sullivan has lived can beat me in a finish fight."[598]

At 8:55 p.m., Professor John Duffy, the referee, entered the ring. Captain Barrett announced that he had a present for Duffy: a silver punch-bowl and ladle.

Corbett was bowing, smiling, and nodding at acquaintances around the ring. He wore an air of confidence. Sullivan sat easily in his corner, appearing perfectly confident as well.

At 9 p.m., the fighters went to ring center to receive instructions from Referee Duffy. Then they returned to their corners to put on the gloves. Sullivan remained standing, but Corbett sat. Sullivan watched him closely. The Californian was laughing and chatting, seeming unconcerned.

The gladiators again were called to ring center, and they shook hands. Although Corbett was taller, the difference in their bulk was very apparent. Between 9:05 and 9:07 p.m., the referee called time to start the fight:

1 - Corbett danced around the entire ring and got away from Sullivan very cleverly. Sullivan missed his right as Corbett ran. When Sullivan tried to corner him, Corbett slipped away like an eel. There was some hissing from the audience. Sullivan glared at the running man before him.

Corbett's tactic was to remain purely defensive, keeping away, ducking, blocking, and circling, to the jeers of the crowd. He had remarkable agility, and Sullivan barely could touch him. Every time Sullivan approached or feinted, Jim would dart back or to the side, or simply run away. Jim ignored the hisses. Sullivan's face was vicious, and he tore after Corbett like a mad bull, but Corbett exhibited surprising quickness.

Neither man landed any blows, but Corbett did not expend energy in attempts the way Sullivan did. Corbett simply smiled. John seemed angry. When he had issued his challenge to all comers, he said he wanted fighting, not foot racing. Yet, that was what Corbett was doing, to John L.'s dismay and frustration. The tame round ended without a blow being landed.

2 - Once again, Sullivan was the aggressor. Corbett continued moving and successfully eluding, or ducking into a clinch. In one clinch, Corbett pressed his forearm under John's chin. After Sullivan rushed Corbett to the ropes, caught him a couple blows and followed with an uppercut, Jim flew "about the arena like a hunted deer." Both landed some punches in the round, mostly to the head. Several Sullivan blows only landed on the shoulder, as Jim was good at rolling away from punches. In a clinch, while his left was around John's neck, Corbett landed a vicious right to the stomach. Jim continued smiling and moving about in a circle, while Sullivan looked serious, anxious, and mean, following him. The man with the pompadour

---

598 Corbett at 187.

haircut appeared happy to be darting about. At the gong, Jim landed a vicious blow to the stomach.

3 - Sullivan continued his attack, smiling disdainfully at Corbett's tactics. It was evident that Corbett was going to make a long fight of it. Jim landed two or three heavy rights to the stomach, as well as some light head shots, all the while evading John's attack. This was the first round that Jim did any meaningful offensive work at all. Sullivan was very aggressive, but cooled down after Corbett landed a heavy punch to his stomach. Jim also landed a heavy right to the ear, knocking John's head back. Mostly, when Sullivan threw, Corbett was not there. His footwork was too fast.

4 - Sullivan continued chasing and rushing Corbett around the ring, but either was hit by lefts or met with a left stiff arm in the face as Jim moved about speedily. Sullivan's blows either were glancing or missed. Once in a while, Corbett would stop and land some punches with both hands, but not with much power. When John missed, Jim laughed and shook his hands mockingly at him. "Corbett's agility was remarkable. He seemed to escape Sullivan's leads with the greatest ease, but he did not work himself, and it was evident that he was playing a waiting game." The crowd once again hissed Corbett's defensive tactics, for he kept matters dull, but, he was making John miss. "It was painful to Sullivan's admirers to admit that he was not the champion of old, being very slow." Corbett walked around with a good-natured smile. He ducked and countered with a left to the neck. "The generalship displayed by Corbett was wonderful." He suddenly lunged forward with a right and left to the head at the gong.

5 - This would be the most exciting round up to that point. Sullivan began landing some hard blows to the neck until Corbett clinched. Sullivan landed some short shots on the inside. They broke and Corbett moved away again.

As Sullivan rushed in, Corbett abruptly switched tactics and brought out his vicious counter attack, quickly stepping in and beating Sullivan to the punch, landing to the body and head, targeting both the nose and mouth with a rapid volley of punches, drawing first blood from Sullivan's nose with his swinging left. Jim had been mostly defensive up to that point, so when Corbett suddenly savagely attacked, he surprised Sullivan.

The champion clinched to save himself. The blood flowed freely from John's nose in streams. After breaking, Sullivan continued pressing, but ate some good lefts and rights as Corbett fought him more. They exchanged viciously like demons. When the gong sounded, Corbett was backing him up and pounding on Sullivan. The men were bathed in Sullivan's blood. It was the first exciting round of the fight.

6 - Corbett hit and moved, particularly targeting Sullivan's bloody nose, but he also landed some occasional body shots. Sullivan began slowing down and became more cautious, though he still occasionally would rush in with some swings that mostly missed. John's nose spilled blood. The bridge of his nose was cut.

Corbett remained elusive and swift, but countered more often, usually with his jab. "Sullivan was slow and appeared to have fully wakened to the realization that Corbett was not wholly adverse to mixing matters whenever the occasion required." Another said, "Corbett's quickness was marvelous, and he landed his left on the broken nose at the call of time." Still another said that Jim jumped around like a cat, but not much was done in the round.

7 - Sullivan tried hard to land, but could not do so. Corbett was more aggressive in this round. He continued jabbing John's bloody nose and became more offensively ambitious, even landing a good right and rushing John to the ropes in a rapid rally. On the inside, Jim landed body shots and an uppercut. He kept landing, avoiding, and countering. Sullivan "was tired when he went to his corner, though he had done nothing in the round but take punishment." Corbett was outboxing him completely. The crowd loudly cheered him.

8 - Corbett continued landing jabs to the body and head, although John landed a bit more than usual in this round, including some jabs, rights, and counters. However, the frisky Corbett usually countered him. He landed a left to the body and head, as well as a left and right to the nose and jaw, sending Sullivan back momentarily. Corbett focused on the stomach, landing some vicious body blows. He also jabbed the bloody nose, "while his excellent judgment of distance prevented Sullivan's well meant blows from doing any damage of consequence." A right to Sullivan's eye appeared to puff it a bit. Sullivan seemed a bit tired.

9 - Corbett kept landing his left to the nose, but his tactics were not quite as successful. Sullivan mostly missed, but when he did land, "it was twice as heavy as his antagonist's." The champion landed some good lefts, a couple punches to the jaw and ear, and a jab to the wind that made Jim more cautious.

Overall though, Corbett's boxing skill prevented Sullivan from landing effectively or very often. There were some clinches. Corbett landed hard body shots during the infighting and continued landing his jab almost at will. Sullivan's lips were swelling. Despite outlanding Sullivan, one writer said that Corbett's blows "did not seem to weaken the big fellow, who appeared only tired."

10 - Corbett was doing most of the hitting at this point, keeping in range more in this round, sending jabs to the nose. Sullivan did land occasionally, and a few of his blows landed well. However, the majority of John's punches fell short or their power was diminished on the quick-moving Corbett, landing only lightly. Corbett kept smiling as Sullivan grew madder. His generalship astonished everyone. Sullivan gathered himself for one of his old-time rushes, but only succeeded in getting jabbed in the nose. Steve Brodie, who had bet on Sullivan, said to the *Evening World* man, "We are done, sure, don't you think so?"

11 - Corbett jabbed the body and head. Sullivan pressed hard for a moment and landed some blows, but Corbett immediately countered with a left uppercut to the chin, right to the ribs near the heart, and left to the side, all of which were effective and hurt. Corbett looked fresh, while Sullivan was bloody and clearly had the worst of the round. Each time that Jim landed, he was able to dance out of harm's way of Sullivan's attempts to counter. He also cleverly stopped an uppercut. A hard left jab to the nose sent Sullivan back for a moment.

12 - Sullivan still seemed strong and steady. Corbett began by landing three lefts to the stomach, each time cleverly getting away. The body blows eventually led Sullivan to lower his guard. Jim then went to the head, but followed to the body again. Sullivan landed some good blows, including a hard right to the ribs, but always was countered. The more effective work overall was being done by Corbett. Jim could quickly move in and out of range, attacking with quick blows when he desired, and smiling and laughing all the while as Sullivan pursued him. However, one observer said, "Great cleverness was shown by Corbett in the way he jabbed and got away, but his blows did not seem to be effective." Tap and move was his strategy.

13 - Corbett exhibited his ability to remain out of Sullivan's range, ducking and moving away whenever John led. The few times that Jim was struck, he always countered. Corbett's style was like water gradually wearing down a stone. He cautiously moved, jumped, walked, and ran about, carefully picked his punches, and then sprung away out of danger after landing. Neither one landed many blows in this round.

14 - Both landed well as they exchanged a number of fierce blows, particularly early in the round. Although Sullivan landed a bit more often than usual in this round, his punches had lost some of their power and were ineffective on the generally moving Corbett, who could step or jump back, or duck, or lean or roll away from punches. Sullivan kept getting hit with jabs. Corbett remained comfortable, almost constantly smiling at John during the bout. It was obvious that Sullivan would need to use his strength to overcome Corbett's great cleverness. One source said Sullivan looked grim and fierce, while Corbett landed on his mouth, which was cut. Another version of the round said that no blow was struck "that would have broken a pane of glass."

15 - Sullivan led hard but continued being countered. Corbett's long reach kept John L. at bay. Sullivan rushed but Corbett clinched, at which point John spoke to Jim. It was not uncommon for them to speak to one another. Corbett landed a right and left to the nose and mouth, bringing out the blood again. He also landed a hard left swing that hurt. They exchanged leads and counters, "mixing it up in lively style." Sullivan landed a blow to the ear and stomach, but looked tired. Jim landed a hard left to the stomach at the bell, to the crowd's cheers. Sullivan had yet to land a really good solid clean blow. Bill Brady was smiling.

16 - With his nose and mouth flowing blood, Sullivan kept trying to rush in, but Corbett used his jab and kept away. Both landed some punches. Sullivan still seemed strong, trying hard to land a good one, but his breathing was labored. Jim jabbed the stomach and escaped returns with ease. Twice in combination, Jim landed his left to the head and right to the body, clinching afterwards each time. During the clinch, John hit Corbett with a half-arm swing and the audience yelled "Foul," but "Corbett refused to have the victory that way." Corbett kept jabbing and ducking.

17 - Sullivan's face was very red. However, he continued pressing and landed some good punches, particularly to the body. Regardless, Jim remained as "spry as a kitten." Corbett stayed away more, but still landed occasional shots. Another account said this round was very tame, as neither man landed any blow of significance.

18 - Corbett landed his left to the body, face, and head, as well as an occasional right to the body or head. John landed a punch to the ribs that "sounded all over the house" like a "bass drum," but Corbett countered with a left to his body. Overall, Corbett was landing more, and he was unmarked. It still was his round. Another account said that John twice landed smashes on the ear, but Jim responded by landing two scorchers to the jaw and following with three more rights. Corbett was fresh and unmarked, while Sullivan was tired and covered with blood.

19 - The *Picayune* said that Sullivan began the round looking dazed, while Jim was "fresh and smiling." The *Times-Democrat* version said that Sullivan still looked strong at the start of the round, but his face and body wore evidence of the jabbing he had suffered. Sullivan remained aggressive and landed on the jaw, but Corbett smiled and danced around. They exchanged, but Corbett always landed.

Corbett was encouraged by his ability to land as Sullivan's defense was weakening, and therefore he attacked more. Jim jabbed a tattoo on him. Sullivan acted as if the blows meant nothing to him, confidently awaiting a well-timed rush. He rallied and rushed, but Corbett again ran away as nimbly as a deer, and then came back and punished him to the body and head with both hands, sending John L. to the ropes.

The *Birmingham Age* said, "Sullivan is winded and has the worst of the fight up to this time." Several papers said Corbett was too clever for him and laughed sarcastically at the champion. Sullivan looked like a beaten man. The *Sun* said the crowd greatly admired Corbett's cleverness in tapping and getting away.

20 - Sullivan looked very tired, but he landed a left to the face, and Corbett grew cautious. However, suddenly Corbett landed a vicious left swing that terribly jarred Sullivan. Jim followed up and went on the attack with several left and right combinations to the body and head. "The champion was nearly knocked down with the left on the stomach and right on the head." Jim's swinging lefts and rights sent Sullivan back to the ropes. John L.

fought back, but Jim had a clear advantage, landing heavily to the stomach and face. When John's guard raised, Jim went to the body. When the guard was lowered a bit, Corbett went back up to the head. Jim landed his double left - to the nose and then to the body.

Sullivan fought back, and they fought fast and furiously. Jim moved away, but inevitably came on again with a rush of blows to the head, sending John backing up to the ropes again. Sullivan landed a left, but was countered with a left to the mouth. John L. was very groggy at the bell.

The crowd was wild, cheering mightily. They sensed that the end was near, for the punishment was telling on Sullivan, who was very tired, groggy, and unable to defend himself.

21 - The *Times-Democrat* said that Sullivan was weak and groggy as a result of the consistent, "seemingly light, but really heavy and jarring jabs," which had been well-directed and landed so often that they finally told. Those punches, combined with the uppercuts to the body, as well as the energy that Sullivan had expended in trying to land his vicious swings, had worn out the champion.

Sullivan was game, but had nothing left. His legs seemed to quiver with weakness. His belly overlapped his trunks at the front, sides, and back. His face was red; his nose, lips, and left eye were swollen; and the blood trickled down, leaving him a sad sight. The *Daily Picayune* agreed that Sullivan's head "seemed but a gory mass of flesh." On the other hand, Corbett was unmarked. Continuing, the *Times-Democrat* said of Corbett,

> His cleverness in dodging, his quickness on his feet and his wonderful amount of wind had stood him in good stead, and though he had traveled four feet to Sullivan's one there was but the slightest possible approach to an impairment of his wind. He seemed as cool and as fresh as when he entered the ring.

Nevertheless, the *Daily Picayune* and *Omaha World-Herald*, which also had reporters at ringside, opined that the one-minute rest seemed to recover Sullivan a bit, and he did not yet seem to be a beaten man, despite the fact that he had been punished severely. As usual, Sullivan led first, landing a left to the chest. He gamely kept trying to land, but was unable to do so with any effect. Jim defended blows for a while. Sullivan kept edging in, but Corbett kept edging away.

Sullivan feinted for the ribs with his right and landed a left swing, but received a similar hard left counter that hurt.

Corbett must have sensed something, because he went on the attack and rushed Sullivan with a number of blows, driving John back. He made a succession of vicious rallies.

Corbett feinted his right for the head but shot the left into the stomach. Sullivan doubled up. Jim then drove the right to the jaw. John's hands dropped for a quick moment and Corbett was all over him with a rain of blows to the head, every punch seeming to land harder than the former.

Sullivan tried to raise his guard, but the blows beat it down. John's head bobbed back and forth from the lefts and rights.

According to the *Picayune*, a Corbett left then right staggered Sullivan. Another left swing landed audibly and sent Sullivan down with a thump. The *Omaha World-Herald* writer said, "A right on the ear and a left on the jaw settled the biz and the championship."

The *Times-Democrat* description of the knockdown said that Corbett landed the left and right to the jaw, jabbed to the stomach with the left, and then finally landed a terrific right uppercut on the chin that dropped Sullivan down to his hands, knees, and then shoulders.

Corbett stood a few feet away, ready to strike should John L. rise again. Sullivan started to rise, getting to his knee, trying to push himself erect, but his body gave out and went limp and he fell back down again with a crash, out cold. The referee counted him out.

James J. Corbett was the new world heavyweight champion, winner of $35,000, and a reputation that would be worth ten times that amount. Donovan and Brady sprang to the stage and flung their arms around him. Tears welled up in Corbett's eyes.

The round had lasted 1 minute 30 seconds. The fight had lasted 1 hour 21 minutes.

Sullivan was out for a couple of minutes. Water was poured over him and ammonia was placed under his nose. Jack McAuliffe fanned him with a towel. When he came to, he asked, "Say, am I licked? Did that young fellow do it?" After being informed that such was the case, Corbett came over and said, "John, will you shake hands with me?" Sullivan replied, "Yes, my boy. I'm glad it was you that won."

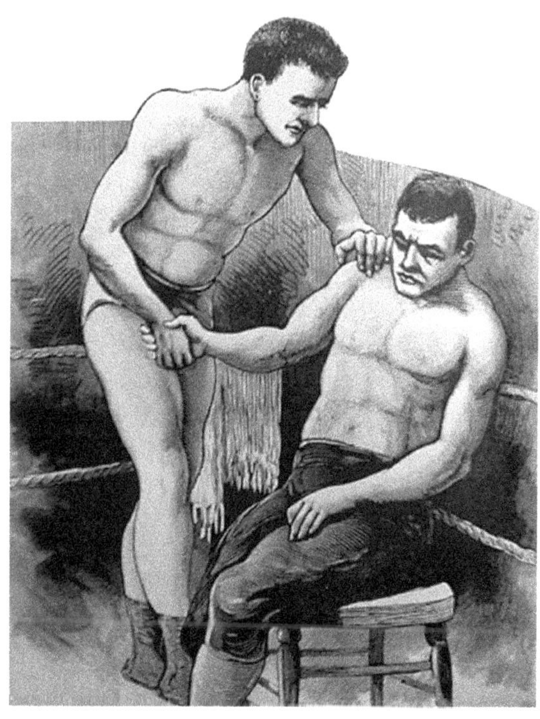

The new champion consoles the ex-champion

Sullivan then addressed the crowd: "Ladies and gentlemen, it is the same old story. The story of a young man against an old one. There are gray hairs in my head and I should have known better. I am only glad that the championship has been won by an American and will remain in America." Sullivan's sportsmanship was admired and his speech brought down the house. Years later, Mike Donovan said, "Here was the man who had stood for twelve years the acknowledged physical king of the human race. In one brief battle his kingdom was swept away from him, but he took his defeat like a man."

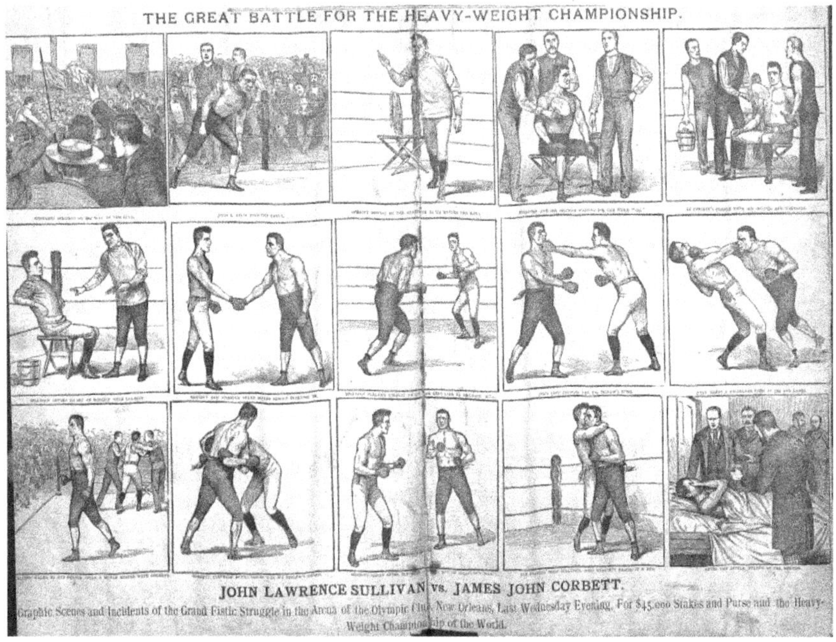

THE GREAT BATTLE FOR THE HEAVY-WEIGHT CHAMPIONSHIP.
JOHN LAWRENCE SULLIVAN VS. JAMES JOHN CORBETT.
Graphic Scenes and Incidents of the Grand Fistic Struggle in the Arena of the Olympic Club, New Orleans, Last Wednesday Evening, For $45,000 Stakes and Purse and the Heavy-Weight Championship of the World.

Bob Fitzsimmons assessed the fight. Early on, he said, "Sullivan will never hit this fellow; he is too shifty for him." After the 5th round, Fitz felt that Sullivan would not last past the 7th round. In the 6th, Fitzsimmons observed, "That's the way Jim will win the fight; those continuous jabs will wear out any man." Of the finish, he said that Corbett hit the mouth and stomach with multiple blows. "Sullivan is gone – right and left on Sullivan's jaws; right and left again – Sullivan is down – just say that it was a rapid succession of right and left hand blows, and Sullivan unable to protect himself."

Summarizing the fight, the local *Daily Picayune* said that early on, the defensive Corbett danced, ducked, and stepped away from blows, and the crowd hissed him. However, as the bout progressed, he took advantage of openings, punished John when the opportunity allowed, and stood his ground more than half the time, mixing it up and constantly changing his plans in order to worry Sullivan. When finally he had weakened Sullivan, Corbett "punched him out like a master," showing that he was a "king of speed and cleverness." The new champion was unmarked.

> [Corbett is] the evolution of the Sullivan era of glove contests…a keen analyst of men and methods. His art consisted not so much in

> the brutal battering down of an adversary, as the parrying of attacks, the accuracy of aim, the discovery of weaknesses, and the skillful acceptance of every opportunity for advantage. He represents the idea of the refinement of the science, of thinking and acting quickly in emergencies, of the perfection of self-defense.

The local *Times-Democrat* said the shifty Californian had landed three blows to one, and sustained his reputation of being one of the quickest and most scientific boxers the world had ever seen. He started off warily, but became aggressive later. Sullivan made a heroic struggle, but finally went down under repeated blows. Jim's skill was too much for John's strength.

The *New York Times* called it a contest between science and strength, saying that Corbett's expert agility in dodging Sullivan's blows and eluding his rushes had won it for him. Corbett was confident from the beginning, demonstrating his ability to stop Sullivan and avoid his punches, all the while looking happy and smiling. Corbett "ducked," "sprung," and even ran out of John's reach, but it was not a fight fought purely for survival. Corbett countered and moved away with "lightning quickness" before John could return his blows. Jim was more defensive early, his tactics designed to get Sullivan to wear himself out. John L. could not reach him. However, over the course of the fight, Corbett "battered his man badly." "The fight was fast and furious and Sullivan nearly fell on the ropes from left hand jabs on the head."

The *New York Sun* said, "From the start, youth, agility, and science were arrayed against advancing years, over-confidence, and strength, and Sullivan had no chance against such odds."

The *San Francisco Chronicle* said that Sullivan was beaten "thoroughly and artistically," being "outsparred, outwinded, outpunched and outgeneraled." Jim won it from first to last.

> He started with a line of defense that he followed perfectly in spite of the jeers of the crowd, and when he had taken the measure of Sullivan's stamina he punched his antagonist to sleep in a hurry. Corbett more than upheld his reputation as a man of exceeding cleverness with the gloves.

The *New York Herald* said that Sullivan was punished brutally, his nose split, mouth swollen and cut, neck enlarged by the blows, and his body battered. He was outclassed in every area but brute strength. Corbett was able to dance away and dash in or out. Either way, there was nothing that Sullivan could do.

Afterwards, Sullivan said,

> I am gone now. I can't fight anymore, and that settles it. I had to go after him from the start to the end. He kept on running away. I swear that through the entire fight he did not hurt me until the last round. Then I felt a smash, and it seemed to me as if I was on a bridge and had fallen into the water. I tried to get out of it, but I couldn't. There

> wasn't a damn punch from him that hurt me until the last round, and that was where I received the knockout blow. That was all. He can't hit hard by any means, and I could not get at him. I had to go for him. …
>
> I went up once too often. Booze is a bad thing, I assure you. I could, seven years ago, at that fellow's age, have licked any one of them in the world, but that time has passed.

He also said, "He hit me forty times and whenever he wanted to. … I tried in every way to hit him, but I couldn't."[599]

One observer said that Corbett coolly eluded Sullivan in the 1st round. He danced about, and when the audience hissed him, "he stopped suddenly, held up his hands deprecatingly and gave the audience a look that seemed to say, 'I came here to do a certain thing, and I mean to do it in my own way.' He had his man gauged after that round." Once Corbett was sure that he could avoid Sullivan when he wanted to, he focused on offense, alternating between the face and stomach.

This observer also said that he had seen Sullivan against Kilrain, and could tell the difference in Sullivan against Corbett. He felt that Sullivan had deteriorated physically, and was badly trained. Ironically, in the loss, Sullivan proved that he could absorb punishment.

Regarding the finish, this observer said that Corbett landed a powerful right to the stomach that pained John L. and caused him to drop his hands. Jim landed a left to the nose that snapped John's head back. He followed with six drives with his left and right, Sullivan's head wobbling about. Then Corbett drew back his right and landed a full-arm swing on the jaw.[600]

In his dressing room afterwards, Corbett tipped the scales at 185 pounds, "showing that he lost five pounds during the fight." He said,

> I knew what I could do. Did I not tell you I could whip him with ease and for you to bet all you could raise on the result? … I am satisfied I could have whipped him sooner had I mixed and gone in for hard infighting, but I was leary. On several occasions I was sorely tempted to close right in on him and do him up quick, but my seconds kept warning me to be a little cautious; that I was doing well and having all the best of it, and that I'd better fight shy of his right hand.

When Mike Donovan entered the room, Corbett said, "Well, Mike, my boy, we are on top at last. Every word you said about Sullivan was right. I followed your advice and here I am winner and champion. I scarcely know how to thank you and express my gratitude."

---

599 *New York Times*, *New York Herald*, *New York Sun*, *Evening World*, *Daily Picayune*, *Times-Democrat*, *San Francisco Chronicle*, *San Francisco Examiner*, *Birmingham Age-Herald*, *Omaha World-Herald*, all September 8, 1892; *Referee*, September 14, 1892; Mike Donovan, *The Roosevelt That I Know* (New York: B.W. Dodge & Co., 1909), 186-187.

600 *Times-Democrat*, September 11, 1892.

Corbett discussed his strategy. He said that he did not throw a punch in the 1st round, just using it to figure out Sullivan.

> He would lunge for me and I would gauge his force and speed and see just where his weak points were, then I would make a feint and try to bring out another weak point. In this way he showed me his entire hand. His best plan would have been to stand stock still and let me come to him. … I would have thought he had something up his sleeve, and I would have been very cautious how I went in.

His tactics were to use his footwork to size up Sullivan, throw off John's rhythm and timing, make him wear himself out in attempts, but also to use his footwork offensively, setting up his own attack. The crowd hissed at first, but he held up his glove to let them know that he was sizing him up, that they needed to wait.

Corbett wanted to keep Sullivan moving and not allow him to rest. "Whenever I would get away too far he would drop his hands in the expectation of getting a rest. Then…I would jump in again and up would go his hands." Sometimes when using this tactic, Corbett "went at him, knowing that he was not ready for me." Thus, Corbett used his in-and-out footwork to make John miss and keep him working, to disrupt his timing, and to surprise him with offense when it wasn't expected.

Jim was careful not to get hit by John's right. When he saw Sullivan setting up to land his right, he either would move away to take him out of proper position for the punch, or Jim would step in with a quicker punch of his own. "I found that it took him some time to get in proper attitude for delivering a blow, and then I either gave it to him on the stomach with the left or on the face, always working around afterwards and keeping him moving his feet."

Corbett generally would roll to the side from Sullivan's chopping left and counter with a left of his own. Corbett was not afraid to engage Sullivan occasionally, noting that whenever Sullivan's "eyes turned green and he looked especially ferocious I would make it a point to go in and mix up with him just to let him know that I was not afraid of him. This, I think, surprised him more than anything else." Jim felt that he could have knocked him out far sooner, but Delaney advised him that Sullivan was still strong, to be careful and hit the body until he got weaker.[601] Corbett also said,

> Sullivan is big and strong but I knew that he could not hit me. In the whole fight he never reached me with a blow. … I kept my right in reserve and cut him down with the left. When I saw I had him safe I ended it as soon as possible. I won by whipping him, not by keeping away.[602]

---

601 *Daily Picayune*, September 13, 1892; *San Francisco Examiner*, September 9, 1892; *Times-Democrat*, September 13, 1892.

602 *San Francisco Examiner*, September 8, 1892.

Regarding the finish, Corbett said, "I really did not know how hard I hit him with my left until I saw the effect of the blow. Then I knew my time had come, and I went at him as hard as I could with both hands."[603]

Corbett later admitted that he had been hit with some good punches, but said that Sullivan was unable to land his hard right cleanly. He noted,

> [Sullivan's blows felt like] kicks from a mule with boxing gloves on his heels. Sullivan does not deliver straight blows, or in fact any kind of blows, like another fighter. He down chops and uses his hand like a club somehow, and the blows make you think that the whole of his weight is in his arms.[604]

Corbett considered quickness of eyesight and ability to judge distance the primary requisites of a good boxer. He relied on ducking and using his legs for defense more so than parrying because he realized early on in his career that punches sometimes could get through his guard in spite of everything. This especially was true with very small gloves.[605] Such tactics were perfect against Sullivan, because for years it was said that Sullivan was so strong that he could beat down any man's guard. Corbett did not rely on his guard as his primary source of defense.

Mike Donovan was in Corbett's corner that night, and years later said that Corbett was a dancing master, too elusive, skipping away, grinning at Sullivan, "making some contemptuous remark" and laughing at him. Corbett landed a left that sent the blood spurting from John's nose, and subsequently "jumped around like a grasshopper." Body shots in the 7th round made Sullivan double up in agony. Donovan told Corbett to finish him, but Jim listened to Bill Delaney, who told him to be cautious and take his time, fearing Sullivan's right. Donovan felt that Sullivan was weak and helpless, and growing weaker from his exertions and the extreme loss of blood from his nose. However, Corbett was content to stab away and move about, showing Sullivan respect, taking his time. "It was more like a game of tag than a fight." Finally, in the 21st round, Corbett rushed at Sullivan and knocked him out.[606]

Bill Delaney backed Donovan's version, saying that Corbett could have finished Sullivan sooner, but agreed that he persuaded Jim to take his time and not take any chances with the powerful puncher.

Corbett echoed his cornermen to a certain extent, saying,

> I don't think Sullivan was himself after the second round. He was decidedly weak. He wanted to rest his arms all the time, but I

---

603 *Daily Picayune*, September 9, 1892.

604 *San Francisco Examiner*, September 9, 1892. There is some existing footage of a much older Sullivan, eighteen years later, in 1910, hitting a speed bag with big swinging punches that had the weight of his body behind them. Corbett's description of how he threw seems apt in light of this short clip.

605 *Referee,* November 1, 1892.

606 Donovan at 177-184.

wouldn't let him; I made him keep them up. He hit me most on the back of the shoulder. Some of his blows were so strange that I did not understand them. … I came very near knocking Sullivan out in the eighth round. He was groggy, and I went in to finish him, and had forced him to the ropes when the bell saved him. … He had recovered by the next round and I determined to wait a little longer for a better opportunity. … Jackson gave me a harder fight. He kept me busy all the time. There is no rest when he is in the ring.[607]

John L. Sullivan had been a dominant champion, undefeated for about 13 - 14 years. His reputation had been built to such mythic legendary proportions that he was considered invincible. He was boxing. Therefore, the world was shocked at his loss.

Mike Donovan said, "[T]he American people have never lost and will never lose their admiration and affection for Sullivan. He was not only the most marvelous fighting machine the world had ever seen, but he was fearless and honest, always on the level. That will never be forgotten of him."[608]

Although Corbett's skill and accomplishment were admired, many felt that his victory was more the result of Sullivan's age, years of inactivity, hard drinking, and improper training. One critic commented,

> Taking into consideration the life he has been leading, Sullivan should have had twelve months steady work instead of twelve weeks. Previous experience had shown him that a 24 foot ring of all places was in no way suited to his style of boxing. … Men who had seen both Sullivan and Corbett fight were agreed that the Californian would have had no show with the Sullivan of ten years back, and on all hands they were loud in praise of the game stand made by John L.

Charley Mitchell, no friend of either, said, "It was not Corbett that beat Sullivan, it was nature and Sullivan himself. A few years back John would have knocked Corbett out inside four rounds."

Frank Slavin said, "Corbett won as I thought he would. He was too young and quick."[609]

Jack Ashton said, "Corbett is much cleverer than we gave him credit for. He hits a very much harder blow than we thought he could do. Sullivan is not the Sullivan of old."

Joe Choynski felt that a good middleweight could have beaten the Sullivan that Corbett fought.

However, Charlie Johnston, Sullivan's backer, said that Sullivan was in excellent condition, but simply was outfought, and that Corbett had earned

---

[607] *New York Sun*, September 9, 1892.

[608] Donovan at 198.

[609] *Referee*, November 16, 1892.

his laurels fairly. Still, Johnston also admitted that although John had retained his punching power, he had lost the speed in his legs.

Pat Duffy said that although John was in good condition, he was not as good a man as he had been in 1889. "He was not prepared, however, to say that he could have beaten Corbett even if he had been at his best."[610]

Steve Brodie believed that Corbett could have whipped the Sullivan of old. Some agreed that Corbett could have whipped Sullivan at his best.

Bat Masterson said Sullivan always was overrated. "I believe Fitzsimmons or Hall could whip him."

A doctor said that Sullivan actually was overtrained. He opined that Sullivan had trained too hard over too short a period of time, rather than gradually working himself back into condition.[611]

One critic later questioned the prudence of losing so much weight so quickly, and training for such a short period of time after such a lengthy period of inactivity. Overtraining likely had an adverse effect.

> No man's strength is so deceptive as that of the athlete who has been trained down to condition in too short a time. Sullivan had not trained for three years. … During all that time he had been drinking like a fish, and his weight never fell below 259 pounds.[612]

The *Omaha World-Herald* writer said that Sullivan had contributed to his own downfall by living a life of dissipation. He was overconfident and contemptuous of the type of training necessary for perfect condition. He simply believed that since he was John L. Sullivan that he could not be defeated.

The next day, Sullivan's eyes were blackened and his face and nose swollen. The club's physician had put three stitches in his nose. Sullivan said,

> I did not run away. … But he licked me – yes he did. He licked me, and let it go at that. I give him all the credit he wants. He licked me square enough, but I'm old, I am. Let him go through what I have. Let him knock 'em all out for twelve years and then see if he can do any better than I did. Yes, he licked the champion and now he's champion. Let him take care of it as good as I did, that's all; I aint kicking.

Sullivan also said that Corbett was "cleverer than any fighter I ever met in my life. I let him hit me one or two body blows purposely, with the idea of catching him as he landed, but I couldn't touch him."[613]

Another newspaper quoted Sullivan as saying,

---

610 *Times-Democrat,* September 9, 1892.
611 *Times-Democrat,* September 15, 1892.
612 *Brooklyn Daily Eagle,* September 11, 1892.
613 *New York Herald,* September 8, 1892.

> Not a single blow that he hit me during the fight until the last round had any more effect than if a featherweight had been sending them in. His body punching annoyed me considerably, and, of course, had something to do with my collapse. In the last round, though, he landed one very hard one somewhere, I can't tell just where, and I experienced the queerest sensation that I ever knew. It seemed to me that I was falling over a precipice into a sheet of water, and I don't remember anything after that until Phil Casey brought me to my senses with ammonia. I am glad, after all, that the title I held so long passes into the hands of one of my countrymen.

Sullivan's eyes then welled up. Speaking to Charley Johnston, he said,

> This has made a great change in my life, Charley. This morning I had thousands of friends, but I don't suppose that many of them will care to recognize me now that I have been beaten. I don't suppose that the people will want to come and see my play now. But if they don't, why, I'll take to some other business.[614]

Analyzing the loss, the *New York Herald* said, "No man, certainly no athlete, can afford to indulge, even spasmodically, in those things which the laws of health and morality forbid, and continue in the full possession of the physical power with which Nature had endowed him." Sullivan's overindulgence had "predisposed him to fleshiness, had caused him the loss of lung power and of the endurance that had once distinguished him."[615]

Jake Kilrain said that Sullivan had lived high and carried too much flesh, and therefore had needed no less than five months of training to be prepared properly. He noted that although Sullivan was in condition, he was not the man that he was three years ago, because no man could do the things he had over the last few years and remain at his best. Even when Jake saw Sullivan at a George Dixon fight on June 27, 1892 in Brooklyn, John was under the influence of liquor, despite his claims that he had stopped drinking. He criticized John's trainers, saying that he had not trained for enough months, and, "They seemed to think only of taking off his weight, without considering at the same time he was losing vitality."

Kilrain also criticized Sullivan's strategy, saying that it was not wise to rush, for doing so had been a fatal tactical error. Jake felt that Sullivan should have been calm, consistent, and methodical in his attack.

> Instead of following Corbett up in this deliberate and worrying manner, Sullivan made those savage rushes at him. … I have always allowed that Corbett was a lot cleverer than Sullivan, who should have known it, too. But apparently he did not, for by his tactics he did not

614 *New York World,* September 14, 1892.

615 *New York Herald, Omaha World-Herald,* September 8, 9, 1892.

appear to give Corbett credit for knowing anything about the business at all.[616]

Years later, Bob Fitzsimmons would employ Kilrain's suggested strategy against Corbett.

The *Times-Democrat* oscillated in its analysis. At one point it said, "How much may have been due to Sullivan's age and, possibly, impaired vitality cannot readily be determined." However, it also remembered a young, prime Sullivan, which stood in sharp contrast to the Sullivan that fought Corbett.

> Sullivan was one of the quickest big men that ever lived; that with all his aggressive ability, which had in reality not been overrated, he was quick as lightning at parrying, ducking, dodging and getting out of the way generally. While his tactics were never to unnecessarily delay a contest, he well knew when it was desirable to rush and when it was prudent to bide his time. In brief, Sullivan, in addition to being probably the hardest hitter that ever stood in a prize ring, was also one of the quickest of big men, a thoroughly scientific boxer by instinct as well as training, and without a superior as a ring general. In this way many boxers of skill and comparatively good sense were ignominiously defeated.

It also said the following day, in more balanced fashion,

> Sullivan certainly did not show the form that was expected of him, and those who always jump at conclusions and then retail them as the most oracular of utterances, at once decided that Corbett is, after all, not entitled to any fame for having vanquished a man upon whom the hand of time and constitutional decadence had been so heavily laid already. On the other hand, there will be people of precisely the same class who will attribute everything to Corbett's marvelous powers. It is probable, though by no means certain, that the truth may be found somewhere between these two extremes.

Those who had seen Sullivan in 1889 and in 1892 felt that he had gone from a man of superior speed to one who was pronouncedly slow. However, the *Times-Democrat* felt that the analysis should take into account that "this was the first time Sullivan's speed had been compared to that of such a phenomenon as Corbett." It believed that it was difficult to tell whether Sullivan had slowed or just seemed slow in comparison to Corbett. "Altogether, it is very difficult to determine how far Corbett's victory was due to his own wonderful capacity as a pugilist and how far to Sullivan's supposed deterioration."[617]

---

616 *Times-Democrat,* September 14, 1892.
617 *Times-Democrat,* September 8, 9, 1892.

A similar debate would be repeated many years later, in the 1920s, when Gene Tunney defeated heavyweight champion Jack Dempsey. Once again, it was a speedy active boxer going up a vaunted and admired heavy puncher who was coming off years of inactivity.

Sullivan's age, lengthy inactivity, loss of interest, heavy drinking, weight gain, combined with overtraining in such a short period of time, and pro career that had lasted around 14 years had left him at less than his best. He really had been at his peak in the early- to mid-1880s. A number of years earlier, Sullivan would have been faster, busier, more reactive defensively, and better conditioned, and it is debatable as to how well Corbett would have dealt with that.

That said, Corbett had been schooled in a boxing club and had developed and honed his skills over many years to become the perfect foil to an aggressive fighter like Sullivan. It required the world's best defensive fighter to defeat a highly aggressive power puncher like Sullivan. Corbett was a skillful defensive master who utilized speedy, well-placed punches, timing, beautiful footwork, elusive head movement, clinching, and relaxation. He was larger and stronger than some of the defensively skilled fighters who had lasted rounds with Sullivan, and it appeared that he had a better chin as well. James J. Corbett had the perfect style to give Sullivan trouble. Therefore, he might have given even a prime Sullivan a very tough fight. After all, Jim had more than held his own with Peter Jackson.

A few years later, Sullivan said, "[H]e licked a man that had tried to drink all the rum there was flowing in the United States, and even then nature went back on me."[618] Sullivan also generally said of the fight that he was never hurt until the end, that Corbett was not a hard hitter, but that he simply tired him out.[619]

However, over a decade later, in 1907, Sullivan in an oddly self-deprecating alleged statement, said,

> The fighting style of today is all shiftiness. … Corbett, it must be given to him was the first of the big exponents of the shifty game. … I didn't know anything about the Corbett stuff before I ran into it. I was warned about it by my friends, but I was bull-headed and incredulous, and I couldn't understand how mere quickness was going to win over me. … I honestly believed that Corbett would be a mark for me, and I trained for the fight on Bass's ale and big black cigars, so to speak. … I was…trimmed good, by the boy who was open-minded enough to study the fighting game from a new angle, and let nobody ever believe that his style of doing it didn't furnish me the surprise of my life. I believe that, even if I had trained faithfully and been in perfect shape for that fight, Corbett, with his panther agility

[618] *Brooklyn Daily Eagle,* December 10, 1895.

[619] *Brooklyn Daily Eagle,* January 21, 1894.

> and his new style of getting in and out again, would have handed it to me that time.[620]

The truth was that a younger Sullivan had dealt with many movers and slick fighters.

Even Corbett years later said of the fight,

> In justice to the man who had reigned so long as champion of the world…I got him when he was slipping; and that goes for all the champions down the line. It is very hard to tell, as you gaze down the list at all the defeated champions of the past, which was supreme. … Like the pitcher that goes too often to the well, the champ will go once too often to the ring, and be broken in the end. And all argument as to their respective merits is foolish and futile.[621]

JOHN L. SULLIVAN, EX-CHAMPION.

[620] *Los Angeles Times,* May 12, 1907.

[621] Corbett at 202.

Appreciation

John L. Sullivan revolutionized boxing. His career represents both the end of the era of bareknuckle fighting, but more importantly, the start of the most lucrative individual sporting profession ever up to that point – gloved Queensberry rules boxing. Sullivan's exciting, awe-inspiring dominance had fostered tremendous explosive growth in the popularity of gloved boxing and made it a legitimate and increasingly legal money-making profession.

Even at the time, the world recognized what he had done for the sport. The *Daily Picayune* summarized Sullivan's importance to boxing, saying,

> [H]e was the virtual inventor of the modern glove contest. He did better with the gloves than all his predecessors with naked fists and did as much execution with padded hands in four rounds as the old time fighter with ungloved battering rams in hours. He Americanized the manly art, deprived it of much of the brutality and made it possible to decide championships before athletic clubs under the best auspices, before classes of people who formerly took little interest in the sport. Nature intended him for a gladiator, and although he abused nature to a considerable extent not even the best trained rivals could defeat him. … He stood out a central figure in the history of pugilism; attracted to him a following from every corner of the country.[622]

Decades later, even James J. Corbett said of Sullivan, "I think he was the most popular pugilist that ever lived."[623]

If world champion since 1882, when he defeated Paddy Ryan, Sullivan made at least 33 successful title defenses. Really, he was the world's best gloved fighter as early as 1880, when he easily stopped Joe Goss. However, since gloved boxing was relatively new, was not considered a real fight, and there were no gloved champions prior to Sullivan, pinpointing an exact start of his gloved reign is challenging. However, at the time, most recognized him as a true world champion once he proved himself against Ryan in an LPR contest. If true, as champion, if one counts his gloved contests masquerading as exhibitions for legal purposes, to this day, he holds more title defenses than any other champion.

Sullivan's skills were far better than many realize. He knew how to feint, get into range, duck and slip punches, block, and land effective knockout blows to the body and head. He was very quick, able to throw

[622] *Daily Picayune*, September 8 - 13, 1892.
[623] Corbett at 117-122.

blazing combinations, and set a fast pace. He had fast feet and could rush in with explosive speed. He had great accuracy, knowing how to find and create openings. He also proved that he could exhibit endurance and poise. The fact is that if Sullivan did not have defense and an iron chin, he simply could not have done as well as he did for as long as he did given that his opponents were firing punches at him with gloves that weighed 2-5 ounces, and sometimes no gloves at all. Bear in mind also that Sullivan was fighting and sparring almost daily and nightly for months on end. Without defense, his face could not have emerged unscathed. He knocked out big men and small men, punchers and movers, skilled and unskilled. As Sullivan said, "I go in to win from the very first second, and I never stop until I have won. Win I must, and win I will, at every stage of the game."[624]

Even Richard K. Fox, his most ardent critic and financial backer of many of his top foes, had to admit that Sullivan was a great fighter after he defeated Kilrain. Fox expected that version of Sullivan, one who had been drinking and coming off a serious illness, to lose to the highly respected Kilrain.

Even when he was no longer at his best, far past his prime, and had been fat and drunk and not serious about boxing for over 3 years, it still took a prime Corbett 21 three-minute rounds with 5-ounce gloves to take him out. Corbett was never close to hurting or dropping men like Jack Burke or Jake Kilrain, men whom Sullivan decked several times years earlier.

The fact is that many of Sullivan's foes had a fair amount of bareknuckle experience in lengthy fights to the finish, and had engaged in gloved bouts and exhibitions as well. Their science usually was commended. Rather than criticizing his opponents' abilities, no matter where he went, observers were unanimous in their acclaim of Sullivan as a rare prodigy, favorably comparing him with history's greatest fighters. John L. Sullivan was such a phenomenon that he could knock out respected veterans of the fight game, often with ease and rapidity.

Although several of Sullivan's foes were much smaller, the fact is that Sullivan took on plenty of men who were as big as or bigger than him, but the biggest fighters Sullivan faced usually were taken out the fastest. The smaller boxers had more speed, endurance, and could move a lot more, and often had more skill. Hence, at the time, they were perceived as bigger threats to Sullivan. Experts believed that it would require a smaller quicker man with crafty footwork and skill as well as great condition to compete with Sullivan. No one could out-strength or outfight him. Great size was seen as a detriment in a lengthy fight to the finish. Most top fighters intentionally trained down in weight for endurance purposes. Few large men today could last for 2 or 3 hours. In fact, few of the big men of today could even last 15 rounds, or one hour. Sullivan fought Mitchell with bare

624 Sullivan at 179.

hands in the cold rain for over 3 hours. He fought Kilrain in over 100-degree heat for over two hours. Such feats require special men.

The biggest criticism of Sullivan's career is the fact that he drew the color line. However, Kilrain defeated Godfrey twice in his career, once before he fought Sullivan and once after. When Jackson was on the scene, Sullivan was not fighting anyone, white or black, and eventually he faced the man who fought Jackson on even terms over 61 rounds.

It is possible, with his skill and endurance, that Jackson might gradually have broken down and defeated Sullivan. However, Jackson struggled with vicious rushers like Farnan and Goddard, who were less talented and skilled than Sullivan, and much smaller than Sullivan as well.

Ultimately, Sullivan was not willing to risk the title against a black man. But one cannot say he was not willing to take on a tough challenge, given that he fought men like Kilrain and Corbett. Corbett might have been more of a stylistic challenge than Jackson. Jackson would not have moved quite as much as Corbett did, so his style would have matched up better with Sullivan's. Also, Corbett had never been down in a fight, whereas Jackson had been down and had been stopped. Even Corbett said,

> I tell you that no one can whip Sullivan who is not as fast as I am. I am not so sure that he wouldn't whip Peter Jackson, for Peter's style would suit him a good deal better than mine. Peter would go and shy with him, and no man can do that with any hope of success.[625]

Towards the end of his career, Sullivan became more concerned with making money. He was content to avoid legal entanglements and instead give short friendly exhibitions and act in plays. That said, if the money was right, and a fighter had sufficient financial backing, he was willing to fight.

When a really big purse finally was offered, he took on Corbett. And despite having not fought in three years, he was willing to do so in a fight to the finish. The fact is that John L. Sullivan had such a huge ego that he could not even conceive of someone being able to defeat him, which is why he made the Corbett bout winner-take-all. He did not care about style matchups. Fear was not in his vocabulary. "I never had stage fright in my life; do not know what it is, and do not suppose I could understand it if somebody would try to explain it to me."[626]

During his prime years, neither punchers nor movers and slick boxers could defeat Sullivan. Mitchell lasted, but he ran around in a large 24-foot ring in muddy conditions under London rules, where he could drop or wrestle down to avoid big shots and get 38 seconds of recovery each time. Under Queensberry rules, Mitchell lasted only 3 rounds. The larger Kilrain used the same tactics, but took severe punishment and went down often. Burke and McCaffrey were knocked down several times. Those who tried

---

[625] Richard K. Fox, *The Life and Battles of James J. Corbett, The Champion Pugilist of the World* (New York: Richard Fox, 1892, 1895), 39-40.
[626] Sullivan at 179.

to win and not simply survive were knocked out quickly or decked multiple times. As Sullivan said,

> Whenever I have boxed with men who have resorted to all the trickery and sharp practices which they or their friends could invent, the match has lasted longer than where the men have come up manfully and fought me.
>
> The length of the match has always depended upon the amount of trickery my opponent could resort to and his sprinting abilities. … Now, in the face of such matches the general public give the man who makes the longest fight the credit of being the best boxer or fighter; whereas such should not be the case by any means, for where one man stands up manfully and fights, and does his best to win and is consequently knocked out in short order, the other man does not attempt to win but attempts to make the fight last as long as possible, depending upon police interference and hoping to make a draw, and knowing that the public will give him credit for having made a long fight.[627]

In 1892, before the Corbett fight, reflecting on his career, Sullivan said that Ryan, Kilrain, Slade, and Flood were the gamest fighters that he had fought. "Slade had the disadvantage that all big men have that I have met with, - the bigger they are the more heavily they fall."

Sullivan said that Mitchell simply was a runner intent on survival rather than fighting to achieve victory. Of the knockdown that Mitchell gave him in 1883, Sullivan said that given the position he was in at that moment, with his feet close together, he had no balance, and he was set down like someone who was going to sit in a chair. "I never have been hit hard enough by anybody to feel it during the fight. I have never felt a man's blow in my life."[628]

In 1908, Billy Madden said, "Jim Jeffries would not have had a chance in the world with John L. Sullivan when the Boston boy was in his prime. I've heard a lot of talk about what Jeff and his mountain of strength would have done against the Old Roman, but let me tell you that I've seen them all and John was the king."

The opposite perspective was that Sullivan was not that clever, never landed on a clever man, and never beat real good men. Jeff Thompson, responding to those two extreme views, said,

> While I am not so cock sure as Madden seems to be that Sullivan would have been able to have taken Jeffries' measure with ease at any time in his career, on the other hand this talk of John L. meeting only third-raters and not being able to land on a clever man, is to laugh.

627 Sullivan at 181.
628 Sullivan at 177.

> I saw Sullivan in practically all of his fights from the time he put Steve Taylor out at Harry Hill's and fought one of the greatest fights with John Flood that I ever saw, up to the time that the wreck of Sullivan was put out by Jim Corbett, and I have seen pretty much all of the good ones in action since. Sullivan was a natural fighter; he could hit the hardest blow of any man I ever saw, and before he was wrecked by drink, I do not believe there was a man that ever lived who could have beaten him.
>
> The idea that he could not land on a clever man is nonsense. They do not grow any cleverer men with their hands and feet than Charley Mitchell was when he met Sullivan first, and Sullivan got to him all right and fought him to a standstill with a punch.[629]

In 1928, William Burns, a fighter and brother of Sullivan opponent Jack Burns, said the following of Sullivan:

> At his best, from 1878 to 1883, in my opinion, he could easily have trimmed Peter Jackson, Jim Corbett, Frank Slavin, Bob Fitzsimmons, Jim Jeffries, or Jack Johnson….
>
> He was as lithe as a cat and his cleverness at dodging was vouched for by the unmarred condition of his face and head after his hectic career. … In the ring, when time was called, he always left his chair like a shot out of a gun, ready and eager for the fray. The impression he gave was one of boundless vitality. Any ordinary man was forced to run to keep pace with his walk. … His whole body seemed to be set on springs. … His hands and head cooperated beautifully at all times. Besides this, he was a natural born fighter, and absolutely fearless. … His left hand was just as deadly as his right and his blows always came straight from the shoulder with the full weight of his body behind them. He was never known to lose his head in a tight place and he always fought a clean fight. …
>
> Sullivan was a strong advocate of glove fighting as he considered bare-knuckle fighting too brutal for true sport. His ambition was to see the ring uplifted and its standards raised to a good deal higher plane than those then prevailing.[630]

John L. Sullivan had elevated and changed the sport. He would be the standard by which future champions would be compared. Few could measure up successfully.

---

[629] *Pittsburg Press*, February 2, 1908.

[630] Burns, William. *Incidents in the Life of John L. Sullivan and Other Famous People of Fifty Years Ago*. 1928, at 25-28.

Afterword

Following his loss to Corbett, John L. Sullivan's boxing career functionally was over. He occasionally engaged in friendly sparring exhibitions to make money, but essentially he was retired. Yet, like Mike Tyson today, he remained a famous curiosity, so he realized that he could continue making money on the stage, in exhibitions, in plays, and in vaudeville performances. People paid to see him and hear him talk. Sullivan often was paid to be a newspaper correspondent, reporting on various fights or offering his opinions and analysis of upcoming bouts. During his fight career, occasionally he had lent his name to various newspapers as an "editor." His name sold newspapers. Readers wanted his insights. Sullivan was present at most big fights. His mere presence remained a draw to fight fans.

On September 17, 1892 at Madison Square Garden in New York, just ten days after they had fought, champion James J. Corbett boxed 3 friendly rounds with the ex-champion at a benefit tendered to Sullivan. Benefits often were held for the losers of fights so that they could make some money. It was Corbett who had won the massive $35,000 purse and stakes from the winner-take-all championship fight, so Sullivan had come up empty-handed. As Mike Donovan said, "Corbett volunteered his services, not only with generosity but with excellent judgment. It is no exaggeration to say that millions of Americans were sore on him because he had beaten the old champion, and the surest way to gain popular favor was to show a kindly interest in the monarch he had toppled off the throne."[631]

When Sullivan entered, the huge crowd cheered for a number of minutes. When Corbett arrived, there was the same. They shook hands in a friendly manner and the cheering continued. Sullivan gave a speech, saying, "I have no excuses to make for my defeat. I was defeated; that is all there is to it, and the defeated man who makes excuses makes the mistake of his life." The crowd cheered wildly.

Writers called the boxing between Corbett and Sullivan "tame" rounds with "light taps," although at one point in the 2nd round, Sullivan hit with a bit more power, Jim gave him a look, and then John ended the round by going to his corner. The final round featured Corbett ducking and countering with light blows, showing what he could do if he desired.

The *New York Sun* said, "Corbett looked young, fresh, buoyant, agile, and vigorous, while Sullivan's gray hair and serious expression of face made him appear very much older. The sparring was light, both men showing science without any attempt to hit hard." Some in the audience called to

[631] Donovan at 197.

John, "Hit him, Sully," but he looked at them contemptuously. "The idea that Sullivan would endeavor to take advantage of a man sparring for his benefit showed that some persons did not understand the man from Boston."[632]

THE GALLERY GODS GO WILD
SULLIVAN MAKES A SPEECH.
THE NEW OLD CHAMPIONS SHAKE HANDS
SULLIVAN IN HIS PRIME—AS THE EX-CHAMPION APPEARED AT THE AGE OF TWENTY-SIX.
THE RUSH TO GET INTO THE GARDEN.

JOHN L. SULLIVAN STILL THE FISTIC IDOL.

The Ex Champion's Grand Testimonial Benefit at Madison Square Garden, New York, at Which Over $12,800 Was Taken In at the Door. The Greatest Ovation Ever Given a Fighter in the History of the World.

---

[632] *New York Sun*, *San Francisco Chronicle*, *San Francisco Examiner*, September 18, 1892.

Champion and Ex-Champion Cheered
John L. Sullivan given a rousing testimonial by over 10,000 enthusiastic admirers in Madison Square Garden, New York on Sept. 17

A couple days after the benefit, in Providence, Rhode Island, Sullivan opened in a play called *The Man From Boston.* Although concerned that no one would want to see a former champion, nevertheless there was a full house. The play included 3 rounds of sparring with Jack Ashton.

In subsequent years, occasionally Sullivan was involved in violent episodes, both with men and women, usually when he was intoxicated. In May 1893, Sullivan struck and kicked a man who only had one arm. Sullivan claimed to be acting in self-defense. He settled the civil suit. In August 1893 in a hotel bar, Sullivan traded words with a man and then punched him to the floor. When the individual pulled a revolver, Sullivan bolted for the door, and the bullet just missed him. In January 1894, allegedly acting in self-defense, a lover smashed Sullivan's head with an Indian club, knocking him unconscious. In June 1894, a barroom argument led to Sullivan requiring stitches to his cheek after being smashed in the face with a bottle. He was fat, his hair gray, and he seemed to be aging rapidly.

Sullivan's friends were dying. In January 1893, Jack Ashton died from a skin infection. In September 1893, Mike Cleary died of consumption. Weeks later, Pete McCoy fell off a boat and drowned.

During 1894 and 1895, Sullivan gave several friendly 3-round exhibitions with Paddy Ryan.

Also in 1894, Thomas Edison attempted to get Sullivan to box Corbett 6 rounds, to be recorded by his new invention – the moving picture camera, but John L. wanted $25,000. Edison instead paid Corbett $5,000 plus royalties to box Peter Courtney.[633]

633 *New York Sun*, September 8, 1894.

Sadly, Sullivan never would be filmed in the ring, although many years later, in 1910, in the days before the Jeffries-Johnson fight, he would be filmed in a formal suit swinging at a speed bag and engaging in a momentary friendly semi-shadow box with Corbett, mostly feinting, showing one punch but then switching to another, but not really throwing. The footage is of limited value because it was brief, Sullivan was 51 years old, had been retired for nearly 18 years, and he appeared to be weighing well over 300 pounds. However, even under all those conditions, one still can get a sense for how quick and reactive he once was.

SULLIVAN "WITH THE WHISKER."
EX-CHAMPION JOHN L. SULLIVAN, OF BOSTON, AS HE APPEARS WEARING "SIDERS."

During the 1894-95 theatrical season, Sullivan performed in the play *A True American*, sparring with Dan Dwyer. He kept drinking and spending all of his money. Occasionally, he had to deal with civil suits for unpaid bills.

In February 1895, a lady cook at a boardinghouse overturned a kettle of boiling fat that set her clothes ablaze. Hearing screams, Sullivan rushed downstairs and tried to extinguish the flames with a mat and his hands, burning himself in the process. Hours later, she died.

In March, a drunken John L. attended the fight between Jake Kilrain and Steve O'Donnell. After 8 rounds, he climbed onto the stage to criticize the referee's officiating.

On June 8, 1895 at Madison Square Garden, at a benefit for Jack Dempsey, Corbett sparred John McVey; Bob Fitzsimmons sparred Frank Bosworth; Joe Choynski sparred Bob Armstrong; and John L. Sullivan sparred Dempsey.[634]

On June 27, 1895 in New York, 28-year-old Corbett and 36-year-old John L. Sullivan gave a sparring exhibition. Jim played with John, "tapping him where and when he pleased," sparring 3 "pretty but short rounds."[635]

On August 9, 1895, Sullivan's brother Michael died of Bright's disease and heart trouble at the age of 28.

Sullivan continued sparring Paddy Ryan as part of *The Wicklow Postman*.

[634] *New York Clipper*, June 15, 1895.
[635] *New York Herald*, June 28, 1895.

In January 1896, Sullivan stepped off a train while it was still moving.

Apparently, the drunken ex-fighter had been looking for a bathroom, opened the back door, and kept walking. The train stopped and Sullivan was found face-down in a muddy ditch, looking worse than he had after any fight. Incredibly, no bones were broken, and he still took the stage that evening. He was nursed by a woman named Maggie Lee, who, like all of his lovers, he called "wife."

On August 31, 1896 in New York, a crowd of 5,000 saw a 278-pound Sullivan spar 3 short friendly rounds (each lasting less than a minute) in a "tapping affair" with Tom Sharkey. Before the bout, when called upon to give a speech, Sullivan said,

> Gentleman: It is not necessary for me to make a speech, for the master of ceremonies has explained to you that this will be only a friendly bout. I've had my day and am too fat to fight again. Now, let me call your attention to this young fellow (pointing towards Sharkey) who is trying to get to the top. He is a worthy young man deserving of your attention.[636]

The following week, Annie Livingston died suddenly from acute gastritis. Sullivan did not attend the funeral.

In March 1897, Sullivan said that all the talk about the supposed new blows invented by Corbett and Fitzsimmons "makes me sick." He said they had not invented anything new, for the punches had existed all along. "Of course it makes good reading, but it is all bombastic talk and nothing more."[637]

After seeing Bob Fitzsimmons defeat Jim Corbett on March 17, 1897, a 38-year-old Sullivan challenged Fitzsimmons to fight. A month later, he confirmed his desire for a fight. "I want the public to know that I never laid down or quit in my life, which is more than Fitzsimmons can say."[638]

Despite his age and inactivity, Sullivan and Fitzsimmons did schedule a 6-round bout to be held on July 5, 1897 in Brooklyn, New York. However, the authorities were determined to prevent it. When Sullivan and

---

636 *National Police Gazette*, September 12, 19, 1896; *New York Sun*, September 1, 1896.
637 *Rocky Mountain News*, March 1, 1897.
638 *San Francisco Examiner*, April 22, 1897.

Fitzsimmons were present to box on the date set, along with 2,000 spectators, the police informed the two that if they put on the gloves and attempted to spar, they would be arrested.[639]

In September 1897, Sullivan performed in *A Trip Across the Ocean.* Jake Kilrain sometimes sparred him during the play.

In 1899, some called for a round-by-round points scoring system for fights. However, John L. Sullivan said there was no need to change the way fights were scored.

> This proposed system of awarding a bout according to rounds amounts to nothing. … What advantage is it to insist on a separate decision after each round? … Only one thing is needed for a fight. That is an honest referee.

Sullivan felt that draws should be abolished, that every fight should have a winner, and that extra rounds should be authorized if needed to determine a definitive winner.

> There should be no draws. There should be a winner in every fight. … If that plan was followed out the scrapping would be more lively, as the uncertainty of the result would force both men to try for a knockout. If two men should be so evenly matched that a referee could not choose at the end of a certain number of rounds, the referee ought to ask them to continue until he is able to say whose fight it is. All of which goes to show how far from right it would be to have a point system. A fight is not decided that way. A referee takes so many things into consideration that he could not award points every round and still give a decision that was at once satisfactory to the spectators and just to the principals.[640]

In the spring of 1899, Sullivan opened a new bar in New York. In November, he purchased an interest in a café.

On August 29, 1900 at New York's Madison Square Garden, a benefit for John L. Sullivan generated $15,000 in ticket sales. About 5,000 to 6,000 were in attendance, including a dozen women. The 41-year-old Sullivan sparred 3 friendly rounds with then 220-pound heavyweight champion James J. Jeffries, who had defeated Fitzsimmons in June 1899; a fight Sullivan had attended. Wearing black trunks (instead of his usual green), Sullivan had gray hair, was very fat, and out of shape. None of the tame 3 rounds lasted even a minute.[641]

In October 1900, a 280-pound Sullivan was operated on for a strangulated hernia.

From 1901 to 1902, Sullivan performed in *Uncle Tom's Cabin* as the villain.

---

[639] *Brooklyn Daily Eagle,* June 29, 30, 1897, July 6, 1897.

[640] *New York Evening Journal,* November 16, 1899.

[641] *New York Journal, Sun, Herald,* August 30, 1900; *National Police Gazette,* September 15, 1900.

Sullivan subsequently engaged in vaudeville, giving monologues. Occasionally, he was drunk on stage.

In November 1902, Sullivan was adjudicated bankrupt.

News of his drunken behavior only stimulated ticket sales. In December 1902 in Detroit, on stage he said, "I'm drunker than a fiddler's bitch." That led to his arrest. Nevertheless, his performances were sold out.

In early 1904, Sullivan was having stomach problems, and his vision was failing him. In August he was arrested for public drunkenness and profanity.

At the 1904 summer Olympics in St. Louis, Sullivan lent his name to a bar which gave him a half-interest in the profits. He had to shake hands with patrons. Eventually, he became a professional greeter in a bar. He later got into a fight with the bartender.

In early 1905, after another drunken spree, Sullivan contracted pneumonia.

Interestingly enough, on March 1, 1905 in Grand Rapids, Michigan, at age 46, weighing 273 pounds, John L. Sullivan boxed in a scheduled 4-round bout with 196-pound Jim McCormick. Sullivan scored a clean knockout at 1 minute 23 seconds of the 2nd round. John L. used his famous rushing right swing to the jaw to do the trick. McCormick dropped unconscious and was out cold for five minutes.

What made his victory over McCormick significant was the fact that in 1900, McCormick went 15 rounds to a no decision with Jack Johnson, and also lost via a 6-round disqualification to Johnson.

Gus Ruhlin KO18 Jim McCormick, August 11, 1905
Sullivan, McCormick, Ruhlin, Billy Jordan

After Sullivan stopped him, in August 1905, McCormick lasted into the 18th round with Gus Ruhlin before being taken out. In February 1906, McCormick would box 10 rounds to a draw with Jack Johnson.

Even at his advanced age, out of shape, and inactive for years, Sullivan showed that he still had some serious power.[642]

McCormick subsequently joined Sullivan's tour as a sparring partner.

Miraculously, on March 5, 1905, three days after his victory over McCormick, Sullivan decided to stop drinking. Sure, he had done it before,

---

642 *Police Gazette*, March 18, 1905; Boxrec.com.

but it never stuck. Only this time it did. Sullivan estimated that he had spent half a million dollars on booze. Finally, his drinking days were over.

In 1906, Sullivan said,

> I could produce sports who will tell you that I could strike more blows in ten seconds than any man living could strike in a minute, and these blows counted some, as they were delivered solidly while I was square on my feet, so that all the heft of my body was in every one of them. I've ducked plenty of them.[643]

On May 9, 1907, Sullivan visited the White House to speak with President Theodore Roosevelt on behalf of his nephew, John L. Lennon, his sister Annie's son. Lennon had been convicted of desertion in Cuba. The 335-pound Sullivan convinced the president to intercede with the Navy to pardon Lennon and allow him to re-enlist and serve out his full military term.

Also during 1907, Jake Kilrain once again joined Sullivan in *A Trip Across the Ocean.* Occasionally, Kid Cutler acted as a sparring partner as well. Usually, Sullivan gave a speech warning about the evils of alcohol.

As of May 1908, a sober Sullivan had not missed any performances.

In December 1908, a 50-year old Sullivan filed for divorce from Annie Sullivan. The judge granted the divorce on the grounds of desertion.

From 1909 to 1910, Sullivan continued giving some sparring exhibitions with Jake Kilrain as part of a theatrical tour. They even performed in the United Kingdom.

When scouting a potential Jim Jeffries vs. Jack Johnson fight, the fans were given quite a jar when Sullivan said that then-champion Johnson would whip retired undefeated ex-champion Jeffries. Sullivan said,

> The negro is not being credited for what he has done. Neither is he given credit for being as good a fighter as he is. I think that when he meets Jeff – if Jeff ever consents to a meeting – that the black boy will beat him to a frazzle. I am a great admirer of Jeff and would be one of the first to bewail the fact that a negro claims the championship, but I fear that Jeff is not the man he was five years ago and that he will be unable to cope with this wily Zulu. I don't like negroes any better than I did twenty years ago, but in this case I think credit must be given to the better man, and I look upon Johnson as being the fighter of the day.[644]

Sullivan knew how hard it was to come back after several years of inactivity, which is why he picked Johnson to defeat Jeffries.

> Take it from me that Jeffries can't come back. I know it, and nobody knows it better than Jeffries himself. I don't care what Corbett says,

---

[643] *Police Gazette*, March 31, 1906.

[644] *San Francisco Examiner*, October 28, 1909.

> his talk to me has the same weight as the ashes on a cigar. He couldn't punch a hole in a pound of butter. With Corbett as his trainer, it would be all off with Jeffries. Corbett, of course, is boosting the game, but that fight, if it ever comes off, will demonstrate what I have said. Jeffries can't come back. If he intended to, he ought to get some husky youngsters, who would punch him around a little.[645]

Sullivan also was quoted as saying, "Will Jeffries lick Johnson? No. Not unless Johnson lays down for him. ... None of the rest of us was able to quit the ring and come back strong ... Jeffries won't have the endurance."[646]

In February 1910, Sullivan married a woman named Catherine Harkins in a civil ceremony. He had been dating and possibly living with her for several years.

On June 21, 1910, 51-year-old Sullivan, acting as a newspaper correspondent, met Jack Johnson and saw him train. Sullivan said, "This is the first time I have ever seen the big black, and to say that he has impressed me favorably would hardly be expressing my meaning. He is a big, husky piece of humanity... [with a] well developed body." Sullivan said Johnson "went at his work with an alacrity that was really surprising, in view of the twelve-mile plug on the road earlier in the day."

---

645 *Richmond Planet*, February 5, 1910.

646 *Freeman*, February 12, 1910.

> What surprised me more than anything else in Johnson's work in the ring was his stealthy method of action. He seemed a good bit like Fitzsimmons in this respect. Apparently he does not move around on his feet and he gives the impression unless you watch him closely that he is not judging distance at all; but when his opponent gets within the proper range, a short straddle gives slight advance forward as the glove goes out and then you can see that he has judged his distance to a nicety.

Sullivan also said that the way Johnson dropped his elbows and held his upper arms loose to his body gave the impression that he had given some thought to a plan of body defense. Still, the ex-champ did not see anything of startling nature that was an improvement over old methods. "I should feel complimented, because these latter-day young fellows have thought sufficiently well of our old methods to adopt a good many of them." [647]

When John L. Sullivan showed up at Jeff's training camp, Jim Corbett barred him and had the gate closed. Sullivan asked "Why?" Corbett replied, "Because you have knocked the big fight and called it a fake. Jeff wants me to say that he will not shake hands with you." Sullivan responded, "That's a mistake. I've been misquoted." Jim replied, "I don't believe you were misquoted." Corbett accused John L. of being jealous because Corbett had beaten him, and said he had held a grudge ever since. "I licked you, and you have never forgiven me." Eventually, Sullivan left.

---

647 *San Francisco Examiner*, June 22, 1910.

CORBETT TELLING SULLIVAN TO LEAVE JEFF'S CAMP

Tex Rickard would attempt to effect reconciliation, saying that John L. would be treated with the same courtesy as any other newspaper correspondent.

On June 25, the Sullivan-Corbett feud came to an end. At Jeff's request, Sullivan visited the camp again, and when John L. met Corbett, they shook hands and engaged in cordial conversation.

SULLIVAN AND CORBETT BECOME FRIENDS AFTER LONG BITTER ENMITY

CORBETT AND SULLIVAN SHAKING HANDS; WILLIAM MULDOON, PEACEMAKER, ACTING AS MASTER OF CEREMONIES, AT HISTORIC RECONCILIATION

Upon meeting him, Jeffries said, "Hello John." Sullivan responded, "How are you, young man?" Jeff told Sullivan that he was willing to take his word for it that John had not knocked him or the bout. Rickard's and Muldoon's peacemaking efforts had been successful.[648]

Tommy Burns, James J. Corbett, James J. Jeffries, John L. Sullivan

[648] *San Francisco Chronicle, Call, Nevada State Journal,* June 26, 1910.

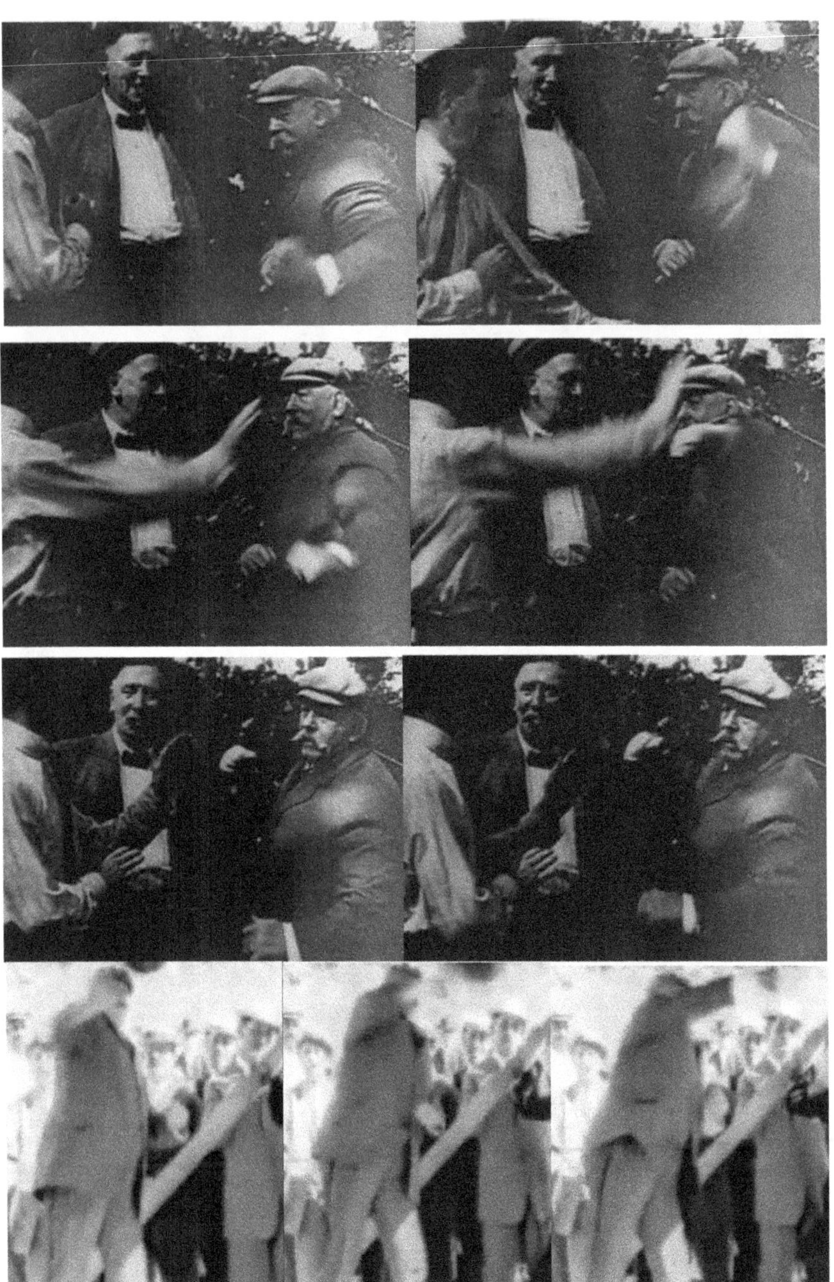

The day of the Jeffries-Johnson fight, on July 4, 1910, Billy Jordan introduced Sullivan to the crowd: "I introduce to you the great and only champion, big hearted John L. Sullivan." The spectators went wild.

After Jeffries lost to Johnson, several writers said pugilism's death seemed imminent. John L. Sullivan said that talk of boxing's future being gloomy was ridiculous. He said the future would take care of itself and the game would be just fine. "It's been the same old story all the time." They said the same things after his big fights, but such was not the case. "Now this Jeffries-Johnson fight marks the end of the sport. BOSH. When they change human nature, and put a mollycoddle's heart in every good, red blooded American citizen then the game might die," but until then, there was scant danger of pugilism ceasing.[649]

Sullivan said Johnson eventually would lose, just like he did. Speaking from experience, he said,

> This colored fellow isn't invincible, you know. He's a great fighter and I predicted two years ago he would beat Jeffries. … But you know when a fellow gets to the top of his profession he falls into many temptations. He finds many who are willing to buy him a drink, and he goes along for a year or two and thinks all the time he's as good as ever. Some day he'll put on the gloves and get into the ring against some clear-headed strong and well trained fellow with young blood running through his veins, and then he'll suddenly awake to the fact that his old activity and spirit have gone and he's bound to be beaten down.[650]

Sullivan purchased a farm in Abington, south of Boston. He occasionally accompanied his wife Kate to church.

In 1913, Sullivan's wife was diagnosed with breast cancer.

In 1915, Sullivan said he was becoming an anti-drinking crusader. He would preach abstinence and explain the pitfalls of alcohol. However, he did not believe in prohibition laws, feeling that the decision to abstain had to come from within. He also realized that if folks wanted alcohol, they would get it, or make it.

Sullivan continued attending and covering fights, including the March 25, 1916 contest between then champion Jess Willard (who had dethroned Jack Johnson) and Frank Moran. George Bellows painted a picture of the moment that Sullivan was introduced, called *Introducing John L. Sullivan.*

On May 25, 1916, Sullivan's wife Catherine Sullivan died from breast cancer at the age of 52.

Sullivan had been having heart problems, owing to his obesity. He claimed to have substituted food for drink.

Eventually, on February 2, 1918, John L. Sullivan died of a heart attack at age 59. He remained a legend whose impact on boxing was and still is indelible.

---

649 *San Francisco Bulletin*, July 11, 1910.

650 *Freeman*, December 17, 1910.

Appendix: John L. Sullivan's Professional Record

1877-1878

?	Jack Scannell	Boston, MA	KO 1

1879

Mar 14	Jack Curley	Boston, MA	Win in

1hr.14min. Likely an LPR fight with gloves.

Mar 14	John "Cocky" Woods	Boston, MA	KO 5?
?	Dan Dwyer	Boston, MA	KO 3?
?	Tommy Chandler	Boston, MA	W 4?

1880

Late '79 or Jan 1880?	John/Jack "Patsy" Hogan	Boston, MA	W 4?
Apr 6	Joe Goss	Boston, MA	TKO 2/EX 3

Actually a KO2, but Goss continued after recovering and Sullivan worked with him.

Jun 28	George Rooke	Boston, MA	KO 3
Dec 11	John Donaldson	Cincinnati, OH	TKO 3/EX 4

Donaldson quit after the 3rd round, but Sullivan convinced him to continue for another round.

Dec 24	John Donaldson	Cincinnati, OH	W 10

London Prize Ring Rules with hard gloves, lasting almost 22 minutes.

1881

Jan 3	Jack Stewart	Boston, MA	TKO 1/EX 3

Sullivan essentially stopped him in each round.

Mar 31	Steve Taylor	New York, NY	KO 2
May 16	John Flood	Yonkers, NY	W 8

London Prize Ring Rules with gloves, lasting 16 minutes.

Jul 11	Fred Crossley	Philadelphia, PA	KO 1
Jul 11	Billy Madden	Philadelphia, PA	EX
Jul 21	John Buckley/Dan McCarty	Philadelphia, PA	KO 1
Aug 13	"Captain" James Dalton	Chicago, IL	KO 4
Sep 3	Jack Burns	Chicago, IL	KO 1
Sep 3	"Captain" James Dalton	Chicago, IL	EX 4

1882

Feb 7	Paddy Ryan	Mississippi City, MS	W 9

London Prize Ring Rules, lasting 10 ½ or 11minutes.

Apr 20	John McDermott	Rochester, NY	KO 3
Jul 4	Jimmy Elliott	Brooklyn, NY	KO 3

Bout fought with gloves, but hybrid rules - the bout lasting 7 minutes 20 seconds.

Jul 17	Joe "Tug" Wilson	New York, NY	EX 4

Wilson was knocked down or dropped down incessantly to last the distance and claim the cash bonus merely for lasting 4 rounds.

Sep 23	Henry Higgins	Buffalo, NY	KO 3
Oct 16	S.P. Stockton	Fort Wayne, IN	KO 2
Oct 30	Charley O'Donnell	Chicago, IL	KO 1
Oct 30	Pete McCoy	Chicago, IL	EX 3
Nov 17	P.J. Rentzler/Rensler	Washington, DC	KO 1
Nov 17	Pete McCoy	Washington, DC	EX

1883

May 14	Charles Mitchell	New York, NY	KO 3
Aug 6	Herbert Slade	New York, NY	KO 3
Oct 17 or 18	James McCoy	McKeesport, PA	KO 1
Nov 3	Jim Miles	St. Louis, MO	KO 1
Nov 3	Steve Taylor	St. Louis, MO	EX
Nov 3	Herbert Slade	St. Louis, MO	EX
Nov 16	Steve Taylor	Chicago, IL	EX 4

Sullivan possibly also boxed a Hoosier and scored a KO3.

Nov 26	Morris Hefey or Hafey	St. Paul, MN	KO 1
Nov 26	Steve Taylor	St. Paul, MN	EX 4
Nov 26	Herbert Slade	St. Paul, MN	EX 4
Dec 4	Mike Sheehan/Shean/Shehan	Davenport, IA	KO 1
Dec 4	Steve Taylor	Davenport, IA	EX
Dec 4	Herbert Slade	Davenport, IA	EX

1884

Jan 12	Fred Robinson	Butte, MT	KO 2
Jan 12	Herbert Slade	Butte, MT	EX
Feb 1	Sylvester La Gouriff	Astoria, OR	KO 1
Feb 1	Steve Taylor	Astoria, OR	EX 3
Feb 1	Herbert Slade	Astoria, OR	EX
Feb 6	James Lang	Seattle, WA	KO 1
Feb 6	Steve Taylor	Seattle, WA	EX
Feb 6	Herbert Slade	Seattle, WA	EX
Mar 6	George M. Robinson	San Francisco, CA	WDQ 4

Robinson went down 28 - 66 times to avoid being knocked out, until disqualified for falling without a blow.

Apr 10	Al Marx	Galveston, TX	KO 1
Apr 10	Steve Taylor	Galveston, TX	EX
Apr 29	Dan Henry	Hot Springs, AR	KO 1
May 1	William Fleming	Memphis, TN	KO 1
May 1	Mike Donovan	Memphis, TN	EX 3
May 1	Steve Taylor	Memphis, TN	EX
May 2	Enos Phillips	Nashville, TN	KO 1/KO 4

Possibly KO 1 if Queensberry rules, but KO 4 if counted in London rules fashion.

Nov 10	John M. Laflin	New York, NY	KO1/KO 4

Laflin was actually knocked out in the 1st round but allowed to continue, in London rules fashion.

Nov 18	Alf Greenfield	New York, NY	W 2

Police stopped the bout when they began slugging.

1885

Jan 12	Alf Greenfield	Boston, MA	W 4
Jan 19	Paddy Ryan	New York, NY	NC 1

Police intervened and the referee declared it no contest.

Jun 13	Jack Burke	Chicago, IL	W 5
Aug 29	Dominick McCaffrey	Cincinnati, OH	W 7

1886

Sep 18	Frank Herald	Alleghany City, PA	W 2

Police stopped the bout, but pre-fight terms allowed for a decision in the event of interference.

Nov 13	Paddy Ryan	San Francisco, CA	KO 3

1887

Jan 18	Patsy Cardiff	Minneapolis, MN	D 6

Sullivan broke a bone in his left arm.

1888

Jan 5	Jack Ashton	Cardiff, Wales	EX
Jan 5	William Samuells	Cardiff, Wales	KO 3
Mar 10	Charley Mitchell	Apremont, France	D 39

London Prize Ring Rules, fight lasting 3 hours 10 minutes 55 seconds.

1889

Jul 8	Jake Kilrain	Richburg, MS	W 75

London Prize Ring Rules, lasting either 2 hours 13 minutes, 2 hours 16 minutes, or 2 hours 18 minutes.

1892

Sep 7	James J. Corbett	New Orleans, LA	LKO by 21

1905

Mar 1	Jim McCormick	Grand Rapids, MI	KO 2

Acknowledgements

Thank you to all those who helped make this book special:

Clay Moyle, prizefightingbooks.com

Steve Westlake, *National Police Gazette,* policegazette.us

Corey Parker

Don Scott, boxingcollectors.com

Tracy Callis

Ray Groh

Bob Yalen

George Rugg, James Cachey, Sara Weber, University of Notre Dame

Department of Special Collections of the Hesburgh Libraries of the University of Notre Dame

Lara Szypszak and Michelle Wright, Library of Congress

University of Iowa

Boxrec.com

Index

Other Books By Adam J. Pollack

In the Ring With James J. Corbett

In the Ring With Bob Fitzsimmons

In the Ring With James J. Jeffries

In the Ring With Marvin Hart

In the Ring With Tommy Burns

In the Ring with Jack Johnson – Part I: The Rise

In the Ring With Jack Johnson – Part II: The Reign

Adam J. Pollack is a professional and amateur boxing judge and referee, a publisher, and a member of the Boxing Writers Association of America. He also is an attorney practicing law in Iowa City, Iowa.

www.ingramcontent.com/pod-product-compliance
Lightning Source LLC
Chambersburg PA
CBHW020407100426
42812CB00001B/241

* 9 7 8 0 9 9 0 3 7 0 3 6 9 *